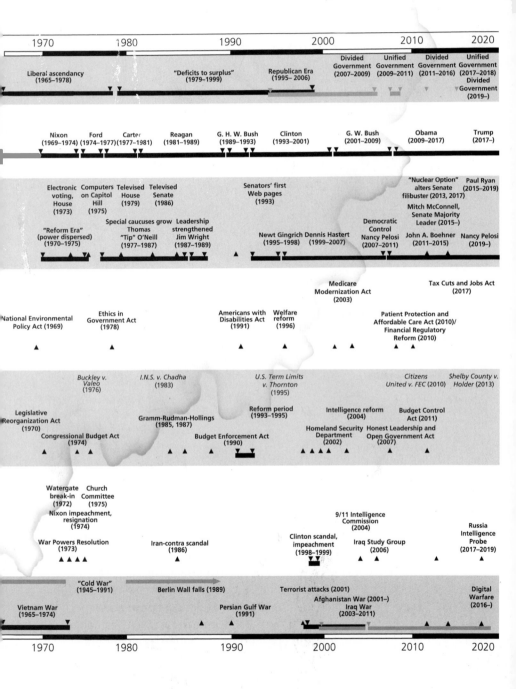

1970　1980　1990　2000　2010　2020

Liberal ascendancy
(1965–1978)

"Deficits to surplus"
(1979–1999)

Republican Era
(1995– 2006)

Divided
Government
(2007–2009)

Unified
Government
(2009–2011)

Divided
Government
(2011–2016)

Unified
Government
(2017–2018)

Divided
Government
(2019–)

Nixon
(1969–1974)

Ford
(1974–1977)

Carter
(1977–1981)

Reagan
(1981–1989)

G. H. W. Bush
(1989–1993)

Clinton
(1993–2001)

G. W. Bush
(2001–2009)

Obama
(2009–2017)

Trump
(2017–)

Electronic
voting,
House
(1973)

Computers
on Capitol
Hill
(1975)

Televised
House
(1979)

Televised
Senate
(1986)

Senators' first
Web pages
(1993)

"Nuclear Option"
alters Senate
filibuster (2013, 2017)

Paul Ryan
(2015–2019)

Mitch McConnell,
Senate Majority
Leader (2015–)

"Reform Era"
(power dispersed)
(1970–1975)

Special caucuses grow
Thomas
"Tip" O'Neill
(1977–1987)

Leadership
strengthened
Jim Wright
(1987–1989)

Newt Gingrich
(1995–1998)

Dennis Hastert
(1999–2007)

Democratic
Control
Nancy Pelosi
(2007–2011)

John A. Boehner
(2011–2015)

Nancy Pelosi
(2019–)

Medicare
Modernization Act
(2003)

Tax Cuts and Jobs Act
(2017)

National Environmental
Policy Act (1969)

Ethics in
Government Act
(1978)

Americans with
Disabilities Act
(1991)

Welfare
reform
(1996)

Patient Protection and
Affordable Care Act (2010)/
Financial Regulatory
Reform (2010)

Buckley v.
Valeo
(1976)

I.N.S. v. Chadha
(1983)

U.S. Term Limits
v. Thornton
(1995)

Citizens
United v. FEC (2010)

Shelby County v.
Holder (2013)

Legislative
Reorganization Act
(1970)

Gramm-Rudman-Hollings
(1985, 1987)

Reform period
(1993–1995)

Intelligence reform
(2004)

Budget Control
Act (2011)

Congressional Budget Act
(1974)

Budget Enforcement Act
(1990)

Homeland Security
Department
(2002)

Honest Leadership and
Open Government Act
(2007)

Watergate
break-in
(1972)

Church
Committee
(1975)

Nixon impeachment,
resignation
(1974)

9/11 Intelligence
Commission
(2004)

Russia
Intelligence
Probe
(2017–2019)

War Powers Resolution
(1973)

Iran-contra scandal
(1986)

Clinton scandal,
impeachment
(1998–1999)

Iraq Study Group
(2006)

"Cold War"
(1945–1991)

Berlin Wall falls (1989)

Terrorist attacks (2001)

Digital
Warfare
(2016–)

Afghanistan War (2001–)
Iraq War
(2003–2011)

Vietnam War
(1965–1974)

Persian Gulf War
(1991)

1970　1980　1990　2000　2010　2020

Sara Miller McCune founded SAGE Publishing in 1965 to support the dissemination of usable knowledge and educate a global community. SAGE publishes more than 1000 journals and over 600 new books each year, spanning a wide range of subject areas. Our growing selection of library products includes archives, data, case studies and video. SAGE remains majority owned by our founder and after her lifetime will become owned by a charitable trust that secures the company's continued independence.

Los Angeles | London | New Delhi | Singapore | Washington DC | Melbourne

Congress and Its Members

17th Edition

For Nancy; Douglas, Victoria, Elizabeth, Thomas, James,
Alexander; Chris, Theo, Emily, and Olivia

—R. H. D.

For Janet, Mark, and Eric

—W. J. O.

For Emery and Beverly

—F. E. L.

For Terri, Sam, and Lea

—E. S.

Congress and Its Members

17th Edition

Roger H. Davidson

University of Maryland

Walter J. Oleszek

Congressional Research Service

Frances E. Lee

Princeton University

Eric Schickler

University of California, Berkeley

FOR INFORMATION:

CQ Press

An Imprint of SAGE Publications, Inc.

2455 Teller Road

Thousand Oaks, California 91320

E-mail: order@sagepub.com

SAGE Publications Ltd.

1 Oliver's Yard

55 City Road

London EC1Y 1SP

United Kingdom

SAGE Publications India Pvt. Ltd.

B 1/I 1 Mohan Cooperative Industrial Area

Mathura Road, New Delhi 110 044

India

SAGE Publications Asia-Pacific Pte. Ltd.

18 Cross Street #10–10/11/12

China Square Central

Singapore 048423

Printed in the United States of America

ISBN: 9781544322957

This book is printed on acid-free paper.

Certified Chain of Custody
SUSTAINABLE FORESTRY INITIATIVE
Promoting Sustainable Forestry
www.sfiprogram.org
SFI-01268

SFI label applies to text stock

Acquisitions Editors: Lauren Schultz and Monica Eckman

Content Development Editor: Scott Harris

Editorial Assistant: Sam Rosenberg

Marketing Manager: Erica Deluca

Production Editor: Veronica Stapleton Hooper

Copy Editor: Karin Rathert

Typesetter: C&M Digitals (P) Ltd.

Proofreader: Dennis W. Webb

Indexer: Jeanne Busemeyer

Cover Designer: Candice Harman

19 20 21 22 23 10 9 8 7 6 5 4 3 2 1

BRIEF CONTENTS

Tables, Figures, and Boxes   xviii

Preface   xxi

About the Authors   xxiv

PART I • IN SEARCH OF THE TWO CONGRESSES

Chapter 1 • The Two Congresses   1

Chapter 2 • Evolution of the Modern Congress   13

PART II • A CONGRESS OF AMBASSADORS

Chapter 3 • Going for It: Recruitment and Candidacy   39

Chapter 4 • Making It: The Electoral Game   69

Chapter 5 • Being There: Hill Styles and Home Styles   107

PART III • A DELIBERATIVE ASSEMBLY OF ONE NATION

Chapter 6 • Leaders and Parties in Congress   137

Chapter 7 • Committees: Workshops of Congress   175

Chapter 8 • Congressional Rules and Procedures   219

Chapter 9 • Decision Making in Congress   261

PART IV • POLICY MAKING AND CHANGE IN THE TWO CONGRESSES

Chapter 10 • Congress and the President   293

Chapter 11 • Congress and the Bureaucracy   321

Chapter 12 • Congress and the Courts   349

Chapter 13 • Congress and Organized Interests   373

Chapter 14 • Congress, Budgets, and Domestic Policy Making 397

Chapter 15 • Congress and National Security Policies 427

PART V • CONCLUSION

Chapter 16 • The Two Congresses and the American People 455

Appendix A: Party Control: Presidency, Senate, House, 1901–2021 A1

Appendix B: Internships: Getting Experience on Capitol Hill A5

Suggested Readings S1

Notes N1

Index I1

DETAILED CONTENTS

Tables, Figures, and Boxes   xviii

Preface   xxi

About the Authors   xxiv

PART I • IN SEARCH OF THE TWO CONGRESSES

Chapter 1 • The Two Congresses   1

The Dual Nature of Congress   3

Legislators' Tasks   4

Popular Images   5

The Constitutional Basis   6

Back to Burke   7

The Two Congresses in Comparative Context   8

Divergent Views of Congress   10

Chapter 2 • Evolution of the Modern Congress   13

Antecedents of Congress   14

The English Heritage   14

The Colonial Experience   15

Congress in the Constitution   17

Powers of Congress   17

Limits on Legislative Power   20

Separate Branches, Shared Powers   20

Judicial Review   23

Bicameralism   25

Institutional Evolution   26

Workload   27

The Size of Congress   28

Conflict With the Executive Branch   29

Partisan Interests   30

Members' Individual Interests   31

Evolution of the Legislator's Job   33

The Congressional Career   33

Professionalization   34

Constituency Demands   36

Conclusion   37

PART II • A CONGRESS OF AMBASSADORS

Chapter 3 • Going for It: Recruitment and Candidacy   39

Formal Rules of the Game   40
     Senate Apportionment   40
     House Apportionment   41
Districting in the House   44
     Malapportionment   45
     Gerrymandering   47
     Majority-Minority Districts   53
Becoming a Candidate   57
     Called or Chosen?   57
     Amateurs and Professionals   59
     Finding Quality Candidates   61
Nominating Politics   64
     Rules of the Nominating Game   64
     Parties and Nominations   65
     Sizing Up the Primary System   65
Conclusion   66

Chapter 4 • Making It: The Electoral Game   69

Campaign Strategies   70
     Asking the Right Questions   70
     Choosing the Message   71
Campaign Resources   72
     Campaign Finance Regulations   74
     Incumbents Versus Challengers   77
     Allocating Resources   79
     Organizing the Campaign   80
Campaign Techniques   81
     The Air War: Media and Other Mass Appeals   81
     The Ground War: Pressing the Flesh and Other Forms of
       Close Contact   83
     The Parallel Campaigns   85
Who Votes?   85
     Reasons for Not Voting   86
     Biases of Voting   88
How Voters Decide   88
     Party Loyalties   88
     The Appeal of Candidates   93
     Issue Voting   96
Election Outcomes   99
     Party Balance   99

Party Alignment and Realignment   103

Turnover and Representation   103

Conclusion   104

Chapter 5 • Being There: Hill Styles and Home Styles   **107**

Hill Styles   108

Who Are the Legislators?   108

Congressional Roles   114

How Do Legislators Spend Their Time?   118

The Shape of the Washington Career   119

Looking Homeward   120

Independent Judgment or Constituency Opinion?   120

What Are Constituencies?   121

Home Styles   125

Office of the Member Inc.   127

Road Tripping   127

Constituency Casework   128

Personal Staff   129

Members and the Media   131

Mail   131

Feeding the Local Press   132

Social Media   134

Conclusion   134

PART III • A DELIBERATIVE ASSEMBLY OF ONE NATION

Chapter 6 • Leaders and Parties in Congress   137

The Speaker of the House   139

The Changing Role of the Speaker   142

The Speaker's Influence: Style and Context   146

House Floor Leaders   149

House Whips   150

Leaders of the Senate   152

Presiding Officers   152

Floor Leaders   154

Selection of Leaders   159

Leadership Activities   160

Institutional Tasks   161

Party Tasks   162

Party Caucuses, Committees, and Informal Groups   164

Party Caucuses   165

Party Committees   165

Informal Party Groups   165

Party Continuity and Change 167
    Intense Party Conflict 167
    The Two-Party System 168
    Advances in Coalition Building 169
Conclusion 171

Chapter 7 • Committees: Workshops of Congress   175

The Purposes of Committees 177
Evolution of the Committee System 177
Types of Committees 179
    Standing Committees 179
    Select, or Special, Committees 184
    Joint Committees 185
    Conference Committees 185
The Assignment Process 186
    The Pecking Order 186
    Preferences and Politicking 188
    How Assignments Are Made 190
    Approval by Party Caucuses and the Chamber 196
Committee Leadership 197
Policy Making in Committee 198
    Overlapping Jurisdictions 199
    Multiple Referrals 202
    Where Bills Go 203
    The Policy Environment 206
Committee Staff 207
Committee Reform and Change 209
    Select Committee on the Climate Crisis 209
    Constricting the Authority of Committee Chairs 211
    Party Task Forces and "Gangs" 213
    Bypassing Committees 214
Conclusion 215

Chapter 8 • Congressional Rules and Procedures   219

Introduction of Bills 222
    Drafting 225
    Timing 226
    Referral of Bills 227
Scheduling in the House 228
    Shortcuts for Minor Bills 229
    The Strategic Role of the Committee on Rules 232

The Emergence of Creative Rules   234
Dislodging a Bill From Committee   239

House Floor Procedures   240
Adoption of the Rule   241
Committee of the Whole   241
General Debate   241
The Amending Phase   242
Voting   243
Recommit and Final Passage   243

Scheduling in the Senate   245
Unanimous-Consent Agreements   246
Ways to Extract Bills From Committee   247

Senate Floor Procedures   249
Normal Routine   250
Holds, Filibusters, and Cloture   251

Resolving House–Senate Differences   257
Amendments Between the Houses   257
The Conference Committee Process   258
Openness and Bargaining   258

Conclusion   259

Chapter 9 • Decision Making in Congress   **261**

The Power to Choose   263

Types of Decisions   263
Specializing   264
Timing of Decisions   265
Taking the Lead   266
Taking Part   267
Offering Amendments   268
Casting Votes   269
What Do Votes Mean?   270

Determinants of Voting   272
Party and Voting   272
Ideology and Voting   277
Constituency and Voting   281
The Presidency and Voting   283
Cue-Givers and Roll Call Votes   285

Legislative Bargaining   285
Implicit and Explicit Bargaining   286
Logrolling   287
Bargaining Strategy   289

Conclusion   289

PART IV • POLICY MAKING AND CHANGE IN THE TWO CONGRESSES

Chapter 10 • Congress and the President   **293**

Constitutional Powers   295
    Veto Bargaining   296
    The Line-Item Veto   299
    The Administrative President   299
Leadership   303
    The President's Power to Persuade   304
    Going Public: The Rhetorical President   307
    Congressional Opinion Leadership   310
    The "Two Presidencies"   311
Sources of Legislative–Executive Conflict and Cooperation   313
    Party Loyalties   313
    Public Expectations   315
    Different Constituencies   316
    Different Time Perspectives   317
The Balance of Power   317
Conclusion   319

Chapter 11 • Congress and the Bureaucracy   **321**

Congress Organizes the Executive Branch   322
    Senate Confirmation of Presidential Appointees   323
    The Personnel System   329
    The Rulemaking Process   333
Congressional Control of the Bureaucracy   338
    Hearings and Investigations   340
    Congressional Vetoes   340
    Mandatory Reports   341
    Nonstatutory Controls   342
    Inspectors General   342
    The Appropriations Process   342
    Impeachment   343
    Oversight: An Evaluation   344
    Micromanagement   346
Conclusion   346

Chapter 12 • Congress and the Courts   **349**

The Federal Courts   350
The Supreme Court as Policymaker   351
    "Judicial Activism"   353
    Federalism   354

Statutory Interpretation 354
Legislative Checks on the Judiciary 356
Advice and Consent for Judicial Nominees 361
Supreme Court Nominations 363
The Lower Courts 368
Conclusion 371

Chapter 13 • Congress and Organized Interests **373**

American Pluralism 374
A Capital of Interests 375
A Nation of Joiners 375
Biases of Interest Representation 377
Pressure Group Methods 379
Direct Lobbying 380
Social Lobbying 382
Coalition Lobbying 383
Grassroots Lobbying 384
Digital Lobbying 385
Groups and the Electoral Connection 385
Groups and Campaign Fund-Raising 386
Groups and Advocacy Campaigns 387
Rating Legislators 387
Groups, Lobbying, and Legislative Politics 388
The Role of Money 388
Lobbying and Legislation 389
Subgovernments 390
Regulation of Lobbying 391
The 1946 Lobbying Law 391
The Lobby Disclosure Act of 1995 392
The Honest Leadership and Open Government Act of 2007 393
Foreign Lobbying 393
Conclusion 395

Chapter 14 • Congress, Budgets, and Domestic Policy Making **397**

Stages of Policy Making 398
Setting the Agenda 398
Formulating Policy 400
Adopting Policy 400
Implementing Policy 401
Types of Domestic Policies 402
Distributive Policies 402
Regulatory Policies 405
Redistributive Policies 405

Characteristics of Congressional Policy Making 406

Bicameralism 406

Localism 407

Piecemeal Policy Making 407

Symbolic Policy Making 408

Reactive Policy Making 408

Congressional Budgeting 409

Authorizations and Appropriations 409

Backdoor Spending Techniques 414

The Challenge of Entitlements 414

The 1974 Budget Act 418

Concurrent Budget Resolution 419

Reconciliation 422

A Revised Budget Process 423

Conclusion 425

Chapter 15 • Congress and National Security Policies **427**

Constitutional Powers 430

The President Proposes 430

Congress Reacts 432

Who Speaks for Congress? 433

Types of Foreign and National-Security Policies 435

Structural Policies 436

The Military–Industrial–Congressional Complex 437

Trade Politics 439

Strategic Policies 443

The Power of the Purse 443

Treaties and Executive Agreements 444

Other Policy-Making Powers of Congress 446

Crisis Policies: The War Powers 447

Constitutional Powers 448

The War Powers Resolution 449

Changes in Warfare 451

Conclusion 453

PART V • CONCLUSION

Chapter 16 • The Two Congresses and the American People **455**

Congress as Politicians 457

Members' Bonds With Constituents 457

Questions of Ethics 459

Congress as Institution   461
    Policy Success and Stalemate   463
    Assessing the Congressional Process   463
    Media Coverage   468
    Citizens' Attitudes Toward Congress   468
Twenty-First-Century Challenges   471
    Security   471
    Checks and Imbalances?   471

Appendix A: Party Control: Presidency, Senate, House, 1901–2021   **A1**

Appendix B: Internships: Getting Experience on Capitol Hill   **A5**

Suggested Readings   **S1**

Notes   **N1**

Index   **I1**

TABLES, FIGURES, AND BOXES

TABLES

Table 4-1 Reelection Rates in the House and Senate, by Decade, 1950s–2000s, Plus 2012–2018   94

Table 6-1 Party Committees in the Senate and House   166

Table 7-1 Standing Committees of the House and Senate, 116th Congress, 2019–2021   180

Table 7-2 House and Senate Committee Comparison   189

Table 8-1 Open, Closed, and Structured Rules, 103rd–115th Congresses (1993–2018)   235

Table 11-1 Growth of the Cabinet   325

Table 12-1 Judgeship Appointments by President, 1933–2018   362

Table 12-2 Supreme Court Nominations Not Confirmed by the Senate   366

Table 16-1 High Approval for Members, Low Approval for Congress   470

FIGURES

Figure 2-1 Length of Service in House and Senate, 1789–2019   35

Figure 3-1 House Apportionment: Change from 2000 to 2010 Census   42

Figure 4-1 The Democratic Congressional Campaign Committee's Recommended Daily Schedule for New Members, 2013   73

Figure 4-2 Average Campaign Expenditures for Incumbents, Challengers, and Open-Seat Candidates: House and Senate, 1974–2016   78

Figure 4-3 Turnout in Presidential and Congressional Elections, 1946–2018   87

Figure 4-4 Seats in Congress Gained or Lost by the President's Party in Presidential Election Years, 1932–2016   91

Figure 4-5	Midterm Fortunes of Presidential Parties, 1934–2018	91
Figure 4-6	Who Were the Voters in 2018?	97
Figure 4-7	Share of Republicans in Congress by State Delegation	101
Figure 5-1	House and Senate Margins of Victory, 1974–2018	123
Figure 6-1	Organization of the House of Representatives, 116th Congress, 2019–2021	141
Figure 6-2	Organization of the Senate, 116th Congress, 2019–2021	153
Figure 8-1	How a Bill Becomes Law	221
Figure 9-1	Party Unity Votes in House, Senate, and Congress, 1953–2018	273
Figure 9-2	Average Party Unity Scores in the House and Senate, 1956–2018	274
Figure 9-3	Ideological Divisions in Congress and the Public	280
Figure 9-4	Presidential Success History, 1953–2018	284
Figure 11-1	The Government of the United States	324
Figure 11-2	Political Appointees by Appointment Type, 2018	330
Figure 11-3	Number of Documents (Final Rules) Published in the Federal Register, 1996–2017	337
Figure 14-1	Federal Spending by Major Category, Fiscal Years 1965 and 2018	415
Figure 16-1	Public Assessments of the Two Congresses, 1992–2018	469

BOXES

Box 3-1	What Is a *Legislature*?	46
Box 3-2	Who Should Be Counted for Political Equality: Total Population or Eligible Voters?	49
Box 3-3	Origins of the Gerrymander	51
Box 7-1	How to Get the Committee Assignment You Want	191
Box 7-2	Party Assignment Committees	195
Box 7-3	Committee Decision Making: A Formal Model	200
Box 8-1	Types of Legislation	223

Box 8-2	Rules and Referral Strategy	230
Box 8-3	Example of a Rule from the Committee on Rules	237
Box 8-4	Examples of Creative Rules	238
Box 8-5	Example of a Unanimous-Consent Agreement	248
Box 8-6	Senate Rule XIV: Bypassing Committee Referral	250
Box 11-1	Lifting of Objection	327
Box 11-2	The Rulemaking Process	334
Box 13-1	Some Theories on Interest Group Formation	378
Box 13-2	The Honest Leadership and Open Government Act of 2007	394
Box 14-1	A Budget Glossary	410
Box 14-2	The Congressional Budget Timetable	420
Box 16-1	Congressional Ethics	462

PREFACE

As authors of the seventeenth edition of a book that first appeared in 1981, we are perforce believers in the maxim that in politics six months is a long time and four years practically a lifetime. Events of recent years surely bear out this wisdom. The roller-coaster reversals of government and politics require frequent updates of any text on the U.S. Congress that aims to be both current and comprehensive.

The 2018 midterm elections brought a new Democratic majority to the House of Representatives. Even as Republicans held onto the Senate, the forty-seat Democratic gain in the House served as a startling reversal for President Donald Trump. Republicans had enjoyed unified party control of government during President Trump's tumultuous first two years in office. Trump and the GOP's congressional leadership entered the 115th Congress (2017–2019) eager to seize their opportunity to transform a range of government policies. While Republicans succeeded in passing a major tax cut, rolling back several Obama-era regulations, and moving the courts in a conservative direction, several other Republican priorities—most prominently repeal of Obamacare—faltered.

Democrats' capture of the House brings about a return to divided government. Since 1980, divided government has been the typical condition, with opposing parties controlling the White House and at least one chamber of Congress nearly 75 percent of the time. Trump's midterm setback fits a recurrent pattern in which a president's opportunity for major policy departures typically declines over time. Each of Trump's three immediate predecessors—Bill Clinton, George W. Bush, and Barack Obama—also endured midterm backlashes that cost their party control of Congress. After an exceptionally productive Congress under unified government in his first two years of office, Obama received what he termed a "shellacking" in the 2010 elections, in which Republicans gained a historic sixty-three seats to retake control of the House of Representatives. Then in 2014 Republicans padded their House majority and recaptured the Senate majority. After 2011, Obama's relations with Congress lurched from crisis to crisis, with impasses threatening to halt federal agency operations or send the government into default. The return of divided government in 2019 has already coincided with an extended government shutdown and the return of aggressive congressional investigations of the president.

The precarious fortunes of recent presidents and congressional majorities are a reminder of the pervasive pluralism of the U.S. political system, with its diverse viewpoints and interests. Presidents and congressional leaders see their perceived mandates collide with the founders' intricate "auxiliary precautions" for preventing majorities from winning quick or total victories. Not the least of the system's attributes is what we call the "two Congresses": Congress is both a conduit for localized interests and a maker of national policy.

In this edition, we discuss new developments and fresh research on nearly every aspect of Congress. When the first edition of this book came out, political scientists were still seeking to explain the decline of party unity in Congress. Today, the strength of partisanship and party leaders is the most salient reality of Capitol Hill. Congress is a vortex of the so-called permanent campaign, in which electioneering is interlocked with the process and content of lawmaking. Individual incumbents work tirelessly for reelection, and just as importantly, the two parties engage in an all-out battle to win or maintain majority control of each chamber. We record shifts in party leaders, the committee system, floor procedures, and the Capitol Hill community. Complex, interdependent relationships with presidents, bureaucrats, and the courts put Congress at the center of the entire federal government.

In the midst of fundamental political change, there remain underlying constants in Congress's character and behavior. Most important is the dual nature of Congress as a collection of career-minded politicians and as a forum for shaping national policy. We employ the two-Congresses theme to explain the details of congressional life as well as scholarly findings about legislators' behavior. Colorful personalities and interesting events are never in short supply when examining Capitol Hill. We strive to describe recent developments and trends; more important, we try to place them in broader historical and conceptual context.

These are troubling times for those of us who believe in representative democracy. True, Congress has, with varying levels of success, absorbed astonishing changes in its membership, partisan control, structural and procedural arrangements, and policy agendas. Yet Congress has all too often retreated from its constitutional mandate to initiate national policy and oversee government operations. Its prerogatives are under siege from executive decision makers, federal judges, and elite opinion makers, who constantly belittle its capacities, ignore its authority, and evade its scrutiny. Lawmakers themselves are to blame for failing to address pressing policy problems, for reinforcing disdain of the institution, and for substituting partisan allegiance for independent judgment and critical thinking. Today's Congress all too often falls short of the founders' vision as the "first branch of government"—for reasons that this book explains.

This edition, like its predecessors, is written for general readers seeking an introduction to the modern Congress as well as for college or university students taking courses on the legislative process or national policy making. We try to present accurate, timely, and readable information, along with insights from scholars and practitioners. Although wrapped around our core theme, the book's chapters are long on analysis. We make no apologies for this. Lawmaking is an arduous, complicated business; those who would understand it must master its details and nuances. At the same time, we hope to convey the energy and excitement of the place. After all, our journalist friends are right: Capitol Hill is the best beat in town.

DIGITAL RESOURCES

SAGE edge for Instructors supports your teaching by making it easy to integrate quality content and create a rich learning environment for students. Learn more at **edge.sagepub.com/davidson17e**.

- **Test banks** provide a diverse range of pre-written options as well as the opportunity to edit any question and/or insert your own personalized questions to effectively assess students' progress and understanding.

- All **tables and figures** from the textbook are included.

ACKNOWLEDGMENTS

We have incurred more debts to friends and fellow scholars than we could ever recount. We thank especially our colleagues at the Congressional Research Service and elsewhere: Christina Bailey, Richard Beth, Ida Brudnick, Maeve Carey, Christopher Davis, C. Lawrence Evans, Louis Fisher, Sam Garrett, Valerie Heitshusen, William Heniff Jr., Henry Hogue, Julie Jennings, Michael Koempel, Emery Lee, Megan Lynch, Jennifer Manning, Elizabeth Rybicki, James Saturno, Judy Schneider, Barbara Schwemle, Jacob Strauss, Jim Thurber, and Donald Wolfensberger. The views and interpretations expressed in this book are in no way attributable to the Congressional Research Service. SoRelle Wyckoff, Emily Hertz, and Sam Trachtman provided valuable research assistance. We wish to thank our reviewers: David A. Bateman, Cornell University; Jim Cottrill, St. Cloud State University; Darin DeWitt, California State University, Long Beach; Harvey L. Schantz, State University of New York, Plattsburgh; Peter L. Francia, East Carolina University; and Linda M. Trautman, Ohio University, Lancaster. The comments of these valued colleagues prompted us to consider new questions, enhance visual presentation of relevant data, and undertake other improvements for the current edition.

Our friends at CQ Press deserve special appreciation. We thank Monica Eckman and Kerstin Christiansen for keeping us on track as we revised the book to reflect the most recent developments. Karin Rathert offered skilled and probing editorial assistance. Veronica Stapleton Hooper supervised the book's production. And we thank Sam Rosenberg for providing photo research.

Our deep appreciation for our families, for their love and support, cannot be fully expressed in words. As a measure of our affection, this book is dedicated to them.

—Roger H. Davidson
Santa Barbara, California

—Walter J. Oleszek
Fairfax, Virginia

—Frances E. Lee
Washington, DC

—Eric Schickler
Berkeley, California
April 2019

ABOUT THE AUTHORS

Roger H. Davidson is professor emeritus of government and politics at the University of Maryland and has served as visiting professor of political science at the University of California, Santa Barbara. He is a senior fellow of the National Academy of Public Administration. During the 1970s, he served on the staffs of reform efforts in both the House (Bolling-Martin Committee) and the Senate (Stevenson-Brock Committee). For the 2001–2002 academic year, he served as the John Marshall chair in political science at the University of Debrecen, Hungary. His books include *Remaking Congress: Change and Stability in the 1990s,* co-edited with James A. Thurber (1995), and *Understanding the Presidency,* 7th ed., co-edited with James P. Pfiffner (2013). Davidson is co-editor with Donald C. Bacon and Morton Keller of *The Encyclopedia of the United States Congress* (1995).

Walter J. Oleszek is a senior specialist in the legislative process at the Congressional Research Service. He has served as either a full-time professional staff aide or consultant to many major House and Senate congressional reorganization efforts beginning with passage of the Legislative Reorganization Act of 1970. In 1993 he served as policy director of the Joint Committee on the Organization of Congress. A former adjunct faculty member at American University, Oleszek is a frequent lecturer to various academic, governmental, and business groups. He is the author or co-author of several books, including *Congressional Procedures and the Policy Process,* 11th ed. (2020), and *Congress Under Fire: Reform Politics and the Republican Majority,* with C. Lawrence Evans (1997).

Frances E. Lee is professor of politics and public affairs in the Woodrow Wilson School and the Department of Politics at Princeton University. She has been a research fellow at the Brookings Institution and an APSA congressional fellow. Most recently, she is the author of *Insecure Majorities: Congress and the Perpetual Campaign* (2016). She is also author of *Beyond Ideology: Politics, Principles, and Partisanship in the U.S. Senate* (2009), which received the Richard F. Fenno Jr. Prize for the best book on legislative politics in 2010 and the D. B. Hardeman Prize for the best book on the U.S. Congress published in 2009. She is co-author, with Bruce I. Oppenheimer, of *Sizing Up the Senate: The Unequal Consequences of Equal Representation* (1999). Her articles have appeared in the *American Political Science Review, Journal of Politics, Legislative Studies Quarterly,* and *American Journal of Political Science,* among others.

Eric Schickler is Jeffrey & Ashley McDermott Professor of Political Science at the University of California, Berkeley. He is the author of three books which have won the Richard F. Fenno Jr. Prize for the best book on legislative politics: *Disjointed Pluralism: Institutional Innovation and the Development of the U.S. Congress* (2001), *Filibuster: Obstruction and Lawmaking in the United States Senate* (2006, with Gregory Wawro), and *Investigating the President: Congressional Checks on Presidential Power* (2016, with Douglas Kriner; also winner of the Richard E. Neustadt Prize for the best book on executive politics). His book, *Racial Realignment: The Transformation of American Liberalism, 1932–1965,* was the winner of the Woodrow Wilson Prize for the best book on government, politics, or international affairs published in 2016, and is co-winner of the J. David Greenstone Prize for the best book in history and politics from the previous two calendar years. He is also the co-author of *Partisan Hearts and Minds,* which was published in 2002.

Representative Joe Crowley, D-N.Y., speaks during a news conference at the U.S. Capitol. Congressional candidate Alexandria Ocasio-Cortez helps get out the vote for the New York progressive ticket. Posters for Ocasio-Cortez's primary challenge against Crowley. Tweet from Ocasio-Cortez after winning her 2018 primary.

2nd, here's my 1st pair of campaign shoes. I knocked doors until rainwater came through my soles.

Respect the hustle. We won bc we out-worked the competition. Period.

2:52 PM - 29 Jun 2018

59,574 Retweets 321,296 Likes

♡ 5.7K   ⟲ 60K   ♡ 321K

THE TWO CONGRESSES

"Congress is too old, they don't have a stake in the game," said 28-year-old Democratic primary candidate Alexandria Ocasio-Cortez.[1] A Congress in which the average House member was nearly 58 years old, she argued, pays insufficient attention to issues affecting young people and future generations, such as climate change and the rising costs of higher education and housing. "They won't have to deal with 20-foot storm surges, but we will," she noted, referring to current members.[2]

Ironically, Ocasio-Cortez's opponent, Rep. Joe Crowley, D-N.Y., was himself seen as a member of a youthful, next generation of congressional leaders. At age 56, Crowley was more than two decades younger than any other top leader of the House Democratic party. First elected to Congress in 1998—when Ocasio-Cortez was eight years old—Crowley had risen to the number four position in the Democratic leadership hierarchy, on track to make a strong bid for House Speaker should those above him in the ranks retire or be edged aside.[3] No doubt with this prospect in mind, Crowley had launched a national travel schedule in 2018, with April appearances in Cleveland, Seattle, and Chicago and plans for further stops through the summer to raise party funds as well as his own national profile.

But Crowley's ambitions were cut short at the end of June 2018 when he lost his Democratic primary election to Ocasio-Cortez. The outcome surprised almost everyone. Only three weeks before the primary, Crowley's team had shown him a poll where he led his rival by 36 percentage points.[4] As a senior member of the House Ways and Means Committee, Crowley had no shortage of campaign money. He outspent Ocasio-Cortez by a ratio of 18 to 1.[5] A Queens party boss who had not even faced a primary opponent since 2004, Crowley was felled by a millennial community organizer who had never held elected office. It was a decisive defeat. Ocasio-Cortez won by a lopsided margin of 15 percentage points. In January 2019, she was sworn in as the youngest woman to ever serve in the U.S. Congress.

Although surprising and extraordinary, the outcome of the 2018 primary in New York's Fourteenth Congressional District highlights fundamental truths about political representation. The work of Congress is conducted not only on Capitol Hill but also in states and districts hundreds or thousands of miles away. Crowley had distinguished himself in Washington, DC. A mainstream Democrat who also managed to cultivate friendly ties with Wall Street, Crowley was a prolific fundraiser. He was also the last remaining member of a group long viewed as up-and-coming leaders of the Democratic party. With other members, such as Rahm Emanuel, D-Ill., and Chris Van Hollen, D-Md., having moved on to elected offices beyond the House, Crowley had few obvious competitors as a future Democratic leader.[6]

But Crowley's ties to his constituents had frayed. Back in 2004, he bought a home in Arlington, Virginia, and his three New York kids attended Arlington public schools.[7] Meanwhile, the demographics of his district were changing. Young, affluent gentrifiers were moving in, transforming communities in Queens, such as Astoria, Sunnyside, and Woodside. In addition, congressional redistricting after 2010 brought in new neighborhoods Crowley had never represented.[8] Crowley's own political base and background were in Queens, but post-redistricting the Bronx made up 40 percent of his district. An old-fashioned Irish American urban politician, Crowley was an awkward fit for his new district, one of the most diverse in the country, in which 70 percent of residents were nonwhite, including substantial communities of Latino, African, and Asian immigrants. Focused on his national ambitions, Crowley had not kept pace building local connections to his changing district. New York City Council Member Danny Dromm said that he tried to warn Crowley, to no avail. The Queens Democratic machine that Crowley headed "does not know this district," Dromm said.[9]

Ocasio-Cortez was able to take advantage of Crowley's underappreciated vulnerabilities. With Crowley unfamiliar to many of his constituents, Ocasio-Cortez made herself ubiquitous. She pounded the pavement for months, shaking hands and building a network of connections. After she won the primary, she tweeted out a picture of her first pair of campaign shoes, a pair of worn out, hole-filled sneakers, with the caption: "Respect the hustle. We won [because] we out-worked the competition." For his own part, Crowley played into the worst stereotypes of an out-of-touch incumbent when he missed two primary debates in the district, sending surrogates in his place. Just before the primary, the *New York Times* ran an editorial titled, "If You Want to Be Speaker, Mr. Crowley, Don't Take Voters for Granted."[10]

Ocasio-Cortez also took advantage of new media and creative marketing to build her visibility in the constituency. On a limited campaign budget, she relied heavily upon social media, including Instagram, Twitter, and Facebook. Meanwhile, Crowley ran a traditional campaign of glossy mailers and flyers. Ocasio-Cortez's campaign video introducing herself went viral. In it, she detailed her Puerto Rican heritage, working class background, and deep roots in New York City. Crowley's campaign video, by contrast, had only been viewed

835 times on YouTube as of the primary. Ocasio-Cortez's colorful, nontraditional, eye-catching campaign flyers echoed those of Cesar Chavez and Dolores Huerta, Latino labor activists of the 1960s.[11] The goal was to brand her as a "revolutionary" leader in contrast to a comfortable political establishment.

Calling her opponent a "corporate Democrat," Ocasio-Cortez eschewed corporate donations and emphasized her reliance on small donors. Whereas Crowley hired consulting firms for canvassing and get out the vote operations, Ocasio-Cortez relied upon activists in organizations such as Bronx Progressives, Black Lives Matter, and Brand New Congress.

Ocasio-Cortez also waged a campaign on an unapologetically progressive set of issue stances. In a district where 41 percent of voters had supported Bernie Sanders in the 2016 presidential primary, Ocasio-Cortez staked out positions in favor of Medicare-for-all, free public college, criminal justice reform, and abolition of the Immigration and Customs Enforcement agency. "If there is any seat in America that is advocating for the abolishment of ICE it should be NY14," she said. "It is a district that is 85 percent Democratic. We have very little to risk by taking bold and ambitious positions."[12] These left-of-center campaign pledges helped to distinguish her from her rival's more mainstream positions and burnished her image for courageous, fresh leadership. After the election, pundits and politicians debated whether her victory signaled a broader leftward shift among Democratic voters. But it is clear that Ocasio-Cortez's victory was based on more than her issue positions. Her district roots, accessibility, style, image, and personal history all bolstered her authenticity as a local representative.

The Crowley/Ocasio-Cortez primary illustrates central themes of this book. No matter how much members of Congress distinguish themselves as lawmakers or Beltway insiders, they also have to distinguish themselves in the eyes of local constituents. There is no question that Crowley had a long career and promising trajectory in Congress, but a successful representative cannot rest on laurels won in Washington. Ambitious potential challengers back in the district are always watching for early signs of weakness. For this reason, lawmakers must win and continually renew bonds of trust with their constituents. These bonds rest on constituents' sense of connection to their representatives. Members must maintain personal relationships and open lines of communication. Constituents may not always understand the details of national policy debates, but they know whom they trust—and whom they doubt.

THE DUAL NATURE OF CONGRESS

Joe Crowley's surprising defeat underscores the dual nature of Congress. Members of Congress must continually inhabit two very different but closely linked worlds. There is the diverse world of New York's Fourteenth Congressional District, one that encompasses both white-ethnic and young hipster communities in Queens as well as Latino and African American communities in the Bronx. Then, there is the world of Washington policy making, where Crowley had cultivated a reputation as one of the Democratic Party's up-and-coming leaders. The balance is often difficult to strike. Such tensions highlight the dual character of the national legislature—Congress as a lawmaking institution and Congress as an assembly of local representatives.

In this sense, there are two Congresses. One is the Congress of textbooks, of "how a bill becomes a law." It is Congress acting as a collegial body, performing constitutional duties, and debating legislative issues that affect the entire nation. This Congress is a fascinating arena in which all of the forces of U.S. political life converge—presidents, cabinet members, career bureaucrats, activists, lobbyists, policy wonks, military leaders, and ambitious political entrepreneurs of every stripe. This Congress is more than a collection of its members at any given time. It is a mature institution with a complex network of rules, organizations, and traditions. Norms mark the boundaries of the legislative playing field and define the rules of the game. Individual members generally must accept Congress on its own terms and conform to its established ways of doing things.

A second Congress exists as well, and it is every bit as important as the Congress portrayed in textbooks. This is the representative assembly of 541 individuals (100 senators, 435 representatives, 5 delegates, and 1 resident commissioner). This Congress includes men and women of many different ages, backgrounds, and routes to office, all doing what is necessary to maintain political support in their local constituencies. Their electoral fortunes depend less on what Congress produces as a national institution than on the policy positions they take individually and the local ties they build and maintain. "As locally elected officials who make national policy," observes Paul S. Herrnson, "members of Congress almost lead double lives."[13]

The two Congresses are, in many ways, separated by a wide gulf. The complex, often insular world of Capitol Hill is far removed from most constituencies, in perspective and outlook as well as in miles. Lawmaking and representing are separate tasks, and members of Congress recognize them as such. Yet these two Congresses are bound together. What affects one affects the other—sooner or later.

Legislators' Tasks

The duality between institutional and individual duties permeates legislators' daily activities and roles. As Speaker Sam Rayburn, D-Tex., once remarked, "A congressman has two constituencies—he has his constituents at home, and his colleagues here in the House. To serve his constituents at home, he must also serve his colleagues here in the House."[14]

No problem vexes members more than that of juggling constituency and legislative tasks. For maintaining local connections, members know that there is no substitute for being present in their states and district. Congressional calendars allow for lengthy recesses, termed district work periods, and most legislative weeks are scheduled from Tuesday to Thursday. "I can tell you based on my experience . . . that time spent in our districts is not 'time off,'" observed Rep. Rob Bishop, R-Utah.[15] On average, between 2010 and 2019, Congress was in session for 104 days a year, about one out of every three days.[16] Members spend much of the rest of their time at home among their constituents.

Reelection is the paramount operational goal of members of Congress. As a former representative put it, "All members of Congress have a primary interest in getting reelected. Some members have no other interest."[17] After all, politicians must win elections before they can achieve any long-range political goals. "[Reelection] has to be the proximate goal of everyone, the goal that must be achieved over and over if other ends are to be entertained," David R. Mayhew observed in *Congress: The Electoral Connection*.[18]

Individual legislators vary in how they balance the twin roles of legislator and representative. Some legislators devote more time and resources to lawmaking while others focus almost entirely on constituency tending. With their longer terms, some senators stress voter outreach and fence mending during the two years before reelection and focus on legislative activities at other times. Yet senatorial contests normally are more competitive and costlier than House races, and many senators now run for reelection all the time—like most of their House colleagues.[19] Most senators and representatives would like to devote more time to lawmaking and other Capitol Hill duties, but the press of constituency business is relentless.[20]

Popular Images

The notion of two Congresses also conforms to the average citizen's perceptions. The public views the U.S. Congress differently from the way it sees individual senators and representatives. Congress, as an institution, is perceived primarily as a lawmaking body. It is judged mainly on the basis of citizens' overall attitudes toward politics, policy processes, and the state of the Union. Do people like the way things are going or not? Do they feel that Congress is carrying out its duties effectively? Are they optimistic or pessimistic about the nation's future?

In contrast with their expectations of Congress as a whole, citizens view their own legislators in great part as agents of local concerns. People judge individual legislators by yardsticks such as communication with constituents, their positions on prominent issues, service to the district, and home style (the way officeholders present themselves in their districts or states). In judging their senators or representatives, voters ponder questions such as "is the legislator trustworthy? Does the legislator communicate well with the state (or district) by being visible in the constituency and offering timely help to constituents? Does the legislator listen to the state (or district) and its concerns?"[21]

The public's divergent expectations of Congress and its members send conflicting signals to senators and representatives. Congress, as a whole, is judged by the processes it uses and the policies it adopts (or fails to adopt), however vaguely voters understand them.[22] But individual legislators are regularly nominated and elected to office on the strength of their personal qualities, the positions they take, and their constituency service. In response to this incongruity, officeholders often adopt a strategy of opening as much space as possible between themselves and those other politicians back in Washington.

The Constitutional Basis

Congress's dual nature—the dichotomy between its lawmaking and representative functions—is dictated by the U.S. Constitution. Congress's mandate to write the nation's laws is found in Article I of the Constitution. By contrast, Congress's representational functions are not specified in the Constitution, although these duties flow from the constitutional provisions for electing senators and House members.

It is no accident that the Constitution's drafters devoted the first article to establishing the legislature and enumerating most of the government's powers. Familiar with the British Parliament's prolonged struggles with the Crown, the authors assumed the legislature would be the chief policy-making body and the bulwark against arbitrary executives. "In republican government, the legislative authority necessarily predominates," observed James Madison in the *Federalist Papers*.[23]

Although, in the ensuing years, the initiative for policy making has shifted many times between the legislative and executive branches, the U.S. Congress remains virtually the only national assembly in the world that drafts, in detail, the laws it passes instead of simply debating and ratifying measures prepared by the government in power.

The House of Representatives was intended to be the most representative element of the U.S. government. House members are elected directly by the people for two-year terms to ensure that they do not stray too far from popular opinion. As Madison explained, the House should have "an immediate dependence on, and an intimate sympathy with, the people."[24] For most representatives, this two-year cycle means nonstop campaigning, visiting, and looking after constituents.

The Senate was initially one step removed from popular voting. Some of the Constitution's framers hoped the Senate would temper the popular passions expressed in the House, so under the original Constitution, state legislatures selected senators. But this original vision was ultimately overruled in favor of a Senate that, like the House, directly expresses the people's voice. In 1913, the Seventeenth Amendment to the Constitution was adopted, providing for direct popular election of senators. Although elected for six-year terms, senators must stay in close touch with the electorate. Like their House colleagues, senators typically regard themselves as constituency servants. Most have transformed their office staffs into veritable cottage industries for generating publicity and handling constituents' inquiries.

Thus, the Constitution and subsequent historical developments affirm Congress's dual functions of lawmaker and representative assembly. Although the roles are tightly bound together, they nonetheless impose separate duties and functions.

Back to Burke

On November 3, 1774, in Bristol, England, the British statesman and philosopher Edmund Burke set forth in a speech the dual character of a national legislature. The constituent-oriented parliament, or Congress, he described as

> a Congress of ambassadors from different and hostile interests, which interests each must maintain, as an agent and advocate, against other agents and advocates.

The parliament of substantive lawmaking he portrayed in different terms. It was

> a deliberative assembly of one nation, with one interest, that of the whole—where not local purposes, not local prejudices, ought to guide, but the general good, resulting from the general reason of the whole.[25]

Burke preferred the second concept and did not hesitate to let his voters know it. He would give local opinion a hearing, but his judgment and conscience would prevail in all cases. "Your faithful friend, your devoted servant, I shall be to the end of my life," he declared. "A flatterer you do not wish for."[26]

Burke's Bristol speech is an enduring statement of the dilemma legislators face in balancing their two roles. Burke was a brilliant lawmaker. (He even sympathized with the cause of the American colonists.) But, as might be said today, he suffered from an inept home style. His candor earned him no thanks from his constituents, who turned him out of office at the first opportunity.

Burke's dilemma applies equally on this side of the Atlantic. U.S. voters tend to prefer their lawmakers to be delegates who listen carefully to constituents and follow their guidance. During an encounter in Borger, Texas, an irate Baptist minister shouted at then-representative Bill Sarpalius, D-Tex., "We didn't send you to Washington to make intelligent decisions. We sent you to represent us."[27] Sarpalius was later defeated for reelection.

Representing local constituents is not the whole story, of course. Burke's idea that legislators are trustees of the nation's common good is still extolled. In a 1995 decision, U.S. Supreme Court Justice John Paul Stevens noted that, once elected, members of Congress become "servants of the people of the United States. They are not merely delegates appointed by separate states; they occupy offices that are integral and essential components of a single national Government."[28]

Many talented individuals seek public office, often forgoing more lucrative opportunities in the private sector, precisely because they believe strongly in a vision of what government should do and how it should do it. For such legislators, winning office is a means to a larger end. It is reasonable to assume that elected officials "make an honest effort to achieve good public policy."[29]

Burke posed the tension between the two Congresses so vividly that we have adopted his language to describe the conceptual distinction that forms the crux of this book. From Burke, we have also drawn the titles for Part II, "A Congress of Ambassadors," and Part III, "A Deliberative Assembly of One Nation." Every member of Congress, sooner or later, must come to terms with Burke's dichotomy; citizens and voters will also have to form their own answers.

THE TWO CONGRESSES IN COMPARATIVE CONTEXT

A look around the world reveals that most democracies differ from the United States in how they elect legislators. Members of Congress are selected by means of the oldest form of elected democratic representation: a plurality vote within geographic constituencies. By contrast, most other advanced democracies elect legislative representatives under systems of proportional representation (PR), a more recent innovation in democratic institutions. Many varieties of PR are in use, but compared with the U.S. electoral system, these systems tend to tie legislators more closely to their political parties than to local constituencies. In this way, PR systems somewhat alleviate the difficult trade-offs that members of Congress face as they attempt to balance national lawmaking with attention to local constituencies.

PR systems rest on the basic principle that the number of seats a political party wins in the legislature should be proportional to the level of support it receives from voters. If a political party wins 40 percent of the vote overall, then it should receive about 40 percent of the seats. In other words, these systems explicitly assume that political parties are more important than geographic locales to voters' values and political interests.[30] Most commonly in these systems, the parties put lists of candidates before the electorate. The number of a party's candidates to be seated in the legislature from those lists then depends on the percentage of voters supporting that party in legislative elections. To a greater extent than is true of members of the U.S. Congress, candidates elected in PR systems thus serve as representatives of their party's policy goals and ideological commitments.

Legislators in PR systems face fewer dilemmas about how to balance local constituency politics with national party platforms. Indeed, some PR systems, such as those in Israel and the Netherlands, do not tie representatives to local geographic constituencies at all; legislators represent the entire nation. Other countries, such as Austria and Sweden, elect multiple representatives from regional districts. Such districts are not captured by a single party on a winner-take-all basis. (This is the system used in the United States, where each constituency has only one representative.) Districts in which more than one political party enjoys a meaningful level of voter support will elect representatives from more than one party, with each legislator representing those voters who supported his or her party. Some countries, such as Germany, Italy, and New Zealand, use a mixed system, with some representatives elected in individual geographic constituencies and others drawn from party lists to ensure proportionality. In all "PR" cases, citizens and legislators alike recognize that the system is primarily designed to ensure that voters' party preferences are proportionally represented.

Members of the U.S. Congress, by contrast, officially represent all residents of their geographic constituency—a difficult task. The constituents grouped together within congressional districts often have little in common. Indeed, constituencies can be very diverse in terms of race, class, ethnicity, religion, economic interests, and urbanization. The largest states are often microcosms of the nation. Some constituencies are narrowly divided in terms of partisanship and ideology, forcing representatives to cope with continual local controversy about their stances on national issues. Some members of Congress face the challenge of representing constituents who lean toward the opposing party.

In attempting to represent their whole state or district, some senators and House members attempt a "lowest common denominator" form of representation, de-emphasizing their party affiliation and their opinions on controversial national issues. Instead, they advertise their personal accessibility to constituents, focus on narrow, localized concerns, and dodge hot-button questions whenever they can.[31] This strategy is most appealing to members representing swing or cross-pressured states and districts. But, to an important extent, the U.S. system of representation encourages a focus on parochial matters among lawmakers generally. Members see themselves, at least to some degree, as attorneys for their constituencies.

Even though the U.S. system of representation does not recognize the importance of political parties in the way that PR systems do, members of Congress have nevertheless become far more closely tied to their parties in recent decades. Lawmakers vote with their parties much more reliably than they did in the 1950s and 1960s. The sources of this increased partisanship are many, but it has corresponded with an increasingly partisan ideological polarization in the activist base of both political parties. "The American public has become more consistent and polarized in its policy preferences over the past several decades," writes Alan I. Abramowitz, "and this increase in consistency and polarization has been concentrated among the most politically engaged citizens."[32] At the same time, the politically engaged public has also sorted itself into more ideologically coherent political parties, with fewer liberals identifying with the Republican Party and fewer conservatives identifying with the Democratic Party.[33] Consequently, relatively few voters split their tickets today by voting for one party's presidential candidate and another party's congressional candidate. These trends have reduced the cross-pressures that members face as they attempt to balance their roles as constituency representatives and national policy makers. More members are able to cooperate with their national party leaders without endangering the support of an electoral majority in their constituency. At the same time, a body of members responding to this more polarized activist base may have a harder time engaging in genuine deliberation and crafting workable legislative compromises.

All members must constantly cultivate the local roots of their power as national legislators. Yet Congress is one body, not two. The same members who attempt to forge national legislation in committee and on the floor must rush to catch planes back to their districts, where they are plunged into a different world of local problems and personalities. The same candidates who sell themselves at shopping centers also shape the federal budget or military weapons systems in the nation's capital. The unique character of Congress arises directly from its dual role as a representative assembly and a lawmaking body.

DIVERGENT VIEWS OF CONGRESS

Congress is subject to intense scrutiny, as the huge array of books, monographs, blogs, and articles devoted to it attest. Many of its features make Congress a favorite object of scholarly attention. For one thing, it is relatively open and accessible, so it can be approached by traditional means—journalistic stories, case studies, normative assessments, and historical accounts. It is also amenable to the analytic techniques of social science. Indeed, the availability of quantitative indicators of congressional work (floor votes, for example) permits elaborate statistical analyses. Its rule-governed processes allow it to be studied with sophisticated formal models. And Congress is, above all, a fascinating place—the very best location from which to view the varied actors in the U.S. political drama.

Writers of an interpretive book on the U.S. Congress thus can draw on a multitude of sources, an embarrassment of riches. In fact, studies of Congress constitute a vast literature. This is a mixed blessing because all of this information must be integrated into a coherent whole. Moreover, the scholarly writing is often highly detailed, technical, and theoretical. We have tried to put such material in perspective, make it accessible to all interested readers, and use illustrative examples wherever possible.

Meanwhile, a gaping chasm exists between this rich scholarly literature and the caricature of Congress prevalent in the popular culture. Humorists from Mark Twain and Will Rogers to Stephen Colbert, John Oliver, Jimmy Kimmel, and Samantha Bee have found Congress an inexhaustible source of raw material. Citizens tend to share this disdain toward the legislative branch—especially at moments of furor over, say, ethics scandals or difficult legislative fights. When legislators are at home with constituents, they often reinforce Congress's poor image by portraying the institution as out-of-touch with reality. As Richard F. Fenno puts it, members "run *for* Congress by running *against* Congress."[34]

The picture of Congress conveyed by the media is scarcely more flattering. Journalistic hit-and-run specialists perpetuate a cartoon-like stereotype of Congress as "a place where good ideas go to die in a maelstrom of bureaucratic hedging and rank favor-trading."[35] News magazines, editorial writers, and nightly news broadcasts regularly portray Congress as an irresponsible and somewhat disreputable gang, reminiscent of Woodrow Wilson's caustic description of the House as "a disintegrated mass of jarring elements."[36]

To comprehend how the two Congresses function—both the institution and individual members—popular stereotypes must be abandoned and the complex realities examined. Citizens' ambivalence toward the popular branch of government—which goes back to the beginnings of the republic—says something about the milieu in which public policy is made. We believe we know our subject well enough to appreciate Congress's foibles and understand why it works the way it does, yet we try to maintain a professional, scholarly distance from it.

According to an old saying, two things should never be viewed up close: making sausages and making laws. Despite this warning, we urge readers to take a serious look at the workings of Congress and form their own opinions. Some may recoil from what they discover. Numerous flaws can be identified in members' personal or public behavior, in their priorities and incentive structures, and in lawmaking processes generally. Recent Congresses especially have displayed troubling tendencies, including rushed legislation, extreme partisanship, frequent gridlock, and abdication of legislative power to the executive branch.[37]

Yet careful observers will also discover much behavior in Congress that is purposeful and principled and many policies that are reasonable and workable. We invite students and colleagues to examine with us what Congress does and why—and to ponder its values and its prospects.

MANDEL NGAN/AFP/Getty Images

Thomas Ustick Walter

Library of Congress

Refreshing Congress. The United States Capitol Dome was constructed more than 150 years ago from a design by architect Thomas U. Walter. The Dome recently underwent a major renovation to restore its original grandeur, which had been gradually eroded by age and weather. Just as the physical appearance of the Capitol has undergone many changes over the years, the institutions of Congress have developed over many decades as members have adapted to new challenges and opportunities.

EVOLUTION OF THE MODERN CONGRESS

The first Congress met in New York City in the spring of 1789. Business couldn't begin until April 1, when a majority of the fifty-nine House members finally arrived to make a quorum. Members then chose Frederick A. C. Muhlenberg of Pennsylvania as Speaker of the House. Five days later, the Senate achieved its first quorum, although its presiding officer, Vice President John Adams, did not arrive for another two weeks.

New York City, the seat of government, was then a bustling port on the southern tip of Manhattan Island. Congress met in Federal Hall at the corner of Broad and Wall Streets. The House of Representatives occupied a large chamber on the first floor and the Senate a more intimate chamber upstairs. The new chief executive, George Washington, was still en route from Mount Vernon, his plantation in Virginia; his trip had become a triumphal procession, with crowds and celebrations at every stop. To most of his countrymen, Washington—austere, dignified, the soul of propriety—embodied a government that otherwise was no more than a plan on paper.

The two houses of Congress did not wait for Washington's arrival. The House began debating tariffs, a perennial legislative topic. In the Senate, Vice President Adams, a brilliant but self-important man, prodded his colleagues to decide on proper titles for addressing the president and himself. Adams was dubbed "His Rotundity" by a colleague who thought the whole discussion absurd.

On inaugural day, April 30, Adams was still worrying about how to address the president when the representatives, led by Speaker Muhlenberg, burst into the Senate chamber and seated themselves. Meanwhile, a special committee was dispatched to escort Washington to the chamber for the ceremony. The swearing-in was conducted on an outside balcony in front of thousands of assembled citizens.[1] Then, the nervous Washington reentered the Senate chamber and haltingly read his inaugural address. After the speech, everyone adjourned to nearby St. Paul's Chapel for a special prayer service. Thus, the U.S. Congress became part of a functioning government.[2]

ANTECEDENTS OF CONGRESS

The legislative branch of the new government was untried and unknown, searching for procedures and precedents. And yet, it grew out of a rich history of development—stretching back more than five hundred years in Great Britain and no less than a century and a half in North America. If the architects of the U.S. Constitution of 1787 were unsure of how well their new design would work, they had firm ideas about what they intended.

The English Heritage

The evolution of representative institutions on a national scale began in medieval Europe. Monarchs gained power over large territories where inhabitants were divided into social groupings, called *estates of the realm*—among them, the nobility, clergy, landed gentry, and town officials. The monarchs brought together the leaders of these estates, not to create representative government but to fill the royal coffers.

These assemblies later came to be called parliaments, from the French *parler,* "to speak." Historians and political scientists have identified four distinct stages in the evolution of the assemblies of estates into the representative legislatures of today. The first stage saw the assemblies representing the various estates gathering merely to vote taxes for the royal treasury; they engaged in little discussion. During the second stage, these tax-voting bodies evolved into bodies that presented the king with petitions for redressing grievances. In the third stage, by a gradual process that culminated in the revolutions of the seventeenth and eighteenth centuries, parliaments wrested lawmaking and tax-levying powers from the king. In the fourth and final stage, during the nineteenth and twentieth centuries, parliamentary representation expanded beyond the older privileged groups to embrace all adult men and women.[3]

By the time the New World colonies were founded in the 1600s, the struggle for parliamentary rights was well advanced into the third stage, at least in England. Bloody conflicts, culminating in the beheading of Charles I in 1649 and the dethroning of James II in the Glorious Revolution of 1688, established parliamentary influence over the Crown.

Out of the struggles between the Crown and Parliament flowed a remarkable body of political and philosophic writings. By the eighteenth century, works by James Harrington (1611–1677), John Locke (1632–1704), William Blackstone (1723–1780), and the Frenchman Baron de Montesquieu (1689–1755) were the common heritage of educated leaders in North America as well as in Europe.

The Colonial Experience

European settlers in the New World brought this tradition of representative government with them. As early as 1619, the thousand or so Virginia colonists elected twenty-two burgesses—or delegates—to a general assembly. In 1630, the Massachusetts Bay Company established itself as the governing body for the Bay Colony, subject to annual elections. The other colonies followed suit.

Representative government took firm root in the colonies. The broad expanse of ocean shielding America from its European masters fostered autonomy on the part of the colonial assemblies. Claiming prerogatives similar to those of the British House of Commons, these assemblies exercised the full range of lawmaking powers: levying taxes, issuing money, and providing for colonial defense.[4] Legislation could be vetoed by colonial governors (appointed by the Crown in the eight royal colonies), but the governors, cut off from the home government and dependent on local assemblies for revenues and even for their own salaries, usually preferred to reach agreement with the locals. Royal vetoes could emanate from London, but these took time and were infrequent.[5]

Other elements nourished the growth of democratic institutions. Many of the colonists were free-spirited dissidents set on resisting traditional forms of authority, especially that of the Crown. Their self-confidence was bolstered by the readily available land, the harsh frontier life, and—by the eighteenth century—a robust economy. The town meeting form of government in New England and the separatists' church assemblies helped cultivate habits of self-government. Newspapers, unfettered by royal licenses or government taxes, stimulated lively exchanges of opinions.

When Britain decided in the 1760s, following the ruinous French and Indian War, to tighten its rein on the American colonies, it met with stubborn opposition. Colonists asked, Why don't we enjoy the same rights as Englishmen? Why aren't our colonial assemblies legitimate governments, with authority derived from popular elections? As British enactments grew increasingly unpopular, along with the governors who tried to enforce them, the locally based legislatures took up the cause of their constituents.

The colonists especially resented the Stamp Act of 1765, which provoked delegates from nine colonies to meet in New York City. There, the Stamp Act Congress adopted a fourteen-point *Declaration of Rights and Grievances*. Although the Stamp Act was later repealed, new import duties levied in 1767 increased customs receipts and enabled the Crown to begin directly paying the salaries of royal governors and other officials, thereby freeing those officials from the influence of colonial assemblies. The crisis worsened in the winter of 1773–1774, when a group of colonists staged a revolt, the Boston Tea Party, to protest the taxes imposed by the Tea Act. In retaliation, the House of Commons closed the port of Boston and passed a series of so-called Intolerable Acts, further tightening royal control.

National representative assemblies in America were born on September 5, 1774, when the First Continental Congress convened in Philadelphia. Every colony except Georgia sent delegates—a varied group that included peaceable souls loyal to the Crown, moderates such as Pennsylvania's John Dickinson, and fire-brands such as Samuel Adams and Paul Revere. Gradually, anti-British sentiment congealed, and Congress passed a series of declarations and resolutions (each colony casting one vote) amounting to a declaration of war against the mother country.[6] After Congress adjourned on October 22, King George III declared that the colonies were "now in a state of rebellion; blows must decide whether they are to be subject to this country or independent."[7]

If the First Continental Congress gave colonists a taste of collective decision making, the Second Continental Congress proclaimed their independence from Britain. When this second Congress convened on May 10, 1775, many colonists had still believed war might be avoided. A petition to King George asking for "happy and permanent reconciliation" was even approved. The British responded by proclaiming a state of rebellion and launching efforts to crush it. Sentiment in the colonies swung increasingly toward independence, and by the middle of 1776, Congress was debating Thomas Jefferson's draft resolution that "these united colonies are, and of right ought to be, free and independent states."[8]

The two Continental Congresses gave birth to national politics in America. Riding the wave of patriotism unleashed by the British actions of 1773–1774, the Congresses succeeded in pushing the sentiments of leaders and much of the general public toward confrontation and away from reconciliation with the mother country. They did so by defining issues one by one and by reaching compromises acceptable to both moderates and radicals—no small accomplishment. Shared legislative experience, in other words, moved the delegates to the threshold of independence. Their achievement was all the more remarkable in light of what historian Jack N. Rakove describes as the "peculiar status" of the Continental Congress, "an extra-legal body whose authority would obviously depend on its ability to maintain a broad range of support."[9]

Eight years of bloody conflict ensued before the colonies won their independence. Meanwhile, the former colonies hastened to form new governments and draft constitutions. Unlike the English constitution, these charters were written documents. All included some sort of bill of rights, and all paid lip service to the doctrine of separating powers among legislative, executive, and judicial branches of government. But past conflicts with the Crown and the royal governors had instilled a fear of all forms of executive authority. So nearly all of the constitutions gave the bulk of powers to their legislatures, effectively creating what one historian termed "legislative omnipotence."[10]

The national government was likewise, as James Sterling Young put it, "born with a legislative body and no head."[11] Strictly speaking, no national executive existed between 1775 and 1789—the years of the Revolutionary War and the Articles of Confederation (adopted in 1781). On its own, Congress struggled to wage war against the world's most powerful nation, enlist diplomatic allies, and manage internal affairs. As the war progressed and legislative direction proved unwieldy, Congress tended to delegate authority to its own committees and to permanent (executive) agencies. Strictly military affairs were placed in the hands of Commander in Chief George Washington, who, at the war's end, returned his commission to Congress in a public ceremony. Considering the obstacles it faced, congressional government was far from a failure. Yet the mounting inability of the all-powerful legislative bodies, state and national, to deal with postwar problems spurred demands for change.

At the state level, Massachusetts and New York rewrote their constitutions, adding provisions for stronger executives. At the national level, the Confederation's frailty led many to advocate what Alexander Hamilton called a more "energetic" government—one with enough authority to implement laws, control currency, levy taxes, dispose of war debts, and, if necessary, put down rebellion. Legislative prerogatives, Hamilton and others argued, should be counterbalanced with a vigorous, independent executive.

In this spirit, delegates from the states convened in Philadelphia on May 25, 1787, authorized to strengthen the Articles of Confederation. Instead, they drew up a wholly new governmental charter.

CONGRESS IN THE CONSTITUTION

The structure and powers of Congress formed the core of the Constitutional Convention's deliberations. The delegates broadly agreed that a stronger central government was needed.[12] But the fifty-five delegates who met in the summer of 1787 in Philadelphia were deeply divided on issues of representation, and more than three months passed before they completed their work. The plan, agreed to and signed on September 17, 1787, was a bundle of compromises. Divergent interests—those of large and small states, landlocked states and those with ports, and Northern and Southern (that is, slaveholding) states—had to be placated in structuring the representational system. The final result was an energetic central government that could function independently of the states but with limited, enumerated powers divided among the three branches.

Powers of Congress

The federal government's powers are shared by three separate branches: legislative, executive, and judicial. Separation of powers was not a new idea. Philosophers admired by the framers of the Constitution, including Harrington, Locke, and especially Montesquieu, had advocated the principle. But the U.S. Constitution's elaborate system of checks and balances is considered one of its most innovative features. The failure of the Articles of Confederation to separate governmental functions was widely regarded as a serious defect, as were the all-powerful legislatures created by the first state constitutions. Thus, the framers sought to create a federal government that would avoid the excesses and instabilities that had marked policy making at both the national and state levels.

Article I of the Constitution embraces many provisions to buttress congressional authority and independence. Legislators have unfettered authority to organize the chambers as they see fit and are accorded latitude in performing their duties. To prevent intimidation, they cannot be arrested during sessions or while traveling to and from sessions (except for treason, felony, or breach of the peace). In their deliberations, members enjoy immunity from any punitive action; for their speech and debate, "they shall not be questioned in any other place" (Article I, section 6).

Despite their worries over all-powerful legislatures, the framers laid down an expansive mandate for the new Congress. Mindful of the achievements of New World assemblies, not to mention the British Parliament's struggles with the Crown, the framers viewed the legislature as the chief repository of the government's powers. Locke had observed that "the legislative is not only the supreme power, but is sacred and unalterable in the hands where the community have placed it."[13] Locke's doctrine found expression in Article I, section 8, which enumerates Congress's impressive array of powers and sets out virtually the entire scope of governmental authority as the eighteenth-century founders understood it. This portion of the Constitution clearly envisions a vigorous legislature as the engine of a powerful government.

Raising and spending money for governmental purposes stand at the heart of Congress's prerogatives. The "power of the purse" was historically the lever by which parliaments gained bargaining advantages over kings and queens. The Constitution's authors, well aware of this lever, gave Congress full powers over taxing and spending.[14]

Financing the government is carried out under Congress's broad mandate to "lay and collect taxes, duties, imposts and excises, to pay the debts and provide for the common defense and general welfare of the United States" (Article I, section 8). Although this wording covered almost all known forms of taxation, there were limitations. Taxes had to be uniform throughout the country; duties could not be levied on goods traveling between states; and "capitation or other direct" taxes were prohibited, unless levied according to population (Article I, section 9). This last provision proved troublesome when the U.S. Supreme Court held in 1895 (*Pollock v. Farmers' Loan and Trust Co.*) that it precluded taxes on incomes. To overcome this obstacle, the Sixteenth Amendment, ratified eighteen years later, explicitly conferred on Congress the power to levy income taxes.

Congressional power over government spending is no less sweeping. Congress is to provide for the "common defense and general welfare" of the country (Article I, section 8). Furthermore, "No money shall be drawn from the Treasury, but in consequence of appropriations made by law" (Article I, section 9). This funding provision is one of the legislature's most potent weapons in overseeing the executive branch.

Congress possesses broad powers to promote the nation's economic well-being and political security. It has the power to regulate interstate and foreign commerce, which it has used to regulate not only trade but also transportation, communications, and such disparate subjects as civil rights and violent crime. The exact limits of the commerce power have been the subject of numerous political and legal battles. As discussed in Chapter 12, the Supreme Court has in recent years sided with conservative foes of an expansive view of the commerce clause, limiting, for example, claims to regulate firearms near schools as affecting commerce. The Commerce Clause does, however, remain a potent instrument for Congress. In addition to its power to regulate commerce, Congress may also coin money, incur debts, establish post offices, build post roads, issue patents and copyrights, provide for the armed forces, and call forth the militia to repel invasions or suppress rebellions.

Although the three branches supposedly are coequal, the legislature is empowered to define the structure and duties of the other two. The Constitution mentions executive departments and officers, but it does not specify their organization or functions, aside from those of the president. Thus, the design of the executive branch, including cabinet departments and other agencies, is spelled out in laws passed by Congress and signed by the president.

The judiciary, too, is a statutory creation. The Constitution provides for a federal judicial system consisting of "one supreme Court, and . . . such inferior courts as the Congress may from time to time ordain and establish" (Article III, section 1). Congress determines the number of justices on the Supreme Court and the number and types of lower federal courts. The outer limits of the federal courts' jurisdiction are delineated in Article III, but Congress must also define their jurisdictions through statute. Moreover, the Supreme Court's appellate jurisdiction is subject to "such exceptions" and "such regulations as the Congress shall make" (Article III, section 2). Congress can also limit the federal courts' discretion in ways other than altering their jurisdiction. Mandatory minimum sentences imposed by statute, for example, limit judges' discretion in imposing prison sentences.

Congress's powers within the federal system were greatly enlarged by the Civil War constitutional amendments—the Thirteenth (ratified in 1865), Fourteenth (ratified in 1868), and Fifteenth (ratified in 1870). The Radical Republicans, who had supported the war and controlled Congress in its aftermath, feared that former Confederate states would ignore the rights of former slaves—the cause over which the war had ultimately been waged. The Civil War amendments were primarily intended to ensure that former slaves would have the rights to vote, to be accorded due process, and to receive equal protection of the laws. Nevertheless, the language of the Fourteenth Amendment was cast broadly, referring to "all persons" rather than only to "former slaves." These amendments also authorized Congress to enforce these rights with "appropriate legislation." As a result, these amendments (and subsequent legislation) greatly expanded the federal government's role relative to the states. Over time, the Civil War amendments effectively nationalized the key rights of citizenship throughout the United States. Through a long series of Court rulings, state governments were eventually required to respect many of the Bill of Rights guarantees that originally applied only to the federal government.

Congress can also be an active partner in foreign relations and national defense. It has the power to declare war, ratify treaties, raise and support armies, provide and maintain a navy, and make rules governing the military forces—including those governing "captures on land and water." Finally, Congress is vested with the power "to make all laws which shall be necessary and proper for carrying into execution the foregoing powers" (Article I, section 8).

Limits on Legislative Power

The very act of enumerating these powers was intended to limit government, for, by implication, those powers not listed were prohibited. The Tenth Amendment reserves to the states or to the people all those powers neither delegated nor prohibited by the Constitution. This guarantee has long been a rallying point for those who take exception to particular federal policies or who wish broadly to curtail federal powers.

Eight specific limitations on Congress's powers are noted in Article I, section 9. The most important bans are against bills of attainder, which pronounce a particular individual guilty of a crime without trial or conviction and impose a sentence, and ex post facto laws, which make an action a crime after it has been committed or otherwise alter the legal consequences of some past action. Such laws are traditional tools of authoritarian regimes.

The original Constitution contained no bill of rights. Pressed by opponents during the ratification debate, supporters of the Constitution promised early enactment of amendments to remedy this omission. The resulting ten amendments, drawn up by the First Congress (James Madison was their main author) and ratified December 15, 1791, are a basic charter of liberties that limit the reach of government. The First Amendment prohibits Congress from establishing a national religion, preventing the free exercise of religion, or abridging the freedoms of speech, press, peaceable assembly, and petition. Other amendments secure the rights of personal property and fair trials and prohibit arbitrary arrest, questioning, or punishment.

Rights not enumerated in the Bill of Rights are not necessarily denied (Ninth Amendment). In fact, subsequent amendments, legislative enactments, judicial rulings, and states' actions have enlarged citizens' rights to include the rights of citizenship, of voting, of privacy, and of "equal protection of the laws."

It should also be noted that the political process itself is a significant limit on the use of government powers, even those clearly granted in Article I, section 8. As Madison noted in *Federalist* No. 51, "A dependence on the people is, no doubt, the primary control on the government."[15]

Separate Branches, Shared Powers

The Constitution not only lists Congress's powers but also sets them apart from those of the other two branches. Senators and representatives, while in office, are prohibited from serving in other federal posts; those who serve in such posts are, in turn, forbidden from serving in Congress (Article I, section 6). This restriction forecloses any form of parliamentary government in which leading members of the dominant party or coalition form a cabinet to direct the ministries and other executive agencies.

Because the branches are separated, some people presume that their powers should be clearly distinct as well. In practice, however, governmental powers are interwoven. Madison explained that the Constitution created not a system of separate institutions performing separate functions but separate institutions that share functions, so that "these departments be so far connected and blended as to give each a constitutional control over the others."[16]

Historically, presidents, Congress, and the courts have reached accommodations to exercise the powers they share. As Justice Robert Jackson noted in 1952, "While the Constitution diffuses power the better to secure liberty, it also contemplates that practice will integrate the dispersed powers into a workable government."[17]

Legislative–Executive Interdependence

Each branch of the U.S. government needs cooperation from its counterparts. Although the Constitution vests Congress with "all legislative powers," these powers cannot be exercised without the involvement of the president and the courts. This same interdependency applies to executive and judicial powers.

The president is a key figure in lawmaking. According to Article II, the president "shall from time to time give to the Congress information on the state of the Union, and recommend to their consideration such measures as he shall judge necessary and expedient." Although Congress is not required to consider the president's legislative initiatives, the president's State of the Union address profoundly shapes the nation's political agenda. In the modern era, Congress has "enacted in some form roughly six in ten presidential initiatives."[18] The Constitution also grants the president the power to convene one or both houses of Congress in a special session.

The president's ability to veto congressional enactments influences both the outcome and content of legislation. After a bill or resolution has passed both houses of Congress and has been delivered to the White House, the president must sign it or return it within ten days (excluding Sundays). Overruling a presidential veto requires a two-thirds vote in each house. Presidential review might seem to be an all-or-nothing affair. In the words of George Washington, a president "must approve all the parts of a bill, or reject it in toto." Veto messages, however, often suggest revisions that would make the measure more likely to win the president's approval. Furthermore, veto threats allow the president to intervene earlier in the legislative process by letting members of Congress know in advance what measures or provisions will or will not receive presidential support. Considering the extreme difficulty of overriding a president's veto, members of Congress know that White House support for legislation is almost always necessary and so will often incorporate presidential preferences into early drafts of legislation.

Carrying out laws is the duty of the president, who is directed by the Constitution to "take care that the laws be faithfully executed" (Article II, section 3). To this end, as chief executive, the president has the power to appoint "officers of the United States." However, the president's appointment power is limited by the requirement to obtain the Senate's advice and consent for nominees, which has been interpreted as requiring a majority vote in the Senate.[19] The president's executive power is further constrained by Congress's role in establishing and overseeing executive departments and agencies. Because these agencies are subject to Congress's broad-ranging influence, modern presidents have struggled to force them to march to a common cadence.

Even in the realms of diplomacy and national defense—the traditional domains of royal prerogative—the Constitution apportions powers between the executive and legislative branches. Following tradition, presidents are given wide discretion in such matters. They appoint ambassadors and other envoys, negotiate treaties, and command the country's armed forces. However, like other high-ranking presidential appointees, ambassadors and envoys must be approved by the Senate. Treaties do not become the law of the land until they are ratified by a two-thirds vote of the Senate. Although the president may dispatch troops on his own, only Congress may formally declare war. Even in a time of war, Congress still wields formidable powers if it chooses to employ them. Congress can refuse to provide continued funding for military actions, engage in vigorous oversight of the executive branch's military operations, and influence public opinion regarding the president's leadership.[20]

Impeachment

Congress has the power to impeach and remove the president, the vice president, and other "civil officers of the United States" for serious breaches of the public trust: treason, bribery, or "other high crimes and misdemeanors." The House of Representatives has the sole authority to draw up and adopt (by majority vote) articles of impeachment, which are specific charges that the individual has engaged in one of the named forms of misconduct. The Senate is the final judge of whether to convict on any of the articles of impeachment. A two-thirds majority is required to remove the individual from office or to remove and also bar the individual from any future "offices of public trust."

Three attributes of impeachment fix it within the separation-of-powers framework. First, it is exclusively the domain of Congress. (The chief justice of the United States presides over Senate trials of the president, but rulings by the chief justice may be overturned by majority vote.) The two chambers are also free to devise their own procedures for reaching their decisions.[21]

Second, impeachment is essentially political in character. The structure may appear judicial—with the House resembling a grand jury and the Senate a trial court—but lawmakers decide whether and how to proceed, which evidence to consider, and even what constitutes an impeachable offense. Treason is defined by the Constitution, and bribery is defined by statute, but the words "high crimes and misdemeanors" are open to interpretation. They are usually defined (in Alexander Hamilton's words) as "abuse or violation of some public trust"—on-the-job offenses against the state, the political order, or the society at large.[22] According to this definition, they could be either more or less than garden-variety criminal offenses. Both presidential impeachment trials (Andrew Johnson, 1868; Bill Clinton, 1998–1999) were fiercely partisan affairs, in which combatants disputed not only the facts but also the appropriate grounds for impeachment.

Finally, impeachment is a blunt instrument for punishing officials for the gravest of offenses. Congress has many lesser ways of reining in wayward officials. As for presidents and vice presidents, their terms are already limited. Although impeachments are often threatened, only sixteen Senate trials have taken place, and only eight individuals have been convicted. Significantly, all eight who were removed from office were judges, who, unlike executive officers, enjoy open-ended terms of office.[23]

Interbranch "No-Fly Zones"

Although the constitutional system requires that the separate branches share powers, each branch normally honors the integrity of the others' internal operations. Communications between the president and his advisers are mostly (though not entirely) exempt from legislative or judicial review under the doctrine of *executive privilege*. Similarly, Article I places congressional organization and procedures beyond the scrutiny of the other branches. This provision was given new meaning in 2007, when the courts determined that an FBI search of the office of Rep. William J. Jefferson, D-La., who was under investigation for bribery, had been unconstitutional under the Constitution's speech and debate clause.[24] The case established a precedent that members of Congress be provided advance notice and the right to review materials before the execution of a search warrant on their congressional offices.

Judicial Review

The third branch, the judiciary, interprets and applies laws in particular cases, when called upon to resolve disputes. In rare instances, this requires the judiciary to adjudicate a claim that a particular law or regulation violates the Constitution. This is called *judicial review*. Whether the framers anticipated judicial review is open to question. Perhaps they expected each branch to reach its own judgments on constitutional questions, especially those pertaining to its own powers. Whatever the original intent, Chief Justice John Marshall soon preempted the other two branches with his Supreme Court's unanimous assertion of judicial review in *Marbury v. Madison* (1803). Judicial review involves both interpretation and judgment. First, "It is emphatically the province and duty of the judicial department to say what the law is." Second, the Supreme Court has the duty of weighing laws against the Constitution, the "supreme law of the land," and invalidating those that are inconsistent—in *Marbury*, a minor provision of the Judiciary Act of 1789.[25]

Despite the *Marbury* precedent, Congress—not the Court—was the primary forum for weighty constitutional debates until the Civil War. Before 1860, only one other federal law (the Missouri Compromise of 1820) had been declared unconstitutional by the Court (in *Dred Scott v. Sandford,* 1857). Since the Civil War, the Court has been more aggressive in interpreting and judging congressional handiwork. For the record, the Supreme Court has invalidated 182 congressional statutes in whole or in part—the vast majority of these since the start of the twentieth century.[26] This count does not include lower-court holdings that have not been reviewed by the Supreme Court. Nor does it include laws whose validity has been impaired because a similar law was struck down.

Who Is the Final Arbiter?

Congress's two most common reactions to judicial review of its enactments are not responding at all or amending the statute to comply with the Court's holding.[27] Other responses include passing new legislation or even seeking a constitutional amendment.

Reconstruction laws and constitutional amendments after the Civil War explicitly nullified the Court's 1857 holding in *Dred Scott v. Sandford.*[28] More recently, a great deal of legislative ferment has followed the Supreme Court's ruling in *Citizens United v. Federal Election Commission* (2010),[29] a 5–4 decision that held that the First Amendment protects corporate, union, and nonprofit funding of independent political speech.

In some cases, Congress reacts to Supreme Court rulings by simply ignoring them. For example, even though legislative veto provisions were largely outlawed by the Court's decision in *Immigration and Naturalization Service v. Chadha* (1983),[30] Congress continues to enact them, and administrators nevertheless feel obliged to honor them out of political prudence.

The Supreme Court does not necessarily have the last word in saying what the law is. Its interpretations of laws may be questioned and even reversed. One study found that 121 of the Court's interpretive decisions were overridden between 1967 and 1990, an average of ten per Congress. The author of the study concluded that "congressional committees in fact carefully monitor Supreme Court decisions."[31] However, as Congress has become increasingly polarized, forging agreements to override important Court decisions has proven increasingly elusive.[32]

Nor are the courts the sole judges of what is or is not constitutional. Courts routinely accept customs and practices developed by the other two branches. Likewise, they usually decline to decide sensitive political questions within the province of Congress and the executive.

In summary, the courts play a leading but not exclusive role in interpreting laws and the regulations implementing them. When Congress passes a law, the policy-making process has just begun. Courts and administrative agencies then assume the task of refining the policy, but they do so under Congress's watchful eye. "What is 'final' at one stage of our political development," Louis Fisher observes, "may be reopened at some later date, leading to revisions, fresh interpretations, and reversals of Court doctrines."[33]

Bicameralism

Although "the Congress" is discussed as if it were a single entity, Congress is divided internally into two very different, virtually autonomous chambers—that is, it is bicameral. Following the pattern that originated with the British Parliament and was then imitated by most of the states, the Constitution created a bicameral legislature. If tradition recommended the two-house formula, the politics of the early Republic commanded it. The larger states preferred population-based representation, but the smaller states insisted on retaining the equal representation they enjoyed under the Articles of Confederation.

The first branch—as the House was called by framers James Madison and Gouverneur Morris, among others—rests on the idea that the legislature should represent "the many," the people of the United States. As George Mason, another framer, put it, the House "was to be the grand depository of the democratic principles of the government."[34]

By contrast, the composition of the Senate reflected the framers' concerns about controlling excessive popular pressures. Senators were chosen by the state legislatures and not by popular vote. This, in theory, would curb the excesses of popular government. "The use of the Senate," explained Madison, "is to consist in its proceeding with more coolness, with more system, and with more wisdom, than the popular branch."[35]

Senate behavior did not necessarily match up with the framers' theories, however. Even though senators were chosen by state legislatures, they were not insulated from democratic pressures. To be selected, Senate candidates "had to cultivate local party officials in different parts of the state and appeal directly to constituents."[36] Once in office, senators voiced their state's dominant economic interests. They also sponsored private bills for pensions and other relief for individual constituents, doled out federal patronage, and sought committee assignments that would enable them to bring home their state's share of federal money. Recent research has shown that senators selected by state legislators were not substantially different from modern, directly elected senators.[37]

Historical evolution finally overran the framers' intentions. Direct election of senators was ushered in with the Seventeenth Amendment, ratified in 1913. A by-product of the Progressive movement, the new arrangement was designed to broaden citizens' participation and blunt the power of shadowy special interests, such as party bosses and business trusts. Thus, the Senate became directly subject to popular will.

Bicameralism is the most obvious organizational feature of the U.S. Congress. Each chamber has distinct processes for handling legislation. According to the Constitution, each house sets its own rules, keeps a journal of its proceedings, and serves as final judge of its members' elections and qualifications. In addition, the Constitution assigns unique duties to each of the two chambers. The Senate ratifies treaties and approves presidential appointments. The House must originate all revenue measures; by tradition, it also originates appropriations bills.

The two houses jealously guard their prerogatives and resist intrusions by the other body. Despite claims that one or the other chamber is more important—for example, that the Senate has more prestige or that the House pays more attention to legislative details—the two houses staunchly defend their equal places. On Capitol Hill, there is no "upper" or "lower" chamber.

INSTITUTIONAL EVOLUTION

Written constitutions go only a short way toward explaining how real-life governmental institutions work. On many questions, such documents are inevitably silent or ambiguous. Important issues of both power and process emerge and develop only in the course of later events. Political institutions continually change under pressures from public demands, shifting political contexts and the needs and goals of officeholders.

Congress has evolved dramatically over time. "Reconstitutive change" is what Elaine K. Swift calls instances of "rapid, marked, and enduring shift[s] in the fundamental dimensions of the institution."[38] During one such period—1809–1829—Swift argues, the Senate was transformed from an elitist, insulated "American House of Lords" into an active, powerful institution whose debates stirred the public and attracted the most talented politicians of the time. Major reform efforts in Congress have also periodically resulted in bold new departures in process and structure.

Yet much of Congress's institutional development has occurred gradually. Early on, Congress had little formal structure. When the first Congress convened, there were no standing committees. Deliberation about policy issues occurred directly on the floors of the House and Senate, where any interested members could participate. After chamber-wide debate had taken place on a broad issue, members would create temporary ad hoc committees to draft bills. The early Congress also had no formal party leadership organization.[39] Prior to the 1830s, the Federalist and Republican coalitions that existed in Congress were "no more than proto-parties."[40]

Today's Congress is a mature institution characterized by complex internal structures and procedures. It is led by a well-defined party apparatus, with each party organized according to its established rules and headed by a hierarchy of leaders and whips, elected and appointed. Party organization extends to policy committees, campaign committees, research committees, and numerous task forces. Minority and majority party leaders command considerable budget and staff resources. Taken together, they employ some four hundred staff aides, and the various party committees employ about an equal number.[41]

The contemporary Congress also has an elaborate committee system bolstered by a vast body of rules and precedents regulating committee jurisdictions and operations.[42] In the 116th Congress (2019–2021), the Senate has sixteen standing committees, and the House has twenty. But these committees are only the tip of the iceberg. House committees have about one hundred subcommittees; Senate committees possess nearly seventy subcommittees. Four joint House–Senate committees have been retained. All this adds up to some two hundred work groups, plus an abundance of informal caucuses.

A basic concept scholars use to analyze the development of Congress's growth and adaptation is *institutionalization*. Political scientist Nelson W. Polsby applied this concept to track the institution's professionalization of the legislative career; its increasing organizational complexity—the growth of more component parts within the institution (committees, subcommittees, caucuses, and leadership organizations); and its elaboration and observance of formal rules governing internal business.[43] Scholars have identified several important factors that have driven institutional development. Among these are legislative workload, institutional size, conflict with the executive branch, and members' partisan interests.

Workload

Congress's workload—once limited in scope, small in volume, and simple in content—has burgeoned since 1789. Today's Congress grapples with many issues that were once considered entirely outside the purview of governmental activity or were left to states or localities. Approximately ten thousand bills and joint resolutions are introduced in the span of each two-year Congress; from 250 to 500 of them are enacted into law.[44] By most measures—hours in session, committee meetings, and floor votes—the congressional workload doubled between the 1950s and the late 1970s. Legislative business expanded in scope and complexity as well as in sheer volume. The average public bill of the late 1940s was two-and-a-half pages long; the average bill now runs to more than fifteen pages.[45]

Changes in workload have been an important driver of institutional change over the course of congressional history.[46] Many of the earliest committees were established to help Congress manage a growing volume of constituent requests. When the nineteenth-century Congress was deluged with petitions requesting benefits, members created committees, such as Claims, Pensions, and Public Lands, to process requests.[47] Similarly, the creation and, occasionally, the abolition of committees reflect shifting perceptions of public problems. As novel policy problems arose, new committees were added.[48] The House, for example, established Commerce and Manufactures in 1795, Public Lands in 1805, Freedmen's Affairs in 1866, Roads in 1913, Science and Astronautics in 1958, Standards of Official Conduct in 1967, Small Business in 1975, and Homeland Security in 2005. An extensive system of committees allows the contemporary Congress to benefit from a division of labor as it strives to manage a far-reaching governmental agenda.

Congress's growing workload does not come only from outside the institution. From the earliest days to the present, members themselves have contributed to their collective burden. Seeking to make names for themselves, members champion causes, deliver speeches on various subjects, offer floor amendments, refer matters to committees for consideration, and engage in much policy entrepreneurship. All of these activities add to the congressional workload.

The Size of Congress

Like workload, the size of a legislative institution profoundly affects its organization. Legislatures with more members face greater problems of agenda control and time management, unless they adopt mechanisms to manage the participation of their members.[49] The U.S. Congress grew dramatically over time, and this growth created pressure for institutional adaptation.

Looking at the government of 1789 through modern lenses, one is struck by the relatively small circles of people involved. The House of Representatives, that "impetuous council," was composed of sixty-five members—when all of them showed up. The aristocratic Senate boasted only twenty-six members, two from each of the thirteen original states.

As new states were added, the Senate grew, from thirty-two senators in 1800 to sixty-two in 1850; ninety by 1900; and, since 1959, one hundred.

For much of the nation's history, the House grew alongside the nation's population. The House membership was raised to 104 after the first census, and it steadily enlarged throughout the nineteenth century. The 1910 census, which counted 92 million people, led to an expansion to 435 members. After the 1920 census, Congress declined to enlarge the House further. And that is the way things stand to this day. With the population continuing to grow, some worry that House districts have grown too large to allow members to maintain close ties to constituents. This has led to renewed calls to increase the size of the House, though critics worry that an enlarged chamber would be harder to manage.[50]

Growth impelled House members to empower strong leaders, to rely on committees, to impose strict limits on floor debate, and to devise elaborate ways of channeling the flow of floor business. It is no accident that strong leaders emerged during the periods the House experienced the most rapid growth. After the initial growth spurt in the first two decades of the Republic, vigorous leadership appeared in the person of Henry Clay (1811–1814, 1815–1820, and 1823–1825). Similarly, the post–Civil War expansion of the House was met with an era of forceful Speakers that lasted from the 1870s until 1910.

In the smaller and more intimate Senate, vigorous leadership has been the exception rather than the rule. The relative informality of Senate procedures and the long-cherished right of unlimited debate testify to the looser reins of leadership. Compared with the House's complex rules and voluminous precedents, the Senate's rules are relatively brief and simple, putting a premium on informal negotiations among senators interested in a given measure.

Conflict With the Executive Branch

Conflict with the president is a perennial impetus for institutional reform. When Congress cannot collaborate on policy with the executive branch, members seek out ways to increase their capacity for independent action. During such confrontations, Congress creates new institutions and procedures that often endure long beyond the specific contexts that gave rise to them.

One of the most important standing House committees, Ways and Means, was first established to provide a source of financial information independent of the controversial and divisive Treasury secretary at the time, Alexander Hamilton.[51] Similarly, the landmark Legislative Reorganization Act of 1946 was adopted amid members' growing concerns about congressional power. Following the massive growth of the administrative state during the New Deal and World War II, members feared that Congress could simply no longer compete with the executive branch. Reformers saw "a reorganized Congress as a way to redress the imbalance of power that had developed between the branches."[52] The act streamlined the legislative process by dramatically reducing the number of committees and regularizing their jurisdictions. Sen. Owen Brewster, R-Maine, argued at the time that the reforms were necessary "to retain any semblance of the ancient division of functions under our constitution."[53] The act was adopted by a sizable bipartisan majority, with both Republicans and Democrats expressing hope that reform would strengthen Congress's power and prestige.

Another major institutional innovation, Congress's budget process, was fashioned in an environment of intense interbranch warfare between President Richard Nixon and a Democratic Congress.[54] President Nixon's unprecedented assertion of authority to withhold funds that Congress had appropriated was a major stimulus for passage of the Congressional Budget and Impoundment Control Act of 1974. Without the power of the purse, Sen. John Tunney, D-Calif., remarked, "we may as well go out of business."[55] However, the act addressed an array of structural issues that went far beyond the particulars of the dispute over the president's impoundment powers. It established a new internal congressional budget process; new budget committees in both chambers; and a new congressional agency, the nonpartisan Congressional Budget Office (CBO). The goal was to allow Congress to formulate a comprehensive national budget on its own, backed by appropriate estimates and forecasts, without relying on the president's budget or the executive branch's Office of Management and Budget.

In *Federalist* No. 51, Madison justified the Constitution as a system to "divide and arrange the several offices in such a manner as that each may be a check on the other." Congress's institutional development bears the indelible stamp of this checking and balancing, as Congress has repeatedly reformed itself to meet challenges from the executive branch.

Partisan Interests

Political parties had no place in the original constitutional blueprint. However, no account of institutional development in Congress can ignore their vital role. Everything about the organization and operation of Congress is shaped by political parties. Indeed, the first thing a visitor to the House or Senate chamber notices is that the seats or desks are divided along partisan lines—Democrats to the left, facing the dais, and Republicans to the right. Although today's congressional parties are remarkably cohesive and energetic, the goals and capacities of the political parties have been a major engine of change throughout congressional history.

Parties began to develop in Congress during the first presidential administration. When Treasury secretary Alexander Hamilton unveiled his financial program in 1790, a partisan spirit swept the capital. The Federalists, with Hamilton as their intellectual leader, espoused energetic government to deal forcefully with national problems and foster economic growth. The rival Republicans, who looked to Thomas Jefferson and James Madison for leadership, rallied opponents of Federalist policies and championed local autonomy, a weaker national government, and programs favoring agricultural or debtor interests. By 1794, Sen. John Taylor of Virginia could write,

> The existence of two parties in Congress is apparent. The fact is disclosed almost upon every important question. Whether the subject be foreign or domestic—relative to war or peace—navigation or commerce—the magnetism of opposite views draws them wide as the poles asunder.[56]

Although these earliest legislative parties lacked formal organizations, conflicts between Federalists and Republicans shaped Congress's deliberations. Parties also flourished throughout the nineteenth century. Regional conflicts, along with economic upheavals produced by rapid industrialization, nurtured partisan differences. At the grassroots level, the parties were differentiated along class, occupational, and regional lines. Grassroots party organizations were massive and militant. In the context of this vibrant nineteenth-century party system, the majority party gained organizational control over the House of Representatives. Ever since the Civil War, the leader of the House majority party has served as Speaker.[57] By the end of the nineteenth century, strong Speakers had tamed the unruly House, and a coterie of state party bosses dominated the Senate.

Even though parties were weaker during the Progressive era and throughout the middle of the twentieth century, they never became irrelevant. Despite the demise of the strong Speakership (1910), the direct election of senators (1913), and profound divisions in the Democratic majority party between the late 1930s and the 1970s, the parties continued to organize Congress down to the present day.[58] All contemporary House and Senate members receive and retain their committee assignments through the two parties. Likewise, members of the majority party chair all of the standing committees of Congress.

Party politics has impelled the development of floor procedure, members' parliamentary rights, leaders' prerogatives, and agenda control devices. The rules of the legislative process at any given time are, in Sarah A. Binder's words, a "result of hard-nosed partisan battles—fought, of course, under a particular set of inherited institutional rules."[59]

A watershed moment in the development of the House of Representatives, the adoption of Reed's Rules in 1890, offers one of the clearest examples of partisan influence on institutional procedure. Prior to 1890, the minority party in the House possessed an arsenal of dilatory tactics to obstruct the majority party's agenda.[60] Reed's Rules, named for then–House Speaker Thomas Brackett Reed, R-Maine, revolutionized House procedure by granting the Speaker secure control over the order of business and strictly curbing the minority party's ability to obstruct the majority party's floor agenda. Majority party Republicans fought for the adoption of Reed's Rules over strong opposition from the Democrats. At that time, Republicans had just won unified party control of the government for the first time in nearly a decade, and they had an ambitious and controversial agenda. Knowing that Democrats would use their resources to obstruct their program, Republicans changed the rules of the House to permit majority party control over the institution, a fact of life in the House of Representatives since. In procedural terms, Reed's Rules permanently transformed the House of Representatives.

The circumstances surrounding the adoption of Reed's Rules offers a blueprint for many partisan rules changes over the course of House history. Based on a study of all procedural rules changes that benefited the majority party at the expense of the minority party between 1789 and 1990, Binder finds that "crucial procedural choices have been shaped not by members' collective concerns about the institution, but by calculations of partisan advantage."[61] When necessary to overcome minority party obstruction, unified majority parties have repeatedly shown themselves willing to alter the institution's rules to ensure the passage of their agenda.

Members' Individual Interests

Institutional development has been driven by more than members' partisan and institutional goals; members also have individual goals. As individuals, members want to build a reputation as effective lawmakers and representatives. To do so, they must be able to point to achievements of their own. When congressional rules or structures inhibit their ability to do so, pressure builds for institutional reform.

In addition to its value as an institutional division of labor, the elaborate committee system in Congress serves members' individual political needs and policy goals. Because of the multitude of leadership positions created by the numerous committees and subcommittees, nearly every member has an opportunity to make an individual contribution. "Whatever else it may be, the quest for specialization in Congress is a quest for credit," observes David R. Mayhew. "Every member can aspire to occupy a part of at least one piece of policy turf small enough that he can claim personal responsibility for some of the things that happen on it."[62]

The congressional reforms of the 1970s are one example of the ways in which members' individual goals have affected institutional development. Over that decade, the two chambers revamped their committee systems to allow more input from rank-and-file members. The streamlined committee systems that had been put in place after the Legislative Reorganization Act of 1946 offered relatively few committee leadership positions, and those were gained on the basis of seniority. Every committee was led by its longest-serving members, who retained their positions until death, defeat, or retirement. The large classes of new members elected in the 1970s, feeling thwarted by this system, began to press for change.[63] Out of this ferment emerged a variety of reforms that opened up new opportunities for junior members. Among these reforms, the seniority system was weakened as committee chairs were forced to stand for election in their party caucus, making them accountable to the party's rank and file.

The persistence of Senate rules that permit unlimited debate is another example of the ways in which individual goals shape institutional rules.[64] Despite the many frustrations unlimited debate has caused for Senate majority parties over the years, senators have generally been unwilling to embrace changes that would allow for simple majority rule. Senators realize that a great part of their own individual power derives from their ability to take advantage of unlimited debate to block votes on matters that have majority support. Senate leaders are forced to negotiate with senators who threaten to obstruct Senate action via unlimited debate.

Reforms that would make it possible for a Senate majority to force a vote have long been in the interest of the Senate's majority party. But such reforms come at a direct, substantial cost to senators' individual power. Not surprisingly, senators have proven very reluctant to trade off so much of their individual influence in favor of collective party goals. In November 2013, majority party Democrats grew sufficiently frustrated with Republican filibusters of judicial and executive-branch nominations to make a substantial change. The Democratic majority imposed a new precedent allowing a simple majority to end debate on all confirmations for offices other than the Supreme Court. Republicans extended this precedent in April 2017, applying it to Supreme Court nominations in order to confirm Donald Trump's first nominee to the Court, Neil Gorsuch. Even so, most senators have proved loath to establish simple majority rule for legislation, suggesting that senators continue to value their individual prerogatives.[65]

Like everything else about Congress, the institution's rules and procedures can only be fully understood in the context of the two Congresses. Members want rules and processes to serve them as individual lawmakers and representatives as well as to facilitate the functioning of the legislature as a whole.

Changing pressures on the institution, congressional–executive conflicts, partisan agendas, and members' individual goals have all been important drivers of Congress's institutional development. Indeed, significant reforms are almost always the result of several of these forces simultaneously buffeting the institution. One broad-ranging study of forty-two major institutional innovations concludes that institutional reforms are typically brought about through *common carriers,* reform initiatives that are, at once, supported by several different groups of legislators for different sets of reasons.[66] The Legislative Reorganization Act of 1946, for example, was espoused by many legislators who wanted to enhance the power and effectiveness of the legislative branch, but it was also supported by members who valued the new pay and pension benefits included in the legislation.[67] Similarly, many members favored the 1970s reforms reducing the power of committee chairs because they wanted access to more policy turf of their own. At the same time, many liberal members backed the reforms because they wanted to reduce the influence of the disproportionately conservative committee chairs.[68]

Because the same reforms are so often backed for several different reasons, no single theory can explain congressional change. Legislative institutions incorporate internal tensions and contradictions rather than maximize the attainment of any particular goal.[69] Furthermore, reforms inevitably fall short of their sponsors' objectives. Instead of achieving stable, effective arrangements, reforms frequently produce "a set of institutions that often work at cross-purposes."[70] At the same time, innovations usually have unanticipated consequences, which may lead to yet another round of reform.

EVOLUTION OF THE LEGISLATOR'S JOB

What is it like to be a member of Congress? The legislator's job, like the institution of Congress, has evolved since 1789. During the early Congresses, being a senator or representative was a part-time occupation. Few members regarded congressional service as a career, and according to most accounts, the rewards were slim. Since then, lawmakers' exposure to constituents' demands and their career expectations have changed dramatically. Electoral units, too, have grown very large. With the nation's population estimated at some 329 million people, the average House constituency since the 2010 reapportionment consists of more than 750,000 people, and the average state of more than 6 million.

The Congressional Career

During its early years, Congress was an institution composed of transients. The nation's capital was an unsightly place, and its culture was provincial. Members remained in Washington only a few months, spending their unpleasant sojourns in boardinghouses.[71]

The early Congresses failed to command the loyalty needed to keep members in office. Congressional service was regarded more as odious duty than as rewarding work. "My dear friend," a North Carolina representative wrote to a constituent in 1796, "there is nothing in this service, exclusive of the confidence and gratitude of my constituents, worth the sacrifice."[72] Of the ninety-four senators who served between 1789 and 1801, thirty-three resigned before completing their terms, only six to take other federal posts.[73] In the House, almost 6 percent of all early nineteenth-century members resigned during each Congress.

Careerism mounted toward the end of the nineteenth century. As late as the 1870s, more than half of the House members at any given time were freshmen, and the mean length of service was barely two terms. By the end of the century, however, the proportion of newcomers had fallen to 30 percent, and average House tenure had nearly reached three terms or six years. About the same time, senators' mean term of service topped seven years, in excess of one full term.[74]

Today, the average senator has served ten years, and the average House member has served nearly nine. Figure 2-1 shows changes since 1789 in the percentages of new members and the mean number of terms claimed by incumbents. In both the House and Senate, members' average length of service has increased over time, and the proportion of first-termers is substantially lower than it was during the first hundred years of the nation's history.

Rising careerism has a number of causes. The increase in one-party states and districts following the Civil War, especially after 1896, enabled repeated reelection of a dominant party's candidates—Democrats in the South and Republicans in the Midwest and the rural Northeast. Members themselves also began to find congressional service more rewarding. The growth of national government during the twentieth century enhanced the excitement and glamour of the Washington political scene, especially when compared with state or local renown.

The prerogatives accorded to seniority further rewarded lengthy service. Beginning in the late nineteenth century in the Senate and in the early twentieth century in the House, members with the longest tenure in office began to dominate positions of power in Congress. Although seniority norms have been considerably eroded since the 1990s, extended service generally remains a criterion for top party and committee posts. The benefits accruing to seniority continue to compound the returns on long service in the contemporary Congress.

Professionalization

During the Republic's early days, lawmaking was not a full-time occupation. As President John F. Kennedy was fond of remarking, the Clays, Calhouns, and Websters of the nineteenth century could afford to devote a whole generation or more to debating and refining the few great controversies at hand. Rep. Joseph W. Martin, R-Mass., who entered the House in 1925 and went on to become Speaker (1947–1949, 1953–1955), described the leisurely atmosphere of earlier days and the workload changes during his service:

> From one end of a session to another Congress would scarcely have
> three or four issues of consequence besides appropriations bills. And
> the issues themselves were fundamentally simpler than those that surge
> in upon us today in such a torrent that the individual member cannot
> analyze all of them adequately before he is compelled to vote. In my early
> years in Congress the main issues were few enough so that almost any
> conscientious member could with application make himself a quasi-expert
> at least. In the complexity and volume of today's legislation, however,
> most members have to trust somebody else's word or the recommendation
> of a committee. Nowadays bills, which thirty years ago would have been
> thrashed out for hours or days, go through in ten minutes.[75]

FIGURE 2-1 ■ Length of Service in House and Senate, 1789–2019

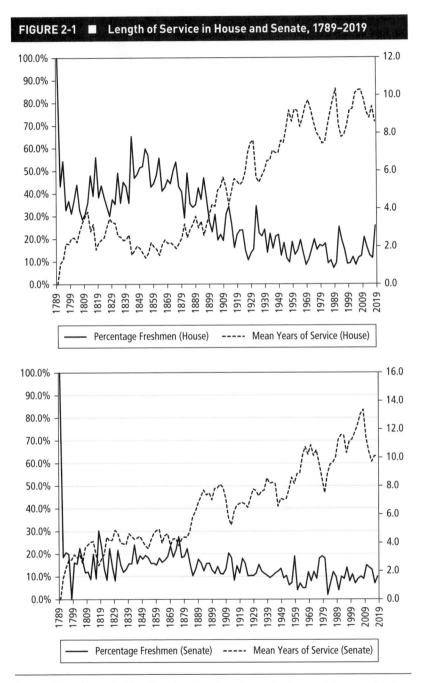

Percentage Freshmen (House) ----- Mean Years of Service (House)

Percentage Freshmen (Senate) ----- Mean Years of Service (Senate)

Sources: Adapted from David C. Huckabee, Length of Service for Representatives and Senators: 1st–103d Congresses, Congressional Research Service Report No. 95-426GOV, March 27, 1995. Authors' calculations for the 104th through 114th Congresses. See also Mildred Amer, Average Years of Service for Members of the Senate and House of Representatives, First–109th Congresses, Congressional Research Service Report RL32648, November 9, 2005. Additional data assembled by the authors.

In recent decades, legislative business has kept the House and Senate almost perpetually in session—punctuated by constituency work periods. Members of the contemporary Congress are—and must be—full-time professional politicians.

Congress has also professionalized in that members now direct a large staff of aides. Until recent decades, members of Congress had access to very limited staff. In the 1890s, only 142 clerks (62 for the House and 80 for the Senate) were on hand to serve members of Congress. Many senators and all representatives handled their own correspondence. It was not until 1946 that Congress began to develop professional staffing. Every member now has employees to handle mail and phone calls, appointments, policy research, speechwriting, and constituent service. With each member directing his or her own staff "enterprise," Congress now sustains a distinct Washington subculture.[76] All told, the legislative branch employs more than 30,000 people, housed in nearly a dozen Capitol Hill buildings.[77]

Constituency Demands

Since the beginning, U.S. legislators have been expected to remain close to voters. Early representatives reported to their constituents through circular letters, communications passed around throughout their districts.[78] But the volume of those demands has increased many times over. Before the Civil War, a member's business on behalf of constituents was confined mainly to awarding rural mail routes, arranging for Mexican War pensions, sending out free seed, and only occasionally explaining legislation. This unhurried pace has long since vanished.

Reflecting on his forty years of congressional service, concluding in 1967, Representative Martin remarked on the dramatic upsurge of constituent awareness:

> Today the federal government is far more complex, as is every phase of national life. People have to turn to their Representative for aid. I used to think ten letters a day was a big batch; now I get several hundred a day. In earlier times, constituents didn't know their Congressman's views. With better communications, their knowledge has increased along with their expectations of what he must know.[79]

Members of Martin's era would be astonished at the volume of constituency work now handled by House and Senate offices. The advent of new communications technologies has increased the volume of congressional mail by an order of magnitude. In 1997, the last year before email use became widespread, members of Congress received 30.5 million pieces of posted mail; by 2007, the volume of mail, email included, had surged to 491 million pieces.[80] Staff surveys suggest that the volume of email has continued to increase, consuming an ever-increasing share of their time.[81] Not only are constituents more numerous than ever before, but they are also better educated, served by faster communication and transportation, and mobilized by lobby organizations. Public opinion surveys reveal that voters expect legislators to dispense federal services and to communicate frequently with the home folks. Even though the more flagrant forms of pork barrel politics are denounced, constituents' demands are unlikely to ebb in the future.

CONCLUSION

While the founders understood the guiding principles of representative assemblies, they could not have foreseen what sort of institution they had created. They wrote into the Constitution legislative powers as they understood them and left the details to future generations.

Just as the Earth's history is marked by periods of intense, even cataclysmic, change—punctuated by equilibrium—so historians of Congress have identified several eras of intensive institutional change, such as the advent of Reed's Rules or the early nineteenth-century transformation of the Senate described by Elaine Swift. But institutional change is not necessarily dramatic. Incremental changes of one kind or another are also always unfolding.

Over time, as a result of changes large and small, Congress became the mature institution of today. The contemporary Congress abounds with norms and traditions, rules and procedures, and committees and subcommittees. In short, the modern Congress is highly institutionalized. How different it is from the First Congress, personified by fussy John Adams worrying about what forms of address to use.

Institutionalization, however, should not be seen as inevitable or irreversible. Indeed, as the parties have strengthened and become more polarized, members have moved away from relying upon seniority as the sole basis for allocating committee leadership roles while other norms and routines that characterized the Congress for much of the past century have come under challenge. Even so, many other indicators of institutionalization—such as the elaborate division of labor represented by the committee system, the prevalence of careerism, and the professionalism of the staff—remain robust.[82]

Institutionalization has a number of important consequences, some good and some bad. It enables Congress to cope with its extensive workload. The standing committee system permits the two houses to process a wide variety of issues simultaneously. Careerism encourages legislators to develop skills and expertise in specific areas. In tandem with staff resources, this specialization allows Congress to compete with the executive branch in absorbing information and applying expertise to public issues. The danger of institutionalization is organizational rigidity. Institutions that are too rigid can frustrate policy making, especially in periods of rapid social or political change. Structures that are too complex can tie people in knots, producing inaction, delays, and confusion.

The institutionalization of the contemporary Congress must be taken into account by anyone who seeks to understand it today. Capitol Hill newcomers—even those who vow to shake things up—confront not an unformed, pliable institution but an established, traditional one that must be approached largely on its own terms.

Electoral Process.
Freshman Representative Lauren Underwood, D-Ill., along with many of her classmates, departs the Capitol office of Senate Majority Leader Mitch McConnell, R-Ky., after urging him to schedule action on legislation to end the partial government shutdown. Newly elected member Dan Crenshaw, R-Tex., takes a photo of the new member lottery process for the selection of his House office as his wife, Tara, looks on. The freshmen members of the 116th Congress (2019–2021) assemble on the East Front of the Capitol for the traditional class photo.

GOING FOR IT

Recruitment and Candidacy

At the start of the 116th Congress in January 2019, 122 new members took the oath of office.[1] Among the ten new senators (eight Republicans and two Democrats), there were two governors, including a 2008 presidential candidate; a state attorney general; two appointive U.S. Senators; a state lawmaker; and four former U.S. House members. Among the 112 new House members (68 Democrats and 44 Republicans) were a CIA analyst; teacher; flight attendant; Navy officer; professional football player; waitress; medical doctor; congressional aide; state lawmaker; professional hockey player; and community organizer.

How did these people get to Congress? This question has no simple answer. In the broadest sense, all legislators are products of recruitment—the social and political process through which people seek and win leadership posts. Recruitment is a key to the effective performance of all institutions, including legislatures. Ideally, the recruitment process should secure the ablest individuals to lead their community, a subject addressed in the first great book about politics, Plato's *Republic*. Sociologists have long observed, however, that recruitment reflects a society's class structure: Privileged members of society are overrepresented in the power structure. Political scientists, whatever their normative concerns, have charted the paths that individuals travel to gain positions in Congress and other institutions of government.

Any recruitment process has both formal and informal elements. For Congress, the formal elements include the Constitution and state and federal laws governing nominations and elections. Equally important are the informal, often unwritten, rules of the game. Ambitions, skills, and resources favor certain aspirants over others; popular moods and attitudes—which are changeable—induce citizens to support some candidates and reject others. Taken together, such elements add up to a series of filters or screens. The recruitment process is a mix of rules, prob-abilities, chance events, and timing. Its biases, both overt and hidden, affect the quality of representation and decision making in the House and Senate.

FORMAL RULES OF THE GAME

The formal gateways to congressional office are wide. There are only three consti-tutional qualifications for holding congressional office: age (twenty-five years of age for the House, thirty for the Senate); citizenship (seven years for the House, nine years for the Senate); and residency (in the state from which the officeholder is elected).

These qualifications cannot be augmented by the states or by Congress. Importantly, the Supreme Court has held that states cannot limit the number of terms their members of Congress can serve. Term limits on members of Congress can only be imposed through a constitutional amendment. The drafters of the Constitution considered but rejected term limits. The authors of *The Federalist Papers* argued that officeholders' desire for reelection would provide a powerful incentive for faithful service. In addition, the framers valued the expertise that experienced lawmakers—people like themselves—could bring to legislative deliberations.

The residency requirement is traditionally stricter in practice than the Constitution prescribes. Typically, constituents expect members to live in the districts they represent, and most do. During the 115th House (2017–2019), only twenty-one lawmakers resided outside the districts they represented.[2] Voters also tend to prefer candidates with long-standing ties to their states or districts and to shun outsiders who move into a state primarily to seek public office (so-called "carpetbaggers"). Nevertheless, Americans' geographical mobility has swollen the "carpetbagger caucus" on Capitol Hill. About a third of the members of both chambers in recent Congresses were born outside the states they represent.

Senate Apportionment

At the 1789 Constitutional Convention, delegates from small states demanded equal representation in the Senate as the price for their support of the Constitution. This arrangement is virtually unamendable because Article V assures that no state can be deprived of its equal voice in the Senate without its own consent. As a result, the Senate is the one legislative body in the nation in which "one person, one vote" emphatically does not apply. By this standard, the Senate is one of the most malapportioned legislatures in the democratic world.[3] The nine most popu-lous states are home to 51 percent of the population but control only 18 percent of the Senate; the twenty-six least populous states elect 52 percent of the Senate but hold only 18 percent of the population.[4] Over time, widening disparities in state population eroded the Senate's representative character. After the first cen-sus in 1790, the spread between the most populous state (Virginia) and the least populous (Delaware) was nineteen to one. Today, the spread between the most populous state (California) and the least populous (Wyoming) is nearly seventy to one.

Populous states complain that they are shortchanged in the federal bargain. Compared with lightly populated states, they contribute more revenue and receive fewer benefits.[5] One study using survey, electoral, and demographic data concludes that the Senate's malapportionment "has increasingly come to underweight the preferences of liberals, Democrats, African Americans, [Asian Americans], and Latinos."[6] Malapportionment of the Senate, an institution known for protecting individual, small-group, and minority party interests in the policy process, underweights those very interests in other important respects; for example, "small states tend to be significantly less racially and ethnically diverse than the nation as a whole."[7]

House Apportionment

The 435 House seats are apportioned among the states by population, with districts averaging more than 747,000 people each. This apportionment process excludes the five delegates (American Samoa, the District of Columbia, Guam, the Virgin Islands, and the Northern Mariana Islands) and one resident commissioner (Puerto Rico). These nonapportioned seats represent populations ranging from 55,441 (American Samoa) to about 3.3 million (Puerto Rico).

Role of the Census

To allocate House seats among the states, the Constitution requires a census of the population every ten years. Once the figures are gathered by the Commerce Department's Census Bureau, House apportionment is derived by a mathematical formula called the method of equal proportions.[8] However, reapportionment does not fully guarantee equality of district population because of two additional requirements: (1) Every state must receive one House member, and (2) congressional districts cannot cross state lines.[9] After the 2010 apportionment, for example, the entire state of Montana, with one representative-at-large for nearly a million people, was the nation's most populous district. Wyoming has the least populous district, with an estimated 574,000 inhabitants. The census also provides a snapshot of who we are as a nation and how the country has changed, such as the rapid growth of the Hispanic and Asian populations between the 2000 and 2010 censuses. The 2020 census is likely to report further increases in the nation's demographic diversity.[10]

Because the size of the House has remained unchanged since 1911, one state's gain now means another state's loss.[11] This reality provoked sharp controversy in the aftermath of the 1920 census. For the first time ever, the results indicated that more Americans lived in urban than in rural areas. With the nation's cities and rural towns sharply at odds over the burning issue of the enforcement of Prohibition, the power struggle over representation was so intractable that

Congress failed to pass a reapportionment bill after the 1920 census.[12] Finally, in 1929, a law was enacted that "established a permanent system for apportioning the 435 seats following each census."[13] Thus, the reapportionment of House seats occurred after the 1930 census and every census since (see Figure 3-1).

For some decades now, older industrial and farm states of the Northeast and Midwest have lost ground to fast-growing states in the South and West—the declining Rust Belt versus the booming Sun Belt. After the 1940 census, states in the East and Midwest commanded 58 percent of all House seats, compared with 42 percent for states in the South and West. With the 2000 census, the ratio was exactly reversed. Over two generations, then, "a huge shift in political power" occurred between the geographic regions.[14] The trend continued with the results of the 2010 census, after which the northeastern and midwestern states once again lost seats to the Sun Belt. Most dramatically, Texas and Florida increased their congressional representation by four and two seats, respectively, while Ohio

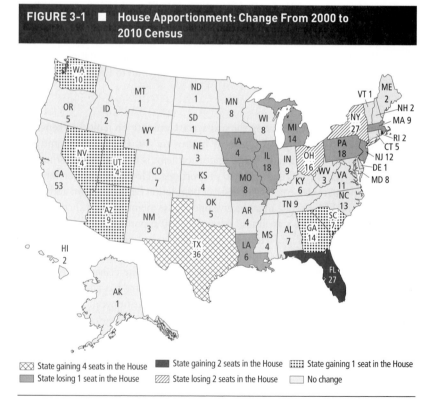

FIGURE 3-1 ■ House Apportionment: Change From 2000 to 2010 Census

☒ State gaining 4 seats in the House ■ State gaining 2 seats in the House ⊞ State gaining 1 seat in the House
■ State losing 1 seat in the House ▨ State losing 2 seats in the House ☐ No change

Source: "Apportionment Population and Number of Representatives, By State: 2010 Census," Census Bureau, U.S. Department of Commerce, December 21, 2010, http://2010.census.gov/news/pdf/apport2010_table1.pdf.

and New York each lost two seats. Population projections again indicate that mainly snow belt states will lose House seats compared with the warmer regions of the nation. Estimates in 2017 suggest that these states will gain seats: Texas with three—a surging Hispanic population—followed by Florida with two and then Arizona, Colorado, North Carolina, and Oregon, with one seat each. States likely to lose a House seat are Alabama, Illinois, Michigan, New York, Ohio, Pennsylvania, Rhode Island, and West Virginia.[15]

Census Politics

The Constitution describes the decennial census as an "actual enumeration" of persons (Article I, section 2). The Fourteenth Amendment adds, "Representatives shall be apportioned among the several States according to their respective numbers, counting the whole number of persons in each State, excluding Indians not taxed." Population figures determine seats and affect power, including each state's share of the Electoral College vote for president and vice president and a state's share of nearly $700 billion of federal grant-in-aid funds, which are based on census counts. Controversy surrounds nearly every aspect of apportionment and districting.

Counting such a large and diverse population is logistically and methodologically daunting. Certain hard-to-contact groups—transients, the homeless, renters, immigrants (legal or not), children, and poorer people generally—elude census takers and are undercounted. College students or others temporarily living away from home are sometimes double-counted (an overcount, in effect).[16] The so-called "tri-caucus" in the House—the Black Caucus, the Hispanic Caucus, and the Asian Caucus—has long been concerned about getting accurate counts of hard-to-reach minorities.[17] The Supreme Court has held that statistical sampling methods that would minimize undercounts of minority populations cannot be used to apportion seats among the states. In 2020, for the first time, people can respond online to the census survey, which has raised concerns about the security ("hacking") of respondents' personal information and access to computer technology.

The immigration issue adds yet another dimension to census politics. Because the Fourteenth Amendment refers to *persons* rather than *citizens,* states with large numbers of both documented and undocumented (such as Arizona, California, Nevada, and Texas) gain House seats at the expense of states with fewer immigrants (such as Michigan and Pennsylvania). "It's one thing if we lose seats simply because of population loss," complained a House GOP lawmaker from Michigan, "but it's another thing if we lose this seat because of illegal immigration, and that's exactly what is happening."[18] The census, however, embraces all residents—whether they are citizens or noncitizens or whether they are qualified to vote. In 2015, the Supreme Court confronted the issue of whom to count for purposes of reapportionment and redistricting: every person in a state or only eligible voters. (For more on this issue, see Box 3-2.)

A controversy emerged in March 2018 when the Trump administration stated that it would add a citizenship status question—"Is this person a citizen of the United States?"—to the 2020 census survey. The ostensible purpose of the question, according to Commerce Secretary Wilbur Ross, is to gather new and updated data on the voting eligibility of the nation's population.

The citizenship question provoked political discord and legal challenges. The U.S. Supreme Court, for example, entered the fray to determine if there was deception as to how and why the citizenship question was added to the 2020 census. Critics noted that many undocumented (non-citizens) and other foreign born people could refuse to participate in the 2020 census for fear of deportation or immigration raids. A possible consequence is significant population undercounts in states and cities with large minority populations. If this occurred, it would affect the apportionment of House seats between different regions (the "frost belt" versus the "sun belt") and among the states (GOP "red" and Democratic "blue") as well as limit federal monies to immigrant-populated areas.

DISTRICTING IN THE HOUSE

Redistricting is fundamentally a state responsibility, but the federal courts increasingly govern the process. Congressional districting is regulated by two federal statutes. The first is a 1967 statute that mandates that all states entitled to more than one seat create districts, each represented by a single member. At-large or multimember districts are prohibited. The second statute is the Voting Rights Act of 1965, as amended; it requires that districts not dilute the representation of racial minorities. In addition to interpreting these statutes, the courts have construed the Constitution to require that districts be nearly equal in population, a standard that they rigorously enforce.

Redistricting is a fiercely political process that affects the fortunes of many people: state legislators, governors, incumbent House members, the congressional leadership, lobbyists, and the leaders of racial and ethnic groups.[19] To insulate the process from politics, a handful of states have turned the job over to some form of independent commission.[20] About a dozen states use some type of commission rather than their legislatures to draw House and state legislative districts. In 2015, the U.S. Supreme Court addressed the constitutionality of the independent-commission approach to district line-drawing (see Box 3-1). In most states, however, redistricting is carried out by the legislature, with the governor able to approve or veto the plan. If a state's politicians become deadlocked on redistricting or if they fail to observe legal guidelines, judges may finish the job—sometimes awarding victory to parties that lost out earlier in the political fracas.

In the redistricting wars, no weapons are left sheathed. Both political parties pour money into state legislative and gubernatorial elections and into postcensus lobbying efforts so they can control the mapmaking process. The shift of only a few seats in a state legislature can thereby determine not only which party dominates its congressional delegation but potentially which party achieves majority control of the House itself. As a GOP consultant said about his role in drawing House seats, "As a mapmaker, I can have more of an impact on an election than a campaign, than a candidate."[21]

Congressional Republicans, more so than Democrats, were strategic in their successful quest to win most state legislative elections in the two years before and after the 2010 census. Their multiyear "Redmap" plan consisted of two steps for tilting the electoral playing field: "take over state legislatures [in 2008] before the decennial Census, then redraw state and Congressional districts [after the decennial census] to lock in partisan advantages."[22] The result was that GOP state legislatures and governors created favorable U.S. House districts through artful line-drawing that contributed to their majority control of the House in the 2012, 2014, and 2016 elections. Partly as a result, Democrats suffered large state-level losses between 2008 and 2015: "69 [U.S.] House seats, 913 state legislative seats, 11 governorships, and 32 state legislative chambers."[23]

The 2018 mid-term election saw Democrats make modest gains in governor and state legislative races. Of 36 gubernatorial races in 2018, Democrats managed to capture seven statehouses previously controlled by the GOP: Illinois, Kansas, Maine, Michigan, Nevada, New Mexico, and Wisconsin. Democrats also made gains in winning more state legislative seats. For example, prior to the November 2018 election, Republicans controlled both state legislative chambers and the governorships of 25 states; Democrats controlled only 8. After the 2018 election, Democrats had total control of redistricting in 14 states; the GOP in 22."[24] Even with the 2018 Democratic gains, the "final verdicts on which party controls redistricting will come during [state] legislative and gubernatorial elections in 2019, 2020, and 2021."[25]

Because congressional seats are political prizes, districting is a tool by which politicians seek partisan, factional, and even personal advantage. Two perennial problems of districting are malapportionment and gerrymandering.

Malapportionment

Before 1964, districts of grossly unequal populations often existed side by side in the same state. As metropolitan areas grew in population, rurally dominated legislatures simply refused to redistrict, holding on to power regardless of population movements and demographic trends—the "silent gerrymander." The courts were slow to venture into this "political thicket." By the 1960s, however, the problem of unequal representation by population was crying out for resolution.[26] In a series of landmark rulings in the 1960s, the Supreme Court held that districting schemes that fell short of standards of population equality violated the Constitution. In *Reynolds v. Sims* (1964), the Court ruled that the Fourteenth Amendment's equal protection clause requires that all state legislative seats be apportioned "substantially on population." That same year, the Court also applied the "one person, one vote" principle to the U.S. House of Representatives. The Court based its decision in *Wesberry v. Sanders* (1964), not on the Fourteenth

BOX 3-1 WHAT IS A *LEGISLATURE*?

In 2000, Arizona voters used the state's initiative process to take the job of redistricting away from partisan state lawmakers and give it to an independent redistricting commission composed of two Democrats, two Republicans, and one independent.[1] "The reason that people push for taking this out of the hands of the Legislature is there is really an inherent conflict of interest here where politicians are getting to custom-design which voters they want in their districts," one reform advocate explained.[2] The independent commission approach to redistricting, then, is a reform idea to discourage partisan gerrymanders and encourage more competitive elections.

The Arizona state legislature sued on the grounds that the independent redistricting commission violated the U.S. Constitution by taking away power reserved to state legislatures exclusively. Specifically, the election clause of the Constitution (Article I, section 4) states, "The Times, Places and Manner of holding Elections for Senators and Representatives, shall be prescribed in each State by the Legislature thereof." The case was first considered by a federal district court. It ruled that removal of the legislature's redistricting authority did not violate the election clause because Arizona's voters were effectively acting as a legislature when they used the initiative process to create the redistricting commission. The Arizona legislature appealed to the Supreme Court. In 2015, the Supreme Court affirmed the lower court's decision, stating that the word *legislature* includes a state's entire lawmaking function (the initiative process and vetoes of the governor, for example). Justice Ruth Bader Ginsburg, who wrote the majority decision, said, "The people of Arizona turned to the initiative to curb the practice of gerrymandering." In dissent, Chief Justice John Roberts said the majority's decision to allow the people, not the state legislature, to decide congressional districts was a "magic trick" of judicial interpretation.

---

[1] In the nearly twenty-five states that use the initiative process, citizens can bypass state lawmakers and governors by placing a proposed law or constitutional amendment on the ballot if they obtain the requisite number of signatures. Commissions come in a variety of forms. For example, some commissions handle only congressional redistricting; others do line-drawing only for state legislative districts. Some are advisory, providing analyses to the state legislature; others, like Arizona, have the authority to redraw House district lines on their own.

[2] Aricia Miller, "Redistricting Reform Is Tough Task Every Time," *Roll Call*, December 14, 2010, online edition.

Amendment but on Article I, section 2, of the Constitution, which directs that House representatives be apportioned among the states according to their respective numbers and chosen by the people of the several states. This language, argued Justice Hugo Black, means that "as nearly as is practicable, one person's vote in a congressional election is to be worth as much as another's."

How much equality of population is "practicable" within the states? The Supreme Court adopted rigid mathematical equality as the underlying standard. In a 1983 case (*Karcher v. Daggett*), a 5–4 majority voided a New Jersey plan in which districts varied by no more than one-seventh of 1 percent. "Adopting any standard other than population equality would subtly erode the Constitution's ideal of equal representation," wrote Justice William J. Brennan for the majority (see Box 3-2 for another perspective). More recently, the Court, in 2012 (*Tennant v. Jefferson County Commission*), established a two-part test to help it to determine the extent of population deviation that is constitutionally acceptable. First, "challengers have the burden of proving that the population differences could have been practicably avoided." Second, if the challengers pass the first test, the state must then demonstrate "that the population differences were needed to achieve a legitimate state objective," such as respecting county boundaries.[27]

Other goals must sometimes be sacrificed to achieve population equality. It is often not feasible to follow other economic, social, or geographic boundaries in drawing districts of equal population. The priority on population equality erodes the values of compactness and contiguity in districting—the idea that districts should bind territory in one tight piece rather than contain a series of disconnected parts that could require a person to leave a district to reach another part of it. As a result, the congressional district tends to be an artificial creation, often bearing little relationship to real communities of interest. "The main casualty of the tortuous redistricting now underway," remarked analyst Alan Ehrenhalt, "is the erosion of geographical community—of place—as the basis of political representation."[28]

Gerrymandering

The term *gerrymander* refers to district line-drawing that purposefully maximizes seats for one party or voting bloc. The gerrymander takes its name from Gov. Elbridge Gerry of Massachusetts, who, in 1812, created a peculiar, salamander-shaped district north of Boston to benefit his Democratic Party (see Box 3-3). Gerrymandering is used not only to gain partisan advantage but also to shape the political prospects of incumbents, particular aspiring politicians, or racial or ethnic groups. For most of its history, Congress has regarded gerrymandering as part of the spoils of partisan warfare.

Two common gerrymandering techniques are *cracking* and *packing. Cracking* splits a party's or a group's strength among several districts, thereby diluting its voting leverage. The objective of placing opposition party members or specific groups in multiple districts is to try to ensure that they lack the votes in any one to elect their preferred candidates. A *packing* strategy takes the opposite approach. Packing draws districts dominated by voters of one party or group. It will thus likely make a district safe for a particular party or group, but it also "wastes" votes in that the favored party or group will win those seats with large margins. If a party's or ethnic group's voters are systematically concentrated in a few "giveaway" districts, it will win fewer seats in the state than its voting strength might otherwise allow.

To sum up, cracking distributes generally like-minded voters—African Americans, for instance—among several House districts in a state so that it is unlikely that they could elect candidates who support their views and values. Packing concentrates like-minded voters in a small number of districts. Neither gerrymandering approach is guaranteed to achieve mapmakers' political objectives. For example, when majority parties spread their voters across more districts in an effort to win more seats by narrow margins, they may also expose their candidates to greater electoral competition. Line-drawers, in short, can make mistakes in allocating like-minded voters among their gerrymandered districts and end up losing seats they expected to win. Some scholars call this unwanted outcome a "dummymander."[29]

Today, gerrymandering is much more easily carried out than it was in the past. With sophisticated computer technology and software, knowledgeable individuals and groups can use census and other data to match people's voting patterns to where they live, even street by street. Political leaders are able to consider various alternative plans until they identify a redistricting map that they believe achieves their objectives. In short, technology and demographic data allow line-drawers to know, with a high degree of accuracy, where Democratic and Republican voters reside. The consequence is that lawmakers select the voters they want in their districts, which predetermines the likely winners on election day.

Gerrymanders also affect the two Congresses in various ways. For example, members who represent predominantly Democratic "blue" or GOP "red" districts are likely to be especially responsive to voters who share their political affiliation and ideology. "Red" and "blue" lawmakers understand that deviations from ideological purity might produce primary opponents further to the right or left of themselves in the next election. As a consequence, lawmakers might be reluctant to collaborate with opposition party lawmakers to forge bipartisan compromises on legislation.

Partisan Gerrymandering

The most common form of gerrymandering is aimed at partisan advantage. This type of gerrymandering occurs in states in which one political party controls the process and draws districts to benefit their members. The Supreme Court held in 1986 that gerrymandering is a justiciable issue—that is, it could be properly raised in court (*Davis v. Bandemer*). Yet despite a number of cases dealing with the issue over the years, the Court has been unable to set out uniform and workable standards for distinguishing permissible from impermissible partisan gerrymandering.

In a 2004 Pennsylvania case (*Vieth v. Jubelirer*), Supreme Court Justice Antonin Scalia wrote the 5–4 plurality decision. (No single opinion received majority support.) Scalia recommended that *Davis v. Bandemer* be overturned because, after 18 years, the Court had found no judicial remedy for adjudicating

BOX 3-2 WHO SHOULD BE COUNTED FOR POLITICAL EQUALITY: TOTAL POPULATION OR ELIGIBLE VOTERS?

Recall that during the reapportionment revolution of the 1960s, the U.S. Supreme Court made a series of decisions that emphasized the constitutional principle of "one person, one vote" in drawing U.S. House and state legislative districts. This principle requires states, after each decennial census, to design House districts that are substantially equal in population. However, left unanswered by the Supreme Court for over fifty years was the definition of a *person*: Does *person* refer to the establishment of legislative districts where everyone is counted, including children, noncitizens, and felons—or does *person* mean that eligible or registered voters are to be used as the population baseline to create substantially equal districts?

In April 2016, the Supreme Court addressed this issue in *Evenwel v. Abbott*, a Texas case involving the redistricting of state senate districts. Sue Evenwel, a registered voter, brought suit against the governor of Texas for signing into law a redistricting plan that used the traditional method for creating districts: total population. Citing the Fourteenth Amendment of the U.S. Constitution—"No State shall deny to any person within its jurisdiction the equal protection of the laws"— Evenwel argued that the Texas redistricting plan unconstitutionally watered down the strength of her vote compared with people living in other districts. Furthermore, the 1964 *Reynolds v. Sims* decision said that "an individual's right to vote for state legislators is unconstitutionally impaired when its weight is in a substantial fashion diluted when compared with votes of citizens living in other parts of the State." Although the Texas districts were substantially equal in population, they varied considerably in the number of eligible voters. Evenwel resided in a rural Texas district with 557,525 eligible voters while another urban district had only 358,205 eligible voters. The "fewer the votes, the more each vote counts."[1]

In a unanimous decision, the Supreme Court decided against Evenwel. Justice Ruth Bader Ginsburg wrote the Court's majority opinion. Ginsburg said that "Texas, like all other States, draws its legislative districts on the basis of total population." Evenwel challenges this uniform method "on the ground that it produces unequal districts when measured by voter-eligible population. Voter-eligible population, not total population," Evenwel argued, "must be used to ensure that [her vote] will not be devalued in relation to citizens' votes in other districts. We hold, based on constitutional history, this Court's decisions, and longstanding practice, that a State may draw its legislative districts based on total population." The Court, however, did not address directly whether a state might use, as Justice Samuel Alito wrote in a concurring opinion, "something other than total population as the basis for equalizing the size of districts."

Two other points about *Evenwel* merit brief mention. First, the case involved the rapid growth of noncitizen populations in states such as Texas, California, Arizona, and Florida. Thus, if Evenwel's argument prevailed, it would have had dramatic nationwide effects, not only in the potential havoc among the states compelled to

(Continued)

(Continued)

redraw their districts but in electoral power as well. Political power would shift from urban Democratic areas where there are more noneligible voters compared with rural and suburban GOP areas that have more eligible voters. Second, scholars and others have stated that, unlike reliable census figures, there is no comparable database of eligible voters. "At best, states would have to use estimates from the American Community Survey, which is collected infrequently, may not exclude all ineligible voters (such as felons) and does not include all eligible voters (such as those voters who are overseas)."[2]

[1]Todd Ruger and Randy Leonard, "Redefining Redistricting," *CQ Weekly*, November 2, 2015, 25.

[2]Richard L. Hasen, "Voting Chaos Ahead?" *Los Angeles Times*, December 10, 2015, online edition.

claims of unconstitutional partisan gerrymandering. But federal courts continue to hear cases of unconstitutional partisan gerrymandering in their search for manageable standards. In November 2016, for the first time, a three-judge federal panel declared that the GOP-controlled Wisconsin Assembly (*Wisconsin v. Gill*) had engaged in unconstitutional partisan gerrymandering.

Federal judges recognize that the political party in control of a state legislature will draw districts advantageous to their party. As a GOP lawmaker in charge of his state's redistricting process bluntly said, "I think electing Republicans is better than electing Democrats. So I drew this map to help foster what I think is better for the country."[30] At issue is what constitutes acceptable rather than unacceptable partisan map-drawing?

To resolve this question, two judges in the three-person judicial panel relied on a mathematical formula developed by two scholars called the *efficiency gap*— the "difference between each party's 'wasted' votes, divided by the total number of votes cast."[31] Under federal law, the losing side in redistricting lawsuits has an automatic right of appeal to the U.S. Supreme Court. "Appeals in cases by [a] three-judge panel go directly to the Supreme Court, which must consider them"—either affirming the judicial panel's decision or scheduling the case for judicial hearings.[32]

The Supreme Court considered these issues in the Wisconsin case of *Gill v. Whitford*. In a unanimous decision on June 18, 2018, the Court rendered a narrow procedural decision that declined to establish a clear standard for determining partisan gerrymanders. The Court said that challengers of Wisconsin's redistricting map lacked "standing" to sue (they had not suffered a concrete, personal injury) because they expressed a "generalized grievance" against the entire statewide plan. Instead, claims of unconstitutional partisan gerrymandering should focus on how individual districts are drawn and the personal injury caused to voters who reside in those particular districts. The Court then voted 7–2 to return

BOX 3-3 ORIGINS OF THE GERRYMANDER

The practice of *gerrymandering*—the excessive manipulation of the shape of a legislative district to benefit certain persons or groups—is probably as old as the republic, but the name for the practice originated in 1812.

In that year, the Massachusetts legislature carved out of Essex County a district that historian John Fiske described as having a "dragon-like contour." When the artist Elkana Tisdale saw the misshapen district at a dinner party, he penciled in a head, wings, and claws. Richard Alsop, a poet, then termed the district a *Gerrymander*—after Elbridge Gerry, then governor of Massachusetts. Federalists reprinted the image widely in newspapers, and the term *gerrymander* gained brief currency as slang for being deceived.

By the 1990s, the term had broadened to include the modern-day practice of drawing maps to benefit racial and ethnic groups. In the past, the term was applied largely to districts drawn to benefit incumbents or political parties.

Source: Michael P. McDonald, "State Legislative Districting," Guide to State Politics and Policy, ed. Richard Niemi and Joshua Dyck (Washington, DC: CQ Press, 2013).

the case to the federal district court to permit the Wisconsin challengers, if they want, an opportunity to establish standing to sue.[33] In short, the 2018 Supreme Court continued to sidestep the fundamental issue of what constitutes an unconstitutional partisan gerrymander. The year 2019 might be different, however. The

Supreme Court will once again consider the issue of partisan gerrymandering involving the congressional maps of North Carolina and Maryland.[34]

Many pundits and politicians complain that the prevalence of partisan gerrymandering inhibits the construction of cross-party coalitions. Research by scholars, however, provides little support for the claim that gerrymandering is an important cause of party polarization in Congress. Political scientist Sean M. Theriault reports that redistricting is responsible for between 10 and 20 percent of the party polarization that has occurred.[35] Other scholars dispute even this relatively modest effect. A study by Nolan McCarty, Keith T. Poole, and Howard Rosenthal concludes that gerrymandering has not contributed to the rise of partisanship to any meaningful extent: "Polarization is not primarily a phenomenon of how voters are sorted into districts. It is mainly the consequence of the different ways Democrats and Republicans would represent the same districts."[36] Moreover, gerrymanders do not affect the U.S. Senate, and it is nearly as party polarized as the House.

Pro-Incumbent Gerrymandering

Bipartisan or "sweetheart" gerrymanders are those with lines drawn to protect incumbents of both parties. The objectives of "incumbent protection" gerrymandering are to encourage predictability in elections and to maintain the political status quo in the legislature. The case of California, home of 12 percent of all House members, illustrates how districting can affect the fate of incumbents. After the 2000 census, California's ascendant Democrats opted to play it safe and adopted an incumbent-friendly districting plan. Under this map, only one California congressional incumbent was defeated over the course of the five election cycles between 2002 and 2010.[37]

Concerned about pro-incumbent redistricting, California voters, like those in several other states, took the job of redistricting away from the state legislature and gave it to an independent bipartisan citizens' commission. The broad objectives of independent commissions are to create compact, contiguous, and competitively balanced districts. It is not at all clear that the reform has had the desired effects. As one analyst stated: "[T]here's scant evidence that members of the Golden State's congressional delegation are any more moderate than before. . . . And it's not clear whether the commission created more competitive districts, or if Donald Trump's polarizing presidency gets the credit for more seats in play than past cycles."[38] Still, taking the redistricting process away from state legislatures remains popular with many voters.

In the end, the competitiveness of congressional elections is shaped at least as much by demography as well by gerrymandering. "The problem is not who draws the legislative lines; it's where people live," notes one observer.[39] As Bruce Oppenheimer of Vanderbilt University explains, "Democrats tend to live next to Democrats. Republicans tend to live next to Republicans."[40] Urban Democrats, in particular, may be victims of what political scientists Jowei Chen and Jonathan Rodden call *unintentional gerrymandering:* natural geographic patterns in which

Democrats live in "dense, urban areas . . . effectively packing themselves into fewer districts."[41] The result is that the "more self-sorted the electorate is, the easier it is for people in charge of redistricting to draw more partisan districts."[42] Because Democratic voters self-segregate in urban areas, they produce an abundance of "wasted votes" that can lead to electoral outcomes where "one party [wins] the popular vote in House races across the country but [ends] up with a minority of House seats."[43]

Majority-Minority Districts

Another form of gerrymandering involves the districting of racial minorities. There is a long history of racial gerrymandering in the United States, meaning "the deliberate and arbitrary distortion of district boundaries for racial purposes."[44]

The earliest forms of racial gerrymandering were designed to disempower African Americans. After the Fifteenth Amendment was ratified to grant former slaves the right to vote, southern states adopted a variety of measures to thwart the law. One of those was the racial gerrymander. In the 1870s, for example, Mississippi opponents of Reconstruction concentrated the bulk of their state's black population in one long, narrow congressional district running along the Mississippi River, leaving five other districts with white majorities. As another example, Alabama lawmakers scattered black voters over six different congressional districts to dilute their influence.[45] In other words, blacks were systematically "packed" into or "cracked" across congressional districts in order to weaken their electoral influence. In addition to racial gerrymandering, a variety of tools, such as literacy tests and poll taxes, were instituted to disenfranchise African Americans across the South, largely denying blacks the right to participate in elections until the civil rights reforms of the 1960s.

The Voting Rights Act (VRA) of 1965, as amended, is arguably the most effective civil rights law ever enacted. It did away with the whole panoply of legal impediments that had been erected in various states and counties to limit minority electoral participation and influence. It simply abolished all voting qualifications or prerequisites that stood in the way of the franchise. Section 4 of the VRA had imposed *preclearance* procedures on the covered states (mainly southern) that historically had discriminated against racial minorities. Preclearance meant that these states had to receive advance approval from either the U.S. District Court for the District of Columbia or the U.S. attorney general for any changes in election rules to ensure that those changes would not deny or abridge the right to vote on account of race or color. Changes to election rules were precleared only if they would not lead to "a retrogression in the position of racial minorities."[46]

With respect to districting, this requirement meant that changes could not lessen the likelihood that minorities would be elected. In *Shelby County v. Holder* (2013), however, the Supreme Court made inoperable the preclearance requirements for specific states, indicating that Section 4 had outlived its purpose and did not reflect current practices in the states covered by the law. As Chief Justice John

Roberts wrote, the preclearance requirements wrongly singled out particular states "based on 40-year-old facts having no logical relationship to the present day."

However, current facts seem to indicate that preclearance has a "logical relationship to the present day." Immediately following the Court's decision, states such as North Carolina and Texas passed legislation that required strict voter identification requirements and imposed other limits on voting, such as curtailing early voting. These types of state laws, which seem directed at racial minorities, spawned a host of court challenges and charges of voter suppression. Noteworthy is that Section 2 of the VRA was not invalidated by *Shelby*. It "prohibits any voting qualification or practice—including congressional redistricting plans—that results in abridgement of the right to vote based on race, color, or membership in a language minority."[47] Redistricting and other changes to voting laws are still subject to judicial oversight and the Voting Rights Act but only as a consequence of legal challenges after the fact rather than via a preclearance process.

In recent decades, race-conscious districting has been employed to help minorities elect candidates of their choice. Unlike in previous eras, when districts had been manipulated to limit minority influence, states after 1990 began to deliberately create *majority-minority districts* to enhance the probability that minorities would be elected to Congress. During 1990s, fifteen new majority African American districts were created, thirteen of them in the South, along with nine new majority Latino districts. Many of these districts were so oddly shaped they made Governor Gerry's 1812 creation look amateurish.

The Supreme Court Enters the Quagmire

Some of these majority-minority districts were later attacked in federal court. Plaintiffs charged that the districts violated white voters' Fourteenth Amendment right to equal protection of the law. The legal battles that resulted progressively deepened the Court's involvement in congressional districting. In a long series of complex, sometimes contradictory cases, the Court attempted to balance two competing values: first, the Fourteenth Amendment's equal protection requirement that states not discriminate on the basis of race, which triggers the strict scrutiny standard (see below), and second, the VRA's protection in Section 2 against redistricting plans that dilute the ability of majority-minority groups to elect candidates of their choice. The balancing act for state legislatures is to accommodate the VRA by creating majority-minority districts in places that practiced racial discrimination without running afoul of the prohibition against the state government's use of race for discriminatory reasons.

In cases dealing with racial gerrymandering, the Court indicated that it will apply a standard of *strict scrutiny* to any district in which race was the "predominant factor" in its creation.[48] To prove racial predominance, it must be shown that "the legislature subordinated to racial considerations traditional race-neutral districting principles, including but not limited to compactness, contiguity, and respect for political subdivisions of communities defined by actual shared interests."[49] Strict scrutiny sets a very high bar that requires a state to demonstrate that it has "a compelling governmental interest in creating a majority-minority district, and that the redistricting plan is narrowly tailored to further that compelling interest."[50]

Considerable uncertainty remains about precisely what majority-minority districting plans will stand or fall upon judicial review. One important clarification is that such plans will be sustained unless race was the *predominant factor* in the creation of the district.[51] Writing for the Court in *Easley v. Cromartie* (2001), Justice Clarence Thomas declared,

> A jurisdiction may engage in constitutional political gerrymandering, even if it so happens that the most loyal Democrats happen to be black Democrats and even if the state were conscious of that fact.[52]

Because of the close correlation between race and partisanship, lawmakers may use race as a way to engage in partisan gerrymandering. Unlike racial discrimination, partisan gerrymandering does not trigger strict scrutiny. The Supreme Court also held that people who challenge a districting plan on the grounds that it amounts to racial gerrymandering must prove that "racial considerations were 'dominant and controlling' in the creation of the districts at issue."

The Supreme Court has demonstrated that it will continue to scrutinize race-conscious districts, even when they are created as part of a broader partisan gerrymander. In the end, the key question is whether the Supreme Court will provide clear guidelines as to what racial (and partisan) redistricting the Constitution will permit. In the quest for a workable standard, the justices seem to adhere to a version of Justice Potter Stewart's 1964 test for defining obscenity: "I know it when I see it." And in view of the closeness of its past decisions on majority-minority districts—nearly every major case on this question has turned on a 5–4 vote—the Court could again shift its direction as its membership changes.

Consequences of Majority-Minority Districts

The growing numbers of majority-minority districts have unquestionably made the House of Representatives more racially and ethnically diverse. Most minority legislators are elected in districts where minority groups make up the majority of the population. Indeed, a recent study confirms that a district's racial composition is by far the most important factor in determining the race of the representative it elects: "Race-conscious redistricting and the creation of effective minority districts remain the basis upon which most African American and Latino officials gain election."[53] Over time, representatives of majority-minority districts have built up a great deal of seniority and institutional clout within the Democratic Party in the House.

Nevertheless, the creation of majority-minority districts comes at some cost to minority voters. Concentrating minorities into districts where they constitute a majority wastes their votes by producing outsized electoral majorities for the winning candidates. Districting plans that pack minority voters together have arguably slowed the diversification of Congress. Packing minority voters into districts simultaneously "bleaches" surrounding nonminority districts, along with whatever leverage minority voters might wield. Even if the share of minority officeholders rises, "the number of white legislators who have any political need to respond to minority concerns goes down as their minority constituents are peeled off to form the new black and Hispanic districts."[54]

Concentrating minority (mostly Democratic) voters in safe (mainly urban) districts tends to strengthen the GOP in outlying suburban and rural areas. Scholar David Lublin has described the outcome as a "paradox of representation" in which packed districts yielded more minority lawmakers but also led to a more conservative House that reduced minorities' leverage and influence over legislative outcomes.[55]

Many doubt that packing districts is the best way to advance minorities' interests. Another strategy for enhancing the political influence of minorities is to maintain substantial minorities of racial and ethnic voters—say, 40 percent or so—in a larger number of districts (so-called *influence districts*) to expand the ranks of officeholders responsive to minority needs.[56] Many Democrats concluded that racial gerrymandering had hurt their party. "For 20 years I've been arguing against the stacking of black voters in districts that has the overall effect of diluting the voting strength of black people," said Rep. James E. Clyburn, D-S.C. "It's better to maintain a 35 to 40 percent black district where [blacks] would have a tremendous influence on elections. I don't think you need 75 percent in order for a black to be elected. That's kind of insulting to me."[57]

Consider the 2015 U.S. Supreme Court case of *Alabama Legislative Black Caucus v. Alabama*. A key issue was whether the GOP-controlled state legislature had created majority-minority districts for the state's House and Senate seats that were, ironically, too safe for African American lawmakers. For example, in 2002, a black Alabama state senator represented a district where 72 percent of the voting-age population was black. Packing a sufficiently high concentration of African Americans into a district so they could elect their preferred candidate was a key objective of the VRA. But when the lines were redrawn in 2012, the Republican state legislature packed another 3 percent of African American voters into that state senate district.[58] This time, however, the Legislative Black Caucus said enough is enough. The political segregation of blacks into a few districts, they said, deliberately diluted the ability of African Americans to compete in and influence other legislative elections in Alabama while, at the same time, facilitating the election of Republicans in the "bleached" districts. The Supreme Court, by a 5–4 vote, returned the case to the federal district court for additional judicial hearings.

In a dissenting opinion concerning the Alabama decision that seemed to sum up the Court's position on minority representation, Justice Clarence Thomas wrote, "We have somehow arrived at a place where the parties agree that Alabama's legislative districts should be fine-tuned to achieve some 'optimal' result with respect to black voting power; the only disagreement is about what percentage of blacks should be placed in those optimized districts." Still, the Alabama case established the claim that racial gerrymandering can now be used to advance minority voting rights rather than only as a challenge to majority-minority districts.[59]

BECOMING A CANDIDATE

Very few of those who are eligible to serve in Congress vie for a seat. Candidates who meet the legal qualifications must weigh a variety of considerations—some practical and rational, others personal and emotional. Candidacy decisions are often the pivotal moments in the entire recruitment process. "The decision to run obviously structures everything else that goes on in the primary process," writes political scientist L. Sandy Maisel. "Who runs, who does not run, how many candidates run. These questions set the stage for the campaigns themselves."[60]

Called or Chosen?

From their Jacksonian heyday in the 1830s to the decline of big-city machines in the 1960s, local party organizations customarily enlisted and sponsored candidates. When these organizations withered, the initiative passed in part to the candidates themselves: self-starters who pulled their own bandwagons. "The skills that work in American politics at this point in history," writes Alan Ehrenhalt, "are those of entrepreneurship. . . . People nominate themselves."

To be sure, candidates consider a host of factors, often with family members and close friends, before deciding whether to run for congressional office. Of course, there are individuals who have an easy time deciding to run, perhaps because they come from political families or they have worked on campaigns. For many, however, the decision to run raises a number of complex issues, such as these five (also see Chapter 4):

- *Time, Money, and Energy.* Campaigning for election is a time-consuming and exhausting process. Candidates constantly must attend meetings and gatherings in their district or state. They must be willing to hit the road nonstop, meet new people, sell themselves, and endure verbal abuse. Moreover, considerable time and energy must be spent raising large sums of money ("dialing for dollars") from friends, relatives, groups and organizations, party committees, political action committees (PACs), and so on. The money is essential for a host of purposes: hiring professional consultants, pollsters, and staff; buying name recognition if not well known; mass and targeted mailings; radio, TV, and digital advertising; and so forth.

- *Privacy.* A sage piece of advice that candidates might receive from campaign veterans is to do opposition research on themselves because opponents will be engaged in this activity. Virtually everything is fair game about the candidate's background from at least high school days forward. Family members are not immune from unwanted publicity in the local media, such as a son or daughter who is arrested for drunken driving or drug infractions. Candidates, in brief, must be prepared to live in a "fish bowl" environment during the entire campaign.

- *A Winnable Contest.* Before entering an electoral contest, a variety of factors influence a candidate's decision to "go or not go." An important variable is whether the election contest involves an *open seat,* a *swing district,* or an incumbent running for reelection. The bottom line is that incumbents are usually difficult to defeat because they have numerous advantages, such as high name recognition, money-raising skill, and legislative staff to assist the needs of their constituents. They can be defeated for various reasons, such as ethical problems, unpopular votes, or *wave elections.* Open or swing contests provide quality candidates with a better chance to win. *Quality* refers to such matters as prior office holding or campaign experience, effective communication and people skills, or being an ambitious "self-starter" with the capacity to create his or her own personal or political organization staffed with professional campaign consultants.

- *Willingness to Be Harsh.* Candidates need to recognize that campaigns are commonly "rough-and-tough" affairs. Elections are zero-sum contests with a winner and a loser. Candidates commonly say they only want to talk about the issues and serve their constituents in an exemplary manner. However, candidates are regularly attacked by their opponents and groups associated with them. The charges may be true, inaccurate, or completely false. Nonetheless, candidates should be aware before entering a race that they will have to engage in these types of activities: refuting personal attacks on their character or background; providing explanations to rebut attacks on their public or personal record; and launching reattacks on their opponents.

- *Policy/Political Message.* A fundamental issue for candidates is to explain why voters should elect them as opposed to the other people, perhaps including an incumbent, in the contest. They will need to draw contrasts based on the competition's policy platform, personality, leadership skills, personal integrity, appeal to significant groups and organizations, talent as a debater, accomplishments, and so on. In the end, the decisive factor is a candidate's ability to convince eligible voters to turn out and vote for him or her over the other candidates. Thus, an important focus of policy and political messaging is to establish clear distinctions between candidates and their opponents.

Congressional aspirants quickly encounter national networks of party committees and their allied interest groups. There are also numerous independent, activist groups that encourage and support potential aspirants to run for the House or Senate. For example, Emily's List encourages and supports the candidacies of Democratic women; a GOP recruitment counterpart is Value in Electing Women.[61] Today, parties are not the exclusive gatekeepers for those who seek public office.

The Republican and Democratic House and Senate campaign committees, however, are active in all phases of congressional elections.[62] They seek out and encourage promising candidates at the local level, sometimes even taking sides to help ensure their nomination. They assist promising candidates with filing deadlines, lining up supporters, and handling finances. In fact, recent research reveals that "recruitment from party leaders, elected officials, and political activists is one of the most important predictors" of who will consider a candidacy for political office.[63] During the recruiting season (generally beginning in early 2017 for the 2018 contests, for example), the leaders and campaign committee staffs of the two major parties "reach out across the country in search of political talent. Like college football coaching staffs in hot pursuit of high-school prospects, they are putting together the lineups" to win House and Senate majorities.[64]

Whether a legislative seat is vacant matters greatly for candidate and party strategy. Open seats—those in newly created districts or those in which incumbents have died or retired—are often less secure and more competitive. To the extent they can, party leaders try to discourage their incumbent colleagues from retiring. If members are going to retire, however, party leaders encourage them to announce their retirement early so that they have time to make preparations to hold the seat.[65]

Most would-be officeholders seek advancement within the two major parties, which boast not only the brand loyalties of a huge majority of voters but also extensive financial and logistical resources. Still, independents and minor-party candidates enter congressional contests. Seldom do these contenders win a sizable number of votes, but they do provide alternatives where only one major party fields a candidate. Only two independents served in Congress in 2019: Vermont senator Bernard Sanders, a self-styled "democratic socialist," and Maine senator Angus King. (Representative Ocasio-Cortez ran in 2018 as a Democrat but referred to herself as a "democratic socialist").

Amateurs and Professionals

How do would-be candidates, whether self-starters or recruited by party leaders, make up their minds to run? The answer often depends on whether the individual is a political amateur or a professional.

Amateurs

Amateur candidates are defined by their lack of previous political experience. Despite inexperience and nonexistent name recognition, many amateurs run for Congress. A few run to bring a specific issue to public attention and are less interested in winning than in advancing their cause. Many politically inexperienced candidates are what David T. Canon calls "hopeless amateurs"—people with little or no chance of winning.[66] Nevertheless, political amateurs regularly compete, and almost every congressional election brings amateurs to Capitol Hill. Two scholars suggest that amateurism is likely to increase as independent groups recruit and "assist unconventional and inexperienced candidates" to run for public office.[67] Potentially, they added, this development might be a "transformative step toward the amateurization of American politics."[68]

Amateurs are more willing than experienced politicians to make a long-shot bid for office. They are frequently the only candidates who will take on seemingly invulnerable incumbents. Amateurs often find that an uncompetitive primary offers their only chance to win a major-party nomination. More attractive political opportunities will generally entice more politically experienced competitors. "I think his chances have gone from absolutely out of the question to extremely remote," remarked the wife of one hopeless contender. "But he's learning a lot, and I think he has enjoyed it."[69] Maisel, a political scientist who wrote candidly about his own unsuccessful congressional primary campaign, described politicians as possessing an "incredible ability to delude themselves about their own chances."[70] One group of amateurs, however, sometimes proves to be the exception: those with highly visible nonpolitical careers. War heroes, entertainers, and athletes are in big demand as candidates. Local or statewide television and radio personalities also make attractive contenders.

Professionals

Professionals are more cautious than amateurs about the races they enter. Those who seek to make a career in politics must consider carefully not just whether to run for a particular political office but when to do so. Political careerists often have more to lose than amateurs from an unsuccessful bid for office because entering one race often means forgoing the office they already hold. An experienced state legislator is unlikely to gamble a safe seat in the state house or senate on a remote chance that he or she might defeat a popular congressional incumbent. Such a candidate will wait for a better opening, when an incumbent retires or is clearly vulnerable. Similarly, a sitting House member will usually wait for an open seat or an exceptional opportunity before attempting to move up to the Senate. In the end, such decisions hinge on "the not-so-simple calculus of winning."[71]

Strategic contenders evaluate their own personal strengths and weaknesses in campaigning, voter appeal, and fund-raising. They consider how well they would personally fit in with the ideological bent of their party in Congress.[72] They weigh the chances of getting the party's nomination in view of the party's ideological bent, leadership, and nominating procedures. They also consider what it will cost to succeed. If there is an incumbent, they identify the incumbent's weaknesses. And they take a look at the broader political environment, including the condition of the economy, the president's standing, and public dissatisfaction with the status quo.

Most successful congressional candidates are professionals—seasoned politicians—before they run for Congress. Grassroots organizations and movements are a breeding ground for candidates. But more often, elective office is the immediate springboard: mayors, district attorneys, or state legislators for the House; governors, lieutenant governors, and attorneys general—who have already faced a statewide electorate—for the Senate. Service in the House has become a common path to the Senate since the 1980s, although such service is no guarantee of electoral success.[73] A majority of senators (fifty) in the 116th Congress had "moved up" from the House.

The circle of people pondering a candidacy (the challenger pool) may be large or small, depending on the office and the circumstances.[74] Any number of elected officials—state legislators (especially if subject to term limits), county officers, mayors, city council members, even governors—are weighing a race for Congress at any given time. "The people who have been successful in the political world are people who know when to strike at the right time," remarked one veteran state legislator contemplating a run against a House incumbent.[75]

Finding Quality Candidates

A party's success in November can hinge on its efforts during the recruitment season. Candidate quality is measured in strategic resources and personal attributes.[76] Quality candidates are skilled in presenting themselves as candidates and are attractive to voters. Previous experience in public office—and the accompanying visibility and credibility—is one of the most important attributes of a quality candidate. In particular, candidates from famous political families have a "brand-name" advantage.[77] Fame or notoriety can sometimes overcome lack of relevant background or experience. Other characteristics of quality candidates include personality, speaking ability, and a talent for organizing or motivating others. Fund-raising ability or potential is essential as well. Today's technology, however, enables astute individuals with little or low name recognition to raise "record-shattering amounts of small-donor cash and [mobilize] unprecedented armies of volunteers."[78]

The Incumbency Factor

Of all the inducements for launching a candidacy, the odds of winning stand at the top. As scholars have found, "experienced candidates (those who have previously run for, and won, an elected office) are more likely to run for the House when national and partisan conditions are more favorable in terms of their likelihood of success." In short, these candidates exhibit strategic behavior in deciding when or whether to run for Congress.[79] A clearly winnable seat seldom lacks for eager quality candidates. Open seats—those without an incumbent running—are especially attractive. As a result, open-seat races are more likely to be competitive and to shift party control than those with an incumbent. Party strategists thus concentrate on these races.

In most House and Senate contests, however, incumbents will be running, and most of them will be reelected. As Gary C. Jacobson writes, "Nearly everything pertaining to candidates and campaigns for Congress is profoundly influenced by whether the candidate is an incumbent, challenging an incumbent, or pursuing an open seat."[80] Less forcibly, the same can be said of the Senate. Since World War II, on average, 94 percent of all incumbent representatives and 82 percent of all incumbent senators running for reelection have been returned to office. In 2016, 97 percent of House members and 87 percent of senators seeking reelection were returned to Congress. Two years later, the reelection rate for House members was 91 percent; for the Senate, it was 84 percent (see www.opensecrets.org).

Because it is difficult to defeat an incumbent, incumbents often face only low-quality opponents. Challengers may be weak fund-raisers, poorly qualified, and unknown to voters. Party leaders sometimes struggle to rouse any candidate at all willing to run against an incumbent. An incumbent's most effective electoral strategy is to scare off serious opposition. "If an incumbent can convince potentially formidable opponents and people who control campaign resources that he or she is invincible," says Jacobson, "he or she is very likely to avoid a serious challenge and so will be invincible—as long as the impression lasts."[81] Any sign of weakness is likely to encourage opponents in the next election.[82] For that reason, incumbents try to sustain wide electoral margins, show unbroken strength, keep up constituency ties, and build giant war chests of reelection money.

Incumbents are hardly invincible, even if their high reelection rates make them seem so. Indeed, in view of the prevalence of strategic retirement—the tendency of incumbents to retire when they perceive themselves to be politically vulnerable—reelection rates are a misleading indicator of incumbent safety. Incumbents keep close tabs on political developments in their constituencies, and many prefer to retire rather than suffer the rebuke of voters. These strategic considerations lurk behind many incumbents' retirements, even when they cite other reasons for their decisions. In short, the chances of success are equally important for incumbents as for challengers when considering future career options.[83]

Female Candidates

High-caliber potential candidates abound in America's communities—even in minority party circles within noncompetitive districts.[84] But all too often, these individuals prefer to remain on the sidelines. The road to public office is increasingly arduous and costly. And the odds are often long, especially when running against a dominant party or an entrenched incumbent. Therefore, quality challengers among women often fail to step forward.

As many past elections demonstrate, women are likely to forgo opportunities to run for political office, even when they have been highly successful in the professions that usually precede public office. Prominent female lawyers, business people, educators, and political activists are less likely than similarly situated males to see themselves as good candidates for political office.[85] U.S. political institutions are more male dominated than those in most other advanced democracies, but the cause appears to lie more with the calculations of prospective candidates than with voters. Women are *not* less likely than men to win races they enter, but they are less likely to consider a candidacy in the first place. In part, this difference reflects the traditional perspective: Many, often male, party leaders, elected officials, and advocacy groups are less likely to recruit women to run. There is also the reality that male lawmakers dominate the membership of the House and Senate, and incumbents are hard to defeat. Broader societal norms and socialization processes can make it more difficult for women to promote themselves and seek political leadership positions. Little surprise that gender parity is not in Congress's immediate future.

On the other hand, there are years like the 2018 mid-term elections that commentators dubbed "The Year of the Woman." A record number of female candidates, overwhelmingly Democratic (89D, 13R), won election to the 116th House. The previous record was 85, set in 2016. Of the newcomers elected in 2018, 37 were Democrats; only one freshman Republican (Carol Miller of West Virginia) won a House seat. The 116th Senate will have 24 females (17D, 7R); the previous record was 23.[86] Of the ten freshman senators elected in 2018, two are Republicans.

Why the record number of females in this election, especially in the House? Three factors, among others, are noteworthy. First, mid-term elections are typically referendums on the incumbent president. Donald Trump's conduct and behavior (e.g., coarse rhetoric) while campaigning for the presidency in 2016 and then in the White House offended numerous women voters across the country. Their anger manifested itself in a number of ways, such as nationwide women's marches the day after Trump's inauguration and the surge of female voters, many suburban Republicans.

Second, a wave of first-time female candidates decided to run for the House, some even challenging their own party's incumbents in primary elections (recall Chapter 1's discussion of Democratic Representative Ocasio-Cortez). They represented the change wanted by many voters. Consider that Democratic women prevailed in 180 primary elections "compared with 52 for the GOP," with "233 women on the House general election ballot."[87] Many women ran for Congress, said an experienced political operative, because they sensed that "no one is going to fight for me or the people like me, so I am going to step up and do it myself."[88]

Third, besides President Trump, the national political context encouraged women's electoral participation and candidacies. They were a driving force that influenced the 2018 election outcome. For example, think of this compelling development: the array of reports about the abuse of power, sexual harassment, and deplorable behavior against women in diverse workplaces, such as business, media, entertainment, and government. Little surprise that such misbehavior gave rise to a countrywide #MeToo movement—women telling their stories about sexual harassment. "This is the year of fired up, female college graduate," said David Wasserman of the *Cook Political Report*. "They have a history of turning out in large numbers. But now, they are even more motivated."[89] According to one account, almost "60 percent of women voted Democratic" in 2018, with the percentage even higher for college graduates.[90]

Many congressional Republicans recognize that they must do much better in recruiting female candidates. In the 116th Congress (2019–2021), 90 percent of House Republicans are white males compared to 38 percent of House Democrats.[91]

Tom Emmers of Minnesota, the 116th Congress's (2019–2021) chair of the House GOP congressional campaign committee, provided a roadmap for improvement. "Women are much less likely than men to consider running for office on their own," he said. "This means two things: Getting more women in office requires infrastructure, like candidate training, on-the-ground recruitment, and fundraising; and political parties have to believe in prioritizing women candidates because they think electing women is important."[92]

NOMINATING POLITICS

Nominating procedures, set forth in state laws and conditioned by party customs, further shape the potential pool of candidates. Historically, these procedures have expanded to ever-wider circles of participants—a development that has diminished the power of party leaders and thrust more initiative upon the candidates themselves. In most states, the direct primary—allowing party voters to choose their party's nominees—is the formal mechanism for selecting congressional candidates.

Rules of the Nominating Game

Every state has election laws that provide for primary elections for House and Senate candidates, but these laws vary widely.[93] The critical question is who should be permitted to vote in a party's primary. The states have adopted varying answers. Party leaders naturally prefer strict rules that reward party loyalty, discourage outsider candidates, and maximize their own influence on the outcome. States with strong party traditions therefore tend to have closed primaries. This arrangement requires voters to declare party affiliation in order to vote in the primary. (Their affiliation is considered permanent until they take steps to change it.) In open primaries, voters can vote in the primary of either party (but not in both) simply by requesting the party's ballot at the polling place.

California, a solid Democratic state, devised a unique primary process. A few other states have something similar. Dubbed a "jungle primary," Democratic and Republican candidates are listed on the primary ballot with the top two vote-getters, regardless of their party affiliation, moving on to the general election. Under this system, the top two might be two Republicans or two Democrats. The concern of Democratic officials is that if their voters split their ballot among many Democratic candidates, two Republicans could advance to the November general elections.[94]

Few primaries are competitive races. According to one study, only about 1 percent of incumbents in the post–World War II period were defeated in a primary.[95] Despite high-profile primary challenges, contested primaries are not becoming more frequent. Instead, primary challenges tend to be more nationally visible because they are funded by more outside groups, centered around larger, ideological controversies, or involve presidential campaigning.[96] Nominations for open-seat races, however, are virtually certain to feature contested primaries. But even including primaries for open seats, the typical primary winner's share is more than 60 percent of the vote.[97]

Parties and Nominations

Despite the prevalence of primaries, party organizations at all levels are hardly without leverage in nominations. They influence nominations indirectly by contacting promising prospects, linking them with campaign contributors, endorsing them, and assisting in other ways. Parties are centrally involved in candidate recruitment. Parties are most active in districts regarded as winnable, and the people they seek out are often respected local officeholders, prominent figures in the community, or someone who has run for or won the seat before.

Mindful of the two Congresses, party leaders tend to be pragmatists—above all, bent on finding winners. They want their party to nominate "electable" candidates. As Senate Majority Leader Mitch McConnell, R-KY stated: "We intend to play in primaries if there's a clear choice between someone who can win in November and someone who can't."[98]

Intraparty rivalries often mark nominating contests. The Tea Party movement, in particular, fueled an unusually high level of internal ideological contention within the Republican Party between 2009 and 2014. In 2010, for example, a Tea Party activist competed in Delaware's special election for the U.S. Senate. She famously began a campaign ad with the phrase "I'm not a witch" because of her early interest in the occult. She won the low-turnout primary contest against a popular GOP former governor, who was also a House member at the time. She lost the special election to the Democratic nominee (Chris Coons).[99]

Congressional Democrats also have their outside insurgent groups who challenge candidates backed by the party establishment. Two 20-year Democratic veterans of the House—representatives Joseph Crowley and Michael Capuano—lost their primaries in 2018 to female candidates (representatives Ocasio-Cortez and Ayanna Pressley).

Sizing Up the Primary System

The direct primary was one of the reforms adopted early in the twentieth century to overcome corrupt, boss-dominated nominating conventions. It has permitted more participation in selecting candidates, and yet, primaries normally attract a narrower segment of voters than do general elections. Primary contests in recent years have drawn less than 25 percent of eligible voters—or less than half the number who voted in the general elections. Less publicized than general elections, primaries tend to attract voters who are somewhat older, wealthier, better educated, more politically aware, and more ideologically committed than the electorate as a whole.[100] Primaries also have hampered the political parties by encouraging would-be officeholders to appeal directly to the public and construct support networks apart from the party machinery. Still, leaders strive to influence who enters their primaries and who wins them. Displaying impressive resilience and adaptability, party organizations have recast themselves as organizations "'in service' to [their] candidates and officeholders but not in control of them."[101] Finally, primaries are a costly way of choosing candidates. Unless candidates begin with overwhelming advantages (such as incumbency), they must mount virtually the same kind of campaign in the primary that they will repeat later in the general election.

CONCLUSION

The rules of the game that narrow the potential field of congressional contenders can be thought of as a series of gates, each narrower than the one before. First are the constitutional qualifications for holding office. Far more restrictive are the personal attributes associated with a successful public career. Next are the complex rules of apportionment and districting. Beyond these are the nominating procedures (usually primaries). These successive gates sharply reduce the number of people who are likely to become real contenders.

Equally importantly, individuals must make up their own minds about running for the House or Senate. Such choices embrace a range of considerations—many personal and emotional but all based on some estimate of the likely benefits and costs of the candidacy. This winnowing process presents voters with a limited choice on election day: two, occasionally more, preselected or self-selected candidates. From this tiny circle, senators and representatives are chosen.

Winners and Losers. Senate candidate Representative Beto O'Rourke, D-Tex., moves through a crowd at a campaign rally in Austin. Senator Ted Cruz, R-Tex., greets supporters in Victoria. Cruz and O'Rourke shake hands before their first debate. O'Rourke logs his campaign appearances on Twitter.

Beto O'Rourke ✔
@BetoORourke   Follow   ⌄

Yesterday, we were block walking in Laredo, meeting with our fellow Texans in McAllen, and coming together again in Brownsville. From skateboarding to a late dinner at Whataburger, here's your recap from day 21 of our road trip:

114K views   1:39 / 2:18

5:44 AM - 19 Aug 2018

2,413 Retweets   7,280 Likes

♡ 208   ⟲ 2.4K   ♡ 7.3K

MAKING IT

The Electoral Game

At the outset of the election cycle, nobody expected the Texas Senate race to be competitive. In a state where presidential candidate Hillary Clinton garnered only 43 percent of the vote and no Democrat had won statewide office since 1994, Republican incumbent Sen. Ted Cruz would likely cruise to reelection. But Beto O'Rourke, a little-known, 45-year-old, three-term congressman from El Paso, made the race one to watch on election night. In fact, the 2018 Texas Senate race would turn out to be one of the most expensive in the country, with the two candidates spending more than $100 million.

O'Rourke waged a campaign that broke all the rules. In one of the most populous states in the country, he ran a person-to-person campaign focused on meeting voters individually. He visited every one of Texas's 254 counties, even though a large majority of the state's voters live in fewer than a dozen. As O'Rourke himself described it, he pursued "the least sophisticated strategy you've ever seen, literally just showing up everywhere all the time, and never discriminating based on party or any other difference."[1] Rather than running as a moderate in a conservative state, O'Rourke campaigned as an unapologetic progressive. He advocated for universal health care, a path to citizenship for undocumented immigrants, an assault weapons ban, abortion rights, and a higher minimum wage.[2] O'Rourke received no help from the national Democratic party, and he disavowed PAC contributions. But relying upon grassroots support, he raised more than $70 million in small donations, nearly twice as much as his opponent.

O'Rourke's unorthodox, rule-breaking campaign elicited a powerful response. His barnstorming attracted large and growing crowds over time. He built a national audience via social media. He livestreamed his campaign on Facebook—showing not just his speeches but himself doing his own laundry or skateboarding in a Whataburger parking lot. His campaign mushroomed to more than 1,000 paid staffers, along with tens of thousands of volunteers, housed in more than 700 "pop-up" offices across the state.[3]

Excitement about O'Rourke's campaign raised Democratic turnout in the 2018 midterms to levels not seen in any Texas midterm election in decades. The turnout in Texas in 2018 was even higher than that in the presidential election of 2000, when Texas governor George W. Bush won the White House. O'Rourke successfully boosted participation even among less politically engaged demographics, including young people and Latinos. The effects extended far beyond O'Rourke's own race, as elevated Democratic turnout helped carry downticket Democratic candidates to victory in several close races.[4]

Idiosyncratic in so many respects, the 2018 Texas Senate race underscores an important element of contemporary congressional elections. In an era when so few voters split their tickets, it is very difficult even for remarkably skilled, hard-working, and charismatic candidates to win against the partisan grain of their states and districts.[5] O'Rourke's persona and message turned what was projected to be a Cruz cakewalk into a barnburner. But even though O'Rourke's campaign offered a compelling message and exciting candidacy, it was not enough to overcome the large imbalance in Texas partisanship. O'Rourke significantly outperformed expectations, falling only 215,000 votes short out of more than 8.3 million votes cast. But Cruz's 2018 reelection attests to a political context in which party allegiances have become an increasingly powerful determinant of election outcomes.

CAMPAIGN STRATEGIES

Campaigns are volatile mixtures of personal contacts, fund-raising, speechmaking, advertising, and symbolic appeals. As acts of communication, campaigns are designed to convey messages to potential voters. The goal is to win over a plurality of those who cast ballots on election day.

Asking the Right Questions

Whether incumbents or challengers, candidates for Congress strive to map out a successful campaign strategy. To that end, each potential candidate must consider the following questions: What sort of constituency do I seek to represent? Are my name, face, and career familiar to voters? What resources—money, group support, and volunteers—can I attract? What leaders and groups are pivotal to a winning campaign? What issues are uppermost in potential voters' minds? How can I reach those voters most effectively? When should my campaign begin, and how should it be paced? And, perhaps most importantly, what are my chances for victory? The answers to such questions define campaign strategy.

The constituency itself shapes a candidate's campaign. In populous states, Senate aspirants must appeal to diverse economic and social groups scattered over wide areas and many media markets. In fast-growing states, even Senate incumbents must introduce themselves to new voters who have arrived since the last election. Only small-state Senate candidates are able to know their constituents as well as House candidates know theirs. But unlike states, House districts often fit within no natural geographic community, media market, or existing political division.[6] In such situations, candidates must find the most suitable forums, media outlets, and organizations to reach voters who may have little in common other than being enclosed within the same district boundaries.

Because incumbents are typically hard to defeat, the incumbent's decision to seek reelection colors the entire electoral undertaking. The partisan leanings of the electorate are also critical. The dominant party's candidates stress party loyalty, underscore long-standing partisan values, and sponsor get-out-the-vote (GOTV) drives. Minority party campaigns highlight personalities, downplay partisan differences, and exploit factional splits within the majority party, perhaps by invoking *wedge issues* designed to pry voters away from their usual party home. As voters' partisan attachments have hardened amid rising polarization, it has become increasingly difficult for candidates to win over enough "defectors" to triumph in a district that tilts toward the other party.

Finally, the perceptions and attitudes of voters must be reflected in campaign planning. Through surveys, focus groups, or old-fashioned informal pulse taking, strategists take account of what is on voters' minds and what, if anything, they know or think about the candidate. Well-known candidates try to capitalize on their visibility; lesser-known ones run ads that repeat their names over and over again. Candidates with a reputation for openness and geniality highlight those qualities in ads. Those who are more introverted (yes, there are such politicians) stress experience and competence. Candidates who are young emphasize their vigor, energy, and new ideas. Candidates who have made tough, unpopular decisions tout themselves as courageous leaders. In the wake of scandals, honesty and openness are on display.

Choosing the Message

The average citizen is barraged with media messages of all kinds—an hour of television commercials per day, among other things. The candidate's overarching challenge is to project an image through this cacophony of media appeals, including those from other candidates. "The only way to cut through this communication clutter," a political marketing executive points out, "is to adopt the strategy proven effective by successful businesses. Create a brand. And manage the message with discipline and impact."[7] In other words, forge a message that will stand out from all of the competing messages in the media marketplace.

A candidate's message is usually distilled into a single theme or slogan that is repeated on radio, TV, billboards, websites, and in campaign literature. "A good message . . . is a credible statement that can be summed up in a few sentences and frequently ends with a kicker slogan."[8] Strategists use these messages to frame the campaign: to set the election's agenda—not by changing people's attitudes but by shifting their attention to issues that favor their candidate or diminish the opponent. "There's only three or four plots," explained Carter Eskew, a Democratic consultant. "Plots for incumbents are Representative X is different from the rest; X can deliver; X stands with you. And the perennial plot for challengers is (fill in the blank) years are long enough; it's time for a change."[9] As challengers seek lines of attack, officeholders often find that incumbency has its liabilities. An extensive public record gives enterprising opponents many potential openings to exploit. Past votes or positions may be highlighted to discredit the officeholder, sometimes fairly and sometimes unfairly. Incumbents may be shackled to unpopular positions or figures, such as an unpopular health care bill, a controversial tax bill, and unpopular presidents or party leaders. Sometimes, incumbents become complacent and take voters' support for granted, a major political mistake. One campaign consultant summed up the lesson of such races: "You have to earn that support every two years. A lot of members of Congress forget how to run."[10]

CAMPAIGN RESOURCES

Even the best campaign strategy will fail if the candidate cannot muster the resources necessary to implement it. The chief resources in congressional elections are money and organization.

"Money is the mother's milk of politics," declared California's legendary assembly speaker Jess Unruh. Money is not everything in politics, but many candidates falter for lack of it, and nearly all expend valuable time and energy struggling to get it. Every candidate, writes Paul S. Herrnson, wages not one but two campaigns: a campaign for resources (the so-called money primary) that precedes and underwrites the more visible campaign for votes.[11] Campaigns in the United States are very costly. In the 2017–2018 electoral cycle, congressional candidates raised $1.7 billion and spent most of it. The average Senate race cost nearly $9 million for each of the two major-party nominees. The average House contest cost $1.9 million per major-party nominee.[12] When modern recordkeeping began some forty years ago, House candidates spent one-sixth as much.[13] Even controlling for inflation, expenditures for congressional campaigns have sextupled over the last forty years.

No mystery surrounds these skyrocketing costs. Stronger competition for majority control of Congress, population growth, and new campaign technologies—electronic media, polling, and consultants of all kinds—account for much of the increase. To be sure, old-fashioned campaigns based on armies of volunteers canvassing door-to-door can be effective in some contests. But candidates raise as much money as they can for good reason.

Fund-raising consumes tremendous amounts of time. In January 2013, the Democratic Congressional Campaign Committee (DCCC) gave a presentation for incoming freshmen about the time they should expect to dedicate to raising money. Figure 4-1 displays a slide from the PowerPoint presentation these new members received. The DCCC prescribed a ten-hour day for members while they are in Washington, DC. Out of each day, four hours should be spent on "call time" and another hour set aside for "strategic outreach," which includes fund-raising as well as media relations. By comparison, three to four hours are set aside for doing the regular work of Congress, including hearings, votes, and meetings with constituents. A subsequent slide specified that members should expect to devote three hours for fund-raising out of every eight-hour workday while they are in their districts during congressional recesses.

In a 2016 interview with on CBS's *60 Minutes,* then-Rep. David Jolly, R-Fla., related what a party leader told him when he came to Congress after a March 2014 special election: "We sat behind closed doors at one of the party headquarter back rooms in front of a white board where the equation was drawn out. You have six months until the election. Break that down to having to raise $2 million in the next six months. And your job, new member of Congress, is to raise $18,000 a day. Your first responsibility is to make sure you hit $18,000 a day."[14] To be sure, fund-raising practices vary. Members from safe districts feel less fundraising pressure than members representing swing seats. Some members raise less money than their party leaders and party campaign committees ask from them. There is no question, however, that fund-raising puts intense year-round pressure on members' daily schedules.[15]

FIGURE 4-1 ■ The Democratic Congressional Campaign Committee's Recommended Daily Schedule for New Members, 2013

☑ **4 hours**   **Call Time**

☑ **1–2 hours**   **Constituent Visits**

☑ **2 hours**   **Committee/Floor**

☑ **1 hour**   **Strategic Outreach**
                          Breakfasts, Meet & Greets, Press

☑ **1 hour**   **Recharge Time**

Source: Ryan Grim and Sabrina Siddiqui, "Call Time for Congress Shows How Fundraising Dominates Bleak Work," *Huffington Post,* politics blog, January 8, 2013, www.huffingtonpost.com/2013/01/08/call-time-congressional-fundraising_n_2427291.html?ncid=edlinkusaolp00000003.

Campaign Finance Regulations

The regulation of campaign finance in the United States is a dauntingly complicated subject. Congress's regulatory efforts have led to a proliferation of entities, many with the sole purpose of raising and spending money in political campaigns, each with its own rules and regulations. In addition, campaign finance law in the United States has been greatly complicated by a variety of Supreme Court rulings. In the landmark case of *Buckley v. Valeo* (1976),[16] the Supreme Court held that campaign contributions and spending are free speech protected by the First Amendment of the Constitution. The Court ruled that Congress may legitimately regulate campaign contributions—to prevent corruption or the appearance of corruption. But the Court held that most campaign spending could not be regulated. Subsequent Supreme Court cases have also had far-reaching effects on the state of the law in this area.

We must distinguish between (1) the rules governing how candidates can raise money for their own campaigns and (2) the rules governing the electioneering activities of organized entities not controlled by candidates. So-called *outside money*—campaign expenditures made by party committees and other organized groups not under candidates' control—has become a much more important feature of campaign financing.

Candidates' Campaigns

Congressional candidates may raise funds from four sources: individual contributors, political action committees (PACs), party committees, and themselves and their families. More than half of the money raised by House and Senate candidates comes from individuals. In the 2017–2018 election cycle, congressional candidates (or their campaign committees) could receive up to $2,700 from each individual contributor for each election (primary, general, or runoff). Individual contributions of more than $200 must identify the contributor's name and employer—information reported to the Federal Election Commission (FEC), the federal agency charged with regulating campaign finance. Although there are caps on the amount of money federal candidates can raise from a single individual, there is no limit to the total amount an individual can contribute across all federal races.[17]

PACs may also contribute directly to congressional candidates. Under current regulations, multicandidate PACs are defined as those registered for more than six months, having fifty or more contributors, and making contributions to five or more candidates for federal office. In the 2017–2018 election cycle, multicandidate PACs could contribute up to $5,000 to a congressional candidate (or the candidate's campaign committee) for each election. For PACs not meeting the definition of multicandidate PACs, contributions to congressional candidates were capped at $2,700 per election. In the 2017–2018 election cycle, PAC contributions topped $505 million. Although they have declined in importance, PACs remain key players in House races: They accounted for a quarter of

House candidates' campaign receipts in 2017–18 and about 10 percent for Senate candidates.

In the 2017–2018 election cycle, party committees—national, state, congressional, and local—could contribute up to $5,000 per election to congressional candidates. As these amounts make clear, party funds cannot begin to cover the costs of today's campaigns. Party organizations of all types account for a relatively small portion of individual candidates' direct funding, even though in recent years, they have greatly increased their efforts and fund-raising capacities. Parties may also use additional funds to pay for services requested by a candidate, such as polling, advertisements, and media time. But these *coordinated expenditures* are also subject to limits set by the FEC.

Another source of campaign money for congressional candidates is the candidate's own funds. Candidates and their families may spend as much of their own money in a campaign as they wish. Candidates who self-fund their races do not have a good track record of success, however.[18] As one particularly stark example, businessman Bob Hugin spent more than $27 million of his own money in a losing challenge to Sen. Bob Menendez, D-N.J., in 2018.

Independent Expenditures

Rather than contribute to candidates' campaigns, parties and organized groups also try to sway election outcomes via independent efforts in campaigns that are formally unconnected to candidates' own efforts. Such groups develop messages, run media ads, and support get-out-the-vote drives. These independent expenditures are not subject to any limits.

A wide array of new organized groups operating outside the control of federal candidates have emerged in the wake of two 2010 court rulings, *Citizens United v. FEC*[19] and *Speechnow.org v. Federal Election Commission*.[20] Exploiting the opportunities opened up by these cases, hundreds of new, big-spending organizations known as *super PACs* have been formed. Super PACs are defined by the FEC as "non-connected political action committees." Such PACs cannot contribute directly to federal candidates' campaigns and cannot spend money in coordination with their campaigns. But they are permitted to make unlimited expenditures to influence the outcome of elections. Before 2010, corporations, nonprofits, and labor unions could not spend funds out of their general treasuries for pro-candidate advertisements. In *Citizens United,* the Supreme Court struck down that limitation as a form of censorship of protected political speech.

The Court expected, however, that such independent expenditures would be subject to the disclaimer and disclosure requirements imposed by existing campaign finance law. In the Court's opinion, Justice Anthony Kennedy wrote, "With the advent of the Internet, prompt disclosure of expenditures can provide shareholders and citizens with the information needed to hold corporations and elected officials accountable."[21] Campaign finance law, however, does not provide for the information that Justice Kennedy assumed would be available. Under the current FEC interpretation, a contribution of $1,000 or more to a group making an electioneering communication—that is, a pro-candidate advertisement in close proximity to an election—is reportable only if the contributor designated it to be used for a particular electioneering communication.[22] In other words, a contributor may avoid disclosure merely by not directing the contribution toward any particular advertisement.

Certain types of groups, moreover, are wholly exempted from disclosure laws. Groups organized under section 501©(4) of the Internal Revenue Code have become much more important players in campaign finance in recent years, in great part simply because of their exemption from disclosure requirements.[23] For example, the National Rifle Association Legislative Action Fund, organized as a 501(c)(4) and thus not required to disclose its funders, spent more than $9 million on 2018 elections. The U.S. Chamber of Commerce, which is organized as a 501(c)(6), does not identify its donors, even though it spent $13 million in 2017–2018. In the 2017–2018 cycle, a total of $151.6 million in outside money was spent with no disclosure of the donors, and another $450 million was subject to only partial disclosure, together constituting more than the total $553.7 million contributed under full disclosure requirements

The upshot of these developments is that the fund-raising efforts of outside groups are far less stringently regulated than those of both candidates and political parties.[24] As a consequence, expenditures by outside groups have surged.[25] As of May 2018, political advertising by nondisclosing outside groups had swelled by nearly 90 percent compared to the same period in the preceding midterm election.[26]

Unlike contributions to super PACs, contributions to the parties are subject to caps, though higher ones than permitted as direct contributions to the candidates themselves.[27] In the 2017–2018 election cycle, the national parties' entities, including the House and Senate campaign committees, spent more than $1.4 billion, accounting for more than a quarter of all campaign spending.[28] The vast majority of this money was spent as independent expenditures in targeted races. This is an impressive figure, considering that the parties face an array of contribution limits that don't apply to outside groups.[29]

The combined effect of independent spending by outside groups and parties is that "candidates are no longer directly in control of financing of their campaigns."[30] Individual candidates accounted for just slightly over half of campaign spending in the 2018 cycle.[31] Outside spending is especially important in the most expensive, hotly contested races: For example, independent expenditures accounted for $90 million of the $114 million spent in the 2018 Florida Senate race in which Republican challenger Rick Scott defeated Democratic incumbent Bill Nelson.

As one former FEC commissioner put it, then, "the money's flowing."[32] When the last major campaign finance reform law was enacted in 2002, skeptics argued that the new law would do little to halt the overall flow of money into political campaigns. "This law will not remove one dime from politics," predicted Sen. Mitch McConnell, R-Ky., the measure's leading GOP foe. McConnell's skepticism has certainly been borne out, both by innovations in campaign finance and by Supreme Court rulings limiting the scope of regulatory restrictions. In the end, campaign finance laws have failed to limit the influence of money in politics. Big money is alive and well in U.S. elections, and it increasingly flows through organized groups and party channels that operate independently of individual candidates.

Incumbents Versus Challengers

Although incumbents need less money than do challengers, they receive more—a double-barreled financial advantage (see Figure 4-2). Incumbents are both better known than challengers and enjoy government-subsidized ways of reaching constituents. Nevertheless, incumbents are able to raise substantially more money. In 2018, House incumbents raised $1.9 million, on average, to defend their seats—more than four times what their challengers could muster. Senate incumbents raised an average of $15.5 million in 2018, outpacing their general-election foes more than seven to one.[33]

Challengers' first hurdle is to raise enough money to make their names and faces known to voters. Because most of them start from a low baseline of name recognition, their campaign dollars tend to be more cost-effective than those of incumbents. Nevertheless, they must raise a great deal of money to defeat an incumbent. As Gary C. Jacobson and Jamie L. Carson point out, "The minimum price tag for a competitive House campaign under average conditions today is probably more than $800,000; 150 of the 160 challengers who defeated incumbents from 1996 through 2014 spent more than that amount."[34]

Incumbents of both parties are able to raise money far more easily than challengers because contributors see them as better investments. Many donors to congressional campaigns seek to cultivate closer relationships with people in positions of power. Donors know that incumbents usually win reelection, so they do not usually waste their money on challengers, even when those challengers might be more appealing in their policy stances or party affiliation. Indeed, "access-oriented" giving follows the shifts in party control of Congress, as donors curry favor with committee chairs and other leaders regardless of party.[35] Challengers obviously cannot attract this type of campaign donation, which gives incumbents a substantial fund-raising advantage.[36]

Challengers have a difficult time convincing donors that they have any reasonable chance of winning. In this arena, as in so many others, nothing succeeds like success. "Failure to raise enough money creates a vicious spiral," explains political analyst Thomas B. Edsall. "Some donors become reluctant to invest their cash, and then state and national parties are less likely to target . . . party building and get out the vote drives in those races."[37]

When challengers are successful in raising money, they typically find that the funds make a significant difference in their electoral chances. Generally speaking, the more challengers spend, the more votes they are likely to attract.[38] The same is not true of incumbents. In fact, for incumbents, there is actually

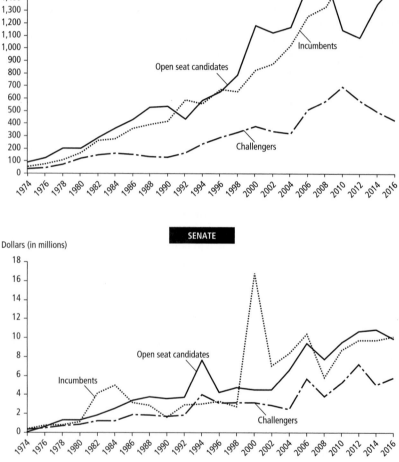

Sources: Federal Election Commission (FEC) figures for campaigns through 2000 are compiled in Norman J. Ornstein, Thomas E. Mann, and Michael J. Malbin, Vital Statistics on Congress 2001–2002 (Washington, DC: AEI Press, 2002), 87–98. Figures through 2014, also derived from the FEC, are found at Center for Responsive Politics, "Election Overview, Incumbent Advantage," www.opensecrets.org.

a negative correlation between campaign expenditures and electoral success. Vulnerable incumbents tend to speed up their fund-raising. As Jacobson points out, "Incumbents can raise whatever they think they need."[39] Endangered incumbents thus raise prodigious sums as they seek to hold onto their seats. Meanwhile, safe incumbents—especially senior members who infrequently face significant electoral challenges—spend much less. Despite the negative correlation between campaign spending and electoral security, incumbents are unquestionably better off with more campaign money than less. But compared with challengers, incumbents' success or failure is much less tied to their fund-raising totals.

Many incumbents raise and spend far more than is necessary. Incumbents' overspending is frequently motivated by a sense of uncertainty and risk. "Because of uncertainty," Jacobson explains, "members tend to exaggerate electoral threats and overreact to them. They are inspired by worst-case scenarios—what would they have to do to win if everything went wrong?—rather than objective probabilities."[40] Not all incumbent fund-raising is actually aimed at the race at hand. Incumbents often have strategic purposes for fund-raising beyond campaign finance. Preemptive fund-raising is aimed at dissuading serious opponents. Sen. Lindsey Graham, R-S.C., for example, sought to fend off challengers by amassing a "staggering war chest" early in the campaign cycle.[41] Some members, especially those with party leadership ambitions, raise money so they can impress their colleagues by distributing funds to needier candidates. Sometimes, longtime incumbents deliberately overspend in pursuit of decisive electoral victories that might establish their claims for higher office.

Allocating Resources

As exercises in communication, campaigns are driven by the need to find a cost-effective way of reaching citizens and getting them to vote. Candidates and their managers face many different trade-offs as they make decisions about allocating resources, depending on the context.

As a rule, statewide Senate races are mass-media contests, with messages conveyed mainly through radio and television. Costs are especially high in densely populated states with large metropolitan media markets. Senate candidates typically spend far more on media advertising and fund-raising than do their House counterparts, who spend more on traditional means of voter contact.

Despite its astronomical costs, television advertising is popular because candidates believe it works. Almost all households in the United States own at least one television, and the average adult watches five hours of television a day.[42] The 2018 congressional elections set new records for television advertising. Between January 1, 2017, and September 17, 2018, over 2.2 million election-related spots aired on television for House and Senate candidates, at a total estimated cost of nearly $1 billion.[43] This level of spending on television advertisements was 70 percent more than the amount spent over the same period for the 2014 congressional races.

Candidates tailor their use of media to their political circumstances. Confident incumbents can channel their money into telephone, Internet and email, or door-to-door appeals that direct their messages to activists, partisans, and supporters. Lesser-known candidates must turn to broad-scale media, such as television, radio, newsletters, and billboards, to promote name recognition. Across the board, digital advertising has surged in importance. Fully $900 million was spent on digital ads to influence the 2018 midterm elections, a 260 percent increase over 2014.[44]

Candidates also have to make decisions about their pace of spending. Especially useful is early money—that is, having funds on hand to organize a campaign at the outset. EMILY's List—Early Money Is Like Yeast ("It makes the 'dough' rise")—a group begun in 1985, was formed on this premise. This group collects (bundles) individuals' donations for Democratic women candidates who support abortion rights. The Republican counterpart is Women in the Senate and House (WISH).

Late-blitz money also can turn the tide, although money alone rarely makes the difference at the end of a race. In the final weeks of a hard-fought race, both sides are trying to reach undecided voters. "You've got to move that 10 or 15 percent, many of whom are not paying much attention," a Democratic consultant explained. "Unfortunately, the way to do that is with negative or comparative ads."[45] Late in a competitive race, opponents frantically attack and—despite the scant time—counterattack.

Organizing the Campaign

Implementing a campaign strategy is the job of the candidates and their organizations. Waging a campaign is not for the fainthearted. Take the case of psychology professor Brian Baird. Having lost to the incumbent by a mere 887 votes in 1996, Baird vowed to run full tilt two years later. He spent almost all of his waking hours campaigning during the peak months (July–October)—more than ten hours a day for 123 days. Travel alone consumed many hours in his average-sized district, Washington's Third (comprising Olympia and southwestern Washington state).[46] Baird won by 10 percentage points in 1998 and went on to hold the seat until his retirement in 2010.

Candidates generally have to put together their own campaign organizations. Few localities today boast strong local parties. In some congressional districts, voter contact is the job of ward, precinct, and block captains. Candidates in some such areas still dispense "walking-around money" to encourage precinct captains to get out the vote and provide small financial rewards for voting. But in most places today, the traditional local parties have been replaced by hybrid organizations that partner with state and national parties and their allied interest groups.

When they can pay the price, today's candidates purchase campaign services from political consulting firms, most of them operating within partisan networks.[47] Consulting firms account for roughly 15 percent to 20 percent of congressional campaign spending.[48] Some firms offer a wide array of services; others specialize in polling, direct mail, phone banks, advertising, purchasing media time, coordinating volunteer efforts, fund-raising, or financial management and accounting. Despite the hype they often receive, it is by no means clear what consultants can really deliver in terms of election results.[49] Consultants cannot turn a campaign around by themselves. At best, they can make the most of a candidate's resources and help combat opponents' attacks. They cannot compensate for an unskilled or lazy candidate or for a candidate whose partisanship or ideology is out of line with the district.

CAMPAIGN TECHNIQUES

Campaigns are designed to convey the candidate's messages to people who will lend support and vote in the election. Campaigns are not necessarily directed at all voters. Often, narrower groups are targeted—most notably, the political party's core supporters.

The Air War: Media and Other Mass Appeals

Candidates reach the largest numbers of voters by running broadcast ads and making televised appearances. Television is the broadest spectrum medium, and its costs eat up half of campaign budgets.

Candidates obviously cannot fully control their media coverage. Some of the most effective appeals—news coverage and endorsements, for example—are determined by persons other than the candidate. Because journalists can raise unwanted or hostile questions, many politicians seek out the friendlier environments of talk shows hosted by nonjournalists. Even more congenial are appeals the candidates themselves buy and pay for—newsletters, websites, media ads, and direct mail. The drawback is that self-promotion is seen as less credible than information from independent sources.

More than half of voters rely on television for their campaign news—network, cable, or local. About four in ten turn to the Internet for news, and 20 percent turn frequently to newspapers.[50] And yet, local news programming largely ignores congressional campaign coverage. In the weeks preceding the 2012 elections, for example, 83 percent of the scheduled half-hour local news programs in a diverse sample of media markets offered no coverage at all of the U.S. House races in the area. For those media markets with a statewide Senate race, the "blackout rate" was also over 80 percent.[51] Most candidates must therefore pay to reach the voters.

Positive Themes

Campaign themes typically seek to evoke positive responses from citizens. Positive ads present candidates in warm, human terms to which citizens can relate. Skillfully done, TV ads can be very effective in bringing home the candidate's themes. A case in point was the series of brilliant, funny—and inexpensive—television ads that helped a little-known Wisconsin state legislator, Russ Feingold, win the Democratic primary, defeat a two-term incumbent senator, and then go on to serve three terms in the U.S. Senate (1993–2011). As his opponents battered each other with negative ads, Feingold ran clever, personal spots describing himself as the "underdog candidate." One showed Elvis, alive and endorsing Feingold. Another showed Feingold walking through his modest home, opening up a closet and saying, "No skeletons."

One of the best positive ads in 2018 was run by Rep. Pete Stauber, R-Minn., one of the only Republican candidates to flip a congressional district from the Democrats in a year where Republicans took widespread losses. In this ad, Stauber's family holds up the series of uniforms he has worn in his life, including a Detroit Red Wings hockey jersey and a Duluth police officer's uniform. The ad ends with Stauber assuring listeners that although he has worn a lot of uniforms in his life, he's "not interested in any political party's uniform" when he gets to Washington, DC.

Negative Themes

Candidates also deploy campaign resources against their opponents. Contrast ads distinguish the candidate from the opponent on the grounds of policy and experience, and attack ads strike at the opponent's record or personal character. The race against Rep. Scott Garrett, R-N.J., featured one of the more striking attack ads of the 2016 cycle. Over a soundtrack playing "Dixie" and visuals of cotton fields, a voice narrates: "His views are perfect for rural Alabama. So why is Scott Garrett representing New Jersey? . . . Scott Garrett's views might sound fine for the land of cotton, but we're not singing his tune in New Jersey." The cheesy soundtrack and the implied joke about southern rednecks lent the ad an undertone of mocking humor. Garrett was defeated for reelection by Josh Gottheimer, a former speechwriter to Bill Clinton.

Negative ads are common in modern campaigning because politicians believe they work. This strategy was forcefully described by Rep. Tom Cole, R-Okla., in a memo to his House colleagues: "Define your opponent immediately and unrelentingly. Do not let up—keep the tough ads running right up to election day. Don't make the mistake of pulling your ads in favor of a positive rotation the last weekend."[52] Although neither positive nor negative ads have much effect on strong partisans, negative ads can sway citizens who have little information to begin with and on those with little or no party allegiance.[53]

Although negative ads do at times stretch or distort the truth, they often serve an informing function. Research has shown that negative ads tend to lift voters' information levels, even if the information conveyed is distorted or trivial. "We should not necessarily see negative ads as a harmful part of our electoral system," argues Kenneth Goldstein, an expert on political advertising. "They are much more likely [than positive ads] to be about policy, to use supporting information, and to be reliable. Few negative ads are on personal issues."[54] As one deterrent to smear tactics, the Bipartisan Campaign Reform Act of 2002 requires that candidates personally appear in and vouch for their advertisements.

Evolving Mass Media

The old-fashioned media—newspapers, radio, and television networks— are on the decline. The newspaper business in the United States, in particular, appears to be in crisis. Just since 2004, the circulation of daily newspapers has dropped by 43 percent.[55] In tandem, the number of newsroom employees fell by 45 percent. The proportion of people who read newspapers continues to fall. Changing media even pose a threat to television, in that young people today rely far less on television news.

Meanwhile, the Internet is an increasingly important news source. In particular, younger adults tend to use social media as a main source of news.[56] In fact, a large majority of U.S. adults—68 percent—now get news on social media, according to a new survey by Pew Research Center.[57]

Since 2010, the use of social media has seen astronomical growth, especially Facebook, Instagram, and Twitter. Given these developments, candidates now recognize that social media has emerged as a vital way of communicating with supporters and cultivating their public image. They are investing increasing efforts in digital advertising and their social media presence.[58] But one of the challenges of the medium is its uncontrollability and decentralization. Any individual or group can generate content that goes "viral." Many of these viral stories turn out not to be true, but there is no recognized authority to warn readers away from disseminators of "fake news." Members of Congress and their staff closely monitor what constituents are saying on social media—even just a handful of comments on social media are enough to attract their attention.[59] As a means of campaign communications, Web outlets are unregulated. In 2006, the FEC decided to treat the Internet "as a unique and evolving mode of mass communication and political speech that warrants a restrained regulatory approach."[60]

The Ground War: Pressing the Flesh and Other Forms of Close Contact

Direct appeals to voters through personal appearances by candidates or their surrogates—at shopping centers, factory gates, or even door-to-door—are part of every campaign. In his successful 1948 Senate campaign, Lyndon B. Johnson swooped out of the sky in a helicopter to visit small Texas towns, grandly pitching his Stetson from the chopper for a bold entrance; an aide was assigned to retrieve the hat for use at the next stop.[61] Other candidates, preferring to stay closer to the ground, stage walking tours or other events to attract attention. Few elected officials get by without doing a great deal of what is inelegantly called *pressing the flesh*.

Recent social science research has demonstrated the importance of retail, as opposed to wholesale, campaigning. TV ads, direct mail, and phone banks are less effective than old-fashioned ways of getting out the vote. An array of experiments has shown that personalized messages delivered face-to-face or in a conversational manner over the phone are far superior to impersonal methods of reaching potential voters.[62] According to Yale political scientists Donald P. Green and Alan S. Gerber, face-to-face canvassing raises turnout by seven to twelve percentage points.[63] One-on-one campaigning is physically and emotionally challenging. But an obvious advantage of so-called *shoe-leather campaigning* is cost, at least when compared with mass-media appeals. "Door-to-door canvassing is the tactic of choice among candidates and campaigns that are short on cash," explain Green and Gerber. "Precinct walking is often described as the weapon of underdogs."[64] Former representative Dan Glickman, D-Kan. (1977–1995), describes his first House campaign as a thirty-one-year-old challenger facing a long-term incumbent:

I walked door-to-door to 35,000 homes over an eight-month period. I walked from 10:30 a.m. to 2 p.m. and again from 5:30 to 8 p.m. I lost 35 pounds and learned to be very realistic about dogs. I met a woman my father had lent $100 or $150 to 30 years before. She embraced me and said, "You saved us." I won by three percentage points.[65]

Face-to-face campaigning is obligatory in smaller communities, where people expect politicians to show up at festivals, parades, or annual county fairs. "If you ain't seen at the county fair, you're preached about on Sunday," remarked a politician as he led his party's Senate candidate around the hog and sheep barns in Ada, Oklahoma.[66] In small states, first-name relationships are often valued. "They want to know you," political scientist Garrison Nelson remarked about Vermont voters. The state's independent senator, Bernard Sanders, has long distributed bumper stickers that simply say, "Bernie."[67] In Bristol, on Rhode Island's coast, the Fourth of July parade—the oldest in the country—is "the first and perhaps biggest event of the campaign season."[68]

Getting Out the Vote

GOTV drives are focused on registering constituents to vote and then getting voters to the polls. Recognizing the importance of personalized voter contact, both parties have developed sophisticated GOTV operations. Each now relies on *microtargeting* to reach sympathetic voters. This approach employs computer models to exploit a wide array of data, such as the groups to which people belong or the magazines they read, to identify potential voters and the issues that are important to them. "Micro-targeting has become so widespread that it is now used by all House and Senate candidates, on both sides, in state legislative races, and in some cases, all the way down the ballot to local school board elections," concludes one journalist.[69] In addition, many groups finance their own field operations in support of favored candidates. In this sense, the parties' GOTV efforts are just part of a broader campaign waged by their allied groups. For example, the Service Employees International Union (SEIU) knocked on 3.6 million potential voters' doors and sent over 700,000 text messages before the 2018 midterm election.[70] For their part, Republicans depend on a wide array of pro-life, evangelical, and socially conservative organizations to undertake GOTV drives for their candidates.

The Parallel Campaigns

The scene is a hospital operating room; the patient is surrounded by surgeons and nurses. One surgeon, in a voice of astonishment, exclaims, "Oh my." A nurse asks, "Colitis?" Another nurse asks, "Hepatitis?" A third, "Diverticulitis?" The surgeon replies, "No, I'm afraid it's Dina Titus. Taxes up the yingyang. Her tax policy is killing us." The target of this television ad was 2008 Democratic House candidate Dina Titus, a former political science professor at the University of Nevada–Las Vegas and current representative for Nevada's First Congressional District. The ad was paid for by Freedom's Watch, a lobbying group bankrolled by wealthy conservatives, notably billionaire casino developer Sheldon Adelson.

The huge increase in spending by outside groups discussed previously means that campaigns no longer resemble boxing matches between two combatants. They have become free-for-alls in which multiple combatants throw punches and land roundhouse kicks. Candidates compete not only against their opponents and their parties but also against scores of groups that join the fray.

Hundreds of such organizations engage in congressional campaigning, most of them favoring one or the other major political party. As allies of a national party, these organizations contribute to the "nationalization" of congressional elections. The ads these organizations run tend to reinforce existing stereotypes about the parties. In 2018, Republican candidates all around the country were lambasted as hostile to health insurance protection for people with preexisting conditions. Democratic candidates everywhere were painted as supporters of "Nancy Pelosi's liberal agenda." Such ads undercut candidates' ability to control their own political image. As outside-group spending becomes a paramount element of campaign finance, it becomes harder for candidates to differentiate themselves from their national parties. Candidates in swing states or districts attempting to carve out distinctive profiles run up against their opponents' super PAC–funded ads that paint with a broad brush, lumping them in with the rest of their party's team.

WHO VOTES?

Although Congress is supposed to be the people's branch of government, less than half of voting-age citizens normally take part in House elections. In the 2014 House elections, just 36.7 percent of the voting-eligible population or VEP (all eligible residents age eighteen and over) participated.[71] In 2018, however, turnout was 50.3 percent—the highest voter turnout for any midterm election since 1914.[72]

As Figure 4-3 indicates, turnout varies according to whether the election is held in a presidential or a midterm year. Midterm races lack the intense publicity and stimulus to vote provided by presidential contests. Since the 1930s, turnout in midterm congressional elections has averaged about twelve percentage points below that of the preceding presidential election. Midterm electorates include a greater share of people who are interested in politics and—not unrelated—who are also more affluent and better educated.[73]

Reasons for Not Voting

Political analysts disagree over the reasons for the anemic voting levels in the United States, which are near the bottom among established democratic countries. Several explanations—not all of them compatible—have been suggested.[74] One explanation for nonvoting is simply demographic. Groups with low voting rates, such as young people, African Americans, and Latinos, have been growing as a share of the U.S. population. Young people (ages eighteen through twenty-nine) are traditional no-shows, perhaps because they have fewer of the life experiences (mortgages, taxes, school-age children, and community ties) that propel older people toward activism. Four out of ten young people have not registered to vote (three times greater than those aged fifty and older).[75] Turnout among young Americans in the 2018 midterms was estimated at 31 percent.[76]

A second explanation stresses legal barriers to voting. More than 20 percent of Americans are not registered to vote.[77] Many democracies automatically register all adults; some even require that people vote. By contrast, U.S. citizens must take the initiative to register and vote.

Other disincentives can be blamed on electoral arrangements. U.S. citizens are asked to vote far more often than are voters in parliamentary regimes; and elections are held on weekdays, not on weekends or national holidays. States have moved in contrary reform directions. A number of states and districts have changed their election procedures to make it easier to register and vote. Absentee balloting and voting by mail have become more common. Some states permit ballots to be submitted over a period of time. Oregon citizens may even vote by telephone. At the same time, lawmakers in other states have raised new barriers through voter ID requirements—such as photo IDs or proof-of-citizenship papers. Although passed under the pretext of combating voter fraud, these are widely understood as partisan measures intended "to depress voter turnout in minority and poor communities."[78] In 2008, the Supreme Court upheld the strictest such law, Indiana's statute that requires all voters to present a valid government ID.[79] The Supreme Court's *Shelby County v. Holder* (2013) decision overturning the Voting Rights Act of 1965's requirement for preclearance of changes in voting rules in states with a history of discrimination opened the door to more states adopting tight

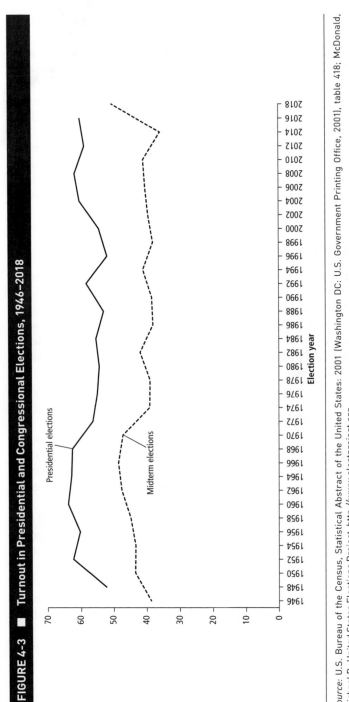

FIGURE 4-3 ■ Turnout in Presidential and Congressional Elections, 1946–2018

Presidential elections

Midterm elections

Election year

Source: U.S. Bureau of the Census, Statistical Abstract of the United States: 2001 (Washington DC: U.S. Government Printing Office, 2001), table 418; McDonald, Michael P., United States Elections Project, http://www.electproject.org.

voter ID laws. Hours after the Supreme Court's ruling, the state of Texas began enforcing a strict photo identification requirement for voting.[80]

Biased or careless election administration can also turn away voters or lead to a miscount of their ballots, as uncovered in voting scandals in Florida and Georgia in 2018. Local election practices often weigh most heavily on minority or socio-economically disadvantaged citizens, who are more likely to encounter insufficient numbers of poll workers, antiquated or badly designed voting machines, and longer lines.

A final explanation for low voter turnout is citizen disaffection, apathy, and cynicism. Many non-voters simply believe that their vote will not make a difference, all candidates make false promises, and elections cannot bring about meaningful change. Noncompetitive elections, poor candidates, and contentious or negative campaigning are also thought to keep people away from the polling booths.

Biases of Voting

Although voting is the simplest and most accessible form of political involvement, it is still biased in favor of people at the higher rungs of the social and generational ladders—those who are older, more affluent, better educated, and more in touch with political events. Social class has a stronger effect on voting participation than race, ethnicity, and gender. According to political scientists Jan E. Leighley and Jonathan Nagler, almost 80 percent of high-income earners vote, compared to barely 50 percent of low-income Americans.[81]

HOW VOTERS DECIDE

What induces voters to cast their ballots for one candidate and not another? As a general rule, voters reach their decisions on the basis of party loyalty. But candidate assessments and salient issues also figure into voters' decisions. The relative strength of these elements varies over time and among specific races.

Although U.S. voters are often uninformed or indifferent about political issues and candidates, they employ what is called *low-information rationality* or gut reasoning to make voting booth decisions. As Samuel L. Popkin explains, people "triangulate and validate their opinions in conversations with people they trust and according to the opinions of national figures whose judgments and positions they have come to know."[82] Thus, voters work through imperfect information to make choices that will often roughly approximate the choices they would have made with more perfect information.

Party Loyalties

Party identification is the single most powerful factor in determining voters' choices. And it remains the strongest single correlate of voting in congressional elections. In recent elections, at least nine in every ten Democrats and Republicans voted for their parties' nominees. Independents tend to split their votes more evenly between the parties. In 2014, independents preferred Republican to Democratic candidates by twelve percentage points.[83] In 2018, however, independents preferred Democrats by thirteen percentage points.[84]

According to surveys, most people who claim to be independents are, in fact, closet partisans who lean toward one party or the other. These independent leaners—about a quarter of the total electorate—hold attitudes similar to those of partisans. Not only do they favor one party over the other, but they also share many (though not necessarily all) of the party's values and will vote for the party's candidates—if they vote at all.

Only a small percentage of citizens (about 13 percent) are true independents; they are unpredictable, however, and have dismal turnout rates.[85] "I would encourage candidates not to play to them," advises David Magleby of Brigham Young University, "because they tend to jump on bandwagons, to follow tides. You're better off [working] on getting your weak partisans and your leaners."[86]

Partisan Resurgence

Today's voters are as loyal to their professed party identification as they have ever been.[87] Few voters who identify as either Republican or Democrat defect from their party when they cast votes in congressional races.

This increase in party loyalty represents a major shift. Between 1950 and 1980, partisan loyalty declined among the U.S. electorate, with voters identifying with one party and often supporting candidates from the other party. These weakened party ties led to an epidemic of split-ticket voting—that is, voters supporting one party's presidential candidate and the opposition party's congressional candidate. Between 1952 and 1988, the number of voters who reported in surveys that they split their ticket between presidential and House candidates rose from 12 percent to 25 percent. Those who split their ballots between different parties' House and Senate candidates grew from 9 percent to 27 percent.[88]

Most of these ticket-splitters, it turned out, were in the throes of moving from one party to another. White southern conservatives made up a large share of ticket-splitters during this era. Targeted by the GOP's so-called southern strategy, these voters were attracted to presidential candidates such as Barry Goldwater, Richard Nixon, and Ronald Reagan. At the same time, southern conservatives continued to back Democrats in congressional and state races, as strong Republican candidates often failed to challenge entrenched incumbents—because the Democratic Party put up conservative candidates and because long-serving Democrats won the "personal vote" of constituents by delivering more benefits back home through their party's control of legislative chambers. The same phenomenon occurred to a lesser degree in the Northeast, where voters were drawn to the Democrats' national policies and candidates but continued to support moderate-to-liberal Republican representatives or senators.[89] Recent party realignment has brought party affiliation into sync with policy and ideological preferences.

In retrospect, the bulge in split-ticket voting seems to have been a by-product of a gradual partisan realignment. Over the last six presidential elections, ticket-splitting has plummeted to less than 10 percent—exactly the same level it was fifty years ago. The number of congressional districts voting for one party's presidential candidate and the other party's House candidate fell as well. In 2016, only around 8 percent of districts voted for one party for the House and the other party for president. Just twenty-three House Republicans won in districts that were carried by Hillary Clinton while twelve Democrats won in districts that voted for Donald Trump.[90]

Midterm and Presidential Election Years

Politicians have long talked about *coattails:* how House and Senate candidates could be pulled into office by the strength of a popular presidential candidate. The idea is that successful presidential candidates will entice new voters, not just for themselves but for their whole party.

In presidential election years, the party that wins the presidency typically does increase its numbers in Congress. As shown in Figure 4-4, the winning presidential candidate's party usually improves its margins in Congress. Over the presidential elections since 1932, the president's party gained, on average, 15.1 seats in the House and 2.1 seats in the Senate. Boosts for the president's congressional party have been considerably more modest in recent election years than they were in the 1930s and 1940s. George H. W. Bush, Bill Clinton, George W. Bush, and Donald J. Trump all began their presidencies with some congressional seat losses for their party. Nevertheless, political scientists who have analyzed the influence of presidential candidates on the outcome of congressional elections have found "nontrivial coattail effects."[91] In 1996, President Clinton's reelection added about 2.6 percentage points to Democrats' House and Senate totals.[92] President Obama began his presidency with the largest increases in his party's numbers in Congress for any president since Reagan in 1980.

As is evident in Figure 4-5, the president's party almost always suffers significant reversals in the congressional elections that take place in nonpresidential election years. In fact, the president's party has lost seats in thirty-seven of the thirty-nine midterm elections since 1860. "This is not quite the certainty of 'death and taxes,' but it is about as dependable as things get in politics," observes political scientist James E. Campbell.[93] Since 1934, the presidential party has lost an average of 28 House seats and 3.6 Senate seats in midterm elections.

The *midterm law* was broken on only three occasions. Democrats gained four seats in the House and held their own in the Senate in 1998, in the midst of impeachment proceedings against President Clinton that were unpopular with the public. In 2002, President George W. Bush's GOP gained eight House seats and one Senate seat, no doubt because of the post-9/11 rally effect. The only other anomaly occurred in 1934, when President Franklin D. Roosevelt's popularity strengthened the Democrats' grip on both chambers. The president party's loss of 40 House seats in the 2018 midterms, Republicans' most serious midterm setback

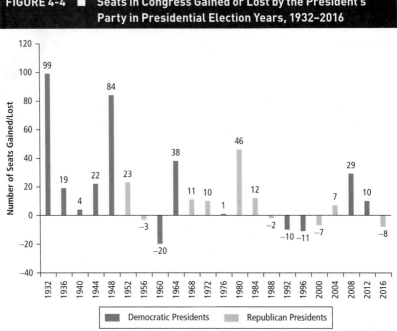

FIGURE 4-4 ■ Seats in Congress Gained or Lost by the President's Party in Presidential Election Years, 1932–2016

Source: Compiled by the authors.

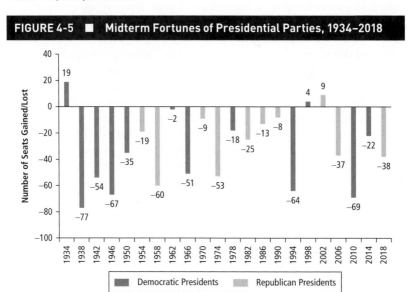

FIGURE 4-5 ■ Midterm Fortunes of Presidential Parties, 1934–2018

Sources: CQ Press Electronic Library, Vital Statistics on American Politics Online Edition, Table 1–17. Originally published in Harold W. Stanley and Richard G. Niemi, eds., *Vital Statistics on American Politics, 2009–2010* (Washington, DC: CQ Press, 2009). Each entry is the difference between the number of seats held by the president's party at the start of Congress after the midterm election and the number of seats held by that party at the start of Congress after the preceding general election. Special elections that shifted partisan seat totals between elections are not noted.

since the elections of 1974, adhered to the usual historic pattern. Unusually, how-ever, Republicans picked up two seats in the Senate in 2018, only the fourth midterm since 1910 in which the president's party gained seats in the Senate while losing seats in the House.

One theory that endeavors to explain the pattern of midterm loss is known as *surge and decline.* This theory posits that the visibility and excitement of a win-ning presidential campaign attracts intermittent voters who tend to support the president's party in down-ticket races. When these presidential candidates are not on the ballot, the shrunken electorate of midterm years contains fewer support-ers of the president's party—that is, a presidential surge, swollen by less moti-vated voters attracted by presidential campaigns, is followed two years later by a decline as intermittent voters drop out of the electorate. But other studies suggest that midterm voters are no more or less partisan than those in presidential years and share most of their demographic characteristics.[94] Another problem with the theory is that, no matter the circumstances, the president's party typically loses more seats at the midterm than it gains during a presidential year. Comparing Figures 4-4 and 4-5, it is also clear that the president's party more consistently loses seats at the midterms than it gains seats during presidential election years.

A second theory argues that midterm elections serve, in part, as a referendum on the president's popularity and performance in office during the previous two years.[95] Voters may hold the president's party responsible for economic reverses, unpopular policies, or military ventures, and the president's party tends to suffer bigger losses when the president is unpopular. Even so, the president's party typi-cally loses seats in Congress at midterms even when approval ratings of the presi-dent exceed 50 percent. The 2010, 2014, and 2018 midterm elections were all seen as referenda on the president's performance. For his part, President Trump simply embraced this reality. "I'm not on the ticket, but I am on the ticket, because this is a referendum about me," Trump said at a rally in Southhaven, Mississippi. "I want you to vote. Pretend I'm on the ballot."[96] In the end, Republicans' 40-seat loss in the House fell directly in line with projections for a midterm election under a president with an approval rating of around 42 percent.

A third theory emphasizes voters' preferences for "balance." By favoring the out-party at the midterm, voters can pull policy back toward the ideological center.[97] Voter behavior may not be driven so much by dissatisfaction with the president as by the desire to check potential presidential excesses. This may seem like an overly sophisticated calculation for the average voter, but even if only a relatively small portion of the electorate follows this logic, it can have a siz-able impact on electoral outcomes. Balance theory helps explain why the shift against the president's party in midterm elections is typically larger than one would expect based on presidents' approval ratings or based on the surge-and-decline thesis.[98] All three schools of thought—surge and decline, referendum theory, and balance theory—can shed light on such dramatic midterm outcomes as the Democrats' 1974 post-Watergate bonus of forty-eight representatives and five senators, the Democrats' retaking of House and Senate majorities in 2006, the Republicans' gain of sixty-three representatives and six senators in 2010, and the Democrats' return to the House majority in 2018.

The Appeal of Candidates

"My theory on politics is ultimately that people vote for the person they like most," declared former senator David Pryor, D-Ark. (1979–1997).[99] Apart from partisan loyalties, the appeal of given candidates is the strongest force in congressional voting. Not surprisingly, candidate appeal normally tilts toward incumbents. When voters abandon their party to vote for House or Senate candidates, they usually vote for incumbents.

Incumbency Advantage

Incumbents rarely lose their bids for reelection, as is evident in Table 4-1. Incumbent reelection rates have consistently been robust. Even in the 2010 watershed election, incumbent winners still included 85 percent of all representatives and 83 percent of all senators who ran for reelection. Likewise in 2018, despite the dramatic congressional turnover and the change of majority control, 90 percent of House incumbents who ran won reelection along with 83 percent of Senate incumbents.

Defeating a House incumbent is an uphill struggle, absent a scandal or misstep. Senate challengers—usually well known and generously financed—have a stronger chance of unseating incumbents than do those seeking House seats. Nevertheless, more than four out of five Senate incumbents win the contests they enter.

Why are incumbents so formidable? Incumbents' electoral success rates have historically exceeded what one should expect based on the partisan character of their constituencies. In other words, incumbents were long able to win by solid margins even in constituencies closely divided between Republicans and Democrats.

This phenomenon led scholars to ask whether the sheer fact of incumbency itself offers advantages: Do candidates fare better running as incumbents than they would running as nonincumbents?[100] To measure this advantage, scholars often look to the *sophomore surge* and the *retirement slump*. The sophomore surge refers to the average gain in vote share by candidates running for reelection for the first time, compared with their performance in their first election. The retirement slump is the average drop in a party's vote share when an incumbent retires and the seat opens up. Scholars then average these two calculations into a single index, known as the *slurge,* which is often used to measure the overall incumbency advantage. According to this measure, incumbents enjoyed about a 6 to 8 percent boost in their share of the vote simply by virtue of being incumbents from the mid-1960s through the 1990s.

The incumbency advantage has fallen dramatically in recent years, as rising levels of partisan voting and conflict in Washington make it hard for individual

TABLE 4-1 ■ Reelection Rates in the House and Senate, by Decade, 1950s–2000s, Plus 2012–2018

Decade	House					Senate				
	Sought reelection	Faced no opponent	Lost primary	General election	Percent reelected	Sought reelection	Faced no opponent	Lost primary	General election	Percent reelected
1950s	402	85	6	25	93.2%	30	4	1	6	77.3%
1960s	404	52	8	26	91.5	32	1	2	4	80.8
1970s	389	57	2	23	92.3	27	1	2	6	67.7
1980s	403	67	13	15	95.7	29	1	0	3	88.0
1990s	385	36	8	18	93.6	26	0	0	3	87.4
2000s	395	40	3	24	93.2	28	1	1	4	87.9
2012	395	37	13	22	91.1	23	0	1	1	91.3
2014	394	32	3	13	95.9	26	1	0	3	88.5
2016	395	29	4	8	97.0	29	0	0	2	93.1
2018	366	17	5	30	90.2	25	0	0	5	82.8
2012–2018	393	33	7	14	93.4	28	0	0	2	84.5

Sources: CQ Weekly

Note: Statistics for each decade are election-year averages for the five elections conducted under that decade's apportionment of House districts. For example, the 1950s include the five elections 1952 through 1960. "Percent reelected" takes into account both primary and general election defeats. "Faced no opponent" means no major-party opponent.

politicians to separate themselves from their parties. The estimated slurge hit a low of three points in 2014 and then fell even lower in 2016 and 2018.[101]

The small edge contemporary members possess by virtue of being incumbents offers only a modest buffer against adverse electoral conditions. The contemporary decline in incumbency advantage is remarkable when one considers the range of assets incumbents possess that challengers do not have. Because many contributors are just seeking access to officeholders, incumbents find it much easier to raise money than challengers (see "Incumbents versus Challengers"). Incumbents are also better known than their opponents. Across American National Election Study (ANES) surveys spanning almost thirty years, nearly all respondents were able to recognize the names of and offer opinions about their Senate and House incumbents running for reelection (means of 97 percent and 92 percent, respectively). Senate challengers were recognized and rated by 77 percent of the respondents, House challengers by only 53 percent.[102]

Incumbents are also able to cultivate constituency support by leveraging their perquisites of office. The typical House member receives staff, office, and travel allocations valued at between $2.5 and $3 million over a two-year term; senators, with six-year terms, command on average $20 million in resources.[103]

Still, in the end, recent elections suggest that none of incumbents' assets matter nearly so much as the underlying partisan tilt of their constituency. As political scientist Gary Jacobson concludes from a study of the 2018 elections: "By virtually every measure the 2018 referendum on the Trump presidency resulted in the most partisan, nationalized, and president-centered midterm elections yet observed."[104] Incumbents' perquisites of office, personal visibility, name recognition, and fundraising capabilities buy them very limited protection in today's electoral circumstances. Indeed, Senate incumbents in 2018 enjoyed no detectable advantage at all.[105]

Senate and House

Senators have long been more vulnerable at the polls than their House counterparts. Senate contests are widely reported, and Senate challengers get a lot of media exposure. Media coverage of House races is more fragmentary than that of Senate races. Senators thus have less ability to shape their image than representatives do. Voters get their information about Senate races largely through the organized media, which senators do not control. Representatives gain exposure through focused means—personal appearances, mailings, newsletters, and social media—which they can fashion to their own advantage. "Somewhat ironically," observes Michael J. Robinson, "powerful senators are less able to control their images than 'invisible' House members."[106]

Strategic Politicians

One should not interpret incumbent reelection rates as a measure of incumbency advantage. Incumbents win a large share of the races they enter in great part because they behave strategically. Many incumbents retire or seek other office when facing a significant likelihood of defeat. In 2018, for example, many Republicans opted to step aside rather than run the risk of losing. Republican retirements were heavily concentrated in districts that had voted for Hillary Clinton or only narrowly for Donald Trump in 2016.[107] All told, forty Republican incumbents declined to run for reelection, a postwar record for the party. Meanwhile, recognizing a favorable electoral environment, only 20 Democratic incumbents retired, nearly half of those to run for higher office. Strategic anticipation of this kind happens in most election years, though not always to such an obvious extent. The clear lesson is that incumbents win at high rates in significant part because they are able to anticipate when they can win, not because they have insulated themselves against electoral accountability.

Issue Voting

Issue preferences and even ideological beliefs figure prominently in voters' decisions. Even if most Americans devote only modest attention to political affairs, a significant number of voters are attuned to issues and base their choices on a specific issue or cluster of issues.[108] Not a few elections turn on those margins.

Congressional Party Platforms

Partisans care deeply about the issues with which their parties are linked. In studying the 1998 House elections, Owen G. Abbe and his colleagues found that "voters are more likely to support candidates whom they deem competent on their issues." They concluded that "party leaders and individual candidates must campaign on a well-defined agenda for party-owned issues to have an impact."[109]

At least since the mid-1970s, congressional parties have forged campaign platforms. The most notable example was the GOP's "Contract with America," the brainchild of then-representative Newt Gingrich of Georgia.[110] The contract was a set of ten proposals that candidates promised to bring to the House floor if Republicans won a majority in the 1994 midterm elections. Similarly, more than a year before the 2006 balloting, House Democrats, led by the minority leader, Nancy Pelosi of California, came up with another list of initiatives known as the "Six for '06" platform, embracing such popular goals as national security, energy independence, and economic strength. In the lead-up to the 2016 elections, congressional Republicans touted a platform called "A Better Way," including tax cuts and tax reform, increased border security, and rollbacks of regulations, among others. Although the effort got only limited media attention, House and Senate Democrats rolled out their "Better Deal for our Democracy" platform in the spring of 2018, a package of voting rights, campaign finance, ethics, and lobbying reforms.

Issues and Partisanship

Voters' responses to political issues show up in the different patterns of choice displayed by demographic groups (see Figure 4-6). Americans sort themselves

FIGURE 4-6 ■ Who Were the Voters in 2018?

Percentage of voters		For Democrat	For Republican
48	Men	47	51
52	Women	59	40
72	White	44	54
11	Black	90	9
11	Hispanic/Latino	69	29
3	Asian	77	23
3	Other	54	42
13	Under 30 years	67	32
22	30–44 years	58	39
39	45–64 years	49	50
26	65 years and older	49	50
23	High school graduate or less	48	51
25	Some college	52	47
24	College graduate	55	43
17	Postgraduate study	65	34
11	Associate's degree	47	50
17	Small city/rural	42	56
51	Suburbs	49	49
32	"Urban"	65	32
55	Protestant or other Christian	42.5	56.5
26	Catholic	50	49
2	Jewish	79	17
7	Something Else	70	28
17	None	70	28
38	Family income < $50,000	59	38
29	$50,000–$99,999	52	47
33	$100,000 or more	47	52
37	Democratic	95	4
30	Independent	54	42
33	Republican	6	94
27	Liberal	91	8
37	Moderate	62	36
36	Conservative	16	83

Source: Data from CNN 2018 election polls at https://www.cnn.com/election/2018/exit-polls.

Notes: National exit poll results from interviews of 18,778 respondents randomly selected voters as they exited voting places across the country on November 6 and previously over the telephone for absentee and early voters. The poll was conducted by Edison Media Research for the National Election Pool, the *Washington Post,* and other media organizations. Typical characteristics have a margin of sampling error of plus or minus four percentage points.

out politically according to their age, sex, income, education, race or ethnicity, region, and even by frequency of attendance at religious services.

A demographic snapshot of the two parties' voters would start at the much-discussed gender gap, the difference in voting between men and women. Women lean toward Democratic candidates; men lean toward Republicans. The gender gap has long been a fact of electoral life. As pollster Celinda Lake remarked, "You'll get [a gender gap] in a race for dogcatcher in Montana, if it's a Republican against a Democrat."[111] But in recent years, the gender gap has surged in importance. While the gender gap was a significant eight points in 2012 and ten points in 2014, it more than doubled to 22 points in 2016 and 23 in 2018.[112] The explanation for the gender gap probably lies in differing responses to political and social issues. Men are more apt to favor military expenditures, tough anticrime laws, and restrictions on welfare recipients and immigrants. Women are more supportive of social programs, such as government-sponsored health benefits, job training, childcare, and assistance to needy families.[113]

A host of similar demographic effects is evident among congressional voters. "There's a family gap, a generation gap, a gender gap," said GOP pollster Neil Newhouse of the fissures among the voting population.[114] Many of the patterns are familiar. The Republicans attract upper-income and conservative voters; the Democrats traditionally engage lower-income and liberal voters. The Republicans draw upon married people, whites, regular churchgoers, gun owners, small-business owners, and older people; the Democrats attract singles and young people, African Americans, Hispanics, Jews, the secular, and occasional churchgoers. Increasingly, Republicans do well with less-educated white voters, while Democrats do better among college educated whites. Such loyalties are built on issues and themes adopted by parties and candidates over the years.

Issues and Campaigns

Legislators and their advisers try to anticipate voters' reactions to their issue stances. They devote much energy to framing positions, communicating them (sometimes in deliberately vague language), and assessing their effect. Moreover, every professional politician can relate cases in which issues tipped an election one way or another. Frequently cited is the electoral influence of single-interest groups. Some citizens vote according to a single issue they regard as paramount—for example, gun control, abortion, or gay marriage. Even if few in number, such voters can decide close contests. For that reason, legislators often shrink from taking positions on such hot-button issues.

Public-policy issues also have powerful indirect effects on election outcomes. Issues motivate *opinion leaders,* who can influence support far beyond their own single vote. Organized interests also carefully monitor lawmakers' behavior and then channel or withhold funds, publicity, and other campaign assistance accordingly. Legislators devote time and attention to promoting and explaining issues to attentive publics because it pays for them to do so.

ELECTION OUTCOMES

The two Congresses are apparent throughout congressional elections. House and Senate contests are waged one by one on local turf but always against a backdrop of national events, issues, and partisan alignments. The involvement of national party entities and their allied interest groups has imposed a greater degree of national coordination on congressional campaigns, especially those in marginal states and districts. The resulting fusion of local and national forces shapes the content and results of congressional elections.

Party Balance

Despite the oft-claimed independence of candidates and voters, almost all races are run under either the Democratic or Republican Party label, fought on playing fields tilted toward one party or the other, and aimed mainly at loyalists who are likely to turn out for their party's candidates.

Shifting Majorities

In some respects, the overall partisan outcome of the 2018 contests was fixed months and even years before the actual balloting. Of the four political science forecasting models published by *P.S.: Political Science and Politics* before the 2018 midterms, all predicted that Democrats would win control of the House of Representatives but that Republicans would retain control of the Senate. The models accurately forecasted the specific seat swing, as well. Models for the House projected that Republicans would lose between 27 and 44 seats, with an average loss of 36 seats across the models. For the Senate, the models forecast that Republicans would either break even or gain up to two seats. These models rely upon simple indicators: Is this a midterm or presidential election year? What is the president's approval rating in public polls? What party do voters say they prefer to control Congress on the "generic ballot." In the end, the 2018 Republicans lost 40 seats in the House and gained two in the Senate, an outcome that was thus expected months in advance of election day.

Taking a longer view, the outcome was predictable in that either the Democrats or the Republicans have controlled Congress since 1855. (See Appendix A for a list of the partisan majorities in the House and Senate since 1901.) For a decade after the Civil War and for the first third of the 20th century, Republicans were the dominant party in American national government. Republicans controlled Congress and the presidency for most of the period between 1896 and 1932.

The New Deal realignment of the 1930s shifted the balance of power to the Democrats. For decades after 1932, the Democrats held sway on Capitol Hill. Across the half-century between 1932 and 1994, Republicans only had a majority in the House of Representatives for two Congresses, (1947–1948, 1953–1954). Democratic sweeps in 1958, 1964, and 1974 padded the party's large majorities on Capitol Hill. Incumbency advantage seemed to make it impossible for congressional Republicans to overcome Democratic dominance, even in election years when voters strongly backed Republican presidential candidates. During the long years of Democratic ascendancy across so much of the twentieth century, conventional wisdom had come to view Democrats as the nation's permanent majority in Congress.

The struggle for party control of national government has been much more competitive in recent decades. Neither party has been able to take control of Congress for granted.[115] Since Republicans won control of the Senate in 1980, no party has controlled a Senate majority for longer than eight years. Control of the House has also been closely competitive since the Republican victory of 1994. Even though Republicans clung to their post-1994 majority in the House for twelve years, Democrats steadily gained seats throughout the 1990s, and Republicans' control of the chamber progressively narrowed. Democrats returned to majority status in both the House and the Senate in 2006 and expanded their margins of control in the 2008 elections.

But in 2010, all the House Democratic gains of 2006 and 2008 were wiped out. Republicans retook House control in 2010, retained their majority in 2012 with minimal losses, and then expanded their majority again in 2014. The 2015–2016 Republicans held their largest House majority since 1927. On Capitol Hill, the 2016 elections were largely a wash, with Republicans retaining a two-seat majority in the Senate and a forty-seven-seat majority in the House. But the Republican House majority could not withstand the backlash against an unpopular Republican president, with Democrats returning back to the House majority in 2019.

Political scientist Mo Fiorina terms our current era of seesawing party control an era of "tenuous majorities." Taking stock of party control of House, Senate, and presidency, he notes that the twelve elections since 1992 "have produced six different patterns of majority control of our three national elective arenas."[116] With another fierce battle for congressional majorities looming again in 2020, two-party competition for control of Congress has yet to come to an end.[117]

Regional Patterns

Recent elections have cemented long-term shifts in the two parties' power bases. Historically, the Grand Old Party was dominant in the populous states of the Northeast and Midwest. "The Democracy," by contrast, owned the solid South from the Civil War era through the 1970s, as well as the large urban political machines. Today, many of the old patterns are precisely reversed, with the Republican Party dominant in the South and the Democratic Party ascendant in the Northeast.[118] The tectonic plates of political alliances move slowly, but they sometimes produce changes of earthquake proportions.

The 1994 earthquake signaled the Republicans' conquest of the South. For the first time in history, the GOP claimed a majority of the South's seats. The party's grip on the region continued to tighten in subsequent election cycles. By

2019, Republicans held 65 percent of House seats and 86 percent of Senate seats belonging to the eleven states of the former Confederacy. The modern-day GOP is currently the party of choice for conservative white southerners.

As shown in the map displayed in Figure 4-7, the South, the Great Plains, and the Mountain West form the backbone of the congressional GOP. Fully 45 percent of the House Republican Conference hails from the South, even though that region accounts for only a third of the chamber's seats. Southerners also make up more than one third of Senate Republicans, even though the region only includes a quarter of Senate seats. In its other regional bastions, the Great Plains and the Mountain West, Republicans claim 79 percent of Senate seats and 63 percent of House districts. Taken together, representatives from the South, Great Plains, and Mountain West regions account for the majority of the GOP's House and Senate contingents. The Great Lakes states constitute a competitive region, with Republicans controlling 53 percent of its House seats but only one-quarter of its Senate seats.

Democrats are strongest on the coastal edges of the national map—the Northeast, the mid-Atlantic, and the West Coast. The eleven states of New England and the mid-Atlantic are overwhelmingly Democratic. In these states—all but one of which were in the Democratic Party's column in the last four presidential elections—the party claims 87 percent of House seats and 91 percent of Senate seats. In New England, Sen. Susan Collins, R-Maine, holds the only

FIGURE 4-7 ■ Share of Republicans in Congress by State Delegation

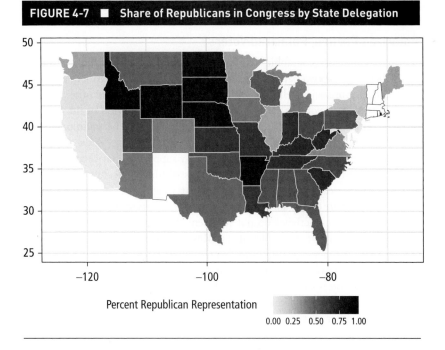

Percent Republican Representation

0.00 0.25 0.50 0.75 1.00

Republican seat in either House or Senate. Similarly, Democrats dominate the country's western coast. All four Pacific Rim states (excluding Alaska) were won by Democratic candidates in the last four presidential elections. In the 116th Congress (2019–2020), Democrats controlled fifty-nine of the region's seventy House seats and all eight of its Senate seats.

Looking beyond such regional patterns, the two parties tend to represent different kinds of districts. Democratic strength lies in cities, inner suburbs, and majority-minority districts, including those in the South and Midwest. Republicans dominate rural, small-town, and exurban areas. Democratic voters tend to be more packed together geographically, with Democrats clustered together in the nation's densely populated urban areas. As a result, Democratic House members tend to win by larger margins than Republicans. Put another way, more Democratic votes are wasted (that is, inefficiently distributed across congressional districts), giving the GOP a structural advantage in congressional elections.[119]

The regional divides between the parties have become more pronounced during the Trump presidency. In particular, Republicans have lost significant support in upscale suburbia. In 2018, Democrats swept Republicans across prosperous suburbs around the country, most notably in New Jersey, Pennsylvania, and Southern California. Districts represented by Republicans now have markedly lower educational attainment than districts represented by Democrats, with three-quarters of Republican districts lagging behind the national average of residents with a college degree. Meanwhile, Democrats now represent more than three-fifths of House districts with a higher than median average income.[120]

Polarized Parties, Polarized Voters?

Underlying this geographic distribution is what might be called a cultural divide between the two parties. Democrats tend to represent urban areas, where most voters favor social welfare spending and environmental and other business regulations. Urban voters also tend to take a more tolerant view of the diversity of racial, ethnic, and sexual identities. Republicans tend to be traditionalists—economic and cultural conservatives who promote businesses large and small, advocate certain religious causes, and generously support military expenditures.

How pervasive are these partisan differences within the electorate? Politically active citizens—candidates, officeholders, party activists, and strong party identifiers—but are clearly sorted by ideology: Democrats to the left, Republicans to the right.[121] Such activists do not represent the majority of citizens, average voters, or even average party identifiers. Most voters either identify as "moderate" or reject any ideological term to describe themselves.[122] Rank-and-file party identifiers have, however, become more ideologically polarized than in the past.[123] Clearly, many voters have responded to the rising amount of ideological rhetoric in the contemporary political arena, including that dispensed by biased cable, Internet, and other partisan communications.

Party Alignment and Realignment

Historically, some political upheavals have shifted party control in the House or Senate with decisive, enduring results. Political scientists and journalists refer to *critical elections* or *critical periods,* in which one party yields preeminence to another, or major voting groups alter the shape of the parties' coalitions, or both. Such watershed eras include the Civil War, the turbulent 1890s, the New Deal of the 1930s, and the Republican revolution of 1994. Each of these upheavals brought to Capitol Hill new lawmakers, new voting patterns, and new legislative priorities.[124]

Between the civil rights upheavals of the 1960s and the mid-1990s, the congressional party system went through a gradual transformation that realigned the parties on ideological lines and brought them into competitive balance. The Republican Party achieved ideological consistency by attracting southern and rural conservatives and by shedding most of its moderate wing, especially members from the northeastern, mid-Atlantic, and Pacific Rim states. In losing most of the South to Republicans, the Democrats also became more ideologically coherent. Long split by divisions between conservative southerners and northern liberals, by the 1990s, the Democratic Party was smaller than in the past but considerably more unified.

Realignments of the party system are only apparent in hindsight. It is now clear that neither the House Democratic majorities of the 110th and 111th Congresses (2007–2010) nor the House Republican majorities of the 112th–115th Congresses (2011–2018) were grounded in any long-term shifts of voter alliances. Today's party system remains in the same tight competitive balance characteristic of the 1990s.

Turnover and Representation

Reelection rates should not be confused with turnover rates. Even in years when few members are turned out of office by the voters, many leave Capitol Hill voluntarily—to retire, to run for another office, or to follow other pursuits. In other words, the natural process of membership change is continuous. Although the vast majority of incumbents seeking reelection won in 2018, the 116th Congress included 88 new House members, one of three largest freshman classes since 1950.[125] In January 2019, more than 40 percent of the House and 30 percent of the Senate had served two Congresses or less. For Congress to be a responsive institution, constant turnover of members is essential—whether by steady increments or by watershed elections. Even when few lawmakers are defeated for reelection, all of them are keenly aware of the possibility of losing. Most take steps to prevent that eventuality by continually monitoring constituents' needs and opinions through personal visits and polls. But are voters' views accurately reflected by the representatives they elect to Congress? This question is not easily answered. Popular control of policy makers is not the same thing as popular control of policies. Constituents' views are not precisely mirrored by legislators' voting behavior or by the laws passed by the legislature.

CONCLUSION

Are voters' attitudes linked to members' voting on issues? In the 1960s, Warren E. Miller and Donald E. Stokes found that constituency attitudes correlated differently depending on the kind of policy.[126] In foreign affairs, constituents' attitudes and legislators' votes exhibited a negative correlation; in social and economic welfare issues, the correlation was moderate; in civil rights issues, the correlation was very high. In other words, in at least one and possibly two major policy areas, the linkage was weak enough to cast some doubt on constituency control of elected representatives.

Nevertheless, there is no doubt that elections reshape Congress and congressional agendas. Winning candidates learn from their campaign experiences, even from issues raised by their opponents. *Issue uptake* is the term coined by political scientist Tracy Sulkin to describe this effect. Sulkin's study shows that House and Senate victors embrace many of their opponents' campaign themes when they return to Capitol Hill. "Congressional campaigns have a clear legacy in the content of legislators' agendas," she writes, "influencing the areas in which they choose to be active and the intensity with which they pursue these activities."[127] Legislative responsiveness is best thought of as a process:

> It begins in campaigns as candidates learn about the salience of issues and their strengths and weaknesses on them; continues throughout winning legislators' terms in office, influencing not just how they vote but also the content of legislation they introduce, cosponsor, and speak about on the floor; goes on to inform their career decisions and future electoral prospects; and leaves a tangible trace on public policy outputs.[128]

If ideological or attitudinal links between voters and their representatives are rough and variable, actual contacts between constituents and individual legislators are numerous and palpable. Much of lawmakers' time and effort while in office is devoted to responding to the folks back home. Constituency politics are ever present in the daily lives of senators and representatives. The two Congresses are distinct but inextricably linked.

Lawmakers on the Hill and at Home. Democrat Montana Senator Jon Tester meets with constituents at the Last Best Outdoors Fest on August 31, 2018, in Livingston, Montana. Tester was running against Republican Matt Rosendale to retain his Senate seat in the 2018 elections. Tester arrives on Capitol Hill in Washington, DC, on Friday, October 5, 2018, for a key vote on Brett Kavanaugh's nomination to the Supreme Court. Members-elect from left, Mikie Sherrill, D-N.J., Abigail Spanberger, D-Va., and Chrissy Houlahan, D-Pa., take a selfie after the freshman class photo on the East Front of the Capitol on November 14, 2018. Congressmen Morgan Griffith, R-Va., greets constituents at the Floyd Country Store in Floyd, Virginia. Griffith was campaigning in Southwest Virginia for the upcoming November election.

BEING THERE

Hill Styles and Home Styles

Rallying his core supporters, campaign volunteers ready to go out canvassing for votes, Sen. Jon Tester, D-Mont., jokingly asked, "What the hell is a field organizer? Do you go out and organize weeds in the field?"[1] Tester often refers to himself as "the only working farmer in the Senate." He returns home every weekend, dividing his time between working the fields and driving to events with constituents. A Democrat in a state that voted overwhelmingly for President Donald Trump, Tester draws on his background as a dirt farmer in rural Montana to persuade voters that he shares their values. His appearance when he travels around the state in his pick-up truck—from his buzz-cut flattop haircut to his jeans and cowboy boots—convey that Tester is not a typical Washington politician.[2]

First elected to the Senate in 2006, Tester's approach to policy making in Washington complements his self-presentation at home. The ranking Democrat on the Committee on Veterans' Affairs, Tester has made advocating for veterans' health care and other benefits a cornerstone of his Washington work. A substantial share of Tester's legislative activity and press releases concerns veterans' issues.[3] When back in Montana, Tester appears at ease at listening sessions held at veterans' clinics, expressing his commitment to fighting benefit cuts and offering constituents help in navigating the Veterans Administration's labyrinthine bureaucracy.[4] Tester also focuses his Washington work on public lands policy, another issue of particular interest to Montana residents and one where the senator is able to build an identity separate from his party. While Republicans have sought to paint Tester as just another vote for liberal party leader Chuck Schumer, D-N.Y., Tester emphasizes his moderation and engagement with issues that are of particular concern to Montanans.[5]

After being elected with less than a 3,000 vote margin in 2006 and surviving another tough race in 2012, Tester was one of the GOP's top Democratic targets in the 2018 midterms. Tester faced off against Montana state auditor Matt Rosendale, and President Trump took a personal interest in the race after Tester had attacked his choice for head of the Department of Veterans Affairs, Ronny Jackson. Trump traveled to the state four times, declaring that, "Democrats have truly turned into an angry mob, bent on destroying anything or anyone in their path. And your senator is one of them."[6] But Tester countered that President Trump had signed 20 of his bills into law, including several measures to help veterans, firefighters, and police officers, and to boost cell service in rural areas.[7] "Washington's a mess," noted Tester, "but that's not stopping me from getting bills signed into law that help Montana."[8] Tester emphasized that his deep Montana roots and continued immersion in the state's daily life gave him a unique understanding of his constituents' needs: "I don't think they can beat who I am."[9] Tester's prediction proved correct, as he survived another tough election battle, defeating Rosendale, 50.3 percent to 46.8 percent.

A local champion and a national leader, Jon Tester personifies the two Congresses. All members live and work in these two worlds: one on Capitol Hill and the other back home in their states and districts.

HILL STYLES

Congress is a body of transplanted locals who naturally speak up for their constituents. However, the ability of Congress to reflect the nation's large and varied population is affected by the diversity of its membership. There is no substitute for having a member of one's own group in a position of influence, and many groups do not receive representation commensurate with their presence in the population.

Who Are the Legislators?

Elections, as Aristotle first observed, are essentially oligarchic affairs that involve few active participants. The active participants are self-starters and risk-takers willing to seek an electoral "contract" for two or six years, with no guarantee of renewal. In addition, by almost any measure, senators and representatives constitute an economic and social elite. They are well educated. They come from prestigious occupations. The pay of senators and representatives ($174,000 since 2009) alone puts them in the top 5 percent of the nation's wage earners, but many members also have earned or inherited considerable wealth.[10] In 2018, nearly 40 percent of House members were millionaires, along with a majority of senators.[11]

The elite character of the congressional membership raises questions of representation. One central purpose of a representative body is to bring together diverse individuals to deliberate on public policy. When the diversity of viewpoints is systematically limited, important interests and concerns are likely to be overlooked or undervalued. As John Stuart Mill argued a century and a half ago, "In the absence of its natural defenders, the interest of the omitted is always in danger of being overlooked."[12] To meet Mill's standards for representation, must Congress closely mirror the demographics of the populace? Hannah Pitkin distinguishes between two types of representation: *descriptive* and *substantive*.[13] *Descriptive representation* refers to whether a legislature's membership reflects the diversity of backgrounds and interests in society. *Substantive representation* occurs when legislators consciously act as agents for constituents and their interests—an activity legislators can perform regardless of their personal background or group memberships. For example, legislators can voice farmers' concerns even if they have never plowed a field. Whites can champion equal opportunities for minorities.

Although descriptive representation and substantive representation are conceptually distinct, a wide range of empirical research has found that they are intertwined in the real world. The social identity of legislators affects representation in myriad ways. Representatives' racial, ethnic, and gender identities shape their priorities, positions, and legislative styles.[14] Whether constituents and representatives share a common identity has also been shown to affect trust and patterns of contact between them.[15]

Education and Occupation

By every measure, Congress is a highly educated body, and it has gradually become better educated over time.[16] When the 116th Congress convened in January 2019, 95 percent of House members and 100 percent of senators held university degrees. More than two-thirds had graduate degrees. Twenty-one representatives and four senators had medical degrees.

Historically, law and politics have been closely linked in the United States. A humorist once quipped that the U.S. government "of laws and not men" is really "of lawyers and not men." And indeed, at the beginning of the 116th Congress, 161 representatives and 53 senators were law school graduates.

That so many members have law degrees does not necessarily mean that they possess extensive experience in the practice of law. "They are not, by and large, successful lawyers who left thriving partnerships to run for public office," observes Alan Ehrenhalt. "Rather, they are political activists with law degrees."[17] Legal training develops skills that are useful in gaining and holding public office, such as verbalization, advocacy, and negotiation. A law degree also serves as a stepping-stone into public service at many levels. Lawyers monopolize elected law enforcement and judicial posts, two main pathways to Congress. Hill staffers are often expected to have law degrees, and many members of Congress start out on Capitol Hill as staff aides. The 116th Congress is home to at least eighty-nine former congressional staffers.

The historical dominance of lawyers on Capitol Hill has nevertheless declined in recent decades. Lawyers are now outnumbered by members from other careers. Today's Congress is filled with professional public servants or, in common parlance, *career politicians.* The 116th Congress includes forty-one former mayors, thirteen former governors, seven former lieutenant governors, sixteen former judges, two former cabinet secretaries, and three ambassadors. Half of senators (fifty) are former House members. Even so, the incoming cohort of new members in the 116th Congress includes an unusually high number of members who lacked prior political experience; indeed, it is the first freshman class elected since 1980 in which a majority of members had not held any elective office.[18]

A significant contingent of Congress members have served in the military, though the veterans' ranks have thinned over time. After World War II, returning veterans surged into Congress. Among them were Reps. John F. Kennedy, D-Mass.; Richard M. Nixon, R-Calif.; Gerald R. Ford, R-Mich.; and Bob Dole, R-Kans. By the 1970s, more than seven of ten members were veterans. As the World War II era receded and draftees were replaced by a volunteer force, fewer veterans were elected.[19] Just 18 percent of the members of the 116th Congress have served in the military. A small group of members currently serves in the Reserves and the National Guard.

Many occupations are and always have been drastically underrepresented in Congress. Low-status occupations—including farm labor, service trades, manual and skilled labor, and domestic service—are extremely rare on Capitol Hill.[20] A recent study finds that the underrepresentation of these lower-status occupations undermines their substantive representation when Congress considers economic issues.[21] Not a few members, however, held menial jobs at some point in their lives. For example, at a hearing on Social Security taxes for household help, Rep. Carrie P. Meek, D-Fla. (1993–2003), a granddaughter of slaves, brought her own vivid experiences to the proceedings. "I was once a domestic worker," she told her colleagues. "My mother was a domestic worker. All my sisters were domestic workers."[22] Such perspectives are valuable for congressional representation and deliberation.

Race

African Americans, who make up 13.4 percent of the nation's population, account for 12.6 percent of the membership of the House of Representatives and 3 percent of the Senate. In 2019, fifty-five African Americans served in the House: fifty-four Democrats and one Republican. One of the three African American senators (Sen. Tim Scott, S.C.) is a Republican. Although African American representation in Congress still does not reflect their proportion of the nation's population, black legislators have gained seniority and congressional influence over time.[23]

Other minorities are more severely underrepresented. Latinos make up 18.1 percent of the U.S. population but only 10.2 percent of the House membership and 5 percent of the Senate. Of the forty-five Latino representatives, most are Mexican Americans. Three of the five Latino senators, however, are Cuban Americans. Of the Latino members of the 116th Congress, thirty-nine are Democrats, and eleven are Republicans. Asian Americans and Pacific Islanders claim seventeen representatives and three senators—all but one are Democrats. There are four Native Americans in the House, two from each party.

The growing presence of racial minorities in Congress has had beneficial effects on representational bonds with minority communities. African Americans represented by black lawmakers, for example, tend to know more about their representatives and hold them in higher esteem.[24] "Even controlling for party affiliation," Katherine Tate's survey of black constituents found that "black legislators received significantly higher ratings on average than their white counterparts."[25] Another study showed that constituents of the same race as the incumbent were 27 percent more likely than constituents of other races to recognize the name of their representative.[26] A growing scholarly literature also suggests that descriptive representation on Capitol Hill yields substantive benefits for minority communities. Black legislators are more active on issues of importance to their constituents of color—that is, they are more likely than their white colleagues to introduce bills on subjects of special concern to black Americans and to attend committee meetings, offer amendments, and participate in deliberations on these issues.[27]

Gender

Neither chamber accurately reflects the nation in terms of gender. Congress historically has been a male bastion. In international comparisons, it still is: The United States ranks seventy-fifth worldwide in the proportion of women serving in the national legislature.[28] Unable to vote nationally until 1920, women have always been underrepresented in Congress. Beginning in 1917 with Rep. Jeannette Rankin, R-Mont., the presence of women in Congress has grown slowly, though the 2018 elections brought about a significant increase. The number of women serving in the 116th Congress set a record for the United States—with one hundred and six representatives (24.2 percent) and twenty-five senators (including two each from Arizona, California, Minnesota, Nevada, New Hampshire, and Washington).[29] More than 80 percent are Democrats. Among them, Nancy Pelosi, D-Calif., is the first female Speaker of the House (2007–2011, 2019–present).

The advent of a critical mass of women has changed Congress. Policy concerns once labeled "women's issues"—which, in truth, affect everyone—now receive a respectful hearing. Gender discrimination, women's health, sexual assault in the military, and issues involving the balance between family and workplace are more seriously addressed. Rep. Nita M. Lowey, D-N.Y., whose mother died of breast cancer, pressed for increased funding for research on the disease. During a debate over family leave policy, Sen. Patty Murray, D-Wash., recalled having to quit a secretarial job sixteen years earlier when she was pregnant with her first child. "When a person in this body gets up and speaks from personal experience, it changes the whole nature of the debate," observed Sen. Chris Dodd, D-Conn. (1981–2011).[30] Referring to the women serving in the Senate, Senator Murray declared, "We've made it okay for men to talk about these [women's] issues, too."[31] Amid the increased attention to sexual harassment and violence with the rise of the #MeToo movement, two female senators revealed that they were victims of sexual assault while serving in the military. The revelations brought renewed focus on what has been called a "silent epidemic."[32] Political science research offers systematic confirmation that the presence of women has had notable effects on Congress. Women legislators are more likely than men to introduce, sponsor, and press for bills of special concern to women and children.[33] Early in the 114th Congress, female Republicans took the lead in sidetracking a leadership-sponsored bill to ban abortions after twenty weeks; most of the female lawmakers favored the general principle behind the bill, but they argued that the bill did not do enough to accommodate rape victims.[34]

One challenge that women lawmakers face is that voters tend to view them as less competent on military and security issues.[35] To counter voters' stereotypes of female politicians in the post-9/11 environment, scholar Michele Swers finds that women legislators have expanded their activity and visibility on defense issues, particularly on homeland security matters.[36] For example, Sen. Susan Collins, R-Maine, played a key role in securing passage of a major intelligence reform bill in 2004.[37] Female senators continued to take active part in debates over security in the Obama and Trump years. As Senate Intelligence Committee chair in the 113th Congress, Dianne Feinstein, D-Calif., became a leading voice in the national conversation on the CIA's post-9/11 interrogation program, releasing a major report that rekindled an intense public debate on torture.[38] In sum, women legislators today are active far beyond the so-called women's issues.

Sexual Orientation

Gays and lesbians passed a milestone in 1998 when Tammy Baldwin, D-Wis., became the first lesbian representative whose sexual orientation was known before her initial election. (Other congressional gays and lesbians revealed their sexuality or were outed after they had served for some time; some remain in the closet.) Baldwin did not shy away from the issue. Her campaign slogan was "A different kind of candidate." In 2013, Baldwin became the nation's first openly gay senator. Elected to the House in 2012 and to the Senate six years later, Kyrsten Sinema of Arizona is the first openly bisexual member of Congress.

As with other types of social identity, electing gay and lesbian representatives matters for the group's representation. Indeed, one recent study found that the presence of lesbian and gay elected officials was the single most important factor affecting local adoption of domestic partner benefits.[39] Still, as former representative Barney Frank, D-Mass., has pointed out, the hardest part of running as a gay man is "convincing voters that you will not disproportionately focus on that minority's issues."[40]

Religion

Ninety-seven percent of all members of Congress cite a specific religious affiliation. By comparison, about 20 percent of Americans do not identify with any particular faith; indeed, the fastest-growing category in recent surveys of American religion is "unaffiliated."[41] Protestants collectively make up a majority of the 116th Congress, but about 30 percent of House and Senate members are Roman Catholics, the largest single religious denomination. Jews account for 6.4 percent. The 116th Congress also includes ten Mormons, three Hindu, two Buddhists, and three Muslims.[42]

Age and Tenure

When the 116th Congress convened in 2019, the average age of members was among the highest in history: fifty-eight for representatives, sixty-three for senators.[43] Tenure, as well as age, has risen since the early days. "Few die, and none retire," it was said as the twentieth century began. Today, the average member of Congress has served for approximately a decade.[44]

Age and tenure levels fluctuate over time. Periods of relatively low turnover (the 1980s, for example) are punctuated by dramatic changings of the guard. The 2010 election was one such moment. Fully 21 percent of the House and 15 percent of the Senate were freshmen in the ensuing 112th Congress. The Democratic wave in 2018 helped bring in another large freshman class, with ninety (20.5 percent) new House members and nine new senators. Similar turnovers occurred in the 1970s and the 1990s, involving both senior and junior members of Congress.[45] Electoral defeats play some role, but the majority of members leave voluntarily. Of course, many departing members retire precisely because they anticipate electoral difficulty.[46]

A balance between new blood and stable membership is undoubtedly optimal for legislative bodies. Rapid turnover—the early 1990s and 2006 through 2018, for example—can sharpen generational conflict. Many newly elected members indulge in Congress-bashing in their campaigns and want to shake up the institution, and not a few of them shun the idea of making a career of public service. The antiestablishment attitudes of members of the Tea Party caucuses on Capitol Hill are not unusual among large classes of relative newcomers. Reflecting on these troublesome freshmen, former Senate majority leader Trent Lott, R-Miss., said, "As soon as they get here, we need to co-opt them."[47] If past is prologue, many will eventually settle into the established power structure on Capitol Hill.

Equal Representation of States

The equal voice that all states have in the Senate is a central feature of congressional representation. The Senate's divergence from population-based representation affects the welfare of many social and economic groups. It enlarges the voice of farmers, ranchers, mining interests, and users of federal lands—all groups that have far more presence in the less populous states than in the nation as a whole. At the same time, racial and ethnic minorities—already underrepresented in Congress relative to their share of the nation's population—are further disadvantaged by the Senate's makeup.[48] The nation's populous states are more racially and ethnically diverse than its less populous ones, and so, one effect of Senate representation is to boost the voting power of the predominantly white residents of lightly populated states and to confer less voting power on the more racially diverse residents of populous states.[49]

Equal state representation in the Senate has other meaningful effects as well. Bonds between senators and their constituents are closer and more personalized in less populous states than in more populous ones.[50] And when Congress makes decisions about distributing federal dollars, less populous states receive more benefits than they pay in taxes, whereas populous states provide more revenue but receive fewer returns. Small-population states are advantaged across most federal spending programs, with the effect most pronounced on the types of programs over which Congress maintains tightest control.[51]

Collective Representation

Representation does not always follow state or district boundaries. It occurs when citizens feel they are served by any member of Congress, not just their local member. Congressional representation is, as Robert Weissberg put it, "collective," not just "dyadic."[52] In other words, representation involves more than the interactions between individual members and the residents of their geographic constituencies. Citizens can feel a sense of connection to Congress when the body as a whole includes members who speak for them. When someone from an ethnic or racial minority background goes to Congress, it is often a matter of pride for an entire identity group. Such legislators speak for people like themselves throughout the nation.[53]

Many constituencies are represented in the same way. One member who suffers from epilepsy defends job rights for other sufferers of the condition; another whose grandson was born prematurely champions funds for medical research into birth defects; members who are openly gay speak out for the rights of homosexuals everywhere. Such causes are close to members' hearts, even though they may pay scant political dividends. Legislators' backgrounds, religious beliefs, social identities, and experiences all shape their views and priorities. Political scientist Barry C. Burden refers to such influences as "the personal roots of representation," and he argues that analysts must take them into account to understand legislators' policy activism in Congress.[54]

Congressional Roles

Members of Congress, as Richard F. Fenno Jr. explains, spend their lives "moving between two contexts, Washington and home, and between two activities, governing and campaigning."[55] The two contexts and the two activities are continuously interwoven. How members govern is deeply affected by their constituency roots and their campaign experiences. In turn, their Capitol Hill activities affect all of their subsequent contacts with people back home. As members carry out their representational functions, it is possible to distinguish three roles undertaken, to some degree, by most members of Congress: legislator, constituency servant, and partisan.

Legislator

The rules, procedures, and traditions of the House and Senate impose many constraints on members' behavior. To be effective, new members must learn their way through the institutional maze. Legislators therefore stress the formal aspects of Capitol Hill duties and routines: legislative work, investigation, and committee specialization. Sen. Charles E. Schumer, D-N.Y., an elected official for most of his life (he was elected to the state assembly at age twenty-three and served nine terms in the U.S. House), explained his commitment as a professional legislator during his successful 1998 Senate campaign:

> I love to legislate. Taking an idea—often not original with me—shaping it, molding it. Building a coalition of people who might not completely agree with it. Passing it and making the country a little bit of a better place. I love doing that.[56]

Legislators pursue information and expertise on issues, not only because of their personal interest in public policy but also because it sways others in the chamber. To influence other members, a legislator must be perceived as credible and knowledgeable—in other words, someone worth listening to.

The legislator's role often dovetails with that of representing constituents. Most members seek committee assignments that will serve the needs of their states or districts. One House member related why he sought a seat on the committee handling flood control and water resource development. "The interests of my district dictated my field of specialization," he explained, "but the decision to specialize in some legislative field is automatic for the member who wants to exercise any influence."[57] Members soon learn the norms, or folkways, that expedite legislative productivity. Examining the post–World War II Senate, Donald R. Matthews identified folkways that restrained and channeled members' legislative activity. Senators were encouraged to serve an apprenticeship, deferring to elders in their early years; to concentrate on Senate work instead of on gaining publicity; to specialize in issues within their committees or affecting their home states; and to extend reciprocity to colleagues—that is, provide willing assistance with the expectation that it would be repaid in kind one day.[58] These folkways have faded in importance in the contemporary Senate. Barbara Sinclair's major reassessment of senators' Hill styles concluded that the restrained activism of the 1950s Senate had given way to unrestrained activism in the contemporary era.[59] New senators now actively take part in most aspects of the chamber's work, ignoring the apprenticeship norm. Many senators, especially those with an eye on the White House, work tirelessly to attract national publicity and personal attention. Committee specialization, although still common, is less rigid than it once was. Senators now have many overlapping committee assignments and are expected to express views on a wide range of issues.

The House relies more on formal channels of power than on informal norms. From interviews, however, Herbert B. Asher uncovered some key House norms.[60]

Among them are the beliefs that the important work of the House should be done in committees and that members should specialize in the issues before their committees. Members should be prepared to bargain and trade votes. Members should learn the procedural rules of the chamber. They should not personally criticize a colleague on the House floor.

As in the Senate, House norms of earlier eras have eroded. New members, impatient to make their mark, assert themselves more quickly, aided by party leaders who worry about getting the freshmen reelected. Leadership comes earlier to members than it used to. Specialization remains more compelling in the House than in the Senate, but many members branch out into unrelated issues. No longer are committees the sole forums for influencing legislation. Many of today's members, more partisan and ideologically driven than their predecessors, shun norms such as reciprocity and compromise. Several of the new progressive Democrats elected to the House in 2018 have challenged prevailing norms in criticizing fellow party members who are seen as too moderate. When one of the new members, Alexandria Ocasio-Cortez, hinted that primary challenges might be in order for Democrats who vote against party priorities, Rep. Emanuel Cleaver, D-Mo., responded that "I'm sure Ms. Cortez means well, but there's almost an outstanding rule: Don't attack your own people." Another veteran Democrat, who shares Ocasio-Cortez's liberal ideology, suggested that, "there's a difference between being an activist and a lawmaker in Congress."[61]

Constituency Servant

As constituency servants, members of Congress attempt to give voice to local citizens' concerns, solve constituents' problems with federal programs, and ensure that their states and districts receive a fair share of federal dollars. Often the task is performed by legislators and their staffs as casework—individual cases triggered by constituent letters or visits. Even though mostly delegated to staff aides, this is a chore that weighs heavily on members. A House member expressed the philosophy of most legislators this way:

> Constituent work: that's something I feel very strongly about. The American people, with the growth of the bureaucracy, feel nobody cares. The only conduit a taxpayer has with the government is a congressional office.[62]

One recent field experiment analyzing members' response time to letters dealing with policy and letters requesting constituent services found that members prioritize service over policy.[63] Sometimes, members stress constituency service to gain breathing room for legislative stands that stray from district norms.

Research has shown that developing a reputation as working hard on behalf of constituents in these ways makes a positive difference for legislators' careers. A recent study found that "a constituent-service reputation generates the most positive notice among citizens . . . [while] policy expertise appears to be less valuable to, or less noticed by, constituents."[64] Procuring pork barrel projects for local constituencies tends to improve representatives' name recognition back home,[65] reduce their likelihood of facing a strong challenger,[66] and enhance vulnerable members' reelection chances.[67] Even while Congress has adopted bans against earmarking special projects for members' constituencies and creating tax breaks for ten or fewer beneficiaries, they recognize that their constituents still expect them to bring home the bacon. An Arkansas lobbyist tells the story of going to visit one of his state's Republican members known for his antipork speeches. "I know you're anti-pork," the lobbyist began, "but I have to tell you about our needs and how to position yourself." "What do you mean?" the representative retorted. "As far as I can tell, it's not pork if it's for Arkansas."[68] Members have especially strong incentives to perform the constituency-servant role whenever Congress considers government programs with highly visible local benefits, such as highway or mass-transit grants, water projects, and homeland security contracts.

Partisan

Members of Congress are elected not just as individual representatives but as members of a political party. Nearly every member of Congress formally affiliates with one of the two major parties, and even the few members elected as independents organize with one of the two parties to receive their committee assignments. Party affiliation is more than a mere label for most members. Members work with and for their parties, and their partisan ties and activities have a pervasive effect on congressional elections, representation, and legislation.

Members have a personal stake in the collective fate of their parties. Whether their party commands a majority of seats in the House or Senate affects their power in the chamber and their ability to achieve personal legislative goals. The majority party elects leaders with agenda-setting responsibilities and controls the chairmanships of all committees and subcommittees in the two chambers. In addition, members know that voters' feelings about the parties will affect their own electoral chances. Former Republican senator Lincoln Chafee of Rhode Island lost his seat in 2006, despite high personal approval ratings, in large part because of his party's unpopularity in Rhode Island. "I give the voters credit," he said. "They made the connection between electing even popular Republicans at the cost of leaving the Senate in the hands of a leadership they had learned to mistrust."[69]

Many members hold posts within their congressional parties. Legislative party organizations are extensive, with whips, deputy whips, regional whips, and a variety of task forces. Elections for party positions are often hotly contested. As discussed in more detail in Chapter 6, members who hold or seek party positions dedicate significant effort to party causes. They do favors for fellow partisans and exhort them to vote the party position. They seek to impress leaders and other party members with their prodigious fund-raising and campaigning on behalf of their party's candidates.[70] Even those members who do not serve as party officers will typically attend and participate in the party caucus. In the contemporary Congress, the House and Senate caucuses of both parties meet at least weekly.

Members engage in internal party communications and party message development. They stage press conferences, reach out to sympathetic groups and opinion leaders, and coordinate floor speeches as they seek to shape media coverage to partisan advantage.[71] A recent study of members' press releases and Facebook posts shows that they get more engagement (likes and shares) when they harshly criticize their partisan opponents than when they discuss bipartisanship, suggesting that many in the public are receptive to such partisan messaging. Members from swing districts are less likely to engage in partisan criticism than are members from districts that lean strongly toward their own parties. As a result, many of the loudest voices in contemporary politics belong to members who represent constituencies that are relatively extreme compared to the United States as a whole.[72] In short, partisan activities today place significant demands on legislators' time and energy. Not only do members seek to enact good policy as legislators and advance local concerns as constituency servants, but they also are partisans, heavily invested in the collective fortunes of their parties.

How Do Legislators Spend Their Time?

For senators and representatives, time is their most precious commodity, and lack of it is their most frequent complaint about their jobs.[73] Allocating time requires exceedingly tough personal and political choices. Members are barraged with requests for meetings with groups and constituents. They are expected to spend considerable amounts of time in their home states and districts.

Scheduling is complicated by the large number of formal work groups—mainly committees and subcommittees but also joint, party, and ad hoc panels. The average senator sits on three full committees and seven subcommittees; representatives average two committees and four subcommittees. With so many assignments, lawmakers are hard-pressed to control their crowded schedules. Committee quorums are difficult to achieve, and members' attention is often focused elsewhere. All too often, working sessions are composed of the chair, the ranking minority member, perhaps one or two interested colleagues, and staff aides.[74]

Repeated floor votes, which lawmakers fear missing, are another time-consuming duty. In a typical Congress, more than a thousand recorded votes may be taken in the House and perhaps six hundred in the Senate. "We're like automatons," one senator complained. "We spend our time walking in tunnels to go to the floor to vote."[75] Rep. Debbie Wasserman-Schultz, D-Fla., shuns the House gym, explaining, "I get my exercise running around the Capitol."[76]

Members are also under relentless pressure to raise campaign funds. As mentioned in Chapter 4, the Democratic Congressional Campaign Committee recommends that new members spend between 40 and 50 percent of their time in Washington on fund-raising. "Call time" takes a large bite out of members' daily schedule. In addition, members must set aside time for fund-raising events and personal meetings with potential donors.

Taken together, lawmakers' daily schedules in Washington are "long, fragmented, and unpredictable," according to a study based on time logs kept by senators' appointment secretaries.[77] "In Congress you are a total juggler," recalls former representative Pat Schroeder. "You have always got seventeen things pulling on your sleeve."[78] Often, members have scant notice that their presence is required at a meeting or a hearing. Carefully developed schedules are frequently disrupted.

Political scientists may claim that Congress runs in harmony with members' needs, but the members know otherwise. In a survey of 114 House and Senate members, *inefficiency* was the thing that most surprised them about Congress (45 percent gave this response).[79] "[Congress] is a good job for someone with no family, no life of their own, no desire to do anything but get up, go to work, and live and die by their own press releases," quipped former representative Fred Grandy, an Iowa Republican who left Congress in 1995. "It is a great job for deviant human beings."[80] The dilemma legislators face in allocating their time is far more than a matter of scheduling; it is a case of conflicting role expectations. Many members want to devote more time to legislative duties than their schedules allow. There are always pressing demands to spend more time on constituency and political chores.[81] The two Congresses pull members in different directions. As a retiring House committee chair remarked,

> One problem is that you're damned if you do and damned if you don't. If you do your work here, you're accused of neglecting your district. And if you spend too much time in your district, you're accused of neglecting your work here.[82]

The Shape of the Washington Career

Once a short-term activity, congressional service has become a career. Accompanying this careerism, or longevity, is a distinctive pattern of Washington activity: the longer members remain in office, the more they sponsor bills, deliver floor speeches, and offer amendments. Despite the democratizing trends of the reform era (1960s and 1970s), senior lawmakers continue to take the lead in legislative activities.[83] Long tenure also tends to pull members toward legislative specialization. Settling into their committee slots, members gain expertise in a distinct policy field, get to know the key interest groups and organizations affected, and spend their time managing legislation and conducting oversight in that field. Seniority tends to boost legislative achievement. Veterans usually enjoy significantly more success than do freshmen in getting their bills passed.[84] The link between members' service and their effectiveness reflects the indispensable role careerists play in the legislative process. As John R. Hibbing observed,

> Senior members are the heart and soul of the legislative side of congressional service. Relatively junior members can be given a subcommittee chairmanship, but it is not nearly so easy to give them an active, focused

legislative agenda and the political savvy to enact it. Some things take time and experience, and successful participation in the legislative process appears to be one of those things.[85]

The wisdom of this statement is repeatedly borne out. A study drawing on the uniquely detailed data available for the North Carolina General Assembly reports that legislators' "effectiveness rises sharply with tenure," and "there is no evidence that effectiveness eventually declines with tenure, even out to nine terms."[86] The study concludes that "the increased effectiveness [of senior legislators] is due to the acquisition of specific human capital, most likely through learning-by-doing."[87] A comprehensive study of U.S. House members' abilities to get their bills past significant stages in the legislative process reports that "as members become more senior they become more efficient at arranging deals with key office-holders."[88] Newcomers bring with them zeal, energy, and fresh approaches. And yet many of them lack patience, bargaining skills, institutional memory, and respect for the lawmaking process.

LOOKING HOMEWARD

Not all of a representative's or a senator's duties lie in Washington, DC. Legislators not only fashion policy for the nation's welfare, but they also act as emissaries from their home states or districts.

Independent Judgment or Constituency Opinion?

Although found in virtually every political system, representation is the hallmark of democratic regimes dedicated to sharing power among citizens. In small communities, decisions can be reached by face-to-face discussions, but in populous societies, such personalized consultation is impossible. Thus, according to democratic theory, citizens can exert control by choosing *fiduciary agents* who will then deliberate on legislation just as their principals, the voters, would do if they could be on hand themselves.[89] But in attempting to serve as a faithful agent for constituents, legislators are faced with a central dilemma of representation: whether to take actions that are popular with constituents or to do what the legislator believes is in their best interest. As Pitkin explains,

> The representative must act in such a way that, although he is independent, and his constituents are capable of action and judgment, no conflict arises between them. He must act in their interest, and this means he must not normally come into conflict with their wishes.[90]

Recent opinion surveys seem to echo Pitkin's formulation. As one analyst puts it, "The public seems to want elected officials to internalize the majority's values and then try to assess how those values come to bear on an issue." No less than

85 percent agreed with the following statement: "The goal of Congress should be to make the decisions that a majority of Americans would make if they had the information and time to think things over that Congress has."[91]

Nonetheless, legislators must do more than register prevailing constituency opinion in order to represent their constituents. Public opinion often changes when controversy arises and constituents become more informed about issues. Legislators have to anticipate constituents' future views if an issue becomes more salient and more broadly understood.

Some representatives reject the idea that they ought to represent public opinion and instead see themselves as Burkean trustees charged with doing what is in constituents' interests. Speaking to a group of newly elected House members, Rep. Henry J. Hyde, R-Ill. (1974–2007), voiced the Burkean ideal:

> If you are here simply as a tote board registering the current state of opinion in your district, you are not going to serve either your constituents or the Congress well. You must take, at times, a national view, even if you risk the displeasure of your neighbors and friends back home. If you don't know the principle, or the policy, for which you are willing to lose your office, then you are going to do damage here.[92]

In short, legislators must instead use their superior information about policy, their broader perspective, and their personal judgment in making decisions. Nearly every member can point to conscience votes cast on deeply felt issues. A few, such as Rep. Mike Synar, D-Okla. (1979–1995), compile a contrarian record, challenging voters to admire their independence, if not their policies. Synar was an unabashed liberal Democrat from a state that now elects mostly conservative Republicans. "I want to be a U.S. congressman from Oklahoma, not an Oklahoman congressman," Synar declared when he arrived in the capital.[93] If turned out of office by hostile sentiment (as Synar later was), the Burkean can at least hope for history's vindication.

In practice, legislators assume different representational styles according to the occasion. They ponder factors such as the nation's welfare, their personal convictions, their party's perspective, and constituency opinions. "The weight assigned to each factor," writes Thomas E. Cavanagh, "varies according to the nature of the issue at hand, the availability of the information necessary for a decision, and the intensity of preference of the people concerned about the issue."[94] Members of Congress are challenged to explain their choices to constituents—no matter how many or how few people truly care about the matter.[95] The anticipated need to explain oneself shapes a member's decisions and is part of the dilemma of choice. A cynical saying among lawmakers asserts that "a vote on anything [is] a wrong vote if you cannot explain it in a 30-second TV ad."[96]

What Are Constituencies?

Senators and representatives cannot respond equally to all of the people within a given state or district. A subset of their constituents elected them, and so, they interact more with supporters than with opponents. The constituencies that legislators see as they campaign or vote are quite different from the boundaries found on maps. Fenno describes a "nest" of constituencies, ranging from the widest (geographic constituency) to the narrowest (personal constituency), which is made up of supporters, loyalists, and intimates.[97]

Geographic and Demographic Constituencies

The average House district today numbers more than 740,000 people. As for senators, fourteen represent states with only one House district; the rest represent multidistrict states with as many as 40 million people.[98] Such constituencies differ sharply from one another. More than half of the people in Manhattan's Upper East Side (New York's Twelfth District) have college degrees, compared with only 6 percent in California's central valley (Twenty-first District). Median family income ranges from $136,000 (California's Thirty-third District, on the coast in Los Angeles County) to less than $28,000 (in New York's Fifteenth District in the South Bronx, where 36 percent of the families live in poverty). Such disparities among districts shape their representatives' outlooks.

Demographically, constituencies may be homogeneous or heterogeneous.[99] Some constituencies, even a few whole states, remain fairly uniform and one-dimensional—mostly wheat farmers or inner-city dwellers or small-town citizens. Because of rising population, economic complexity, and educational levels, however, virtually all constituencies, House as well as Senate, have become more heterogeneous than they used to be. The more diverse a constituency, the more challenging is the representative's task. Fenno suggests that a representative's challenge is easier to the extent that the member can identify a single "lowest common denominator" that characterizes their constituency.

Another attribute of constituencies is electoral balance, especially as manifested in the incumbent's reelection chances. Heterogeneous districts tend to be more competitive than uniform ones. Incumbents predictably prefer safe districts—that is, those with a high proportion of groups leaning toward their party. Not only do safe districts favor reelection, but they also imply that voters will be easier to please.[100] Truly competitive districts are not the norm, especially in the House of Representatives. Even though the big Democratic tide of 2018 generated a larger number of competitive districts than usual, only 76 races (17.5 percent of the total) were considered either toss-ups or leaning toward one party, and a solid majority of victors won by twenty points or more.[101]

As Figure 5-1 shows, competitiveness varies over time. Senate seats are more likely to be closely contested than House races, but most incumbents still win by a substantial margin.

Whatever the numbers might show, few incumbents regard themselves as truly safe. The threat of losing an election is very real. Even with incumbent reelection rates at above 90 percent, incumbent officeholders understandably fear even a 10 percent chance of losing a job they have worked so hard to win. Most lawmakers have a close call at some time in their congressional careers, and many

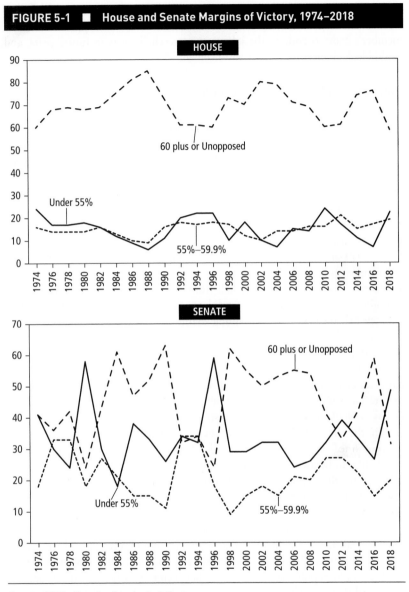

FIGURE 5-1 ■ House and Senate Margins of Victory, 1974–2018

Sources: *CQ Weekly* and authors' calculations.

Notes: Percentages may not add to 100 because of rounding. "Unopposed" includes districts or states where only one major-party candidate was on the ballot.

of them eventually suffer defeat.[102] In addition to the incumbents who went down to defeat in 2018, a number of others—including 13 senators and some 59 House members—survived while receiving what might be called warning signs from the home folks.[103] Incumbents thus worry not only about winning or losing but also about their margins of safety. Downturns in normal electoral support narrow the member's comfort zone in the job, may invite challengers in future years, and could block chances for further advancement.[104]

Political and Personal Constituencies

As candidates or incumbents analyze their electoral base, three narrower constituencies can be discerned: supporters (the reelection constituency), loyalists (the primary constituency), and intimates (the personal constituency).[105] Supporters are those who generally are expected to back the candidate in the November general election. Candidates and their advisers constantly monitor these voters, reassessing precinct-level political demography—registration figures, survey data, and recent electoral trends. The more elections incumbents have survived, the more precisely they can identify supporters. Areas and groups with the biggest payoffs are usually targeted.

Loyalists are the politician's staunchest supporters. They may share ties with the member from preelectoral ventures—civil rights, environmental, or Tea Party activists, for example. They may hail from the same religious or ethnic groups or political or civic clubs as the candidate. They may be friends and neighbors. Whatever their source, they are willing volunteers who can be counted on to lend a hand in reelection campaigns.

Candidates dare not ignore these loyalists. A favorite story of House Speaker Thomas P. "Tip" O'Neill Jr., D-Mass. (1953–1987), emerged from his first campaign for city council (at which he failed). A neighbor told him, "Tom, I'm going to vote for you even though you didn't ask me." "Mrs. O'Brien," replied a surprised O'Neill, "I've lived across the street from you for 18 years. I shovel your walk in the winter. I cut your grass in the summer. I didn't think I had to ask you for your vote." To this the lady replied, "Tom, I want you to know something: people like to be asked."[106] Expressions of gratitude are equally important. The elder George Bush reportedly "always carried a box of note cards with him on the campaign trail and penned a personal note immediately following each event to the volunteers and hosts."[107]

Even entrenched officeholders worry about keeping their core supporters energized. Loyalists are a politician's defenders in times of adversity. "There's a big difference between the people who are for you and the people who are excitedly for you," an Iowa politician told Fenno, "between those who will vote if they feel like it and those for whom the only election is [your] election. You need as many of that group as you can get."[108]

Intimates are close friends who supply political advice and emotional support. They may be members of the candidate's family, trusted staff members, political mentors, or individuals who shared decisive experiences early in the candidate's career. The setting and the players differ from state to state and from district to district. Tip O'Neill's inner circle was made up of the "boys" of Barry's Corner, a local clubhouse in Cambridge, Massachusetts, whose families O'Neill had known intimately over more than fifty years of political life. When Rep. David E. Price, D-N.C., first decided to run for Congress, he relied on what he called the "Wednesday night group," which he described as "an inner circle without whom the effort would never have gotten off the ground."[109] Such intimates play an indispensable role. Beyond their enthusiastic support, they provide unvarnished advice on political matters and serve as sounding boards for ideas and strategies.

Home Styles

Legislators evolve distinctive ways of presenting themselves and their records to their constituents—what Fenno calls their *home styles*. These styles are exhibited in members' personal appearances, mailings, newsletters, press releases, radio and television spots, Twitter feeds, and websites. Little is known about how home styles coalesce, but they are linked to members' personalities, backgrounds, constituency features, and resources. The ways members interact with constituents have a powerful effect on their electoral success.[110]

Presentation of Self

A successful home style will elicit trust—constituents' faith that legislators are who they claim to be and will do what they promise.[111] Winning voters' trust does not happen overnight; it takes time, persistence, and consistency. Members must establish their qualification for office—that is, the belief that they are capable of handling the job. Members also strive to convey identification—the impression that legislators resemble their constituents—and empathy—the sense that legislators understand constituents' problems and care about them.

Because of the variations among legislators and constituencies, the use of many different home styles can effectively build the trust relationship. The legendary Speaker "Mr. Sam" Rayburn represented his East Texas district for nearly fifty years (1913–1961) as a plain dirt farmer. Once he was back in his hometown of Bonham, his drawl thickened; his tailored suits were exchanged for khakis, an old shirt, and a slouch hat; and he traveled not in the Speaker's limousine but in a well-dented pickup truck. His biographer relates,

> If Rayburn ever chewed tobacco in Washington, a long-time aide could not recall it, but in Bonham he always seemed to have a plug in his cheek. He made certain always to spit in the fireplace at his home when constituents were visiting, so that if nothing else, they would take away the idea that Mr. Sam was just a plain fellow.[112]

The aim of a member's home style is to become "one of us" in constituents' estimation. Accomplishing this is a "difficult feat—far more difficult than establishing a reputation as a fine constituency servant or policy expert."[113]

Today's legislators are no less inventive in fashioning home styles. Some embrace what Fenno calls a *person-to-person style* that relies upon knowing constituents by name and meeting with them in small, face-to-face groups. Such an approach can forge a sense of deep connection between the member and his home community. Others adopt an *issue-oriented approach,* which typically involves holding many town hall events where the member articulates and defends her or his stances across a range of hot-button topics. The issue-oriented member conveys the impression that she or he is an activist, engaged in issues that her or his constituents view as important. Still other members rely upon their personal background to help forge a connection with constituents, such as the military veteran, who uses national defense issues to symbolize his or her oneness with a district supportive of the military. The repertoire of home styles is virtually limitless.

Although members retain some choice as they devise their home style, the most effective style will depend, in part, on how well the member's ideology and party fit with district dynamics. A recent study drawing upon thousands of member press releases to categorize types of home styles found that members from districts filled with out-partisans tend to emphasize credit-claiming for spending in the district rather than articulating policy positions. By contrast, members from districts that are dominated by their copartisans adopt home styles that emphasize taking positions on a range of policies. This difference in strategies means that policy debates in Washington tend to be shaped by the more extreme voices of members from one-party districts.[114] Voters are likely to remember style long after they forget issue statements or voting records. Even so, legislators know full well that they must explain their decisions to others.[115]

Explaining Washington Activity

Explaining is an integral part of decision making. In home district forums, constituents expect members to be able to describe, interpret, and justify their actions. If they do not agree with the member's conclusions, they may at least respect the decision-making style.

Although few incumbents fear that a single vote can defeat them, all realize that voters' disenchantment with their record can be fatal—more so in these days of Internet communications, when lobby groups publicize voting records. Although local news media coverage of Congress is often uncritical, it can promote political accountability. Local media devote more time and resources to monitoring representatives who are "out of step" with their district's presidential vote than those who are perceived to be in step. Such members face additional media scrutiny and must therefore account for their Washington decisions more frequently.[116] Members stockpile reasons for virtually every position they take, often more than are needed. Facing especially thorny choices (for example, on health care reform, immigration, or the appropriate reach of surveillance policy), they might seek a middle-of-the-road route. More often, they huddle under the umbrella of their party's line. Whatever course they choose, they will find that inconsistency is mentally and politically costly. A recent study showed that when senators' position on an issue differs from their constituents, they tailor their explanations to their audience by highlighting aspects of their behavior that fit with their constituents' preferences. Even so, they avoid statements that are inconsistent with their true position.[117]

Constituency Careers

Constituency bonds evolve over the course of a lawmaker's career. Constituency careers have at least two recognizable stages: expansion and protection. In the expansion stage, the member builds a reelection constituency by solidifying the help of hard-core supporters and reaching out to attract additional blocs of support. Aggressive efforts to reach out to new voters—exploiting the perquisites of incumbency, such as fund-raising and an election year avalanche of messages to constituents—partly account for the *sophomore surge,* in which newcomers typically boost their margin in their first reelection bid. In the protection stage, the member stops expanding the base, content with protecting support already won. Once established, a successful home style is rarely altered.

Certain developments, however, can lead to a change in a member's home style. One is demographic change in the constituency, as population movement or redistricting force a member to confront unfamiliar voters or territory. A second cause is a strategic reaction, such as when a fresh challenger or a novel issue threatens established voting patterns. Because coalitions may shift over time, members and their advisers pour over the results of the most recent election (and available survey results).

Finally, home styles may change with new personal goals and ambitions. Achieving positions of power in Washington can divert a member's attention from home-state business. This can ultimately lead to serious problems in the home district. Rep. Joe Crowley's, D-N.Y., primary loss to Alexandria Ocasio-Cortez owed in part to Crowley spending more of his time and attention in Washington as he sought to position himself for a top leadership position in the Democratic Party.[118] Family responsibilities or the need to improve one's financial situation may also lead to a shift in priorities. Faced with new aspirations or shifting constituency demands, some members decide to retire. Others struggle ineffectively and are defeated. Still others survive by rejuvenating their constituency base.

OFFICE OF THE MEMBER INC.

Home style includes the way a member answers day-to-day questions: How much attention should I devote to state or district needs? How much time should I spend in the state or district? How should I keep in touch with my constituents? How should I deploy staff aides to handle constituents' concerns?

Road Tripping

During the nineteenth century, legislators spent most of their time at home, traveling to Washington only when Congress was in session. However, after

World War II (and the advent of both air travel from home and air-conditioning on Capitol Hill), congressional sessions lengthened until they spanned most of the year.

By the 1970s, both houses had adopted parallel schedules of sessions punctuated with district work periods (House) or nonlegislative periods (Senate). At the same time, members were permitted more paid trips to states or districts. Today, senators and representatives are allowed as many trips home as they want, subject to the limits of their official expense allowances. While about 38 percent of members went home nearly every weekend in 1973, 78 percent did so in 2013. In this earlier period, about two-thirds of members' families lived in Washington; today, a full 85 percent of members' families live in their home district. Today's home styles thus entail almost continual commuting.[119]

Seniority is also a factor. Senior members tend to make fewer trips to their districts than do junior members, perhaps reflecting junior members' greater attentiveness to their districts or senior members' greater Washington responsibilities. Finally, members' decisions to retire voluntarily are usually accompanied by large drops in trips home.

Constituency Casework

"All God's chillun got problems," exclaimed Rep. Billy Matthews, D-Fla. (1953–1967), as he pondered mail from his constituents.[120] In the early days, lawmakers lacked staff aides and wrote personally to executive agencies for help in matters such as pension or land claims and appointments to military academies. The Legislative Reorganization Act of 1946 provided de facto authority for hiring caseworkers, first in Senate offices and later in the House.

What are these cases all about? As respondents in a nationwide survey reported, the most frequent reason for contacting a member's office (16 percent of all contacts) is to express views or obtain information on legislative issues. Requests for help in finding government jobs form the next largest category, followed by cases dealing with government services, such as Social Security, veterans' benefits, or unemployment compensation. Military cases (for example, transfers, discharges, or personal hardships) are numerous, as are tax, legal, and immigration problems. Constituents often ask for government publications. And there are requests for flags that have flown over the U.S. Capitol.

Many citizen appeals, moreover, betray a hazy understanding of the officeholder's duties. Rep. Luis V. Gutierrez, D-Ill. (1993–2009), reported being barraged with all manner of complaints and requests when he shopped in his North Side Chicago neighborhood. Examples of what he has heard are as follows: "They haven't picked up my trash!" (the city's job). "Can you get my son a scholarship to the state university?" (a state matter). Or "I can't pay my child support" (personal). Representative Gutierrez's personal favorite was this: "I own property in Puerto Rico and someone is blocking my driveway."[121] Cases arrive in legislators' offices by letter, phone, email, fax, or in person at district or mobile offices. All representatives and senators now have email addresses and websites with contact information. Occasionally, members themselves pick up cases from talking to constituents. Indeed, many hold office hours in their districts for this purpose. When a constituent's request is received, it is usually acknowledged promptly by a letter that either fulfills the request or promises that an answer will be forthcoming.

Keeping up with incoming communications is a priority for all congressional offices. If the constituent's request requires contacting a federal agency, the contact in the executive agency is usually a liaison officer. When the agency reaches a decision, a reply is forwarded to the congressional office. The reply is then sent along to the constituent, perhaps with a cover letter signed by the member. If the agency's reply is deemed faulty, the caseworker may ask for reconsideration; in some cases, the member may personally intervene to lend weight to the appeal.[122]

The volume of casework varies from state to state and from district to district. Demographic variation affects casework volume because some types of citizens simply are more likely to have contact with government agencies. Senators representing the smallest states often have casework loads that exceed those of House members because their greater institutional clout makes them even more attractive to small-state residents than their state's House members. When Jon Tester travels around Montana, he routinely brings casework staff, and he is quick to connect constituents with them to handle their problems.[123] By contrast, large-state senators are perceived as being more distant, so constituents in those states are more likely to turn to their House members for casework requests.[124] From all accounts, casework pays off in citizen support for individual legislators. In one National Election Study survey, 17 percent of all adults reported that they or members of their families had requested help from their own representatives. Eighty-five percent said they were satisfied with the response they received.[125] "Casework is all profit," contends Morris P. Fiorina. Unlike the positions members take on issues, casework wins friends without alienating anyone.

Some criticize constituency casework as unfair or biased in practice. Citizens may not enjoy equal access to senators' or representatives' offices. Political supporters or cronies may receive favored treatment at others' expense. But in the great bulk of cases, help is universally dispensed.

Personal Staff

Legislators head sizable office enterprises that reflect their responsibilities within the institution and toward their constituents. Staff members assist with legislative and constituency duties. Constituent representation is deemed so essential that when a member dies, resigns, or is incapacitated, the staff normally remains on the job (supervised by the secretary of the Senate or the clerk of the House, as the case may be).

Each House member is entitled to a member representational account that ranges from $1.3 to $1.5 million annually. From this account, members pay the salaries of no more than eighteen full-time and four part-time employees. The average House member's full-time staff actually numbers about fifteen. Representatives also use the member representational account for travel, telecommunications, district office rental, office equipment, stationery, computer services, and mail.[126] Senators' personal staffs range in size from thirteen to seventy-one; the average is from thirty to thirty-five full-time employees. Unlike the House, the Senate places no limits on the number of staff a senator may employ. A senator's office expense account depends on factors such as the state's population and its distance from Washington, DC. Congressional offices depend heavily on unpaid help, mainly college-age interns. On average, each House and Senate office uses about nine interns every year. (See Appendix B for information on internships.)

Staff Organization

No two congressional offices are exactly alike. Each is shaped by the personality, interests, constituency, and politics of the individual legislator. State and district needs also influence staff composition. A senator from a farm state likely will employ at least one specialist in agricultural problems; an urban representative might hire a consumer affairs or housing expert. Traditions are important. If a legislator's predecessor had an enviable reputation for a certain kind of service, the new incumbent will dare not let it lapse.

The member's institutional position also affects staff organization. Committee and subcommittee chairs have committee staff at their disposal. Members without such aides rely heavily on personal staff for their committee work.

Staff Functions

Most personal aides in the House and Senate are young, well educated, and transient. Senate and House aides have served, on average, less than three years in their posts. Their salaries, although somewhat above the average for full-time workers in the United States, fall well below those for comparably educated workers.[127]

The mix of personal staff functions is decided by each member. Most hire chiefs of staff, legislative assistants, caseworkers, and press aides, as well as a few people from the home state or district. Chiefs of staff supervise the office and impart political and legislative advice. Often, they function as the legislator's alter ego, negotiating with colleagues, constituents, and lobbyists. Legislative assistants work with members in committees, draft bills, write speeches, suggest policy initiatives, analyze legislation, and prepare position papers. They also monitor committee sessions that the member is unable to attend.

To emphasize personal contacts, many members have moved casework staff to their home districts or states. Virtually all House and Senate members have home-district offices. Some members have as many as five or six such offices. Field offices have lower staff salaries, cheaper rents, and less overhead. They also are more accessible to constituents, local and state officials, and regional federal officers. Members' district staffs fill the role once performed by local party workers and simultaneously enhance members' reelection prospects. The share of personal staff for House members based in the district has increased from 35 percent in 1979 to 47 percent in 2016; the climb in the Senate has been even steeper, with 24 percent of staff based in the home state in 1979, as compared to 43 percent in 2016.[128]

This organizational division reflects the fundamental duality of legislative roles. Legislative functions are centered on Capitol Hill, whereas constituency functions are based in field offices. In other words, "Office of the Member Inc." is increasingly split into headquarters and branch divisions—with the Capitol Hill office handling legislative duties and the state or district office dealing with constituents.

Because members' resources—offices, staffs, and allowances—are funded by the taxpayers, they are restricted to the conduct of official business. "Any campaign work by staff members must be done outside the congressional office, and without using any congressional office resources," states a 2006 House ethics memorandum.[129] This distinction may seem cloudy; after all, members' offices are suffused with electoral concerns, and what constitutes "campaign activity" is unclear. During the campaign season, certain aides go on leave and transfer to the campaign organization's payroll.

MEMBERS AND THE MEDIA

Office allowances in both chambers amply support lawmakers' unceasing struggle for media attention. A member's office bears some resemblance to the communications division of a medium-size business. Nearly every day, messages are released for wide distribution. In addition to turning out press releases, newsletters, and individual and mass mailings, members communicate through telephone, interviews, radio and TV programs, email and text messages, official and personal websites, and through online social networking services. Most of the time, these publicity barrages are aimed not at the national media but at individuals and media outlets back in the home state or district.

Mail

The traditional cornerstone of congressional publicity is the franking privilege—the right of members to send out mail at no cost with their signature (the frank) instead of a stamp. This practice, which dates from the First Continental Congress in 1775, is intended to facilitate official communication between elected officials and the people they represent (a rationale accepted by federal courts in upholding the practice).

Critics point out that franked mail is largely unsolicited and often politically motivated. The fact that the volume of mail is much higher in election years than in nonelection years seems to bear that criticism out. Most items are mass mailings, such as general-purpose newsletters blanketing home states or districts or special messages targeted to certain categories of voters. Recipients are urged to share their views or contact local offices for help. Sometimes, the newsletter may feature an opinion poll asking for citizens' views on selected issues. Whatever the results, the underlying message is that the legislator cares what folks back home think.

Current law forbids franked mail that is "unrelated to the official business, activities, and duties of members." It also bars the frank for a "matter which specifically solicits political support for the sender or any other person or any political party." In addition, Congress has placed caps on newsletters and on total outgoing mail. Chamber rules forbid mass mailings (five hundred or more pieces) sixty days (Senate) or ninety days (House) before a primary, runoff, or general election. In the lead-up to the beginning of each cutoff period, streams of U.S. Postal Service trucks are seen pulling away from the loading docks of the congressional office buildings.

The advent of email poses the problem of whether or how the much-debated franking restrictions should apply. The Senate has generally applied the franking rules to electronic mail. The House, however, has declined to adopt such strict rules.

Feeding the Local Press

News outlets are decentralized and dispersed across the United States. These include daily and weekly newspapers, radio and TV stations, and cable systems. Virtually all of these media outlets are locally based, centered on local issues, and funded by local advertising.

Most local media outlets have inadequate resources for covering their congressional delegations. In fact, very few have their own Washington reporters. Most rely on syndicated or chain services that rarely follow individual members consistently. "If they report national news it is usually because it involves local personalities, affects local outcomes, or relates directly to local concerns," stated a Senate report.[130] The inadequate resources enjoyed by local press outlets create opportunities for members of Congress to ensure that they receive mostly positive attention.

Most legislators have at least one staffer who serves as a press aide; some have two or three. Their job is to generate coverage highlighting the member's work. Executive agencies often help by letting incumbents announce federal grants or contracts awarded in the state or district. Even if the member had nothing to do with procuring the funds, the press statement proclaims, "Senator So-and-So announced today that a federal contract has been awarded to XYZ Company in Jonesville." Many offices also prepare weekly or biweekly columns that small-town newspapers can reprint under the lawmaker's byline. More generally, a substantial share of local newspaper coverage is based on press releases issued by members of Congress.[131]

Given these tendencies, it should be no surprise that most stories about incumbents are uncritically positive: only 6 percent of the news stories compiled by R. Douglas Arnold in his study of local congressional press coverage cited anyone who criticized the incumbent's performance.[132] The House, the Senate, and the four Capitol Hill parties (House and Senate Republicans and Democrats) have fully equipped studios and satellite links where audio or video programs or excerpted statements can be produced for a fraction of the commercial cost.[133] Some incumbents produce regular programs that are picked up by local radio or television outlets. More often, these local outlets insert brief audio or TV clips on current issues into regular news broadcasts—to give the impression that their reporters have gone out and obtained the story. Members also create their own news reports and beam them directly to hometown stations, often without ever talking to a reporter. With direct satellite feeds to local stations, members regularly go "live at five" before local audiences.

Like printed communications, radio and TV broadcasts pose ethical questions. House and Senate recording studios are supposed to be used only for communicating about legislation and other policy issues, but the distinction between legitimate constituent outreach and political advertising remains blurred. (The studios run by the parties have no such limits.) Some radio and television news editors have qualms about using members' programs. "It's just this side of self-serving," said one television editor of the biweekly *Alaska Delegation Report*.[134] Others claim to see little difference between these electronic communications and old-fashioned press releases. Local editors and producers still have to decide whether to use the material, edit it, or toss it.

Local radio and television's weakness for congressionally initiated communications magnifies the advantages incumbents enjoy. ABC News commentator Cokie Roberts observed, "The emergence of local TV has made some members media stars in the home towns and, I would argue, done more to protect incumbency than any franking privilege or newsletter ever could, simply because television is a more pervasive medium than print."[135] Studies have confirmed a link between the expansion of local television stations across the country and the rise of incumbency advantage in the post-1960s era.[136] Reports on Congress from the national press corps are far more critical than those from local news organizations. Following the canons of investigative journalism, many national reporters are on the lookout for scandals or evidence of wrongdoing. The national press reports primarily on the institution of Congress, whereas the local press focuses mostly on local senators and representatives. The content and quality of press coverage in local and national media underscore the differences between the two Congresses. Congress as collective policy maker, covered mainly by the national press, appears in a different light from the politicians who make up Congress, covered mainly by local news outlets.

Social Media

Americans increasingly rely on the Internet for news. It is no wonder, then, that lawmakers have set up active websites, Facebook presences, and Twitter feeds to reach constituents.[137] Most websites feature the member's biography, committee assignments, and votes on major issues but vary in their content, usability, and interactivity.[138] Some members' websites include streaming audio or video of members' speeches or appearances on news programs. Few of them include such potentially sensitive information as the member's financial disclosure reports, travel spending, and meetings with lobbyists.

Members have been quick to embrace new communications technologies. In 2018 alone, members of Congress posted over 500,000 times on official Twitter, Facebook, Instagram, and YouTube accounts.[139] The audience for these messages varies considerably across members. While most focus primarily on staying in touch with constituents back home, a number of members have used social media to cultivate national followings. Alexandria Ocasio-Cortez's ability to shape the agenda in Congress is enhanced by her 6 million Twitter and Instagram followers.[140] For example, Ocasio-Cortez used her Twitter feed to draw attention (and cosponsors) for her Green New Deal resolution. A handful of other new Democrats who appeal to liberal voters across the country have also built large social media followings, including Ilhan Omar, D-Minn., Rashida Tlaib, D-Mich., and Ayanna Pressley, D-Mass. By contrast, Democrats from swing districts who have sought to put forward a more moderate image tend to have much smaller social media followings nationally but nonetheless use the medium to reach core and potential supporters in their districts.[141]

There is little doubt that the burgeoning use of social media by members provides a tool for members to reach a broader audience. Yet building coalitions in Congress nonetheless continues to require gaining the support of members who are most concerned with ensuring that voters at home will view their actions favorably.

CONCLUSION

How members of Congress manage the two-Congresses dilemma is reflected in their daily tasks on Capitol Hill and in their home states or districts. Election is a prerequisite to congressional service. Legislators allocate much of their time and energy—and even more of their staff and office resources—to the care and cultivation of voters. Their Hill styles and home styles are adopted with this end in mind.

Yet senators and representatives do not live by reelection alone. Many bemoan the need for constant campaigning. "What drives me nuts about this place is that, when I came here, it used to be that you had at least a year after you were elected where you could get the people's business done before the next election intruded," complained former representative David Obey, D-Wis. (1969–2011). "Now the way politics has been nationalized, the election intrudes every day."[142] For those who remain in office, reelection is not usually viewed as an end in itself but as a lever for pursuing other goals—policy making or career advancement. Fenno once remarked to a member that "sometimes it must be hard to connect what you do here with what you do in Washington." "Oh no," the lawmaker replied, "I do what I do here so I can do what I want to do there."[143]

Party Leaders. Incoming House Speaker Nancy Pelosi (D-Calif.) surrounded by children and grandchildren of lawmakers, takes the oath at the opening of the 116th Congress at the U.S. Capitol in Washington, DC, on January 3, 2019. Speaker Pelosi is flanked by House Majority Leader Steny Hoyer (D-Md.), Senate Minority Leader Charles Schumer (D-N.Y.), and Senator Dick Durbin (D-Ill.) while speaking to the media at the White House after meeting with U.S. President Donald Trump about ending the partial government shutdown on January 9, 2019, in Washington, DC. Schumer and Senate Majority Leader Mitch McConnell (R-Ky.) walk side by side to the Senate Chamber at the U.S. Capitol on February 7, 2018, in Washington, DC; the two leaders announced they had reached agreement on a two-year budget deal that will raise strict caps on military and domestic spending. McConnell speaks during a news conference following a Senate Republicans policy luncheon on Capitol Hill, January 15, 2019 in Washington, DC.

6

LEADERS AND PARTIES IN CONGRESS

Democrats had just gained 40 House seats, decisively winning back their majority after eight years of Republican control, yet the party's leader Nancy Pelosi appeared to be in trouble in the immediate aftermath of the 2018 midterm elections. Twenty-one Democratic members of the incoming 116th Congress had promised not to back Pelosi as Speaker of the House.[1] This would be sufficient to block her election if they all stood firm. Many of these members were elected in Republican-leaning districts in which the liberal Pelosi was viewed as a political liability. In addition, several other new members were suggesting that they wanted to see new, younger leadership and refused to commit to support Pelosi's election. The 78-year old Pelosi had served in the House for more than thirty years and had been Democratic leader since 2003. Admired by many in the party for her skill in holding the membership together and for her fundraising prowess, Pelosi was not viewed as a particularly effective public messenger and her reputation with voters had suffered after years of GOP attacks. Although even Democratic rebels understood the troubling symbolism of replacing the first female Speaker in a year in which female candidates and voters propelled Democrats to a majority, Pelosi critic Tim Ryan, D-Ohio, commented that "there's plenty of really competent females that we can replace her with."[2]

Pelosi's critics, however, soon found themselves overmatched. One key job of a congressional party leader is to understand how to win over dissident party members, using a mix of pressure and concessions to gain their support. Pelosi's long years in the leadership had given her plenty of experience in doing just that. One of Pelosi's tactics was to draw on a network of outside supporters—including Democratic governors, labor union leaders, and liberal interest groups. These supporters aggressively lobbied lawmakers to back Pelosi, making several of the freshmen reluctant to sign on to the effort to dump the Speaker, despite their campaign promises.[3] When it appeared that Rep. Martha Fudge, D-Ohio, might run against her for Speaker, Pelosi's allies orchestrated a public relations campaign questioning Fudge's record. Within days, Fudge announced she would not run and instead backed Pelosi's election.[4] Pelosi also played the inside game of quiet negotiation to win over members. Rep. Brian Higgins, D-N.Y., had signed a letter circulated by Pelosi foes committing to vote against her, but he backed down after Pelosi promised to try to get his Medicare bill a vote on the House floor. Higgins expressed regret for his earlier criticisms, noting "I shouldn't have signed the letter."[5]

With the rebels' support eroding, one of the leading dissidents, Rep. Ed Perlmutter, D-Colo., met with the Speaker to try to negotiate a resolution. In their conversations, Pelosi offered to back term limits for top leadership positions, paving the way for a leadership change within two to four years. Pelosi promised to serve no more than four more years as Speaker, with a two-thirds caucus vote required for her to serve beyond the current two-year term. As one of the rebels recalled, "When [Pelosi] started floating specific concepts involving term limits for top leadership positions, that was the first time we saw a path to success on the negotiations." The resulting agreement clinched Pelosi's reelection, avoiding an embarrassing floor fight. An aide for a rebel Democrat noted ruefully that "we were shocked" by the skill and speed with which Pelosi had defeated their challenge.[6] About six weeks later, the planned House Democratic Caucus vote on leadership term limits was quietly and indefinitely postponed "for further study."[7] Clearly, Pelosi's victory was rooted in decades of experience navigating the personalities and politics of the Democratic Caucus.

The job of top congressional party leaders is extraordinarily difficult. Their array of duties is large and complex, and their goals and objectives are often hard to achieve. They have their share of both setbacks and successes. Pelosi's successful battle for reelection as Speaker provides a window into ways that party leaders in both chambers might react in the face of difficult circumstances. Party leaders strive to comprehend the mood and sentiment of their members so they are not blindsided by the unexpected.

Pelosi's efforts relied on her deep knowledge of what each Democratic member wanted and how that member might be reached in order to gain their support. At times, this meant relying on outside allies whom the member views as important to their reelection. In other cases, it meant identifying the right concession to win over the member. Pelosi's reputation for toughness also helped her cause: As it became more likely to observers that Pelosi would be reelected, the fear set in that being on the wrong side of the Speaker would lead to negative consequences. Pelosi ally Jon Soltz, the chairman of the liberal lobbying group VoteVets, advised the potential rebels to "Think about the long game. To be an effective legislator, you will have to work with the next Speaker—which more likely than not would be Pelosi."[8]

In addition to managing internal party politics, the wide-ranging duties of congressional leaders include building electoral majorities and passing legislation. These responsibilities must be carried out with careful attention to the two Congresses. Leaders must facilitate lawmaking while, at the same time, attending both to party members' representational ties with their constituents and to the party's public image. Making national policy means finding ways of persuading members who represent different constituencies, regions, ideologies, values, and interests to support legislation that addresses national concerns. "The only thing that counts is 218 votes, and nothing else is real," a House leader declared. "You have to be able [to attract a majority of the House] to pass a bill."[9] Implicit in this party leader's statement is recognition that mobilizing winning coalitions is not easy.

Party leaders encounter what scholars call a *collective-action dilemma*.[10] How can leaders mobilize majorities to legislate for the public good when it is in the self-interest of rank-and-file lawmakers to focus solely on their own individual electoral needs? Such members often prefer to free ride on the efforts of their colleagues. In many cases, they want to avoid the difficult trade-offs that are frequently required for successful legislation. Legislative deal-making can be especially painful during conditions of divided government, in which neither party is able to achieve many of its partisan aims. Of course, if there are too many free riders, little lawmaking will get done at all.

Taking account of the two Congresses requires party leaders to assume roles both inside and outside the institution. In their inside role, party leaders formulate policy agendas and use their procedural and organizational authority to advance them. In their outside role, party leaders articulate and publicize issue positions designed to galvanize partisan support and swing voters. In today's era of ideological polarization, sharp partisanship, and intense electoral competition, leaders try to generate public momentum either to force legislative action on party priorities or to create issues to take to the voters in the next election. Leaders' inside and outside roles are inextricably intertwined. They serve as their party's link to the president, the press, the public, and the party faithful.

Congressional leadership is fundamentally partisan. Indeed, Congress itself is a partisan institution—that is, parties organize the legislature. The majority party in the House and Senate controls not only the top leadership posts but also the chairs and majorities on committees and subcommittees. With these tools, the majority party is generally able to control the legislative agenda.

THE SPEAKER OF THE HOUSE

No other congressional leader possesses the visibility and authority of the Speaker. "Because the Speakership is the only leadership position in Congress whose existence and method of selection is mandated by the Constitution," writes political scientist Matthew N. Green, "the office possesses considerable prestige."[11] Although the Constitution does not require the Speaker to be a House member, all of them have been. Under the Presidential Succession Act of 1947, the Speaker is next in line behind the vice president to succeed to the presidency.

The office of Speaker combines procedural and political prerogatives with policy and partisan leadership. Speakers preside over the House, meaning that they rule on points of order, announce the results of votes, refer legislation to committees, and maintain order and decorum in the House chamber. In addition to these procedural prerogatives, they exercise important political powers. They set the House's agenda of activities, control the Committee on Rules, chair or influence the decisions of their party's committee assignment panel, bestow or withhold various rewards, coordinate policy making with Senate counterparts, and, in this age of television and Internet communications, expound party and House positions to the public at large. In practice, Speakers today seldom actually preside over the House because they focus so much attention on external activities, such as campaigning for party members, fund-raising, and message development.

Speakers are formally elected by the members of the House, but in practice, the key step is to be selected by a majority of the majority party when it caucuses to select leaders. Today's Speakers have served long careers in the House, over which they have built relationships with fellow members and risen through the ranks of their party. Speakers elected since 1899 served, on average, more than twenty years before their election to the post. Speakers John Boehner, R-Ohio (2011–2015), and Nancy Pelosi, D-Calif. (2007–2011, 2019–), each served twenty years before becoming Speaker. Pelosi's immediate predecessor, Republican Paul Ryan of Wisconsin, served nearly twenty years before being elected Speaker in unusual circumstances (see later discussion).

Once in office, Speakers traditionally have been reelected as long as their party has controlled the House. Members typically vote for the Speakership along straight party lines. Not since 1923 has there been a genuine floor battle over the Speakership because, since that time, one party has always enjoyed a clear majority in the House, and that party has been able to work out, internally, disagreements over control of the Speakership.[12] In 2015, however, Boehner suffered twenty-five Republican defections in his election as Speaker, the most for any sitting Speaker in more than a century. This challenge to Boehner was poorly organized in that his disaffected conservative opponents were unable to coalesce around a single candidate as an alternative. The challenge to Pelosi's election as Speaker in 2019 was similarly disorganized, and the 15 Democratic dissidents who opposed her cast their votes for a variety of different individuals.

As chief parliamentary officer and leader of the majority party (see Figure 6-1), the Speaker enjoys unique powers in scheduling floor business and in recognizing members during sessions. Occasionally, Speakers will relinquish the gavel to join in the floor debate and to vote on issues. The Speaker is also in charge of administrative matters. The current administrative structure was established after Speaker Newt Gingrich officially took office in 1995. Gingrich's reforms streamlined and modernized management, undertook an independent audit of the accounting systems, and assigned responsibility to a new chief administrative officer—elected by the House at the start of each Congress—for running the House's administrative operations in a professional manner.[13]

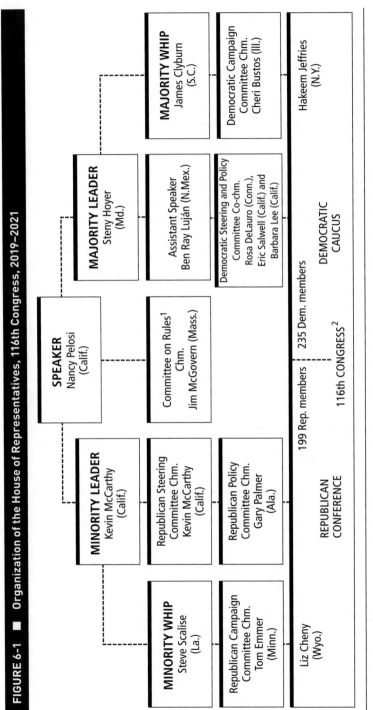

FIGURE 6-1 ■ Organization of the House of Representatives, 116th Congress, 2019–2021

SPEAKER
Nancy Pelosi
(Calif.)

MAJORITY LEADER
Steny Hoyer
(Md.)

MAJORITY WHIP
James Clyburn
(S.C.)

MINORITY LEADER
Kevin McCarthy
(Calif.)

MINORITY WHIP
Steve Scalise
(La.)

Committee on Rules[1]
Chm.
Jim McGovern (Mass.)

Assistant Speaker
Ben Ray Luján (N.Mex.)

Democratic Campaign
Committee Chm.
Cheri Bustos (Ill.)

Republican Steering
Committee Chm.
Kevin McCarthy
(Calif.)

Democratic Steering and Policy
Committee Co-chm.
Rosa DeLauro (Conn.),
Eric Salwell (Calif.) and
Barbara Lee (Calif.)

Republican Campaign
Committee Chm.
Tom Emmer
(Minn.)

Republican Policy
Committee Chm.
Gary Palmer
(Ala.)

Hakeem Jeffries
(N.Y.)

Liz Cheny
(Wyo.)

199 Rep. members

235 Dem. members

REPUBLICAN
CONFERENCE

DEMOCRATIC
CAUCUS

116th CONGRESS[2]

[1]Although not strictly a party panel, the Rules Committee, in modern times, functions largely as an arm of the majority leadership.

[2]The number of representatives as of January 2019.

The Changing Role of the Speaker

The Speaker's power derives, in great part, from the House's majoritarian rules. A determined House majority can achieve its policy objectives via majority rule. But it was not always so. Before 1890, intense battles were fought over the minority's right to delay—and even stop—legislative action. Throughout most of the nineteenth century, the House minority possessed a variety of stalling tactics that often frustrated House decision making.[14] In the 1890s, however, Republican Speaker Thomas "Czar" Reed of Maine finally curtailed the minority's capacity for obstruction. The House adopted procedures (the famous Reed Rules) to facilitate action on the basis of majority rule, including an 1890 House rule, still in effect: "No dilatory motion shall be entertained by the Speaker."

By 1910, Speaker Joseph G. Cannon, R-Ill., dominated the House—assigning members to committees, appointing and removing committee chairs, referring bills to committee, regulating the flow of bills to the House floor as chair of the Committee on Rules, and controlling floor debate. Taken individually, Cannon's powers were little different from those of his immediate predecessors, but taken together and exercised to their limits, they bordered on dictatorial. The result was a revolt. Progressive Republicans joined with discontented minority Democrats to reduce the Speaker's authority.

The House forced Cannon to step down from the Rules Committee in 1910 and required the House to elect the committee's members. The next year, when Democrats took control of the House, the new Speaker, James B. "Champ" Clark of Missouri, was denied the authority to make committee assignments, and his power of recognition was curtailed. The Speakership then went into long-term eclipse, as power flowed briefly to party caucuses and then to the committee chairs.

Over time, after the 1910 revolt, committees became more powerful relative to party leaders. Power in Congress was diffused among a relatively small number of committee chairs, who were often called the "barons" of Capitol Hill. These chairs rose to power by means of a nearly inviolable seniority system, in which each committee's longest-serving majority party member served as chair until death, resignation, or retirement. This system tended to elevate to top committee posts the long-serving conservative southern Democrats or midwestern Republicans from safe seats, a process that eventually yielded committee chairs that were out of step with the preferences of party leaders. But Speakers of this era had little ability to discipline the powerful, independent committee chairs, whom they did not appoint and could not remove.

Working from this more constricted office, Speakers after Cannon exhibited various leadership styles. The longest-serving Speaker in history, Democrat Sam Rayburn of Texas (1940–1947, 1949–1953, 1955–1961), functioned largely as a broker or mediator, who negotiated with committee chairs to report out legislation supported by the Democratic majority. Rayburn used his personal prestige as well as his long political experience and immense parliamentary skills to lend coherence to a decentralized chamber. As he explained, "The old day of pounding on the desk and giving people hell is gone. A man's got to lead by persuasion and kindness and the best reason—that's the only way he can lead people."[15]

The distribution of power in the House of Representatives changed fundamentally during the 1970s. Frustrated by the conservative tilt of the committee barons, activist, liberal lawmakers elected during the Vietnam War and the Watergate era joined forces with other longtime members disgruntled with the status quo to curb the power of committee chairs. These reformist Democrats took a two-pronged approach toward transforming the distribution of power in the House.

First, the reformers limited the ability of committee chairs to act independently. Rather than allowing chairs to hold their positions regardless of their adherence to the party's agenda, new party rules adopted in 1973 required that committee chairs be elected by secret ballot of the Democratic Caucus. Committee chairs were also obligated to share power with subcommittee chairs.

Second, the reformers strengthened the hand of the party leadership. The Speaker, for example, gained the right to name all of the majority party members of the Rules Committee, including the chair. The Speaker was also permitted to refer measures to more than one committee.

Although the reforms enhanced party leaders' powers, Speakers did not exploit them to the fullest degree immediately. Instead, power was gradually centralized in the majority party leadership over many subsequent Congresses. Longtime Speaker Thomas P. "Tip" O'Neill Jr., D-Mass. (1977–1987), strengthened the office by drawing Democratic rank-and-file members into the leadership orbit, expanding the whip structure, and creating leadership task forces to allow them input on party priorities.[16]

O'Neill's successor, Speaker Jim Wright, D-Tex. (1987–1989), pushed the prerogatives of the office further. His unyielding personal style and knack for making "minority status more painful," as one House GOP leader put it, embittered Republicans (and even some of his own party).[17] Wright's tenure in office ended in the wake of ethics charges successfully initiated against him by an energetic up-and-coming Republican, Newt Gingrich. Although Wright's successor, Speaker Thomas S. Foley, D-Wash. (1989–1995), had a reputation for being a judicious, low-key, and consensus-oriented leader, he began to make far more extensive use of the Rules Committee to shape the floor agenda and restrict amending opportunities.[18]

The Contemporary Speaker

Speaker Newt Gingrich, R-Ga., took the office of Speaker to new heights. In the lead-up to the 1994 elections, Gingrich had spearheaded a ten-point party platform called "The Contract with America." Almost all House Republican candidates pledged to act on every item in the platform within the first hundred days of the 104th Congress if their party won a majority. Gingrich was widely credited with the GOP's sweeping victory in the 1994 elections: "[Gingrich is] the one responsible for leading the Republican Party out of the wilderness of the minority to the promised land of the majority," said one GOP House member.[19] In the immediate aftermath of the Republicans' taking control of the House, GOP lawmakers observed a parliamentary model of governance marching in lockstep with their "prime minister." Everything in the ten-point contract, except term limits for lawmakers, passed the House within a hundred days. Gingrich also adopted a wide array of institutional changes that centralized power in his office. He curbed the independence of committees by personally selecting committee members and chairs who would strongly support his agenda—and, when necessary, ignored seniority in the process. In addition, he required the GOP members of the Committee on Appropriations to sign a written pledge that they would heed the leadership's directives for spending reductions. Most significantly, he changed the House rules to impose a six-year term limit on all committee and subcommittee chairs, so no chair could accumulate enough influence to challenge the central party leaders. In short, party power came to dominate committee power.

But Gingrich did not remain Speaker for long. Two extended face-offs with President Bill Clinton in late 1995 and early 1996 resulted in highly unpopular shutdowns of ongoing government operations, for which the public blamed the Republicans, not President Clinton.[20] In 1996, the House voted overwhelmingly to reprimand and fine Gingrich in response to ethics charges related to inaccurate financial information he had given to the House Ethics Committee. When the 1998 midterm results came in, many Republicans blamed Gingrich for their poor showing. He then left the Speakership and resigned from the House.

Gingrich's successor as Speaker, Rep. Dennis Hastert, R-Ill. (1999–2007), played a less visible role outside the House, but inside the institution, he was no less powerful than Gingrich. The longest-serving GOP Speaker, Hastert exercised "top-down" command of the House and followed a partisan governing strategy on party-preferred measures. "The job of the Speaker," he said, "is not to expedite legislation that runs counter to the wishes of the majority of his majority."[21] Hastert and his leadership team were not reluctant to direct rank-and-file members or committee chairs to toe the line on issues important to the party. For example, during a GOP conference meeting, Veterans' Affairs chair Christopher H. Smith of New Jersey criticized the Republicans' budget resolution and the spending proposals for veterans. Speaker Hastert "got up and shut him down," said a witness to the tongue-lashing. "I've never seen anything like that. It was scathing."[22] When Smith refused to curb his advocacy of more spending for veterans, GOP leaders removed him as Veterans' Affairs chair and even from the committee itself.

The trend toward centralization of power in the Speaker's office was not reversed under Hastert's successor, Nancy Pelosi (D-Calif., 2007–2011). Her elevation to the Speakership was groundbreaking in that she was the first woman to rise so high in U.S. politics, but Speaker Pelosi's leadership style tracked the same "top-down," centralized model of her immediate predecessors. Of her leadership style, a Brookings Institution report concluded that "a pattern of tighter, more centralized control . . . continues unabated."[23]

Pelosi's Republican successor John Boehner of Ohio (2011–October 2015) continued the pattern of centralized leadership, despite entering with promises of a more inclusive, committee-oriented manner. By selecting loyal Republicans as committee chairs, Boehner ensured that committees served the leadership's broader interests.[24] Boehner also informed rank-and-file members that the leadership monitors their voting behavior and makes committee assignments accordingly.[25] In 2012, Boehner's Steering Committee stripped four members of their committee assignments as punishment for their intransigence and willingness to criticize fellow Republicans.[26] Boehner tried to hold his Tea Party–infused ranks together on high-stakes issues, but conservatives refused to go along with bipartisan deals, especially if Boehner worked to negotiate compromises with President Obama and Democratic leaders, such as Nancy Pelosi. Nonetheless, to avoid unwanted national crises, Boehner had to rely, at times, on Democratic votes to pass important legislation, such as to raise the debt ceiling or to keep the government operating. Successful efforts at compromise enraged the Speaker's most conservative members.

Disgruntlement with Boehner's leadership among hard-core conservatives culminated in the summer of 2015 when Tea Party leader Rep. Mark Meadows, R-N.C., introduced a resolution in the House that, if taken up, would force a vote declaring the Speakership vacant. In the midst of the intraparty conflicts, Boehner unexpectedly announced that he was stepping down as Speaker, pending election of a replacement. This was a rare mid-session departure of a Speaker, with Boehner's resignation from the House to be effective October 30, 2015.

Majority Leader Kevin McCarthy, R-Calif., was strongly favored to succeed Boehner. However, McCarthy resigned amid conservative complaints that he was too moderate and too much like Boehner. McCarthy also made a serious gaffe in a television interview, implying that the House's real purpose in creating a select committee to investigate the Benghazi [Libya] tragedy was to damage Hillary Clinton's 2016 presidential aspirations. (The Benghazi attack occurred when Clinton was secretary of state.) As GOP Rep. Dana Rohrabacher of California said to his majority leader, "Kevin, you just made a verbal blunder that has dramatically damaged our [GOP] cause. I just cannot support you for speaker—just a few days after you said something so harmful to that cause."[27]

With McCarthy's withdrawal, the GOP's attention turned to Paul Ryan, the chair of the Committee on Ways and Means and former vice presidential nominee. A popular and well-respected nine-term lawmaker, advocates for his candidacy argued that Ryan was the only House Republican who could unite the party and win the support of every key faction in the party. After some reluctance, Ryan agreed to seek the Speakership. However, he successfully insisted that prior to his commitment to run, he receive the support of the three main GOP groups: the Freedom Caucus, the conservative Republican Study Committee, and the moderate Tuesday Group.[28] All three groups endorsed Ryan, and he was elected Speaker on October 29, 2015.

Ryan's hold on the Speakership became uncertain when, in October 2016, he informed House Republicans that he no longer would defend GOP presidential nominee Donald Trump's embarrassing behavior and damaging statements. Instead, his principal focus would be on retaining control of the 115th House by electing congressional Republicans.[29] Conservatives inside the House and outside expressed dismay with Speaker Ryan's declaration, accusing him of "stabbing" Trump in the back and "sabotaging" his campaign.[30] Despite clashes between Trump and Ryan, the Speaker kept the gavel in the 115th Congress (2017–2019), winning every GOP vote (240), except for one defection.

Ryan worked assiduously to cooperate with President Trump in 2017–2019 as the GOP enjoyed a brief period of unified control. Although Trump at times criticized Ryan for not delivering on his agenda, the Speaker did not break with the White House. He did, however, decide not to run for reelection, paving the way for McCarthy to succeed him as party leader. The GOP's loss of the House majority meant that McCarthy would be minority leader rather than Speaker.

After turning back the challenge to her election as Speaker, Nancy Pelosi enjoyed a major early success in the battle over funding the government that dominated the early months of 2019. President Trump vowed not to sign a spending bill that failed to provide $5.7 billion for his proposed border wall. From the start, Pelosi made it clear that the House would not approve a bill with such funding—and that she would not negotiate a broader deal on immigration until the government was opened. Pelosi kept Democrats unified during the record-long shutdown that lasted from December 22 through January 25. Amid nervousness among Senate Republicans and poor poll numbers, the president eventually relented, signing spending bills that were no better than Pelosi and the Democrats had offered in December 2016. President Trump, however, followed this action by declaring a national emergency on the border, invoking executive powers to shift funds to the border wall that had not been appropriated for that purpose. Pelosi promised to attempt to reverse these actions legislatively; in the meantime, Trump's declaration also faces court challenges. Even as the border fight continues to unfold, Democrats perceived Pelosi's leadership in the funding fight as a success, as she both held her party together and appeared to win the broader public relations fight with President Trump.

The Speaker's Influence: Style and Context

Congressional analysts disagree about the extent to which congressional leaders can influence policy outcomes. Compared with legislative party leaders in many other democracies, party leaders in Congress unquestionably have fewer tools to induce party loyalty among lawmakers. Nevertheless, congressional leaders enjoy more institutional authority at some times than at others. In general, political scientists stress context over personal style as the main factor affecting the Speaker's institutional clout. Political scientists have developed a theory—conditional party government—to explain why congressional leaders appear to be stronger during some eras than others.[31]

Conditional party government theory posits that if partisans share common policy views and confront an opposition party with sharply different policy preferences, then these dual conditions favor strong, centralized leadership. Rank-and-file partisans (the principals) will empower their party leaders (agents) to advance an agenda that nearly all of them support. According to the two leading proponents of this theory,

> These two considerations—preference homogeneity [or policy agreement within parties] and preference conflict [or policy disagreement between parties]—together form the "condition" in the theory of conditional party government. As these increase, the theory predicts that party members will be progressively more willing to create strong powers for leaders and to support the exercise of those powers in specific instances. But when diversity grows within parties, or the differences between parties are reduced, members will be reluctant to grant greater powers to leaders. This is the central prediction of [conditional party government].[32]

Conditional party government theory provides an explanation for the changing role of the Speaker. Speaker Sam Rayburn's role as cautious broker and negotiator, for example, makes sense in light of fractures within the Democratic Party during the 1950s. During Rayburn's era—and for many years afterward—congressional Democrats were deeply divided between their northern and southern wings. Southern Democrats tended to be more conservative than their northern colleagues on significant political issues, particularly civil rights and labor regulations (such as minimum-wage laws, union organizing, and business–labor relations). On such matters, southern Democrats often allied with Republicans in a voting pattern known as the *conservative coalition*. Recognizing these divisions, Rayburn had to lead cautiously. Just bringing the Democratic Caucus together could be politically explosive, so Rayburn rarely convened the caucus.[33] Instead, he dealt with members on a personalized, individual basis.

According to conditional party government theory, Rayburn's leadership style was not merely a personal stylistic choice; it was also a way of coping with intractable conflict within the party. Under such conditions, rank-and-file Democrats simply would not trust their Speaker with expansive procedural and political powers.

By the same token, conditional party government theory attributes the forceful leadership of recent Speakers to changes in the political context. Since the 1960s, regional realignments have created (1) far more ideological consensus *within* each of the two congressional parties and (2) considerably less ideological agreement *between* the two parties than existed during the 1950s and 1960s. Partisan realignment is an important part of the story. After the enfranchisement of southern African Americans in the 1960s, the Democratic Party in the South began to elect Democrats (such as John Lewis of Georgia) who were more responsive to African American constituents and more ideologically compatible with their party colleagues from the rest of the country. Meanwhile, conservative southern whites gradually moved into the Republican Party. Because the South is now largely in the GOP camp, today's Democratic Party lacks the deep regional divisions that characterized the earlier era. The conservative coalition is no longer an important voting bloc in Congress. Constituency change in the North reinforced this ideological homogenization of the parties. Moderate Republicans have largely disappeared in the Northeast. As a result of these constituency changes, the two parties are more internally coherent in their policy preferences.

This new context helps explain the assertive styles of contemporary Speakers. The rank-and-file members of both parties are more willing to trust their leaders with institutional authority. Contemporary Speakers of both parties have been given more influence over committee assignments, allowing them to appoint like-minded members to coveted committees. By stacking important committees with loyal partisans, a Speaker raises the likelihood that they will report legislation that the Speaker favors. Individual members also recognize that they owe their committee assignments, in part, to the Speaker. Given the greater willingness of members to tolerate hierarchical leadership, recent Speakers have been able to direct committee chairs, advance party agendas, and take procedural actions to hamstring the minority party. In short, leaders' personal talents have been augmented by formal and informal procedural changes that have enhanced their influence.

Not all scholars accept the conditional party government account. An alternative theory—the pivotal voter theory—eschews a focus on parties and leaders as a way to understand Congress. Instead, this perspective emphasizes the power of rank-and-file members, particularly the critical members whose votes are necessary to form a majority or to clear other thresholds, such as the two-thirds supermajority needed to override a presidential veto. Proponents of this theory argue that policy outcomes on the floor rarely diverge from what is acceptable to the pivotal voter—in the House, the member who casts the 218th vote.[34] Why would members vote to support a policy with which they disagree? After all, leaders have only limited tools with which to discipline members, who cannot be "fired" except by the voters back home. Leaders are ultimately accountable to their party members and to the chamber for their actions.

When a majority party is internally unified, there will be no difference between what it prefers and what is acceptable to the chamber majority. But when the majority party is divided, it is unable to enforce its agenda unless it can command a majority. In pursuit of their desired outcomes, members will coalesce across party lines to form a winning coalition, just as conservative southern Democrats once did with conservative Republicans—the conservative coalition that shaped legislative policy making for a good part of the twentieth century. From this vantage point, the important question for understanding Congress is simply the distribution of policy preferences in the chamber as a whole, not the activities and powers of party leaders and party organizations.

Other critics of conditional party government emphasize that leadership is by no means entirely determined by the political context. "Leadership in Congress occurs within an institutional context that imposes limits," writes Randall Strahan, "but some leaders take advantage of those opportunities and others do not. Leadership involves not only the conditions that make leadership possible but also the choice of the leader to act."[35] Adroit and forceful Speakers can lead by molding circumstances and seizing opportunities favoring their own objectives.[36] In short, Speakers' personal capacities allow them to exercise that elusive quality called leadership—that is, an ability to persuade others to follow even when they disagree with their leaders' views.

House Floor Leaders

The Speaker's principal deputy—the majority leader—is the party's floor leader. Elected every two years by secret ballot of the party caucus, the floor leader is not to be confused with a floor manager. Floor managers—usually two for each bill and frequently the chair and ranking minority member of the committee that reported the bill—are responsible for steering particular bills to a final vote.

The House majority leader is usually an experienced legislator. The current majority leader, Rep. Steny Hoyer, is no exception, having served in the House for more than thirty-five years. Hoyer has occupied a series of party leadership positions since 1989, including Democratic Caucus chair and party whip (see below). He is seen as relatively moderate, compared to the more liberal Pelosi. Although Hoyer and Pelosi have been rivals at times, their roles require them to work as a team to keep their party unified. While their extensive experience is clearly an asset, many younger members have expressed concern that the party needs to have an influx of new leadership given that the top three leaders—including Whip James Clyburn, D-S.C.—are each over 75 years old. House and party rules are largely silent about the majority leader's duties. By tradition, the primary duties are to organize the House's floor schedule, serve as principal strategist and spokesperson for the party, and to monitor the House floor. By modern custom, neither the Speaker nor the Democratic or Republican leaders chair committees,[37] but they may serve on formal or informal task forces or panels.

To plan the daily, weekly, and annual legislative agendas, Hoyer must consult widely. He meets regularly with committee chairs to discuss their schedule of activities, review pertinent legislative issues, and coordinate chamber action with the party's floor managers. He also gauges sentiment on legislation among rank-and-file members and urges them to support or reject measures. As one majority leader said, "The Majority Leader has prime responsibility for the day-to-day working of the House, the schedule, working with the committees to keep an eye out for what bills are coming, getting them scheduled, getting the work of the House done." He added that the majority leader must also "articulate to the outside world" what his or her party stands for and is trying to do.[38]

The minority leader is the floor leader of the opposition party. Like the majority leader, the minority leader promotes unity among party colleagues, monitors the progress of bills through committees and subcommittees, and forges coalitions in support of proposals. However, the minority leader is more often in a reactive position, criticizing the majority party's initiatives and developing alternatives to them. Bertrand Snell, R-N.Y., minority leader from 1931 to 1939, described the duties:

> He is spokesman for his party and enunciates its policies. He is required to be alert and vigilant in defense of the minority's rights. It is his function and duty to criticize constructively the policies and program of the majority, and to this end employ parliamentary tactics and give close attention to all proposed legislation.[39]

With Paul Ryan's retirement, former Majority Leader Kevin McCarthy, R-Calif., was in line to become minority leader in the 116th Congress. McCarthy faced a challenge from the right by Jim Jordan of Ohio but triumphed easily on a 159–43 vote. McCarthy rose to leadership quickly. After entering the House as a freshman in 2007, he was elected the party's majority whip in 2011. In a short time frame, he had distinguished himself as a party activist. For instance, he was lead author of the House Republican "Pledge to America," a party platform document for the pivotal, Tea Party–imbued 2010 elections that returned the House to GOP control. McCarthy was also a strong advocate for Trump when he was a candidate, fostering a close relationship that has helped him win over hard-core conservatives in the GOP caucus.[40]

The minority leader must forge party unity by managing internal conflicts and resolving intraparty disagreements. Perhaps the most important job of the minority leader is to craft a strategy to win back majority control of the House. In this respect, the minority leader must decide whether to cooperate with or to confront the majority party. By working with the majority, the minority party can often influence legislation more to its followers' liking. However, cooperation entails supporting the majority party's legislation on the floor—an often unpleasant task.

A minority party can instead pursue a strategy of confrontation. By consistently offering an alternative vision on issues of the day, the minority party can build the case for its return to power. There is no set formula for how to win back majority control of the House because many of the electoral and political forces and events that influence majority status are beyond party leaders' control.[41] But in an era of slim majorities, where control of the chamber appears up for grabs, minority leaders may be more likely to spurn compromises that might end up making the majority party look capable of effective governance and instead to pursue a strategy of confrontation and communication (messaging) that would persuade the public it is time for a change.[42]

House Whips

Another top elective party post is that of chief whip. The current Majority Whip, James Clyburn of South Carolina, has served in the House since 1993. Clyburn has occupied a series of leadership positions, including serving as Whip the last time Democrats were in the majority (2007–2011). As the term implies, the whip and the whip's team of deputies and regional whips encourage party discipline, count votes, and, in general, mobilize winning coalitions on behalf of partisan priorities. To do so, the chief whip serves as liaison between the party's rank-and-file membership and its leaders. The whip assembles and communicates political and policy intelligence, assigns deputy whips to take the "temperature" of the various factional groups within the party, and provides the party's members with scheduling information.

Accurate vote counting is a whip's most important skill. Several veteran former whips advised one newly elected whip, "You need to know your count, and you don't share your count."[43] Members' voting predilections on important procedural and substantive issues are typically classified as "yea," "leaning yea," "undecided," "leaning no," and "no." Clyburn used a fishing metaphor to explain his procedure for forging winning coalitions:

> When it comes to working with the Democratic Caucus I have to fish in a lot of ponds. I go fishing with the Blue Dogs [fiscally conservative Democrats]. I go fishing with the New Dems [moderate Democrats]. I go fishing with the Hispanics and I go fishing with the Asian Pacific Islanders, trying to cobble together the 218 votes I need.[44]

The parties' whip teams meet regularly to discuss issues and strategy. These large whip teams involve many members in leadership decision making and give them incentives to back their top leaders. With several dozen members, the Democratic whip organization is able to reach every Democrat in the Caucus. A large whip team also ensures leadership representation for important party groups and broadens the party's appeal to outside constituencies while allowing for a division of labor. "Grunt work is subcontracted out to whip team members: Each is typically assigned two or three House colleagues. . . . [W]hip team members take cards from the . . . cloakroom, approach their assigned colleagues and check the appropriate box on the card reflecting the lawmaker's intentions."[45]

At times, party leaders disagree on how aggressively to pressure members to toe the line. Democrats faced repeated challenges in 2019 from Republicans' use of a procedural motion—called a motion to recommit—to add politically embarrassing amendments to bills. Some leaders, including Pelosi, advocated treating the motion to recommit like other procedural votes and thus to enforce strict party discipline. An aide noted, "She thinks the caucus should vote together. The more you act afraid of these things, the more Republicans seize on it."[46] Republicans had imposed such discipline on motion to recommit votes when they were in the majority. But Hoyer and Clyburn advocated for allowing members to vote for the motions if they believed it would help at home: "My position has always been, if it does no harm, and members feel that's a vote they need to cast, then it's fine with me."[47] But once some Democrats defect, it becomes harder for others to hold the line. The GOP even succeeded in using the tactic to add language condemning anti-Semitism to an unrelated bill, the first time a motion to recommit had been approved since 2010. After a second GOP success—amending a bill to require background checks on all gun sales to include a provision that the Immigration and Customs Enforcement be told of any undocumented immigrant who attempts to purchase a gun—Democrats met in a party caucus to debate how to respond to such GOP motions. Pelosi threatened defectors with the prospect of less party help in their campaigns, but moderates countered that they need to cast votes in line with their constituents' expectations.[48] The conflict underscores the two Congresses—the pressure to vote the district versus acting on behalf of broader shared policy goals—and points to the internal tensions of a Democratic majority dependent on the votes of many members elected from GOP-leaning districts.

LEADERS OF THE SENATE

Unlike the House, today's Senate is an institution that tolerates and even promotes individualism. Candidate-centered elections, the proliferation of policy and ideological interest groups, the outsized role of money in campaigns, generous staff resources, and senators' efforts to win news media coverage are among the factors that gave rise to today's individualistic Senate. Senators cherish and assert their independence, which intensifies the challenges faced by those elected to lead them. Unlike their House counterparts, Senate leaders must lead an institution with few institutional prerogatives and procedures to facilitate majority rule on legislation.

Presiding Officers

The House majority's highest elected leader, the Speaker, has the authority to preside over the House. By contrast, the Senate's majority leader, the majority party's highest leader, almost never presides in the Senate chamber.

The Senate has three kinds of presiding officers. First, the constitutional president of the Senate is the vice president of the United States (see Figure 6-2). Except for ceremonial occasions, the vice president seldom presides over Senate sessions and can vote only to break—not make—a tie. When votes on major issues are expected to be close, party leaders make sure that the vice president is presiding so he can break the tie. Vice President Mike Pence made history because he cast the tie-breaking vote (51 to 50) for Betsy DeVos to be secretary of education. Pence's tie-breaker was the first time that such a vote was needed to confirm a cabinet secretary.[49] And as a former six-term House member, Pence has played an important legislative liaison role based on his knowledge of Congress and friendship with many lawmakers.

Second, the Constitution provides for a president pro tempore to preside in the vice president's absence. In modern practice, this is the majority party

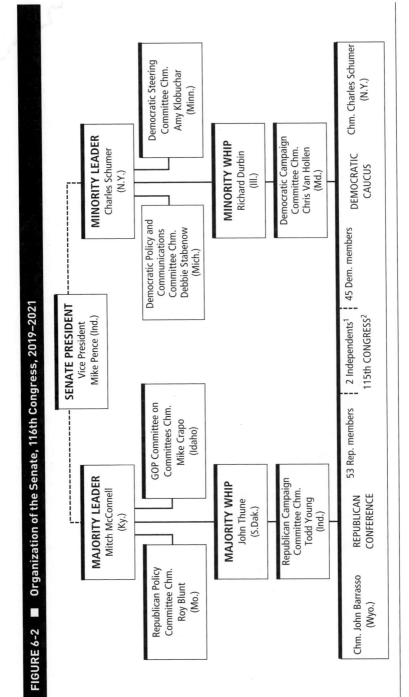

FIGURE 6-2 ■ Organization of the Senate, 116th Congress, 2019–2021

SENATE PRESIDENT
Vice President
Mike Pence (Ind.)

MAJORITY LEADER
Mitch McConnell
(Ky.)

Republican Policy
Committee Chm.
Roy Blunt
(Mo.)

GOP Committee on
Committees Chm.
Mike Crapo
(Idaho)

MAJORITY WHIP
John Thune
(S.Dak.)

Republican Campaign
Committee Chm.
Todd Young
(Ind.)

MINORITY LEADER
Charles Schumer
(N.Y.)

Democratic Policy and
Communications
Committee Chm.
Debbie Stabenow
(Mich.)

Democratic Steering
Committee Chm.
Amy Klobuchar
(Minn.)

MINORITY WHIP
Richard Durbin
(Ill.)

Democratic Campaign
Committee Chm.
Chris Van Hollen
(Md.)

Chm. John Barrasso
(Wyo.)

REPUBLICAN
CONFERENCE

53 Rep. members

2 Independents[1]

115th CONGRESS[2]

45 Dem. members

DEMOCRATIC
CAUCUS

Chm. Charles Schumer
(N.Y.)

[1] Align with Democrats.

[2] As of January 2019.

senator with the longest continuous service. Sen. Charles Grassley is president pro tempore of the Senate of the 116th Congress (2019–2021). By passing a simple resolution, the Senate sometimes appoints a deputy president pro tempore. This majority party official presides over the Senate in the absence of the vice president and president pro tempore.

Third, a dozen or so senators of the majority party, typically junior members, serve approximately one-hour stints each day as the presiding officer. The opportunity to preside helps newcomers become familiar with Senate rules and procedures.

Floor Leaders

The majority leader is the head of the majority party in the Senate, its leader on the floor, and the leader of the Senate. Similarly, the minority leader heads the Senate's minority party. (Today, minority leaders prefer to be called *Republican leader* or *Democratic leader,* as the case may be.) The majority and minority leaders are elected biennially by secret ballot of their party colleagues. Neither position is mentioned in the Constitution; they are relatively recent creations that date from the early 1900s. Although serving as a party leader in the House is typically a full-time position, every party leader in the Senate sits on one or more committees. The smaller size of the Senate allows leaders to participate in committee work while discharging their leadership duties.

Emergence of the Floor Leader

Historically, the Senate has always had leaders, but no single senator exercised central management of the legislative process in the fashion of today's floor leader. During the Senate's first century or so—especially in the 1790s and early 1800s, when there was no system of permanent standing committees or organized senatorial parties—leadership flowed from the personal talents and abilities of individual legislators. The small size of the early Senate promoted an informal and personal style of leadership. Throughout the nineteenth century, scores of prominent senators were called "leaders" by scholars and other observers. Some were sectional or factional leaders; others headed important committees (by the mid to late 1840s, committees and their chairs were centers of power); and still others (such as Henry Clay, John C. Calhoun, and Daniel Webster) exercised wide influence because of their special political, oratorical, or intellectual gifts. Even as late as 1885, however, Woodrow Wilson could write, "No one is *the* Senator. No one exercises the special trust of acknowledged leadership."[50]

By the turn of the twentieth century, the political landscape had changed. Party structures and leaders emerged as clearly identifiable forces for organizing and managing the Senate's proceedings. This important development occurred, according to a historian of the Senate, because of the influx of a "new breed" of senators who valued party unity and "the machinery of [party] organization," especially the party caucus.[51] In addition, fierce interparty competition may have spurred the parties to formalize their leadership.[52] Soon, those senators who chaired their respective party caucuses acquired levers of authority over senatorial affairs. They chaired important party panels, shaped the Senate's agenda of business, and mobilized party majorities behind important issues. By 1913, the position of majority leader had informally emerged out of the caucus chairmanship.[53]

Not until Lyndon B. Johnson (LBJ) became majority leader in 1955 was the post transformed into one of great authority and prestige.[54] Considered by many analysts to be the most influential majority leader ever, the Texas Democrat had an extensive network of trusted aides and colleagues who gave him better information about more issues than any other senator. Opposition party control of the White House under President Dwight D. Eisenhower gave the aggressive Johnson the luxury of choosing which policies to support and which strategies to employ to get them enacted. Armed with a pragmatic outlook, domineering style, and legendary arm-twisting abilities, Johnson became the premier vote-gatherer in the Senate. The majority leader's display of face-to-face persuasion was called the "Johnson Treatment":

> The Treatment could last ten minutes or four hours. It came, enveloping its target, at the LBJ Ranch swimming pool, in one of LBJ's offices, in the Senate cloakroom, on the floor of the Senate itself. Its tone could be supplication, accusation, cajolery, exuberance, scorn, tears, complaint, the hint of threat. It was all of these together. It ran the gamut of human emotions. Its velocity was breathtaking, and it was all in one direction. Interjections from the target were rare. Johnson anticipated them before they could be spoken. He moved in close, his face a scant millimeter from his target, his eyes widening and narrowing, and his eyebrows rising and falling. From his pockets poured clippings, memos, statistics. Mimicry, humor, and the genius of analogy made The Treatment an almost hypnotic experience and rendered the target stunned and helpless.[55]

Buttressing Johnson was an inner club, a bipartisan group of senior senators. A particularly important ally within this inner club was Sen. Richard B. Russell of Georgia. The leader of southern Democrats and a lawmaker of immense influence, Russell endorsed Johnson as Democratic leader. (The Russell Senate Office Building on Capitol Hill is named for the Georgia senator.) The club, observers said, wielded the real power in the Senate through its dominance of most of the Senate's key committees and leadership positions.[56] Furthermore, unwritten rules of behavior (for example, junior members should be seen and not heard) encouraged new senators to defer to the establishment.

Today's majority leaders encounter a Senate that is much different from the one led by Johnson. Gone is the seniority-ruled, club-like, relatively closed Senate of old. It was ended largely by three key developments: the influx of independent-minded and activist senators who wanted and expected to be major policy participants; internal senatorial changes that promoted egalitarianism, such as the provision of staff resources to all members; and external developments in the broader political environment (such as the twenty-four-hour news cycle).

Together, these developments led to an individualistic Senate where leaders were expected to serve members' personal needs and advance their individual agendas. As former majority leader Robert C. Byrd, D-W.Va. (1977–1981, 1987–1989), once remarked about the egalitarian, individualistic, and C-SPAN-covered Senate, "Circumstances don't permit the Lyndon Johnson style. What I am saying is that times and things have changed. Younger Senators come into the Senate. They are more independent. The 'establishment' is a bad word. Each wants to do his 'own thing.'"[57]

The current majority leader, Mitch McConnell of Kentucky (2015–), reinforced Senator Byrd's observations. He emphasized that the contemporary Senate is "a body of a hundred strong-willed men and women, each with his or her own interests and views." Thus, being the majority leader "requires deep understanding [of the members], an ability to listen, great patience in the interest of achieving long-term goals later on. It means viewing the legislative process as the best means we have for making good decisions collectively."[58] A talented and skilled parliamentarian, Senator McConnell employs his many leadership qualities—patience, focus, determination, discipline, procedural expertise, and more—to mobilize the votes to achieve his party, policy, and procedural goals.

Senator McConnell can also act unilaterally to make decisions. A dramatic example occurred when U.S. Supreme Court Justice Antonin Scalia died in early 2016. A few hours after Scalia's death became known, Senator McConnell, acting alone, with no consultation with GOP senators, declared that any replacement nominee of President Obama's (Judge Merrick Garland) would not be considered by the Senate until the U.S. electorate determined who would be president (Trump or Hillary Clinton). McConnell's strategic decision turned out as he wanted and proved to be critically significant—"helping hold the Senate majority, aiding a Republican takeover of the White House and keeping a conservative majority on the Supreme Court."[59]

McConnell's job as leader has been complicated by the need to work with the often-mercurial President Trump. For example, McConnell had been skeptical of Trump's willingness to have the government shut down during the border wall fight. But McConnell understood that abandoning Trump publicly would divide the party and jeopardize his standing with the party's base. As a result, McConnell went along with the fight for several weeks, but quietly signalled to Trump that his Senate support was wavering as the shutdown dragged on. When the final deal was reached to fund the government for the rest of the year in mid-February 2019, McConnell rushed to the floor to announce that the president had agreed, so that there would be less of a chance of a reversal from the White House.[60]

Limits on Today's Leadership: Individualism and Partisanship

If individualism characterizes the post-Johnson Senate, another development has added to leaders' difficulties in managing and processing the Senate's business:

escalating partisanship. Unlike in the House, having a strong and cohesive party does not necessarily enable a Senate majority leader to govern. Comparing his job with a groundskeeper at a cemetery, Senator McConnell said, "Everybody's under you, but nobody's listening."[61]

As discussed in more detail in Chapter 8, the Senate's rules do not permit the majority party leadership to set the agenda without input from the minority party. It is common (often many times during a session day) for the majority leader to negotiate with the minority leader in scheduling legislation for floor consideration. To lead the Senate successfully, then, Senate leaders must achieve considerably more cross-party consensus than is necessary in the House.

As in the House, the two Senate parties have become more cohesive internally and more ideologically distinct from one another. Differences between the parties are also grounded in the two parties' electoral interests, as each party strategizes to communicate clear reasons for voters to prefer it to the opposition.[62] Groups allied with the parties also contribute to the widening divide. The two Congresses are very much in evidence, as Democratic senators champion policies favored by their core national constituencies (such as environmentalists, gays, minorities, and unions), and Republican lawmakers do the same for their constituency base (such as religious conservatives, Trump-backing immigration hawks, business owners, gun owners, and antiabortion advocates).

Majority Leader

Party polarization makes it extraordinarily difficult for the Senate majority leader to achieve the consensus needed to make the Senate function. Any senator has significant parliamentary powers to stymie action, which puts a premium on the leader's skill in negotiating and deal-making. In order to move legislation, Senate leaders rely heavily on patience, perseverance, personal ties, and procedural hardball. If one or more senators object to moving forward on a matter, the majority leader faces an even higher hurdle: acquiring the sixty votes needed to end debate (that is, invoking a procedure called *cloture*) so the Senate can vote on the measure or matter. As a former majority leader reminisced,

> It's a tough job [being majority leader], and it has gotten tougher and tougher. Part of it is that now you don't need 50 votes—you've got to have 60 votes. The filibuster and cloture used to be used occasionally for big issues. [In more recent years] it has become an instrument used on almost every bill. You can have 51 votes, you can have 55 votes, but if you don't get 60 votes, [the bill] can die. And it is very hard to dredge up 60 votes.[63]

"The biggest challenge I have is results," said another former majority leader. "If you have more than half [in the Senate], that doesn't mean you are going to win."[64] The Senate majority leader frequently finds it impossible to push legislation past the procedural hurdles erected by the Senate minority.

Minority Leader

The job of the minority leader is to build party consensus, craft policy alternatives, and devise tactics to block or modify the majority's initiatives. The minority leader also acts as his or her party's representative in any dealings with the president. When the minority leader is a member of the president's party, he or she has the traditional duties of pushing the administration's program and responding to partisan criticisms of the president. When in opposition, the minority leader has to calculate when to cooperate with and when to confront the president.

The minority leader is always striving to win back control of the Senate. In pursuit of that goal, it is often useful for a minority leader to shun compromise. Bipartisan deals tend to blur the differences between the parties, and a minority party seeking to win more seats needs a clear argument against the majority in its campaign for change. While in the minority during President Obama's first two years in office (2009–2011), Republican leader McConnell made much use of this approach. Reflecting on the party's strategy of frequent opposition, McConnell observed, "It was absolutely critical that everybody be together because if the proponents of the bill were able to say it was bipartisan, it tended to convey to the public that this is O.K."[65] McConnell's objective achieved many of its desired effects: It excited the Republican base, intensified media controversy, defined party lines, and weakened public confidence in President Obama and the Democratic congressional leadership.

The Senate's Democratic minority leader in the 116th Congress (2019–2021) is Chuck Schumer of New York. A hardworking, pragmatic, and skillful deal-maker, Schumer has many responsibilities, but two, in particular, stand out. First, with Republicans in charge of the Senate and White House, Senator Schumer must work with Speaker Pelosi to decide when to compromise with President Trump as well as with Senate Republicans. Senate Democrats, he said, will "stand in the way of Republicans when necessary."[66] With the Senate divided fifty-three to forty-seven, if Senator Schumer can keep at least forty-one Democrats united, they can block the enactment of unwanted measures because most bills must attract at least sixty votes to stand a chance of passage (see Chapter 8 on legislative procedures). As Majority Leader McConnell wrote, "The Senate is the only legislative body on earth where a majority is not enough—most things require sixty votes to pass."[67]

Second, Schumer has to find ways to protect vulnerable Democrats seeking reelection in 2020, while forcing Senate Republicans to take tough votes that they would prefer to avoid. Democrats need to net three seats (and win the White House) to gain unified control in 2020. With Republicans defending 22 seats to Democrats' 12, the Senate map is more favorable for Democrats than in 2018, when the party was defending numerous seats in states that had voted for President Trump. Schumer, like Pelosi, did an effective job in keeping Democrats unified during the government funding showdown in early 2019, which in turn put considerable heat on Republicans to find a compromise that the president could accept.

At the same time, Schumer often finds himself on the defensive, given McConnell's ability to force votes on issues that divide Democrats. For example, McConnell announced in February 2019 that the Senate would vote on Rep.

Alexandria Ocasio-Cortez, D-N.Y., and Sen. Edward Markey's, D-Mass., resolution to create a "Green New Deal" to combat climate change. The proposal had attracted an initial wave of Democratic endorsements and grassroots support but had come under fire when Ocasio-Cortez's office released (and subsequently replaced) a summary of it that "called for an end to air travel and cows."[68] McConnell calculated that the proposal would divide and embarrass Democrats, as many would face the competing pulls of energy-producing interests in their states and progressive activists. Schumer responded, "Bring it on. You think it might embarrass Democrats to vote on a nonbinding resolution that some of us support but not others. Trust me, we'll be fine because the American people know that our entire party actually believes that climate change is happening." Schumer vowed to try to attach amendments that will mean that Republican senators will "also have to take a public position on climate change."[69] Schumer and the Democrats eventually settled on a strategy of voting "present" on the Green New Deal resolution, so that party members could stick together without directly repudiating or endorsing the proposal. In this case and others, Schumer is expected to provide a legislative strategy and message that position the party for electoral success. In sum, the challenge for Minority Leader Schumer is determining when to cooperate with President Trump and Senate Republicans because their goals coincide and when to confront the opposition for proposing bad, dangerous, or unworkable ideas. As one account noted, Schumer's "first step in trying to manage this internal tension was to expand the Democratic leadership team to include more geographic and ideological diversity, from the more conservative Joe Manchin of West Virginia to progressive powerhouse Bernie Sanders of Vermont."[70]

Party Whips

The Senate's whip system carries out functions similar to those of the House, such as counting noses before crucial votes, monitoring floor activity, and fostering party consensus.

Sen. John Thune, R-S.Dak., is the Senate's majority whip in the 116th Congress, the Republicans' second in command. Thune had served as chair of the Senate Republican Conference from 2012–2018 and moved up to whip when John Cornyn, R-Tex., was term limited from the post.

Sen. Richard J. Durbin, D-Ill., is the minority whip of the 116th Congress. Durbin, quite knowledgeable about procedure, has a reputation for being "very good at taking issues and making them resonate with the public."[71] As Sen. Patty Murray, D-Wash., said, "He puts issues we're dealing with in real American language. I think he's really a good face for our party."[72]

SELECTION OF LEADERS

Before the opening of each new Congress, senators and representatives elect their top leaders by secret ballot in their party caucuses. Candidates for party leadership positions usually wage elaborate campaigns to win support from their partisan colleagues. Occasionally, last-minute entrants successfully bid for leadership positions. But whether brief or lengthy, campaigns for party leadership positions are intense. Members understand that a party leadership post can be a "career launching pad either within the [Congress] or outside it."[73]

Both House and Senate leaders are generally chosen from the mainstream of their respective parties. As political scientist David Truman observed in 1959, party leaders tend to be "middlemen" in their parties—in ideological terms, from neither the far-left nor the far-right fringes.[74] A recent study examining all open leadership contests over the past hundred years determined that leaders tend to be closer to their party's ideological median than would happen by chance but also that Democratic leaders tend to come from the left of the party median and Republican leaders from the right of the party median.[75] It also appears that these patterns are evident early in the selection process, suggesting that candidates with these profiles are more likely to seek leadership positions in the first place.

Seniority in Congress is one of many criteria that influence the election of party leaders. Another consideration is geographical balance within the leadership. In his contest for House Republican whip, Rep. Steve Scalise, R-La., made his successful case for the position partly on the basis of the dearth of other southerners in top Republican leadership positions.[76] Other factors influencing the choice of leaders include the following: parliamentary expertise; competency in organizational matters; skill in forging winning coalitions; fund-raising prowess; communication skills; sensitivity to the mood of the membership; and personal attributes, such as intelligence, fairness, persuasiveness, political shrewdness, and media savvy. Gender balance may be becoming a more important consideration, as the number of women lawmakers rises. For example, female representation was a prominent consideration in the most hotly contested leadership battle of 2012, as Republicans selected Rep. Cathy McMorris Rodgers, R-Wash., for the number-four leadership slot over then-representative Tom Price, R-Ga.[77] Representative McMorris Rodgers has held her leadership position since she first won it.

LEADERSHIP ACTIVITIES

Leadership duties can be broadly described as institutional maintenance (ensuring that Congress and its members perform their lawmaking and oversight duties and preserving Congress's reputation and integrity) and party maintenance (crafting winning coalitions among partisan colleagues and providing assistance to their members).[78] These two tasks are often blended, as leaders perform their institutional tasks in ways that simultaneously serve their party. Nevertheless, congressional leaders have responsibilities for the basic functioning of Congress that transcend party politics.

Institutional Tasks

From an institutional perspective, party leaders have various obligations. To help them carry out these diverse responsibilities, their chamber gives them extra staff resources.

Organizing the Chamber

Party leaders select the top administrative officers of both houses of Congress, such as the clerk of the House and the secretary of the Senate. These officers are important for the day-to-day functioning of the chambers, even if they are invisible to the public. Party leaders also oversee committee jurisdictional revisions and revise congressional rules. A few examples make the point. Speaker Gingrich backed the abolition of three standing committees in 1995; Speaker Hastert supported a major recodification of House rules in 1999, the first since 1880; Speaker Pelosi championed the 2008 creation of the Office of Congressional Ethics and supported the creation of a select committee to consider ways to modernize Congress in 2019.

Scheduling Floor Business

"The power of the Speaker of the House is the power of scheduling," Speaker O'Neill once declared.[79] Or as Gingrich put it, "When you are Speaker you get to set the agenda. . . . [Y]ou get to decide what legislation is up."[80] After broad consultation, House and Senate party leaders decide what, when, how, and in which order measures should come up for debate. Setting the chamber's agenda and schedule—determining what each chamber will debate—is perhaps the single most important prerogative of the Speaker and Senate majority leader. Scheduling legislation is a basic task that must be managed for the institution to function at all, but leaders also act strategically in their party's interests as they make these decisions.

Once a bill is scheduled for action, the job of the leaders is to see that members vote—a task more difficult than merely herding bodies into the chamber. Party leaders may seek out certain members to speak on an issue because their endorsement can persuade other legislators to support it. Or they may delay action until the bill's sponsors are present. "The leadership must have the right members at the right place at the right time," said Robert Byrd, D-W.Va., when he was the Senate majority whip.[81] Although leaders generally seek to influence members of their own party and chamber, they also try to win cooperation from the other chamber and from the opposition party.

Leaders' scheduling prerogatives mold policy outcomes. The point at which a bill reaches the floor can seal its fate. A week's delay in scheduling a controversial White House initiative, for example, may give the president, lobbying groups, and others additional time to muster votes for the proposal. Depending on the circumstances, delay may also afford the opposition an opportunity to mobilize its forces.

Legislative business is also scheduled with forthcoming elections in mind. Measures are postponed to avoid an electorally embarrassing defeat, or they may be brought to the floor to satisfy groups allied with the party. What better time to take up legislation revamping the Internal Revenue Service than on or around April 15, the filing deadline for federal income taxes? Reflecting the two Congresses, both parties use the floor as an election platform to raise issues that appeal to external audiences. After passing measures advocated by its electoral base, a party can say, "Look what we did for you." Even a party that fails to pass a measure can say to its bedrock supporters, "Look what we tried to do."

Consulting the President

A traditional duty of party leaders is to meet with the president to discuss the administration's goals and to convey legislative sentiment about what the executive branch is doing or not doing. Although presidents spend more time dealing with leaders of their own party in Congress, they also consult with opposition leaders. Presidents journey to Capitol Hill to meet with party leaders or attend annual party meetings. For example, President Trump and Vice President Pence participated in a bicameral GOP retreat in 2017 in Philadelphia. The House and Senate leaders, Speaker Ryan and Senator McConnell, led "a discussion on the GOP's plan for Trump's first 200 days."[82] With Democrats in control of the House, President Trump and his team were forced to consult with Speaker Pelosi in seeking progress on a government funding deal and other measures. But when the House is controlled by the opposing party, such encounters are often highly adversarial and give way to messaging battles before the public.

Party Tasks

From a party perspective, congressional party leaders have a number of formal and informal responsibilities. Each party's rules formally specify certain functions and responsibilities for their leaders. Parliamentary precedents and chamber rules assign additional duties to party leaders. Party leaders have also assumed a wide range of duties on an informal basis.

Organizing the Party

Congressional leaders help to organize their party by selecting partisan colleagues for standing committees, revising party rules, choosing other party leaders, and appointing party committees. A few examples illustrate the point. Senate Republicans' rules authorize their leader, Senator McConnell, to appoint party colleagues to certain committees. In the House, Speaker Boehner ensured that many freshmen elected in 2010 received plum committee assignments.[83] As a reward for his help in regaining majority control of the Senate in the 2006 midterms, Democratic leader Reid brought Sen. Schumer into party leadership as chair of the Democratic Policy and Communications Center (DPCC). Similarly, when Senator McConnell first became majority leader in 2015, he recruited as "counselors" four senators from across the ideological spectrum: senators Mike Lee, R-Utah; Rob Portman, R-Ohio; Deb Fischer, R-Neb.; and Shelley Moore Capito, R-W.Va.[84] Also, in 2015, when he first became Speaker, Paul Ryan revamped the membership and operation of the GOP's Steering Committee (the committee assignment panel). For example, six standing committee chairs were replaced with new rank-and-file Republicans elected by the GOP Conference.[85]

Promoting Party Unity

Another leadership responsibility is to encourage party unity in Congress on priority legislation. Sen. Everett Dirksen, R-Ill. (minority leader, 1959–1969), used social gatherings to accomplish this goal:

> Dirksen brought party members together in a series of social affairs. He held cocktail parties at a Washington country club, inviting all Republican senators and sometimes their wives too. These were calculated by Dirksen to improve party harmony and to build a friendly feeling for himself with the Republican senators.[86]

Party leaders' efforts to foster party cohesion go far beyond extending social invitations. Leaders perform many services for their party rank and file that build goodwill and a sense of common purpose. They schedule members' bills, provide them with timely political information, advise them on electoral issues, visit with their constituents, help them obtain good committee assignments, and work with them to forge policy agendas. "You really have to make people feel part of the process," remarked a Senate Democratic leader.[87] Periodically, leaders organize partisan retreats where members discuss party and policy goals, consider specific legislative initiatives, air differences, and resolve disputes.

Party leaders do not have to rely solely on their powers of persuasion. Informal political networks and access to strategic information give them an edge in influencing colleagues:

> Because members will respond more candidly to leadership polls than to lobbyist or White House polls, [leaders] have perhaps the most important information in a legislative struggle—information on where the votes are and (sometimes) what it will take to win certain people over.[88]

Top leaders also can bestow or withhold a variety of tangible and intangible rewards, such as naming legislators to special or select committees, influencing assignments to standing committees, aiding reelection campaigns, and smoothing access to the White House or executive agencies.

Publicizing Party Views

Leaders are expected to publicize their party's policies and achievements. To do so, they give speeches in various forums, appear on radio and television talk shows, write newspaper and journal articles, hold press conferences, organize town meetings around the country, and maintain an active presence online via websites and social media platforms. Leaders are also expected to develop public relations strategies to neutralize the opposition's arguments and proposals.[89] The advocacy role has increased in importance in recent years, in part because of the twenty-four-hour news cycle. "We've created a situation," noted a scholar, "where the real way you drive the legislative process is by influencing public opinion, rather than by trading for votes."[90]

Party leaders also provide members with talking points for meetings with journalists or constituents. Parties often create communications teams that meet regularly to discuss message development and delivery and to recommend their more telegenic members to present party positions. "We're focused on making sure we deliver the [party] message both here in Washington and out in the hinterlands," said a chair of the Senate Republican Conference.[91]

Providing Campaign Assistance

Leaders must be energetic campaigners and fund-raisers on behalf of their partisan colleagues. As then-House majority leader McCarthy stated, raising campaign funds is "what I've always done." It's "about traveling, helping candidates and incumbents" collect the fiscal resources needed to win elections. They campaign for incumbents and challengers from their party. They encourage outside groups to contribute to the party's electoral efforts. They also help vulnerable colleagues gain a higher profile by giving them a lead role on a major issue.[92]

In both the House and the Senate, the ability to raise funds for colleagues is an increasingly important criterion for judging prospective party leaders.[93] Pelosi's skill and energy as a fundraiser propelled her ahead of Steny Hoyer when they first competed for party leadership in 2002 and has helped Pelosi maintain members' support over the years.[94] Members anticipating a run for a leadership post distribute campaign funds as standard operating practice. According to one account, "It seems that the job of fundraiser is becoming more important to senators' expectations of what a majority leader should do. . . . [They] are not trying to buy votes so much as to demonstrate how well they can fulfill that role."[95] Leaders stand at the intersection of the two Congresses—the representative assembly, where money is needed to win elections, and the lawmaking body, where power calls the shots.

PARTY CAUCUSES, COMMITTEES, AND INFORMAL GROUPS

House and Senate leaders operate in diverse institutional settings. In the larger, more impersonal House, majority party leaders sometimes ignore the wishes of the minority party. But this seldom happens in the Senate, where leaders must cope with the extensive rights of individual senators and the minority party. Despite these differences between the House and the Senate, parties in the two chambers are organized into the same three components: caucuses, committees, and informal party groups.

Party Caucuses

The organization of all partisans in a chamber is called the caucus or the conference. Party caucuses or conferences elect leaders, approve committee assignments, provide members with services, debate party and legislative rules and policies, appoint task forces or issue teams, develop themes to keep members on message, enable members to vent their frustrations, and discuss outreach programs that appeal to voters. In an explanation that applies equally well to both parties and chambers, a senior House Democrat said,

> The caucus is the place where a great deal of freewheeling debate over an issue takes place and where sometimes a consensus develops. . . . You don't take a vote, but you try to develop a consensus and make concessions where they're necessary and develop the strongest possible position that can be supported by the maximum number of Democrats.[96]

In brief, party caucuses are useful forums where party members and leaders can assess sentiment on substantive or procedural issues and forge party unity. On rare occasions, party caucuses consider whether to strip particular members of their committee seniority or to oust committee leaders. Sometimes, presidents attend their party's House or Senate caucus to rally the troops, as President Obama did just before the House of Representatives voted on health care reform in 2010.[97]

Party Committees

Each of the four congressional party groups—Senate and House Democrats, Senate and House Republicans—establishes committees to serve partisan needs and objectives (see Table 6-1). The four party groups on Capitol Hill have policy committees, for example.[98] Party committees do not directly make policy, but they do provide advice on scheduling, study substantive and political issues, distribute policy papers, track votes on issues, and discuss and implement party policy. Their influence has varied over the years, assuming greater importance when the party does not control the White House and thus needs policy and oversight assistance. The policy committees also maintain websites that party members and staff can access for information. Other important party panels are the campaign committees (discussed in Chapter 4) and the committee assignment committees (discussed in Chapter 7).

Informal Party Groups

In addition to party committees, a variety of informal partisan groups operate on Capitol Hill. Among party groups in the House are the conservative

TABLE 6-1 ■ Party Committees in the Senate and House	
Committee	**Function**
Senate Democratic	
Policy and Communications	Considers party positions on specific measures and assists the party leader in scheduling bills; facilitates communication between Senate Democrats and to external audiences
Steering	Assigns Democrats to committees
Campaign	Works to elect Democrats to the Senate
Outreach	Galvanizes people to get involved in the political process; mobilizes outside support for Democrats
Senate Republican	
Policy	Provides summaries of GOP positions on specific issues; researches procedural and substantive issues; drafts policy alternatives
Committee on Committees	Assigns Republicans to committees
Campaign	Works to elect Republicans to the Senate
House Democratic	
Steering and Policy	Assists the leadership and Democratic Caucus in establishing, implementing, researching, and communicating party priorities; assigns Democrats to committees
Campaign	Works to elect Democrats to the House
House Republican	
Policy	Considers majority party proposals and works for consensus among Republican members
Steering	Assigns Republicans to standing committees
Campaign	Works to elect Republicans to the House

Note: The official names of the parties' campaign committees are as follows: Democratic Senatorial Campaign Committee, National Republican Senatorial Committee, Democratic Congressional Campaign Committee, and National Republican Congressional Committee.

Freedom Caucus and the Republican Study Committee; the liberal Progressive Caucus; the centrist New Democrat Coalition; and the Tuesday Group of moderate Republicans. Members of these groups commonly reserve time at the end of the legislative day to spotlight their priorities and successes and to challenge the views of the other party, as the case may be. A prominent party group in the other body is the Senate Steering Committee, whose members are staunch GOP conservatives. There are hundreds of informal groups on Capitol Hill that are not explicitly partisan. Instead, they typically have a policy focus—such as cybersecurity, food safety, cancer, coal, biomedical research, or municipal finance—and promote public awareness of issues. Some are bicameral and others are solely House or Senate in membership.

PARTY CONTINUITY AND CHANGE

Several features of the contemporary party system on Capitol Hill stand out: the intensity of party conflict, the persistence of the two-party system, and the advent of new coalition-building practices.

Intense Party Conflict

By any test one can use, the four Capitol Hill party groups are flourishing. The organizational elements are healthy and active, their leaders are increasingly prominent, and party voting is at very high levels. The congressional parties are well assisted by professional staff.

The strength of today's parties has definite virtues. For one, it enables voters to better comprehend the divergent views, values, and principles of the two parties, and it may even encourage voter turnout. "Confrontation fits our strategy," said Richard B. "Dick" Cheney when he was in the House (1979–1989). "Polarization often has very beneficial results. If everything is handled through compromise and conciliation, if there are no real issues dividing us from Democrats, why should the country change and make us the majority?"[99] The public's awareness and understanding of differences between the parties has increased as a result of party polarization.[100]

Nevertheless, the intensity and extent of partisan conflict raises questions about the body's ability to engage in meaningful bipartisan deliberation and mutual accommodation. Compromise is a traditional hallmark of legislative decision making. Observers and members alike decry the dearth of legislative give and take in the contemporary Congress. As a senior GOP lawmaker pointed out, "Compromise is seen as weakness by many of your constituents, and by all your potential opponents in the next primary."[101] The goal of bipartisanship is an oft-heard refrain on Capitol Hill—but it is an elusive one. As former senator Olympia J. Snowe, R-Maine, observed, "The whole Congress has become far more polarized and partisan so it makes it difficult to reach bipartisan agreements. The more significant the issue, the more partisan it becomes."[102]

The conflicts between the two parties reflect more than just their ideological, cultural, or racial differences. Intense and passionate electoral competition should be added to the mix. Democrats and Republicans engage in combative clashes to retain or win majority control of the House or Senate. As one of the authors of this book has written,

> In seeking to advance their collective interests of winning elections and wielding power, legislative partisans stir up controversy. They impeach one another's motives and accuse one another of incompetence and corruption, not always on strong evidence. They exploit the floor agenda for public relations, touting their successes, embarrassing their opponents, and generally propagandizing for their own party's benefit. They actively seek out policy disagreements that can be politically useful in distinguishing themselves from their partisan opponents.[103]

Unsurprisingly, campaigning by legislating is a fixture in both legislative chambers. Another legislative feature requires mention: Not all issues arouse the ideological or partisan passions of the two parties. Bipartisan majorities to pass important measures—veterans' benefits, medical research, or legislation to counter the opioid crisis are examples—occur regularly in the House and Senate.

The Two-Party System

The Democratic and Republican parties have dominated U.S. politics and Congress since the mid-nineteenth century. Scholars have advanced various theories for the dualistic party politics of a country as diverse as the United States. Plurality elections in single-member congressional districts encouraged the creation and maintenance of two major parties. Under the winner-takes-all principle, the person who wins the most votes in a state or district is elected to the Senate or House. This principle tends to discourage the formation of third parties. However, other countries using this system of representation, such as Canada and the United Kingdom, have nonetheless had a tradition of successful third parties. Some scholars also trace the origins of the national two-party system to early conflicts between Federalists (advocates of a strong national government) and Antifederalists (advocates of limited national government).[104] In addition, many states have laws that make it difficult to create new parties. Constitutional, political, and legal arrangements all contribute to the existence and maintenance of the two-party system.

Whatever mix of causes produced the two-party system, one thing is clear: Few third-party or independent legislators have been elected to Congress during the last century. The high-water mark was the Sixty-third Congress (1913–1915), which had one Progressive senator and nineteen representatives elected as Progressives, Progressive-Republicans, or independents. Since World War II, only a handful of lawmakers have been elected from minor parties or as independents.[105] Most of these legislators have converted to one of the major parties or have voted with them on procedural and substantive matters. In the 116th Congress, Sen. Angus King of Maine is an independent but affiliates with the Democratic Party. Vermont senator Bernie Sanders was elected as an independent but competed as a Democrat for the 2016 Democratic presidential nomination. Third-party or independent members participate in Democratic or Republican affairs by invitation only.

Advances in Coalition Building

In Capitol Hill's highly competitive environment, party leaders are constantly searching for new ways to get the legislative results they want. Fierce competition has prompted continual innovation in media, public relations, and legislative strategies.

Media and Public Relations

Party leaders understand that media strategies—that is, the use of the press, television, radio, polls, the Internet, speeches, and so on—are essential to advance or block legislation as well as to shape the party's public image. Leaders form issue teams, message groups, "war rooms," or theme teams to orchestrate, organize, and coordinate political events and communications strategies that promote the party's message to the general public. No longer is the inside game—working behind the scenes to line up votes—sufficient to pass major legislation.

Also necessary is the outside game—influencing public opinion, coordinating with advocacy groups, and creating grassroots support for policy initiatives. Little surprise that congressional leaders have increased their hiring of staff experienced in public relations. Today, both parties use all types of media (print television, radio, and online) to complement their parliamentary strategies in order to raise issues, define and frame priorities, and respond to partisan criticisms. Both congressional parties understand the importance of words as political weapons. GOP consultants found, for example, that characterizing the tax on inheritances as the "death tax"—and having GOP officeholders repeat it again and again over several years—aroused public ire against the tax. The identical strategy was employed to turn public opinion against President Obama's signature legislation: the Patient Protection and Affordable Care Act, shortened to the Affordable Care Act.

From the health law's beginning in 2009, congressional Republicans and allied outside groups waged a multiyear battle to repeal, replace, repair, and modify the Affordable Care Act. And their messaging campaign to castigate the law proved to be quite successful at first. The GOP coined "Obamacare" as a pejorative term, yet it gained such wide acceptance that President Obama even called the law "Obamacare." In 2009, a GOP consultant wrote a twenty-eight-page memo to GOP lawmakers urging them "to use the phrase 'government takeover' when referring to the Democrats' health care package."[106] "Death panels" was another phrase used over and over by critics of Obamacare—that is, end-of-life counseling by trained individuals implied that this panel would determine when a person should die. The messaging success of Republicans linking Obamacare to "big government," "big spending" Democrats, combined with over $100 million spent by outside groups on negative ads, contributed to the 2010 election of eighty-seven GOP freshmen "whose victories enabled the party to retake the House."[107]

With the 115th Congress and the White House in GOP hands, Republicans found that it is not easy to develop consensus health care legislation to dismantle the Affordable Care Act. The GOP drive to repeal Obamacare ran aground when party members could not agree on a replacement—and when polls and town hall meetings suggested heated public opposition to repeal. While the House narrowly passed a repeal-and-replace bill after numerous compromises and setbacks, the bill failed in the Senate when three Republicans—John McCain of Arizona, Susan Collins of Maine, and Lisa Murkowski of Alaska—defected on the key showdown vote. Republicans did eventually succeed in including a provision repealing Obamacare's requirement that individuals purchase insurance (the "individual mandate") as part of their major tax overhaul bill in 2017. But party members increasingly emphasized that their goal was to "repair," not get rid of Obamacare. Even so, many Republicans spent much of the 2018 campaign defending themselves against accusations that they had supported doing away with many of the law's popular provisions, such as its protections for individuals with preexisting conditions.

Worth mention is that many GOP lawmakers confront the two Congresses when it comes to "repairing" the health care law. Many less-well-off people in states such as West Virginia and Kentucky, who voted for Trump and congressional Republicans in November 2016, depend heavily on the benefits provided by Obamacare, especially its expansion of Medicaid. Yet many GOP leaders advocated health care legislation that could reduce the medical benefits provided to many of their constituents. To fashion a compromise health overhaul approach that resolves such disagreements proved too deep a challenge for GOP party leaders and the Trump administration.

Democrats own messaging efforts also played an important role in preventing the repeal of Obamacare in the 115th Congress. House minority leader Pelosi, for example, urged her party members to hold events in their districts highlighting the benefits of the Affordable Care Act and the dangers of GOP plans to repeal the law. Senate minority leader Schumer worked to frame the GOP's health care overhaul as a "war on seniors," by requiring them to pay more for health care.[108]

In sum, congressional party leaders hold press conferences, appear on diverse media outlets, organize town meetings, prepare talking points for the press (and their own members), develop party themes, write newspaper editorials, circulate data and statistics, organize policy forums, and engage in a variety of other activities to promote their legislative agenda to the public and to criticize the opposition's proposals.

Omnibus Bills

A phenomenon of modern lawmaking is the rise of megabills—legislation that is hundreds or thousands of pages in length, encompassing disparate policy topics. Many of Congress's most significant recent policy departures have been enacted through omnibus bills.

Joining several bills in a single package can help leaders garner support. In such megabills, sweeteners can be added to woo supporters, and provisions that could not win majority support in stand-alone bills can be tucked out of sight. Bundling popular programs with painful spending cuts limits the number of difficult votes lawmakers must cast and provides them with political cover. Members can explain to angry constituents or groups that they had to support the indivisible whole because its discrete parts were not open to separate votes. Leaders, however, must be wary of the reverse concern that a megabill can attract a coalition of opponents with the votes needed to reject the measure.

Megabills can also strengthen Congress's leverage with the executive branch. Measures that a president might veto if presented separately can be folded into megabills and signed in that fashion. "I assure you that in the spending bill, we will be pushing back against this bureaucracy by doing what's called placing riders," said Republican majority leader McConnell of his strategy for negotiating with then-president Obama over appropriations. "We're going to go after them on health care, on financial services, on the Environmental Protection Agency, across the board."[109] Party leaders command the resources and authority to influence the packaging process. "Omnibus bills place a huge amount of power in the hands of a few key leaders and their staffs," pointed out one House member.[110] Rank-and-file members look to party leaders to formulate a package acceptable to a majority, if not all, of its members. Nevertheless, these megabills often arouse lawmakers' suspicions and complaints. "These omnibus bills . . . are abominations," one member complained. "No one member of Congress has a chance to read much of them, let alone understand them, before they are voted on."[111]

CONCLUSION

Congressional parties have elaborate organizations, and their leaders fulfill a multiplicity of roles and duties. As Sen. Robert Byrd explained when he held that post, the Senate majority leader performs many duties: "He facilitates, he constructs, he programs, he schedules, he takes an active part in the development of legislation, he steps in at crucial moments on the floor, offers amendments, speaks on behalf of legislation and helps to shape the outcome of the legislation."[112] And yet, typically, party leaders cannot command their colleagues. The House party leader, according to Pelosi, is a "weaver of a loom, just pulling together all the threads of different opinion in our caucus."[113] But leaders' success rests chiefly on their skill in giving others reasons to follow them. "A leader without followers is simply a man taking a walk," remarked former Speaker Boehner.[114] Republican Bob Michel of Illinois, the longest-serving (fourteen years) House minority leader in history (1981–1995), used musical terms to explain the fundamental task of any congressional party leader. "My job," he said to his colleagues, "is to orchestrate your many talents. I know some of you prefer to speak quietly, like woodwinds, and some very loudly, as brass and percussion. But our measure of success is how well we harmonize."[115]

Parties have organized Congress from its earliest days. Yet the power of party leaders to harness the energies of individual members to pass legislation has varied considerably over time. Today's Congress features much more vigorous leadership than was the case for much of the twentieth century. This revival is rooted in both the shared policy goals of partisans and the intense battle for majority control of Congress. Even so, in keeping with the Two Congresses, contemporary party leaders have to contend with individual members' local concerns. Party leaders are stronger than in the past, but maintaining their influence requires carefully navigating a diverse array of competing forces and incentives.

Party Leaders. Senate Judiciary Committee chairman Lindsey Graham, R-S.C., and the ranking Democrat, Diane Feinstein, Calif., listen to the testimony of William Barr to be the U.S. Attorney General. Senate Finance Chairman Chuck Grassley, R-Iowa, and the panel's ranking Democrat, Ron Wyden, Ore., prepare for a hearing that features testimony by Treasury Secretary Steve Mnuchin. The chair of the House Financial Services Committee, Maxine Waters, D-Calif., talks with Representative Joyce Beatty, D-Ohio, during a meeting of the committee. Representative David Price, D-N.C., who heads an Appropriations Subcommittee, reviews documents concerning border security handed to him by a professional staff aide.

COMMITTEES

Workshops of Congress

Committees have been fixtures of the House and Senate from its earliest days. Sometimes they dominate policymaking. In his classic 1885 study, Woodrow Wilson, wrote that "Congress in session is Congress on public exhibition, whilst Congress in its committee-rooms is Congress at work."[1] Wilson described committees as autonomous "little legislatures." Wilson's view held true throughout much of the twentieth century when powerful committee chairs, selected by a rigid system of seniority, exercised significant independent power. During this period, party leaders exercised limited authority, as lawmakers primarily looked to committees to achieve their legislative and political goals.

Today, Wilson would have to modify his characterization of committees. At least since 1995, political parties and leaders (Chapter 6) have become the principal actors on many of the most significant matters that come before the Congress. Committees still play an important role, but their influence has waned over time. Power has become so concentrated in top party leaders that many committee chairs as well as rank-and-file lawmakers would like to see reform. Party leaders today often bypass committee consideration of legislation, craft priority legislation in secret, limit or prevent debate and amendment opportunities on the floor, and constrain the policymaking role of rank-and-file lawmakers. Frustration with the centralization of power in party leaders is especially evident in the House. Committee leaders, caucuses (e.g., the House's bipartisan Problem Solver's Caucus), and individual lawmakers advocate and support changes to strengthen their policy-making role (e.g., see below, the Select Committee on the Modernization of Congress). Congress's committees serve two broad purposes: individual and institutional. Individually, lawmakers are able to use their committee assignments to benefit their constituents. "As far as I can see, there is really only one basic reason to be on a public works committee," admitted a House member. "Intellectual stimulation" is not it. "Most of all, I want to be able to bring home projects to my district."[2]

Legislators fully understand the connection between their committee assignments and their influence over the funding of federal projects that can help their reelection. Lawmakers can claim credit back home for obtaining federal funding for projects (roads and bridges, for example) in their district or state. At the start of the 116th Congress (2019–2020), sixteen freshmen (12 Democrats and 4 Republicans) obtained assignment to the Transportation and Infrastructure Committee, an excellent vantage point for delivering tangible benefits to constituents.

Committees also enable legislators to utilize or develop expertise in areas that interest them. A former teacher, for example, may seek assignment to the committee overseeing education policy. And some panels, such as the tax and appropriations committees, enable members to wield personal influence among their colleagues. In particular, the Appropriations panel controls the distribution of discretionary federal money (over $1 trillion in 2019). For much of congressional history, members sought seats on the House Committee on Appropriations because, as one GOP leader explained, they "instantaneously . . . have a host of new friends."[3]

Institutionally, committees are the centers of policy making, oversight of federal agencies, and public education (largely through the hearings they hold). By utilizing division of labor, the House and Senate are able to consider dozens of proposed laws simultaneously. Without committees, a legislative body of 100 senators and 441 House members[4] could not handle biennially the roughly 10,000 bills and nearly 100,000 nominations, a $4.1 trillion national budget, and a limitless array of controversial issues. Although floor actions often refine legislation, committees are the means by which Congress sifts through an otherwise impossible jumble of bills, proposals, and issues.

Congressional committees serve another important institutional function in the political system: They act as safety valves—that is, they are outlets for national debates and controversies. Military and economic challenges, demographic shifts, trade agreements, global environmental concerns, the social dislocations caused by technological advances, and the cost of health care place enormous strains on the political system. As forums for public debates, congressional committees help to vent, absorb, and perhaps resolve these strains. The safety valve function also gives citizens a greater sense of participation in national decision making and helps educate members about public problems.

At times, the individual and institutional purposes of the committee system come into conflict. Because members tend to gravitate to committees for constituency or career reasons, they are not the most impartial judges of the policies they authorize. "It's one of the weaknesses of the system that those attracted to a committee like Agriculture are those whose constituents benefit from farm programs," acknowledged Sen. Charles E. Schumer, D-N.Y. "And so they're going to support those programs and they're not going to want to cut them, even the ones that are wasteful."[5]

THE PURPOSES OF COMMITTEES

Senator Schumer's comment highlights an ongoing debate about the development and fundamental purposes of the committee system. To explain the organizational logic of legislatures and the behavior of their committees, scholars have advanced theories emphasizing distributional, informational, and partisan motives.

Distributive theory suggests that legislatures create committees to give lawmakers policy influence in areas critical to their reelection. Members seek committee assignments to "bring home the bacon" (public goods and services) to their constituents. Because lawmakers self-select onto these kinds of committees, the committees become filled with what scholars call *preference outliers*—members whose homogeneous preferences for benefits to their constituents put them out of step with the heterogeneous views of the membership as a whole. Chamber majorities may need to restrain overreaching committees by rejecting or amending their recommended actions.[6]

Because good public policy may be impeded by the parochial orientations of individual members, Congress has a small number of control—or centralizing—committees that promote institutional and policy integration. For example, each house has a budget committee, which proposes limits on how much Congress can spend on designated functional areas.[7]

Informational theory proposes that legislative bodies establish committees to provide lawmakers with the specialized expertise required to make informed judgments in a complex world. Furthermore, the division of labor under the committee system augments Congress's role in relation to the executive branch. Instead of being composed primarily of preference outliers, committees, under this model, have a diverse membership with wide-ranging perspectives. The basic goal of committees, then, is to formulate policies that resolve national problems.[8]

Partisan theory views committees as agents of their party caucuses. According to this perspective, committee members are expected to support their party's programs or, at minimum, not advance policies opposed by a majority of their own party.

Each of these perspectives captures an aspect of the committee system. Certain issues may lend themselves more to the distributive than to the informational or party theory of policy making. More broadly, all lawmakers are concerned both with local issues of immediate concern to constituents as well as broad national issues, such as the condition of the economy or the natural environment. From any perspective, committees must be understood as vital centers that structure the policy, oversight, and representational activities of individual lawmakers.

EVOLUTION OF THE COMMITTEE SYSTEM

Committees in the early Congresses were generally temporary panels created for specific tasks. Proposals were considered on the House or Senate floor and then were referred to specially created panels that worked out the details—the reverse order of today's system. The Senate, for example, would "debate a subject at length on the floor and, after the majority's desires had been crystallized, might appoint a committee to put those desires into bill form."[9] About 350 ad hoc committees were formed during the Third Congress (1793–1795) alone.[10] The parent chamber closely controlled these temporary committees. It assigned them clear-cut tasks, required them to report back favorably or unfavorably, and dissolved them when they had completed their work.

By about 1816, the Senate—and the House a bit later—had developed a system of permanent—or standing—committees, some of which are still in existence. Standing committees, as historian DeAlva Stanwood Alexander explained, were better suited than ad hoc groups to cope with the larger membership and wider scope of congressional business. Another scholar, George H. Haynes, pointed out that the "needless inconvenience of the frequent choice of select committees" taxed congressional patience. Lawmakers recognized that debating bills one at a time before the whole chamber was an inefficient way of processing Congress's legislative business. Perhaps, too, legislators turned to standing committees as counterweights to presidential influence in setting the legislative agenda.[11] Permanent committees changed the way Congress made policy and allocated authority. The House and Senate now reviewed and voted on recommendations made by specialized, experienced committees. Permanent committees also encouraged oversight of the executive branch. Members have called them "the eye, the ear, the hand, and very often the brain" of Congress.[12]

As committees acquired expertise and authority, they became increasingly self-reliant and resistant to chamber and party control. After the House revolt against domineering Speaker Joseph G. Cannon, R-Ill., in 1910, power flowed to the committee chairs. Along with a few strong party leaders, committee chairs held sway over House and Senate policy making during much of the twentieth century. In rare instances, committee members rebelled and diminished the chair's authority. But most members heeded the advice that Speaker John W. McCormack, D-Mass. (1962–1971), gave freshmen: "Whenever you pass a committee chairman in the House, you bow from the waist. I do."[13]

The chairs' authority was buttressed by the custom of seniority that flourished with the rise of congressional careerism. The majority party member with the most years of continuous service on a committee virtually always became its chair. As a result, committee chairs owed little or nothing to party leaders, much less to presidents. This automatic selection process produced experienced, independent chairs but concentrated authority in a few hands. The have-nots wanted a piece of the action and objected that seniority promoted the competent and incompetent alike. They objected, too, that the system promoted members from safe one-party areas—especially conservative southern Democrats and Midwestern Republicans—who could ignore party policies or national sentiments.

The late 1960s and the 1970s saw a rapid influx of new members, many from the cities and suburbs, who opposed the conservative status quo. (In the House, this surge was abetted by U.S. Supreme Court–mandated reapportionments, as discussed in Chapter 3.) Allying themselves with more senior members seeking a stronger voice in Congress, these reformers sponsored changes that diffused power and shattered seniority as an absolute criterion for leadership posts. Today, House and Senate committee chairs (and ranking minority members) are elected by their party colleagues. No longer free to wield arbitrary authority, they must abide by committee and party rules and be sensitive to majority sentiment within their party's caucus or conference. As Rep, Mike Simpson, R-Idaho (1999–), a subcommittee leader on the Appropriations Committee, stated: "Times aren't like they used to be. Yeah, leadership needs to give direction, but the committee chairmen aren't what they used to be."[14] A somewhat similar situation exists in the Senate, "where party leaders have also become far more powerful at the expense of committee chairmen."[15] Sen. Lamar Alexander, R-Tenn. (2003–) shares this view. He chairs both an authorizing committee (Health, Education, Labor and Pensions) and an Appropriations subcommittee. He said:

> In the Senate, too much has become centralized in the leadership. Part of that is a function of the media and the world you live in because [party leaders] have to respond four, five times a day, unlike 50 years ago. Republican senators can't do that as a unit, so to be effective in your political activity, you need a highly centralized leader. That does tend to diminish the influence of committees, and that's not healthy for the Senate.[16]

TYPES OF COMMITTEES

Today, Congress boasts a shopper's bazaar of committees—standing, subcommittee, select, joint, and conference—and within each of these general types are variations. Standing committees, for example, can be classed as either *authorizing* or *appropriating* panels. Authorizing committees (such as Agriculture, Armed Services, and Judiciary) are the policy-making centers on Capitol Hill. As substantive committees, they propose solutions to public problems and advocate what they believe to be the necessary levels of spending for the programs under their jurisdictions. The House and Senate Committees on appropriations recommend how much money agencies and programs will receive. Not surprisingly, the two types of panels, authorizing and appropriating, tend to come into conflict. Typically, authorizers press for full funding of their recommendations, whereas appropriators usually recommend lower spending levels, especially in an era of spending austerity.

Standing Committees

A standing committee is a permanent entity created by public law or House or Senate rules. Standing committees continue from Congress to Congress, except in rare instances when they are eliminated or new ones are created. Table 7-1 identifies the standing committees in the 116th Congress.

TABLE 7-1 ■ Standing Committees of the House and Senate, 116th Congress, 2019–2021	
House	**Senate**
Agriculture	Agriculture, Nutrition, and Forestry
Appropriations	Appropriations
Armed Services	Armed Services
Budget	Banking, Housing, and Urban Affairs
Education and Labor	Budget
Energy and Commerce	Commerce, Science, and Transportation
Ethics	Energy and Natural Resources
Financial Services	Environment and Public Works
Foreign Affairs	Finance
Homeland Security	Foreign Relations
House Administration	Health, Education, Labor, and Pensions
Judiciary	Homeland Security and Governmental Affairs
Natural Resources	Judiciary
Oversight and Reform	Rules and Administration
Rules	Small Business and Entrepreneurship
Science, Space, and Technology	Veterans' Affairs
Small Business	
Transportation and Infrastructure	
Veterans' Affairs	
Ways and Means	

Sources: House and Senate committee webpages.

Standing committees process the bulk of Congress's daily and annual agenda. Typically, measures are considered on the House or Senate floor after first being referred to and approved by the appropriate committees. At the same time, committees are the burial ground for most legislation—that is, committees select from the thousands of measures introduced in each Congress those that merit floor debate. Of the hundreds of bills that clear committees, fewer still are enacted into law.

Sizes and Ratios

The biennial congressional election results frame the party negotiations over setting committee sizes and ratios (the number of majority and minority members on a panel). At the beginning of each new Congress, each chamber adopts separate resolutions, offered by Democrats and Republicans, electing party members to the committees and thus setting their sizes and ratios. In practice, committee sizes and ratios are established in the House by the majority leadership. Because the majority party has the votes, it is the final arbiter if the minority protests its allotment of seats.

At the opening of the 116th Congress, the House ratio of Democrats to Republicans was 54 percent to 46 percent. In the main, this was the approximate ratio (often 56 to 44) on most of the twenty House standing committees. Important to note is that the majority party commonly assigns a higher percentage of their members to certain committees, such as Appropriations (57 to 43) and Ways and Means (60 to 40) because of their critical responsibilities for spending and taxing. Other committees traditionally have disproportionate partisan ratios, such as the House Committee on Rules (two to one plus one) and the Committee on House Administration (two to one) because of the important role they play in internal chamber operations. The Rules Committee establishes the conditions for debating and amending legislation; the House Administration Committee exercises jurisdiction over, for instance, House facilities and services, committee funding recommendations, and campaign financing. The House Committee on Ethics has an equal number of majority and minority members, with the Speaker designating the chair.

In the Senate, sizes and ratios are negotiated by the majority and minority leaders. (Senate rules, unlike those of the House, establish the sizes of the standing committees, but these can be adjusted up or down with the agreement of the majority and minority leaders.) Senators are assigned to committees through Senate adoption of organizing resolutions (one for each party). The resolutions can be filibustered (60 votes are required to break a talkathon). This circumstance encourages a spirit of cooperation and accommodation between the two party leaders.

Once it became clear after the 2018 elections by what margin the Republicans had won Senate control (fifty-three to forty-seven), the two party leaders—Republican Mitch McConnell, Ky., and Democrat Charles Schumer, N.Y.—met and negotiated committee sizes and ratios. As Senator McConnell noted, "We'll be negotiating committee ratios, the two of us."[17] Given the Republican edge of three seats in the 116th Senate, Senators McConnell and Schumer agreed that of the fifteen standing committees, six would have a two-seat margin and the other nine a one-seat advantage. Panels with a two-seat edge were mainly those with jurisdiction over key priorities of Senate Republicans and President Trump: for example, the Committee on Finance (tax, health, and trade) and the Committee on Judiciary (federal judgeships and immigration).

Senate leaders may change party ratios on committees "by shifting seats between the parties, rather than by adding seats to panels."[18] Or they might add seats to committees. For instance, at the start of the 116th Congress, there was large concern that because of ratio changes Democratic senator Kamala Harris of California, a 2020 contender for the presidency, might lose her seat as the most junior Democrat on the Committee on Judiciary. Senate GOP gains in the November 2018 elections meant more seats for Republicans on committees and fewer slots for Democrats. Outside progressive groups lobbied for Senator Harris's retention on Judiciary, and Minority Leader Schumer made it a priority. He succeeded by persuading Senator McConnell to add another seat to Judiciary.[19] Senator McConnell, mindful of Judiciary's all-male GOP contingent, appointed the first Republican women ever to serve on that committee: Senators Marsha Blackburn, Tenn., and Joni Ernst, Iowa. (The Senate Select Committee on Ethics always has an equal number of majority and minority party members. It is chaired by a majority member.)

Party leaders also enlarge panels to accommodate lawmakers competing for membership on the same committees. They recognize that intraparty harmony can be maintained by boosting the number of committee seats. There was concern among Hispanic Democrats at the start of the 116th Congress that the House Ways and Means Committee had only one Latino on the panel. The size of Ways and Means was increased to accommodate this concern, as well as a request from Republicans to add a seat from their side.[20] There are occasions, too, when House committees are downsized to boost productivity and to cut costs. Biennial House and Senate election results largely determine whether the majority party expands or reduces its margins on committees.

Subcommittees

Subcommittees perform much of the day-to-day lawmaking and oversight work of Congress. Like standing committees, they vary widely in rules and procedures, staff arrangements, modes of operation, and relationships with the full committee, as well as its other subcommittees. They are created for various reasons, such as lawmakers' need to subdivide a committee's wide-ranging policy domain into manageable pieces, their wish to chair these panels and to have a platform to shape the legislative agenda, and their desire to respond to the policy claims of specialized constituencies.

Under House rules, most standing committees are limited to no more than five subcommittees, though exceptions for specific committees commonly occur at the start of a new Congress. For example, when the 116th Congress (2017–2019) adopted new House rules, several standing committees were authorized to have additional subcommittees, largely because of workload demands.[21]

Another House rule limits members to serving on no more than four subcommittees. Such limits—on the number of subcommittees for each standing committee and subcommittee assignment restrictions for each member—are designed to make Congress "more deliberative, participatory, and manageable by reducing scheduling conflicts and jurisdictional overlap."[22]

Democratic Caucus rules outline the process for determining subcommittee chairs. Rule 27 states that committee caucuses (the Democrats on the respective standing committees) "shall establish the number of subcommittees, fix the jurisdiction of each subcommittee, and determine the size of each subcommittee." Rule 28 stipulates a detailed selection process for subcommittee chairs. Briefly, four key provisions define the process.

First, Democratic members, "in order of full committee seniority" (or seniority on the Appropriations subcommittee), bid for the positions of subcommittee chair, subject to majority approval by secret ballot of the Democratic committee members. Second, if members are rejected, they "may bid for any remaining position of Chair of a subcommittee." Third, subcommittee chairs on four of the most influential committees—Appropriations, Energy and Commerce, Financial Services, and Ways and Means—also require approval of the Steering and Policy Committee. Fourth, the full Democratic Caucus votes by secret ballot to approve or reject the subcommittee chairs of the four standing committees.

House Republicans have their own set of procedures for determining the ranking members of the various standing committees. GOP Rule 15 states that "the method of selection of chairs [or ranking member] of the Committee's subcommittees shall be at the discretion of the full Committee chair [or ranking member], unless a majority of the Republican Members of the full Committee disapprove the action of the chair [or ranking member]." Unlike for the other committees, nominations for ranking member on the twelve appropriations subcommittees are submitted to the GOP Steering Committee for approval (or rejection). If someone is rejected, the Appropriations Committee ranking member will submit a new nomination.

The two Congresses are also evident in the composition of subcommittees. A good example occurred a few Congresses ago when the GOP won back control of the House, and the Judiciary Committee chair passed over Steve King, R-Iowa, for the chairmanship of the Judiciary Subcommittee on Immigration and Citizenship. King had been the ranking GOP member on the panel in the previous Congress. But worried that King's inflammatory statements about immigrants would alienate Latino voters in the upcoming November elections, the Judiciary chair selected a committee Republican "who has a lower profile and a less strident tone than King" to head the subcommittee.[23] (Representative King continued over the years to make what many interpreted as racially charged comments. Thus, at the start of the 116th Congress, GOP leaders decided not to assign King to any committee, effectively removing him from his service on the Agriculture and Judiciary committees.)[24]

Although silent on the number of subcommittees that standing committees may establish, Senate and party rules set subcommittee assignment limits for senators and prohibit them from chairing more than one subcommittee on any given committee. The number of subcommittees, not surprisingly, often equals the number of majority party members on a committee eligible to chair a subcommittee. Subcommittee chairs and assignments are determined in one of two ways: by the committee chair in consultation with the ranking member or by senators' order of seniority on the full committee. It is traditional in both chambers for committee members to defer to the chair on organizational matters, such as the number of subcommittees and their respective jurisdictions.

Unlike in the House, where every standing committee except Budget, Ethics, and House Administration has subcommittees, in the Senate, four standing committees customarily function without subcommittees—Budget, Rules and Administration, Small Business, and Veterans' Affairs—as do four other permanent panels—Indian Affairs, Ethics, Intelligence, and Aging. These panels are able to process their legislative business without subcommittees because of their relatively small workloads compared with those of other Senate committees.

Select, or Special, Committees

Select, or special, committees are temporary panels that typically go out of business after the two-year life of the Congress in which they are created. But some select committees take on the attributes of permanent committees. The House, for example, has a Permanent Select Committee on Intelligence. Select committees usually do not have legislative authority (the right to receive and report out measures) unless it is granted by their authorizing measure; they can only study, investigate, and make recommendations. The membership of select committees is the prerogative of the Speaker. In practice, he or she names the majority members, including the chair, and the minority leader appoints lawmakers from her or his side of the aisle.

Select panels are created for several reasons. First, they can accommodate the concerns of individual members. Indeed, the chairs of these panels may attract publicity that enhances their political careers. For example, Democrat Harry S. Truman of Missouri came to the public's (and President Franklin D. Roosevelt's) attention as head of a special Senate committee investigating World War II military procurement practices. Second, special panels can be an access point for interest groups (e.g., the Senate Special Committee on Aging reflects the concerns of the elderly). Third, select committees supplement the standing committee system by overseeing and investigating issues for which the permanent panels may lack adequate time or prefer to ignore. At other times, majority party leaders may spur the creation of a select committee to draw attention to a compelling issue or problem.

For example, on the opening day of the 116th Congress (January 3, 2019), the House created a fifteen member (9D, 6R) Select Committee on the Climate Crisis (informally called the "Green New Deal" panel). Its mandate is to "investigate, study, make findings, and develop recommendations on policies, strategies, and innovations to achieve substantial and permanent reductions in pollution and other activities that contribute to the climate crisis." The work of the select panel concludes at the end of the 116th Congress (see the following section, Overlapping Jurisdictions, for more on this select panel).

The House also responded to member and public concern with congressional operations ("broken" or "dysfunctional" are oft-used characterizations) by creating a bipartisan (6D, 6R) Select Committee on the Modernization of Congress. Its mandate is to study and make recommendations on a number of specific topics, such as rules and procedures; schedules and the calendar of business; leadership development; and staff recruitment, diversity, and retention. The Select Committee on Modernization terminates on February 1, 2020.

Finally, select committees can be set up to coordinate consideration of issues that overlap the jurisdictions of several standing committees. A good example occurred following the tragic 9/11 terrorist attack on the United States. In 2003, the Department of Homeland Security (DHS) was formed by merging twenty-two federal agencies with a workforce at the time of 180,000 employees. Because numerous House committees exercised jurisdiction over parts of DHS, Speaker Dennis Hastert, R-Ill., created a select homeland security panel to determine whether a new, single-focused standing committee should be created to oversee DHS. Interesting to note is that the select panel was dominated by committee chairs keen on protecting their jurisdiction rather than transferring any significant portion to a new standing committee on homeland security. As a result of the select panel's review, Speaker Hastert backed the creation of a new standing Committee on Homeland Security, which did not receive as much jurisdiction as advocates wanted. (The Senate also created a counterpart panel: Homeland Security and Governmental Affairs.)

Joint Committees

Joint committees, which include members from both chambers, have been used since the First Congress for study, investigation, oversight, and routine activities. Unless the composition of a joint committee is prescribed in statute, House members of these committees are appointed by the Speaker; senators are appointed by that chamber's presiding officer. There are now four joint committees that have been in existence for many decades: Joint Committee on Economics, Joint Committee on the Library, Joint Committee on Printing, and the Joint Committee on Taxation. The Joint Committee on the Library and the Joint Committee on Printing oversee, respectively, the Library of Congress and the Government Printing Office. The Joint Committee on Taxation is essentially a holding company for staff who work closely with the tax-writing committees of each house. The Joint Economic Committee conducts studies and hearings on a wide range of domestic and international economic issues. The chair of the joint committees rotates each Congress between House and Senate members.

Conference Committees

Before legislation can be sent to the president to be signed, it must pass both the House and the Senate in identical form. One way this result is obtained is to create a conference committee (see Chapter 8 for more on conferences). Sometimes called the third house of Congress, these bicameral panels reconcile differences between similar measures passed by both chambers. They are composed of members from each house.

THE ASSIGNMENT PROCESS

Every congressional election sets off a scramble for committee seats. Legislators understand the linkage between winning desirable assignments and winning elections. Newly elected representatives and senators quickly make their preferences known to party leaders, to members of the panels that make committee assignments, and to others—such as friendly lobbyists or generous contributors. They may be able to help the newcomers obtain their preferred committee seats. At the same time, incumbents may try to move to more prestigious panels.

Elections trigger "musical chairs" on Capitol Hill, mainly because of reelection defeats. For example, committee and subcommittee chairs and ranking minority positions are shuffled as lawmakers vie for the vacant leadership positions. The scramble can set off a chain reaction of roster changes. For example, the 2018 election defeat of veteran Sen. Bill Nelson, D-Fla. (by GOP senator Rick Scott) prompted discussions about who would replace Nelson as the top Democrat on the Commerce, Science and Transportation Committee. Sen. Maria Cantwell, D-Wash., was next in line, but she also was ranking on Energy and Natural Resources. She had to choose between them and decided to be ranking on Commerce, which opened the ranking post on Energy. Sen. Joe Manchin, D-W.Vir., fourth in seniority on Energy following Nelson's defeat, became ranking on Energy. Three Democratic senators with more seniority than Manchin on Energy opted to stay ranking on other committees.[25] Committee and subcommittee shuffles also occur for other reasons beside elections (e.g., term limit rules, death, or resignation).

Assignment to the most important committees is generally "exclusive." House Democrats who serve on exclusive committees (Appropriations, Energy and Commerce, Financial Services, Rules, and Ways and Means) may serve on no other standing committees unless they are granted an exemption—or waiver—from this requirement. Waivers are commonly granted, for instance, to permit members to sit on an extra committee that they deem important to their reelection prospects. This is another example of the two Congresses—the institution bending to suit the preferences and constituency needs of individual members. House Republicans also have generally exclusive panels, such as Appropriations, Energy and Commerce, and Ways and Means.[26]

The Pecking Order

The most powerful—and thus, most desirable—standing committees are House Ways and Means and Senate Finance, which pass on tax, trade, Social

Security, and Medicare measures. The House and Senate appropriations committees, which hold the federal purse strings, are also influential panels and usually much sought after. Mindful of the two Congresses, lawmakers seek assignment to committees where they have the opportunity to try to ensure that federal funds are funneled to their districts or states.

Nonetheless, the attractiveness of the appropriations committees waned somewhat in recent years, given the escalating challenge of distributing fiscal resources between domestic and defense priorities; the now-routine inability of lawmakers to fund the government by the statutory deadline of October 1 each year; wider use of omnibus appropriations bills (often written in secret by a few lawmakers and party leaders); and the moratorium on earmarks (congressionally directed spending for projects in members' districts or states, often called "pork,"), which Republicans successfully imposed on Congress when they controlled the legislative branch.[27] Periodically, lawmakers urge the return of earmarks, such as House majority leader Steny Hoyer, D-Md., "I think earmarks worked" to facilitate (or "grease") the passage of appropriations bills. He added, "Republicans eliminated earmarks altogether," which weakened Congress's power of the purse.[28] Democrats have yet to revive the practice of earmarking when they assumed control of the 116th House.

In today's contentious partisan environment, where fiscal clashes occur constantly between Democrats and Republicans over taxes, expenditures, and the size of government, party leaders have taken a much larger role in shaping appropriations measures and in mobilizing the votes to win their enactment. The consequence of these developments is to make some lawmakers wary of either chairing or serving on the appropriating panels. These lawmakers recognize the potential perils of the two Congresses: They could be challenged electorally either by conservative-leaning voters for not cutting enough or by liberal-leaning constituents angry at spending cuts to favorite programs. Although the attractiveness of committees can change over time, the House and Senate appropriations committees remain desirable assignments for many lawmakers.

The budget committees, established in 1974, have an important role in economic and fiscal matters and their guardianship of the congressional budgeting process. Members with a fiscal background or who want to fix what many consider to be a "broken" (e.g., missed deadlines) budget process, may be attracted to this panel. The House and Senate commerce committees, along with each chamber's banking and financial services committees, are also coveted panels: Not only do they command broad jurisdictional mandates, but the many interest groups they affect can supply cash donations for the committee members' future election campaigns. For example, it is usual for Democratic and GOP leaders to boost the reelection chances of their freshmen lawmakers by naming them to committees where it is relatively easy to raise campaign funds, such as Financial Services, Energy and Commerce, Appropriations, and Ways and Means. "The amount of money you can raise is almost entirely determined by committee membership," said a GOP insider.[29]

On the other hand, several of the seven liberal Democratic freshmen assigned to the Financial Services Committee in the 116th Congress (2019–2021) refuse to accept corporate campaign funds. They raise campaign donations in other ways. "I don't take corporate PAC [political action committee] money," said freshman representative Katie Porter, D-Calif. These members hope "to change the perspective of the committee and the issues it chooses to focus on" from banking and financial institutions to middle-class concerns about affordable housing and consumer protection.[30]

Among those panels that seldom have waiting lists are the House and Senate ethics committees. These committees are not popular because legislators are reluctant to sit in judgment of their colleagues. "Members have never competed for the privilege of serving on the ethics committee, and I am no exception," remarked a House Democrat after his party's leader prevailed on him to join the Ethics panel. Or as one GOP member grumbled after serving as Ethics chair, "I've paid my debt to society. It's time for me to be paroled."[31]

Preferences and Politicking

In his analysis of six House committees, Richard F. Fenno Jr. found that three basic goals of lawmakers—reelection, influence within the House, and good public policy—affected the committee assignments that members sought. Reelection-oriented members were attracted to committees such as Natural Resources (e.g., lawmakers whose districts had significant mineral resources, forest reserves, or coastal zones.) Appropriations and Ways and Means attracted influence-oriented members. Policy-oriented members sought membership on the Education and Labor Committee and the Foreign Affairs Committee. Members with similar goals found themselves on the same committees, Fenno concluded. Such homogeneity of perspectives may result in harmonious but biased committees (see Table 7-2).[32]

Since Fenno's study, scholars have elaborated on the link between members' goals and committee assignments. They have divided House committees into reelection (or constituency), policy, and power panels, and they concur that some mix of the three goals motivates most of the committees' activities. They agree, too, that members' goals "are less easily characterized in the Senate than in the House."[33] After all, most every senator has the opportunity to serve on one of the top committees, such as Appropriations, Armed Services, Commerce, and Finance. Thus, the power associated with a particular committee assignment is less important for senators than for representatives.

Members do not always get assigned to the committees they prefer. Although both parties try to accommodate assignment preferences, some members are inevitably disappointed. A classic case was that of Democratic representative Shirley Chisholm of Brooklyn (1969–1983), the first African American woman elected to Congress. Initially, she was assigned to the House Agriculture Committee. "I think it would be hard to imagine an assignment that is less relevant to my

TABLE 7-2   ■   House and Senate Committee Comparison

Category	House	Senate
Number of standing committees	20	16
Committee/ subcommittee assignments per member	About 6	About 11
Power or prestige committees	Appropriations, Budget, Commerce, Financial Services, Rules, Ways and Means	Appropriations, Armed Services, Commerce, Finance, Foreign Relations[1]
Treaties and nominations submitted by the president	No authority	Committees review
Floor debate	Representatives' activity is somewhat confined to the bills reported from the panels on which they serve	Senators can choose to influence any policy area regardless of their committee assignments
Committee consideration of legislation	More difficult to bypass	Easier to bypass[2]
Committee chairs	Subject to party and Speakership influence that can limit the chair's discretionary authority over committee operations	Freer rein to manage committees
Committee staff	Active policy and oversight role; often shorter tenure and lower salary	Influential policy making role; often longer tenure and higher salary
Subcommittee chairmanships	Representatives of the majority party usually wait at least one term	Majority party senators, regardless of their seniority, usually chair subcommittees

[1]Almost every senator is assigned to one of these committees.

[2]For example, by allowing riders—unrelated policy proposals—to measures pending on the floor.

background or to the needs of the predominantly black and Puerto Rican people who elected me," she said. Chisholm's protests won her a seat on the Veterans' Affairs Committee. "There are a lot more veterans in my district than there are trees," she later observed.[34]

Yet some urban lawmakers welcome service on the Agriculture Committee, where they can fuse metropolitan issues with rural issues through food stamp, consumer, and other legislation. A number of newly elected Democrats to the 116th House "have a food, agriculture, or restaurant background" and may welcome assignment to the Agriculture Committee. As freshman representative Alexandria Ocasio-Cortez observed, "You'd be hard-pressed to find a political issue that doesn't have food implications."[35]

Members campaign vigorously for the committees they prefer. In *Hit the Ground Running,* his 115th Congress guidebook for GOP newcomers to Congress, House majority leader Kevin McCarthy, R-Calif., outlined the key steps for securing committee assignments (see Box 7-1). Although McCarthy is the Republican minority leader of the 116th House, his analysis is relevant for Democratic members as well.

How Assignments Are Made

Each party in each house has its own panel to review members' committee requests and dispense assignments to standing committees: the House Republican Steering Committee, the House Democratic Steering and Policy Committee, the Senate Republican Committee on Committees, and the Senate Democratic Steering Committee. (These panels will be referred to as "steering" committees in this chapter.) The decisions of these panels are the first and most important step in a three-step procedure. The second step involves approval of the assignment lists by each party's caucus. Finally, there is a pro forma election by the full House or Senate.

Formal Criteria

Both formal and informal criteria guide the assignment panels in choosing committee members. One formal rule of the House Democratic Caucus is that recommendations for "committee posts need not necessarily follow seniority." Similarly, House GOP rules stipulate that the lawmaker nominated by the Steering Committee to be the chair or ranking member "need not be the Member with the longest consecutive service on the Committee." Senate GOP conference rules state that two Republicans from the same state should not serve on the same committee.

Since 1953, when Senate Democratic leader Lyndon B. Johnson of Texas announced his "Johnson rule," all Senate Democrats have been assigned one major committee before any party member receives a second major assignment. In 1965, Senate Republicans followed suit. Senate rules also classify committees into different categories, popularly called *A, B,* and *C.* There is even a separate category of

BOX 7-1   HOW TO GET THE COMMITTEE ASSIGNMENT YOU WANT

The first step is to decide which committee assignments are right for you and your district. Soon after the organizational conference, you will receive a Dear Colleague letter from your leadership requesting that you submit your committee preferences. Expect this form by the first week of orientation. Your personal policy interests, the needs of your district and state, and your future goals are important factors in deciding which committees to request.

Obtaining a seat on your preferred committee may be a multi-year process depending on vacancies and which committees you select. This applies especially to the "A" committees, which usually take several terms before gaining appointment.

Secondly, be prepared to make your case as to why you should be selected to your committee of choice. The competition for "B" committees such as Transportation and Infrastructure and Armed Services can be intense, and you'll need to clearly state your argument.

Successful arguments may include highlighting your professional experience or policy expertise within the committee's jurisdiction, the critical needs of your district or state or the fact that your region of the country may be underrepresented on the committee. Bottom line: This is about marketing yourself, your experience, your abilities, and your district.

Finally, you should engage the Steering Committee [the committee assignment panel]. First, reach out to your class representative and then to your regional representative [on the Steering Committee]. They will be your primary voice on the Steering Committee, and it is important that they be an advocate for your request. Keep in mind that your class representative must prioritize and balance the needs of your entire class. This means being responsive to their questions.

You should also discuss your committee choices with the elected leaders. They hold a substantial bloc of votes on the Steering Committee. In addition, you may want to reach out to other Members of the Steering Committee. Ideally, you want to have someone other than your class and regional representative speak in support of your request when the Steering Committee convenes.

prestigious *Super A* committees. Senators may sit on only one of the four Super A panels: Appropriations, Armed Services, Finance, and Foreign Relations (unless they are granted a waiver of party rules. A noteworthy waiver concerning Super A committees occurred in 2019, something that had not happened since 1944. Two GOP Senators (Steve Daines, Mont., and James Lankford, Okla.) who served on the Appropriations Committee were also assigned to the Finance Committee. Senate Rule XXV states that members must serve on no more than two committees in the A category, which includes the four Super A panels; one in the B grouping (such as Budget, Rules and Administration, and Small Business);

and any number of C committees (Joint Economic, Ethics, Indian Affairs, Joint Library, Joint Printing, and Joint Taxation).

Informal Criteria

Many informal criteria affect committee assignments—including party loyalty, geography, substantive expertise, gender, and electoral vulnerability. House Democratic rules instruct the Steering Committee to consider "merit, length of service on the committee, degree of commitment to the Democratic agenda, and the diversity of the Caucus, including appropriate representation of the Caucus' ideological and regional diversity," in granting committee assignments.

When House Republicans completed their selection of committee chairs for the 113th Congress (2013–2015), there were no women committee leaders. As a result, female GOP members made it known to their Speaker, John Boehner, R-Ohio, that he must rectify this situation by naming women to head committees (Ethics and House Administration) with leadership vacancies for which he had appointment authority. The Speaker complied with this request. Noteworthy is that in the 116th Democratic House (2019–2021), five standing committees and the Joint Economic Committee are chaired by women. (Additionally, over thirty subcommittees are also headed by women.)

Members' own wishes are another criterion. Lawmakers who represent districts or states with large military installations may seek assignment to the Armed Services Committee. Or lawmakers with a specific policy interest (education, health, and so on) may strive to win appointment to panels that deal with those topics. Finally, the committee assignment panels of each congressional party typically respect what is referred to as a *property norm*. Returning lawmakers of each party are generally permitted to retain their committee seats (unless they are bumped because of committee ratio changes) before new members bid for vacant committee positions. Lawmakers who do lose their committee positions because of ratio changes could be returned to those panels in the next or subsequent Congresses.

The two Congresses are always intertwined in committee assignment decisions. Each party seeks to boost the electoral resources of its members. House Democratic and GOP leaders, for example, sometimes grant electorally vulnerable freshmen an extra committee assignment to broaden their appeal as they head toward their reelection contests. "All of these committees have constituents," said Democratic leader Steny Hoyer of Maryland. "And all of these [freshmen Democratic appointees] have people in their districts who are members of these constituencies."[36]

More seasoned members who could face tough electoral competition may seek plum assignments as well, in order to boost their influence and capacity for fund-raising. Democratic senators Joe Manchin of West Virginia and Claire McCaskill of Missouri each won assignments to top committees because they were up for reelection in 2018 in states carried by President Trump in the 2016 elections. Manchin won a seat on the Appropriations Committee, which enabled him to procure federal funds for his state, and McCaskill landed on the Finance Committee, with its jurisdiction over major topics of interest to voters, such as Social Security, Medicare, trade, and taxation. Senate Democratic leader Charles Schumer of New York even gave up his own seat on Finance to make room for McCaskill.[37] Senator Manchin emerged victorious in the 2018 mid-term election; McCaskill lost her race to Republican Josh Hawley.

Another important assignment consideration for some lawmakers is to serve on committees that boost their aspirations to compete for the presidency. This factor helps explain the appeal of defense and foreign policy committees among senators. Press reports indicated that when Barack Obama launched his first presidential campaign in 2008, freshman Senator Tim Kaine, D-Va., was on his short list to be considered as a vice presidential candidate. Kaine's lack of foreign policy experience was a factor in Obama's selection of Joe Biden, a chair of the Foreign Relations Committee, as his running mate. Several Democratic senators mentioned as 2020 presidential prospects serve on the Armed Services or Foreign Relations committees to bolster their international or defense policy credentials. Party leaders also promise committee assignments to congressional candidates to help them win election.

Another informal, controversial, and little-known criterion that might affect members' committee assignments is their fund-raising prowess. As Joseph Califano, a decades-long Democratic official who served in the Pentagon, on the White House staff, and as a cabinet secretary, wrote, "Committee assignments are accompanied by fund-raising [or "pay to play"] taxes, euphemistically called party dues."[38] Both parties in the House expect their members to pay dues to their respective party campaign committees, and the amount of these financial contributions varies according to whether they are the chairs or ranking members of the top committees. Califano's research found the "Democratic fund-raising price tags that its members had to pay for each House committee assignment in 2013."[39] Rep. Ken Buck, R-Colo., revealed in 2017 "that top tier [GOP] committee chair positions cost $875,000 each in party dues."[40] Other lawmakers dispute the assertion that there is a direct connection between members' contributions to party coffers and their committee assignments.[41]

Seniority

Normally, the assignment panels observe seniority when preparing committee membership lists. The member of the majority party with the longest continuous committee service is usually listed first as the incoming chair. In general, the House and Senate parties observe seniority in the assignment process, more so in the Senate than the House. Senate Republicans apply seniority rigidly when two or more GOP senators compete for either a committee vacancy or chairmanship. The longest-serving senator typically prevails. As a senator noted, "When I first came to the Senate, I was skeptical [of the seniority tradition]. But as I've become more senior, I've grown more fond of it."[42] (By party rule, the Senate GOP leader fills half of all vacancies on the A committees; seniority determines the other half.)

By contrast, the two House party groups do not observe seniority as strictly as Senate Republicans typically do. Recall that House Democratic rules even state that members of their assignment panel are not bound by seniority in nominating members for committee posts (see Box 7-2 on party assignment committees). A noteworthy case when seniority came into play occurred when Henry Waxman, D-Calif., the former chair and ranking member of the Energy and Commerce Committee, chose not to run for reelection to the 114th Congress (2015–2017). His departure provoked a contentious intraparty succession contest.

Two Democrats on the panel wanted to assume Waxman's spot: Anna Eshoo, Calif., who was fifth in seniority, and Frank Pallone, N.J., first in seniority. Leader Pelosi, a close friend of Eshoo, strongly endorsed her candidacy in a "Dear Colleague" letter to all Democrats. On the other hand, Steny Hoyer of Maryland, the Democratic whip at the time, backed Pallone. (Pelosi and Hoyer have long had a competitive relationship.) The battle lines were drawn, and the contest for Energy's top spot was intense. Pelosi's firm control of the Steering and Policy Committee ensured that Eshoo would prevail over Pallone, but the Democratic Caucus reversed that decision and voted to make Pallone the ranking member on the Energy panel.

A number of factors contributed to Pallone's victory, including the issue of seniority. On the one hand, Pelosi contended that "seniority makes you a contender, but it does not make you a chairman. It is a consideration, not a determination." Hoyer disagreed with Pelosi's view: "I have historically been for the ranking member, the senior member, if that member is capable and able, and if that member has contributed significantly to the legislative product. I think Frank Pallone has done all those."[43] (Pallone chairs the Energy and Commerce panel in the 116th Congress, 2019–2021).

The Eshoo-Pallone contest triggered an internal party debate about the value of seniority in determining the top Democratic posts on committees. Many House Democrats advocate a three-term limit for chairs following the Republican model. The November 2018 elections sparked another term limit discussion among Democrats. A new generation of House Democrats wanted the opportunity to be committee leaders without waiting, possibly decades, for that chance. The rotation of chairs could also bring new energy and ideas to committee decision making. On the other hand, many senior Democrats opposed the three-term limit for committee chairs. The "haves" suggested that term limits would produce the loss of substantive experience and institutional memory. Various Democratic groups, such as the Black Caucus and the Hispanic Caucus, opposed term limits and voiced firm support for a seniority-based system that "helps elevate minority representatives to positions of power."[44] As Rep. Cedric Richmond, N.Y., the leader of the Black Caucus, said, six-year terms limits for chairs "would hurt the seniority system, which we're adamant supporters of. [Term limits] is something I would not support."[45] To date, the six-year term limit proposal has not been adopted by House Democrats.

BOX 7-2   PARTY ASSIGNMENT COMMITTEES

House Republicans. Before the official convening of the 104th Congress in January 1995, incoming Speaker Newt Gingrich, R-Ga., revamped his party's Committee on Committees, which he would chair. Gingrich renamed it the Steering Committee, transformed it into a leadership-dominated panel, and eliminated a weighted voting system whereby a GOP member of the assignment panel casts as many votes as there were Republicans in his or her state delegation. Instead, Gingrich granted the GOP leader (himself in this case) the right to cast the most votes (five); every other Steering Committee member could cast only one vote, except the majority leader, who got two votes. These changes have continued in subsequent Congresses, except that Minority Leader Kevin McCarthy now casts four rather than five votes. The Republican leader also appoints all GOP members of the Rules, House Administration, Ethics, and Permanent Select Intelligence Committees.

House Democrats. Democrats on the House Ways and Means Committee functioned as their party's committee on committees from 1911 until 1974, when the Democratic Caucus voted to transfer this duty to the Steering and Policy Committee. The Steering Committee, cochaired by Rosa DeLauro of Connecticut, Eric Swalwell of California, and Barbara Lee of California, recommends Democratic assignments to the caucus, one committee at a time. Speaker Nancy Pelosi names the chairs and members of her party to the Ethics, House Administration, Rules, and Permanent Select Intelligence committees.

Senate Republicans. The chair of the Republican Conference appoints the assignment panel of five or so members. The floor leader is an ex officio member. Idaho senator Mike Crapo chairs the panel during the 116th Congress.

Senate Democrats. The Steering Committee makes assignments for Democrats. Its size may fluctuate from Congress to Congress. The party's floor leader appoints the members of this panel and its chair. In the 116th Senate, the chair is Sen. Amy Klobuchar of Minnesota.

On the Senate side, Republicans adopted, in 1997, a party rule restricting committee chairs (or ranking members) to six years of service. Specifically, Senate GOP term-limit rules state that "time served as a ranking member doesn't count as time served as chairman." However, "once a lawmaker serves six years as a chairman on a committee," that member cannot then serve as a ranking member on that committee.[46] "The whole thrust behind this," said the Senate author of the term-limit change, "is to try to get greater participation, so new members of the Senate don't have to wait until they've been here 18 years to play a role."[47]

This goal is not easy to achieve because long-serving Republicans are often senior on more than one committee. Thus, when they hit the six-year limit, party rules permit them to seek the chair (or ranking minority position) of another committee and leapfrog over a party member with less committee seniority.

Senate Democrats have no term-limit rule for their committee leaders. Their long-standing tradition is to allow seniority on a panel to determine who will be either the chair or ranking minority member of a standing committee. But Senate rules also limit members to one full committee chair. Senate Rule XXV states, in part, that "no Senator shall serve at any time as chairman of more than one" standing committee.

Biases

The decisions made by the assignment panels inevitably determine the geographical and ideological composition of the standing committees. Committees can easily become biased toward one position or another. Farm areas are over-represented on the agriculture committees and small-business interests on the small business committees. It is no wonder, then, that committees are policy advocates. They propose laws that serve the interests of their members and the outside groups and agencies that gravitate toward them.

Both who gets on a panel and who does not affect committee policy making. Committees that are carefully balanced between liberal and conservative interests can be tilted one way or the other by new members. New committee leaders, as when party control changes hands, can shift a panel's policy agenda and out-look. The agenda priorities of liberal representative Maxine Waters, D-Calif., the new chair of the Financial Services Committee in the 116th Congress, are very different from those of the GOP chair in the previous Congress, conservative Jeb Hensarling of Texas. Waters, for example, favors affordable housing, rental assistance, and assertive oversight of the Consumer Financial Protection Bureau. A committee's political philosophy influences its success on the House or Senate floor. Committees ideologically out of step with the House or Senate majority are more likely than others to have legislation defeated or significantly revised by floor amendments.

Approval by Party Caucuses and the Chamber

For most of the last century, each chamber's party caucuses either simply rati-fied the assignment decisions of their committees on committees or took no action on them at all. Beginning in the 1970s, however, party caucuses became major participants in the assignment process. Chairs and ranking minority members were subjected to election by secret ballot of their party colleagues. Committee leadership in both houses and parties is no longer an automatic right. For many decades of the twentieth century, a committee's most senior member of the major-ity party would become chair regardless of the individual's ability or senility.

Each chamber's rules require that all members of standing committees, including chairs, be elected by the entire House or Senate. The practice is for each party's leaders to offer their caucus-approved assignment lists to the full chamber. Normally, these are approved quickly and without controversy by voice vote. Neither party wants the other to interfere in its assignment decisions.

COMMITTEE LEADERSHIP

Committee chairs call meetings and establish agendas, hire and fire committee staff, arrange hearings, maintain order and decorum in committee proceedings, recommend conferees, act as floor managers, allocate committee funds and rooms, develop legislative strategies, chair hearings and markups, function as the committee's spokesperson, devise committee rules, and regulate the internal affairs and organization of their committees. For example, as the Senate Judiciary chair told a journalist, "I've always set the agenda in Judiciary."[48]

Among other things, chairs may also organize partisan or bipartisan retreats to identify their panel's legislative and oversight priorities; revamp subcommittee jurisdictions; coordinate with the administration if of the same party; block unwanted minority party priorities; work with their party leaders to develop a legislative agenda for the months ahead; consult with the chairs of other committees on policy issues that overlap their respective jurisdictions; or establish new roles for panel members, such as naming committee majority whips to muster the votes to pass legislation in committee and on the floor.

Committee chairs may also empower less senior members to take on special policy assignments, such as management of issues within the panel's jurisdiction. A House Armed Services chair viewed himself as the "delegator-in-chief." "The point is," he said, "that we have a huge amount of talent and resources on the committee and it is better for the country when we take advantage of it."[49]

A chair's procedural advantages are hard for even the most forceful minority members to overcome. The chair may be able to kill a bill simply by refusing to schedule it for a hearing. Or a chair may convene meetings when proponents or opponents of the legislation are unavoidably absent. The chair's authority derives from the support of a committee majority and a variety of formal and informal resources, such as substantive and parliamentary experience and control over the agenda, communications, and financial resources of the committee. When told by a committee colleague that he lacked the votes on an issue, then-House Energy and Commerce chair John Dingell, D-Mich., reminded him, "Yeah, but I've got the gavel."[50] Dingell banged his gavel, adjourned the meeting, and the majority had no chance to work its will before the legislative session ended.

The Dingell example highlights the formidable ability of chairs to stymie action on legislation they oppose. However, committee chairs also are among the most substantively and strategically knowledgeable members of their panel and of the chamber. They are advantageously positioned to advance ideas into law. Chairs are well-situated to mobilize winning coalitions in committee, in the chamber, and in reconciling bicameral differences on legislation. House chairs, for instance, may discuss with counterparts in the Senate how to draft legislation in their chamber to maximize its chances of adoption by the Senate.

The ranking minority party members on committees are also influential figures, but they are often reacting to the plans of the majority, especially in the House. Among their powers are nominating minority conferees, hiring and firing minority staff, influencing the committee's agenda, managing legislation on the floor, and acting as committee spokespersons for their party. Ranking members, as appropriate, present minority alternatives to majority proposals, challenge the chair on procedural and policy matters, develop tactics and strategies to foil the majority's plans, and highlight party goals and views to the attentive public.

In 2011, Rep. Elijah Cummings, D-Md., won the ranking position on the then named Committee on Oversight and Government Reform over other competitors because he was viewed as more able than others to challenge and confront the aggressive and media-savvy GOP chair of the panel. Eight years later, following the 2018 mid-term elections, Cummings became the chair of Oversight and Reform. His ranking minority member is Jim Jordan of Ohio. Jordan, the assertive founder of the conservative Freedom Caucus, was selected for the ranking post to challenge the committee's investigations of the Trump administration and related activities of the Cummings-led panel. "I love [Jordan] defending me on television," said President Trump. "He is a bulldog. He doesn't give a damn."[51]

Consider, too, the role of Sen. Bernie Sanders of Vermont, the ranking Democrat on the Budget Committee in the 116th Congress. After the national recognition he received campaigning for the 2016 presidential nomination against Hillary Clinton, Senator Sanders (who is a contender for the 2020 presidential nomination) uses his Budget Committee position as a platform to advance policies that appeal to working-class and middle-class families as well as younger, female, and other Democratic-leaning groups. As he once said, the ranking post is "a heavy responsibility. It helps shape the priorities of the United States government and I am going to do everything that I can to make sure the budget that leaves the United States Congress is a budget that represents the needs of working families and a shrinking middle class and not billionaires, who are doing phenomenally well."[52] Sanders's national message reflects a two-Congresses perspective: encourage the election of Democratic congressional candidates in the November 2020 elections and seek enactment of policies different in many ways from Republican and President Trump's priorities.

POLICY MAKING IN COMMITTEE

Committee decision making tends to be deliberate, collegial, and strategic, encouraging bargaining and accommodation among members. To move bills through Congress's multiple decision points from subcommittee to committee, authors of bills and resolutions typically make compromises in response to important committee members, among others. These gatekeepers may exact numerous alterations in a bill's substance. The proliferation of committees also multiplies the points of access for outside interests.

Overlapping Jurisdictions

The formal responsibilities of standing committees are defined by the rules of each house, various public laws, and precedents. Committees do not have watertight jurisdictional compartments. Any broad subject—energy, health, homeland security, and transportation are examples—overlaps numerous committees. A number of Senate committees, for instance, handle surface transportation issues. The Commerce, Science and Transportation Committee considers railroads, buses, trucks, and highway safety; the Environment and Public Works Committee has jurisdiction over highway construction and maintenance; Banking, Housing, and Urban Affairs is responsible for mass transit; the Finance Committee for fuel taxes; and the Appropriations Subcommittee on Transportation for spending on transportation projects. Jurisdictional overlap also is true in the House. These House bodies, along with a brief sketch of some of their environmental responsibilities, are as follows:

Agriculture: pesticides; soil conservation; some water programs

Appropriations: funding for environmental programs and agencies

Energy and Commerce: health effects of the environment; environmental regulations; solid-waste disposal; clean air; safe drinking water

Financial Services: open-space acquisition in urban areas

Foreign Affairs: international environmental cooperation

Natural Resources: water resources; power resources; land management; wildlife conservation; national parks; nuclear waste; fisheries; endangered species

Oversight and Reform: federal executive-branch agencies for the environment

Science, Space, and Technology: environmental research and development

Small Business: effects of environmental regulations on business

Transportation and Infrastructure: water pollution; sludge management

Ways and Means: environmental tax expenditures

Jurisdictional overlaps can have positive results. They enable members to develop expertise in several policy fields, prevent any one group from dominating a topic, and promote healthy competition among committees. Committees with overlapping jurisdictions sometimes formulate a written memorandum of understanding that outlines how policy topics are to be referred among them.[53] But healthy competition can quickly turn into intercommittee warfare. Various House and Senate committees periodically clash over issues that do not fit neatly into any single panel's area of responsibility (energy and environmental issues

BOX 7-3 COMMITTEE DECISION MAKING: A FORMAL MODEL

Political scientists use a variety of sophisticated techniques to understand legislative decision making. Employing concepts from economics such as rational choice—the notion that individuals (or lawmakers) have preferences or desires and that they will act in their self-interest to achieve their goals—these scholars utilize a number of analytical tools to consider how lawmakers devise strategies to accomplish their policy objectives. One such analytical approach is called spatial theory. The term *spatial* refers to a mathematical idea that theorists rely on called a policy space. An easy-to-understand example is that certain policy preferences can all be arrayed along a single dimension. For example, one end of the line might be labeled "more spending" and the other "less spending." Different spending preferences could be placed at different points or spaces along the line.

In employing spatial theory to model legislative decision making, scholars make a number of assumptions. Two are especially important: (1) Lawmakers hold consistent preferences, and (2) members have an ideal policy outcome that they prefer. Put differently, lawmakers will vote for policy alternatives that bring them closer to their policy ideal and oppose those that do the reverse. The work of these scholars highlights the importance of institutional rules and procedures in determining which of several policy alternatives will prevail. Analysts have also found that the median voter—the midpoint lawmaker with an equal number of other members to his or her left or right—is the ultimate determiner of majority-rule outcomes in unidimensional cases. Another way to view the median voter is the 218th vote in the House, the Supreme Court justice who casts the fifth vote in a 5–4 decision, or the member who casts the sixth vote in a committee of eleven members.

To depict this graphically, assume that a House appropriations subcommittee has sent to the floor a spending bill that reflects its committee median (CM). The subcommittee also must take into account a floor median (FM) if it wants its majority position to carry the day on the floor. The current policy status quo (Q) means that if the bill does not pass, last year's funding level remains in force. If the subcommittee's bill is brought to the floor under a no-amendment rule, then the House membership can either accept or reject the panel's position. If the House rejects the subcommittee's policy recommendation, it has agreed to retain the status quo. Whether the subcommittee's position prevails on the floor can be depicted using these two examples.

If the subcommittee's position is to win on the House floor, it must devise a strategy that takes account of the majority preferences of the membership. Furthermore, the subcommittee must have some way to acquire information about the policy options likely to be accepted by at least a majority of the House. These types of considerations are commonplace in the real world of Capitol Hill policy making.

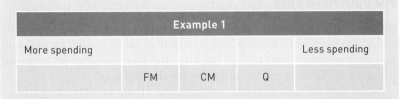

Example 1			
More spending			Less spending
	FM	CM	Q

In Example 1, the preferences of a majority of the House clearly are closer to the committee's position than the status quo. Thus, the committee's position prevails.

Example 2			
More spending			Less spending
	FM	Q	CM

In Example 2, a majority of the House clearly favors the policy status quo instead of the committee's position, which loses in an up-or-down floor vote.

Most bills concern not a single dimension, such as more or less spending, but a multitude of dimensions. For example, a bill might be close to a member's ideal point on the spending dimension but be far away on another dimension, such as which governmental level (federal or state) should handle the issue. The introduction of additional dimensions (multidimensionality) produces greater difficulty in analyzing legislative decision making. By employing spatial theory and other analytical approaches, political scientists strive to better understand and explain congressional politics and decision making.[1]

[1]See, for example, Kenneth Shepsle and Mark Boncheck, *Analyzing Politics* (New York: Norton, 1977); Charles Stewart, *Analyzing Congress* (New York: Norton, 2001); and Gerald Strom, *The Logic of Lawmaking: A Spatial Theory Approach* (Baltimore: Johns Hopkins University Press, 1990).

or cybersecurity, for example). Committees' formal jurisdictional mandates have not kept pace with change—nor can they, given the constant emergence of new issues (such as climate change). Another trigger of turf battles is forum shopping by outside interests, who want their carefully drafted bills referred to sympathetic committees and to work with committee staff to secure a favorable referral from the House or Senate parliamentarian, as the case may be.

The expansionist tendency of some committees also can create intercommittee tussles. The "bold jurisdictional power grab" by the House Energy and Commerce Committee for an intellectual copyright bill will not stand, declared the bipartisan leaders of the Judiciary Committee. "Rest assured, we will wholeheartedly oppose this move in a bipartisan fashion, as we would expect Energy and Commerce leaders to do if we attempted to write energy legislation."[54]

Multiple Referrals

When a bill is introduced in the House, it usually is referred to a single committee. But when legislation falls within more than one committee's jurisdiction, legislation will be *multiply referred,* meaning that more then one committee will act on the bill before it will be reported to the chamber floor.

When Republicans assumed control of the House in 1995, they streamlined multiple referrals and placed them firmly under the Speaker's control. The Speaker must "designate a committee of primary jurisdiction upon the initial referral of a measure to a committee." The primary committee concept increases accountability for legislation while retaining for the Speaker flexibility in determining whether, when, and for how long other panels can receive the measure.

At the time of initial referral, the Speaker identifies the primary committee. It has predominant responsibility for shepherding the legislation to final passage. The Speaker may also send the measure to secondary panels. The House parliamentarian calls this practice an *additional initial referral.* In the following example of referral language, the Energy and Commerce Committee is the primary committee and Judiciary is the additional initial panel:

> H.R. 650. A bill to establish reasonable legal reforms that will facilitate the manufacture of vital, life-saving vaccines, and for other purposes; to the Committee on Energy and Commerce, and in addition to the Committee on the Judiciary, for a period to be subsequently determined by the Speaker, in each case for consideration of such provisions as fall within the jurisdiction of the committee concerned.

Multiple referrals may promote integrated policy making, broader public discussion of issues, wider access to the legislative process, and consideration of alternative approaches. They also enhance the Speaker's scheduling prerogatives. The Speaker can use the referral power to intervene more directly in committee activities and even to set deadlines for committees to report multiply referred legislation. The reverse is also possible: The Speaker can delay action on measures by referring them to other committees. Thus, multiple referrals can be employed to slow down legislative decision making. (Around 20–30 percent of measures introduced in the House are multiply referred.)

The Senate usually sends measures to a single committee—the committee with jurisdiction over the subject matter that predominates in the legislation. Although multiple referrals have long been permitted by unanimous consent, they are used infrequently, mainly because senators have many opportunities to influence policy making on the floor. Senate procedures provide lawmakers with relatively easy ways either to bypass the referral of legislation to committees or to raise issues for chamber consideration (see Chapter 8).

Where Bills Go

Many bills referred to committee are sent by the chair to a subcommittee. Others are retained for review by the full committee. In the end, committees and subcommittees select the measures they want to consider and ignore the rest. Committee consideration usually consists of three standard steps: public hearings, markups, and reports.

Hearings

When committees or subcommittees conduct hearings on a bill, they listen to a wide variety of witnesses. Hearings are an important way for lawmakers to learn and to keep abreast of the policy and oversight issues that come before the committees on which they serve. Witnesses who testify include the bill's sponsors, federal officials, pressure group and think tank representatives, business leaders, academics, state and local officials, and private citizens—sometimes even celebrities. Celebrity witnesses can help give a bill national visibility. As a senator put it, "Quite candidly, when Hollywood speaks, the world listens. Sometimes when Washington speaks, the world snoozes."[55]

Equally important are witnesses who add drama to hearings because of their firsthand experience with an issue or problem. The Senate Committee on Finance, for example, attracted national headlines with its hearings on alleged wrongdoings by the Internal Revenue Service (IRS). Taxpayers recounted their horrendous experiences, and IRS agents donned black hoods to tell about the organization's mistreatment of taxpayers.[56] Testimony by employees who lost their jobs and retirement savings because of corporate scandals and mismanagement helped to galvanize congressional enactment of corporate accounting and accountability laws, such as the landmark Dodd-Frank Wall Street Reform and Consumer Protection Act (P.L. 111–203).[57] Hearings, then, are often orchestrated as political theater in which witnesses put a human face on a public problem and tell stories that may generate public momentum for or against legislation.[58]

Hearings also provide opportunities for committee members to be heard on issues. Frequently, lawmakers present their views on legislation in their opening statements and in the guise of questioning witnesses. By revealing the patterns and intensity of support or opposition and by airing substantive problems, hearings indicate to members whether a bill is worth taking to the full chamber. Most hearings follow a traditional format. Each witness reads a prepared statement. Then, each committee member has a limited time (usually five minutes) to ask questions before the next witness is called. To save time and promote give and take, committees occasionally use a panel format in which witnesses sit together and briefly summarize their statements.

Committees will sometimes convene joint hearings with other relevant House or Senate panels. They also may organize field hearings in cities around the country to generate and solicit public support for an issue or, in a two-Congresses theme, schedule hearings in the chair's state or district to win him or her favorable publicity and visibility prior to the November elections. Party committees, ad hoc legislative groups, or individual lawmakers also may conduct informal hearings of their own. Since the 1970s, committee proceedings have become significantly more open to public observation.

Committee hearings and markups (see below for markups) are regularly televised over C-SPAN (the Cable Satellite Public Affairs Network) and by other broadcasting networks. Committees utilize diverse technology to make the legislative process "fully accessible and transparent" to the public.[59] House and Senate panels employ interactive video, teleconferencing, and other technology to collect testimony from witnesses who may be located in other parts of the nation or the world. The Internet is used to transmit testimony to members, staff, and the interested general public and cable television viewers email or fax questions to witnesses.[60] Many committees also designate digital staff to keep members and the public informed about upcoming hearings. And, in a first, an astronaut became the only person to deliver testimony from outer space to a committee hearing on Capitol Hill.[61] Some of the overlapping purposes served by hearings are the following:

- To explore the need for legislation

- To build a public record in support of legislation

- To publicize the role of committee chairs

- To stake out committee jurisdictions

- To review executive implementation of public laws

- To provide a forum for citizens' grievances and frustrations

- To educate lawmakers and the attentive public on complex issues

- To raise the visibility of an issue

Hearings are shaped mainly by the chairs and their top staff, with varying degrees of input from party leaders, the ranking minority member, and others. Chairs who favor bills can expedite the hearings process; conversely, they can kill with kindness legislation they oppose by holding endless hearings. When a bill is not sent to the full chamber, the printed hearings are the end product of the committee's work. Committee chairs, mindful of the two Congresses, can also use hearings to try to win reelection by addressing issues that appeal to various voting groups in their state or district.

Noteworthy is that at the start of the 116th Congress, frustration over the years with top-down legislating led the House to adopt a series of rules changes to enhance the role of committees and individual members. For example, bills and joint resolutions are not to be made in order for chamber consideration unless they have been subject to committee hearings and markups. Every House committee is also required to hold "Member Day Hearings" during the first session (2019). The purpose is to allow any interested member the opportunity to present their ideas for legislation.

Markups

After hearings are held, committee members decide the bill's actual language—that is, they mark up or amend the bill (see Box 7-3 on committee decision making). Chairs may circulate their "mark" (the measure open for amendment) to committee colleagues and solicit their comments and suggestions.

Some panels adhere closely to parliamentary rules during the committee amending phase; others operate by consensus with few or no votes taken on the issues; and still others have *conceptual markups*. A senator explained that Finance Committee markups "are not about legislative language. They are concept documents that are then put into legislative language and brought to the floor."[62] Concepts may include, for example, whether going to school counts as work for welfare recipients or what kind of tax plan best fosters economic growth. Proponents try to craft a bill that will muster the backing of their colleagues, the other chamber, lobbyists, and the White House.

Not surprisingly, the bill that emerges from markup is usually one that can attract the support of most members. As a former chair of the House Ways and Means Committee stated, "We have not written perfect law; perhaps a faculty of scholars could do a better job. A group of ideologues could have produced greater consistency. But politics is an imperfect process."[63] Or as Sen. Pat Roberts, R-Kans., said about a bill revamping the intelligence community, "While this is not the best possible bill, it is the best bill possible."[64]

Outside pressures often intensify during markup deliberations. Under House and Senate sunshine rules, markups must be conducted in public, except on national security or related issues. Compromises can be difficult to achieve in markup rooms filled with lobbyists watching how each member will vote. Thus, committees sometimes conduct premarkups in private to work out their positions on various issues.

After conducting hearings and markups, a subcommittee sends its recommendations to the full committee. The full committee may conduct hearings and markups on its own, ratify the subcommittee's decision, take no action, or return the matter to the subcommittee for further study.

Reports

If the full committee votes to send the bill to the House or Senate, the staff prepares a report, subject to committee approval, describing the purposes and provisions of the legislation. Reports emphasize arguments favorable to the bill, summarizing selectively the results of staff research and hearings. Reports are noteworthy documents. The bill itself may be long, highly technical, and confusing to most readers. "A good report, therefore, does more than explain—it also persuades," commented a congressional staff aide.[65] Furthermore, reports may guide executive agencies and federal courts in interpreting ambiguous or complex legislative language.

The Policy Environment

Executive agencies, pressure groups, party leaders and caucuses, and the entire House or Senate form the backdrop against which a committee makes policy. (To be sure, outside groups, the 24/7 media, and the broad issue context of a particular period all influence committees' policy environment.) These environments may be consensual or conflictual. Some policy questions are settled fairly easily; others are bitterly controversial. Environments also may be monolithic or pluralistic. Some committees have a single dominant source of outside influence; others face numerous competing groups or agencies.

Environmental factors influence committees in at least four ways. First, they shape the content of public policies and thus the likelihood that these policies will be accepted by the full House or Senate. The judiciary committees are buffeted by diverse and competing pressure groups who feel passionately about volatile issues such as abortion, immigration, and gun control. The committees' chances for achieving agreement among their members or on the floor depend, to a large extent, on their abilities to deflect such issues altogether—or to accommodate diverse groups through artful legislative drafting and political accommodation.

Second, policy environments foster mutual alliances among committees, federal departments, and pressure groups—the *iron triangles.* The House and Senate veterans' affairs committees, for example, regularly advocate legislation to benefit veterans' groups, the second point in the triangle. This effort is backed by the Department of Veterans Affairs, the third point in the triangle. At the very least, issue networks emerge. These are fluid and amorphous groups of policy experts who try to influence any committee that deals with their subject area.[66]

Third, policy environments establish decision-making objectives and guidelines for committees. Clientele-oriented committees, such as the House and Senate small business committees, try to promote the policy views of their clientele groups: small-business enterprises. Alliances between committees and federal departments also shape decisions, such as the traditional support given to the military by the House and Senate armed services committees.

Finally, environmental factors influence the level of partisanship on committees. Some committees are relatively free of party infighting, but other committees consider contentious social issues that often divide the two parties. The House and Senate judiciary committees are filled with conservative Republicans and liberal Democrats; ideological clashes are not uncommon. To try to reduce the intense partisanship on various committees, chairs may organize informal gatherings or bipartisan retreats as a way for committee members "to find common ground despite the strong feelings on a lot of issues."[67]

COMMITTEE STAFF

Staff aides play a big role in the three principal stages of committee policy making: hearings, markup, and report. Representatives and senators (the latter to a greater degree because there are fewer of them) cannot handle their large workloads on their own, so they must rely heavily on their unelected employees. Indeed, Congress needs qualified professional staff to counter the expertise lodged in the executive branch and in the lobbying community. In the House, committee resources are roughly divided between the majority and minority parties on a two-thirds to one-third basis; in the Senate, it is a 60 to 40 percent ratio. Informally, both parties rely on a network of outside experts to help them evaluate proposals from the executive branch, forge policy proposals, or provide strategic advice. For example, think tanks provide lawmakers and their staff with numerous domestic, defense, and foreign policy options and proposals.

The discretionary agenda of Congress and its committees is influenced by congressional staff. Their effectiveness can be direct or indirect, substantive or procedural, visible or invisible. In the judgment of one former senator, "Most of the work and most of the ideas come from the staffers. They are predominantly young men and women, fresh out of college and professional schools. They are ambitious, idealistic, and abounding with ideas."[68] However, staff tenure is relatively short. Studies of selected House and Senate committee staff positions indicate the relatively short service of these aides. For example, the average tenure in years of House committee staff directors was 2.4, and for the Senate, it was 2.7. For minority staff directors for the House, it was two years, and for the Senate, it was 1.3. And for chief counsels of House committees, it was 3.1 years, and for the Senate, it was 2.8 years. Many top committee staff as well as personal and party leadership aides use their experience as a stepping-stone to other jobs, such as lobbying.[69]

There is some concern in Congress that staff working conditions (low salary and long hours) require remediation to improve the recruitment and retention of talented personnel to balance that in the executive branch and lobbying community. Staff reductions at the committee and other levels have arguably weakened the legislative branch's capacity to carry out its policy making and oversight responsibilities. During the Newt Gingrich, R-Ga., speakership (1995–1998), for example, committee staff shrunk by a third, and a nonpartisan legislative support agency (the Office of Technology Assessment) was abolished. In the view of Rep. Bill Pascrell Jr., D-N.J., "our policy staffs, the brains of Congress, have been so depleted that we can't do our jobs properly."[70] Leadership offices in both parties and chambers, however, have seen hikes in their staff resources.

Policy proposals emanate from many sources—lawmakers, the White House, administrative agencies, interest groups, state and local officials, scholars, and citizens, among others—but staff aides are strategically positioned to advance or hinder these proposals. As one Senate committee staff director recounted,

"Usually, you draw up proposals for the year's agenda, lay out the alternatives. You can put in some stuff you like and leave out some you don't. I recommend ideas that the [chair is] interested in and also that I'm interested in."[71]

Many committee staff members are active in outside communications and issue networks (health or the environment, for example) that enhance lawmakers' abilities to make informed decisions.[72] Staff aides negotiate with legislators; lobbyists; their counterparts in the offices of party leaders, other committees, and individual members; and executive officials on issues, legislative language, and political strategy. Staff members do the essential spadework, such as drafting legislation that can lead to changes in policy or new laws. Staff aides sometimes make policy decisions. Consider their crucial role on a defense appropriations bill:

> The dollar figures in the huge piece of legislation [were] so immense that House–Senate conferees, negotiating their differences, . . . relegated almost every item less than $100 million to staff aides on grounds that the members themselves did not have time to deal with such items, which [a senator] called "small potatoes."[73]

In preparation for hearings, aides recruit witnesses, on their own or at the specific direction of the chair, and plan when and in what order they appear. In addition, staff aides commonly accompany committee members to the floor to give advice, draft amendments, and negotiate compromises. The number of aides who can be present on the floor is limited, however, by House and Senate regulations.

For information, analyses, policy options, and research projects, committee staff can turn to the three legislative support agencies: the Congressional Research Service, established in 1914; the Government Accountability Office, established in 1921 (as the General Accounting Office and renamed in 2004); and the Congressional Budget Office, established in 1974. Unlike committee or personal aides, these units operate under strict rules of nonpartisanship and objectivity. Staffed with experts, they provide Congress with analytical talent matching that in executive agencies, universities, and specialized groups.

Staffing reflects members' dual roles in the two Congresses: national policy maker and constituency representative. Lawmakers understand the importance of hiring staff that reflect the diversity and demographics of the nation and the states or districts they represent. Called "descriptive representation" by scholars, both chambers have staff diversity initiatives to recruit and retain a congressional workforce that reflects racial, ethnic, and other demographic characteristics of the people who elect office seekers to Congress. The 116th House even created an Office of Diversity and Inclusion. A diverse staff, like a diverse membership, can broaden the spectrum of views and issues considered during the lawmaking process. During the electoral season, staffers frequently take unpaid leave to work as campaign volunteers for their boss or "to boost their party's prospects in pivotal races."[74]

COMMITTEE REFORM
AND CHANGE

Since passage of the Legislative Reorganization Act of 1946, Congress has made numerous attempts to reform the committee system but has succeeded mainly with limited rather than comprehensive approaches to change. In brief, because of strong opposition from members who stood to surrender subcommittee chairmanships or favored jurisdictions, Congress has had only mixed success in reorganization efforts. One change to the committee system—the creation of the aforementioned House select climate panel—illustrates some of the usual difficulties associated with changes to the committee structure of the House or Senate.

The fundamental point is that proposals that affect committee jurisdictions, such as forming new panels, arouse considerable controversy because jurisdictional "turf" represents power over subject areas. Committees, even on a bipartisan basis, oppose the diminishment of their policy-making authority.

Select Committee on the Climate Crisis

The 116th House created a select committee to address global climate change, a key priority of many senior and newly elected Democrats. Extreme worldwide weather events and the proliferation of studies and academic conferences on the implications of earth's rising temperatures provoked demands that the House address what many viewed as an urgent issue of major international importance. Speaker Nancy Pelosi supported the panel's creation. She said: "Inspired by the energy and activism of the many young organizers and advocates leading the way on the climate crisis, the new Democratic Majority will act decisively to combat the crisis."[75] When Democrats last controlled the House (2007–2011), Speaker Pelosi won chamber approval of a Select Committee on Energy Independence and Global Warming despite opposition from several of her committee chairs.

Fast forward to the 116th House to see a repeat of this pattern. Several committee chairs and members of the standing committees with jurisdiction over global warming pushed back against the Speaker's proposal to re-establish another select climate panel. To reemphasize, jurisdictional "turf" is something that standing committees protect against perceived invaders of their legislative responsibilities. Prominent among the standing committees unenthusiastic about the need for the select committee were Energy and Commerce, Natural Resources, and Science, Space and Technology. The chairs of these committees had their own ideas and plans to make climate change a priority. Members of these panels expressed strong opposition to the proposed select climate committee.

A senior lawmaker of the Energy and Commerce Committee exclaimed: "It's a slap in the face for some of us who have been fighting on this issue for the last eight years. It's going to be confusing at best. Is this a message committee? Why are we wasting the resources just to have a messaging committee? Is this some kind of way to appease certain newly elected members of Congress? I think that's wrongheaded."[76] On the other hand, Peter DeFazio, D-Ore., the chair of Transportation and Infrastructure, backed formation of the select committee. Climate change is "the existential threat to the future of the planet," he said. "I don't think we can have too many members actively involved."[77]

Speaker Pelosi met several times with the skeptical chairs to address their concerns, to stress the need for a climate change select committee, and to reach a consensus on its formation. The Speaker's power to assuage the critics was significant, as indicated by these four points.

First, the Speaker determined the mandate of the select committee—it would have no legislative authority (the right to receive and report legislation)—a key demand of the three chairs. The panel's mission is to investigate, study, and make recommendations on "policies, strategies, and innovations" concerning climate change. Second, all policy recommendations "shall be submitted to the relevant standing committee of jurisdiction not later than March 31, 2020." This provision underscores the primacy and policy-making authority of the standing committees.

Third, House rules authorize the Speaker to appoint members to select committees. In this case, Speaker Pelosi named members to the climate panel from the committees unsupportive of the select panel's formation. Such appointments ensured that these members could defend their home committee's prerogatives. Speaker Pelosi named Rep. Kathy Castor of Florida, one of her allies, as chair of the climate panel. Castor serves on Energy and Commerce and, coming from a state vulnerable to climate change, is well-versed on the topic.

Fourth, the select panel's authorizing resolution stipulated that the panel would not have subpoena power. Opponents of the select panel's creation rejected the idea that a "study and recommend" committee required subpoena authority. To accommodate both proponents and opponents, a compromise was reached. The Select Committee on the Climate Crisis could recommend to the relevant standing committees that they should issue subpoenas to compel the attendance of witnesses at hearings and the production of specific documents.

As for House Republicans, Minority Leader McCarthy encountered difficulties in selecting six from his party to serve on the select climate panel. Republicans were divided as to whether the GOP leader should appoint lawmakers supportive of bipartisan solutions to climate change or those who are likely to challenge costly and economically damaging Democratic climate policies.

On one side was Rep. Francis Rooney of Florida. He said: "I hope [GOP] leaders realize that we need to regain a role in the environmental debate . . . [A]lmost every large company CEO realizes the CO_2 in the industrial era has had an impact on changes in the climate—not maybe the only impact, but a substantial one."[78] On the more skeptical side was Minority Whip Steve Scalise of Louisiana. "I'm not sure what [Democrats are] trying to achieve except to raise the cost of energy in America and make it harder for us to provide for ourselves." He added that Democrats have a "radical agenda" that would "raise energy costs and make it harder for Americans to manufacture and create jobs."[79] With the select committee just getting underway, it is not possible at this juncture to assess its successes, failures, or something in-between.

Committees are remarkably durable, resilient, and stable institutions, despite the periodic forces for change that buffet them (such as public criticism of Congress and reformist sentiment among institutionally minded lawmakers). Major committee restructuring plans often arouse considerable controversy and may produce only marginal adjustments in committees' jurisdictional mandates, policy-making influence, or method of operation. Scholars and lawmakers posit various theories to explain why it is difficult to accomplish major jurisdictional realignment. For example, Speaker Thomas P. "Tip" O'Neill Jr., D-Mass., explained the House's rejection of a major 1973–1974 committee realignment plan in this succinct manner: "The name of the game is power, and the boys don't want to give it up."[80] A political scientist offered an electoral explanation for the demise of committee reshuffling plans that embodies the two-Congresses concept:

[A] primary and constant force hindering committee restructuring movements has been the electoral objectives of members of Congress. Under pressure to bolster their reelection prospects in order to achieve long-term legislative and personal goals, rational politicians with the ability to shape legislative structures utilize the arrangement of rules and procedures to secure targeted government benefits for needy constituents and voting blocs. Any widespread change in the established order of policy deliberation—particularly its centerpiece—the committee system—would create far too much uncertainty in members' electoral strategies and therefore would be broadly opposed from the start.[81]

Whatever other factors (such as interest group, party leadership, or committee member and staff opposition) impede major committee overhaul, these workshops of Congress evolve in response to new events and circumstances. Several recent developments highlight the dynamic quality of the committee system. These include ebbs and flows in the authority of committee chairs, the use of task forces, and the circumvention of the committee process.

Constricting the Authority of Committee Chairs

The contemporary Congress is largely a party-centric institution, compared to the earlier committee-centric era. Rep. John Dingell's lengthy years of service (1955–2015) spanned both periods. Dingell succinctly defined the fundamental difference between the two eras: "It used to be that the chairman would call the Speaker up and say, 'I want this bill on the floor at this time.' Now, it's the opposite."[82]

A host of internal and external factors contributed to this power shift (see Chapter 6). House Democratic reforms of the 1970s weakened seniority and required chairs to be elected by secret vote of their partisan peers (several chairs lost their posts). Second, at least since the 1980s, a volatile and closely divided electorate has led to frequent changes in party control of the House and Senate. This development has heightened the focus of the two parties on winning or retaining majority control. In this political environment, congressional party leaders became more influential in directing committee activities. Centralized control over committees was plainly evident during the speakership of Newt Gingrich (1995–1999), who sometimes circumvented committee consideration of legislation; dictated legislative changes to committees; used the Rules Committee to redraft committee-reported measures; and engaged in other actions that undermined the committee system, such as creating partisan task forces to draft legislation. Two changes made during the Gingrich era that remain in place today require emphasis because they demonstrate party control of the GOP's committee leaders. First, the aforementioned term limits for committee chairs prevent the return of powerful committee barons, like Representative Dingell, who could challenge the Speaker's leadership. Second, Gingrich took control of the committee assignment process, set aside seniority as the principal criterion in choosing committee leaders, and stressed qualities such as party loyalty and fund-raising in naming committee chairs.

Speaker Dennis Hastert, R-Ill. (1999–2011), was not reluctant to rein in committee chairs. He decided to use an interview process to determine replacements for full committee chairs who had completed their six years.[83] Hastert also made it known that there was no guarantee that chairs would be permitted to serve their full six-year term if they aroused the ire of party leaders. In an unprecedented event, Hastert ousted a colleague in 2004 (Christopher Smith of New Jersey) as chair of the Veterans' Affairs Committee, removed him from the panel, and named another member as chair. Smith's offense was this: his outspoken advocacy of more spending on veterans' benefits. The message of Smith's removal was plain to every Republican: Toe the party line, and be a team player, or you will be benched.

As a former committee chair, Speaker John Boehner, R-O. (2011–2015) wanted to follow the "regular order" and allow committees to produce legislative products by observing the usual deliberative process of hearings, markups, and reports. He promised that "no more bills [would be] written behind closed doors in the speaker's office. Bills should be written by legislators in committee in plain public view."[84] The reality was different, however. Significant measures were the product of private negotiations among the top House party leaders, particularly the Speaker, Senate leaders (with Senate GOP leader Mitch McConnell often playing a key role), Vice President Joe Biden, and President Barack Obama.

Like the previous Speakers, Paul Ryan, R-Wisc. (2015–2019), also promised to rely on committees. When he gave his first address to the House as Speaker-elect on October 29, 2015, he declared, "Let's be frank. The House is broken. . . . The committees should retake the lead in drafting all major legislation." Ryan did have some successes in fulfilling his promises in the 114th Congress by mainly bringing measures to the chamber reported from committee and by allowing a relatively open floor amendment process.[85] On the other hand, deference to committees and open floor procedures, especially on appropriations bills, created some pushback from rank-and-file Republicans who had to cast difficult votes—providing campaign ammunition to Democratic challengers. The result: a surge in structured and closed rules for the remainder of Ryan's time as Speaker (see Chapter 8).

With the opening of the 116th Congress (2019–2021), it is too soon to assess whether Speaker Pelosi's centralized leadership style, often manifested during her first speakership, would continue or change to reflect new legislative conditions and House rules. She would like to "make the House more bipartisan and empower the rank-and-file."[86] Whether and to what extent significant decentralizing changes occur (e.g., empowering committees) is uncertain, especially with a divided Congress and the critical 2020 elections ahead.

Senate committee chairs also are subject to direction from their party leadership. For example, when Harry Reid, D-Nev., was Senate majority leader (2007–2015), he told the Finance chair to "stop chasing Republican votes on [President Obama's] massive health care reform bill."[87] When political momentum began to build for enactment of an earlier health measure, another majority leader took the issue away from the chair of the Health, Education, Labor, and Pensions Committee and "created a [party] task force . . . to write the . . . bill."[88] The point is that on measures of utmost party importance, congressional leaders will often override the prerogatives of committee chairs to take control of crucial agenda items.

To sum up, the ability of today's party leaders, particularly in the House, to exercise significant control over committee leaders represents a major change in how Congress works. Committee chairs are subject to centralized leadership direction on the party's top priorities and might face sanctions if their performance does not comport with party expectations. On the one hand, this development ensures that the chairs (and ranking minority members) are ultimately accountable for their actions to the Democratic Caucus or Republican Conference. On the other hand, tight leadership control, combined with term limits for House and Senate Republicans, attenuates the traditional role of committees as the policy specialization system for the legislative branch. Why bother to devote years of effort to becoming substantive experts, some committee members might ask, if policy on major issues is decided at the top and GOP committee leaders are forced to relinquish their posts after six years (if not sooner)?

Party Task Forces and "Gangs"

Speaker Gingrich was noted for creating numerous party task forces, in part because he could determine their mandate and timetable, appoint the chair and members, and assign a deadline for drafting a product. Many of these task forces did little, but some wrote legislation. Indeed, task forces can forge consensus, draft legislation, coordinate strategy, promote intraparty communication, and involve noncommittee members and junior members in issue areas. Speakers also have created partisan or bipartisan task forces to conduct studies, investigate matters, or propose measures.

Senate leaders also form party task forces, sometimes to showcase senators up for reelection (the "two Congresses") and to promote party priorities. For example, a senator up for reelection was named by Republican leader McConnell to head the GOP's high-tech task force.[89] Party task forces are also created to develop legislative plans or ameliorate internal party conflict. Senate GOP leader Bob Dole of Kansas (1985–1996) established a party task force to cool the passions of junior Republicans who wanted to oust the Appropriations chair (Mark Hatfield of Oregon) because he did not vote in 1995 for a top GOP priority, a constitutional balanced-budget amendment. The task force came up with term limits for committee chairs.

A variation on task forces in both chambers is what commentators call "gangs." They are lawmakers of both parties in each house who come together to advance major issues that the relevant committees of jurisdiction are hard-pressed to resolve because of ideological, partisan, or other divisions. In the view of an insightful commentator, "With polarization increasingly clogging the conventional paths to agreement (either at the committee level or through leadership), [lawmakers] convene a coalition of the willing to chart a bypass." Another analyst noted that committees "have been bypassed so many times by the leadership that they are not [always] the venue [for deal-making] anymore."[90] The "gang of eight" in the 113th Senate—composed of four Democrats and four Republicans—is a good example of this phenomenon. This gang played a major role in securing Senate passage, in 2013, of a comprehensive immigration reform measure. At the same time, the House also created a bipartisan gang of members, led by Rep. Mario Diaz-Balart, R-Fla., who met in secret to craft an immigration reform bill that might pass the House. By early 2014, they began to share the contents of their proposed bill with lawmakers they trusted. The two Congresses soon ended hopes for House enactment of immigration reform. In a stunning upset, Majority Leader Eric Cantor, R-Va., was defeated in a party primary by a little-known challenger (former two-term Rep. David Brat, who was defeated in the 2018 midterm elections), who castigated Cantor as a secret advocate of "amnesty" for illegal aliens. The outcome was this: support faded quickly among Republicans for immigration reform.[91]

Bypassing Committees

It has not been unusual in recent years for House and Senate party leaders to bypass some or all of the stages of committee consideration of legislation. In general, the circumvention of committees reflects the dominance of party power over committee power. It also represents Congress's focus on partisan gain over cooperative policy making. Specific reasons for bypassing committees are noteworthy. For example, heightened partisanship in certain committees encourages party leaders to take charge of priority measures to avoid negative media coverage of committee markups. Or factional disputes within committees may prevent them from reaching agreement on measures deemed important to party leaders. Time is a factor as well. Party leaders may believe there is not enough time for committees to hold hearings and markups on major bills they want to consider within a certain time period. Wanting fast action early in the 115th Congress to overturn unwanted regulations promulgated by the Obama administration—a top campaign promise of President Trump's—House Republicans brought a number of regulatory repeal bills to the floor absent any committee hearings and markups and under a closed amendment floor process. While some analysts contend that "there are few consequences if [committees are bypassed] because nobody outside Congress cares whether a bill went through committee or not,"[92] many committee chairs and rank-and-file lawmakers are frustrated as the careful legislating made possible by committees takes a back seat to other considerations, such as political messaging.[93]

CONCLUSION

Several generalizations can be made about congressional committees today. First, they shape the House and Senate agendas. Not only do they have negative power—pigeonholing legislation referred to them—but they have positive power as well. The bills they report largely determine what each chamber will debate and in what form. As one House chair stated in his testimony before the Joint Committee on the Organization of Congress, committees

> provide Congress with the expertise, skill, and organizational structure
> necessary to cope with the increasingly complex and technical questions
> in both the domestic and international arenas. They also ensure a
> forum for the broadest possible participation of diverse interests and
> constituencies in the formative stages of the legislative process. They are,
> in short, the window through which much of the democratic participation
> in lawmaking is made possible.[94]

Second, committees differ in their policy-making environments, mix of members, decision-making objectives, and ability to fulfill individual members' goals. Recruitment methods reinforce committees' autonomy; they frequently are imbalanced ideologically or geographically. And they are likely to advocate policies espoused by agencies and outside groups interested in their work.

Third, some committees still have an *esprit de corps* that flows across party lines, in part because these panels have developed a culture of bipartisanship. The military panels are a good example. Despite intermittent partisan clashes, for the past fifty-five years, the House and Senate armed services committees have never failed to win enactment into law of the annual National Defense Authorization

Act. Committee members usually will defend their panels against criticisms or jurisdictional trespassing and criticize attempts to bypass them.

Fourth, committees typically operate independently of one another. This long-time custom fosters an attitude of mutual noninterference in the work of other committees. However, multiple referrals of bills spawn broader interrelationships among committees.

Fifth, the committee system contributes fundamentally to policy fragmentation, although a few committees—such as the House's Rules and Budget committees—act as policy coordinators for Congress. "This is one of the anomalies here," remarked a House member. "In order to attain legislative efficiency, we say that we have to break down into committees with specialized jurisdictions. When you do that, you lose your ability to grapple with the big problems."[95] As a result, party leaders are more involved than ever in coordinating policy making and forging winning coalitions in committees and on the floor.

Finally, committee autonomy is far weaker today than it was before the 1970s, as assertive party leaders strive to move the party's agenda forward and promote party cohesion—with or without the committee leaders' cooperation. Gone are the days when committee chairs were known as the "dukes" and "barons" of Capitol Hill. In brief, the balance of power in Congress has shifted to party leaders.

House and Senate Chambers. Senators sit at assigned desks in the elegant Senate chamber. The House Speaker's chair is in front of the flag and to the left of the Mace—a symbol of the authority of the Sergeant at Arms that, on rare occasions, may be hoisted and displayed to quell disturbances in the chamber. The seats below are for clerks, and the box in the foreground is the "hopper," where members may place amendments for House consideration. The House chamber, seen from the rear, shows the Speaker's rostrum as well as the galleries and lawmakers' seats. Members do not have assigned seats, but the majority and minority committee leaders' tables are seen to the right.

CONGRESSIONAL RULES
AND PROCEDURES

Congress needs written rules to do its work. Compiling the Senate's first parliamentary manual, Thomas Jefferson stressed the importance of a known system of rules:

> It is much more material that there should be a rule to go by, than what the rule is; that there may be uniformity of proceeding in business not subject to the caprice of the Speaker or captiousness of the members. It is very material that order, decency, and regularity be preserved in a dignified public body.[1]

If Jefferson returned to view lawmaking in today's House and Senate, he might wonder why some of his parliamentary precepts, such as uniformity and regularity in lawmaking, are sometimes followed and sometimes not. Compared to earlier periods, legislative processes in today's Congress are more flexible and unpredictable. Legislation today follows a variety of procedural paths, sometimes traditional and at other times highly improvisational.[2]

No matter the process employed, lawmaking is seldom easy, given the "checks and balances" constitutional design and the diversity of the nation. Compounding the difficulty of legislating are the two parties' intense policy differences and their fiery electoral battles for control of the House and Senate. The minority party employs procedural maneuvers to block the majority party's priorities in order to run against a "do nothing" Congress. To "get control of the process" and win enactment of their legislative priorities, the majority party may employ, in the words of a congressional scholar and former aide to a Senate majority leader, "exotic procedures that are incomprehensible" to all but a few parliamentary experts.[3]

Extraordinary processes are used in lawmaking because they might be the only way to achieve policy results. For instance, unable to enact into law each of the dozen appropriations bills in the required yearly time period, the outstanding spending measures are bundled together in lengthy omnibus measures—often right before an impending government shutdown—and enacted with little time for scrutiny, debate, or amendment. Omnibus bills are not new to Congress (more on this below). What is different is their frequency—provoked by sharp partisan, bicameral, and legislative-executive conflicts—and, importantly, how they are used.

Since the mid-1990s, the threat or reality of government shutdowns or credit defaults—the government's failure to pay its debts in a timely manner—have become part of the procedural and political toolkit to influence policy making. Deadline lawmaking has long been commonplace on Capitol Hill. Each side waits until the last days (or hours) to heighten their bargaining leverage in order to win the compromises they want. What is new today is that many contemporary lawmakers, even the president, employ brinkmanship tactics to inflict domestic, financial, and global pain in their attempt to compel capitulation by the other side. Sometimes the "my way or the highway" works and sometimes not.[4] Whatever the outcome, this form of governance undermines public confidence in our elective branches.

Jefferson preferred an orderly and deliberative lawmaking process, but legislating is often messy, untidy, or disjointed. A noted House member wrote that no diagram or figure can depict "the difficulties facing any member [or party] of Congress who wants to shepherd an idea into law" because legislating is "dynamic, fluid, and unpredictable."[5] The dynamic character of lawmaking inheres in the Constitution (Article I, section 5): "Each House may determine the Rules of its Proceedings." In practice, this means that procedural revisions reflect the majority (or supermajority) preferences of the House or Senate membership.

House and Senate rules serve diverse purposes, such as to protect majority and minority rights, divide the workload, help contain conflict, encourage fair play, and distribute power among members. Because formal rules cannot cover every contingency, precedents—accumulated decisions of House Speakers and Senate presiding officers—fill in the gaps. These precedents are codified by House and Senate parliamentarians, published in many large volumes and distributed to lawmakers. Members are also constrained by informal expectations or norms of behavior, such as honoring commitments to colleagues.[6] Such norms are commonly transmitted from incumbent members to newcomers.

Before bills become laws, they typically pass successfully through several stages in each house. Figure 8-1 offers a simplified view of the traditional lawmaking process. Although this traditional process is less often used than in the past, many bills still do traverse the steps laid out here.

As shown in Figure 8-1, bills face a procedural obstacle course. Bills that fail to attract majority (sometimes supermajority) support at any critical juncture may never be passed. In short, the legislative process favors opponents of legislation

FIGURE 8-1 ■ How a Bill Becomes Law

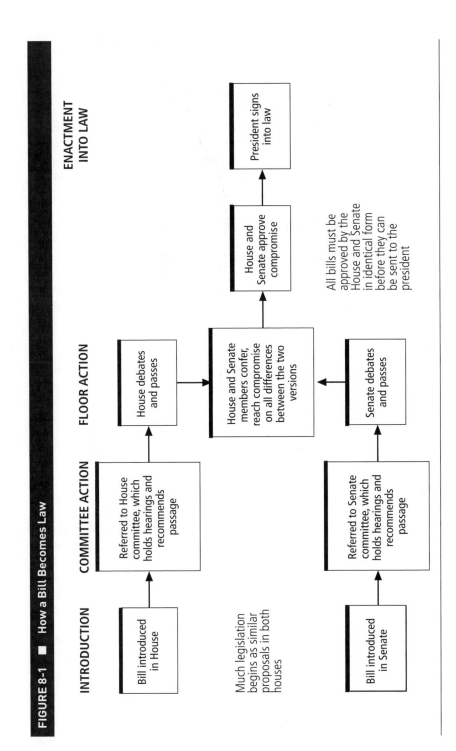

INTRODUCTION   COMMITTEE ACTION   FLOOR ACTION   ENACTMENT INTO LAW

Bill introduced in House

Referred to House committee, which holds hearings and recommends passage

House debates and passes

House and Senate members confer, reach compromise on all differences between the two versions

House and Senate approve compromise

President signs into law

Much legislation begins as similar proposals in both houses

Bill introduced in Senate

Referred to Senate committee, which holds hearings and recommends passage

Senate debates and passes

All bills must be approved by the House and Senate in identical form before they can be sent to the president and hinders proponents. This defensive advantage encourages bargaining and compromise at each decision point.

Congressional rules are not independent of the policy and power struggles that lie behind them. The process shown in Figure 8-1 may be circumvented in favor of a more streamlined approach that bypasses committee consideration altogether. Indeed, there is very little the House and Senate cannot do under the rules so long as the action is backed by votes and inclination. And yet votes and inclination are not easily obtained, and the rules persistently challenge the proponents of legislation to demonstrate that they have both resources at their command.

INTRODUCTION OF BILLS

Only members of Congress can introduce legislation. Often embedded in these measures are a number of assumptions—for example, that a problem exists, that it can best be resolved through enactment of a federal law instead of allowing administrative agencies or state and local governments to handle it, and that the proposed solution contained in the bill ameliorates rather than exacerbates the problem.

Lawmakers introduce legislation for many reasons: personal, political, and policy. When gasoline prices rise, members respond in two-Congresses fashion by introducing numerous energy-related bills. Members introduce bills for reasons that go beyond their desire to pass laws. They introduce bills to lay claim to an issue; to spark public debate; to respond to constituent concerns; to suggest alternative approaches to problem solving; or to send political or policy "messages" to various entities, including the White House, federal agencies, the other legislative chamber, and interest groups.

Another motivation for bill introduction is a personal brush with adversity. Congress is an intensely human place, where personal experience sometimes has powerful repercussions.[7] As a senator stated, "Each of us, as United States senators, comes to . . . this public place with the sum of our beliefs, our personal experience and our values, and none of us checks them at the door."[8] Representative Lucy McBath, D-Ga., is a forceful advocate for gun control. Why? Her 17-year old son was shot and killed at a gas station after a confrontation with a man who complained about the loud music in the teen's SUV. As one journalist observed, "Much is made of the so-called intersection of policy and politics. Hardly noticed, but perhaps more important to lawmakers themselves, is the intersection of policy and personal affairs, the bills that directly play a role in the lives of lawmakers and their loved ones."[9] Beyond personal experience, members get ideas for bills from numerous sources, such as the executive branch, interest groups, scholars, state and local officials, constituents, the media, and their own staff.

A member who introduces a bill becomes its sponsor. He or she may seek cosponsors to demonstrate wide support for the legislation. Outside groups also may urge members to cosponsor measures. "We were not assured of a hearing," said a lobbyist of a bill that his group was pushing. "So it was very important

BOX 8-1 TYPES OF LEGISLATION

Bill

- Most legislative proposals before Congress are in a bill form.
- Bills are designated H.R. (House of Representatives) or S. (Senate) according to where they originate, followed by a number assigned in the order in which they were introduced, from the beginning of each two-year congressional term.
- Public bills deal with general questions and become public laws if approved by Congress and signed by the president.
- Private bills deal with individual matters, such as claims against the government, immigration and naturalization cases, and land titles. They become private laws if approved and signed by the president.

Joint Resolution

- A joint resolution, designated H. J. Res. or S. J. Res., requires the approval of both houses and the president's signature, just as a bill does, and has the force of law.
- No significant difference exists between a bill and a joint resolution. The latter generally deals with limited matters, such as a single appropriation for a specific purpose.
- Joint resolutions are used to propose constitutional amendments, which do not require presidential signatures but become a part of the Constitution when three-fourths of the states have ratified them.

Concurrent Resolution

- A concurrent resolution, designated H. Con. Res. or S. Con. Res., must be passed by both houses but does not require the president's signature and does not have the force of law.
- Concurrent resolutions generally are used to make or amend rules applicable to both houses or to express their joint sentiment. A concurrent resolution, for example, is used to fix the time for adjournment of a Congress and to express Congress's annual budgeting plan. It might also be used to convey the congratulations of Congress to another country on the anniversary of its independence.

Resolution

- A simple resolution, designated H. Res. or S. Res., deals with matters entirely within the prerogatives of one house.
- It requires neither passage by the other chamber nor approval by the president and does not have the force of law.
- Most resolutions deal with the rules of one house. They also are used to express the sentiments of a single house, to extend condolences to the family of a deceased member, or to give advice on foreign policy or other executive business.

to line up a lot of cosponsors to show the over-all concern."[10] A two-Congresses dimension is also evident in signing (or not signing) on to legislation. For example, a lawmaker may cosponsor a labor bill to win the support of union workers back home. Conversely, the lawmaker may decide against cosponsoring the labor bill because it would mobilize business groups to oppose his or her reelection. Vulnerable lawmakers up for reelection may cosponsor measures offered by opposition members to broaden their appeal to voters in both major parties.

Equally important as the number of cosponsors is their identity, especially their leadership status and ideological stance. Members often seek out cosponsors from the opposing party to signal that the bill transcends partisan politics. In an unusual cosponsorship pairing, the former House chairs of their respective party campaign committees joined to introduce bipartisan legislation on campaign finance.[11] When Sen. Ted Kennedy, D-Mass., an outspoken liberal, served in the Senate with Sen. Strom Thurmond, R-S.C., a southern conservative, he exclaimed, "Whenever Strom and I introduce a bill together, it is either an idea whose time has come, or one of us has not read the bill."[12]

Although identifying a bill's sponsors is easy, pinpointing its real initiators may be difficult. Legislation is "an aggregate, not a simple production," wrote Woodrow Wilson. "It is impossible to tell how many persons, opinions, and influences have entered into its composition."[13] President John F. Kennedy, for example, usually is given credit for initiating the Peace Corps. But Theodore Sorensen, Kennedy's special counsel, recalled that the Peace Corps was

> based on the Mormon and other voluntary religious service efforts, on an editorial Kennedy had read years earlier, on a speech by General [James] Gavin, on a luncheon I had with Philadelphia businessmen, on the suggestions of [Kennedy's] academic advisers, on legislation previously introduced and on the written response to a spontaneous late-night challenge he issued to Michigan students.[14]

In short, many bills have complex origins.

Required legislation, particularly funding measures, make up much of Congress's annual agenda. Bills that authorize programs and specify how much money can be spent on them (authorization bills) and bills that provide the money (appropriations bills) appear on Congress's schedule at about the same time each year. Other matters recur at less frequent intervals, every five years perhaps. Emergency issues require Congress's immediate attention. Activist legislators also push proposals onto Congress's program.

Bills not acted on die automatically at the end of each two-year Congress. "Anybody can drop a bill into the hopper [a mahogany box near the Speaker's podium where members place their proposed bills]," said a House GOP leader. "The question is, Can you make something happen with it?"[15]

In many cases, the ideas in bills that are never passed can still become law in other ways. For example, a twenty-three-year veteran of the House who was criticized for introducing 640 unsuccessful measures during his service refuted the contention that he was "the nation's least successful lawmaker of the past two decades" by pointing out that many of his ideas "were a seed planted . . . in a larger bill." In fact, the member estimated that 110 of his ideas became law "after being stuck in somebody else's bill."[16]

Drafting

"As a sculptor works in stone or clay, the legislator works in words," observed one member.[17] Words are the building blocks of policy, and legislators frequently battle over adding, deleting, or modifying terms and phrases. One word, such as *may* or *shall,* can have significant implications in forging legislative coalitions. For instance, a crucial bloc of members might support a measure if it is drafted to allow certain requirements to be permissive rather than mandatory.

Members increasingly give their bills eye-catching titles to attract media attention and for partisan message purposes. For example, when Barack Obama was president, GOP lawmakers introduced bills with titles such as the Reducing Barack Obama's Unsustainable Deficit Act.[18] Titles, such as the Violence Against Women Act, also have a two-Congresses dimension. "Obviously, you want to be for [that] title," remarked Sen. Roy Blunt, R-Mo. "If Republicans can't be for it, we need to have a very convincing alternative."[19] Creative acronyms are also increasingly popular on Capitol Hill because they attract public attention. Consider the DREAM Act (Development, Relief, and Education for Alien Minors), the STOP Act (Synthetics Trafficking and Overdose Prevention), or a bill addressing government shutdowns titled the STUPIDITY Act (Stop Shutdowns Transferring Unnecessary Pain and Inflicting Damage In The Coming Years).

Although bills are introduced only by members, anyone can draft them.[20] Expert drafters in the House and Senate offices of the legislative counsel assist members and committees in writing legislation. Executive agencies and lobbying groups also often prepare measures for introduction by friendly legislators. Many home-state industries, for example, draft narrowly tailored tariff or regulatory measures that enhance their business prospects. These proposals are then introduced by local lawmakers—another instance of the two-Congresses linkage. As a senatorial aide explained, the senator sometimes "just introduces [bills] as a courtesy to his constituents."[21] (See Box 8-1 outlining the four basic types of legislation: bills, joint resolutions, concurrent resolutions, and simple resolutions.)

Regularly, as noted, Congress frequently acts on comprehensive (omnibus) bills or resolutions (sometimes called packages or megabills by the press). Packages contain an array of issues that were once handled as separate pieces of legislation. Their increasing use stems, in part, from members' reluctance to make hard political decisions without a package arrangement. A House Budget Committee chair once explained their attractiveness. As he stated,

> Large bills can be used to hide legislation that otherwise might be more controversial. By packaging difficult issues in measures that command broad support, they enable members to avoid hard votes that they

would have to account for at election time and allow members to avoid angering special-interest groups that use votes [to decide] contributions to campaigns. Leaders can also use them to slam-dunk issues that otherwise might be torn apart or to pressure the President to accept provisions that he objects to.[22]

The packaging process strengthens the hand of majority party leaders because they can influence the megabill's substance—what it contains and what is left out—as well as the procedures for its consideration (often limited time for debating and amending). Majority party leaders might also use deadline lawmaking to minimize dilatory tactics by opposition lawmakers. The strategy is this: Bring a "must-pass" package to the floor near a critical deadline that, if missed, could provoke a bad outcome (a government shutdown). Or majority party leaders could forestall a planned adjournment of their respective chambers and require lawmakers to stay in continuous session to resolve the outstanding matter, thus missing important constituency commitments and events back home.

Conversely, majority party leaders might want to avoid drafting megabills and instead opt for a series of piecemeal measures. Mindful of the two Congresses during the lead-up to the November 2018 mid-term elections, House GOP leaders urged party colleagues facing tough reelection to introduce bills dealing with the opioid crisis, a priority issue for numerous voters. Many of the opioid bills had Democratic cosponsors, which enabled vulnerable Republicans to highlight their willingness to work in a bipartisan manner to solve critical national problems.[23]

Timing

"Everything in politics is timing," Speaker Thomas P. "Tip" O'Neill Jr., D-Mass. (1977–1987), used to say. A bill's success or failure often hinges on when it is introduced or brought to the floor. A bill that might have succeeded early in a session could fail as adjournment nears. However, controversial legislation can sometimes be rushed through during the last hectic days of a Congress. "You do learn that everything has its time," noted, a former chair of the Committee on Foreign Relations. You "just wait for the moment which is going to be the best environment."[24]

Elections greatly influence the timing of legislation. Policy issues can be taken off or kept on Congress's agenda because of electoral circumstances—a good illustration of how the two Congresses are inextricably connected. For example, coming off of major electoral successes, parties will usually try to capitalize on their momentum with quick action early in the new Congress. Noteworthy examples are the House's action, in 1995, on the ten-point, hundred-day Contract with America agenda heralded by Speaker Newt Gingrich, R-Ga., and the hundred-hour legislative agenda pushed in 2007 by Speaker Nancy Pelosi, D-Calif.

The majority party's plans for a fast legislative start following a November election victory sometimes fail to materialize. This was the case for Democrats after they reclaimed control of the House in the November 2018 elections after eight years as the minority party. The 116th Congress convened on January 3, 2019, but committee hearings on their top priority—the "For the People" Act (H.R. 1), a comprehensive reform package dealing with campaign finance, ethics, voting rights, and other matters—did not get underway until late January. The record-setting 35-day partial government shutdown stalled legislative action on other issues. The shutdown consumed much of the time and focus of the House and made it impossible for the new majority to advance an ambitious legislative agenda in the early weeks of 2019.

Referral of Bills

After bills are introduced, they are referred formally to the appropriate standing committees by the Senate presiding officer or the House Speaker. (In practice, however, measures are referred by the Senate or House parliamentarian, who is the official procedural adviser to each chamber's presiding officer.)

A bill's phraseology can affect its referral and therefore its chances of passage. This political fact of life means that members use words artfully when drafting legislation. The objective is to encourage the referral of their measures to sympathetic, not hostile, committees. If a bill mentions taxes, for example, it invariably is referred to the tax panels. In a classic case of circumventing the Committee on Finance, GOP Senator Pete Domenici of New Mexico avoided the word *tax* in a bill proposing a charge on waterborne freight:

> If the waterway fee were considered a tax—which it was, basically, because it would raise revenues for the federal treasury—the rules would place it under the dominion of the Senate's tax-writing arm, the Finance Committee. But Finance was chaired by Russell B. Long, of Louisiana, whose state included two of the world's biggest barge ports and who was, accordingly, an implacable foe of waterway charges in any form. Domenici knew that Long could find several years' worth of bills to consider before he would voluntarily schedule a hearing on S. 790 [the Domenici bill]. For this reason, [Domenici staff aides] had been careful to avoid the word *tax* in writing the bill, employing such terms as *charge* and *fee* instead.[25]

Domenici's drafting strategy worked. His bill was jointly referred to the commerce and the environment committees, on which he served. Because committees' jurisdictional mandates are ambiguous and overlap, it is not unusual for legislation to be referred to two or more committees—the concept of "one bill, many committees." So-called *multiple referrals* are common in the House, less so in the Senate. In the Senate, they require unanimous consent to implement. Furthermore, all senators have many opportunities to influence committee-reported measures or matters, regardless of whether they serve on the panel of jurisdiction (see Box 8-2, which describes how parliamentary convention affects the reference of legislation).

Of the thousands of bills introduced each year, Congress takes up relatively few. During the 115th Congress (2017–2018), 11,416 public bills and joint resolutions were introduced, but only 338 (2.9 percent) became public laws, many naming post offices and federal buildings. Many more public laws were enacted in earlier Congresses: for example, 640 in the 90th (1967–1969) and 590 in the 99th (1985–1987). Part of the general decline in the number of laws enacted can be explained by the use of omnibus or megabills. The decline may also stem from the widespread congressional sentiment that more laws may not be the answer to the nation's problems. But the decline also reflects political stalemates resulting from the complexity of issues, the intensity of partisanship, legislative–executive and bicameral conflicts, and the narrow party divisions in Congress. Lawmakers understand that most of the bills they introduce are unlikely, as stand-alone measures, to become law. Members know that the ideas encapsulated in their legislation can be "added as amendments to a larger bill or negotiated into a markup or conference report."[26]

Lawmaking is an arduous and intricate process. As a Senate GOP leader noted, "That's the way Congress works. You work for two years and finally you get to the end and either it all collapses in a puddle or you get a breakthrough."[27] Or as former representative John Dingell, D-Mich., the longest-serving (59 years) lawmaker in U.S. history in either chamber, phrased it, "Legislation is hard, pick-and-shovel work," and it often "takes a long time to do it."[28]

Once committees complete action on the bills referred to them, the House and Senate rules require a majority of the full committee to be physically present to report (vote) out any measure. If this rule is violated and not waived, a point of order can be made against the proposal on the floor. (A point of order is a parliamentary objection that halts the proceedings until the chamber's presiding officer decides whether the contention is valid.)

Bills reported from committee have passed a critical stage in the lawmaking process. The next major step is to reach the House or Senate floor for debate and amendment. The discussion that follows begins with the House because tax and appropriations bills originate there—the former under the Constitution, the latter by custom.

SCHEDULING IN THE HOUSE

All bills reported from committee in the House are listed in chronological order on one of several calendars. Bills that raise or spend money directly or indirectly are assigned to the Union Calendar. The House Calendar contains non-money-related public measures, such as proposed constitutional amendments. Private bills, such as immigration requests or claims against the government, are assigned to the Private Calendar. A new "Consensus Calendar" was created by Democrats on January 3, 2019, the start of the 116th Congress. Its purpose is to provide another avenue to the floor for measures that meet two criteria: They have 290 cosponsors, and the primary committees of jurisdiction have not reported the bills.[29] (See a discussion of the Discharge Calendar, which follows.)

There is no guarantee that the House will debate legislation placed on any of these calendars. The Speaker, in consultation with party and committee leaders, the president (under unified government), and others largely determine whether, when, how, and in what order bills come up. In recent years, the majority leader has assumed the role of managing the day-to-day schedule of the House. The Speaker, however, remains the ultimate decider.

The Speaker's agenda-setting authority is bolstered by rules and precedents upholding the principle of *majority rule,* a fundamental House characteristic. Majority rule means that in the House, a united and determined voting majority—whether partisan or bipartisan—will prevail over resolute opposition. In the polarized environment of the contemporary House, majority rule typically means extensive control of decision making by the majority party.

As for the minority party's role in today's hyperpartisan House, it is often limited to messaging and obstructing. Reflecting on his time as a minority lawmaker, Patrick McHenry, R-N.C., exclaimed that "being in the minority in the House is the absolute worst, most painful position to be in" because the majority party controls the levers of institutional power: committee chairmanships, control of the agenda, dominance of the Rules Committee, larger committee staffs, and so on.[30]

Shortcuts for Minor Bills

Whether a bill is major or minor and controversial or noncontroversial influences the procedure employed to bring it before the House. Most bills are relatively minor and are taken up and passed through various shortcut procedures.

One especially important routine and time-saving procedure for considering minor or relatively noncontroversial measures is suspension of the rules. The procedure is in order Monday, Tuesday, and Wednesday of each week but controlled by the Speaker through the power of recognizing who may speak. ("Mr. Speaker, I move to suspend the rules and pass H.R. 1234.") The vote on this motion simultaneously suspends House rules and enacts (or rejects) the measure. Most public laws enacted by the House are accomplished through this procedure. An analysis of the 115th Congress (2017–2018) found that 63 percent of lawmaking vehicles (bills and joint resolutions) reached the floor via suspension-of-the-rules procedure.[31] Legislation considered under suspension of the rules does not have to be reported from committee before the full House takes it up. Importantly, the suspension procedure permits only forty minutes of debate, allows no amendments, and requires a two-thirds vote for passage. The procedure is often favored by bill managers who want to avoid unfriendly amendments and points of order against their legislation. Bills that fail under suspension can return again to the floor by a rule issued by the Rules Committee (discussed later in this chapter). The majority leadership "does not ordinarily schedule bills for suspension unless confident of a two-thirds vote."[32]

BOX 8-2   RULES AND REFERRAL STRATEGY

Sometimes, the Senate's rules can be so arcane that it takes major strategy sessions to get even the most routine bills through the legislature.

That was the case when Sen. Bob Graham, D-Fla. (1987–2005), drafted a bill (targeted only at Florida) to permit the Forest Service to sell eighteen tracts of land and use the proceeds to buy up patches of private lands within the Apalachicola National Forest. To ensure that such a low-profile bill moved, Graham wanted it to go through the Energy and Natural Resources Committee, on which he sat.

Instead, Parliamentarian Alan S. Frumin told Graham's aides that the bill, which was soon to be introduced, would be referred to the Agriculture, Nutrition, and Forestry Committee. Because Graham was not a member, such a move could have guaranteed the bill a quiet death.

Why the Agriculture Committee? For at least four decades, the jurisdiction over land bills has been split between the two committees. Bills affecting land east of the 100th Meridian—which runs through North Dakota and South Dakota and the middle of Texas—are assigned to Agriculture while bills that affect lands west of it go to Energy.

Graham's bill dealt with the wrong side of the country. To change Frumin's mind, Graham's aides needed to turn the rules to their advantage.

They found their opportunity by uncovering the roots behind the 100th Meridian rule. The idea was to divide jurisdiction between public lands and privately owned lands. Because most land on the East Coast is privately owned, that side of the country went to Agriculture, which had jurisdiction over private lands. Everything in the West fell to Energy, which had jurisdiction over public lands.

Graham's aides, however, found out that a majority of tracts in Florida were always public lands. That persuaded Frumin that the bill belonged to the Energy panel.

Source: Adapted from David Nather, "Graham Turns Rules to His Advantage," *CQ Weekly,* June 8, 2002, 1494.

The heightened partisanship in the closely divided House raises the question of why the suspension procedure, which requires bipartisanship to attract the two-thirds vote, is being employed more and more in such a polarized institution. The answer seems to involve a trade-off. "As members are increasingly being denied opportunities in special rules to offer amendments to more substantive bills on the floor," explained Donald R. Wolfensberger, former staff director of the House Committee on Rules, "the leadership is providing alternative mechanisms to satisfy members' policy influence and reelection needs through the relatively non-controversial and bipartisan suspension process."[33] Thus, greater use of suspensions serves two prime purposes: It provides an outlet for members to achieve their policy and political goals, and it keeps the lid on members' frustration with limited or closed amendment procedures.

The current rules of the House Democratic Caucus establish specific guidelines for using the suspension procedure. Under Caucus Rule 38, bills and resolutions are not to be scheduled using the suspension procedure if, for example, they have not been cleared by the Speaker and chair(s) of the committee(s) of jurisdiction; cost in excess of $100 million in a fiscal year (October 1 to September 30); or one-third of the committee of jurisdiction opposed reporting the measures. Members are kept informed about the measures being considered under the suspension procedure through daily and weekly whip notices and leadership announcements. Lawmakers often refer to measures on the "suspension calendar" even though there is no formal calendar for this purpose.

To accommodate lawmakers' constituency and legislative activities (the two-Congresses concept), the House instituted a cluster-voting rule. The Speaker announces that record votes on a group of bills debated under the suspension procedure will be postponed and clustered until later that day or within the next two days. The bills are then brought up in sequence and disposed of without further debate. Cluster voting accommodates lawmakers returning from weekends in their district. It also minimizes interruptions of committee or constituency meetings when the House is in session throughout the week. Absent cluster voting, members would be required to run back and forth to the chamber scores of times throughout the day to vote on issues.

At times, the minority party gets upset with the majority leadership for not scheduling enough of their bills via the suspension procedure. To protest, minority party members may vote against suspension bills until more of their routine measures are taken up on the floor. They also may castigate the majority leadership for using the suspension-of-the-rules procedure on bills that, in their estimation, merit more debate than forty minutes and require the offering of amendments.

Another expedited procedure is unanimous consent. The Speaker will recognize a lawmaker to call up bills or resolutions by unanimous consent "only when assured that the majority and minority floor leadership and the relevant committee chairs and ranking minority members have no objection."[34] Without these clearances, unanimous consent is not a viable avenue to the floor. Only 11 percent of legislation passed the 115th House by unanimous consent.[35] Major measures reach the floor by different procedures. Budget, appropriation, and a limited number of other measures are considered *privileged*[36]—meaning that the House rulebook grants them a "ticket," or privileged access, to the floor. Privileged measures may be called up from the appropriate calendar for debate at almost any time. (Remember, the Speaker sets the agenda, even for privileged business.)

Most major bills, however, do not have an automatic green light to the floor. Before they reach the floor, they need to be granted a rule (a procedural resolution) by the Rules Committee. These procedural resolutions, known as *rules* or *special rules,* are how virtually all major bills reach the House floor. Special rules also establish the terms for debating and amending legislation.

The Strategic Role of the Committee on Rules

The House Rules Committee has existed since the First Congress. During its early years, the committee prepared or ratified a biennial set of House rules and then dissolved. As House procedures became more complex because of the growing membership and workload, the committee became more important. In 1858, the Speaker became a member of the committee and, the next year, its chair. In 1880, Rules became a permanent standing committee. Three years later, the committee launched a procedural revolution. It began to issue rules, privileged resolutions granting measures priority for floor consideration.[37]

Arm of the Majority Leadership

The Speaker and the majority party leadership have not always had firm control over the House Rules Committee. After the House rebelled against the arbitrary decisions of Speaker Joseph G. Cannon, R-Ill., and removed him from the Rules Committee in 1910, the committee became independently powerful. As such, it extracted substantive concessions in bills in exchange for rules, blocked measures it opposed, and advanced those it favored, often reflecting the wishes of the House's conservative coalition of Republicans and southern Democrats.

For example, the chair of the Rules Committee from 1955 to 1967, Howard W. "Judge" Smith, D-Va., was a diehard conservative who regularly resisted pressure from Democratic leaders and constituencies to act on liberal agenda items, especially civil rights. Smith was a master at devising delaying tactics. He might abruptly adjourn meetings for lack of a quorum, allow requests for rules to languish, or refuse to schedule meetings. House consideration of the 1957 civil rights bill was temporarily delayed because Smith absented himself from the Capitol, and his committee could not meet without him. Smith claimed he was seeing about a barn that had burned on his Virginia farm. Retorted Speaker Sam Rayburn, D-Tex., "I knew Howard Smith would do most anything to block a civil rights bill, but I never knew he would resort to arson."[38] Liberals' frustration with the bipartisan coalition of conservatives who dominated the committee finally boiled over. After John F. Kennedy's election as president in 1960, Speaker Rayburn recognized that he needed greater control over the Rules Committee if the House was to advance the president's activist New Frontier program. Rayburn proposed enlarging the committee from twelve members to fifteen. This proposal led to a titanic struggle between Rayburn and the archconservative Rules chair:

> Superficially, the Representatives seemed to be quarreling about next to nothing: the membership of the committee. In reality, however, the question raised had grave import for the House and for the United States. The House's answer to it affected the tenuous balance of power between the great conservative and liberal blocs within the House. And, doing so, the House's answer seriously affected the response of Congress to the sweeping legislative proposals of the newly elected President, John Kennedy.[39]

In a dramatic vote, the House agreed to expand the Rules Committee. Two new Democrats and one Republican were added, loosening the conservative coalition's grip on the panel.

During the 1970s, the Rules Committee came under even greater majority party control. In 1975, the Democratic Caucus authorized the Speaker to appoint, subject to party ratification, all Democratic members of the committee, including the chair. (Thirteen years later, Republicans authorized their leader to name the GOP leader and members of the Rules Committee.) The majority party maintains a disproportionate ratio on the panel (currently nine Democrats and four Republicans in the 116th Congress). The Rules Committee, in short, has once again become the Speaker's committee. As a GOP Rules member said about the panel's relationship with the Speaker, "How much is the Rules Committee the handmaiden of the Speaker? The answer is, totally."[40] Democratic representative Jim McGovern of Massachusetts heads the panel in the 116th Congress.

The Rules Committee is effectively a "traffic cop" for the House floor. In the absence of a special rule, bills in the House would have to be taken up in the chronological order listed on the calendars, and many substantial bills would never reach the floor before Congress adjourned. The Rules Committee can put major bills first in line.

Equally importantly, a rule from the committee sets the conditions for debate and amendment. Special rules are as or more important to a bill's fate as a favorable committee vote. A request for a rule is usually made by the chair of the committee reporting the bill. The Rules Committee conducts hearings on the request in the same way that other committees consider legislation, except that only members testify. The House parliamentarian usually drafts the rule after consulting with majority Rules Committee leaders and staff. The rule is considered on the House floor and is voted on in the same manner as regular bills (see Box 8-3 for an example of a structured rule from the Rules Committee.)

Rarely are rules rejected by the House. In part, the majority party's success reflects the efforts of majority Rules Committee members (and the party's whip system) to win support for their procedural packages, often by strategically permitting wavering members to offer their amendments.[41] At the same time, majority party members also understand the importance of maintaining party discipline on procedural matters. As Speaker Thomas "Tip" O'Neill once said, "Defeat of the rule on the House floor is considered an affront to the [Rules] Committee and to the Speaker."[42] Majority party members who fail to support their leaders on rules may be subject to retribution, such as removal from leadership positions.[43] The Speaker's influence over the Rules Committee thus ensures that the Speaker can both bring measures to the floor and shape their procedural consideration.

Types of Rules

Traditionally, the Rules Committee has granted open, closed, and modified rules, as well as waivers. An open rule means that any lawmaker may propose germane amendments that are in compliance with House rules and the 1974 Budget

Act. A closed rule prohibits the offering of amendments by rank-and-file members. A modified rule comes in two forms: modified open and modified closed (today commonly called a *structured rule*). When used, the distinction hinges, in part, on the number of amendments made in order by the Rules Committee—few or only one under modified closed, more under modified open.

The term "structured" is used by either majority party as a replacement for "modified closed" rules. Why? "Closed" has negative connotations; "structured" implies an orderly amendment process. Structured rules are designed to prevent a free-wheeling floor amendment process, once frequent in earlier periods when there were many more open rules.

Structured rules restrict the number of amendments to those specified in the special rule or in the report of the Rules Committee accompanying the special rule; prohibit alterations to the specified amendments; restrict the time for debating each amendment; and identify the specific lawmaker who is authorized to offer an amendment to the pending bill. The increase in structured rules, compared to the dramatic decline of open rules, is a prime example of nontraditional lawmaking (see Box 8-3). Waivers of points of order are commonly included in the different types of rules. Waivers set aside technical violations of House rules to allow bills or other matters to reach the floor.

The Emergence of Creative Rules

The Rules Committee has long been creative and imaginative in designing new rules. As a result, it has numerous choices in the way it constructs tailor-made special rules to advance majority party objectives. Table 8-1 focuses on the three main types of rules: open or modified open, structured, and closed. Box 8-4 identifies several creative rules that the committee has crafted over the years. A recent innovation of the Rules Committee not mentioned in Box 8-4 is the so-called *compound rule,* a nontraditional rule that can serve the interests of both parties.

The uniqueness of this rule is that one rule makes in order two or more discrete measures for chamber consideration; moreover, a compound rule specifies for each measure whether it will be considered under open, structured, or closed procedures. In the minority, Democrats criticized the rule as a "grab bag" procedure because the several bills made in order by a compound rule may not have any substantive relationship to one another. Members' views on procedural matters tend to shift as they move from the minority to the majority.

Compound rules save the time of the House, rank-and-file lawmakers, and Rules members. Debate on a compound rule is one hour—identical to that for an open, closed, or structured rule—but its adoption brings several bills to the floor one after the other. In contrast, the one-hour debate on a traditional rule governs floor consideration of only one bill. A compound rule also saves the time of the House by limiting the number of times that the minority party can try to amend a special rule before its adoption by the usual party-line vote of the full House.

TABLE 8-1 ■ Open, Closed, and Structured Rules, 103rd–115th Congresses (1993–2018)

Congress	Open/Modified Open		Structured		Closed		Totals	
	Number	Percentage	Number	Percentage	Number	Percentage	Number	Percentage
103rd (1993–1995)	46	44%	49	47%	9	9%	104	100%
104th (1995–1997)	83	58	40	28	19	14	142	100
105th (1997–1998)	74	53	42	30	24	17	140	100
106th (1999–2000)	91	51	49	27	39	22	179	100
107th (2001–2002)	40	37	44	41	23	22	107	100
108th (2003–2004)	34	26	62	47	37	28	133	100
109th (2005–2006)	24	19	61	49	40	32	125	100
110th (2007–2008)	23	14	81	50	59	36	111	100
111th (2009–2010)	0	0	73	65	38	34	111	100
112th (2011–2012)	25	18	65	46	50	36	140	100
113th (2013–2014)	12	8	65	43	72	48	149	100
114th (2015–2016)	8	5	82	53	65	42	155	100
115th (2017–2018)	0	0	77	44	98	56	177	100

Source: Don Wolfensberger, resident scholar, Bipartisan Policy Center, Washington, DC. Wolfensberger is a former decades-long professional staff aide and staff director of the House Rules Committee. Information for the 114th Congress was provided by Christopher Davis, CRS expert on Congress; Wolfensberger for the 115th.

Note: The table applies only to special rules providing for the initial consideration for amendment of bills, joint resolutions, and significant concurrent resolutions (e.g., budget or war related). It does not apply to privileged resolutions considered in the House, to subsequent rules for the same measure, to conference reports, or to special rules that only waive points of order against appropriations bills but do not provide for consideration in the Committee of the Whole. Rules making in order more than one bill are counted as a separate rule for each measure made in order (e.g., a rule providing for the consideration of four bills under closed rules is counted as four closed rules).

Whether Democrats or Republicans control the House, it is common today for the Rules Committee to announce in advance that it will provide a structured (i.e., "restricted") rule and require lawmakers to submit their proposed amendments to the committee. The committee will then review the amendments and determine which to make in order for chamber consideration. The requirement that all amendments be either preprinted in the *Congressional Record* or submitted in advance to Rules aids the majority party in preparing its floor strategy.

The shift to creative, or nontraditional, rules reflects several developments. Among the most important are the wider use of multiple referrals, which requires Rules to play a larger coordinating role in arranging floor action on legislation; the rise of megabills hundreds of pages in length that contain priorities the Speaker does not want picked apart on the floor; the desire of majority party leaders to exert greater control over floor procedures; members' impatience with dilatory floor challenges to committee-reported bills; members' demand for greater certainty and predictability in floor decision making; and efforts by committee leaders either to limit the number of amendments or to keep unfriendly amendments off the floor.

The rise of partisan acrimony has also triggered an increase in nontraditional rules. Although Speakers since the mid-1990s have promised that they would provide greater opportunities for all lawmakers to offer floor amendments to pending legislation, that pledge has been hard to keep. When Paul Ryan, R-Wisc., gave his 2015 inaugural address as Speaker, he said: "Let's open up the process. Let people participate." It wasn't too long before a minority Rules Democrat criticized the majority's overuse of closed rules. "[T]oday we have another closed rule, or, as I call them now, Putin rules. This is the kind of process they have in Russia: no amendments, no debate, no nothing, completely shut down. It is your way or the highway."[44]

It is too soon to assess whether the Democratic-led 116th House will provide greater amendment opportunities for members or continue with procedures that limit or prevent changes to its agenda priorities (see Table 8-1 for data on special rules). Noteworthy is that Rep. Tom Cole of Oklahoma, the ranking GOP member on Rules, commended McGovern for "giving members on both sides of the aisle an opportunity to present the case for their amendments to the Rules Committee and, in many cases, to the full House."[45] However, a key concern of the majority party is that the minority will use an open process primarily to offer so-called "gotcha" amendments, such as politically charged proposals crafted to cause reelection issues for majority members or to offer amendments designed to eviscerate the majority's policy priorities.

As Table 8-1 reveals, there were no open rules in the 115th Congress continuing a decades-long trend restricting or preventing opportunities for members to offer amendments.[46] This pattern, provoked by acrimonious partisanship and fierce electoral competition, occurs regardless of which party is in the majority. Whether the majority is Democratic or Republican, restrictive rules prevent troublesome amendments from being offered, debated, and voted upon. As

BOX 8-3 EXAMPLE OF A RULE FROM THE COMMITTEE ON RULES

This is a structured rule (H. Res. 27) that sets the terms for debating and amending the Regulatory Accountability Act of 2015 (H.R. 185). This often-used rule by either party when it controls the House limits the number of amendments, even naming the members in the Rules Committee report on H. Res. 27 who may offer the relatively few amendments made in order. The House adopted H. Res. 27 on January 13, 2015, by a vote of 242 to 180.

Resolved, That at any time after the adoption of this resolution the Speaker may, pursuant to clause 2(b) of rule XVIII, declare the House resolved into the Committee of the Whole House on the state of the Union for consideration of the bill (H.R. 185) to reform the process by which Federal agencies analyze and formulate new regulations and guidance documents. The first reading of the bill shall be dispensed with. All points of order against consideration of the bill are waived. General debate shall be confined to the bill and shall not exceed one hour equally divided and controlled by the chair and ranking minority member of the Committee on the Judiciary. After general debate the bill shall be considered for amendment under the five-minute rule. The bill shall be considered as read. All points of order against provisions in the bill are waived. No amendment to the bill shall be in order except those printed in part A of the report of the Committee on Rules accompanying this resolution. Each such amendment may be offered only in the order printed in the report, may be offered only by a Member designated in the report, shall be considered as read, shall be debatable for the time specified in the report equally divided and controlled by a proponent and an opponent, shall not be subject to amendment, and shall not be subject to a demand for division of the question in the House or in the Committee of the Whole. All points of order against such amendments are waived. At the conclusion of consideration of the bill for amendment the Committee of the Whole shall rise and report the bill to the House with such amendments as may have been adopted. The previous question shall be considered as ordered on the bill and amendments thereto to final passage without intervening motion except one motion to recommit with or without instructions.

Source: Congressional Record, 114th Cong., 1st sess., January 13, 2015, H237–H248.

Wolfensberger, explained, "Majority status brings with it new responsibilities to pass the party's priority legislation in a timely and successful manner, and that often entails severely restricting the amendment process on major legislation to avoid minority party obstruction and weakening or politically embarrassing amendments."[47]

In summary, rules establish the conditions under which most major bills are debated and amended. They determine the length of general debate, permit or prohibit amendments, and often waive points of order. Writing the rules is the majority party's way of ensuring that measures reach the floor under terms

BOX 8-4   EXAMPLES OF CREATIVE RULES

Queen-of-the-Hill Rule

- Under this special rule, a number of major alternative amendments—each the functional equivalent of a bill—are made to the underlying legislation, with the proviso that the substitute that receives the most votes is the winner.

- If two or more alternatives receive an identical number of votes, the last one voted upon is considered as finally adopted by the membership.

Self-Executing Rule

- This special rule provides that when the House adopts a rule, it has also agreed simultaneously to amend the underlying bill made in order by the special rule.

- This rule is used for various reasons, such as reconciling the policies recommended by multiple committees, correcting procedural or Budget Act violations, or making changes in the base bill to pick up votes to enact the measure.

- Whether this rule is controversial or not usually depends on the nature of the policy being agreed to in the "two-(or more)-for-one" vote.

Structured Rule

- The essential feature of the structured rule is that it limits the freedom of members to offer germane amendments to the bills made in order by those rules. The only amendments permitted are those designated in the special rule or in the Rules Committee report to accompany the procedural rule (see Box 8-3 for an example of a structured rule). The number of structured rules has increased since the 1980s. The majority party uses these rules to minimize debate, prevent unwanted amendments, and maximize its ability to mobilize winning majorities.

- Rank-and-file members often rail against these rules because they restrict their opportunities to amend committee-reported measures or majority party initiatives.

Multiple-Step Rule

- This type of rule facilitates an orderly amendment process.

- One variation is for the Rules Committee to first report a rule that regulates general debate on a bill and then report another follow-on rule to govern the amending process to the measure.

- Another variation is for the Rules Committee to state publicly that if a measure encounters difficulties on the floor, the panel will report a subsequent rule that limits time for further debate or further amendments.

Suspension Day Rule

- This type of rule authorizes the Speaker to entertain motions to suspend the rules on days other than Monday, Tuesday, or Wednesday.

favorable to the party's preferred outcomes. Put differently, the majority party limits and structures the votes to get the legislative and political results it intends, keeping the two Congresses in mind. In this era of message politics and partisan polarization, innovative, nontraditional rules can both protect majority party members from casting electorally perilous votes or, alternatively, make amendments in order that appeal to diverse party constituencies.

Dislodging a Bill From Committee

Committees do not necessarily reflect the point of view of the full chamber. What happens when a standing committee refuses to report a bill or when the Rules Committee does not grant a rule? To circumvent committees, members have at least three options: the discharge petition, the Calendar Wednesday rule, and the ability of the Rules Committee to extract a bill from committee. However, these tactics are rarely employed and seldom successful. (As of this writing, the aforementioned Consensus Calendar has yet to be used in the 116th House.)

The discharge petition permits the House to relieve a committee of jurisdiction over a stalled measure. This procedure also provides a way for the rank and file to force a bill to the floor, even if the majority leadership, the committee chair, and the Rules Committee oppose it. If a committee does not report a bill within thirty legislative days after the bill was referred to it, any member may file a discharge motion (petition), which requires the signature of 218 members, a majority of the House. Once the signatures are obtained, the discharge motion is placed on the Discharge Calendar for seven days. House rules then stipulate that the Speaker is required to schedule consideration of the privileged discharge motion within two legislative days after a member who signed the petition announces to the House his or her intention to offer the motion. Since 1910, when the discharge rule was adopted, only rarely (fewer than five times) have discharged measures ever become law. Its threatened or actual use, particularly as the number of signatures closes in on 218, may stimulate a committee to act on a bill and the majority leadership to schedule it for floor action. In mid-June 2015, when an immigration reform discharge petition appeared certain to attract the required signatures, Speaker Paul Ryan's office announced that the House will consider "two bills next week that will avert the discharge petition and resolve the border security and immigration issues."

The discharge rule also applies to the Rules Committee. A motion to discharge a rule (a simple resolution) from the Rules Committee is in order after seven legislative days, instead of thirty days, as long as the legislation made in order by the rule has been in the committee of jurisdiction for thirty days. House adoption of the discharged rule establishes the conditions for debating and amending—if any are permitted—the measure made in order by the discharge procedure.

The discharge procedure is rarely successful as a lawmaking device largely because members are reluctant to second-guess committees, to write legislation on the floor without the guidance of committee hearings and reports, and to use a procedure that may one day be used against committees on which they serve.

Moreover, 218 signatures are not easy to obtain. The Speaker, too, is not reluctant to pressure majority party members who sign discharge petitions to remove their names because their actions could jeopardize the majority's control of the floor schedule. If majority lawmakers add or refuse to remove their names, the message being sent, according to Representative Cole, is that "you're thumbing your nose at your own leadership."[48] Unwanted consequences might result for majority members who refuse to heed their leader's advice, such as being bypassed for a committee chairmanship. Occasionally, the minority party will use discharge petitions for campaign purposes, castigating vulnerable majority-party members for failing to sign these petitions, which are supported by many voters in their district.[49]

Adopted in 1909, the Calendar Wednesday rule provides that on Wednesdays, committees may bring up from the House Calendar or Union Calendar their measures that have not received a rule from the Rules Committee. However, the clerk will not call committees on Wednesdays unless the committee chair gives notice on Tuesday that he or she will seek recognition to call up a measure under the rule. Calendar Wednesday is cumbersome to employ, seldom used, and generally dispensed with by unanimous consent. Since 1943, fewer than fifteen measures have been enacted into law under this procedure.[50]

Finally, the Rules Committee has the power of extraction. The committee can propose rules that make bills in order for House debate even if the bills have been neither introduced nor reported by standing committees. Based on an 1895 precedent, this procedure is akin to discharging committees without the required 218 signatures. It stirs bitter controversy among members who think it usurps the rights of the other committees, and therefore, it is seldom used.

HOUSE FLOOR PROCEDURES

The House meets Monday through Friday, often convening at noon. In practice, it conducts the bulk of its committee and floor business during the middle of the week (to accommodate the so-called Tuesday to Thursday Club of members who go home to their constituencies every weekend). At the beginning of each day's session, bells ring throughout the Capitol and the House office buildings, summoning representatives to the floor. The bells also notify members of votes, quorum calls, recesses, and adjournments. Typically, the opening activities include a daily prayer; approval of the *Journal* (a constitutionally required record of the previous day's formal proceedings); recitation of the Pledge of Allegiance; receipt of messages from the president (such as a veto message) or the Senate; announcements, if any, by the Speaker; and one-minute speeches by members on any topic. On Mondays through Thursdays, a period of morning-hour debate takes place after the opening preliminaries but before the start of formal legislative business.

After these preliminaries, the House generally begins considering legislation. For a major bill, a set pattern is observed: adopting the rule, convening in the Committee of the Whole, allotting time for general debate, amending, voting, and moving the bill to final passage.

Adoption of the Rule

The Speaker, after consulting other majority party leaders and affected committee chairs, generally decides when the House will debate a bill and under what kind of rule. Speakers rely on their majority leader to help draft and manage the floor agenda. When the scheduled day arrives, the Speaker recognizes a majority member of the Rules Committee for one hour to explain the rule's contents. By custom, the majority member yields half the time for debate only to a minority member of the Rules Committee. At the end of the debate, which may take less time than the allotted hour, the House votes on the previous-question motion. Its approval brings the House to an immediate vote on the rule. Rejection of the previous question (a rare occurrence) could allow the minority party an opportunity to amend the rule.

Opponents of a bill can try to defeat the rule and avert House action on the bill itself. But rules are rarely defeated because majority party members generally vote with their leaders on procedural votes, and the Rules Committee is sensitive to the wishes of the House. Nancy Pelosi never lost a rule during her first years as Speaker (2007–2011), nor did Speaker Boehner (2011–Oct 2015) or Speaker Ryan (2015–2019). During the lengthy Speakership of Dennis Hastert, R-Ill. (1999–2007), the House rejected only two rules offered by the Rules Committee, largely because of divisions within the majority party. Procedural votes are usually party line votes. Once the rule is adopted, the House is governed by its provisions. Most rules state that "at any time after the adoption of [the rule] the Speaker may declare the House resolved into the Committee of the Whole."

Committee of the Whole

The Committee of the Whole House on the state of the Union is a parliamentary artifice that the House borrowed long ago from the British House of Commons. Its function in the contemporary House is to expedite consideration of legislation and to promote member involvement in general debate and the amendment process, if amendments are permitted by the special rule. It is simply the House in another form with different rules. For example, a quorum in the Committee of the Whole is only one hundred members, compared with 218 for the full House. Debate on amendments is governed by the five-minute rule rather than the one-hour rule that applies in the House. By custom, Speakers never preside over the committee; they always appoint a majority party colleague to act as chair of the committee, which then begins general debate of a bill.

General Debate

A rule from the Rules Committee specifies the amount of time, usually one to two hours, for a general discussion of the bill under consideration. Controversial bills require more time, perhaps four or more hours. Control of the time is divided equally between the majority and minority floor managers—usually the chair and ranking minority member of the committee that reported the legislation.

(When bills are referred to more than one committee, a more complex division of debate time is allotted among the committees that had jurisdiction over the legislation.) The majority floor manager's job is to guide the bill to final passage; the minority floor manager may seek to amend or kill the bill.

After the floor managers have made their opening statements, they parcel out several minutes to colleagues on their side of the aisle who wish to speak. General debate rarely lives up to its name. Most legislators read prepared speeches. Give-and-take exchange occurs infrequently at this stage of the proceedings.

The Amending Phase

The amending process is the heart of decision making on the floor of the House. It allows interested lawmakers an opportunity to amend proposed legislation. Amendments determine the final shape of bills and often dominate public discussion. Former representative Henry J. Hyde, R-Ill., for example, repeatedly and successfully proposed amendments barring the use of federal funds for abortions. Hyde's 1977 antiabortion amendment remains today a regular provision of many public laws.

If there is an open process in the Committee of the Whole, amendments are considered under the five-minute rule, which gives the sponsor five minutes to defend it and an opponent five minutes to speak against it. The amendment then may be brought to a vote. Amendments are routinely debated for more than ten minutes, however. Legislators gain the floor by saying, "I move to strike the last word," or, "I move to strike the requisite number of words." These pro forma amendments, which make no alteration in the pending matter, simply serve to give members five minutes of debate time. An open process permits amendments ("sweeteners") that attract bipartisan support from many lawmakers; conversely, offering many amendments can be an effective dilatory tactic of the minority party.

To "filibuster by amendment" is virtually impossible today given the Rules Committee's prerogative of issuing closed, structured, or other clamp-down rules. To allow controversial and politically charged amendments on the floor would require the Speaker's approval. Gone are the days when measures, such as defense authorization bills, would be subject to many days of debate as well as an open, bipartisan amendment process.

Consider "that from 1991 through 2010, amendments approved with bipartisan majorities made up one of every six amendment votes in the House. Since 2011, they have been only one of every 20 such votes."[51] This change highlights a significant decline in the influence of cross-party amending activity, a reflection of the prominence of partisan polarization in the chamber. The House Parliamentarian *emeritus* wrote that the majority party's intent is to "minimize spontaneous debate" and amendments and "to maximize [m]ajority party voting majorities" in "furtherance of time and issue certainty."[52]

In the amending phase, the interconnection of the two Congresses is evident: Amendments can have electoral as well as legislative consequences. Floor amendments enable lawmakers to take positions that enhance their reputations with the folks back home, put opponents on record, and shape national policy. For example, "put-them-on-the-spot amendments," as one representative dubbed them, can be artfully fashioned by minority lawmakers to force the majority to vote on controversial issues, such as gun control, immigration reform, or climate change that can be used against them in the next campaign.[53] The majority party's control of the Rules Committee minimizes the use of this tactic because the panel "scripts" the amendment process by issuing structured rules. Recall that structured rules block spontaneous amendments and debates on issues that might stymie passage of the majority party's priorities.

Voting

Before passage of the 1970 Legislative Reorganization Act, the Committee of the Whole adopted or rejected amendments by voice votes or other votes with no public record of who voted and how. Today, any legislator supported by twenty-five colleagues can obtain a recorded vote. (The member who requested a recorded vote is counted as one of the twenty-five who rise to be counted by the chair.)

Since the installation of an electronic voting system in 1973, members can insert their personalized cards (about the size of a credit card) into one of more than forty voting stations on the floor and press the "Yea," "Nay," or "Present" button. A large electronic display board behind the press gallery provides a running tally of the total votes for or against a motion. The voting tally, said a representative, is watched carefully by many members:

> I find that a lot of times, people walk in, and the first thing they do is look at the board, and they have key people they check out, and if those people have voted "aye," they go to the machine and vote "aye" and walk off the floor.

> But I will look at the board and see how [members of the state delegation] vote, because they are in districts right next to me, and they have constituencies just like mine. I will vote the way I am going to vote except that if they are both different, I will go up and say "Why did you vote that way? Let me know if there is something I am missing."[54]

After all pending amendments have been voted on, the Committee of the Whole rises. The chair hands the gavel back to the Speaker, and a quorum once again becomes 218 members.

Recommit and Final Passage

As specified in the rule, the full House must review the actions of its agent, the Committee of the Whole. The Speaker announces that under the rule, the previous question has been ordered, which means, in this context, that no further debate is permitted on the bill or its amendments. The Speaker then asks whether any representative wants a separate vote on any amendment adopted in the Committee of the Whole. If not, all of the amendments agreed to in the committee will be approved.

The next important step is the motion to recommit, which provides a way for the House to return, or recommit, the bill to the committee that reported it. The motion to recommit has two forms: (1) the rarely used "straight" motion to return the measure to committee (which effectively kills it) and (2) a motion to recommit with instructions that the committee report "forthwith," which means the bill never really leaves the House. If this form of the motion is adopted, the bill, as modified by the instructions, is automatically before the House again. By precedent, either form of the motion is always made by a minority party member who opposes the legislation. Each form of the motion is also subject to ten minutes of debate, five per side. Recommittal motions are usually not successful because they are so heavily identified as an opposition party prerogative, but they do serve to protect the rights of the minority.

Recent Congresses have seen a change in the major purposes of the motion to recommit. Although still employed by the minority party to force the House to vote on its alternative policy proposal (the "instructions" in this motion), the motion to recommit is now frequently employed to achieve two political purposes: (1) to defeat, delay, or weaken majority party policies, and (2) to force vulnerable majority lawmakers to vote on amendments that might damage their reelection chances back home if they do not vote for the minority proposal. These motions are usually rejected on party-line votes.

In the early days of the 116th House, however, the GOP minority had some success politically in offering motions to recommit. To the dismay of Speaker Pelosi, a strong advocate of party unity, about two dozen of her newly elected members voted several times for GOP motions to recommit early in 2019. The motions were targeted strategically to encourage vulnerable Democrats from swing districts to vote with the Republicans. Majority Leader Hoyer and Majority Whip James Clyburn, S.C., "personally told freshmen they may side with Republicans [on recommittal motions], as long as Democrats don't lose the overall vote—breaking a years-long precedent among party leaders in the majority."[55] Republicans even scored a big win when one of their motions to recommit was adopted, something that had not occurred since 2010.

The winning GOP motion declared that it is in "the national security interest of the United States to combat anti-Semitism around the world."[56] The motion was adopted overwhelmingly by the House (424 yeas to 0 nays). This example illustrates how motions to recommit, whether proposed by a Democratic or Republican minority, can be politically weaponized. In this instance, a freshman Democrat, six years before she was elected to the 116th House, had written a tweet critical of Israel. Once the tweet was disclosed, the freshman lawmaker publicly apologized for her comments. Even so, GOP campaign strategists began to use the member's tweet, as well as controversial comments by other newly elected Democratic freshmen, "to demonize Democrats well in advance of the 2020 elections by painting them" as radicals who support risky policies.[57] When a second minority motion to recommit was adopted concerning background checks for gun sales, it provoked significant consternation within Democratic ranks. Newspaper headlines, for instance, referred to the intraparty disharmony as a "blowup," "rebellion," or "struggles over party unity."[58]

If the motion to recommit with instructions is adopted, the minority proposal is incorporated into the bill. If it is rejected, as usually occurs, the Speaker will declare, "The question is on passage of the bill." Passage of the measure, by the House in this case, marks about the halfway point in the lawmaking process. The Senate must also approve the bill, and its procedures are strikingly different from those of the House. It is an institution noted for protecting the rights of the minority—hence its reliance on the unanimous consent of all senators to accomplish much of the chamber's business.

SCHEDULING IN THE SENATE

Compared with the larger and more clamorous House, which needs and follows well-defined rules and precedents, the Senate operates more informally. And unlike the House, where the rules permit a determined majority to make decisions, the Senate's permissive rules emphasize individual prerogatives (freedom to debate and to offer amendments, including nonrelevant amendments) and minority rights (those of the minority party, a faction, or even a single senator). "The Senate," said one member, "is run for the convenience of one Senator to the inconvenience of 99."[59] No wonder some commentators say the Senate has only two rules (unanimous consent and exhaustion) and three speeds (slow, slower, and slowest). As a former senator said, "The only thing it's easy to do in the Senate is slow things down. The Senate is 100 human brake pads."[60]

In brief, the Senate's rules, practices, and traditions, especially its sixty-vote requirement under Rule XXII to bring debate to a close on measures or matters (e.g., nominations or treaties) make it a *supermajority rule* institution compared with the majority rule House. Stated differently, minority rule (by one senator, a small group, or the minority party) is a core feature of the Senate.

The scheduling system for the Senate appears relatively simple. There is a Calendar of Business on which are listed public and private bills reported by the committees and a separate Executive Calendar for treaties and nominations. The Senate has nothing comparable to the scheduling duties of the House Rules Committee, and the majority and minority leadership actively consult about scheduling. The Senate majority leader is responsible for setting the agenda. "If there's any power in this job," said Senate majority leader Mitch McConnell, R-Ky., "it's the power to schedule, to decide what you're going to do or not do."[61] The majority leader is aided in controlling scheduling by the priority given him when he seeks recognition on the floor. What this means is that if several senators are seeking recognition from the presiding officer and the majority leader is among them, the chair will always give preference to the majority leader.

Despite the Senate's smaller size, establishing a firm agenda of business is harder in the Senate than in the House. As a majority leader once said,

> The ability of any Senator to speak without limitations makes it impossible to establish total certainty with respect to scheduling. When there is added to that the difficulty and very demanding schedules of 100 Senators, it is very hard to organize business in a way that meets the convenience of everybody.[62]

Legislation typically reaches the Senate floor in two ways: by unanimous consent or by motion. But senators, too, can also force Senate consideration of their proposals by offering them as nonrelevant amendments to pending business. Unanimous-consent agreements are of utmost importance to the smooth functioning of the Senate.

Unanimous-Consent Agreements

The Senate frequently dispenses with its formal rules and instead follows negotiated agreements submitted to the Senate for its unanimous approval (see Box 8-5 on unanimous-consent agreements). The objectives are to expedite work in an institution known for extended debate, to impose some measure of predictability on floor action, and to minimize dilatory activities. As a party floor leader observed,

> We aren't bringing [measures] to the floor unless we have [a unanimous consent] agreement. We could bring child-care legislation to the floor right now, but that would mean two months of fighting. We want to maximize productive time by trying to work out as much as we can in advance [of floor action].[63]

It is not uncommon for party leaders to negotiate piecemeal unanimous-consent agreements—limiting debate on a specific amendment, for example—and to hammer them out in public on the Senate floor.

Unanimous-consent agreements (also called time limitation agreements) limit debate on the bill, any amendments, and various motions. Occasionally, they specify the time for the vote on final passage and typically impose constraints on the amendment process. The Senate's unanimous-consent agreements are functional equivalents of special rules from the House Rules Committee. Both waive the rules of their respective chambers and must be approved by the members—in one case by majority vote and in the other by unanimous consent. These accords are binding contracts and can be terminated or modified only by another unanimous-consent agreement. The Senate's two party leaders and their top aides often negotiate, draft, and circulate unanimous-consent agreements privately before they are propounded on the floor. The House Rules Committee hears requests for procedural rules in public sessions, but the rule itself is the product of the majority leadership.

Ways to Extract Bills From Committee

If a bill is blocked in committee, the Senate has several ways to obtain floor action. Senators could transform a bill stuck in committee into a relevant or nonrelevant floor amendment and offer it to a measure pending on the floor; employ Senate Rule XIV to bypass the committee stage by placing a measure on the Senate's legislative calendar; suspend the rules; or discharge a bill (or nomination) from committee. Only the first two procedures are effective; the other two are somewhat difficult to employ and seldom succeed. Motions to suspend the rules require one-day's notice in writing (published in the *Congressional Record*) specifying the precise rule to be suspended. The motion is debatable and requires a two-thirds vote for adoption. The Senate's formal discharge procedure is little used because of its cumbersome requirements, such as a layover stipulation.

A widely used prerogative of senators is offering nongermane amendments to legislation under floor consideration. Because the Senate has no general germaneness (or relevancy) rule, senators can take an agriculture bill that is stuck in committee, draft it as a nonrelevant floor amendment, and offer it to a pending health bill. "Amendments may be made," Thomas Jefferson noted long ago, "so as to totally alter the nature of the proposition." Unanimous-consent agreements can limit or prohibit nonrelevant amendments. There are other circumstances under which senators may not offer nongermane amendments, such as during consideration of reconciliation legislation as prescribed by the Budget Act of 1974. But the ability to offer nongermane amendments has long afforded individual senators far greater ability to bypass committees than their House counterparts enjoy.

Senators can also bypass the referral of measures to committee by invoking one of the chamber's formal rules (Rule XIV). Typically, when senators introduce bills or joint resolutions (or when bills or joint resolutions are passed by the House and sent to the Senate), they are referred to the appropriate committee of jurisdiction. Rule XIV specifies that those measures are to be read twice by title on different legislative days before they are referred. If a senator interposes an objection after the first reading and again the next day after the second reading, the bill or joint resolution is automatically placed on the Senate's Calendar of Business (see Box 8-6 for how Rule XIV works). Although not used for the vast majority of measures, Rule XIV is increasingly invoked on party issues of high priority. The majority leader, for example, may employ it to circumvent committees because no time is available for a lengthy committee review or because he wants an issue ready to be called up at his discretion. As Sen. Lamar Alexander, R-Tenn., noted, "From the 103rd to the 109th Congress, Rule XIV to bypass [committees] was

BOX 8-5 EXAMPLE OF A UNANIMOUS-CONSENT AGREEMENT

Ordered, That on Wednesday, January 28, 2015, at 2:30 p.m., the Senate resume consideration of S. 1, a bill to approve the Keystone Pipeline, and proceed to vote in relation to the following amendments in the order listed:

—Cardin Amdt. No. 75;

—Peters Amdt. No. 70;

—Sanders Amdt. No. 23;

—Cruz Amdt. No. 15;

—Merkley Amdt. No. 125;

—Moran Amdt. No. 73;

—Whitehouse Amdt. No. 148;

—Daines Amdt. No. 132;

—Coons Amdt. No. 115;

—Collins Amdt. No. 35;

—Carper Amdt. No. 120;

—Murkowski Amdt. No. 166;

—Heitkamp Amdt. No. 133;

—Gillibrand Amdt. No. 48;

—Barrasso Amdt. No. 245;

—Cardin Amdt. No. 124;

—Daines Amdt. No. 246;

—Burr Amdt. No. 92, as modified.

Ordered further, That all amendments listed above be subject to a 60 vote affirmative threshold for adoption and that no second degree amendments be in order to the amendments; provided, that there be 2 minutes of debate equally divided between each vote; provided further, that all votes after the first in the series be 10 minute votes.

Ordered further, That with respect to S. 1, the filing deadline for first degree amendments be 3 p.m. on Monday, January 26, 2015, and the filing deadline for second degree amendments be 5 p.m. on Monday, January 26, 2015.

Ordered further, That with respect to the motions to invoke cloture on Amendment No. 2, offered by the Senator from Alaska (Ms. Murkowski), to S. 1 . . . the mandatory quorum required under Rule XXII be waived. (Jan. 23, 26, 27, 2015.)

Source: U.S. Senate, Calendar of Business, January 28, 2015, p. 2.

used on average 24 times per Congress. This was shattered in the 110th Congress when it was used 57 times."[64]

SENATE FLOOR PROCEDURES

The Senate, like the House, often convenes at noon, sometimes earlier, to keep pace with the workload. Typically, it opens with a prayer, followed by the Pledge of Allegiance and then leaders' time (usually ten minutes each to the majority leader and the minority leader to discuss various issues). If neither leader wants any time, the Senate typically either permits members who have requested time to make their statements, or it resumes consideration of old or new business under the terms of a unanimous-consent agreement. The Senate, too, must keep and approve the *Journal* of the previous day's activities. Commonly, the *Journal* is "deemed approved to date" by unanimous consent when the Senate adjourns or recesses at the end of each day.

Normal Routine

For most bills, the Senate follows four steps:

1. The majority leader secures the unanimous consent of the Senate to an arrangement that specifies when a bill will be brought to the floor and the conditions for debating it.

2. The presiding officer recognizes the majority and minority floor managers for opening statements.

3. Amendments are then in order, with debate on each amendment regulated by the terms of the unanimous-consent agreement.

4. A roll call vote takes place on final passage.

As in the House, amendments in the Senate serve various purposes. For example, floor managers might accept "as many amendments as they can without undermining the purposes of the bill, in order to build the broadest possible consensus behind it."[65] Some amendments are drafted with the two Congresses in mind. Such amendments are often designed to embarrass members who must vote against them. "My amendment can be characterized as a 'November amendment,'" remarked a Republican senator, "because the vote . . . will provide an opportunity for Senators to go home and say, 'I voted to reduce Federal taxes' and 'I voted to cut Federal spending.'"[66] Senate Democrats, like their GOP colleagues, make "use of amendments to strike a contrast with [the other party's] policies."[67]

Unless constrained by some previous unanimous-consent agreement or filibusters that block the offering of amendments, senators generally have the right to offer an unlimited number of floor amendments. In recent Senates, however, there has been a drop-off in the number of Senate amendments considered. Democratic and Republican majority leaders have taken steps to inhibit Senators of their party

BOX 8-6 SENATE RULE XIV: BYPASSING COMMITTEE REFERRAL

MEASURES READ THE FIRST TIME—S. 338 AND S. 339

Mr. CORNYN. Mr. President, I understand that there are two bills at the desk, and I ask for their first reading en bloc.

The PRESIDING OFFICER. The clerk will report the bills by title for the first time.

The assistant legislative clerk read as follows:

A bill (S. 338) to permanently reauthorize the Land and Water Conservation Fund.

A bill (S. 339) to repeal the Patient Protection and Affordable Care Act and the Health Care and Education Reconciliation Act of 2010 entirely.

Mr. CORNYN. Mr. President, I now ask for a second reading, and I object to my own request en bloc.

The PRESIDING OFFICER. Objection having been heard, the bills will be read for the second time on the next legislative day.

Source: Congressional Record, February 2, 2015, S702.

MEASURES PLACED ON THE CALENDAR—S. 338 AND S. 339

Mr. MCCONNELL. I understand there are two bills at the desk due for a second reading.

The PRESIDING OFFICER. The clerk will read the bills by title for the second time.

The legislative clerk read as follows:

A bill (S. 338) to permanently reauthorize the Land and Water Conservation Fund.

A bill (S. 339) to repeal the Patient Protection and Affordable Care Act and the Health Care and Education Reconciliation Act of 2010 entirely.

Mr. MCCONNELL. Mr. President, in order to place the bills on the calendar under the provisions of rule XIV, I object to further proceedings en bloc.

The PRESIDING OFFICER. Objection is heard. The bills will be placed on the calendar.

Source: Congressional Record, February 2, 2015, S702; *Congressional Record,* February 3, 2015, S707.

from offering amendments.[68] Various reasons account for the drop-off, such as the leader's preference to concentrate on nominations rather than legislative issues as well as the desire to protect vulnerable party members from taking difficult votes in a period of close competition for majority control of the Senate.

Recent majority leaders have increasingly used their right of first recognition on the floor to "fill the amendment tree," an important departure from Senate tradition and practice. The amendment tree refers to a chart that imposes a limitation on the number of amendments to a measure that may be offered and pending at the same time. Using the right of first recognition, the majority leader can offer amendment after amendment until the so-called "amendment tree" is filled. Once the amendment tree is filled, no other senator may offer amendments—that is, the amending process is frozen "until action is taken to dispose of one or more of those already pending."[69]

This practice is controversial and angers many lawmakers, especially those in the minority. When he was majority leader (2007–2015), Harry Reid, D-Nev., employed tree-filling far more than his Democratic or Republican predecessors. Majority Leader McConnell also employs tree-filling. Tree-filling largely reflects two general and overlapping developments: heightened partisan conflict in the chamber and wider use of amendments by the minority party for political message sending.

Understandably, members of the minority party (as well as some in the majority) criticize the majority leader for undermining the unique deliberative character of the Senate by preventing Senators of either party from offering their amendments. From the majority leader's perspective, tree-filling is done for several specific purposes, such as blocking unwanted, nonrelevant amendments; protecting vulnerable party colleagues from voting on amendments crafted to cause them electoral problems; or promoting negotiations with the opposition so an accord might be reached on the number of amendments each side is willing to vote on. If an accord is reached, the majority leader would drop some or all of his amendments, opening places on the tree for others to offer their amendments.

In the Senate, a bill is brought to a final vote whenever senators stop seeking recognition to talk. Unlike the House, the Senate has no motion to end debate and bring a measure or matter to a vote. This can be a long process, particularly in the absence of a unanimous-consent agreement. On some bills, unanimous-consent agreements are foreclosed because of deliberate obstructive tactics, particularly the threat or use of the filibuster (extended debate). In these instances, bills cannot be voted upon until the filibuster has ended through, for instance, use of Rule XXII's cloture (closure of debate) procedure.

Holds, Filibusters, and Cloture

The old-style filibuster has long been associated with the 1939 movie *Mr. Smith Goes to Washington,* which featured a haggard Jimmy Stewart conducting a dramatic solo talkathon on the floor of the Senate to inform the public about political wrongdoing. In its new incarnation, the filibuster is usually threatened more than executed. Filibuster threats gain a senator bargaining power and negotiating leverage.

Today, the mere threat to filibuster is sufficient to block action on many bills or nominations, in large measure because it is so hard to mobilize sixty votes to invoke cloture (closure of debate). Moreover, cloture is a time-consuming procedure (three to five days) that impedes the Senate's ability to process its extensive workload.

Filibustering techniques involve many blocking tactics besides extended debate in which senators might hold the floor for hours of endless speeches. In today's polarized Senate, senators skillfully exploit rules to wage filibusters. For example, senators might offer scores of amendments, raise many points of order, or demand numerous and consecutive roll call votes. Holds also function as a form of "silent filibuster."

Holds

Long an informal custom, a hold permits one or more senators to block floor action on measures or matters by asking their party leaders not to schedule them. A hold, explained Sen. Charles E. Grassley, R-Iowa, is "a notice by a Senator to his or her party leader of an intention to object to bringing a bill or nomination to the floor for consideration."[70] The majority leader decides whether or for how long to honor a colleague's hold. The power of holds is grounded in the implicit threat of senators to conduct filibusters or to object to unanimous-consent agreements.

Holds have come under criticism because they often lead to delays or even the death of measures or nominations. Originally intended as a way for senators to get information about when the majority leader planned action on a measure, holds have become devices for senators to delay or kill measures and nominations or to extract concessions on other matters. For instance, Sen. Joe Manchin, D-W.Va., placed a hold on a nominee to serve on the Federal Communications Commission (FCC). The senator wanted the FCC to expedite the wiring of high-speed broadband service to homes in his state's rural areas. Senator Manchin lifted his hold when the FCC complied with his request.[71]

Filibusters and Cloture

The right of extended debate is unique to the Senate. Any senator or group of senators can talk continuously in the hope of delaying, modifying, or defeating legislation. In the view of Sen. Robert C. Byrd, D-W.Va., one of the foremost parliamentary experts in the history of the Senate, the filibuster is the "main cornerstone of the Senate's uniqueness." It is a "necessary evil," he said, but it "must be tolerated lest the Senate lose its special strength and become a mere appendage of the [majority rule] House of Representatives."[72] To be sure, there are Senators and many others, including President Donald Trump, who advocate for abolishing or greatly restricting the filibuster.

Most measures can be subject to at least two primary filibusters: the first on the motion to take up the legislation and the second on the consideration of the bill itself. *Double filibusters* underscore the expansive scope of minority rights that characterizes Senate procedure. Importantly, however, a number of laws, including trade and budget reconciliation measures, restrict a senator's right to extended debate. As a former Senate parliamentarian explained, "We have on the books probably a couple hundred laws that set up specific legislative vehicles that cannot be filibustered or only amended in a very restricted way."[73]

The success of a filibuster depends not only on how long it takes but also on when it is waged. A filibuster can be most effective late in a session because there is insufficient time to break it.[74] Even the threat of a filibuster can encourage accommodations or compromises between proponents and opponents of legislation.

During most of its history, the Senate had no way to terminate debate except by unanimous consent, exhaustion, or compromise. In 1917, the Senate adopted Rule XXII, its first cloture (debate-ending) rule. After several revisions, Rule XXII now permits three-fifths of the Senate (sixty members) to shut off debate on substantive issues or procedural motions. (A two-thirds vote is required to invoke cloture on a proposal to change the rules of the Senate.)

Once cloture is invoked, thirty hours of debate time remain before the final vote occurs on the matter identified in the cloture motion. There might also be multiple cloture votes on a measure: on the motion to proceed, on the bill itself, and on amendments. If the Senate is in a procedural "hardball" situation, opponents of a measure will consume the entire thirty hours of postcloture debate on each clotured item. These actions "can grind legislative business to a halt and leave the Senate in an interminable purgatory."[75]

Senators complain about the frequent use of filibuster threats and cloture attempts. In the past, filibusters generally occurred on issues of great national importance. Today, they occur on a wide range of less momentous topics. As one majority leader pointed out,

> Not long ago the filibuster or threat of a filibuster was rarely undertaken in the Senate, being reserved for matters of grave national importance. That is no longer the case. . . . The threat of a filibuster is now a regular event in the Senate, weekly at least, sometimes daily. It is invoked by minorities of as few as one or two Senators and for reasons as trivial as a Senator's travel schedule.[76]

Unsurprisingly, many commentators call it the "sixty-vote Senate." Or as a senator observed, "It isn't good enough to have the majority. You've got to have 60 votes," which is a dramatic departure from traditional practice.[77] Majority votes to pass measures were once common, except for supermajority requirements specified in the Constitution, statute, or Senate rules. Sixty votes are now required for enacting all types of measures or matters. It has become a common practice for unanimous consent agreements to simply stipulate that a bill or amendment must attract sixty votes for passage. The interests of both sides are served by this development. Majority advocates get a vote, and the supermajority threshold protects minority opponents. Moreover, this accord saves the Senate's time by avoiding use of the cloture procedure, which can consume three or more days.

Attempts to invoke cloture also have increased, particularly in recent Congresses. For example, in the decade from 1961 to 1971, there were 5.2 cloture votes per Congress, but during the 109th Congress (2005–2007), there were fifty-two cloture votes.[78] From the 110th Congress through the 113th Congress (2013–2015), there were 494 cloture votes.[79] The 114th Congress (2015–2017) alone took 124 votes on cloture and the 115th, 168.

Importantly, a cloture vote does not mean a filibuster is underway. Cloture is sometimes employed for purposes unrelated to ending a filibuster. For example, if the sixty votes are obtained under Senate Rule XXII, there is the requirement that all amendments must be germane to the clotured measure. Or the majority leader may schedule repeated cloture votes, knowing that he or she will fail, in order to tar the other party as "obstructionists" in the next election.

There is little question that contemporary senators wield their procedural prerogatives for partisan advantage. It is not surprising, then, that majority and minority partisans typically provide different interpretations of the circumstances that provoke their dismay and frustration with Senate proceedings. When Democrats held the Senate majority for eight years (2006–2014), they often lamented that minority Republicans provided "less cooperation and more determination to block almost anything than at any time I have seen in the 30 years I have served here."

> We have a noncontroversial issue, a motion to proceed [to the consideration of] something on which there is no controversy, and it is subject to a filibuster, and then a cloture motion has to be filed. Then 2 days have to pass before it ripens. We have a cloture vote, and then following the cloture vote, the minority says: Well, we insist that the 30 hours postcloture be used. So 30 hours has to be burned off. Only then can you get a vote on a noncontroversial issue [that may pass 98 to 1].[80]

Today, we have partisan reversal: Republicans controlled the 115th and now the 116th Senate (2019–2021). It is Democrats who are deciding when to "weaponize" Senate procedures to block GOP priorities, using such parliamentary tools as filibuster threats, holds, objections to unanimous-consent requests, and so on. In the midst of the explosion in obstruction by both parties a number of senators have proposed to change Senate rules. Rule XXII provides that invoking cloture on a rules change requires a two-thirds vote. However, one reform group has argued that a newly elected Senate should not be bound by Rule XXII or any preexisting rule. Like the House does every two years, reform-minded members argue that the Senate has the constitutional right "to determine the rules of its proceedings" by majority vote at the start of a new Congress, notwithstanding any inherited (or continuing) rules from the previous Congress.

Another approach to changing Senate rules is what has become known as the *nuclear option*. Rather than amending the text of Rule XXII at the start of a new Congress, the nuclear option—which can be invoked at any time—involves establishing a new precedent of majority cloture by overturning rulings of the presiding officer. Because overturning (or upholding) rulings of the presiding officer requires, with few exceptions, only a simple majority vote, the majority party can take such an action without any support from senators of the minority party. (The word *nuclear* is employed because of the parliamentary fallout expected from an angry minority party.) The effect is the same as a formal rules change because precedents trump Senate rules until they are modified or repealed at some later date.

On November 21, 2013, the nuclear option was triggered and produced a major procedural change in the Senate. A congressional scholar called the development "among the three or four most important events in the procedural history of the Senate." By permitting majority cloture, the nuclear option "reshaped the strategic calculations of presidents and senators involved in the nomination and confirmation process. The reform-by-ruling approach to establishing a new procedure had been used before, but the approach had never been used to directly and explicitly undermine Rule XXII."[81]

Majority Leader Reid, long frustrated by his party's inability to attract sixty votes to overcome Republican obstruction and approve President Obama's executive and judicial nominees, successfully invoked the nuclear option to establish majority cloture on executive and judicial nominees, excepting only nominees to the Supreme Court.

The procedural maneuver went as follows: When the Senate voted (fifty-seven yeas to forty-three nays) against cloture on a judicial nominee of President Barack Obama, Senator Reid raised a point of order (a parliamentary objection) that "the vote on cloture under Rule XXII for all nominations other than the Supreme Court of the United States is by majority vote." The presiding officer rejected Reid's point of order, mindful of Rule XXII's sixty-vote requirement to invoke cloture. Reid appealed the chair's ruling, which the Senate reversed on a 52–48 partisan vote. The Senate's authoritative new precedent "reinterpreted the provisions of Rule XXII to require only a simple majority to invoke cloture on most nominations."[82] To be sure, any majority party could use the nuclear option to change, by majority vote, the interpretation of Senate rules that impede favorable action on party-preferred priorities.

To say that the minority Republicans were upset is an understatement. For example, GOP senator Charles Grassley of Iowa called it a "naked power grab and nothing more than a power grab."[83] For the remainder of the 113th Congress, Republicans continued to delay action on presidential nominees by, ironically, using a Rule XXII procedure left unchanged by the new precedent: They consistently used all of the thirty hours allowed for postcloture debate before permitting votes on the nominees (see additional discussion that follows). Despite these delays, the nuclear option increased substantially Senate approval of the president's nominees.[84]

Four years later, on April 6, 2017, with Republicans now in control of the Senate, they expanded rather than reversed the move to majority rule for considering nominations. Senate Republicans invoked the nuclear option to permit a majority to invoke cloture for Supreme Court nominees. The Senate's decision cleared the way for Judge Neil Gorsuch and future nominees to the highest federal court to be confirmed by majority vote. That majority might include only members of the controlling party.

Senate Democratic distress at many of President Trump's cabinet and other nominees provoked Democrats to battle against their approval and to "slow walk" the confirmation process through dilatory actions. The minority was powerless to block the appointments unless they could win over a handful of Republicans. Consider the "57 straight hours [of Democratic speeches] in protest of Education Secretary Betsy DeVos and Attorney General Jeff Sessions," as well as a 2 a.m. vote on "Health and Human Services Secretary Tom Price."[85] The all-night speeches were filibusters in the usual sense: using prolonged speechmaking to prevent votes on the nominees. Senate Democrats realized, however, that it would be difficult to block the president's nominees. Instead, the Democratic speechmaking was an attempt, for example, "to call more attention to the vote, and increase public pressure on GOP senators who already received tens of thousands of calls and emails from people who oppose [Betsy] DeVos" as education secretary.[86]

Meanwhile, majority leader McConnell and GOP senators worked to circumvent the dilatory actions of Democrats. For example, he scheduled a rare 6:30 a.m. Senate session to vote on the DeVos nomination. He worked with his committee chairs to foil dilatory actions at the committee stage. Despite committee rules that require Democratic participation to report nominations, "Republicans changed [or suspended] committee rules so they could jam [the nomination] through committee" and onto the floor.[87] Many Senate Republicans, as well as President Trump, castigated Senate Democrats for delaying votes on the nominees.

The castigation increased when Senate Democrats began to use the thirty hours of postcloture debate to consume scarce floor time and to stymie action on Trump's executive and judicial branch nominees. On April 3, 2019, the Senate triggered the nuclear option for the third time. The new precedent reduces to two hours, from thirty, the time allowed for postcloture debate for most executive branch nominees and for federal district court nominees.[88] Senator McConnell favored the change to expedite Senate action on these nominees because his self-proclaimed top priority is to fill the judicial branch with life-time judges nominated by President Trump.

Political fights over the nuclear option put the procedural quandary facing the Senate in stark terms. Most senators value the benefits provided by unlimited debate to them as individuals. Many senators also believe that it would be a grave mistake for the Senate to "become just like the House" with its majority party dominance. But in an atmosphere of bitter partisan warfare in which the minority regularly uses all of the tactics available to it to obstruct the majority, the Senate may not be able to continue to function with a set of rules and precedents that assume a degree of restraint and comity. Some senators worry that if partisan conditions worsen, the nuclear option might be used to establish majority cloture for legislation (bills and resolutions). If this should occur, it would represent a nontraditional procedural change of momentous import.

RESOLVING HOUSE–SENATE DIFFERENCES

Before bills can be sent to the president, they must be passed by the House and the Senate in identical form (the same text and bill number). Conference committees are the best-known method used to resolve bicameral differences when the two chambers pass dissimilar versions of the same bill. Under each chamber's rules and precedents, conference committees meet only to resolve the matters in bicameral dispute; they are not to reconsider provisions already agreed to, and they are not to write new law by inserting matter that neither house considered. However, parliamentary rules are not self-enforcing, and either chamber can waive or ignore them. Conference committees, however, are not the only way of resolving interchamber differences. In fact, they have declined in importance in recent years.

Amendments Between the Houses

An increasingly common means of resolving House–Senate differences is to "ping-pong" House and Senate amendments between the chambers until each house is satisfied with the product.[89]

Recent congresses have turned to the ping-pong procedure more frequently (from about 20 percent of the time previously to upwards of 40 percent today—e.g., 38 percent in the 113th Congress). Indeed, there has been a precipitous decline in the convening of conference committees. For instance, in the 104th Congress (1995–1997), there were fifty-three conference reports; in the 112th, (2011–2013), seven; in the 113th, three; in the 114th, seven; and in the 115th, five. Various reasons account for this drop-off: the difficulty of passing legislation in a partisan era; the rise of megabills that contain numerous discrete measures previously handled individually; the Senate's problems in overcoming obstruction to convene a conference; and certain advantages to party leaders that inhere in the amendment exchange approach.

First, the amendment exchange process enhances the negotiating power of the top majority party leaders in each chamber. They can meet in secret and craft bicameral compromises likely to be agreed to in both chambers. Second, the ping-pong route minimizes the role of committees. Committee chairs and members might not be part of the reconciling process. Third, minority party members could be completely excluded from the negotiating process. Lastly, many formal House and Senate rules that apply to conferences do not apply to the amendment exchange process. For example, the designation of House and Senate conferees is public information. The identity of the participants in the ping-pong process is secret unless the names are revealed by, for example, party leaders.

The Conference Committee Process

When conference committees are employed to resolve House–Senate differences, conferees usually are drawn from the committee or committees that reported the legislation. Although congressional rules state that the Speaker and the Senate presiding officer select conferees, that decision typically is made by the relevant committee chairs and the ranking minority members. But House and Senate party leaders will get involved in naming conferees on major legislation to ensure that the conferees will back leadership positions on the legislation.

House and Senate party leaders are sometimes named as conferees—a sign that they want to direct conference negotiations on high-stakes issues important to their party. When the top majority party leaders of either chamber are named as conferees, this signals, as one senator declared, a "majority-party driven" conference.[90] Each chamber may name as many conferees as it wants. The ratio of Democrats to Republicans on a conference committee generally reflects the proportion of the two parties in the House and Senate.

In conference, each chamber has a single vote determined by a majority of its conferees, who are generally expected to support the legislation as it passes their body. A standard objective of conferees is to fashion a compromise product—the conference report—that will be acceptable to a majority of the membership of both chambers and that the president will sign into law.

A conference ends when its report (the compromise bill) is signed by a majority of the conferees from each chamber. House and Senate staff then prepare the conference report and the accompanying joint explanatory statement, which summarizes the conferees' recommendations. The House and Senate then vote on the conference report without further amendment. If either chamber rejects the conference report—an infrequent occurrence—a new conference may be called or another bill introduced. Once passed, the compromise bill is sent to the president for approval or disapproval.

Openness and Bargaining

Secret conference meetings were the norm for most of Congress's history. In 1975, both houses adopted rules requiring open meetings unless the conferees from each chamber voted in public to close the sessions. Two years later, the House went further, requiring open conference meetings unless the full House agreed to secret sessions. Sometimes, C-SPAN televises conference proceedings.

The open conference is yet another instance of individual–institutional cleavage. Under the watchful eye of lobbyists, conferees fight harder for provisions they might have dropped quietly in the interest of bicameral agreement. And yet private bargaining sessions still permeate conference negotiations.

If senators and representatives expect certain bills to go to conference, they plan their bargaining strategy accordingly. For example, whether to have a recorded vote on amendments in either chamber can influence conference bargaining. In the absence of a recorded vote, amendments may be easier to drop in conference. Bargaining techniques in conference cover a range of approaches: from logrolling ("you accept my chamber's position on this provision, and I'll accept yours on another provision") to threats to walk out of the negotiations unless the other side compromises. One side may fight hard for a position on which it plans to yield, so the conferees can tell their parent chamber that they put up a good battle, but the other side would not relent. Conference committees sometimes make changes or additions to legislation that neither chamber ever reviewed or considered in committee or on the floor.

CONCLUSION

The philosophical bias of House and Senate rules reflects the character of each institution. Individual rights are stressed in the Senate, majority rule in the House. In both chambers, however, members who know the rules and precedents have an advantage over procedural novices in affecting policy outcomes. Sen. Robert Byrd, D-W.Va.—the longest-serving Senate member in history—was the acknowledged procedural expert in the Senate. Byrd understood that passing measures often involved unorthodox processes and procedures (for example, foregoing committee hearings or markups or even floor debate).[91]

In addition to congressional rules, persistence, strategy, timing, compromise, and pure chance are important elements in the lawmaking process. To make public policy requires building winning coalitions at successive stages where pressure groups and other parties can advance their claims. Political, procedural, personal, and policy considerations shape the final outcome. Passing laws, as one former representative said, is like the "weaving of a web, bringing a lot of strands together in a pattern of support which won't have the kind of weak spots which could cause the whole fabric to fall apart."[92]

The First Step Act.
President Donald J. Trump, with Senator Chuck Grassley, R-Iowa, by his side, participates in a signing ceremony for S. 756, First Step Act, and H.R. 6964, Juvenile Justice Reform Act, in the Oval Office at the White House on Friday, December 21, 2018, in Washington, DC. Senate Judiciary Committee Chairman Chuck Grassley (R-Iowa) speaks on the passage of the First Step Act. Grassley, (R-Iowa), Senator Cory Booker (D-N.J.), Senator Dick Durbin (D-Ill.) and Senator Mike Lee (R-Utah) chat before a press conference on December 19, 2018, in Washington, DC.

DECISION MAKING IN CONGRESS

"This is a great bi-partisan achievement for everybody," declared President Donald Trump in a tweet as he prepared to sign the First Step Act criminal justice reform bill. "When both parties work together we can keep our Country safer." Although the lopsided votes in favor of the bill in 2018 might suggest otherwise, the act had only barely survived a long trek through both chambers. "This bill was declared dead at least a dozen times . . . This has been a battle," noted a leading outside advocate for reform.[1] The First Step Act changes sentencing laws that govern the federal prison system. Among other provisions, it eases mandatory minimum sentences, increases "good time credits" that inmates can earn to reduce their prison sentences through good behavior, and encourages inmate participation in vocational and rehabilitation programs.[2] The first major criminal justice overhaul in decades, the act will allow thousands of individuals to earn an earlier release from federal prison and is expected to reduce the length of sentences in the future.[3]

The carefully crafted compromise was the product of years of negotiations involving conservative Republican and liberal Democratic members of Congress, along with a diverse array of interest groups and White House officials. The unlikely coalition began as a partnership between die-hard conservative Mike Lee, R-Utah, and liberal Democrat Richard Durbin of Illinois. Lee, a former prosecutor, had been outraged by what he viewed as an excessive sentence for a minor drug offense and recalled the judge telling him that "only Congress can fix this problem." Soon after entering the Senate in 2010, Lee began looking for allies to change those laws. He teamed with Durbin, who had long regretted his vote, as a junior House member, for a 1986 bill that stiffened sentences for drugs, particularly crack cocaine. Durbin noted that working with Lee was a "terrific alliance because it really puzzled people why Durbin and Lee would be doing something together." But the unlikely pairing faced numerous obstacles, including the opposition of several powerful conservative Republicans who were reluctant to support legislation that might be perceived as soft on crime. By 2015, Durbin and Lee had gained the cosponsorship of Sen. Judiciary Chair Chuck Grassley for a sentencing reform bill, but opposition from other conservatives, such as Tom Cotton, R-Ark., and Jeff Sessions, R-Ala., sunk the measure.[4]

With legislation stalled in the Senate, Rep. Doug Collins, R-Ga., and Hakeem Jeffries, D-N.Y., decided to work on a narrower bill. They gained critical support from President Trump's son-in-law, Jared Kushner, who had become an advocate of sentencing reform in the wake of his father, Charles Kushner's imprisonment for tax evasion and illegal campaign contributions. With Kushner's help, Collins and Jeffries persuaded House Republican leaders to greenlight a modest bill which did not reduce mandatory minimums.[5]

The measure easily passed the House, but Senate advocates for stronger reform were furious. "We basically said we're going to do everything we can to defeat this bill," declared Cory Booker, D-N.J., who had joined the criminal justice reform effort when he entered the Senate in 2013. Advocates feared that passage of a less ambitious bill would sap the energy behind more meaningful changes. The Senate reformers' united opposition forced Kushner and the Trump administration, which wanted some sort of bipartisan legislative accomplishment to point to, back to the bargaining table. The reformers' efforts were boosted by a lobbying campaign that included the ACLU and the Leadership Conference on Civil and Human Rights on the left, and the Koch Brothers and Heritage Action on the right. After weeks of negotiations, a compromise was reached that expanded the scope of the House bill sufficiently to win over reform backers in the Senate without alienating the White House.[6]

Even then, bill supporters faced one final obstacle: Majority Leader Mitch McConnell did not want to schedule legislation that was still opposed by a small group of hard-core conservatives in his party. To win over McConnell, outside advocates mobilized supporters in his home state of Kentucky, generating 30,000 calls to McConnell's office. "Hear from us is what he got," noted one organizer. McConnell remained on the fence until Grassley persuaded President Trump to pressure the Senate leader with a tweet, "Hopefully Mitch McConnell will ask for a VOTE on Criminal Justice Reform . . . Go for it Mitch." Four days later, McConnell announced that the bill would come to a vote in a few days.[7] It then passed the Senate 87–12 and the House by a 358–36 vote.

The legislative journey of the First Step Act underscores several elements of lawmaking in today's Congress. Legislative success required a long process in which policy entrepreneurs negotiated compromises with members who initially were opposed to the legislation. Success ultimately required the cooperation not only of senior committee leaders but also of party leaders and the White House. Rather than seeing committees and party leaders simply as rivals for power, collaboration is often necessary for the success of both groups. A further key to success was that the reform coalition attracted outside support from both the left and the right. Liberal groups concerned with the effects of mass incarceration on their communities joined forces with conservative groups that were largely motivated by concerns about excessive spending. The breadth of this advocacy coalition allowed a diverse set of members to vote for the same bill, even as they did so for a range of different reasons. As the First Step Act illustrates, legislative assemblies are deliberative bodies, and in the United States, this deliberation takes place in the context of the two Congresses. Individual members confront thousands of choices: how and when to participate, how to decide, how to find allies, and how to explain their actions to constituents back home.

THE POWER TO CHOOSE

All members of Congress have the ability to shape public policy, although some members are far more influential than others. At a minimum, every legislator has the right, indeed the obligation, to vote. Legislators must cast their own votes; no colleague or staff aide may do it for them. To exchange their votes or other official acts for money or for any other thing of value is a federal crime. But aside from bribery or corruption, there are no legal grounds for challenging legislators' deliberations or decisions. As discussed in Chapter 2, the U.S. Constitution specifies that "for any Speech or Debate in either House, [members of Congress] shall not be questioned in any other place."

Policy making in Congress involves far more than casting roll call votes. Matters that come before Congress for a vote have already been shaped by the participation of members at prior stages. Some of this work, like members' votes, is a matter of public record: formal meetings, markups, debates, and amending activities. Of equal importance are the less visible informal negotiations that surround nearly every enactment—away from the eyes and ears of reporters and the general public. In a study of members' committee activity, Richard L. Hall found that members' formal and informal activities do not always coincide.[8] Sometimes, members use formal actions to signal concern to constituents and other groups but then do not follow through with the hard informal work needed to shape the legislation.

A full accounting of lawmakers' performance, then, would embrace not only how members participate in floor and committee deliberations but also how much effort they expend overall. How much attention do they pay to issues? How do they gain expertise? Whom do they consult for information on legislative decisions? How much do they rely upon party leaders for information? How do they hire, deploy, and supervise their staffs? Countless such decisions define what it means to be a member of Congress.

TYPES OF DECISIONS

One basic decision facing legislators is how to spend their time and energy while in the nation's capital. Some try to digest the mountains of studies and reports that cross their desks. They "do their homework," in Capitol Hill parlance. Others seem to know or care little about legislative matters. They pursue other duties—communication, outreach, visits with constituents or lobby groups, partisan politics, and fund-raising. Such members may rarely contribute to committee or floor deliberations. Their votes usually follow cues from party colleagues, staff aides, the White House, or interest groups. Some are found in the ranks of the "Obscure Caucus," a list of unnoticed members compiled periodically by *Roll Call,* a Capitol Hill newspaper. These members "spend time on parochial concerns or constituent service" rather than "staff a PR portfolio with press releases, television appearances and photo ops."[9]

Specializing

Within the legislative realm, members may dig deeply into a particular area or range widely across issues and policies. Senators are more apt to be generalists while representatives tend to cultivate a few specialties. Former senator Jim DeMint, R-S.C., once explained why members should specialize:

> If you've got twenty things you want to do, see where everything is. You'll find that maybe ten of those are already being worked on by people, and that while you may be supportive in that role, you don't need to carry the ball. But you can find those two or three things that are important to you that no one seems to be taking the lead on. But if you try to play the lead on everything, you'll be wasting your time.[10]

In both houses, key policy-making roles are played by those whom Rep. David E. Price, D-N.C., a political scientist, calls *policy entrepreneurs*—that is, those recognized for "stimulating more than . . . responding" to outside political forces on a given issue.[11] Often nearly invisible to the mass of citizens, these legislators are known to specialized publics for their contributions to specific policies—for example, Sen. Rob Portman, R-Ohio, on human trafficking; Sen. Jon Tester on public lands; and Rep. Mac Thornberry, R-Tex., on cybersecurity.

Members' policy reaches can go beyond their committee assignments—through speeches, floor amendments, caucuses, and task forces, to name a few. When only in his second term, Rep. Dick Armey, R-Tex. (1985–2003), who was not a member of the Armed Services Committee, devised an ingenious scheme to employ an outside commission—the Base Realignment and Closure (BRAC) Commission—to decide which unneeded military bases should be closed. His proposal smoothed political sensitivities regarding base closures in members' constituencies and won bipartisan support for its enactment into law (P.L. 100–526). Such feats are not everyday occurrences, but the fluidity of legislative procedures makes even the most junior member a potential policy entrepreneur.

A member's knowledge and perceived expertise on issues is a vital source of legislative influence. As Sen. Edmund S. Muskie, D-Maine (1959–1980), put it,

People have all sorts of conspiratorial theories on what constitutes power in the Senate. It has little to do with the size of the state you come from. Or the source of your money. Or committee chairmanships, although that certainly gives you a kind of power. But real power up there comes from doing your work and knowing what you're talking about. Power is the ability to change someone's mind. . . . The most important thing in the Senate is credibility. Credibility! That is power.[12]

This sort of credibility generally comes from immersion in a particular set of issues rather than aiming to speak authoritatively across the sweep of congressional business.

Timing of Decisions

Lawmakers do more than specialize in a particular policy field. They are constantly forced to make decisions on issues, many far from their areas of specialization. Timing is key. *When* members make decisions has important consequences for the deliberative process, a point that Richard F. Fenno Jr. discussed in his work on the "politics of timing."[13] Fenno identified three types of decision makers: early deciders, active players, and late deciders.

Early deciders are fervent supporters who want to get out front in the debate. "I'd rather come out early and be part of the fight," said Rep. Peter T. King, R-N.Y., of his ready support for granting the president fast-track trade authority.[14] These members are buoyed by friendly lobbyists but ignored by others because their commitments are known at the outset from declarations, bill sponsorship, or prior voting records.

Active players, by contrast, delay their commitments, inviting bids from various sides of the issue at hand and often gaining leverage over the final language of legislation.

Late deciders delay their decision until the very last moment. They forfeit influence over the basic framework of the measure. But late deciders are eagerly courted by all sides and may gain specific concessions. With every vote critical to Senate passage of President Obama's health care overhaul plan and pressure mounting to conclude action, Sen. Byron Dorgan, D-N.D., informed Majority Leader Reid that he would not vote for the Patient Protection and Affordable Care Act unless it included Native American health care. "That's not a threat, just a statement of fact," he said.[15] (Dorgan, now retired, was chair of the Committee on Indian Affairs.) Native American health care was included as part of the larger bill. In other cases, late deciders gain intense publicity—both positive and negative—by delaying a decision on a showdown vote until the last moment, as occurred in July 2017 when Sen. John McCain came out against Republicans' Obamacare repeal bill at the last moment, casting the decisive vote alongside Republican defectors Susan Collins of Maine and Lisa Murkowski of Alaska.[16]

Taking the Lead

Senators and representatives differ widely in the rate at which they introduce and sponsor bills. Some lawmakers are inveterate initiators of bills and resolutions. Others shy away from sponsoring measures. Still others commonly take the lead in sponsoring legislation because of the position they occupy, such as the chair of the relevant committee of jurisdiction. A study by Wendy Schiller found that bills in the Senate are most likely to be introduced by senior senators, those who are chairs or ranking members of high-volume committees (such as Commerce), and those who represent large, diverse states.[17]

Sponsoring legislation can provide members with valuable credit-claiming opportunities. In the lead-up to the 2018 election, Republican leaders scheduled floor votes on an array of relatively minor bills to address the opioid crisis. Many of these bills were sponsored by the party's most vulnerable members, providing them with an opportunity to tell constituents that they were working hard to fight this urgent problem. Rep. Mary Bono noted that bringing dozens of small bills to the floor instead of a single comprehensive measure allows members to show their individual contribution: "It's hard to go out on the campaign and say I negotiated this provision in the bill . . . Leadership recognizes they should give credit where credit is due."[18]

Senate and House rules do not limit the number of members who can cosponsor bills or resolutions. Thus, cosponsorship has become common. Most bills are cosponsored; in a recent Congress, the average Senate bill had 4.1 cosponsors, and the average House bill had 15.5 cosponsors.[19] Authors of measures often circulate a "Dear Colleague" letter detailing the virtues of the bill and soliciting cosponsors to demonstrate broad support and urge committee action. A researcher found that more than twelve thousand such letters were sent electronically by House members in 2009, an average of more than twenty-five letters per member.[20] Do legislators favor the bills and resolutions they introduce? Normally they do, but as Sportin' Life, the *Porgy and Bess* character, said, "It ain't necessarily so."[21] Members may introduce a measure to stake out jurisdiction for their committee or to pave the way for hearings and deliberations that will air a public problem. Or they may introduce measures they do not personally favor to oblige an executive agency or to placate an important interest group. In rare cases, this results in members backtracking if a measure actually reaches the floor for a vote. For example, many House Democrats responded to outrage over the Trump administration's family separation policy at the border by cosponsoring the "Abolish ICE" bill. But with polls showing the proposal to eliminate the Immigration and Customs Enforcement Agency lacked majority support—and with Democrats yet to agree on what would replace ICE—GOP leaders saw an opportunity to put Democrats on the spot by scheduling a vote on the measure. In the end, Democrats announced they would vote against the bill but use the floor debate to criticize the administration's policy. Republican leaders then cancelled the vote.[22]

Taking Part

As members in any organization, some lawmakers take a passionate interest in what goes on; others pay selective attention to issues; a few seem just to be going through the motions. In a detailed study of three House committees, Richard L. Hall uncovered great variation in members' levels of participation. Although members' attendance at committee and subcommittee sessions was respectable (about three quarters of the members showed up for at least part of each session), active participation—taking part in markup debate, offering amendments, and the like—was far less common. Perhaps half of a subcommittee's members could be considered players, by a generous counting. The rest were nonplayers. As a sub-committee staffer remarked, "On a good day half of [the members] know what's going on. Most of the time it's only five or six who actually mark a bill up."[23]

Constituency interests strongly propel members to participate in committee business. In formal subcommittee markup sessions, "the public forum has the benefit of allowing members at once to promote—through their votes, argu-ments, amendments, obstructionism—constituency interests and be seen doing so."[24] But even when negotiations are not visible to the public, legislators will have an incentive to advocate for constituent interests.

Constituency-driven activity was especially common in the House Committee on Agriculture, a panel historically buffeted by regional and commodity pres-sures. Because of the committee's composition, its membership is more favor-able to agriculture programs than the House as a whole. Furthermore, only a subset of the committee's members participates in most matters, and those who choose to take part tend to be more predisposed to favor the programs under consideration than even the rest of the Agriculture Committee. Hall found in his late-1990s study that members representing constituencies with large numbers of dairy farmers and peanut growers, for example, were the most active in influenc-ing policy affecting dairy and peanut interests. Neither the full committee nor floor deliberations counterbalanced the enthusiastic advocacy of the dozen or so lawmakers from districts that produced those commodities. Participation on Agriculture was the most biased toward members with a constituency stake in the legislation being considered. In debates over job-training legislation in another committee, participating members tended to represent areas with higher unem-ployment rates than those of nonparticipants, but the gap was less stark than on Agriculture. No participatory biases were found when concentrated district benefits were not at stake.

Members in formal leadership positions are also more likely to take an active part in committee deliberations. Members often forgo participation because there are so many demands on their time that they must prioritize issues that are impor-tant to their constituents. Committee and subcommittee leaders, however, face fewer obstacles to participation because their seniority and authority "[place] them at the epicenter of the communications network in which most important leg-islative interactions take place."[25] In other words, holding leadership posts puts members "in the know" and enables them to be major players on legislation even when they do not personally have a significant constituency stake in the outcome.[26] Judiciary Chair Grassley's prominent role in pressuring McConnell to advance the First Step Act is an example of committee leaders' active engagement in legislation with broad-reaching implications. More generally, a recent study demonstrates that majority party members holding senior committee or party leadership posts are the most effective representatives in enacting their preferred legislation.[27]

Participation in House or Senate floor debates is equally varied: Members who do not serve on the relevant committees or who have only peripheral interests in the matter are tempted to speak simply "for the record." Floor speeches vary greatly in the quality of their informational content. A study of three major congressional debates determined that it is "typically no better than moderately informed." Gary Mucchiaroni and Paul J. Quirk concluded, "Legislators frequently assert claims that are inaccurate or misleading, and reassert them after they have been effectively refuted."[28] The good news about floor debates is that opposing members often—though not always—counter erroneous or distorted arguments.

Offering Amendments

Another important way of participating is to offer amendments to bills or resolutions. Amendments propose specific changes in legislative language: They delete or add words or substitute one provision for another. They are a chief means of shaping legislation during committee and floor deliberations. However, amendments are not always intended to enact policy changes. They can instead be used as a tool of obstruction or to derail legislation. They also can serve political purposes by putting members on the record on specific issues. For example, Sen. Claire McCaskill, D-Mo., who won reelection in a tight 2012 contest, exclaimed that in the lead-up to the election, Senate GOP leader Mitch McConnell, R-Ky., had been "trying to figure out what amendments he could put on the floor to make my life miserable." McConnell's goal, she said, was "to figure out some way to put something on the floor that would get me to vote against my own mother."[29]

House majority leaders, who control the floor agenda, regularly employ special rules to limit the amendments that members can offer to particular bills. By so doing, the leaders often can engineer favored policy outcomes, expedite floor action, and prevent politically difficult issues from being raised on the floor. In November 2017, for example, Speaker Paul Ryan came under criticism from Democrats and dissident Republicans for using a restrictive amendment rule to block a vote on a proposal to phase out the 2001 Authorization for Use of Military Force, which had passed in the wake of 9/11 but was still being used to justify a range of military actions. The amendment had bipartisan support but was opposed by the Trump administration and GOP leaders. Republican dissident Justin Amash of Michigan complained "We're supposed to have a speaker who keeps the House open and reflecting the will of the people . . . There's a lot of protection happening right now, where leaders are trying to shield their members from votes."[30]

Compared with the House, in the Senate—because of individual senators' prerogatives—amendments are more freely offered and form a central part of floor debate. Senate amendments are often designed to force members to declare themselves on issues that command public attention. Sen. David Vitter's, R-La., amendment to an omnibus appropriations bill to end automatic cost-of-living increases in congressional salaries is an example. Lawmakers who vote for salary increases, especially during hard economic times, risk having the voters turn them out of office.

Other amendments are poison pills. A so-called killer amendment is intended to make a bill so unpalatable that, if adopted, it will kill the underlying measure. Although killer amendments upset the sponsors and managers of bills, they rarely alter a measure's ultimate fate. Examining seventy-six killer amendments considered in the mid-1990s, a scholar concluded that they "rarely, if ever, cause bills to fail. . . . Most were easily defeated."[31]

Casting Votes

Lawmakers' most visible choices are embodied in the votes they cast. Members know that their voting records communicate a great deal of information about their policy and political commitments to their constituents. Reflecting on his vote on a financial institutions bailout package, a House member said, "This is a legacy vote; these are the votes you have to live with for the rest of your life."[32] Several months after the 112th Congress convened, many Tea Party-supported congressional Republicans found themselves facing a legacy vote. These lawmakers, having promised in the 2010 elections to cut and curb government spending, now faced an unavoidable vote: the electorally painful decision to raise the national debt ceiling. A failure to raise the debt ceiling when needed would risk global financial instability, but voting to increase it is never popular with constituents, particularly those most concerned about government debt. Raising the "must-pass" debt ceiling is "beautiful politics—the brutal kind," declared former senator Alan Simpson, R-Wyo. (1979–1997).[33]

Members anticipate that constituents will review their votes at reelection time. Outside groups closely follow members' votes on specific measures and publicize them during campaigns. Special interests want to know whether members' promises on the campaign trail tracked their voting decisions in Congress. Groups may grade lawmakers as "heroes" or "zeros" based on their votes for environmental or business measures. Nevertheless, members' own personal judgments sometimes outweigh political expedience. Members may be willing to risk their reelection chances by casting a vote contrary to the strong preferences of many of their constituents (for example, voting for gun control in a state or district with a pro-gun culture), especially if they have explained to voters in advance the reasons for their decision.

Senators and representatives strive to be recorded on as many floor and committee votes as possible. On 708 roll call votes on the House floor in 2017, members voted 96 percent of the time. Senators recorded a participation rate of 98 percent on the 325 votes taken in 2017.[34] Members seek to compile a record of diligence to forestall charges of absenteeism by potential opponents. They also want to compile a good voting record to demonstrate their commitment to the voters back home. Just before casting her five thousandth consecutive vote, Sen. Susan Collins, R-Maine, said, "While I recognize that not every vote is a critical vote, at this time when the public's confidence is so low, casting every single vote sends a strong signal to one's constituents of dedication to the job and to respect for the high privilege that we have been given."[35] House and Senate leaders make it easier for members by trying to schedule votes at predictable times: stacking votes back to back in midweek or holding fewer votes on Mondays, when lawmakers are returning to Capitol Hill from their states or districts, and Fridays, when many members are anxious to depart for their constituencies.

If members cannot vote in person, they can still be recorded on an issue by announcing their views in floor statements or in press releases. A member who wishes to be recorded on an issue but cannot be present for the roll call vote may also ask another member who plans to vote on the other side for a "pair" arrangement in which both announce their positions in the *Congressional Record* but neither casts a vote. (They cancel each other out.) Members often grant such requests as a courtesy to their colleagues. Members might also vote "present" for various reasons. For example, Sen. Charles Schumer, D-N.Y., cast a rare "present" vote on a judicial nominee because the nominee was married to his sister.[36]

What Do Votes Mean?

Like other elements of the legislative process, votes are open to multiple interpretations. House and Senate floor votes do not perfectly register members' views. Members sometimes vote against a bill that they prefer to the status quo because they hope that a better bill on the matter might emerge later. Members know that a weak reform can deplete political will for bolder action. Killing a modest measure may lead to action on a more wide-ranging proposal later. Politicians may also refuse to accept a compromise when they can force a confrontation that will sharpen the differences between the parties. At times, members prefer to keep the issue alive rather than to pass a bill.[37]

Members also may vote for a bill that they do not favor because they fear that if they fail to support it the end result will be something even worse. For example, some conservative Republicans voted for a federal program providing prescription drug coverage for elderly Americans because they believed it was the best bill they could get. "I don't think we'll write a better bill if we defeat this," explained a conservative senator.[38] Members may also go along with legislation because on the whole, they deem the bill a step forward, even though they dislike specific provisions.

In some cases, recorded votes are wholly misleading. Given the multiplicity of votes—procedural as well as substantive—on many measures, lawmakers can come out on more than one side of an issue—or at least appear to do so. For example, members may vote to authorize a program and later vote against funding it. Or they may vote against final passage of a bill but for a substitute version. This tactic, which may open a lawmaker to the charge of being a "flip-flopper," assures the bill's backers that the lawmaker favors the concept while pleasing voters who oppose the bill. Such voting patterns may reflect either a deliberate attempt to obscure one's position or a thoughtful response to complex questions. As in so many aspects of human behavior, lawmakers' motivations are often difficult to discern.

Members can also take advantage of "free votes" when their own individual vote will not affect the final outcome. Some members delay voting until the outcome of the vote is already assured. For example, during the debate on a constitutional amendment to prohibit flag burning, there was *strategic waiting* on the part of members.[39] Democratic members were cross-pressured on the issue—Democratic leaders opposed the anti-flag-burning amendment, but it was very popular with constituents. Before it was clear that the amendment was going to fail, only 28 percent of the voting Democrats supported the amendment. Once enough votes had been cast to defeat the amendment, 73 percent of the remaining Democrats voted in favor of it. After the amendment had failed, members could take the popular position without any legislative consequences. Opportunities for insincere votes proliferate in the U.S. separation-of-powers system. Members can deliberately vote for measures that they believe will fail in the other chamber of Congress or be vetoed by the president. And they can support popular measures that they expect the courts will strike down as unconstitutional.

Lawmakers' voting rationales are sometimes hard to explain to outsiders. In some cases, members face a dilemma: either vote their convictions and deal with the consequences or swallow their misgivings and vote for appearance's sake. A GOP House member chose the former course when he joined fourteen other Republicans in voting against a popular bill authorizing U.S. sanctions against nations that persecute religious minorities—an appealing idea but fraught with problems. "This was an awfully awkward vote, and I know I'll hear from the folks back home," he explained. "But the devil was in the details."[40] More often, lawmakers decide to go with the crowd. Regarding a highly appealing constitutional amendment requiring a balanced budget, a senator admitted that he planned to vote for it because he got "tired of explaining" its deficiencies. It was easier "just to say put it in."[41] It no doubt eased the member's conscience to know that the chances were slim that the amendment would ultimately be ratified.

Scholars and journalists often mistakenly treat votes as if they were unambiguous indicators of legislators' views. Lobbyists, too, are prone to assess lawmakers on the basis of floor votes. Many groups construct voting indexes that label legislators as "friendly" or "unfriendly." Citizens should be cautioned to examine such indexes closely. How many votes does the index include? Are they a fair sample of the group's concerns? Does the index embody a partisan or ideological agenda, hidden or otherwise? The bottom line is this: Beware of an interest group's voting scorecards, even if you agree with its policy leanings.

DETERMINANTS OF VOTING

Votes, particularly on single issues, should be examined, interpreted, and categorized with care. Party affiliation, ideological leanings, constituents' views, presidential leadership, and cues from trusted fellow members are among the factors that shape congressional voting.

Party and Voting

Party affiliation is the strongest single correlate of members' voting decisions. In a typical year, from half to three quarters of all floor votes could be called party unity votes, defined as votes in which a majority of voting Republicans oppose a majority of voting Democrats. Figure 9-1 depicts House and Senate party unity votes from 1953 to 2018. Party voting is far more prevalent today than it was in the 1970s or early 1980s. Indeed, contemporary levels of party voting recall the militant parties of the late-nineteenth century.

In the GOP-controlled House, party voting set a new record in 2017.[42] A majority of Republicans voted against a majority of Democrats on 76.0 percent of the 709 roll calls. House party votes were common in large measure because Republican leaders worked hard to "settle disputes and rally support" as they set the legislative agenda.[43] Speaker Ryan had also promised to refuse to bring to a vote measures lacking support from at least a majority of the Republican party, thereby restricting the occurrence of intra-party vote splits.[44] In the Senate, a near-record 69 percent of votes split along party lines in 2017.[45] The share of party votes fell in both chambers in 2018—to 59 percent in the House and 49.6 percent in the Senate—as the Republican majority pursued a narrower agenda ahead of the midterm elections.

Figure 9-2 depicts unity scores for the two parties in each chamber from 1956 to 2018. Both House Republicans and Democrats achieved extremely high cohesion in 2017: 92 percent of Republicans and 93 percent of Democrats voted with their own party when the two parties disagreed. The Democrats' unity level was at an all-time high. Senate Democrats achieved similar unity, with 92 percent of party members sticking with their party on party votes in 2017. The Senate GOP had even greater success holding its troops together, recording a record 97 percent unity rate in 2017. While party unity dipped slightly in both chambers in 2018, the vast majority of members continued to stick with their party.

Party cohesion stems from a number of roots. Members of a political party vote similarly because they are elected by many of the same sorts of constituencies and organized interests throughout the country. As one study noted, on a wide range of unrelated issues—"gun control, the economy, war, same-sex marriage, abortion, the environment, the financial bailout—the views of Republicans and Democrats have become increasingly monolithic."[46]

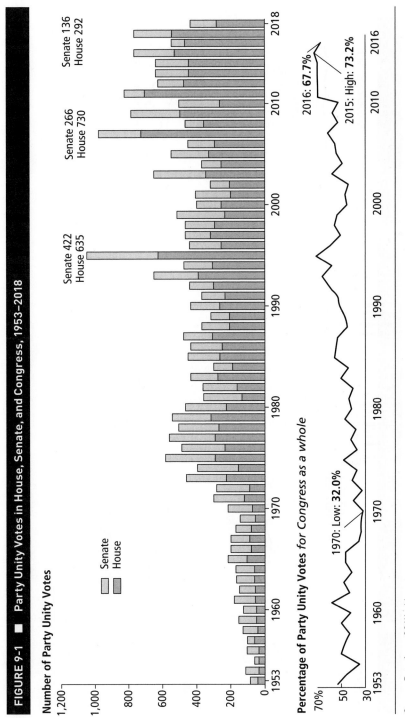

Source: Data from *CQ Weekly*.

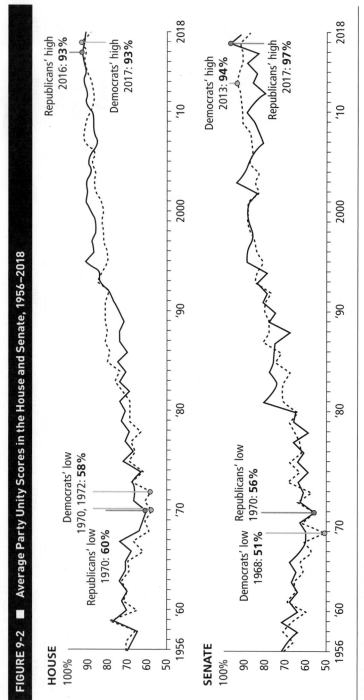

FIGURE 9-2 ■ **Average Party Unity Scores in the House and Senate, 1956–2018**

HOUSE

Republicans' high
2016: **93%**

Democrats' high
2017: **93%**

Democrats' low
1970, 1972: **58%**

Republicans' low
1970: **60%**

SENATE

Democrats' high
2013: **94%**

Republicans' high
2017: **97%**

Democrats' low
1968: **51%**

Republicans' low
1970: **56%**

Source: Data from *CQ Weekly.*

Party members also vote together because of their shared ideological commitments. Changes in the ideological composition and the constituency base of the two congressional parties have contributed to the increased levels of partisanship in the contemporary Congress. Each of these sources of party unity—constituency and ideology—is discussed here. However, it is important to note that congressional party unity also has a source in explicitly *partisan* motives, meaning party members' shared political interests in helping their party win elections and control Congress.[47] These interests bring fellow partisans together despite the diversity of their policy preferences. Indeed, even when interparty conflict in Congress was at a low ebb in the late 1960s and early 1970s, the parties still successfully organized the committees and leadership of Congress, and party affiliation remained the strongest single predictor of members' voting behavior.

Members of Congress cooperate with their fellow partisans, in part, because their personal fate as politicians is bound up with their party's public image and collective reputation. Members know that they do not win or lose elections solely as individual legislators. Voters' attitudes about the national parties affect their choices in particular congressional elections.[48] As a result, members have reason to take into account how their individual actions will affect public perceptions of their party as a whole.

Members also care about the collective image of their party because they want their party to command a congressional majority. Members gain power personally when their party is in the majority. Members of the majority party chair all committees and subcommittees, and majority leaders set the floor agenda. It is easier for members to advance their personal policy initiatives when they are in the majority. This interest is likely to be especially salient in periods—such as the past two decades—when majority control is seen as up for grabs.[49]

Members concerned with winning elections and wielding influence will therefore pay attention to their party's collective reputation. To foster positive public impressions of their party, fellow partisans work to find common ground. They collaborate in efforts to construct an appealing policy agenda and then cooperate in promoting it. They also exploit opportunities to call into question the other party's competence and integrity.

Common political interests nurture bonds of trust and communication among fellow partisans. To deepen these bonds, the congressional parties now hold regular lunches, conferences, and retreats for members. In addition, the socialization of new members largely takes place in partisan settings. Thus, fewer friendships cross party lines these days. As one senator explained, "If the only knowledge you have of 'the other side of the aisle' is what you have read in an attack press release written by the party operatives, you wouldn't want to talk to them, and you certainly wouldn't want to be friends."[50] Majority and minority party leaders regularly appeal to their members' common partisan interests in order to rally their troops behind the party agenda. The leaders of both parties strive to give the electorate a favorable view of the party's "brand." They hire consultants to devise messages and strategies crafted to generate broad public support for their policy goals and objectives. Reflecting on these partisan motives, political scientists Gary Cox and Mathew McCubbins wrote, "Modern political parties facing mass electorates, similar to corporations facing mass markets, have a strong incentive to fashion and maintain a brand name."[51]

The common political interests of Democrats and Republicans mean they are predisposed to support their party. Political scientists who have studied members' voting decisions have found that members decide mainly by consulting the views of their partisan colleagues.[52] The typical member of Congress feels "duty bound to ascertain the views of the party leaders and [to] go along in the absence of contrary inclinations."[53] In other words, members cooperate with their parties unless they have a reason to defect. Wavering members who have reservations about the party's position may be subject to heavy pressure from party leaders. A classic example involved House Speaker Newt Gingrich, R-Ga. (1995–1999), and his lieutenants. During the GOP's first year in power after forty consecutive years of Democratic control, a junior Republican described the leadership's approach at persuasion:

> They pull us into a room before almost every vote and yell at us. . . . They say, "This is a test of our ability to govern," or "This is a gut check," or "I got you here and you hired me as your coach to get you through, but if you want to change coaches, go ahead."[54]

Party leaders in both chambers can usually rely on a high level of reflexive support from fellow partisans, especially on procedural matters. Political scientists have repeatedly shown that members are more likely to vote with their parties on procedural motions than directly on the substance of legislation.[55] Indeed, members often support their party leaders on procedural matters related to a bill, even when they do not intend to support the bill on final passage. Procedural votes, in brief, are usually partisan votes. As a senator once observed, "This is a procedural vote, and in the Senate we traditionally stick with the leadership on such votes."[56]

House leaders have broad authority to exploit procedures to strengthen party unity. Through their control of key committees, scheduling powers, and use of special rules, majority party leaders arrange for votes they are likely to win and avoid those they are apt to lose. For example, the majority leadership can use their agenda-setting prerogative in positive and negative ways. They can bring legislation to the floor under procedures that advantage the majority party, or the leaders can block unwanted measures (or amendments) from even being brought up for chamber consideration.

Senate leaders have fewer procedural tools than do House leaders, but majority leaders can use their right to be recognized first on the floor to regulate the timing, order, and content of debates to partisan advantage. For example, then-Senate majority leader Reid deliberately scheduled a series of votes he knew he would lose in fall 2010. Why? He wanted to portray Republicans as "obstructionists," to indicate to the bill's supporters that he tried, to demonstrate that Senate rules need revision (the measures were blocked by filibuster threats), and to direct the public's attention to these issues. Minority Leader McConnell viewed the entire exercise as political theater: "Are we here to perform, or are we here to legislate?"[57] At the same time, minority party members also have strong incentives to stick together on procedural and other matters, forcing vulnerable majority party members to cast difficult votes and making it increasingly difficult for the majority party to pursue its program.

Ideology and Voting

Most lawmakers today hold strong ideological views on such topics as the proper role and purpose of government. Indeed, many members of Congress entered politics through various ideological causes. Support for President Obama's health care reform and concern about the huge income disparity between the rich 1 percent and the other 99 percent spurred political activism for members on the left of the political spectrum. Many members on the right entered politics because of their small-government views or traditionalist social values. Long before they take their first oath of office, members bring ideological loyalties that inspire voting decisions throughout their political careers.

Both political parties encompass ideological diversity, which reflects their demographic and behavioral differences. The Republican Party, for example, embraces both economically conservative voters—educated, higher-income cohorts who are often associated with business—along with less educated, lower- or middle-income people who are drawn to the party's traditional social and cultural values, its emphasis on national and border security, and a hard line on crime. Balancing the party's ideological wings is not an easy assignment for GOP congressional leaders. They work to accommodate both the party's social and religious conservatives as well as its economically conservative business wing, not to mention the hard-core conservative Freedom Caucus.

Thus, even as Republicans enjoyed unified party government after the 2016 election, the journey to an acceptable compromise among House Republicans often proved difficult, sometimes impossible. Indeed, Speaker Ryan's legislation to repeal Obamacare in March 2017 initially foundered when he was unable to hold onto the support of the three dozen Freedom Caucus members who believed the bill did not go far enough; concessions intended to win over the Freedom Caucus eroded support among moderate conservatives. President Trump pressured dissident Republicans to back the repeal effort, but party leaders struggled to hold the contending factions together and had to temporarily pull the bill from the floor.[58] Party leaders eventually negotiated a compromise that passed the House by a 217–213 margin, with 20 Republicans defecting. The bill went to the Senate, where the concessions to win over House conservatives created problems for more moderate Republicans who believed the bill went too far. In the end, three GOP Senate defectors were sufficient to sink the repeal.

The Democratic Party also embraces ideological variety. In brief, Democrats include across-the-board liberals who are committed to a vigorous government redressing economic grievances, to tolerant stances on social and lifestyle issues, and to international treaties and institutions guiding foreign policy. But the party also includes factions advocating for a more conservative position on economic issues or on social issues, such as abortion. For example, the New Democrat Coalition brings together nearly 100 House Democrats who generally tack left on social issues but favor pro-business policies that could appeal to independent and moderate voters.[59] The 2018 midterms brought to Washington several young, progressive Democrats committed to aggressive action on climate change, immigration, and economic redistribution. But those same midterms also brought a large number of Democrats elected from upscale suburbs who are not likely to support radical policy departures. The party's diversity reflects its voters, who range from union members—who are concerned with economic issues but less liberal on social causes—to the "creative class" of professionals in university towns and urban enclaves who are far more libertarian on social issues but often less concerned with "bread-and-butter" issues like jobs, housing, and the minimum wage.[60] Free-trade pacts also tend to split these groups: Union members fear losing jobs to low-wage foreign labor while educated professionals tend to be more open toward globalization. Democratic leaders have to navigate these ideological divisions, often by avoiding issues that fracture the party.

When political scientists began seriously to analyze congressional roll call voting in the 1950s, ideological diversity within each of the two parties was far greater than it is today. Conservatives and liberals had a meaningful presence in both legislative parties. Although members often voted along party lines, at other times, they would unite across parties in recognizable ideological coalitions. Frequently, Republicans and southern Democrats would cooperate in a voting pattern known as the conservative coalition.[61] The coalition's success rate was impressive in both chambers during the 1939 to 1965 period—no matter which party controlled the White House or Capitol Hill.

Since the 1960s, the two legislative parties have sorted themselves out along ideological lines, with almost all conservatives in the Republican Party and liberals exclusively in the Democratic Party. Scholars have found that "the most conservative Democrat is more liberal than is the most liberal Republican," with Republicans moving further to the right than Democrats to the left (called *asymmetric polarization*).[62] As a consequence, the cross-party conservative coalition surfaces so rarely these days that the respected *CQ Weekly* stopped scoring it.[63] Bipartisan conservatism fell victim to the increasing ideological consistency of both political parties. In short, "Democrats are perched on the left, Republicans on the right, in both the House and the Senate as the ideological centers of the two parties have moved markedly apart."[64] The polarization of the contemporary Congress—in which partisanship and ideology are closely intertwined—can be shown spatially on a left–right (liberal–conservative) continuum. Using the congressional roll call voting record, political scientists Keith T. Poole and Howard

Rosenthal have devised a scaling methodology to generate ideological scores for all members of Congress.[65] Their data show marked divergence between the parties in recent years.

Figure 9-3 displays the distribution of ideological preferences for Republicans and Democrats among activists and the general public and within Congress. When voters are asked to locate themselves on the ideological spectrum, the result roughly follows a normal bell-shaped curve. As shown in Panel A, the greatest number of citizens are at or near the middle of the ideological spectrum, with relatively few respondents identifying themselves as very liberal or very conservative.[66] The same centrist pattern appears when voters are asked to position themselves on specific policy issues, even on hot-button topics such as taxes and abortion. By contrast, political activists are more likely to identify as either liberal or conservative. The survey results displayed in Panel A of Figure 9-3 reveal Republican and Democratic activists clustering to the left or right of the median, with far less overlap between the two parties at the elite level than exists in the mass public.

In 1968, the ideological divisions in the House of Representatives (displayed in Panel B in Figure 9-3) looked similar to those of the party elites. Democrats appeared in almost every ideological niche, from far left to far right. Although Republicans were more tightly clustered on the right, a number spilled over to the liberal side of the scale.[67] Political moderates—members at or near the midpoint between the parties—constituted a substantial bloc.

The contemporary Congress (represented by Panel C) is almost completely polarized along party lines. Only a handful of members fall at the midpoint—not a single Republican falls on the liberal side of the scale, and no Democrats stray into the conservative category.

In today's Congress, members' party affiliation and ideological views overlap almost perfectly. (These figures are for the House; patterns in the Senate are similar.) This polarization and the resulting collapse of the middle (the *shrinking center*) have produced clear ideological battle lines between the parties. Although partisan rigidity gets a bad rap from commentators, one must consider how closely political convictions are linked to partisanship in the minds of lawmakers and their activist supporters. "If you can't find common ground, that doesn't mean you're partisan," explained Nancy Pelosi. "It just means you believe different things."[68]

The proportion of political moderates—conservative-leaning Democrats or liberal-leaning Republicans—hovered at about 30 percent in the 1960s and 1970s. Today, however, fewer than one in ten lawmakers fall into this centrist category.[69] Conservative Democrats, traditionally the larger of the two centrist groupings, once represented a third of their party's members; today, they could caucus around a single conference table. The fiscally conservative "Blue Dog" Democrats, as they called themselves, saw their ranks cut in half (from a little over fifty to twenty-six) in the November 2010 elections. After dwindling to just fourteen members in 2015–2016, the 2018 midterms brought in several new moderates, bringing the

FIGURE 9-3 ■ Ideological Divisions in Congress and the Public

A. Ideological distribution of general public and party activists, 2016

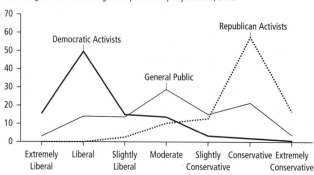

B. Ideological distribution in the U.S. House: Pre-realignment, 1967–1968

C. Ideological distribution in the U.S. House: Post-realignment, 2017–2018

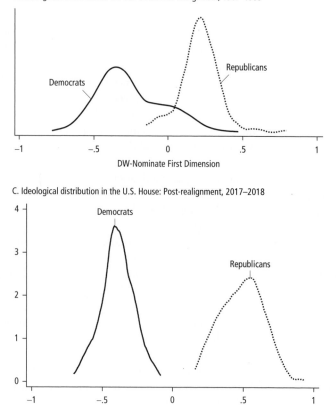

Sources: Panel A: Cooperative Congressional Election Survey, 2012. Data compiled by Rob Van Houweling. Panels B and C: These data are derived from Keith T. Poole and Howard Rosenthal's DW-NOMINATE ideology scores (voteview.com). See Keith T. Poole and Howard Rosenthal, *Congress: A Political-Economic History of Roll-Call Voting* (New York: Oxford University Press, 1997).

Blue Dogs' membership back up to twenty-four or just over 10 percent of House Democrats. Even rarer are moderate Republicans, who account for about 8 percent of all House GOP members and 4 percent of senators.[70]

Constituency and Voting

Constituency context is another powerful influence on members' vote choices. Constituencies control lawmakers' choices in two ways. First, people usually elect representatives whose views mirror their own. In this sense, representatives vote their constituency because they are transplanted locals. Second, members listen to constituents because it is politically imperative to do so. Representatives feel great electoral pressure to respond to the dominant political interests and opinions in their constituencies. For example, pleas for stronger gun control laws are unlikely to resonate with members from Idaho, where the culture embraces the right of individuals to purchase guns.

Constituency concerns can either reinforce or undermine party unity in Congress. For much of the twentieth century, it was not unusual for conservative-leaning states to elect Democrats and for liberal-leaning states to elect Republicans. During that period, constituency influence often led members to buck their party. But since the 1960s, constituencies have gradually sorted themselves out according to ideological and policy preferences. In the current era, constituency pressure tends to bolster party unity.

Relatively few Democrats in the 116th Congress represent conservative districts or states. In 1960, all senators from the South were Democrats, and they constituted a large conservative bloc that often resisted Democratic Party leaders and cooperated across party lines with Republicans. But in the 116th Congress (2017–2019), only three southern Democrats are in the Senate.[71] By the same token, many areas once represented by GOP liberals have been captured by Democrats. New England, an area of the country that was once a moderate Republican stronghold, now elects Democrats almost exclusively. The decline of conservative Democrats and moderate Republicans underlies much of the ideological cohesion within and the chasm between today's Capitol Hill parties.[72] Partisans in the contemporary Congress vote together, in great part, because they reflect the same kinds of states and districts. Republicans tend to represent rural areas and outer suburbs. Democrats tend to represent urban areas, inner-ring suburbs, and majority-minority districts.[73] Two interrelated demographic trends are worth noting briefly. First, today the GOP is strongest among white voters and older citizens while Democrats fare much better among minority groups and young voters. Democrats also hold an advantage among women while Republicans attract a greater share of men.

Second, diversity characterizes Democrats more than Republicans and House Democrats more than Senate Democrats. Starting with the 113th Congress (2013–2015), white males have been—for the first time in U.S. history—a minority in the House Democratic caucus.[74] The consequences of having a white-male-dominated, heavily "southernized" House Republican Party and a minority and female-dominated House Democratic Party are not self-evident. However, it is reasonable to suggest that compromises on significant issues may be harder to obtain, disagreements over the role of government are likely to be more contentious, and conflicts over social issues are likely to increase. In the judgment of a political scientist, "When you have parties so divergent in views, regions, and genders, the culture wars could escalate from conventional to nuclear weapons."[75] The few remaining party mavericks in today's Congress tend to come from parts of the country where their party generally does not do well electorally. This is especially the case among Democrats; the least loyal Democratic senators in the 115th Congress (2017–2018) all came from states that voted Republican for president, such as Joe Manchin of West Virginia, Heidi Heitkamp of North Dakota, and Joe Donnelly of Indiana.[76] The most independent Republicans likewise typically represent Democratic-leaning constituencies, such as Susan Collins of Maine. But Republican mavericks also include some hardline conservatives who, at times, differentiate themselves from the party mainstream by defecting. Hardcore conservative Justin Amash of Michigan was thus among the Republicans with the lowest unity scores in the 115th Congress.[77]

Constituency affects congressional decision making, as politicians take both attentive and inattentive publics into account. Political scientist R. Douglas Arnold has tracked how both groups can influence members' electoral calculations.[78] Attentive publics are those citizens who are aware of issues facing Congress and hold decided opinions about what Congress should do. It is thus relatively easy for politicians to consider their views. A politician's natural instinct is to yield to the strongly voiced preferences of an attentive public, unless the issue in question mobilizes two equally vociferous but opposing interests. Especially feared are single-interest groups that threaten to withhold electoral support if their preferences—for example, on abortion or gun control—are ignored.

Inattentive publics are those who lack extensive knowledge or firm preferences about a specific issue. Frankly, this definition describes most people most of the time. People pay attention to only a small fraction of the issues before Congress, yet a reelection-minded legislator dare not ignore those who seem indifferent to an issue. "Latent or unfocused opinions," Arnold cautions, "can quickly be transformed into intense and very real opinions with enormous political repercussions. Inattentiveness and lack of information today should not be confused with indifference tomorrow."[79] Legislators are well advised to approach even the most minor choices with this question in mind: Will my decision be defensible if it were to appear on the front pages of major newspapers in my state or district?

Calculating the electoral consequences of a lawmaker's multitude of daily decisions is no easy task. Arnold summarizes the components of such calculations:

> To reach a decision, then, a legislator needs to (1) identify all the attentive and inattentive publics who might care about a policy issue, (2) estimate the direction and intensity of their preferences and potential preferences, (3) estimate the probability that the potential preferences will be transformed into real preferences, (4) weigh all these preferences according

to the size of the various attentive and inattentive publics, and (5) give special weight to the preferences of the legislator's consistent supporters.[80]

Fortunately, lawmakers need not repeat these calculations every time they face a choice. Most issues have been around for some time. The preferences of attentive and even inattentive publics are fairly well known. Moreover, Congress is well structured to amass information about individual and group preferences. And prominent officials—party leaders and acknowledged policy experts, for example—can often legitimize members' choices and give them cover in explaining those choices to voters.

The Presidency and Voting

Although Congress often pursues an independent course and members differ in their feelings toward the occupant of the White House, presidents can persuade members to support their agendas. Figure 9-4 depicts the percentage of the time presidents—from Dwight D. Eisenhower to Donald Trump—have prevailed in congressional roll call votes on which they announced a position. Presidents take positions on a wide range of issues, from the momentous (tax cuts and immigration, in Trump's case) to large numbers of routine and noncontroversial matters (most Senate confirmations of executive nominations, for example).[81]

During President Trump's first two years in office, he enjoyed substantial success in winning congressional support on those issues where he took a clearly stated position. In fact, in 2017, he had a 98.7 percent success rate.[82] Although his success dipped a bit in 2018, it was a still robust 93.4 percent. These numbers reflect, in part, the President's triumphs on a series of controversial executive and judicial nominations, which were made easier by recent rules changes requiring a simple majority for confirmation (see Chapter 12). But Trump's high success rate also resulted from Republican leaders' use of agenda control: Speaker Ryan and Leader McConnell were "loath to hold votes when facing the prospect of defeat."[83]

Trump's high success rate in his first two years resembled the experience of President Obama, who also enjoyed unified control at the start of his administration. After losing control of the House in November 2010, Obama's success rate declined substantially. For the next four years, Obama enjoyed an overall success rate that hovered in the 50 to 60 percent range. But this masked a huge gap between the Republican House and Democratic Senate. In 2014, for example, the president won on just 15 percent of the roll call votes in the House where he took a position; by contrast, he succeeded on 93 percent of the Senate roll calls where he took a stand. Since legislation must pass both chambers, the battles between the president and House Republicans meant that "Obama signed fewer new laws than any president this century, or in the half-century before that."[84] Republicans' takeover of the Senate in the 2014 midterms further dampened Obama's opportunities for legislative success in his final two years. Facing a Democratic House in 2019–2020, President Trump will likely also see his success rate fall substantially as compared to his first two years.

FIGURE 9-4 ■ Presidential Success History, 1953–2018

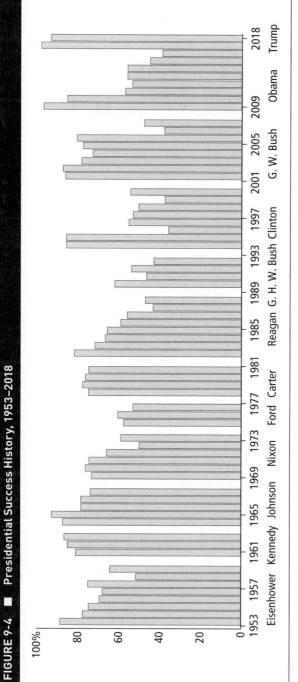

Source: Data from *CQ Weekly.*

Note: Presidential success is defined as the percentage of the time the president won his way on roll call votes on which he had taken a clear position.

Indeed, party control of Congress dramatically affects presidential success rates. As long as their party controls Congress, presidents win at least three of every four votes on which they take a position; when the government is divided, presidents fall well below that level.[85] Another important pattern evident in Figure 9-4 is that presidents tend to lose congressional support as their administrations age. Presidents' best years in dealing with Congress are usually their first. This could be due to a *honeymoon effect,* in which legislators are more likely to side with a popular president, though it also may result from presidents tackling issues where the opportunity for success is strongest early in their terms and being left with harder problems as their term continues.

Cue-Givers and Roll Call Votes

It is impossible for a single member to make an informed decision on the hundreds of roll call votes confronted in each Congress. As a result, members rely heavily upon their colleagues and other informants as a source of cues as they make up their minds. A good cue-giver will tend to be a member with expertise on the issue under consideration who shares the partisan, ideological, and perhaps regional affiliations of the member seeking out help in making a decision. Exchanges of voting cues are endemic in both chambers. The exchange not only saves the recipient the time and trouble of mastering the subject matter, but it also can provide credible cover in defending the vote. Cue-giving is a key element in John W. Kingdon's model of representatives' decisions, derived from interviews with members immediately after their votes on specific issues.[86]

Legislators have little difficulty making up their minds when they receive no conflicting cues from party leaders, respected fellow members, constituents, or key interest groups. If all of the cue-givers in their field of vision concur, members operate in a consensus mode of decision making. If the actors are in conflict, the lawmaker will have to weigh the alternatives.

Fellow members emerge in Kingdon's study as the most influential cue-givers, with constituencies ranking second. As one lawmaker observed,

> I think that the other members are very influential, and we recognize it. And why are they influential? I think because they have exercised good judgment, have expertise in the area, and know what they are talking about.[87]

When members deviate from a consensus stance among their cue-givers, it is usually to follow their own conscience or their constituencies.

LEGISLATIVE BARGAINING

Whatever their sources of influence, in the end, individual legislators have only a single vote on any given bill or, more typically, on an amendment. At that moment, the vote is reduced to a "yea" or "nay" question, with no hedging or nuance allowed. Legislators have to decide how to cast these binary votes on a bewildering array of issues. They rarely have adequate—or even much—information on any particular bill or amendment. Legislators must weigh their goals—which often may conflict—and process their limited information in a relatively short period of time to arrive at a decision.[88]

Such a state of affairs—disparate goals and widely scattered influence—is hazardous. Stalemate is a constant threat. The *collective-action problem* is the way political scientists refer to the challenge of merging individual goals into group achievements. To overcome this predicament, members have to resort to politicking—that is, they must trade off goals and resources to get results. It is no wonder, then, that Congress is "an influence system in which bargain and exchange predominate."[89]

Implicit and Explicit Bargaining

Bargaining is a general term that refers to several related types of behavior. It describes, in an overall sense, the process by which two or more actors arrive at a mutually beneficial exchange. Such processes may be implicit or explicit.

Implicit Bargaining

Implicit bargaining occurs when legislators take actions designed to elicit certain reactions from others, even though no negotiation has taken place. For example, legislators often introduce bills or sponsor hearings not because they expect the measure to pass but to prod someone else—an executive-branch official or a committee chair with broader jurisdiction on the question—to take action. Or a bill's managers may accept a controversial amendment knowing full well that the objectionable provision will be dropped in the other chamber or in conference. At other times, a committee's judgment about the merits of a bill may receive deference from noncommittee members, with the expectation that the committee members will reciprocate when it comes to other committees' proposals. These are examples of the so-called law of anticipated reactions.[90]

Explicit Bargaining

Explicit bargains also take several forms. In making compromises, legislators may agree to split their differences. Compromises are straightforward on issues dealing with quantitative elements that can easily be adjusted upward or downward—for example, funding levels or eligibility criteria. Compromise on substance is also possible. For example, members who favor a major new program and members who oppose any program at all may agree to a two-year pilot project to test the idea.

"You cannot legislate without the ability to compromise," declared former senator Alan Simpson, R-Wyo., who often found fault with militant junior members of his own party. He recounted the following tale:

> On a recent bill, I went to [conservative House members] and said: "Here's what I'm doing. I've got six senators who will vote this far, and then the next time if you go any further, they will not be there." So [my GOP colleague] and I delivered on this singular bill, and they said, "We want you to get more." And we said, "There is no more to get." Next vote on this bill, we lost six votes. Then they came in and said, "We are going to probably kill the whole thing. . . ." [A]nd they got nothing.[91]

The lesson is that compromise is inevitable in crafting laws; those who are unwilling to give ground are bound to be disappointed. On occasion, both parties avoid compromise and engage in brinksmanship, with each expecting the other to "blink" first before the interparty deadlock produces bad political and policy repercussions. Winning concessions from the opposing side is a key aim of this form of strategic bargaining.

The classic compromise—a "win–win" for the contending sides—has been hard to achieve in recent Congresses. A significant number of lawmakers have instead preferred a "no-compromise" stance. There was simply an unwillingness on their part to engage in the traditional "give-and-take" negotiating process: Members give up legislative provisions or positions but take others they find acceptable enough to move legislation forward. A view expressed by a House Republican reflected one shared by many others on Capitol Hill: "When it comes to compromise, half of a bad deal is still a bad deal."[92] Effective governance is challenged when issues provoke high-stakes brinksmanship and compromise implies political weakness, a sellout, or a betrayal of principle.

Logrolling

Logrolling is bargaining in which members exchange support so that all parties to the deal can attain their individual goals. The term originated in the nineteenth century when neighbors helped each other roll logs into a pile for burning. Its most visible form is a something-for-everyone enactment, sometimes called a "Christmas tree" bill. Such bills are prevalent in legislative areas such as public works, omnibus taxation, or tariffs and trade. Farm legislation is an area traditionally conducive to logrolling, as representatives gain subsidies for crops grown locally in exchange for supporting subsidies for crops in other states and districts. In a rare major bipartisan legislative accomplishment, Congress passed an $867 billion farm reauthorization act in 2018 that renewed support for a wide range of subsidies and for food stamps, while winning over a handful of additional votes by legalizing hemp and supporting organic farming. In the words of one conservative critic, "classic logrolling" is at work as "the marriage of food stamps and farm subsidies (creates) common cause for urban Democrats and rural Republicans."[93]

Logrolling draws lawmakers into the finished legislative product by embracing their special interests, proposals, or amendments. Henry M. "Scoop" Jackson, D-Wash. (House, 1941–1953; Senate, 1953–1983), when asked how he had assembled a majority for a new proposal, responded this way: "Maggie [Sen. Warren Magnuson of Washington] talked to Russell, and Tom promised this if I would back him on Ed's amendment, and Mike owes me one for last year's help on Pete's bill."[94] Such reciprocity especially pervades the Senate, dominated as it is by individuals. Sponsors of a Senate bill often must placate most or all interested legislators to gain clearance to bring a bill to the floor.

Lawmakers who enter into and stand to profit from a logroll are expected to support the final package, regardless of what that package looks like. A broad-based logroll is thus hard to stop. "It's not a system of punishment. It's a system of rewards," explained a House member.[95] Logrolling can turn narrowly targeted programs into broad-scale ones, as many lawmakers want a piece of the policy pie. This development can dilute a program's impact by spreading funds throughout the nation rather than in targeted areas. Similarly, if resources are spread too thinly among too many sites, the program may not make a noticeable difference in any single area.

When faced with an austere fiscal environment, logrolling is often aimed at equalizing sacrifices instead of distributing rewards. Broad-spectrum bills—authorizations, omnibus tax measures, continuing resolutions, and budget resolutions—may include numerous less-than-optimal provisions, many of which would fail if voted on separately. Such a negative logroll enables lawmakers to support the measure as "the best deal we can get."

In a time logroll, members agree to support one measure in exchange for later support for another measure. A time logroll was important to Senate passage of President Trump's $1.4 trillion tax cut in December 2017. Sen. Susan Collins, R-Maine, was worried that the tax cut's repeal of the individual mandate to purchase health insurance would further erode the Obamacare system. To gain Collins' vote, Majority Leader Mitch McConnell promised to help pass two bills by the end of the year that Collins believed would stabilize the Obamacare exchanges. In explaining her decision to back the tax cut, Collins declared "I feel certain that the agreement that I negotiated will be kept this year." As it turned out, the Senate did not end up considering the bills proposed by Collins, suggesting the risks inherent in a time logroll.[96] Sometimes, logrolls can be constructed on the basis of side payments to members. A lawmaker's support is exchanged for benefits on an unrelated issue—for example, a federal project for the state or district, a better committee assignment, inclusion in an important conference, help with fund-raising, or access to the White House. Although such side payoffs may seem trivial or parochial, they can enable members to achieve valued goals.

Bargaining Strategy

For bargaining to take place, participants in the House and Senate must be able to rely on one another's future actions. Rep. John P. Murtha, D-Pa. (1974–2010), a master deal-maker, cited two elements of power on Capitol Hill: "Develop expertise on an issue that makes you vital to colleagues, and keep your word."[97] Relying on his expertise and contacts within the defense community, he often cut deals quietly in the back corner of the Democratic side of the House. On the Senate side of the Capitol, the same kind of deal-making occurs. Democratic leader Reid, for example, was not reluctant to provide senators Ben Nelson, D-Neb., and Mary Landrieu, D-La., with what each wanted in order to win their votes for President Obama's controversial health overhaul plan. The press soon called the special health benefits each received for their states, respectively, the "Cornhusker Kickback" and the "Louisiana Purchase."[98]

For bargaining to succeed, the participants must agree on the need for a legislative product—that is, the benefits of reaching a decision must exceed the costs of failing to do so. In many cases, politicians may prefer a course of strategic disagreement, the "efforts of politicians to avoid reaching an agreement when compromise might alienate supporters, damage their prospects in an upcoming election, or preclude getting a better deal in the future."[99] According to bargaining theory, a measure's sponsors will yield only what they absolutely must to gain a majority of supporters. "Parties wish to use their votes efficiently, winning victories at the cheapest possible price."[100] By this logic, if bargainers act rationally and have perfect information about one another, minimum winning coalitions should predominate.[101] Recounting Senate majority leader Lyndon B. Johnson's meticulous vote counting before a floor fight, a top Senate aide concluded, "And once a sufficient majority had been counted, Johnson would seldom attempt to enlarge it: Why expend limited bargaining resources which might be needed to win future battles?"[102] Most legislative strategists, however, lack Johnson's extraordinary skills. Uncertainty about outcomes leads them to line up more than a simple majority of supporters. Moreover, at many points in the legislative process, supermajorities are required—for example, in voting under suspension of the rules, in overriding vetoes, or in ending Senate filibusters. Not surprisingly, therefore, minimum winning coalitions are not typical of Congress, even in the majoritarian House of Representatives.[103] Yet coalition size is the crux of legislative strategy. Bargainers repeatedly face the dilemma of how broadly or how narrowly to frame their issues and how many concessions to yield in an effort to secure passage.

CONCLUSION

Congressional deliberation is at risk today. With both parties unified and seemingly uninterested in debate or compromise, life on Capitol Hill has become, in

Thomas Hobbes's words, "nasty" and "brutish" (though hardly "short"). Take-no-prisoners strategies are encouraged by today's highly competitive, polarized party system. As a senator observed,

> The pressure on congressional leaders both from interests in the party and from outside groups is severe. Many would rather fight and lose, rather than reach out and find common ground. Congress should not be like the Super Bowl, in which one team always has to win and the other team inevitably loses. There's nothing wrong with reaching legitimate compromise and getting something done for the American people.[104]

Political scientist Sarah Binder's findings echo this sentiment. "The decline of the political center," she writes, "has produced a political environment that more often than not gives legislators every incentive not to reach agreement."[105] The result is often legislative inaction, which may be criticized as stalemate or gridlock.

Yet the enterprise of lawmaking rests on the premise that, at least where urgent matters are concerned, bargainers will normally prefer some sort of agreement to none at all. As Everett M. Dirksen, R-Ill., the legendary Senate Republican leader (1959–1969), once remarked, "I am a man of fixed and unbending principle, and one of my principles is flexibility."[106] While bargaining has become more treacherous in today's polarized Congress, it not an entirely lost art. A case in point is the First Step Act, in which conservative Republicans and liberal Democrats meticulously constructed a broad, bipartisan coalition that made meaningful changes to sentencing laws without alienating members concerned about remaining "tough" on crime. Bargaining is a necessary part of legislative life. It shapes the character of bills, resolutions, and other forms of congressional policy making. It also underlies many attributes of the legislative process: delay, obfuscation, compromise, and norms such as specialization and reciprocity.

Deliberation is the hallmark of legislative decision making. Coalitions are constructed as diverse views are voiced and a variety of members, executive officials, and interest groups participate. It is yet another point of contact and conflict between the two Congresses—the Congress of individual wills and the Congress of collective decisions.

House Minority Leader Nancy Pelosi and Senate Minority Leader Chuck Schumer speak at a news conference as a possible government shutdown looms. Senate Majority Leader Mitch McConnell stands with President Trump to affirm Republican unity during the shutdown. Demonstrators protest the government shutdown as it stretches into its 21st day.

CONGRESS AND
THE PRESIDENT

"We've been down this path before," Senate majority leader Mitch McConnell, R-Ky., warned President Trump in December 2018. "There's no education in the second kick of a mule."[1] Frustrated by Congress's refusal to appropriate funds for a southern border wall, the president was considering withholding support for a continuing resolution. Failure to pass this continuing resolution would trigger a funding lapse affecting many federal departments and agencies, forcing a partial shutdown of the federal government.

McConnell, a veteran of previous government shutdowns, did not favor such a course of action. One of McConnell's close allies, Sen. John Cornyn, R-Texas, explained that McConnell "thinks shutdowns don't work. Nobody wins."[2] For his part, outgoing Speaker of the House Paul Ryan, R-Wisc., also advised the president against a government shutdown.[3] Despite Republican leaders' opposition, however, Trump balked and refused to sign appropriations that did not include funding for a border wall.

The result was a 35-day partial shutdown, the federal government's longest to date. Throughout, the president maintained that he would not reopen the government unless Congress relented on wall funding. More than a month into the impasse, the president tweeted, "Without a Wall it all doesn't work. . . . We will not Cave!"[4] Meanwhile, new Speaker of the House Nancy Pelosi insisted that Democrats would not be held hostage to the president's demands and would not negotiate on border security as long as the government was shut down: "What we are saying is, 'Open up the government. And then we can discuss.'"[5]

As the shutdown persisted, its effects multiplied. Furloughed federal workers missed two paychecks and a month's income. So-called essential personnel—such as air traffic controllers, Transportation Security Agency workers, border patrol agents, prison guards, FBI agents, Coast Guard services—were required to show up for work despite not being paid. Meanwhile, other government services deemed less essential were shuttered, keeping government scientists, park rangers, regulators, and others home. Anxiety began to grow about whether tax returns would be processed in a timely manner. When delays began to mount at airports due to staff shortages, pressure grew on Congress to act.

With the president taking the lion's share of the blame for the shutdown in public opinion polls, these pressures were more severe for Republicans than Democrats. Democrats held firm to Pelosi's stance, with moderate Democrats refusing the White House's invitation to discuss border security during the shutdown.[6] But Republican resolve began to crumble. On January 24, 2019, McConnell called the president to let him know that Republicans would not hold out much longer and that some senators were in revolt.[7] Describing the mood among Senate Republicans, one senator reported, "A lot of the conference wanted to end the shutdown by any means possible."[8] "Shutdowns are miserable," said Sen. Shelley Moore Capito, R-W.Va., "and this one was double miserable."[9]

With deteriorating support behind the scenes, Trump simply reversed his position and agreed to reopen the government for three weeks so as to allow a conference committee to explore an agreement on border security funding. Meeting with conservative groups afterwards, Trump reportedly complained that Paul Ryan had "screwed him" by not getting border wall funding while Republicans still controlled the House.[10] In the end, the president got essentially the same deal from Congress that he had initially rejected in December, with nothing to show for the 35-day shutdown.

The tensions between Trump and Republican leaders throughout the controversy illustrate an enduring truth about presidential relationships with Congress. Unified government does not guarantee cooperation between Congress and the president. In this case, the Republican Congress had not been eager to provide funding for the border wall even when they had power to do so. Congressional Republicans questioned how such a program would be paid for and whether it was a good use of funds. Throughout the first two years of the Trump presidency, Republican leaders repeatedly demurred when the president asked about the wall, giving other agenda items higher priority. Despite having unified government in 2017 through 2018, the president thus made little progress toward funding for the wall, his most visible campaign promise. Conflict between the president and Congress intensified once Democrats took control of the House of Representatives in January 2019. But the policy outcome under divided government with Democrats in control of the House of Representatives—no large-scale funding for a wall on the southern border—differed little from what Trump had previously gotten from the Republican Congress in 2017 through 2018.

A shared party label by no means guarantees close coordination between presidents and members of Congress. Congress has long served as a site of fierce opposition to presidents, regardless of the partisan configuration of national institutions.[11] Presidential interactions with Congress are often contentious and difficult, even when the same party controls both branches of government.

More than diverging policy priorities complicate the president's relationship with Congress. Congress and the presidency are simply very different institutions. The executive branch is more hierarchical and vertical in decision making while Congress is more collegial and horizontal—with power spread among 535 independent-minded lawmakers. The legislative branch's great strength is that it is able to give voice and visibility to diverse viewpoints, but its dispersion of power slows down decision making and tends to make congressional policy making more incremental and cautious.[12] By contrast, the president's great strength is, in the words of Alexander Hamilton, its "decision, activity, secrecy, and dispatch."[13] Congress's ponderousness can promote public acceptance of the nation's policies, but it can also render decisive action impossible. These institutional differences alone are an enduring source of interbranch conflict.

Understanding the chief executive's relations with Congress is no easy task. The founders did not clearly define the legislative–executive relationship, and it remains a work in progress. Presidents always bring their own style to the relationship, which political scientist Charles O. Jones characterizes as ranging from a *partnership model* to an *independent model*. The partnership model means that presidents consult regularly with lawmakers and involve them directly in the policy and political affairs of the White House. On the independent model, presidents minimize their involvement with Congress and strive on their own to accomplish their top priorities.[14] President Trump has employed a mix of approaches depending on the subject matter. On tax cuts and health care initiatives, he employed a partnership approach, allowing Congress to take the lead in policy formulation. On foreign policy and trade, however, he has taken a much more independent course. Regardless of how presidents approach Congress, they confront the basic constitutional fact that the legislative and executive branches of government can each block the other, and each needs the support or acquiescence of the other to accomplish most objectives.

In this chapter, we will examine the relationship between Congress and the president from three perspectives: (1) the president's constitutional powers relative to Congress, (2) each institution's capacity for public leadership, and (3) the persistent sources of conflict and cooperation between the two institutions.

CONSTITUTIONAL POWERS

Article II of the Constitution reflects the framers' ambivalence about executive power. Although Article I specifies the powers of Congress in considerable detail, Article II is very brief and general. Broadly speaking, the most important feature of the constitutional relationship between Congress and the president is the extent to which these two separate institutions, each independently elected, share powers. Rather than segregating executive and legislative functions in different branches of government, the Constitution blends them together. The Congress and the president each possess critical powers over legislation and administration.

Article II begins by stating, "the executive power shall be vested in a President of the United States." But the document does not then go on to define the executive power with much specificity. The first administrative power mentioned in the Constitution is to "require the opinion, in writing, of the principal officers" of the executive departments, an obscure clause of the Constitution that has seen little judicial interpretation. Any executive's most important administrative tool is the ability to hire and fire personnel. The president is empowered to nominate appointees to executive-branch departments and agencies. But under the Constitution, these appointments are subject to the "advice and consent of the Senate" or to other processes as Congress may designate by law. In other words, Congress is able to check the president even in the exercise of the president's most basic administrative functions.

The president's powers extend beyond administration. The president is also a legislative leader. Presidents have a critical power over lawmaking: the veto. Article I, section 7, of the Constitution requires the president to approve or disapprove bills passed by Congress. When the president disapproves (vetoes) a measure, it dies unless it "shall be repassed by two thirds of the Senate and House of Representatives." Because vetoes are so difficult to override, the veto power transforms the president into, in Woodrow Wilson's words, a "third branch of the legislature."[15] The Constitution also enjoins the president to take an active leadership role in proposing policy. The president is instructed to "give to the Congress information on the State of the Union and recommend to their consideration such measures as he shall judge necessary and expedient." Soon after delivering the annual State of the Union address, the president will typically send to Congress draft administration bills for introduction. What Congress chooses to do with these recommendations, however, rests entirely on its own discretion.

Veto Bargaining

The presidential veto is a powerful bargaining tool. In most cases, a presidential veto will stop a bill because presidents can usually attract enough of their supporters in Congress to prevent a congressional override. From 1789 through the end of 2018, presidents exercised their veto authority on 2,574 occasions. Congress successfully overrode these vetoes on only 111 occasions (4.3 percent).[16]

Most presidents have employed the veto. In fact, no president since Thomas Jefferson (1801–1809) has served two full terms without vetoing a bill. Interestingly, recent presidents have employed the veto less often than most twentieth-century presidents. Presidents Obama and George W. Bush, for example, each vetoed just twelve bills during their presidencies. Not since Warren Harding (1921–1923) had a president issued as few as twelve vetoes.[17] After two years in office, President Trump has yet to veto a bill.

When contemplating a veto, presidents seek advice from numerous administration sources, such as agency officials, the Office of Management and Budget, and White House aides, as well as allied lawmakers and interest groups. When issuing a veto, presidents commonly offer legal and policy justifications for their action, such as the bill is unconstitutional, it encroaches on the president's independence, it is unwise public policy, it cannot be administered, or it costs too much.

But both president and Congress also exploit the veto for political reasons. A veto fight with Congress often allows presidents to underscore how their views differ from the other party's. By the same token, Congress may deliberately send the president of the opposite party a measure that lawmakers want and expect him to veto, so they can use the issue on the campaign trail—a "winning-by-losing" strategy.[18]

Veto Processes

After receiving a bill from Congress, a president has ten days (excluding Sundays) in which to exercise one of four options:

1. Sign the bill. Most public and private bills presented to the president are signed into law. The president also may issue a signing statement that expresses an interpretation of the new law's provisions.

2. Return the bill with a veto message to the originating house of Congress.

3. Take no action, and the bill will become law without the president's signature. This option, which is seldom employed, is reserved for bills the president dislikes but prefers not to veto. Presidents may take this course when they disapprove of a bill but expect Congress to override a veto.

4. Pocket veto the bill. Under the Constitution, if a congressional adjournment prevents the return of a bill, the bill cannot become law without the president's signature.

Veto Threats

The veto is much more than a negative power to stop unwanted legislation. Presidents frequently issue threats to veto while legislation is being developed. Because vetoes are almost always successful in stopping legislation, a veto threat creates incentives for Congress to accept presidential input.

Veto threats are used for many reasons, such as protecting administration priorities, defining party differences and positions, or encouraging negotiations. Veto threats will typically spur legislative–executive bargaining. In the process, legislators will often choose to substantially accommodate executive preferences and objections. "We try to use the veto threat wisely, to change votes or to change the language of the underlying document," explained a top White House legislative aide. "And we succeed."[19] In February 2018, President Trump threatened a veto of a Senate-negotiated bipartisan immigration compromise that would have provided a path to citizenship for young, undocumented immigrants in exchange for $25 billion for border security, including the president's border wall. By threatening this veto, the president hoped to induce Congress to accept an administration-supported alternative imposing new limits on legal immigration.[20] In the end, no immigration measure could garner sufficient support to clear the Senate in 2017–2018.

Veto threats are a pervasive feature of divided government. For its part, Congress will sometimes try to dissuade the president from vetoing provisions the president dislikes by adding them to must-pass legislation (such as appropriations bills) or to measures the president strongly favors.

Research shows that veto threats are frequently successful in getting Congress to alter legislation, even when presidents threaten to veto must-pass measures. Based on an analysis of riders added to appropriations bills, political scientists Hans J. G. Hassell and Samuel Kernell find that presidents achieve a nearly 60 percent success rate in removing provisions they threaten to veto.[21]

Presidential veto threats commonly spur the president's partisans in the Senate to filibuster or put up other resistance. Such actions then frequently result in the controversial riders being dropped from the legislation.[22] President Obama, for example, seldom needed to follow through on threatened vetoes during his first six years, in large measure because the Democratic Senate could block anti-administration bills coming out of the GOP House.[23] But even after Democrats lost their Senate majority in the 2014 elections, Democrats could still use holds and filibusters to block or force concessions and would often do so on legislation the president threatened to veto. However, President Obama had to make greater use of the veto during his final two years in office when Democrats no longer controlled either chamber of Congress.

The Pocket Veto

Pocket vetoes occur when the president receives a bill but does not sign or reject and return it to Congress within ten days of a congressional adjournment. Such bills neither become law nor are subject to a congressional veto override. There has been legal controversy over exactly when a congressional adjournment prevents the return of a president's veto.[24] Until the Supreme Court makes a definitive ruling involving the use of the pocket veto both during and between legislative sessions, it is likely that legislative–executive conflicts over the pocket veto will continue to occur periodically. Up to now, the scope of the pocket veto power, as public-law scholar Louis Fisher has written, "has been left largely to practice and to political understandings developed by the executive and legislative branches."[25]

Postveto Action

Congress need not act at all on a vetoed bill. If party leaders lack the votes to override, the chamber that receives a vetoed measure may refer it to committee or table it. Even if one house musters the votes to override, the other body may do nothing. A vetoed bill cannot be amended—it is all or nothing at this stage— and the Constitution requires that votes on overriding a veto be recorded. On occasion, Congress may feel intense political heat after it receives a veto message.

A week after President Nixon's televised veto of a 1970 bill funding welfare programs, House members received more than fifty-five thousand telegrams, most of them urging support for the veto. And Congress did uphold the veto, in part because of Nixon's televised appeal. Presidential pressure does not necessarily dissuade Congress from a veto override, of course. Despite a massive telephone campaign to congressional offices (as many as eighty thousand calls an hour) urging members to sustain President Reagan's veto of a 1988 civil rights bill, the House and Senate easily overrode the veto.[26]

The Line-Item Veto

Congress's habit of combining numerous items into a single measure obliges the president to accept or reject the entire package. Presidents and supporters of executive power have long advocated allowing the president to veto items selectively. After much debate, Congress passed a line-item veto in 1996. This measure would allow the president to cancel dollar amounts specified in appropriations, strike new entitlement programs or expansions of existing programs, and delete limited tax breaks. In 1998, however, the Supreme Court held the Line-Item Veto Act unconstitutional, because it gave the president "unilateral authority to change the text of duly enacted statutes."[27]

Since the Court's decision, some lawmakers and presidents have expressed interest in enacting a constitutionally valid line-item veto. President Trump asked for a line-item veto in March 2018 when signing an omnibus spending bill he criticized for containing "things that are really a wasted sum of money."[28] But many lawmakers oppose the line-item veto because they believe it would cede too much power to the president. Critics also maintain that presidents already have the only tool they need to control spending: the veto. For his part, President Trump said he would never again sign another bill like the March 2018 omnibus appropriation.[29] However, the alternative to signing appropriations bills—a government shutdown—often does not achieve a president's objectives, either.

The Administrative President

As the chief executive officer under the Constitution, presidents possess a range of powers to act unilaterally to advance their objectives. Presidents can announce executive orders, meaning instructions to government officials and administrative agencies to take specific actions as they carry out policies and programs within their jurisdiction.[30] They can also issue proclamations stating administration policy to groups outside government. Proclamations have been employed for many purposes, such as to establish new national monuments, make modifications to tariffs, and explain how the administration intends to interpret a new law. Presidents can negotiate executive agreements with other countries, enabling them to circumvent the treaty process and unilaterally commit the United States to international deals on trade, navigation, environmental standards, and immigration, among many other issues. In the area of national security, presidents can issue presidential directives establishing administration policy across a vast range of issues, including cybersecurity, terrorism, nuclear weapons, and foreign policy toward particular countries and regions.

The president does not need support from Congress to use these administrative powers. Presidents make use of their unilateral powers in numerous ways, such as naming loyal political appointees to supervise and monitor agency activities, reorganizing executive departments to advance presidential goals, and using the budget process to reduce unwanted programs or increase priority activities. At times, they are able to use these powers to achieve outcomes blocked by Congress.[31]

Presidents have repeatedly employed executive orders and reorganization plans to create entirely new administrative entities. For example, in the immediate aftermath of the attacks of September 11, 2001, President George W. Bush unilaterally created an Office for Homeland Security in the White House; constructed a prison for suspected terrorist noncitizens at Guantánamo Bay, Cuba; and instituted a new legal system for handling cases involving *unlawful enemy combatants*.[32] Presidents establish new government agencies unilaterally with some frequency. In 2018, for example, President Trump ordered the Defense Department to establish a new branch of the armed forces, a Space Force that would protect the nation's interests in space.[33] Based on a study of all of the administrative agencies established between the end of World War II and 1995, William G. Howell and David E. Lewis report, "presidents have unilaterally created over half of all administrative agencies in the United States."[34]

Through the use of these powers, presidents have sometimes been able to institute policies that Congress would not have created of its own accord. For example, President Harry S. Truman issued an executive order racially integrating the armed services in 1948, an action that could not have passed Congress at that time. When Congress resisted his proposals to close the Guantánamo Bay military prison, President Obama responded by using prisoner transfers to steadily reduce the population held there to as low as sixty.[35]

When presidents circumvent Congress by establishing new agencies and policies, they are often able to pressure Congress into acceptance. When presented with new "facts on the ground," Congress must get organized to mount a response. Congress may not succeed in doing so, even when majorities of the House and Senate are unhappy with a president's actions. In particular, it is harder for Congress to defund or abolish an existing agency or policy than it is to institute them in the first instance. For example, when President Kennedy encountered significant opposition in Congress to the Peace Corps idea, he opted to create the agency by executive order. By the time Congress got around to reviewing the president's actions, the Peace Corps already had 362 employees and 600 volunteers at work in eight countries.[36] The administration's action had created a fait accompli that Congress was hard pressed to undo. Generally speaking, Congress rarely attempts to overturn executive orders—and even when it tries, it often fails.[37]

Presidents' use of their unilateral powers has been a pervasive source of inter-branch conflict. Stymied by the GOP-controlled Congress on issues such as antismoking legislation, a patients' bill of rights, and subsidies for school construction, President Bill Clinton made extensive use of executive orders. "His formula include[d] pressing the limits of his regulatory authority, signing executive orders and using other unilateral means to obtain his policy priorities when Congress fail[ed] to embrace them."[38] Congressional Republicans railed against Clinton's "go-it-alone" governing at the time.

All the presidents since Clinton have attempted to use unilateral powers to achieve policy goals blocked in Congress. When the Senate blocked action on Bush's faith-based initiative (assisting religious groups in winning government grants for charitable and social service work), the president ordered his administration to implement the program through executive orders and changes in agency regulations.[39] When Congress failed to act on comprehensive immigration reform, the Obama administration crafted the Deferred Action for Childhood Arrivals (DACA) program to grant work permits to young undocumented immigrants and protect them from deportation. Similarly, when Congress deadlocked on legislation addressing climate change, the Obama administration's Environmental Protection Agency developed the Clean Power Plan to reduce carbon dioxide emissions from electrical power plants.

If anything, President Trump has wielded unilateral powers even more boldly than his predecessors. He unilaterally withdrew the United States from the Paris Climate Agreement, a landmark accord reached in 2015 among 195 countries seeking to stave off the effects of climate change.[40] Trump also pulled out of a major Cold War-era arms control agreement with Russia, the 1987 Intermediate-Range Nuclear Forces (INF) Treaty.[41] Claiming threats to national security, Trump imposed tariffs on steel and aluminum imports from Europe, Canada, Mexico, China, and other countries.[42] Trump's so-called "travel ban" indefinitely suspended the issuance of visas to applicants from the Muslim-majority countries Libya, Iran, Somalia, Syria, and Yemen, as well as North Korea and Venezuela.[43] When Congress refused to provide funding, Trump repeatedly threatened to use the president's emergency powers to begin construction of the border wall with Mexico.[44] As of this writing, many of these actions remain subject to litigation in the federal courts. But it is clear that President Trump has continued and even escalated recent presidents' bold use of unilateral authority.

A key vulnerability of the administrative presidency is that the president's unilateral actions can be more easily reversed by their successors than legislation. Changes in party control of the presidency can thus lead to reversals of some orders. However, when an administration issues a formal regulation, a new executive order is generally not sufficient to repeal it. Administrative rulemaking is a rule-bound process governed by the Administrative Procedure Act (discussed in Chapter 11). Presidents who seek to rescind existing regulations must go through a process of notice and public comment on new proposed rules, as well as navigate possible litigation over the changes they seek to implement.[45] Compared with reversing rules already in place, it is easier for a new president to issue a stop-work order on pending regulations still in the process of agency development or to refrain from defending regulations blocked in court.

A president's best-case scenario is usually to get Congress to enact laws rather than to use administrative actions. Unilateral action often indicates that the president has failed to win congressional support for his policies. Winning congressional support for new laws is almost always a major hurdle. Even when Congress is not actively opposed, getting Congress to pass even relatively uncontroversial legislation is an arduous process. But in the event Congress will not move forward in a manner consistent with presidential priorities, presidents can often achieve some of their aims via administrative action. In short, presidents seeking significant policy change should work to enact legislation whenever feasible, but when such an effort falls short, they can advance their aims through organizational or managerial techniques.

Faced with powerful congressional resistance to most of his agenda, Obama did not shy away from using executive power on numerous issues. But Obama's actions have been targeted for reversal under Trump. Within the president's first year in office, the Trump administration's EPA moved to repeal Obama's Clean Power Plan and replace it with a rule allowing states to write their own, weaker regulations for power plants.[46] Also during 2017, the Trump administration's Justice Department rescinded Obama's DACA program. Both of these moves have faced judicial challenge. The federal courts required the administration to fully restore the Obama-era DACA program protecting "Dreamers," and the program remains in limbo awaiting resolution at the Supreme Court.[47] In response to the administration's action against the Clean Power Plan, attorneys general in seventeen states banded together to bring suit in federal court to block the Trump administration from enforcing the regulation. This ongoing litigation illustrates that even presidents' unilateral actions are subject to limits and potential reversal.

Signing Statements

At times, presidents issue proclamations called *signing statements* to accompany bills they have signed into law. Even though they are not mentioned in the Constitution, signing statements have been used since James Monroe's presidency (1817–1825). George W. Bush, however, employed them more often than any other president.[48] Bush issued signing statements to override laws that he claimed would impinge upon his constitutional prerogatives as commander in chief. When Congress banned torture of war prisoners, for example, the president held that the law trespassed on his powers as commander in chief. It is not clear how much signing statements actually affect the administration of laws. Studies have shown that "federal agencies seem to have generally complied with thousands of legislative provisions that [Bush] had questioned."[49] Both Obama and Trump continued to use signing statements, albeit with less public controversy.[50]

Patronage

Patronage is another administrative asset presidents can employ to advance their aims. Presidents often grant or withhold their patronage resources to cultivate support and goodwill in Congress. Broadly conceived, patronage involves not only federal and judicial positions but also federal construction projects, location of government installations, campaign support, access to strategic information, plane rides on *Air Force One,* White House tours for important constituents, and countless other favors, large and small. Some presidents even keep records of the political favors they grant to lawmakers, IOUs that they can cash in later for needed support in Congress. There are limits, however, to the persuasive power of patronage. As one White House congressional-relations chief said, "The problem with congressional relations is that with every good intention, at the end of the day you can't accommodate all the requests that you get."[51] Although patronage may make a marginal difference in some cases, other considerations—public opinion as well as lawmakers' constituency interests, policy preferences, and ideological dispositions—are more important in shaping congressional outcomes.

LEADERSHIP

Beyond the constitutional powers possessed by Congress and the president, both also have the ability to engage in public leadership. Presidents and members of Congress are players in a "public sphere," which David R. Mayhew defines as "a realm of shared . . . consciousness in which government officials and others make moves before an attentive stream of the public."[52] Within this public sphere, institutional leaders "persuade, connive, hatch ideas, propagandize, assail enemies, vote, build coalitions, shepherd legislation, and in general cut a figure in public affairs."[53] All of these activities shape the public's concerns, attention, perceptions, opinions, and support. Momentarily, we will consider how these institutional leaders can engage in public leadership.

The president's capacity for leadership is powerfully driven by expectations. Everyone—including Congress, the press, and the public—expects the president to take the lead in proposing legislative initiatives.[54] Despite the president's limited powers specified in the Constitution, the president has come to be called the chief legislator. Over time, Congress has delegated increasingly more agenda-setting power by requiring the president to submit annual budgets and other reports. The legislative presidency emerged after World War II when this new presidential role was institutionalized, meaning it was established in institutional arrangements and standard operating procedures not merely because of some unique combination of personality and circumstance.

As a collegial body of 535 members, Congress does not provide a focal point for leadership comparable to the president. Nevertheless, one should not underestimate Congress's capacity to engage in public leadership. When issues prove to be highly controversial in Congress, the news media covers them more intensely. Political scientist W. Lance Bennett refers to this phenomenon as *indexing*, meaning that the news media systematically benchmark the amount and intensity of their issue coverage against the degree of controversy that occurs among political elites, especially in Congress.[55] When Congress collectively makes decisions about what topics to debate, to consider for legislation, and to serve as the subjects for hearings, Congress is also engaging in public leadership.

The President's Power to Persuade

"Presidential power is the power to persuade," wrote Richard E. Neustadt, a former staff aide in the Truman White House and adviser to President-elect John F. Kennedy.[56] This power of persuasion, Neustadt asserted, meant more than the executive's ability to persuade Congress to enact a bill. "Strategically, the question is not how he masters Congress in a peculiar instance, but what he does to boost his chances for mastery in any instance."[57] Presidents striving to be successful are urged to employ all of their resources—constitutional, political, bureaucratic, personal, and more—to persuade Congress and others to follow their lead.

Presidents are better able to persuade other Washington political elites when they are perceived as possessing both *skill* and *will*.[58] Skillful presidents recognize the limits of their political capital and have a good sense for what is politically possible. Backing proposals for which he cannot win sufficient support depletes a president's reputation for skill. "If [a president's] failures seem to form a pattern," writes Neustadt, "the consequence is bound to be a loss of faith in his effectiveness next time."[59] Perceptions of a president's *will* focus on whether the president is seen as being strongly committed to advancing a specific agenda. A president who has realistic ambitions and is strongly committed to them stands a better chance of success in persuasion.

From this analysis, it follows that presidents are more persuasive when they advance a clear, focused, achievable agenda. There is a limit to how much Congress can tackle at once. President Jimmy Carter (1977–1981) offers an instructive case of problematic agenda setting. As President Ronald Reagan (1981–1989) was taking office, his staff studied the difficulties his predecessor had faced in dealing with Congress. Reagan found that Carter quickly overloaded Congress's agenda and never made clear what his priorities were:

> There was little clarity in the communication of priorities to the American public. Instead of galvanizing support for two or three major national needs, the Carter administration proceeded on a number of fronts. . . . [P]erhaps more important, the lack of priorities meant unnecessary waste of the President's own time and energy.[60]

By contrast, agenda control was the hallmark of Reagan's leadership during his first year in office. By limiting his legislative priorities, Reagan focused Congress's and the public's attention on one priority issue at a time. Most were encapsulated as "Reaganomics"—tax and spending cuts. He exploited the usual honeymoon period for new presidents by moving his agenda quickly, during a moment of widespread anticipation of a new era of GOP national political dominance.

Even when presidents set agendas skillfully, persuading Congress is not easy. Even when the president's party possesses majority control of Congress, it is difficult to marshal action from a bicameral body of 535 members. Research has shown that presidents typically craft their legislative agenda in consultation with party leaders in Congress. During what Matthew N. Beckmann terms the *early game* of a legislative drive, presidents work most closely with congressional party leaders rather than with rank-and-file members or with moderate, potentially pivotal members.[61] Presidential lobbying for individual votes may become increasingly important in the later stages of the legislative process. Although commonly employed, this sequence offers no guarantee of success. Early in the Trump presidency, for example, the administration worked closely with Speaker Ryan and House committee chairs to craft a replacement for Obamacare. But when it came time to marshal the votes for the bill, neither extensive lobbying from the president nor pleading from congressional leaders was sufficient to bring on board rank-and-file Republicans on the conservative and moderate flanks of the party.[62] Defections from these two factions dealt the new president a stunning early defeat.

Deft congressional relations can sometimes make a difference. Reagan, for example, dealt skillfully with Democratic Speaker Thomas P. "Tip" O'Neill Jr. of Massachusetts, including a private dinner with the Speaker and his wife. Enjoying a Republican majority in the Senate, the Reagan White House focused primarily on lobbying the Democratic House to pass the president's economic program— the "greatest selling job I've ever seen," said Speaker O'Neill. As critical roll call votes approached, Reagan reached out to numerous rank-and-file lawmakers. He personally called or telegraphed all of the "Boll Weevils," the forty-seven southern Democrats in the Conservative Democratic Forum.[63] He persuaded several governors to meet with members from their states who were opposing the program. Top executive officials were dispatched to targeted Democratic districts to drum up public support. On the key House vote on Reagan's budget, all 191 GOP members and 63 Democrats backed the president's budget plan.

Presidents recognize the importance of maintaining informal contacts with Congress as a means of facilitating trust and open lines of communication. As Lyndon Johnson—who had served as Senate minority leader (1953–1955) and majority leader (1955–1960)—once declared, "Merely placing a program before Congress is not enough. Without constant attention from the administration, most legislation moves through the congressional process at the speed of a glacier."[64]

Some presidents deal with Congress more adeptly than others. Lyndon Johnson assiduously courted members. He summoned legislators to the White House for private meetings, danced with their wives at parties, telephoned greetings on their birthdays, and hosted them at his Texas ranch. He also knew how to twist arms to win support for his programs. "There is only one way for a President to deal with the Congress," he said, "and that is continuously, incessantly, and without interruption."[65] Johnson regularly (and sometimes crudely) admonished his aides and departmental officers to work closely with Congress. "[Get off] your ass and see how fast you can respond to a congressional request," he told his staff. "Challenge yourself to see how quickly you can get back to him or her with an answer, any kind of an answer, but goddamn it, an answer."[66]

Critics of President Obama charge that he did not make effective use of informal contacts to persuade members of Congress to support his programs. Obama showed limited interest in socializing with members, and his office of legislative liaison did not enjoy especially close ties to legislative leaders and rank-and-file members. "My friend the president isn't a great people person in terms of reaching out," said former senator Tom Coburn, R-Okla. "What you have to do is invest in relationships. And I think that's probably one of his biggest failings, is not investing enough in the relationships in the Congress."[67] Even some Democrats expressed exasperation.[68] Obama frequently outsourced the congressional liaison role to Vice President Joe Biden, who had close ties to many House and Senate members, given his more than three decades of Senate service.

President Trump has had a strained relationship with both congressional Republicans and Democrats. The president's unpredictability and tendency to reverse himself has undermined trust with both parties. In a televised meeting with congressional leaders, for example, Trump denounced the National Rifle Association's influence and stated that he wanted tougher gun control measures, including the ability to seize weapons from mentally disturbed people without due process.[69] He reversed his position shortly afterwards. On another occasion, Democratic leaders Chuck Schumer and Nancy Pelosi thought they had a deal with Trump on comprehensive immigration reform,[70] only to discover later that the president was not prepared to support a wall-for-Dreamers deal.[71] Likewise, in December 2018, Senate majority leader Mitch McConnell thought the president had agreed to support a continuing resolution without funding for the border wall only to have the president refuse support after the Senate had passed it.[72]

Mistrust between Congress and the president is a two-way street in this case. For his part, Trump remembers vividly that most Republican leaders were ready to abandon him at controversial moments during his presidential campaign. "We all remember the fact that Kevin McCarthy was the only member of leadership to not run away from Trump—the only one," said a White House aide.[73] On numerous occasions, Trump has criticized his congressional allies for what he sees as their failures to deliver on their promises. "Can you believe that Mitch McConnell, who has screamed Repeal & Replace for 7 years, couldn't get it done," Trump wrote in one of numerous tweets aimed at the Senate majority leader.[74]

Despite the difficulties in his relationship with Congress, President Trump does have some close congressional allies. He has golfed with senators Lindsey Graham, R-S.C., Rand Paul, R-Ky., and David Purdue, R-Ga. He regularly turns for advice to Freedom Caucus leader Rep. Mark Meadows, R-N.C. He has also brought congressional allies into the administration, notably former Rep. Mick Mulvaney, R-S.C., who has held a large number of administration posts, including most recently acting Chief of Staff. Similar to Obama's reliance upon Vice President Biden, Trump has also tasked vice president and former long-time House member Mike Pence with congressional negotiations. "We served with Pence. We know him. He's predictable," said House minority whip Steny H. Hoyer, D-Md. So, to that extent, one could say it's easier to work with Pence."[75]

Informal and personal relationships between the president and members of Congress promote but do not guarantee productive problem solving. "These kinds of relationships just don't pop up out of the air or out of necessity," observed a former aide to Speaker Boehner. "They require trust, and they take time. You just don't grow that necessary trust and relationship overnight."[76]

Going Public: The Rhetorical President

"With public sentiment, nothing can fail; without it nothing can succeed," Abraham Lincoln once observed.[77] Lincoln's idea is the essence of the rhetorical presidency: how and when a chief executive strategically employs contemporary campaign techniques and media technology to promote "himself and his policies in Washington by appealing to the American public."[78] The rhetorical president's ultimate objective is to produce an outpouring of public support that encourages lawmakers to push his ideas through the congressional obstacle course. Presidents often turn to these strategies when they find that they do not have the votes they need to pass their favored initiatives. As one analyst observes, "If [the president] had the votes he would pass the measure first and go to the public only for the bill-signing ceremonies."[79]

Going public on an issue is not without its risks. Political scientist Samuel Kernell argues that the strategy may alienate legislators who feel that the president is going over their heads, cutting them out of the process, and disregarding their constitutional role.[80] As opposed to bargaining and exchange, presidents who "go public" are not offering Congress anything. Instead, they are implicitly trying to threaten members' public standing or reelection if they block the president's agenda. As such, going public is often interpreted as a zero-sum game, a matter of winning or losing rather than working toward a compromise outcome. For these reasons, going public has a tendency to make enemies in Congress. Going public can also limit presidents' bargaining flexibility by putting the details of their proposals on display in advance of negotiations. The president can also raise expectations that cannot be met, make inept appeals, or stiffen the opposition.

Even so, the president's supporters typically expect and demand that the administration mount media campaigns to bring the public on board with their agenda. Reagan's adroitness with the media is a legacy that has loomed large for subsequent presidents and Congresses. The Hollywood actor turned president was at home in front of cameras and microphones, and he had a keen sense of public ritual and symbolism as means of rallying support. After an assassination attempt on his life on March 30, 1981, Reagan quickly recovered and, a month later, made a dramatic public appeal for his economic program. "The White House shrewdly tied Reagan's return to action to the budget and tax debate, scheduling an April 28 comeback speech before a joint meeting of Congress. It was a triumph, and people began to call him the 'Great Communicator.'"[81]

Not unlike Reagan, President Obama was an exceptionally skilled speaker. But despite his eloquence, Obama—by many accounts—was not able to employ the "bully pulpit" to move public opinion toward supporting his ambitious agenda. Obama himself agreed with this criticism: "What I have not done as well as I would have liked to is to consistently communicate to the general public why we're making some of these decisions."[82]

President Trump seeks to maintain a close, unmediated relationship with his supporters in the mass electorate. Although this may serve his own political interests, it often gets in the way of relationships with Congress. "I think sometimes the president undermines his own effectiveness because of his tweeting, and things like that," said Sen. John Cornyn, R-Texas. "He communicates in an unconventional way for a president, as you might have noticed, and I think that sometimes he steps on his own message."[83] Trump's rhetoric is often repetitive, simplistic, and grammatically awkward. "He is interesting to me linguistically because he speaks like everybody else," said linguistics scholar Jennifer Sclafani. "And we're not used to hearing that from a president. We're used to hearing somebody speak who sounds much more educated, much smarter, much more refined than your everyday American."[84]

Systematic research raises questions about presidents' capacity to use campaign techniques and speeches to change public opinion on issues. An important factor affecting members' willingness to support a presidential proposal is the president's popularity in their own states and districts.[85] But in an era where the parties' supporters are sorted along geographic lines, a president's popularity varies widely across the country. A president can be reasonably popular nationally and yet simultaneously very unpopular in many states and districts, as was often the case with both presidents Barack Obama and George W. Bush. By the same token, President Trump entered office with historically low approval ratings in national polls, but he maintains solid support among his base voters concentrated in many Republican members' states and districts.[86] A president's ability to wield public opinion against Congress declines when many legislators are more popular than the president in their own districts or states.

Political scientist George Edwards's work demonstrates that presidents rarely succeed in moving public opinion to favor their agenda.[87] Numerous obstacles get in the way of effective presidential opinion leadership. Presidents struggle to command large audiences. Given the increased range of choices available to consumers of news and entertainment today, presidents garner a declining audience share for their major speeches. Ironically, those most likely to tune in to a presidential address tend to be already highly informed and opinionated and thus very hard to persuade. Furthermore, many of those who watch will not remember what the president said. Compounding presidents' difficulties in persuasion, partisanship powerfully structures how viewers respond. Presidents struggle to shift the views of those who align with the opposing party while a president's fellow partisans often do not need to be persuaded. Edwards's data even reveal that the public often reacts against presidents' issue campaigns rather than moving toward the president. Generally speaking, Democratic presidents tend to provoke conservative backlashes, and Republican presidents provoke liberal backlashes.

Rather than trying to move public opinion, presidents do better when they champion issues that the public already favors.[88] Successful presidents are often skilled in timing their media campaigns with moments when the public is especially open to presidential leadership.[89] For example, President Bill Clinton (1993–2001) capitalized on a battle over funding for flood relief to make a positive case for the role of government against House Republican "revolutionaries." The public already found flood victims sympathetic and wanted to see them helped. Preexisting public opinion thus set the stage for Clinton to use the issue to push his own agenda.

Similarly, George W. Bush (2001–2009) came into his own as a communicator in the aftermath of the 2001 terrorist attacks on the World Trade Center in New York City and on the Pentagon. In the context of a public outraged about the attacks and eager to see an effective response, Bush's direct and confident manner resonated with Americans and boosted both public and congressional support for his antiterrorism and war plans. These examples point to how presidents can use public campaigns to rally support for their proposals most effectively when the public already, in principle, supports the president's efforts. In these cases, presidents do not change public opinion so much as capitalize on it for their own purposes.

With mixed success, presidents continually strive to shape their public image in the news media. They employ aides with expertise in lighting, camera angles, and backdrops. The most elaborately staged event during the Bush presidency was his flight to and speech on the aircraft carrier *Abraham Lincoln* during which he prematurely announced "mission accomplished" and the end of major military combat in Iraq.[90] President Obama continually experimented with different media technologies to reach audiences. He recognized that "in a fragmented media universe, presidents must communicate nearly constantly across an array of platforms, both traditional and new."[91] President Obama held fewer press conferences than his predecessors,[92] but he was a guest on various "soft news" and entertainment programs. He experimented with a live Internet "town hall" meeting in which he fielded questions in the White House from citizens across the nation, as well as from a live audience in the East Room.[93] Obama also held town hall meetings using Twitter, YouTube, and Facebook.[94] In the Internet age, with its 24/7 media cycle, presidents "must exploit an array of traditional and nontraditional communication methods if they are to influence and shape the public conversation."[95]

The Trump presidency demonstrates the effectiveness of a new communications model relying heavily upon social media. Trump's tweets serve as powerful agenda-setting devices. A Trump tweet is disseminated first to his millions of followers and then frequently discussed extensively in traditional media, both in newspapers and on cable news. The candid, spontaneous quality of Trump's tweets forges a connection with his supporters. Tweeting allows him to break through with his own message and thereby forces news media gatekeepers to pay attention.

Advancing administration priorities requires skill at both the inside game of mobilizing winning coalitions on Capitol Hill and the outside game of stirring popular support for the president's agenda. President Richard Nixon made a keen observation on how administrations can win favorable congressional action on their policies: "In the final analysis, [legislative successes] are not won or lost by programs. They are won or lost on how these programs are presented to the country, and how all the political and public relations considerations are handled."[96]

Congressional Opinion Leadership

Like the president, Congress's influence over U.S. politics extends beyond its formal powers under the Constitution. Congress is far more than a legislative institution. As a representative body, members deploy debate, hearings, resolutions, media events, interviews, and other types of public action to great effect. Congress has numerous informal ways to mobilize political opposition and thereby shape both the political context and the president's strategic options. Congress can engage in all of these influential activities, even when it is unable to coalesce around any particular legislative enactment.

Based on a survey of actions taken by members of Congress that receive coverage in major texts of U.S. history, David R. Mayhew finds that only about half of the actions for which members are known in public-affairs history were associated with legislating.[97] To a great extent, members of Congress have instead made their mark on U.S. history by investigating, taking stands, making major speeches, writing books and articles, and disclosing information. Members' ability to engage in opinion leadership has by no means declined. Instead, Congress is perhaps more potent in this regard than ever. Developments in media technology have enabled even backbench members of Congress to cultivate national constituencies. Today's members have public-speaking opportunities that extend well beyond the House or Senate floor. They can tweet, post on Facebook, appear on cable news, and make themselves social media celebrities.[98]

Congressional opinion leadership has significant consequences for presidents. First, congressional controversy undercuts the president's standing with the public. Research has shown that congressional investigations of presidents and their administrations tend to drive down the president's approval ratings.[99] Low public-opinion ratings then harm presidents' ability to advance their agenda in Congress.[100] Second, the presence of congressional opposition constrains presidents' choices. Presidents who are facing intense criticism in Congress are less tolerant of additional political risk. For example, research has shown that presidents facing tougher investigatory scrutiny from Congress take fewer and more limited military actions when faced with international crises.[101] Third, the content and intensity of congressional discourse has significant effects on public opinion. Indeed, political scientist John Zaller regards elite discourse—of which Congress is a key component—as the key driver of public opinion more generally.[102]

Put simply, Congress has considerable capacity to "go public," just as the president does. Congress is not just a passive entity that presidents seek to bend to their will. In the constitutional system of checks and balances, Congress is a formidable opinion leader in its own right.

The "Two Presidencies"

"The United States has one president, but it has two presidencies; one presidency is for domestic affairs, and the other is concerned with defense and foreign policy."[103] According to this formulation by political scientist Aaron Wildavsky, presidential proposals achieve markedly more success with Congress in the international arena than in the domestic arena. This differential success does not stem so much from the president's formal constitutional powers, such as being designated commander in chief of the armed forces. Instead, the reason is political: "Presidents prevail [more often in foreign affairs] not only because they may have superior resources but because their potential opponents are weak, divided or believe that they should not control foreign policy."[104] Put simply, Congress tends to assert itself more in domestic policy making than in foreign policy.

The *two-presidencies thesis* seems especially relevant to the presidency of George W. Bush. Bush's presidency was transformed by the terrorist attacks of September 11, 2001. Before the attacks, Bush was embattled. Democratic control of the Senate after May 2001 had generated significant problems for the administration. Democrats were holding hearings to spotlight their agenda and critique Bush's, as well as modifying and blocking administration bills coming from the GOP House.[105] By June 2001, Bush's public standing had fallen "to a tepid 50 percent approval, the lowest presidential approval rating in more than five years."[106] But Bush soon benefited from a rally-around-the-flag effect. Images of the president consoling firefighters and others at the site of the World Trade Center, his calm and confident demeanor, and his eloquent statements to the public—including an address before a joint meeting of Congress on September 20, 2001—rallied the nation to fight a global war on terrorism. Bush's public approval ratings soared to a record-level 91 percent, breaking his father's record of 89 percent during the 1991 Persian Gulf War.[107] Meanwhile, Congress moved on a bipartisan basis to authorize the president to employ "all necessary and appropriate force" against those groups or nations involved in the terrorist attacks. Subsequently, the military ousted the Taliban regime in Afghanistan, which had provided safe haven for Osama bin Laden, the al Qaeda leader behind the September 11 attacks.

President Bush's focus then turned to Iraq, a nation he declared to be part of the "axis of evil" that threatened the world. In October 2002, the administration persuaded Congress to enact a joint resolution granting the president unilateral authority to launch a preemptive military strike against Iraq. On March 19, 2003, President Bush went on national television and informed the nation of the start of the war in Iraq. Three weeks later, on April 9, U.S. forces entered Baghdad, ending the regime of longtime dictator Saddam Hussein. The free hand Bush enjoyed in launching all of these major foreign-policy initiatives contrasts strongly with the constraints with which he had to contend on the domestic front both before and after 9/11.

Consistent with the two presidencies thesis, President Trump encountered no obstacle either in Congress or public opinion when he decided to launch a cruise missile strike against Syria in response to a chemical weapons attack directed at civilians. Trump even saw a small uptick in his approval rating, though the effect did not persist.[108] Although the United States has not engaged in a major new military mission since 2017, Trump clearly possesses a wide scope of action in military affairs, consistent with his predecessors.

Since its emergence, Wildavsky's analysis has been the subject of much reexamination and comment. One recent study has found continued support for the central thesis.[109] Comparing federal agencies dealing with defense and foreign affairs with agencies dealing with domestic issues, political scientists Brandice Canes-Wrone, William Howell, and David E. Lewis find that presidents achieve greater success in obtaining their requested appropriations for agencies dealing with defense and foreign affairs. In addition, presidents tend to possess more centralized administrative control over agencies dealing with defense and foreign affairs. A key challenge for the two-presidencies thesis, however, is differentiating the two arenas in a world in which the international and domestic constantly overlap. Scores of issues are both domestic and transnational in character, including climate change, refugee flows, global economic crises, and the struggle against terrorism.

Even if presidents can better shape foreign than domestic policy, it is important not to underestimate Congress's influence over foreign affairs. When Congress is displeased with a president's foreign policy, it has many means of expressing itself. Mayhew finds that fully a quarter of all the significant congressional actions mentioned by historians were in foreign affairs, an underappreciated fact about the institution's role in U.S. politics.[110] Most of the time, members' significant foreign-policy actions did not take the form of legislation. Instead, members of Congress exert their influence by investigating, making speeches, and engaging in other forms of public criticism. In turn, controversy in Congress strongly influences media coverage, generating more press scrutiny and skepticism of administration policy. Even though Congress has almost never used legislation to force the president's hand in foreign policy, such as by cutting off funds for a military operation, Congress's capacity for leadership extends far beyond its formal legislative powers.[111]

SOURCES OF LEGISLATIVE–EXECUTIVE CONFLICT AND COOPERATION

Unlike the legislative assemblies of many nations where executive authority is lodged in the leader of parliament—called the prime minister or premier—Congress truly is separate from the executive branch. Legislative–executive conflicts were evident in 1789, and they are pervasive today.

Yet the executive and legislative branches are also mutually dependent in policy making. The structure of the U.S. government, with its elaborate system of checks and balances and veto points, generally means that policy making requires cooperation across branches and across parties. Legislation is rarely achievable when the two parties emulate parliamentary systems in which one party governs (or tries to) and the other is united in opposition. Bargaining and compromise are thus essential to public policy making in the United States. In recent years, compromise has proven to be exceptionally difficult. Many factors account for this development, including the ideological divide between the two political parties and intense party competition for control of national institutions.[112]

But now, as in the past, the interdependence of the U.S. system gives each branch of government an incentive to bargain. The 125 volumes of the *United States Statutes at Large* testify to the cooperative impulses of the two branches. Each volume contains the joint product of Congresses and presidents over the years, from the 108 public laws enacted by the First Congress (1789–1791) to the 442 enacted by the 115th Congress (2017–2018).

In the following sections, we consider four key factors that affect interbranch bargaining: partisan ties, public expectations, institutional constituencies, and time horizons.

Party Loyalties

Party ties can, at times, bridge the institutional differences that separate presidents from Congress. Both the president and his party in Congress tend to be judged together by voters, giving them incentive to cooperate in their common political interest. But these same party ties pull in opposing directions when different parties control the White House and Congress. Party is thus a source of both collaboration and conflict between the branches.

The best predictor of presidential success with Congress is the number of seats his party controls.[113] The skills individual presidents bring to bear make only a modest difference beyond this brute institutional circumstance.[114] Obviously, much of presidents' support from their copartisans reflects the fact that party members agree more with one another than with members of the opposing party. Politicians who share a party label also cater to many of the same interest groups. But party affects the relationship between Congress and the president for reasons that go beyond the extent to which copartisans agree among themselves and disagree with their party opposition on policies and priorities.

Members of Congress benefit politically and fare better in elections when a president of their own party is popular and perceived as successful. Congressional Democrats wanted President Obama to succeed in moving his agenda, even when they did not always share his priorities. As Rep. Chris Van Hollen, D-Md., once said, "Our political fortunes are tied to Barack Obama's."[115]

In a two-party system, however, political benefits to one party are necessarily political harms to the other. As such, members of the president's opposition party are better off politically when the president is not popular or seen as successful. The party not controlling the presidency normally gains seats in midterm elections, but it typically gains even more when the public disapproves of the president. These basic facts create powerful political incentives for both parties.

Members of the president's party have political reason to go along with the president's proposals. Put differently, members of the president's party have incentive to seek out reasons to support the president, even if they have policy or ideological reservations about the president's proposals. In considering President George W. Bush's No Child Left Behind legislation, for example, House minority whip Roy Blunt, R-Mo., said, "I always had misgivings about it. . . . But I did vote for it on the basis that maybe [President Bush] was right and this was his big domestic initiative, and let's give him a chance."[116] Along the same lines, many Republicans who staunchly opposed President Obama's requests for additional investment in infrastructure are much more open to supporting infrastructure projects proposed by President Trump.[117] Likewise, Republicans in Congress—long supporters of free trade agreements—would not likely have tolerated a Democratic president imposing sweeping new tariffs on steel, aluminium, and imports from China, though they have largely held their fire in response to Trump's tariffs.

By the same token, members of the president's opposition have political reasons to resist the president's leadership. Rather than looking for reasons to go along with the president, opposing partisans are inclined to seek out reasons to withhold their support. They have little incentive to give the president the benefit of the doubt. Members of the president's opposition do not gain in political terms (and likely will suffer political harm) if the president wins broad bipartisan approval of his initiatives and is seen as a successful, consensus-building leader. As Senate minority leader Mitch McConnell, R-Ky., explained in dealing with President Obama's agenda, "It was absolutely critical that everybody be together because if the proponents of the bill were able to say it was bipartisan, it tended to convey to the public that this is O.K., they must have figured it out. . . . It's either bipartisan or it isn't."[118] As the presidential out party in 2009–2010, there was strategic reason for Republicans to deny bipartisan legitimacy to the president's efforts. Looking toward the 2010 midterms, McConnell went on to say, "I think the reason my members are feeling really good is they believe that the reward for playing team ball this year was the reversal of the political environment and the possibility that we will have a bigger team next year."[119] Undoubtedly, McConnell's strategy was vindicated by the election outcome, a historic landslide in favor of Republicans.

Under conditions of divided government, partisan incentives create additional hurdles to interbranch cooperation, in addition to the policy differences that already exist between the parties. The president's opposition, in control of the legislative branch, wants to build an argument against the president's reelection or against the president's party's continuation in office. They cannot do so, if they are working cooperatively with the president and demonstrating that both parties are able to achieve their objectives under such conditions.

Partisan interests thus powerfully shape the relationship between Congress and the president. Because one party has a stake in the president's success and the other party has a stake in the president's failure, presidential leadership often tends to exacerbate partisan divisions and polarize the parties further. Research has shown that most types of policy issues become more controversial when incorporated as part of a president's agenda.[120] For example, the COPS program, a grant-in-aid program to assist local law enforcement in hiring police officers, was a hugely controversial program during the Clinton administration, when it was a signature initiative championed by the president. During the Clinton years, there were numerous straight party line votes as Republicans sought to defund the COPS program. But once Clinton was no longer president, the issue faded from the political agenda, though the program continues to exist. At times, parties even exchange positions in reaction to presidential leadership. For example, when the president is a Democrat, Republicans have tended to oppose federal education standards and Democrats to support them. When the president is a Republican, Democrats have tended to oppose federal education standards and Republicans to support them.[121]

Partisanship shapes congressional–presidential relations in foreign and military policy as well as on domestic issues. "When the opposition party holds a large number of seats or controls one or both chambers of Congress, members routinely challenge the president and step up oversight of foreign conflicts; when the legislative branch is dominated by the president's party, it generally goes along with the White House," conclude political scientists William G. Howell and Jon C. Pevehouse.[122] Generally speaking, presidents enjoy a freer hand in managing military operations when their party controls Congress.[123] Controversy over a president's foreign policy is especially likely under conditions of divided party control.

Partisan incentives can help smooth the operation of separation of powers under circumstances of unified party control. But in a political system characterized by divided party control two-thirds (69 percent) of the time between 1954 and 2021, partisan ties are more often an obstacle to interbranch cooperation.

Public Expectations

Despite the political incentives that work against bipartisan cooperation under conditions of divided government, political scientist David Mayhew concluded that with respect to productivity of laws and investigations, it "does not seem to make all that much difference whether party control of the American government happens to be unified or divided."[124]

Subsequent research has concluded that divided government makes some difference for legislative productivity.[125] Reexamining Mayhew's data from 1947 through 2012, R. Douglas Arnold concludes that unified governments enacted 23 percent more bills that contemporary observers deemed important than did divided governments.[126] But divided government by no means brings the operation of U.S. government to a halt. Generally speaking, it is fair to say that even in light of subsequent analysis, Mayhew's findings remain an important corrective. Other factors shaping interbranch relations often attenuate or counterbalance the effects of party control of governing institutions.

Most importantly, the public expects government to function under conditions of both divided and unified government. Politicians have incentives to respond to public expectations at all times. Members of Congress continually seek credit-claiming opportunities as individual lawmakers, not just as partisans. This is especially true of legislators with presidential ambitions. Individual credit can be won from legislating regardless of conditions of party control.

The public also expects the president and Congress to work together in response to crises. Interbranch agreement is often achieved as a result of events. At times, the Washington community comes to focus on a particular problem, and wide agreement can often be forged when this happens. The bipartisan response to the September 11, 2001, terrorist attacks offers an example.

Finally, there is much that is just not understood about lawmaking over time. The most salient pattern in any analysis of legislative productivity in the modern Congress is a "huge surge of legislative activism that began in the Eisenhower years and peaked with the Great Society but continued well into the Nixon administration."[127] This surge has a larger effect on legislative productivity than the circumstances of party control of governing institutions. Mayhew attributes this remarkable surge of legislation to an activist public mood characterized by the era's "interlocking civil rights, consumer, antiwar, labor, student, women's liberation, environmental, and 'public interest' movements."[128] Congress and the president responded to the public expectations of this time period with much important new legislation expanding the role of the federal government to a host of new areas, including the rights of women and minorities, as well as a wide range of new environmental, consumer, and business regulations. The bottom line is that when the public seems to demand action from the federal government, presidents and Congress have incentives to respond.

Different Constituencies

The different constituencies presidents and Congress represent are often a source of conflict between the branches. Presidents and their vice presidents are the only public officials elected nationally. To win, they must create vastly broader electoral coalitions than are necessary for legislators, who represent either states or districts. Presidents and legislators tend to view policies and problems from different perspectives. Members of Congress often subscribe to the view that "what's good for Portland is good for the nation." Presidents are apt to say that, "what's good for the nation is good for Portland."

In other words, public officials are likely to view issues differently when they represent diverging interests. For example, a president might wish to reduce international trade barriers. A representative from a district where a manufacturer is threatened by imported products is likely to oppose the president's policy, whereas retailers of imported products are likely to support the president. The challenge to national policy making is to forge consensus within an electorate that simultaneously holds membership in two or more competing constituencies.

Disparities in constituencies are underscored by differences in the ways voters judge presidents and members of Congress. Studies of presidential popularity suggest that presidents are judged on the basis of broad policy outcomes: economic boom or bust, the presence or absence of wars or other crises, and the impact of policies on given groups.[129] Individual legislators, by contrast, cannot be held accountable for the overall outcomes of government. Instead, they tend to be assessed on the basis of their personalities, their communication with constituents, the positions they take, and their service in material ways to the state or district. Not only do presidents and legislators serve different constituencies, but they also labor under divergent incentives.

Different Time Perspectives

Finally, Congress and the president operate on different timetables. Presidents have four years, at most eight, to win adoption of their programs. They are usually in a hurry to achieve all they can before they leave office. In practice, they have even less time because of the typical falloff in presidential support after the initial "honeymoon." Indeed, presidents and their advisers actually often have a year, perhaps less, to sell their basic programs to Congress and the public. "A president's most effective year is his first," explained Sen. Richard Durbin, D-Ill. "After the first year, an election year is under way and people look at [a president] differently."[130]

On major, long-standing issues, however, Congress typically moves slowly. Seldom does it pass presidential initiatives quickly unless an emergency or crisis of some sort is looming. Moreover, many legislators are careerists. Once elected, House members are likely to be reelected, and senators serve six-year terms. Most members hold office a good deal longer than the presidents they deal with. Skeptical legislators, reluctant to follow the president, realize that if they resist long enough, someone else will occupy the White House.

THE BALANCE OF POWER

"The relationship between the Congress and the presidency," wrote Arthur M. Schlesinger Jr., "has been one of the abiding mysteries of the American system of government."[131] Part of the mystery inheres in the Constitution, which enumerates many powers for Congress, as well as those "necessary and proper" to carry them out, while leaving the president's powers largely unstated. Where does the balance of power lie?

Generally speaking, presidents have grown in power relative to Congress over the course of U.S. history, just as executives have increased their power relative to legislatures around the world. Even so, periods of presidential ascendancy have often been followed by eras of congressional assertiveness. The First Congress of "its own volition immediately turned to the executive branch for guidance and discovered in [Treasury Secretary Alexander] Hamilton a personality to whom such leadership was congenial."[132] Two decades later (by 1825), the "initiative in public affairs remained with [Speaker Henry] Clay and his associates in the House of Representatives" and not with the president.[133] Thus, dominance in national policy making can pass from one branch to the other. Strong presidents sometimes provoked efforts by Congress to reassert its own authority and to restrict that of the executive. Scholars have even identified periods of *congressional government* or *presidential government*.[134]

However, even during periods in which one branch appears to dominate, the actual balance of power varies widely across policy areas. The mid-1960s and early 1970s, for example, are often cited as a time of *imperial presidents* and compliant Congresses.[135] But Congress was an important instigator of policy during this time period, not just a rubber stamp for presidents. Although Congress enacted much of President Johnson's Great Society program, it also initiated scores of laws, including consumer, environmental, health, and civil rights legislation. Nor did executive actions go unchallenged. Nationally televised hearings conducted in 1966 by the Senate Foreign Relations Committee helped to mobilize congressional and public opposition to the Vietnam War.

The refrain "imperial presidents" and "compliant Congresses" was heard regularly when President George W. Bush presided over unified Republican government from 2001 to 2007. More recently, a House majority leader called President Obama an imperial president for using his regulatory and executive authority to govern without Congress.[136] When Democratic leader Nancy Pelosi regained the Speakership in 2019, she proclaimed the end of the "rubber stamp Congress" that President Trump had enjoyed under unified government in 2017–2018.[137] Yet all recent presidents faced numerous setbacks on domestic policy throughout their terms in office, including Bush's failed push for Social Security privatization, Obama's inability to persuade Congress to enact immigration reform or legislation combatting climate change, and Trump's failure to repeal and replace Obamacare.

Legislative–executive relationships are not zero-sum games. If one branch gains power, the other does not necessarily lose it. The expansion of the federal government since World War II has augmented the authority of both branches. Their growth rates were different, but each expanded its ability to address complex issues, initiate legislation, and frustrate the proposals of the other. Conflict between Congress and the president is embedded in the system of separation of powers and checks and balances. But the founders also expected their governmental arrangement to promote accommodation between the branches. Historical patterns have veered between these two extremes. The two branches worked together in the early days of Woodrow Wilson's progressive New Freedom (1913–1916); during the New Deal (1933–1937) and World War II (1941–1945); during the brief Great Society years (1964–1966) following John F. Kennedy's assassination in 1963; for the even briefer "Reaganomics" juggernaut during Ronald Reagan's first year in office (1981); during most of George W. Bush's first six years in office (2001–2007); and during Barack Obama's first two years (2009–2011). At other times, the two branches fought fiercely—during Wilson's second term (1919–1921); after 1937, during the Franklin Roosevelt administration; after 1966, during the Lyndon Johnson administration; and for much of the Nixon, Reagan, George H. W. Bush, and Clinton administrations, the final two years of George W. Bush's presidency, and Obama's presidency after 2010.

Finally, a wide gap often separates what presidents want from what they can achieve. Congress can influence what, when, how, or even whether executive recommendations are sent to Capitol Hill. Expectations of what will pass Congress frequently shape White House agendas. At times, this indirect priority-setting power of the House and Senate will discourage presidents from even attempting to get Congress to consider certain proposals. At other times, the White House will forward and endorse recommendations because they are known to have broad legislative support. "The president proposes, Congress disposes" is an oversimplified adage.

CONCLUSION

Conflict would seem to be the inevitable result of a system that intentionally divides lawmaking and other powers between the executive and legislative branches. But neither branch is monolithic. Presidents find supporters in both chambers even when presidents are opposed by congressional majorities. Likewise, presidents encounter resistance even when their parties control both House and Senate. To achieve common goals, Congress and the president must find ways to work together. Much of the time, the relationship between Congress and the executive is better characterized as accommodation rather than conflict. Both branches seek support for their policy preferences from each other and from outside allies.

Nevertheless, confrontation is a recurring element in dealings between Capitol Hill and the White House. The framers of the Constitution consciously distributed and mixed power among the three branches. They left it unclear how Congress or the president would assert control over the bureaucracy and over policy making. Even when both houses of Congress are controlled by the same party as the White House, the two branches have different constituencies and political incentives and often become adversaries.

Tasos Katopodis/Getty Images

AP Photo/Andrew Harnik

Bill Clark/CQ Roll Call

Bureaucracy: The Fourth Branch. U.S. Attorney General nominee William Barr testifies at his confirmation hearing before the Senate Judiciary Committee on January 15, 2019, in Washington, DC. Barr, who previously served as Attorney General under President George H. W. Bush, was confronted about his views on the investigation being conducted by special counsel Robert Mueller. Senator Kamala Harris, D-Calif., right, accompanied by Senator Cory Booker, D-N.J., left, questions Barr. Secretary of Energy nominee and former Governor Rick Perry, R-Tex., speaks with Senator Catherine Cortez Masto, D-Nev., as he arrives for his confirmation hearing in the Senate Energy and Natural Resources Committee on January 19, 2016.

CONGRESS AND THE BUREAUCRACY

"Look what's happening with every agency—waste, fraud, and abuse. We will cut so much, your head will spin," declared presidential candidate Donald Trump on the campaign trail. Trump is hardly the first successful presidential candidate to target the federal bureaucracy in his speeches. But with Republicans in control of both chambers of Congress during his first two years in office, the new president appeared to have the opportunity to force major changes across a slew of government agencies.

In order to fulfill this agenda, Trump appointed die-hard conservatives to run several key departments and agencies. In more than a few cases, he put well-known critics of an agency's mission in charge of its direction. Former Texas governor Rick Perry had called for the Energy Department to be abolished when he ran for president in 2012; he now leads the department. Trump's selection to head the Environmental Protection Agency, Scott Pruitt, spent much of his time as Oklahoma's attorney general suing the EPA to block its enforcement of climate change regulations. Although Pruitt resigned in July 2018 after months of scandals, his successor, acting EPA head Andrew Wheeler, shares his hostility toward aggressive environmental regulation. Trump's education secretary, Betsy DeVos, is a noted advocate for private-school vouchers.[1] An adviser to Trump observed that "he wants them to totally shake these agencies up. . . . He doesn't want them to do business the same old way."[2] A particular target for Trump and his team are the many new Obama-era regulations that they charge have hobbled businesses and undermined economic growth.

But cutting government bureaucracy is not simply a matter of appointing program critics to lead agencies. As they seek to roll back bureaucratic regulations, Trump and his congressional Republican allies "have their work cut out for them," noted conservative analyst Andy Koenig. Once enacted, the process for reversing government regulations is time-consuming and cumbersome, requiring several stages, including time for public review and comment. Assaults on regulations also often spark lawsuits that, at a minimum, create delay. And most agencies are staffed by veteran civil servants who can be counted on to resist changes that they believe undermine programs that they have dedicated their careers to implementing. With Democrats' takeover of the House majority in the 2018 midterms, assaults on regulations will see more challenges in committee hearing rooms and, possibly, through legislation.

More broadly, efforts to scale back federal agencies often turn out to be more popular in principle than in practice. Although they profess to want to get the government off their backs, Americans of virtually all ideological persuasions often turn to the government to help fulfill their goals and to provide assistance during times of need. As William S. Cohen, former GOP senator from Maine (1979–1997), put it, "The government is the enemy until one needs a friend."[3] Trump himself promised voters that they would continue to receive many of the same benefits they have been accustomed to receiving from the federal government but with greater efficiency.

The paradox, then, is that citizens and various groups oppose the general idea of big government, but they support many of the government's specific roles in ensuring clean air and water, a strong national defense, access to quality health care, the safety of food products and prescription drugs, providing assistance after national disasters, and well-functioning transportation networks. Understandably, lawmakers typically defend government programs supported by their constituents. In brief, many people may dislike or resent government, but they usually support federal programs that benefit themselves.

To implement any government program, an organized bureaucracy is required—often federal *and* state bureaucracies. Importantly, Washington relies on the states to administer many national programs. By the same token, states rely on federal resources to fund many of their health care, transportation, and education priorities. Each level of government needs the other. Although the federal–state relationship is rife with tensions and turf battles, today's federal–state relationship is usually more symbiotic than confrontational.

The two Congresses contribute to an expanding bureaucracy. In today's complex and interdependent world, constituents typically look to the national government rather than the private sector to secure collective goods, such as security, justice, and protection. Similarly, nationwide corporations often lobby for federal regulation so they do not have to contend with the different rules of the fifty states. Members of Congress respond to such demands.

CONGRESS ORGANIZES THE EXECUTIVE BRANCH

Just as the president and Congress share influence over lawmaking, they share responsibility for the executive branch of government: the bureaucracy. The

Constitution requires the president to implement the laws, and by implication, it empowers him to manage the executive branch. But Congress "has at least as much to do with executive administration as does an incumbent of the White House."[4] Congress is constitutionally authorized to organize and fund the executive branch.

The framers, of course, did not foresee the huge federal bureaucracy that has arisen from their sparse references to "executive departments." George Washington supervised only three departments (State, War, and Treasury); Donald Trump heads fifteen. Beyond the cabinet departments, the federal bureaucracy also includes independent agencies (such as the Central Intelligence Agency), independent regulatory commissions, and government corporations (see Figure 11-1).

Congress has extensive influence over the structure and composition of the federal bureaucracy.[5] Among other things, it can enact statutes that establish or abolish executive agencies and departments (see Table 11-1). The most recent cabinet creation is the Department of Homeland Security (DHS), established in 2002 in the wake of the terrorist attacks of September 11, 2001. Other ways Congress can influence the structure of the executive branch include the following: instructing departments and agencies to reorganize themselves, establishing an outside commission to make recommendations, or authorizing the president to reorganize on his own or to develop reorganization plans that will then be subject to some form of congressional review. Congress extends its long arm into the bureaucracy in many different ways. The Senate confirms (or not, as the case may be) presidential appointments of high-level officials. Congress authorizes the basic personnel systems of federal entities. It also grants rulemaking authority to administrative agencies.

Senate Confirmation of Presidential Appointees

High-level federal appointments—executive, diplomatic, and judicial—are subject to the Senate's "advice and consent" under Article II, section 2, of the Constitution. After the president has decided whom to nominate, the Senate decides whether to confirm.

Senators use their confirmation power to wield influence over executive-branch priorities. Senate committees usually elicit the following promise from departmental and agency nominees they have confirmed: "The above nomination [a cabinet secretary, for example] was approved subject to the nominee's commitment to respond to requests to appear and testify before any duly constituted committee of the Senate."[6] Or as Sen. Charles Grassley, R-Iowa, declared, "I'm going to hit every [Obama] nominee with the question, 'Are you open to congressional oversight?'"[7] Senators also use confirmation hearings to extract promises on important pending issues. In January 2019, Democrats on the Senate Judiciary Committee pressed William Barr, Trump's nominee to be his new attorney general, for assurances that he would allow Special Counsel

FIGURE 11-1 ■ The Government of the United States

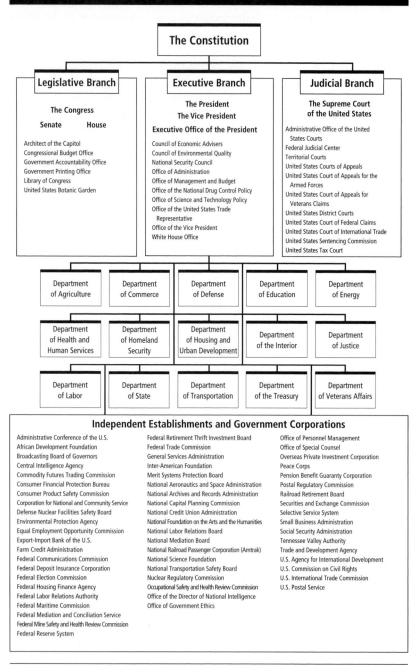

The Constitution

Legislative Branch

The Congress

Senate   House

Architect of the Capitol
Congressional Budget Office
Government Accountability Office
Government Printing Office
Library of Congress
United States Botanic Garden

Executive Branch

The President
The Vice President

Executive Office of the President

Council of Economic Advisers
Council of Environmental Quality
National Security Council
Office of Administration
Office of Management and Budget
Office of the National Drug Control Policy
Office of Science and Technology Policy
Office of the United States Trade
   Representative
Office of the Vice President
White House Office

Judicial Branch

The Supreme Court of the United States

Administrative Office of the United
   States Courts
Federal Judicial Center
Territorial Courts
United States Courts of Appeals
United States Court of Appeals for the
   Armed Forces
United States Court of Appeals for
   Veterans Claims
United States District Courts
United States Court of Federal Claims
United States Court of International Trade
United States Sentencing Commission
United States Tax Court

Department of Agriculture	Department of Commerce	Department of Defense	Department of Education	Department of Energy
Department of Health and Human Services	Department of Homeland Security	Department of Housing and Urban Development	Department of the Interior	Department of Justice
Department of Labor	Department of State	Department of Transportation	Department of the Treasury	Department of Veterans Affairs

Independent Establishments and Government Corporations

Administrative Conference of the U.S.
African Development Foundation
Broadcasting Board of Governors
Central Intelligence Agency
Commodity Futures Trading Commission
Consumer Financial Protection Bureau
Consumer Product Safety Commission
Corporation for National and Community Service
Defense Nuclear Facilities Safety Board
Environmental Protection Agency
Equal Employment Opportunity Commission
Export-Import Bank of the U.S.
Farm Credit Administration
Federal Communications Commission
Federal Deposit Insurance Corporation
Federal Election Commission
Federal Housing Finance Agency
Federal Labor Relations Authority
Federal Maritime Commission
Federal Mediation and Conciliation Service
Federal Mine Safety and Health Review Commission
Federal Reserve System

Federal Retirement Thrift Investment Board
Federal Trade Commission
General Services Administration
Inter-American Foundation
Merit Systems Protection Board
National Aeronautics and Space Administration
National Archives and Records Administration
National Capital Planning Commission
National Credit Union Administration
National Foundation on the Arts and the Humanities
National Labor Relations Board
National Mediation Board
National Railroad Passenger Corporation (Amtrak)
National Science Foundation
National Transportation Safety Board
Nuclear Regulatory Commission
Occupational Safety and Health Review Commission
Office of the Director of National Intelligence
Office of Government Ethics

Office of Personnel Management
Office of Special Counsel
Overseas Private Investment Corporation
Peace Corps
Pension Benefit Guaranty Corporation
Postal Regulatory Commission
Railroad Retirement Board
Securities and Exchange Commission
Selective Service System
Small Business Administration
Social Security Administration
Tennessee Valley Authority
Trade and Development Agency
U.S. Agency for International Development
U.S. Commission on Civil Rights
U.S. International Trade Commission
U.S. Postal Service

Source: The United States Government Manual, 2015 (Washington, DC: Office of the Federal Register, Government Printing Office).

TABLE 11-1 ■ Growth of the Cabinet	
Department	**Year created**
State	1789
Treasury	1789
War (reorganized and renamed Defense in 1947)	1789
Interior	1849
Justice (position of attorney general created in 1789)	1870
Agriculture	1889
Commerce (created as Commerce and Labor)	1903
Labor (split from Commerce and Labor)	1913
Health, Education, and Welfare (reorganized and renamed Health and Human Services in 1979)	1953
Housing and Urban Development	1965
Transportation	1966
Energy	1977
Education	1980
Veterans Affairs	1989
Homeland Security	2002

Source: CQ Daily Monitor, January 10, 2003, 3.

Robert Mueller's Russia investigation to proceed without interference and that he would make Mueller's report public when complete.[8] The confirmation process also reflects the two-Congresses principle. As a top Senate official once remarked, "It looks very, very good in California or some place to put out a press release that says, 'Today, I questioned the new Secretary of Transportation about the problems of our area.'"[9]

Nominees for high-level executive posts generally face a rigorous vetting process to ensure against conflicts of interest or serious ethical lapses. In standard practice, each nominee must fill out several lengthy questionnaires and undergo security checks. According to political scientist Norman Ornstein, "Each security check is a massive operation, involving up to 40 face-to-face interviews, and is basically the same for the assistant secretary of Education for public affairs as it is for the secretary of State."[10] Investigators from the White House, Federal Bureau of Investigation (FBI), IRS, and Senate ask nominees difficult and uncomfortable questions about their personal and professional lives. "I have never been subjected to such personally insulting and expensive scrutiny in my life," said one Obama nominee, who was asked for receipts for furniture he donated to charity more than a decade ago.[11] Democrats and ethics advocates criticized Senate Republicans in January 2017 for scheduling confirmation hearings for several Trump administration cabinet nominees who had not yet completed their financial-disclosure forms. In the end, Republican committee leaders agreed to postpone several nominees' confirmation hearings in order to allow time for a more complete vetting process.[12] Nonetheless, administration critics complained that Senate Republicans went ahead with several confirmation cases despite the kind of conflict-of-interest concerns that might have sunk nominees during the Bush or Obama administrations.

Once a candidate moves beyond the vetting process, the confirmation hearings themselves can be extremely difficult, particularly in these polarized times. Many nominees are subjected to rough treatment. For example, Trump's nominee to be his first secretary of state, Exxon CEO Rex Tillerson, faced tough questions from Democrats about his company's ties to Russia. Even Republican senator Marco Rubio of Florida aggressively challenged Tillerson on his reluctance to declare Russia's president Vladimir Putin to be a war criminal. Tillerson ultimately was confirmed by the Senate, though he departed the administration in March 2018 when Trump soured on his performance. Sometimes, the purpose of Senate confirmation hearings "seems less to ensure that nominees are fit than to cripple the chief executive's political leadership."[13]

Delay is another concern about the state of the confirmation process. Although the Senate eventually confirms most nominees, it often takes a long time to fill the full-time cabinet and agency positions requiring Senate confirmation. Public administration expert Paul C. Light studied five hundred of Obama's nominees for full-time jobs in his administration and found that they "waited an average of more than nine months to be confirmed, longer than at any time since the 1960s."[14] Additional delays are caused by the administration's slowness in nominating people to serve in high federal positions.[15] Indeed, two months into the Trump administration, no one had yet been nominated to fill 492 of 553 key positions requiring Senate confirmation, and approximately one hundred positions awaited nominees as the administration hit the two-year mark.[16]

Individual senators regularly threaten filibusters or place holds on nominations—that is, senators notify party leaders that they oppose floor consideration of certain nominees (see Box 11-1). The Senate may also refuse to consider a nominee if members invoke senatorial courtesy. This tradition, dating from the nation's earliest years, means that the Senate will usually delay or not act on nominees for offices in a state if opposed by a senator of the president's party from that state.

Increasingly frustrated with the delays facing President Obama's executive-branch and judicial nominees, the Democratic Senate voted, in November 2013, to require only a simple majority to end debate on all executive-branch

BOX 11-1   LIFTING OF OBJECTION

Mr. GRASSLEY. Madam President, on June 27, I provided notice of my intent to object to proceeding to the nominations of Mark J. Mazur, to be an Assistant Secretary of the Treasury, and Matthew J. Rutherford, to be an Assistant Secretary to the Treasury. My support for the final confirmation of these nominees depended on receiving information from both the Treasury Department and the Internal Revenue Service regarding their implementation of the tax whistleblower program. Since I have received the responses, I no longer object to proceeding to these nominations. . . .

I began asking questions about the program's implementation in 2010. I wrote again in 2011 and then again on April 30 of this year. Unfortunately, I did not get complete answers until I objected to proceeding to the nominations of Mr. Mazur and Mr. Rutherford. . . .

It is unfortunate that objecting to these nominees, both of whom were approved by the Finance Committee by unanimous, bipartisan votes, was the only way I could get information about the whistleblower program. At least there is now more information than ever before about the IRS whistleblower program.

Source: An excerpt from the *Congressional Record*, July 30, 2012, S5655–S5656.

appointments and all judicial nominees other than to the Supreme Court (see Chapter 8 for a detailed discussion). Although Republicans objected vociferously to the change at the time, Senate GOP leaders retained the provision when they gained control of the Senate in the 114th Congress. As a result, executive-branch nominees no longer need to overcome filibuster threats. This greatly reduced Senate Democrats' leverage as they fought several of Trump's nominees to lead federal agencies. Indeed, Democratic complaints about several Trump cabinet nominees' alleged conflicts of interest, extremism, and inexperience were easily set aside by GOP leaders, who had little to fear from Democratic opposition so long as they could keep their own party's members on board. Nonetheless, while the president was successful in seeing his nominees confirmed, numerous top officials continued to be dogged by questions about conflicts of interest and questionable decision making after their confirmation, undermining the administration's effectiveness in pursuing its agenda.[17]

Bypassing Advice and Consent

The challenges posed by the confirmation process create an incentive for presidents to bypass the Senate's advice-and-consent role entirely. The Constitution (Article II, section 2) provides that "[t]he President shall have Power to fill up all Vacancies that may happen during a Recess of the Senate, by granting Commissions which shall expire at the End of their next Session." For example, a recess appointee named in 2016 could serve until late 2017. Presidential recess appointments are not unusual, and they have occurred during intersession—the interval between the first and second sessions of a Congress—and intrasession breaks. For example, a 2013 study by the Congressional Research Service found that since the inauguration of President Ronald Reagan in 1981, "presidents have made 329 intrasession recess appointments and 323 intersession appointments."[18] Over time, presidents came to rely more on recess appointments in response to the wider use of Senate filibusters and holds to block the confirmation of presidential appointments.

Senators have long resented presidential use of the recess appointment option, especially if the chief executive is not of their party because it undermines their constitutional advice-and-consent role. In response, the Senate sometimes adopts a simple formula to block recess appointments: no Senate recesses, no presidential recess appointments. The Senate meets in *pro forma* session, convening for only a few seconds and seldom conducting any official business. Use of these sessions prevented President Obama from employing recess appointments for people opposed by Senate Republicans. By precedent, presidents respected the fiction that the Senate was in session during *pro forma* meetings and did not make recess appointments.

In 2012, President Obama broke precedent, ignored the Senate's *pro forma* sessions, and recess-appointed Richard Cordray as chair of the new Consumer Financial Protection Bureau as well as three members of the National Labor Relations Board (NLRB). The president contended that the Senate was not actually in session because nearly every senator, except for a few Republicans, had departed for the winter holidays. Senators protested that Obama had exceeded his authority, and the dispute prompted review by the Supreme Court.

In *NLRB v. Noel Canning*,[19] the Supreme Court unanimously invalidated President Obama's 2012 recess appointments to the National Labor Relations Board. The Court also concluded that a vacancy must be of "substantial length"— meaning, in historical practice, more than ten days—before a recess appointment by the president could be made. Finally, the Court held that whether the Senate is in session for a few seconds or minutes, *pro forma* sessions mean that the president cannot make recess appointments.

The president has other ways to bypass the Senate's advice-and-consent role. The president can name individuals, on a temporary acting basis, to fill vacant positions that require confirmation by the Senate. For example, President Trump named Matthew Whitaker as acting attorney general to replace Jeff Sessions, who had angered Trump by recusing himself from the Russia investigation and thereby paving the way for the appointment of Special Counsel Robert Mueller. Trump critics filed suit against Whitaker's appointment, arguing that the advice-and-consent clause in the Constitution requires acting appointees to have been confirmed by the Senate to an official role in the administration. Whitaker had previously been Sessions' chief of staff.[20] The issue was rendered moot in February 2019 when William Barr was confirmed as attorney general, replacing Whitaker.

Furthermore, many prominent officials, such as White House advisers, are not subject to the advice and consent of the Senate. President Obama named many individuals, informally called *czars,* to head up important policy initiatives—the *environmental czar,* the *economic czar,* the *Ebola czar.*[21] Czars oversee and coordinate the forming of policies that cut across the jurisdictions of several departments and agencies. For example, the economist Peter Navarro has played an important role as President Trump's *trade czar,* pushing a hard-line in negotiations with America's trade partners.

The appointment of numerous czars reflects the amassing of further power in the White House. Yale law professor Bruce Ackerman contends, "We need to seriously consider requiring Senate approval of senior White House staff positions."[22] And yet the slow pace of confirmations no doubt provides incentives for presidents to name policy czars as a way to avoid lengthy Senate approval.

Donald Trump named several of his most controversial advisers to positions in the White House that do not require Senate confirmation, including chief strategist Steve Bannon, National Security Adviser Michael Flynn, and his son-in-law Jared Kushner. Confirmation hearings on Bannon and Flynn would have surely featured intense fireworks, given their controversial statements; Flynn ended up resigning after less than one month in his position, amid accusations that he lied about his contacts with Russia during the transition. The current national security adviser, John Bolton, also has a long record of controversial statements and thus benefited from avoiding a Senate confirmation fight. Kushner, who is not taking a salary, serves as a senior adviser to the president; ethics watchdogs warned that his business dealings and family ties to the president raise important conflict-of-interest issues, but as a White House adviser, he was not subject to Senate confirmation.[23]

The Personnel System

Congress wields constitutional, legal, and informal authority over the federal personnel system. The civil service itself was created after a disgruntled job seeker assassinated President James A. Garfield in 1881. That event prompted Congress to curb the abuses of the spoils system, the practice of handing out federal jobs to supporters of the party that had won the presidency. In 1883, Congress passed the first civil service law that substituted merit for patronage. But those patronage practices have a modern equivalent: the political appointee system. The latest figures show that the executive branch is home to more than 4,000 political appointees (see Figure 11-2).[24] The number of political appointees, however, is small compared with the number of federal employees: As of 2017, there are nearly 2.1 million civil servants and 1.3 million active uniformed personnel. But these political appointees nonetheless give presidents the opportunity to reward personal loyalists and to staff key positions with individuals with a demonstrated commitment to the president's policy programs.[25]

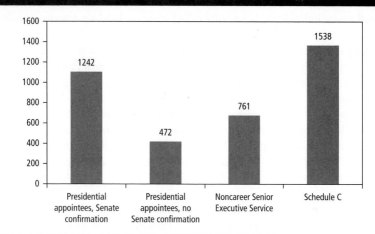

FIGURE 11-2 ■ Political Appointees by Appointment Type, 2018

Source: Bonnie Berkowitz and Kevin Uhrmacher, "It's not just the Cabinet: Trump's transition team may need to find about 4,100 appointees," *Washington Post,* updated Dec. 5, 2018, https://www .washingtonpost.com/graphics/politics/trump-transition-appointments-scale/.

Not all political appointees have the requisite experience to meet the challenges of their office. A classic example involved Hurricane Katrina, which devastated the Gulf Coast in late August 2005. At the time, the chief of the Federal Emergency Management Agency (FEMA) was Michael Brown. A former commissioner of the International Arabian Horse Association, Brown had little experience in emergency management. Despite President George W. Bush's praise—"Brownie, you're doing a heck of a job!"—FEMA's response to this crisis was widely viewed as inept and inadequate. One response by Congress was to pass the Post-Katrina Emergency Management Reform Act of 2006 (P.L. 109–295), which requires that any nominee named to head FEMA must meet certain qualifications.[26]

Periodically, various lawmakers recommend a reduction in the number of political appointees. They contend that there are simply far more appointees than the president can manage effectively. Far from enhancing responsiveness, said one senator, the large number of political appointees undermines "presidential control of the executive branch."[27] Not everyone agrees. Amid rising partisanship, one scholar argued, "presidents need to stock departments with people who understand politics and the importance of interaction with Congress, lobbyists and the media."[28]

Pay and Other Legal Standards

By law, Congress has wide control over federal employees. It can establish retirement programs; special requirements for holding office; personnel ceilings;

employee performance standards; wages, benefits, and cost-of-living adjustments (COLAs); and protections from reprisals for whistle-blowers (employees who expose waste and corruption).

Importantly, the 1939 Hatch Act, named for Sen. Carl Hatch, D-N.M. (1933–1949), restricts federal employees' partisan activity. The act was passed during the New Deal after reports that civil servants were being bullied to back President Franklin D. Roosevelt in his reelection efforts. The purposes of the Hatch Act are "to ensure that federal programs are administered in a nonpartisan fashion, to protect federal employees from political coercion in the workplace, and to ensure that federal employees are advanced on merit and not based on political affiliation."[29] Today, civil servants can engage in political activity in accord with regulations prescribed by the U.S. Office of Special Counsel. For example, most career civil servants can run for nonpartisan office, contribute money to political organizations, or attend political rallies. They may not run for partisan office, use their authority to exert influence over an election, or wear political buttons while on duty.[30] The special counsel's office has also issued guidelines for federal employees on the use of social media, such as Facebook and Twitter, in election campaigns.[31] Other limits are placed on bureaucrats as well. After leaving public office, many executive officers, top legislative staffers, and legislators themselves pass through the "revolving door" to jobs with private firms that deal with the government. Various laws impose a "cooling-off" period before these officials and employees may lobby their former agencies, departments, or branches of government.[32] Nevertheless, government officials regularly move to the private sector and vice versa. Soon after enactment of the landmark Dodd-Frank Wall Street Reform and Consumer Protection Act (P. L. 111–203) in 2010, many government regulators walked through the revolving door to join Wall Street firms.[33] Similarly, top White House officials have often left public service to take high-paying jobs in business, law, and public-relations firms, though an executive order issued by President Trump forbids former officials from lobbying the federal agency where they worked for five years.[34]

Size of Government

Americans have debated the size and reach of the federal government since the nation's founding. Then, as well as now, many Americans tend to think: "That government governs best that governs least." Others have long taken a more expansive view. Alexander Hamilton famously favored a strong national government and an energetic chief executive. In the view of Abraham Lincoln, "Government is people coming together collectively to do that which they could not do as well, or at all, individually."[35]

The national government's role has expanded dramatically since the turn of the twentieth century—from the Progressive Era to World War I, from the New Deal to the Great Society, to today's governmental interventions in the private sector. Growth has been driven by overlapping factors. Wars and crises, of course, expand federal obligations and centralize authority in the national government. The intelligence community mushroomed during the Cold War as the United States faced a major threat from another nuclear-armed superpower, the Soviet Union. It also expanded dramatically after the September 11, 2001, terrorist attacks. As a result, some 1.4 million people, including many private contractors, hold top secret clearances.[36] Complexity is another factor triggering governmental growth. New problems and issues repeatedly demand national action. Today, the federal government must address issues with global dimensions, from trade to migration flows to climate change. As the nation's population grew to over 320 million and government expanded its responsibilities and capacities, it was only natural that individuals and groups would look to their national officeholders to solve problems in health care, transportation, law enforcement, energy, and so on.

People often complain about the overly large federal establishment, but what does "too big" really mean? There is considerable disagreement about how the federal government's size should be measured: the share of the gross domestic product (GDP) devoted to federal expenditures, the magnitude of the federal budget, or the number of federal employees. As to the first standard, federal spending relative to the size of the U.S. economy is a mixed picture, from 21.2 percent of GDP in 1990 to 17.6 percent in 2000, 23.4 percent in 2010, and 20.8 percent in 2017.

Another measure of the government's size is the federal budget. The federal government spent over $4.1 trillion in fiscal year 2018, with a deficit of $779 billion. The large federal deficit represents, to a significant degree, the disconnect between what citizens want and what they are willing to pay for.

Contrary to what many people believe, the federal workforce has remained relatively constant in size. How can the government continue to perform services while generally keeping its size down? One answer is that much of what the federal government does is transfer money to eligible recipients, such as the elderly who receive Social Security. This function does not require large numbers of federal workers. Another answer is that federal work has been outsourced to contract firms or privatized. The Pentagon, for example, reached a milestone in 2001 when the number of its private-sector employees (734,000) exceeded its civilian workforce (700,000). Although it is difficult to obtain a precise count of contractors, there continue to be more private-sector employees in DoD than civilian workers.[37] These contract employees "perform service jobs from mowing lawns to testing weapons systems."[38] As one analyst explained, "Everybody wants the federal government to look smaller than it really is. By contracting out jobs rather than having civilian workers in those jobs, you can say, 'Look, the government's smaller.'"[39] Another scholar has put the true personnel size of the government at about 9.1 million employees: the 3.8 million civilian, military, and postal workers plus the 5.3 million "shadow" employees who work under federal contracts or grants.[40]

Whatever the outcome of this debate about government size, privatizing (or outsourcing) the federal government's work has certain benefits and costs. Contractors often can be faster, more flexible, and cheaper than the career bureaucracy. They can provide security services, technological skills, intelligence capabilities, and other benefits that government agencies are unable to fulfill. However, many analysts believe that certain functions are inherently governmental, which means they are "so intimately related to the public interest as to require performance by a federal government employee."[41] Because contractors are not directly responsible to Congress, the so-called third-party (or shadow) government raises serious questions of accountability, resulting in fraud, waste, and cost overruns.

The Rulemaking Process

Congress creates and funds executive agencies and defines their legal mandates, but rarely can it specify the details needed to implement policies and programs. By statute, Congress delegates to federal entities the task of implementing rules and regulations (the terms are interchangeable) for carrying out the mandates contained in laws. As Senator Grassley explained, "All regulations are based ultimately on the authority granted by this Congress. When an agency promulgates a rule, it is engaging in a legislative task—in effect, filling in the gaps on the implementation that we in Congress have established through statute."[42] Executive agencies, through their rule-writing authority, enact more "laws" annually than the legislative branch (their final regulations have the full force and effect of statutes). In other words, executive-branch officials who write regulations are lawmakers operating in a bureaucratic context. Congress delegates such authority to federal agencies largely because lawmakers lack the time and technical expertise to devise the detailed language required to implement the goals of complex statutes. Moreover, Congress retains broad legislative power to amend, modify, or repeal regulations.

For example, lawmakers can employ procedures specified in the Congressional Review Act (CRA) to try to nullify, one at a time, unwanted regulations promulgated by executive agencies. The CRA requires regulators to submit all proposed major rules and regulations—those with an economic impact over $100 million in any one year—to the House and Senate. Lawmakers then have sixty legislative days from the time a regulation is published in the *Federal Register*—the government's daily publication of regulatory activities—to reject it via a joint resolution of disapproval, considered under expedited procedures (meaning, for example, restrictions on the length of debate).[43] Important to note is that the president can veto joint resolutions of disapproval, and mustering the two-thirds vote needed to override the chief executive is a high hurdle. Since the CRA's enactment in 1996 through the end of 2016, there were forty-nine attempts to disapprove a rule, with only one success (in 2001 on an ergonomics rule to curb workplace injuries).[44] President Obama successful vetoed all five disapproval resolutions that passed Congress during his time in office.[45] But President Trump and the GOP Congress used the act to repeal 16 rules adopted by the Obama administration.[46] For example, in late March 2017, congressional Republicans succeeded in rolling back two workplace safety rules that they charged imposed an undue burden on business.[47]

Even when CRA challenges are unsuccessful, an aide to a former Senate GOP majority leader noted that it nonetheless "provides an important public relations tool to highlight real concerns and perhaps force the administration to make some changes [to the challenged regulation] that they would otherwise not be willing to make."[48] Disapproval resolutions also signal to regulatory agencies that Congress is keeping a close eye on their work.

Statutory Standards for Rulemaking

In the Administrative Procedure Act (APA) of 1946 and later amendments to it, Congress established standards for rulemaking by government agencies. Under the APA, regulatory agencies are required to publish a notice in the *Federal Register* of their proposed rulemaking. The notice includes such information as where and when "interested parties" can comment on the proposed rule. Typically, the public comment period runs for at least thirty days. Interested parties can take part in the process by testifying in public about the merits or demerits of proposed regulations. Citizens can comment on federal rulemaking through the government's official websites—www.federalregister.gov or www.reginfo.gov—as well

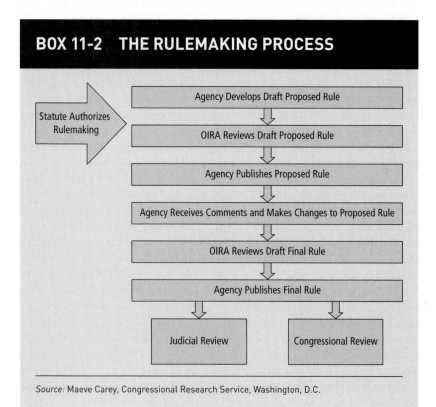

BOX 11-2 THE RULEMAKING PROCESS

Statute Authorizes Rulemaking

Agency Develops Draft Proposed Rule

OIRA Reviews Draft Proposed Rule

Agency Publishes Proposed Rule

Agency Receives Comments and Makes Changes to Proposed Rule

OIRA Reviews Draft Final Rule

Agency Publishes Final Rule

Judicial Review

Congressional Review

Source: Maeve Carey, Congressional Research Service, Washington, D.C.

as through comparable sites. Record numbers of public comments on proposed regulations are being received by government agencies, both because comments can be made easily on federal websites and the issues provoke controversy among businesses, outside groups, and other stakeholders:

> The State Department received more than 2.5 million comments on whether to permit construction of the Keystone XL oil pipeline. More than 1.26 million have weighed in this summer [2014] on Federal Communications Commission rules on how broadband providers treat traffic on their networks. At the Environmental Protection Agency, officials are sorting through hundreds of thousands of comments on new emission rules for power plants.[49]

The federal courts also ensure that executive officials do not repeal rules by fiat. A federal appeals court has held that once a rule is published in the *Federal Register,* "it cannot be reversed without a lengthy administrative process, even if [the rule] has not yet taken effect."[50] Although presidents can overturn executive orders with the stroke of a pen, they cannot treat regulations the same way. "It is not easy for a president to stop a final rule that has been published in the *Federal Register* short of putting the whole process [as prescribed in the Administrative Procedures Act of 1946] in reverse and beginning the process of rulemaking anew—with public notices, comment periods and agency reviews that could take years."[51]

An alternative to formally repealing regulations is to appoint agency officials who will slow down implementation and try to minimize enforcement. But there are internal checks on this strategy as well: Career staff tend to resist efforts that they view as undercutting their agency's mission, and advocacy groups often stand ready to take agencies to court when they fail to implement regulations that they issued.[52] As a result, enacting new legislation through Congress is often the most effective way to reverse agency regulations.

Legislative–Executive Clashes

Congress and the White House frequently skirmish over rulemaking. GOP administrations tend to have a pro-business regulatory perspective favoring voluntary compliance and giving key regulatory jobs to corporate and industry officials who are keen on reducing regulation. Democratic presidents appoint individuals to head agencies who support worker safety and consumer and environmental protections. Inevitably, these disparate party views of federal regulation produce sharp disagreements. Congressional Republicans accused the Obama administration of issuing job-killing regulations that stifled economic growth by imposing expensive costs and red tape on businesses. For his part, President Obama countered that Republicans want the end of regulations "that protect Americans from risky financial deals and other reckless behavior that crashed our economy."[53]

A critical controversy between Congress and the executive agencies in recent years centered on the authority of the Environmental Protection Agency (EPA) to regulate carbon emissions. Under President Obama, the EPA used its authority under the Clean Air Act (P.L. 101–549) to require power plants, electric utilities, and oil refineries to employ the best available technologies to reduce their carbon emissions. In response to the EPA's actions, House and Senate members from energy-producing states immediately went on the offensive to limit or strip the EPA's climate change authority. "We are not going to let this administration regulate what they've been unable to legislate," declared House Energy and Commerce chair Fred Upton, R-Mich.[54] Upton also promised that the EPA administrator would be testifying so frequently before his committee "that he'll guarantee her a permanent parking space on Capitol Hill."[55] However, after several years of committee hearings and passing bills in their chamber repealing EPA regulations, House Republicans started to recognize that their chances of curbing environmental regulations were not good. As Joe Barton, R-Tex., former chair of the House Committee on Energy and Commerce, explained, "Congress can do something [about EPA regulations], but you need a majority in the House and 60 percent in the Senate, plus the president to avoid a veto. In this environment, we don't have that." Instead, mindful of the two Congresses, Barton said Republicans should push messaging bills. "Message bills are different. I'm open to that," he said.[56] "Over-regulation is always a good message for us," added a spokesperson for the Republican National Committee.[57] Cutting federal red tape was a theme employed regularly by GOP candidates in the 2014 and 2016 elections.

Although Republicans enjoyed unified control of Congress and the White House after the 2016 elections, they were unable to adopt major legislation targeting environmental regulations. Instead, Trump focused on administrative action, issuing an executive order in March 2017 instructing the EPA to dismantle Obama-era climate-change regulations.[58] The EPA followed up a year later by proposing an alternative to Obama's Clean Power Plant regulatory framework.[59] However, if the EPA gives final approval to the alternative approach, it will face lengthy court challenges. And with Democrats gaining control of the House in the 2018 midterms, Trump's anti-regulatory agenda faces another important obstacle.

Regulatory Review

Hundreds of rules and regulations issued each year by executive agencies must be reviewed by the White House regulatory "czar" before agencies may publish them in the *Federal Register*. (For a summary of the rulemaking process, see Box 11-2.) This czar is the chief of the Office of Information and Regulatory Affairs (OIRA) within the Office of Management and Budget. OIRA devotes considerable time to analyzing economically significant regulations, those that would impose more than $100 million in costs on affected industries. OIRA can reject these major rules, require their revision, or approve them in line with the president's priorities. (For a list of the number of final federal rules published in recent years, see Figure 11-3.)

FIGURE 11-3 ■ Number of Documents (Final Rules) Published in the Federal Register, 1996–2017

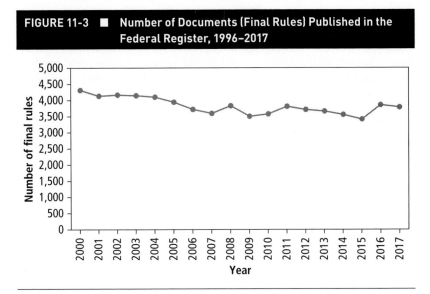

Source: Mercatus Center at George Mason University. Data compiled by Jonathan Nelson and Patrick McLaughlin from the federal register database produced by QuantGov.

Proposed rules and regulations are typically subject to cost–benefit review. Measuring costs and benefits is, at best, a tricky undertaking. Risk analysis experts hold that this traditional tool should be used "to sort through a complex world of threats to human and environmental health so we can identify the choices that will do the most people the most good at the least cost."[60] Critics of this approach, however, point out that measuring costs is usually easier than estimating benefits; costs are more easily quantified, whereas benefits are often intangible and long term. How valuable are regulations? Lawmakers, like their constituents, are of two minds. Some, such as former senator Barbara Boxer, D-Calif., emphasize their positive aspects:

> The purpose of the Federal regulatory process is to improve and protect the high quality of life that we enjoy in our country. Every day, the people of our Nation enjoy the benefits of almost a century of progress in Federal laws and regulations that reduce the threat of illness, injury, and death from consumer products, workplace hazards, and environmental toxins.[61]

Other lawmakers call for regulators to issue "smarter, more cost-effective regulations."[62] Meanwhile, corporations complain that federal rules and regulations require them to spend billions in compliance costs. A difficult challenge is to distinguish between inflexible, pointless, or overly burdensome regulations and the beneficial regulations that are necessary to promote and protect the public's health and safety.

Whatever their view of the regulatory process, legislators must act as intermediaries between their constituents and federal agencies. Constituents' problems are handled within members' offices by personal staff aides called caseworkers. In addition to courting the electoral payoff of effective casework—evidence of the two Congresses once again—some members appreciate its value as oversight. "The very knowledge by executive officials that some Congressman is sure to look into a matter affecting his constituents acts as a healthy check against bureaucratic indifference or arrogance," wrote a former senator.[63]

CONGRESSIONAL CONTROL OF THE BUREAUCRACY

"Congressional power, like chastity," explained a scholar, "is never lost, rarely taken by force, and almost always given away."[64] Because no law can be sufficiently detailed to cover every conceivable circumstance, Congress allows executive officials wide discretion in implementing the laws it passes. This delegation of authority occurs because legislators lack the time, knowledge, or expertise to address the complexities of contemporary administration.

Congress is often sharply criticized for drafting vague or sloppy legislation that gives executive officials and judges too much interpretive leeway. "Administration of a statute is, properly speaking, an extension of the legislative process," pointed out political scientist David B. Truman; therefore, Congress must watch over its programs lest they undergo unintended change.[65] Because of the size and reach of the executive establishment, Congress's oversight role is even more important today than when Woodrow Wilson wrote in 1885, "Quite as important as lawmaking is vigilant oversight of administration."[66] The Constitution does not refer explicitly to the oversight role, but it implicitly flows from Congress's right, among other things, to make laws, raise and appropriate money, give advice and consent to executive nominations, and impeach federal officials. The Supreme Court has explicitly recognized Congress's oversight authority. For instance, the Supreme Court held in *Watkins v. United States* (1957) that Congress's investigatory power "is inherent in the legislative process. That power is broad. It encompasses inquiries concerning the administration of existing laws as well as proposed or possibly needed statutes." Two years later, in *Barenblatt v. United States,* the Supreme Court stated, "The scope of [Congress's] power of inquiry . . . is as penetrating and far-reaching as the potential power to enact and appropriate under the Constitution."

Congress has formalized its oversight duties in laws and House and Senate rules. The Legislative Reorganization Act of 1946 directed all House and Senate committees to exercise "continuous watchfulness" over the programs and agencies under their jurisdiction. Subsequent statutes and House and Senate rules have extended Congress's authority and resources for oversight. The Government Accountability Office (GAO), the chief investigative arm of the legislative branch, provides the House and Senate at the start of each new Congress with "high-risk" reports on the management and accounting practices of federal agencies and departments. The reports specifically identify "areas in need of broad-based transformation."[67] Overall, GAO issues annually more than a thousand audits and reports on administrative management.

Members understand their review responsibilities. "Congress's duty didn't end in passing this law," remarked a senator. "We have to make sure the law works." Another senator said, "I have always felt that one-third of the role of Congress should be in oversight."[68] Or as then-Speaker John Boehner emphasized, "I think the biggest part of Congress's job is to provide proper oversight of the executive branch of government."[69]

The purposes of oversight are many, but three are especially important: (1) to check the power of the executive branch, (2) to determine how laws are being implemented and whether they need adjustments and refinements, and (3) to shine the spotlight of public attention on significant executive actions and activities. As Woodrow Wilson wrote in 1885, "The informing function of Congress should be preferred even to its legislative [lawmaking] function." He went on to say,

> Unless Congress [has] and use[s] every means of acquainting itself with the acts and dispositions of the administrative agencies of government, the country must be helpless to learn how it is being served; and unless Congress both scrutinize[s] these things and sift[s] them by every form of discussion, the country must remain in embarrassing, crippling ignorance of the very affairs which it is most important it should understand and direct.[70]

Political purposes are served by oversight as well, such as generating favorable publicity for programs, urging the elimination or reduction of agencies, responding to requests from special interests to influence agency decisions, winning electoral support from constituents, or undermining the standing of an administration led by the opposing party. Oversight thus occurs in a political context, within which Congress's relationship with administrative agencies can range from cooperation to conflict.

To ensure that laws are working, Congress relies on a varied array of formal and informal processes and techniques. Each has its strengths and weaknesses, and it is often necessary to use several in combination if the House and Senate are to challenge or assess executive-branch performance. Many oversight activities are indirect, ad hoc, and not subject to easy measurement or even recognition. "Oversight isn't necessarily a hearing," said John D. Dingell, D-Mich., a noted and feared House overseer when he chaired the Committee on Energy and Commerce. "Sometimes it's a letter. We find our letters have a special effect on a lot of people."[71]

Hearings and Investigations

Many of Congress's most dramatic historical moments have occurred during legislative probes into administrative or business misconduct. Examples include the Teapot Dome inquiry (1923), the Senate's Watergate hearings (1973–1974), the Iran-Contra investigation (1987), the hearings on the Iraq war (2007), and the hearings into taxpayer-funded bonuses for Wall Street executives (2009). The mere threat of a congressional hearing is often enough to keep agencies in line. But Congress's investigative authority is not without limits. Earl Warren, when he was chief justice of the U.S. Supreme Court, wrote in the aforementioned *Watkins v. United States* (1957),

> There is no general authority to expose private affairs of individuals without justification in terms of the functions of Congress. . . . Nor is the Congress a law enforcement or trial agency. These are functions of the executive and judicial departments of government. No inquiry is an end in itself; it must be related to, and in furtherance of, a legitimate task of the Congress.[72]

By collecting and analyzing information, House and Senate inquiries can clarify whether new laws are needed to address public problems. They also sharpen Congress's ability to scrutinize executive branch activities, such as the expenditure of funds, the implementation of laws, and the discharge of duties by administrative officials. Investigations inform the public by providing "a forum for disclosing the hidden aspects of governmental conduct," wrote two senators. It allows a "free people to drag realities out into the sunlight and demand a full accounting."[73]

This informing role often places congressional investigators in direct opposition to the White House. Hearings can be used to highlight shortcomings that will damage a president's public standing, which can redound to the political or policy benefit of the opposing party in Congress.[74] But hearings do not have to be adversarial in order to be influential. A recent study found that there is often a burst of oversight when unified party government arrives in Washington: In these cases, the congressional majority works in tandem with ideological allies in the executive branch to uncover ways to pursue their shared policy goals through the bureaucracy.[75] Hearings and investigations are, in short, valuable devices for making government accountable to the people. They can spawn new laws or their functional equivalent: change in bureaucratic operations.

Congressional Vetoes

Congress has little choice but to delegate sweeping authority to administrative agencies. The question, then, is how can Congress control those agencies? One answer historically has been the legislative veto (or congressional veto), a statutory enactment that permits presidents or agencies to take certain actions subject to later approval or disapproval by one or both houses of Congress (or in some cases by committees of one or both houses). Legislative vetoes are arrangements of convenience for both branches. Executives gain decision-making authority they otherwise might not have, and Congress retains a second chance to examine decisions.

In 1983, many forms of the legislative veto were declared unconstitutional by the Supreme Court (*Immigration and Naturalization Service v. Chadha*). The Court's majority held that the device violated the separation of powers, the principle of bicameralism, and the presentation clause of the Constitution. (Legislation passed by both chambers must be presented to the president for his signature or veto.) Yet despite the *Chadha* ruling, legislative vetoes of the committee variety continue to be enacted into law. Public-law scholar Louis Fisher has summed up the status of legislative vetoes:

> Are they constitutional? Not by the Court's definition. Will that fact change the behavior between committees and agencies? Probably not. An agency might advise the committee: "As you know, the requirement in this statute for committee prior-approval is unconstitutional under the Court's test." Perhaps agency and committee staff will nod their heads in agreement. After which the agency will seek prior approval of the committee.[76]

Self-interest impels agencies to pay close attention to the wishes of members of Congress, especially those who sit on their authorizing or appropriating panels.

Mandatory Reports

Congress can require the president, federal agencies, or departments to assess programs and report their findings.[77] Reports can act "as a mechanism to check that laws are having the intended effect." Moreover, they can "drive a reluctant bureaucracy to comply with laws it would otherwise ignore."[78] Each year, executive agencies prepare several thousand reports for submission to Congress. Because of the massive size and important role of the Defense Department, it is not surprising that the Pentagon is tasked with preparing numerous reports for Congress. At a 2010 departmental briefing, Defense Secretary Robert Gates noted, "In 1970, the Pentagon produced a total of 37 reports for the Congress, a number that topped off at more than 700 reports in last year's cycle."[79] Trying to reduce the number of outdated or duplicative reports—which Congress does periodically—often comes with the requirement that agencies be more responsive to committees' requests for information. A spokesperson for the former chair of the House Armed Services Committee said his boss would be happy to work with the secretary of defense to eliminate various reporting requirements if the Pentagon would do "a better job of providing specific programmatic and policy information in a timely manner" to the committee.[80]

Nonstatutory Controls

Congressional committees also use informal means to review and influence administrative decisions. These range from telephone calls, letters, personal contacts, and informal understandings to statements in conference reports, hearings, and floor debates.[81] Committee reports frequently contain phrases such as "the committee clearly intends that the matter be reconsidered" or "the committee clearly intends for the Secretary to promote" or "the committee clearly expects."

On occasion, OMB directors tell federal agencies to ignore report language because it is not legally binding. Lawmakers of both parties and chambers (and even executive officials), however, may seek to thwart such directives. Sometimes, members threaten to make all report language legally binding on agencies, thereby limiting the agencies' flexibility and discretion in resolving issues.[82] Although their usage is not measured, nonstatutory controls may be the most common form of congressional oversight.

Inspectors General

In 1978, Congress created a dozen independent offices for inspectors general (IGs). Since then, Congress has established inspectors general offices in nearly every federal department and agency. IGs conduct audits and investigations of agency programs and operations, prevent and detect fraud and abuse in such programs and operations, and keep Congress and agency heads fully informed on a timely basis about problems and the need for corrective actions. Granted wide latitude and independence, IGs are "the government's first line of defense against fraud."[83] Inspectors general testify frequently before congressional committees and submit directly to Congress reports on their efforts to root out waste, fraud, and abuse. For example, the Department of Defense IG reported in 2018 that the military's poor software management practices were putting its network at grave risk of cyberattack.[84] The House Committee on Oversight and Government Reform responded to such critiques with hearings and reports of its own focusing increased attention on cybersecurity in government agencies.[85]

The Appropriations Process

Congress probably exercises its most potent oversight of agencies and programs through the appropriations process. By cutting off or reducing funds (or threatening to do so), Congress can abolish agencies, curtail programs, or obtain requested information. Upset that the secretary of the Department of Housing and Urban Development (HUD) was flying off to various conferences rather than dealing with the housing foreclosure crisis, appropriators eliminated the secretary's travel budget. "Frankly, I want to cause [HUD] officials a little personal pain," declared one legislator. He said he wanted them to "just plant their butts at their desks and do the job that they were appointed to do."[86] In another case, a House Appropriations subcommittee chair, angry because the Homeland Security Department had not provided reports on its spending priorities, declared, "They've just been ignoring us. They'll pay for that."[87] By the same token, Congress can build up a program by increasing its appropriations—sometimes beyond the levels that the administration has requested.

The appropriations power is exercised mainly through the House and Senate appropriations committees, especially through each panel's twelve standing subcommittees. These panels annually recommend funding levels for federal agencies and departments so that they can carry out their program responsibilities. The budgetary recommendations of the appropriations subcommittees are generally accepted by their parent committees and by the House or Senate.

The appropriations committees and their subcommittees or members from the House or Senate floor may offer amendments that limit the purposes for which money may be spent (*limitation riders*) or that impose other spending limits on federal agencies. Funding bills also may contain various policy directives to federal agencies—for example, prohibiting agencies from using funds to promulgate or issue certain regulations. Such directives are often in the form of floor amendments. "These amendments," wrote two GOP senators, "are an important way for Congress to save taxpayers from wasteful agency spending, and they enjoy a long-standing precedent because of their use by Republican and Democratic Congresses alike to rein in the excesses of Republican and Democratic administrations."[88] Political scientist Jason A. McDonald has underscored the legislative importance of such limitation amendments in influencing agency actions. They provide "Congress with much more influence than scholars have appreciated over not only everyday policy decisions within agencies . . . but also over the substance of regulations about which members of Congress, and their constituencies, care for political and policy reasons."[89]

Impeachment

Article II, section 4, of the Constitution states, "The President, Vice President, and all Civil Officers of the United States, shall be removed from office on Impeachment for, and Conviction of, Treason, Bribery, or other high Crimes and misdemeanors." This removal power is the ultimate governmental check vested in Congress.[90] The House has the authority to impeach an official by majority vote. It then tries the case before the Senate, where a two-thirds vote is required for conviction.

Only impeached federal judges have been convicted by the Senate. The most recent case occurred on December 8, 2010, when the Senate voted for only the eighth time to convict and remove a federal district judge.[91] The lack of impeachment cases against presidential appointees likely reflects the effectiveness of political mechanisms for holding them accountable. Numerous lower-level federal officials have been pressured to resign amid scandals—or have been directly fired by the president.

Oversight: An Evaluation

Congress's willingness to conduct regular and meaningful oversight stems from several factors: public dissatisfaction with government, revelations of executive-agency abuses, the influx of new legislators skeptical of government's ability to perform effectively, concern about the growth of a regulatory state, the availability of seasoned congressional staff, and recognition by Congress that it must make every dollar count.[92]

The perspective of the two Congresses highlights the electoral, political, and policy incentives that encourage members to oversee the bureaucracy. One of these incentives is the opportunity to claim credit for assisting constituents and to receive favorable publicity back home. Another is the prodding by interest groups and the media. Committee and subcommittee chairs "seek a high pay off—in attention from both the press and other agencies—when selecting federal programs to be their oversight targets."[93] Members on the relevant committees of jurisdiction are also motivated to induce favorable agency and departmental action on pet policies or programs.

Divided government—the president of one party, with Congress (or one chamber) controlled by the other—encourages vigorous congressional oversight. Oversight simultaneously enables majority party lawmakers in Congress to monitor closely agency activities and look for ways to undermine the administration's policy goals or public reputation. Simply responding to scores of subpoenas issued by committees controlled by the opposition party can sap the time and energy of the White House and agency officials. By comparison, under unified government, the majority party in Congress tends to engage in less adversarial oversight. As one senior GOP lawmaker said of the unified period (2003–2007) when Republicans were in charge of the elective branches, "Our party controls the levers of government. We're not about to go out and look beneath a bunch of rocks to cause heartburn."[94] In the 115th Congress, House Intelligence chair Devin Nunes of California was criticized by many Democrats and even some Republicans for his efforts to defend President Trump as his committee investigated charges of Russian efforts to influence the 2016 election.[95] Party loyalty, in short, may overcome institutional responsibility.

One of Democrats' key promises in the run-up to the 2018 midterms was that they would provide more assertive oversight of the Trump administration. After the election, incoming chair of the House Judiciary Committee Jerrold Nadler, D-N.Y., warned Homeland Security Secretary Kirstjen Nielsen, "I want to put you and the department on notice: the time for accountability has arrived."[96] Since 2017, Democrats had criticized the DHS's border enforcement policies under Trump; the election put them in a position to use oversight to bring enhanced scrutiny to those policies. House Democrats are also likely to use their oversight power to explore allegations of conflicts of interest against several senior Trump officials as well as against the president himself and to protect the Robert Mueller special counsel probe if the administration seeks to limit its reach. At the same time, Democratic leaders recognize the risk of backlash if it appears that they are too focused on uncovering scandals rather than legislating. While many Democratic voters and activists are eager for House investigators to generate revelations that might lead to impeachment, some representatives are wary of overreach. As Rep. Gerry Connolly, D-Va., observed, "For it to have credibility and to stick, [oversight has] got to be methodical and fact-based. It can't just be about emotion, that's a balancing act we're going to have to figure out here."[97]

Whether there is unified or divided government, congressional oversight of important programs may not probe as deeply as some might wish. Friendly alliances can develop among the committees that authorize programs, the agencies that administer them, and the interest groups that benefit from governmental services. Many committees are biased toward the programs or agencies they oversee. They want to protect and nurture their progeny and make program administration look good. This kind of cooperative relationship can dissuade committees from conducting meaningful inquiries that require agencies to justify their existence and contribution to the public's well-being. Without concrete allegations of fraud or mismanagement, committees may lack the incentive to scrutinize and reevaluate their programs.

A standard rationale for oversight is that it ensures that laws are carried out according to congressional intent. But because many laws are vague and replete with multiple objectives, they are difficult to assess. Moreover, proof that programs are working as intended may not emerge for years. Congressional patience may wane as critics conclude that there are no demonstrable payoffs for the taxpayer. Alternatively, oversight may identify program flaws but not reveal what would work or even whether there is any ready solution. To address these issues requires sustained efforts by congressional committees to determine if programs are working effectively, efficiently, and economically. A key oversight objective is to link program performance to the funding decisions of the House and Senate. Thus, the House and Senate employ an array of oversight techniques to evaluate federal programs.

Each oversight technique has limitations. Hearings may provide dramatic episodes, but they often result in minimal follow-up. The appropriations process is usually hemmed in by programmatic needs for financial stability. And statutes are often blunt instruments of control. Other obstacles to effective oversight include inadequate coordination among committees sharing jurisdiction over a program; sporadic review by committees of departmental activities; and frequent turnover among committee staff aides, a situation that limits their understanding of the programs created by Congress.

Critics who fault Congress's oversight may be erecting unattainable standards. Many analysts are looking for what scholars have come to call "police patrol" oversight—active, direct, systematic, planned surveillance of executive activities. Instead, Congress often waits until the "fire alarms" sound—set off by interest groups, the press, and others concerned about administrative violations—before it begins to review, in detail, agencies' activities.[98]

Congress may be benefitting from some extra police patrol assistance offered by a combination of individual lawmakers, civic-minded individuals, and technology. A current trend is the "public as watchdog." A good example is the enactment, in 2006, of the Federal Funding Accountability and Transparency Act, informally called the "Google-your-government" law because it required OMB "to provide a user-friendly, searchable database" of nearly $1 trillion in federal grants and contracts.[99] Government websites, such as USASpending.gov, allow citizens to monitor the projects that receive taxpayer dollars. The GAO has a website and hotline to enable citizens to report allegations of waste, fraud, or mismanagement of federal funds. A House chair established a whistleblower website where agency employees could alert committee staff of fraud and abuse in their agency. A House party leader's website contained a feature dubbed YouCut that allowed the public to vote on "which government programs should be cut."[100]

There are even informal "citizen regulators" who test children's toys and clothing to protect them from harmful chemicals. "I'm not going to rely on an agency that changes personnel based on administrations and takes years to make any kind of change," remarked the mother of a three-year-old.[101] The promise of these actions is that they enable any interested person or watchdog group to monitor federal spending or products available in stores across the nation and make their evaluations known to congressional lawmakers. Evolving communications technologies, in short, add millions of extra eyes to congressional oversight.

Micromanagement

Because oversight often means legislative intrusion into administrative details, executive-branch officials sometimes complain about congressional micromanagement. Even though the executive bureaucracy may react with dismay, Congress's focus on administrative details is as old as the institution itself. The structural fragmentation of the House and Senate encourages examination of manageable chunks of executive actions. Members realize that power inheres in details, such as prescribing personnel ceilings for agencies. "It is one of the anomalies of constitutional law and separated powers," writes Louis Fisher, "that executive involvement in legislative affairs is considered acceptable (indeed highly desirable) while legislative involvement in executive affairs screams of encroachment and usurpation."[102]

CONCLUSION

Modern governance is impossible without bureaucracy. Yet Americans remain deeply ambivalent about the role played by executive agencies in regulating their everyday lives and decisions. Americans favor many of the specific programs that the government provides, even as they remain skeptical of the overall size of the federal role. The question of who controls the bureaucracy is equally fraught: The

Constitution provides a role both for Congress and the president in directing agencies. The balance of power between the branches has shifted over time, with the president gaining important advantages. Yet Congress retains a critical role in supervising the bureaucracy and has, on important occasions, used investigations and other tools to force agencies to respond to congressional views.

Judge Brett Kavanaugh offers emotional testimony before the Senate Judiciary Committee in response to claims that he had sexually assaulted Christine Blasey Ford when they were high school students. Senator Amy Klobuchar, D-Minn., questions Kavanaugh about his recollections. U.S. Supreme Court Associate Justice Brett Kavanaugh attends his ceremonial swearing in at the White House.

12

CONGRESS AND
THE COURTS

It was day five of his Senate confirmation hearing, and the president's Supreme Court nominee, Brett M. Kavanaugh, had lost any remaining patience with Democratic senators' questions. The fifth day of testimony was a last-minute addition to the schedule, called hastily to examine allegations that a drunken Kavanaugh had attempted to sexually assault another student while in high school. Sen. Amy Klobuchar, D.-Minn., was asking Kavanaugh about his history with alcohol and memory.

"So you're saying there's never been a case where you drank so much that you didn't remember what happened the night before, or part of what happened," Klobuchar asked.

Clearly losing his composure, Kavanaugh stammered, and then blurted, "It's—you're asking about, you know, blackout. I don't know. Have you?"

This remarkable exchange—for which Kavanaugh apologized to Klobuchar shortly after—encapsulates the vitriol and anger that roiled these confirmation hearings and spilled over, far beyond the Senate hearing room. For a couple of weeks in the autumn of 2018, Democrats and Republicans sparred over President Trump's nomination of the conservative judge Kavanaugh to replace the Supreme Court's retiring "swing justice," Anthony M. Kennedy. Few events in recent history have illustrated so well the contentiousness of confirmation politics and the mounting effects of polarization on the relationship between the courts and Congress.

Conflicts between Congress and the federal courts over constitutional and statutory interpretation have been common in U.S. history. The most famous episode occurred during the New Deal, when the Supreme Court invalidated thirteen acts of Congress in one term (1935–1936). Frustrated, President Franklin D. Roosevelt proposed legislation to increase the number of justices, providing him the opportunity to nominate judges more sympathetic to his program.

Widespread legislative and public opposition, however, defeated Roosevelt's Court-packing scheme. Nevertheless, the Court, perhaps sensitive to the changes underway in the country, became more accommodating in interpreting key constitutional provisions. In 1937, the Court handed down a decision that upheld a state minimum-wage law similar to one that it had previously ruled unconstitutional.[1] In that same year, the Court also upheld a federal law governing management–labor relations, recognizing a far greater congressional power to regulate commerce than the Court's precedents had permitted. This abrupt turnaround by the Court was, as a wit of the period put it, "the switch in time that saved nine."

With the recent history of Supreme Court nominations, including Senate Republicans' refusal to consider President Obama's nomination of Merrick Garland in 2016, some Democratic activists have actually resurrected the idea of Court-packing as a response to the perceived GOP effort to dominate the Supreme Court for another generation.[2] On the other hand, although nomination contests can become quite heated, over time passions often cool. After the Kavanaugh hearings, Senate majority leader Mitch McConnell, R-Ky., commented, "These things always blow over." Time will tell whether the majority leader's prediction is correct.

THE FEDERAL COURTS

In contrast to the Constitution's detailed provisions specifying the structure and authority of Congress, Article III leaves the creation of the federal courts other than the Supreme Court wholly to the discretion of Congress. Thus, the judicial branch owes less to constitutional mandates and more to the legislation establishing its structure and the rulings of the early justices, such as Chief Justice John Marshall (1801–1835). As a noted legal scholar explained,

> Congress was created nearly full blown by the Constitution itself. The vast possibilities of the presidency were relatively easy to perceive and soon, inevitably materialized. But the institution of the judiciary needed to be summoned up out of the constitutional vapors, shaped and maintained.[3]

The most important constitutional provision related to the courts is the guarantee of lifetime tenure for Article III judges. The framers of the Constitution wanted an independent judiciary—that is, a judiciary insulated from political pressure. This independence is an important part of the U.S. system of separation of powers and also the source of the courts' ability to frustrate congressional policy objectives.

The federal court system today comprises district courts, courts of appeals, and the Supreme Court. The district courts are the federal trial courts, which deal with a range of civil matters and federal criminal cases. In addition to Article III district judges, the district courts are staffed by magistrate judges, who serve a fixed term and assist the district judges in handling their civil and criminal caseloads. The district courts also house the federal bankruptcy courts, which are staffed by specialized judges serving a fixed term.

District courts are analogous to congressional committees in the sense that most of the work of the federal courts is done at that level. District courts are organized by state, in a manner similar to congressional districts. Each state and the District of Columbia have at least one, with larger states (such as Texas and California) having as many as four. The primary function of the district courts is *norm enforcement*—that is, applying relatively settled law to disputes.

Above the district courts are the courts of appeals, organized in eleven regional circuits. There is also a circuit for the District of Columbia and one additional circuit, the Federal Circuit, with a nationwide, specialized jurisdiction centering mainly on appeals of administrative-agency rulings and patent cases. Parties unhappy with the outcome of a case at the district court level typically have an automatic right of appeal to the appellate level. These courts are staffed by judges typically called circuit judges. The courts of appeals hear oral arguments and decide cases in three-judge panels. In rare circumstances, a three-judge panel's decision will be reviewed by a larger number of circuit judges, sitting *en banc.* The primary function of the courts of appeals is *error correction*—that is, reviewing the work of lower courts and some executive branch agencies for mistakes of law or fact.

Parties unhappy with the outcome of an appeal can seek Supreme Court review of their cases, but unlike at the court-of-appeals level, Supreme Court review is almost never automatic. Instead, the Court has discretion to decide which cases from the courts of appeals and the state courts of last resort to hear. Typically, the Supreme Court will hear and decide about 1 percent of the cases in which one or both parties have requested review. As a result, the Court's docket is dominated by cases raising important questions of constitutional and statutory interpretation. Unlike the lower federal courts, the Supreme Court rarely takes a case for the sole purpose of correcting an error committed by a lower court. Instead, its policy-making role is paramount.

THE SUPREME COURT AS POLICY MAKER

"Scarcely any political question arises in the United States that is not resolved, sooner or later, into a judicial one," wrote Alexis de Tocqueville in *Democracy in America,* his classic 1835 study of early U.S. life.[4] No recent controversy has illustrated Tocqueville's truism so perfectly as continuing litigation over the Patient Protection and Affordable Care Act of 2010 ("Obamacare").

The federal courts have considered multiple challenges to Obamacare. The first case to reach the Supreme Court—*National Federation of Independent Business v. Sebelius*[5]—involved challenges to the constitutionality of the law's mandate requiring individuals to purchase health insurance and to its expansion of Medicaid. When the justices finally handed down their decision in 2012, hundreds of demonstrators had gathered outside the Supreme Court building. In the end, the Court, in a rather convoluted fashion, upheld the individual mandate, the most controversial aspect of Obamacare.

The ruling in *NFIB v. Sebelius* was not to be the Court's last word on Obamacare. A second challenge to the law—based on the statute's language rather than its constitutionality—subsequently made its way to the high court. The plaintiffs in *King v. Burwell*[6] argued that, given the plain language of the statute, the tax credits to assist low-income persons in buying health insurance should not be available in the states that did not set up their own health insurance exchanges. Because thirty-six states declined to set up their own exchanges, a Supreme Court holding in favor of the plaintiffs in this case would have crippled Obamacare. In 2015, a six-justice majority sided with the Obama administration, holding that the ambiguity in the statutory language must be interpreted to provide tax credits even in the states that had not established their own exchanges.[7]

The most recent case involving Obamacare, *Texas v. United States,* was filed after passage of the Tax Cut and Jobs Act (TCJA) of 2017. The TCJA eliminated the tax penalties enforcing the ACA individual mandate to purchase health insurance but did not address the other provisions of Obamacare, including the regulations related to preexisting conditions. Twenty state attorneys general from states including Texas filed suit, asserting that the zeroing out of the tax penalties for failing to maintain health insurance rendered the entire statute unconstitutional. Their novel argument was that, because the Supreme Court in *NFIB v. Sebelius* had upheld the constitutionality of the ACA's individual mandate as an exercise of Congress's power to tax, the elimination of the tax penalties deprived the individual mandate of its constitutional basis. Moreover, they argued, the rest of the statute's regulations would have to fall at the same time, as Congress intended for the statute's provisions to work together. In statutory interpretation terms, the issue here is one of the "severability" of the unconstitutional parts of a statute from the parts that would pass constitutional muster separately. The *Texas* plaintiffs argued that Congress in 2010 did not intend for the rest of the ACA, including provisions related to preexisting conditions, to be severable from the individual mandate. The statutory framework must stand—or fall—as a unified whole.

Sixteen states and the District of Columbia intervened in the *Texas* litigation to defend Obamacare from this challenge. The intervenors argue that the individual mandate is still constitutional, despite the TCJA, and that even if it is not, the individual mandate is severable from the rest of the ACA because, had the Congress in 2017 intended to repeal all of the ACA, it would have done so, and it did not.

On December 14, 2018, District Judge Reed O'Connor, a George W. Bush appointee, granted summary judgment, adopting the *Texas* plaintiffs' arguments and striking down the entire ACA. That decision is stayed pending appeal, as of this writing. The court of appeals and the Supreme Court are likely to rule on this litigation before all is said and done.

As in *NFIB v. Sebelius,* the Supreme Court's interpretations of the Constitution are final and authoritative—a power referred to as *judicial review.* The U.S. Supreme Court first asserted the prerogative of judicial review in the landmark case of *Marbury v. Madison* (1803).[8] But as the *Burwell* case demonstrates, the Supreme Court also plays an important role in interpreting statutes passed by Congress. In interpreting statutes, the Supreme Court, and the lower courts as well, can have wide-ranging policy effects.

"Judicial Activism"

Ever since the Supreme Court claimed the power of judicial review in 1803, it has considered a large number of separation-of-powers and federalism issues. In both roles, the Supreme Court is often attacked for usurping the prerogatives of the other national branches or of the state and local governments. Members of Congress "often reserve their most vituperative criticism of federal courts for decisions that, in their view, unduly limit the prerogatives of state and local governments to regulate such matters as abortion, school prayer, prison overcrowding, school busing, local elections, and so on."[9]

A common refrain in criticism of the courts is that judges are acting as a "super legislature" in their rulings—that is, they are legislating from the bench. The charge of *judicial activism* is premised on the view that, at least in some cases, judges are overreaching and making decisions based on their personal values rather than the dictates of law. Critics of such decisions argue that such questions should be settled by the elective branches of government and not unelected and politically unaccountable judges.

Judicial activism, however, is frequently in the eye of the beholder. When, for example, the Supreme Court ruled 5–4 in *District of Columbia v. Heller*[10] that the Second Amendment protects an individual's right to own firearms—thereby overturning long-standing D.C. law and, by implication, elsewhere—relatively few conservative commentators charged the Court with judicial activism. Many liberals, by contrast, saw the *Heller* case as a clear example of conservative judicial activism.[11] On the other hand, when the Supreme Court ruled, also 5–4, in *Kelo v. City of New London* that the power of eminent domain could be used to condemn a private residence to promote local economic development, liberals praised the Court's judicial restraint in permitting democratically accountable local governments to make such decisions free from judicial second-guessing.[12] Meanwhile, conservatives denounced the case as "liberal activism."[13] The charge of judicial activism often serves as a way of denouncing judicial decisions that politicians and opinion leaders oppose on other grounds.

In the broader context of partisan and ideological polarization, the judiciary has come in for harsh attacks from many quarters. Retired Supreme Court justice Sandra Day O'Connor commented that "the breadth and intensity of rage currently being leveled at the judiciary may be unmatched in American history. The ubiquitous 'activist judges' who 'legislate from the bench' have become central villains on today's domestic political landscape."[14]

Federalism

When there is a dispute between states and the federal government, the Supreme Court ultimately determines the scope of powers possessed by each. This role has also been front and center in the Obamacare litigation. One controversial aspect of the law was its expansion of the state mandates under the federal Medicaid program. Medicaid is a health insurance program for low-income Americans in which the federal government provides funding to states to establish their own Medicaid programs, provided that the states comply with federal rules that create minimum standards for who and what is covered. States thus have a choice to participate in the Medicaid program or not, in keeping with their residual sovereignty. Medicaid funding has become an important part of many state budgets, and by the 1980s, all fifty states participated in the program. From time to time, however, state governors complain that the regulations imposed as a condition of receiving Medicaid funding are onerous on the states.

The Obamacare legislation imposed new Medicaid guidelines on the states to expand health insurance coverage to the uninsured poor not previously covered. To encourage all states to adopt these new guidelines, the legislation provided that states rejecting the new Medicaid coverage requirements would lose not only the Medicaid dollars covering the expansion of the program to new beneficiaries but also the support they currently received for their Medicaid programs. Several states argued this was federal coercion—that is, because Medicaid has become such an important part of state budgets, a threat to deprive states of all Medicaid revenue would leave the states with no choice at all but to accept the expansion of the program. In the *NFIB v. Sebelius* ruling, a seven-justice majority of the Court agreed that the conditions attached to the Medicaid expansion were unconstitutional. Rather than overturning the Medicaid expansion in its entirety, the Court instead permitted states to choose whether or not to expand their Medicaid rolls to cover those newly qualified under Obamacare without losing all federal support for their existing Medicaid program.[15] Because many conservative states used the authority granted under *NFIB v. Sebelius* to decline Obamacare's Medicaid expansion, this ruling significantly limited the reach of the program and left a much larger uninsured population than lawmakers had intended. In this case, as in many others, the Court regulated the balance between federal and state power.

Statutory Interpretation

The distinction between statutory and constitutional interpretation is very important. In statutory interpretation, federal judges construe the meaning or intent of the often vague language embedded in laws. Constitutional interpretation occurs when federal or state laws are challenged as violating the U.S. Constitution.

The major difference between statutory and constitutional interpretation is the relative ease with which Congress can reassert its understanding of the law against the Supreme Court. When the Court misinterprets a statute, Congress can amend or clarify the law, as it did in *Ledbetter v. Goodyear Tire and Rubber*[16] (2007). Lily Ledbetter had long received less pay than her male counterparts at Goodyear. After twenty years on the job, she learned of Goodyear's discriminatory treatment and sued on the grounds of gender-based pay and employment discrimination. Based on its interpretation of the relevant federal statute's language, the Supreme Court ruled, in a 5–4 decision, that Ledbetter's lawsuit was not timely because she did not file the suit within 180 days of the date on which the lower pay had been agreed to by the parties. The Court majority rejected the argument that the deadline for filing such a claim restarted with every discriminatory paycheck. A vigorous dissent by Justice Ruth Bader Ginsburg chided the Court's majority for their ignorance of workplace realities and noted that Congress could clarify the law. As one of its first actions, the 111th Congress (2009–2011) passed legislation, which President Obama signed into law, overturning *Ledbetter* and resetting the statutory deadline with every discriminatory paycheck, making it easier for workers to challenge gender-based employment discrimination.[17]

By contrast, a constitutional decision of the Court is binding on Congress and can be undone only by a subsequent constitutional amendment—which is very rare—or by the Court itself when it overrules one of its precedents.

Judicial interpretation of federal statutes is fraught with difficulty because communication between Congress and the federal courts is highly imperfect. Neither branch understands the workings of the other very well.[18] Ambiguity, imprecision, or inconsistency can often be the price of winning enactment of legislative measures. The more legislators try to define precisely the language of a bill, the more they may divide or dissipate congressional support for it. Abner J. Mikva, a four-term House Democrat from Chicago who went on to become a federal judge and later counsel to President Bill Clinton, recounted an example from his Capitol Hill days. The issue involved a controversial strip-mining bill being managed by Arizona Democrat Morris K. Udall, then chair of the House Interior (now called Natural Resources) Committee:

> They'd put together a very delicate coalition of support. One problem was whether the states or the feds would run the program. One member got up and asked, "Isn't it a fact that under this bill the states would continue to exercise sovereignty over strip mining?" And Mo replied, "You're absolutely right." A little later someone else got up and asked, "Now is it clear that the Federal Government will have the final say on strip mining?" And Mo replied, "You're absolutely right." Later, in the cloakroom, I said, "Mo, they can't both be right." And Mo said, "You're absolutely right."[19]

Called upon to interpret statutes, judges may not appreciate the efforts required to get legislation passed on Capitol Hill or understand how to examine legislative history, as manifested in hearings, reports, and floor debate. Within the courts and among legal scholars, there is a lively debate over the proper way to approach statutory interpretation. Should judges focus only on the plain meaning of the statutory language, or should they delve into legislative history to ascertain what Congress intended when it employed certain statutory phrases? A group of legal thinkers, led until his death by Supreme Court Justice Antonin Scalia, argues that legislative history is unreliable as an indicator of legislative intent because it is open to manipulation by lawmakers, executive officials, and congressional staffers.

Rather than relying on legislative history, Scalia contended that justices should follow a textualist approach, examining the wording of laws or constitutional clauses and interpreting them according to what they meant at the time of enactment.[20] Former Justice John Paul Stevens took a contrary view, saying that a "stubborn insistence on 'clear statements' [in the law] burdens the Congress with unnecessary reenactment of provisions that were already plain enough." The chief counsel of the Senate Committee on the Judiciary observed that difficulty in textual interpretation "encourages us to write clearer legislation. But unclear bills are still written."[21]

King v. Burwell[22] (2015) highlights how these differing approaches to statutory interpretation matter in terms of policy outcomes. The statutory scheme in Obamacare providing for tax credits to assist the purchase of health insurance assumed, to some extent, that states would set up their own insurance *exchanges,* online marketplaces where people can select among a variety of health insurance plans. But the law also provided for a federal exchange in the event that particular states declined to set up their own. Due in part to political opposition to the law, a large majority of states declined to establish their own exchanges. The *King* challengers focused on the section that authorizes the Internal Revenue Service (IRS) to provide tax credits for exchanges "established by the State." The challengers argued that, given the plain meaning of this phrase, a "State" cannot be the federal government. Thus, the IRS regulations providing tax credits for insurance purchased on both state and federal exchanges go beyond what the statute permits. Obamacare's defenders at first found this challenge hard to fathom. The removal of the tax subsidies would likely doom the federal exchange, frustrating Congress's intent in enacting the law and setting up the federal exchange in the first place. A major tenet of statutory interpretation is that the language of a statute should not be read in isolation from the overall purpose of the law. And there can be no doubt that a Supreme Court decision limiting the subsidies to the fourteen states that established their own exchanges would have frustrated the 111th Congress's policy goals in enacting Obamacare. In the end, six justices sided with the Obama administration's interpretation of the statute, while "textualist" Justice Scalia wrote a blistering dissent calling the majority opinion's result "quite absurd."[23]

Legislative Checks on the Judiciary

Many factors promote conflict between Congress and the courts. With federal judges serving life tenure, turnover on the courts is far slower than in Congress.

Meanwhile, the ideological and partisan composition of Congress can diverge widely from that of the federal courts. In addition, some Supreme Court rulings have direct and profound effects on Congress and its members. Cases involving partisan gerrymandering, campaign finance, and voter identification laws are recent examples. Scores of interest groups also monitor court decisions, and when they disagree with them, these groups are not reluctant to lobby Congress to seek their statutory reversal.

Congress has a variety of tools by which it can influence the Supreme Court and lower federal courts. In addition to the Senate's constitutional advice-and-consent role regarding judicial nominations, four legislative powers merit discussion: (1) withdrawal of jurisdiction; (2) impeachment of judges; (3) changing the size, procedures, and pay scales of the courts; and (4) constitutional amendment.

Withdrawal of Jurisdiction

The jurisdiction of the federal courts, including the Supreme Court, is delimited by both Article III and federal statute. Congress can thus alter the jurisdiction of the federal courts to achieve policy goals.

In some circumstances, Congress may seek to expand federal-court jurisdiction—usually at the expense of state courts—to achieve particular policy goals. In the post–Civil War period, for example, Congress expanded federal-court jurisdiction in an effort to protect the civil rights of African Americans.[24] Republican Congresses in the latter half of the nineteenth century also expanded federal-court jurisdiction in order to protect commercial interests against state controls.[25] Similarly, the Class Action Fairness Act of 2005 expanded federal jurisdiction over many large class action lawsuits, a key goal of business groups that had been frustrated by plaintiff lawyers' "forum shopping" to find the most friendly state courts.

But Congress's power over the jurisdiction of the federal courts also serves as a potential check on judicial overreach. Under its constitutional authority to determine the Supreme Court's appellate jurisdiction, for example, Congress may withdraw the Court's authority to review certain categories of cases. But more commonly, members of Congress will threaten efforts to do so. Responding, for example, to a Ninth Circuit decision that inclusion of the phrase "one Nation under God" to the Pledge of Allegiance was unconstitutional, on First Amendment grounds, then-House Majority Leader Tom DeLay, R-Tex., remarked, "I think that [legislation limiting the court's jurisdiction] would be a very good idea to send a message to the judiciary [that] they ought to keep their hands off the Pledge of Allegiance."[26] Other topics—such as same-sex marriage and the public display of the Ten Commandments—have evoked similar responses in Congress.[27] Such threats may actually affect judicial decision making. One study found that the Supreme Court responds to the introduction of court-curbing legislation by striking down fewer laws in subsequent years.[28] Despite the ongoing conflicts between Congress and the courts, on only one occasion in U.S. history did Congress prevent the Supreme Court from deciding a case by removing its appellate jurisdiction:

> This extraordinary action was taken by a Congress dominated by Radical Republicans who wanted to prohibit the Supreme Court from reviewing the constitutionality of the Reconstruction Acts of 1867. The acts substituted military rule for civilian government in the ten southern states that initially refused to rejoin the Union and established procedures for those states to follow to gain readmittance and representation in the federal government.[29]

Congress simply passed legislation repealing the Supreme Court's right to hear appeals involving these matters, thereby preventing "a possibly hostile Court from using the power of judicial review to invalidate a piece of legislation."[30] Various scholars have identified a variety of reasons why court-curbing legislation is so rarely adopted: "the historically broad consensus in Congress to protect, or at least tolerate, an independent judiciary; judicial opponents' reluctance to emasculate an institution that they may someday need as an ally; . . . and resistance by the organized bar."[31]

Impeachment of Judges

Federal judges, like other national civil officers, are subject to impeachment under Article II of the Constitution. They are appointed "during good behavior," effectively for life. Only one Supreme Court justice, Samuel Chase, has ever been impeached by the House. This occurred in 1804, during bitter partisan battles between the Federalists and Jeffersonian Republicans. The judiciary was the last bastion of Federalist influence after Thomas Jefferson won the presidency in the 1800 election. Chase's intemperate and arrogant behavior—he even campaigned for John Adams's reelection in 1800—raised the ire of Jefferson and his allies in Congress. On March 12, 1804, the House voted 73–32 along party lines to impeach Chase. The Senate, however, failed to convict (and thus remove) him. The importance of Chase's acquittal by the Senate was underscored in a book by Chief Justice William Rehnquist:

> The acquittal of Samuel Chase by the Senate had a profound effect on the American judiciary. First, it assured the independence of federal judges from congressional oversight of the decisions they made in the cases that come before them. Second, by assuring that impeachment would not be used in the future as a method to remove members of the Supreme Court for their judicial opinions, it helped to safeguard the independence of that body.[32]

Fifteen federal judges, including Chase, have been impeached, and eight have been removed by a two-thirds vote in the Senate.[33] Most recently, the 111th Congress (2009–2011) saw active impeachment proceedings against two district judges. In May 2009, Judge Samuel B. Kent of the Southern District of Texas had been convicted of obstruction of justice, resulting from an investigation of claims that he had sexually abused two female court staffers, and sentenced to prison. Following this conviction, the House voted to impeach, but Kent resigned before the Senate could try him. In 2010, Judge Thomas Porteous Jr. of the Eastern District of Louisiana was impeached and removed from the bench based on charges of corruption and making false statements on his financial-disclosure reports.

These recent examples of judicial impeachments are representative of such cases throughout U.S. history. Judges have been impeached for unethical and illegal acts rather than because of their legal and policy judgments. Congressional norms weigh against impeachment as a mechanism to exert political influence over the judiciary, despite the "Impeach Earl Warren" billboards and bumper stickers that appeared all across the South in the 1960s in the wake of *Brown v. Board of Education*.

Size, Procedure, and Pay

Historically, the size of the Supreme Court has ranged from six to ten members. "Generally, laws decreasing the number of justices have been motivated by a desire to punish the president; increases have been aimed at influencing the philosophical balance of the Court itself" (such as Roosevelt's Court-packing plan).[34] But since 1869, Congress has not changed the Court's size from its current nine justices.

Procedurally, lawmakers have occasionally proposed that Supreme Court decisions overturning federal laws be accomplished by a supermajority vote of the justices.[35] None of these proposals has been adopted. Instead, they serve as signals to the judiciary that lawmakers disapprove of certain court decisions. Lawmakers have also communicated complaints to the judicial branch by calling for stronger ethical guidelines for judges to ensure their impartiality, though the judicial branch claims that such legislation would violate judicial independence.[36]

Another legislative proposal that has generated interbranch controversy is opening federal courtrooms to television cameras. Several justices have opposed televising Supreme Court proceedings, in part because the cameras might alter decision making, intrude on the privacy of the justices by making them public celebrities, and threaten their personal security. During an appearance before the Senate Judiciary Committee, then-Justice Anthony Kennedy implored senators not to pass legislation mandating the televising of their open proceedings.[37] His concern was that televised Court sessions would eventually undermine the collegial character of the Court and encourage the justices to speak in sound bites. Attitudes toward cameras in the courtroom may be changing, however. In her confirmation hearings, Elena Kagan said that she thought "it would be a great thing for the institution and for the American people" to be able to watch Supreme Court arguments on television.[38] In his confirmation hearings, Justice

Kavanaugh stated that he would keep an open mind on the issue of cameras in the Supreme Court but noted, "I know nominees who've sat in this chair in the past have expressed the desire for cameras in the courtroom, only to get to the Supreme Court and really change their positions fairly rapidly."[39]

A recent concern has been that fewer aspirants are seeking federal judgeships. Part of the reason is pay: "Salaries are far lower [for federal judges] than what fresh-faced law-school grads can make at big corporate firms."[40]

In the current legislative environment, it is unlikely that Congress will approve any substantial judicial pay increase. The chief justice currently receives an annual salary of $267,000; associate justices, $255,300; appeals court judges, $220,600; and federal district judges, $208,000.[41]

A related concern about pay is that "low" judicial salaries encourage judges, even highly respected ones, to leave the bench for other, better paying positions. Judges' earnings lag behind other high-status legal professionals. Law school deans, for example, can earn over $400,000 a year, and top law firm partners earn $1 million or more a year.[42] Moreover, former judges are in high demand as arbitrators in large-scale commercial disputes. Some judges may leave the bench to become, in effect, high-paid "private judges" for large corporations.[43]

Constitutional Amendments

On four occasions, Congress successfully used the arduous process of amending the Constitution to overturn decisions of the Supreme Court. In *Chisholm v. Georgia* (1793), the Court held that citizens of one state could sue another state in federal court.[44] To prevent a rash of citizen suits against the states, Congress oversaw passage of the Eleventh Amendment to reverse this decision and protect states' sovereign immunity from lawsuits brought by citizens of other states and foreign countries. The *Dred Scott v. Sandford* (1857) decision[45]—denying African Americans citizenship under the Constitution—was nullified by the Thirteenth Amendment (abolishing slavery) and Fourteenth Amendment (granting African Americans citizenship). The Sixteenth Amendment overturned *Pollock v. Farmer's Loan and Trust Co.* (1895), which struck down a federal income tax. The Twenty-Sixth Amendment invalidated *Oregon v. Mitchell* (1970), which held that Congress had exceeded its authority by lowering the minimum voting age to eighteen for state elections.[46]

Lawmakers are generally reluctant to amend the Constitution. The view of former representative Melvin Watt, D-N.C., reflects that of many members: "I just think the Constitution has served us very well over a long, long period of time, and one needs to make a compelling case before we start amending the Constitution to do anything."[47] However, certain constitutional amendments have appeared repeatedly on the legislative agenda, for example, proposals to ban desecration of the American flag, in response to a 1989 Supreme Court ruling that flag burning is protected by the First Amendment right of free speech.[48] The House passed anti-flag desecration amendments several times, but the Senate never mustered the two-thirds majority needed to send the resolution to the states for ratification.

Eliminating life tenure for federal judges is another proposal that increasingly surfaces on the Internet, if not on Capitol Hill. Bitter judicial-nomination battles have prompted calls for term limits (such as fifteen years) for federal judges. "If the Senate can't figure out how to reach a [partisan] truce in its battles over these all-important jobs," wrote one analyst, "maybe the best solution is to make the jobs not quite so important."[49] Others argue against life tenure because justices strategically retire so as to engineer their replacement by a president of their preferred party. Others simply contend that Supreme Court justices serve too long. Aging justices may become arrogant and out of touch with contemporary values—or perhaps too impaired to serve. To avoid the difficulties of winning approval of a constitutional amendment, some have proposed a legislative approach that, instead of term limits *per se,* would move "justices into senior status after roughly eighteen years on the high court."[50]

ADVICE AND CONSENT FOR JUDICIAL NOMINEES

Article II, section 2, of the Constitution states that the president "shall nominate, and by and with the Advice and Consent of the Senate, shall appoint . . . Judges of the Supreme Court." The founders rejected giving the power to appoint judges solely to the executive, to Congress as a whole, or to the Senate. In the end, they compromised and required joint action by the president and the Senate. The president has the sole prerogative to nominate, but the power to confirm (or not) belongs to the Senate. Alexander Hamilton, in *Federalist* No. 66, viewed this division of responsibility in stark terms: "There will, of course, be no exertion of CHOICE on the part of the Senate. They may defeat one choice of the Executive and oblige him to make another; but they cannot themselves CHOOSE—they can only ratify or reject the choice he may have made."

Hamilton's perspective, however, requires some refinement. Giving two elective institutions a voice in the appointments process necessarily means that the Senate is able to influence the president's choice of nominees. Indeed, individual senators, House members, interest groups, bar associations, the Federalist Society, the press and media, and even sitting judges can all influence both the choice of judicial nominees and Senate action, if any, on those nominees. The fact that federal district and appellate court jurisdictions are geographically based means that senators representing those states (especially if they are of the president's party) commonly have input in recommending judicial candidates to the White House (see Table 12-1 for judgeship appointments by presidents).

The norms and procedures that have historically governed judicial nominations have been under great pressure in recent congresses. This is perhaps most

TABLE 12-1	■ Judgeship Appointments by President, 1933–2018				
President	Supreme Court	Regional Court of Appeals	USCAFC[1]	District Courts	Total
F. Roosevelt (1933–1945)	9	52	—	136	197
Truman (1945–1953)	4	27	—	102	133
Eisenhower (1953–1961)	5	45	—	127	177
Kennedy (1961–1963)	2	20	—	102	124
L. Johnson (1963–1969)	2	41	—	125	168
Nixon (1969–1974)	4	48	—	182	231
Ford (1974–1977)	1	12	—	52	65
Carter (1977–1981)	0	56	—	206	262
Reagan (1981–1989)	3	78	5	292	378
G. H. W. Bush (1989–1993)	2	37	5	149	193
Clinton (1993–2001)	2	62	4	306	374
G. W. Bush (2001–2009)	2	61	2	261	326
Obama (2009–2017)	2	48	7	268	325
Trump[2] (2017–	2	30	0	53	84

Sources: Adapted from "Judgeship Appointments by President," *The Third Branch,* newsletter of the federal courts, February 2009. Data for the Obama administration are from the Federal Judicial Center, www.fjc.gov/history/home.nsf/page/research_categories.html. The work of CRS experts Steven Rutkus and Barry McMillion and FJC expert Jake Kobrick is gratefully acknowledged.

[1]The U.S. Court of Appeals for the Federal Circuit (USCAFC) was established in 1982.

[2]Data are through January 1, 2019.

clear in the GOP Senate majority's treatment of President Obama's third Supreme Court nominee Merrick Garland, who received no formal consideration.

Supreme Court Nominations

When Supreme Court justice Antonin Scalia died unexpectedly in early 2016, conservatives quickly took to social media demanding that the Senate Republican majority block any nominee Obama put forward. An Obama nominee to replace Scalia would have potentially shifted the court—which often divided 5–4 on controversial matters, with five reliable conservative votes—in a markedly liberal direction. In an unprecedented step, Majority Leader Mitch McConnell, R-Ky., issued a blanket statement on the very day of Scalia's death: "The American people should have a voice in the selection of their next Supreme Court Justice. Therefore, this vacancy should not be filled until we have a new president."[51]

Despite McConnell's statement, President Obama nominated Chief Judge Merrick Garland of the U.S. Court of Appeals for the District of Columbia Circuit for the vacancy. President Bill Clinton had appointed Garland to the D.C. Circuit in 1997, after, among other things, his leading role in the prosecution of the Oklahoma City bombers. Many saw him as a moderate nominee. At the age of sixty-three, Judge Garland was an "old" nominee by contemporary standards. Some interpreted this as an attempt by President Obama to make him more acceptable to the GOP Senate majority, as he would not likely serve as long as a younger nominee. The Senate GOP majority, however, refused to hold hearings on the nomination. Democrats loudly criticized the obstruction, pointing to past confirmations in the final year of a president's term and Garland's extensive qualifications for the seat.

The Garland nomination and its aftermath illustrates how the traditional norms and practices governing judicial nominations have eroded. The GOP-controlled Senate never formally considered the Garland nomination. President Trump was thus able to choose Scalia's successor. On February 1, 2017, President Trump nominated Judge Neil Gorsuch of the Tenth Circuit Court of Appeals to the Scalia seat. Senate Democrats opposed Gorsuch's nomination—not based on his qualifications, but based on partisan and ideological concerns. Sen. Charles E. Schumer, D-N.Y., now Democratic leader, led a filibuster of his nomination. In response, Senate Majority Leader McConnell deployed a simple-majority process to change Senate precedents, a maneuver widely termed the *nuclear option*. This move allowed Republicans to defeat the Democratic filibuster, even though they could not get sixty senators to support cloture on the Gorsuch nomination. It also set a new precedent permitting confirmation of future Supreme Court justices by simple majority vote in the Senate.

Before selecting Gorsuch, President Trump considered a short list of potential nominees holding political and policy views consistent with his party as well as a reputation for competence and relevant experience. The Garland, Gorsuch, and Kavanaugh selections all followed the trend toward viewing prior judicial experience, especially experience as an appellate judge, as an essential qualification for the Supreme Court. Of current members of the Court, only Justice Elena Kagan never served as a federal appellate judge.

Moreover, recent presidents have avoided nominating justices with prior experience in elective office. During the 2016 campaign, candidate Trump released not one but two "short" lists of the kinds of potential nominees he would consider for the Supreme Court—the lists together totaled twenty-one names, making for an extensive "short" list.[52] The Trump lists included a number of federal and state appellate judges, including Judge Gorsuch, but also elected officials, including Sen. Mike Lee, R-Utah. It was once more typical for the Court to include members steeped in legislative or executive experience. Chief Justice Warren, for example, was sitting governor of California when he was appointed to the Court. Some legal scholars have argued that a wider range of occupational experiences on the Court would serve an important representational function and enhance decision making "with a variety of issues in the electoral and legislative spheres."[53] In the Court's recent history, only Supreme Court Justice Sandra Day O'Connor ever held an elective office; she was an Arizona state senator.

The contemporary selection process typically includes careful vetting of potential nominees' personal and professional lives, as the recent experience of the Kavanaugh nomination illustrates. The research process conducted for the nominees scours "the real estate transactions, taxes, ethics, the backgrounds of spouses and adult children, as well as a particularly close look at the early jobs held right after law school."[54] Once the president selects his nominee, he sends a written nomination to the Senate, which is then, typically, referred to the Judiciary Committee. The nominee is then escorted to various Hill offices with minders sometimes called "sherpas" to meet with key senators.

Confirmation hearings for Supreme Court nominees have been routine since the 1950s. But the 2018 Kavanaugh hearings were more contentious than typical, even for recent nominations. When Supreme Court associate justice Anthony M. Kennedy announced his retirement from the Court, "a furious fight over the future of the Supreme Court" ensued.[55] Kennedy was widely seen as the swing vote on the Court, most notably in cases involving social issues such as gay rights and abortion. His replacement with a reliable socially conservative justice would potentially shift the Court's already conservative majority in an even more rightward direction, potentially for a generation. After considering a short list of potential nominees, President Trump announced his decision to nominate Kavanaugh.

Given the stakes, the Kavanaugh nomination was always going to be contentious, and the first round of hearings featured the nominee facing tough questions from Democratic members of the Senate Judiciary Committee. But the nomination fight ratcheted up when allegations were made public that Kavanaugh had sexually assaulted another student while in high school.[56] Psychology professor Christine Blasey Ford emerged as Kavanaugh's reluctant—and credible—accuser.[57] Eventually, two other accusers also came forward. The Kavanaugh nomination appeared to be in serious trouble. Sen. Jeff Flake, R-Ariz., a member of the committee, pressured his party's leaders to schedule an additional day of hearings to consider Blasey Ford's allegations.

Even by contemporary standards, the Kavanaugh–Blasey Ford hearing became a national political spectacle. The *New York Times* described it as "an extraordinary, emotional day of testimony that ricocheted from a woman's tremulous account of sexual assault to a man's angry, outraged denial, all of which played out for hours before a riveted nation and a riven Senate."[58] The drama, however, did not derail the nomination, as the Judiciary Committee voted along party lines to recommend confirmation, although floor consideration was delayed a week. The week's delay was to provide time for the Federal Bureau of Investigation (FBI) to file a supplemental report on the Blasey Ford allegations, which senators were then permitted to view in secret. The supplemental FBI report was also forced on the GOP leadership by Senator Flake and two Senate colleagues.

In general, the Senate majority leader decides when to call up a Supreme Court nomination for chamber consideration after consultation with various lawmakers, including the minority leader. Since the 2017 nuclear option precedent, only a majority vote is required to invoke cloture on Supreme Court nominations. After debate ends, the Senate then decides whether to confirm the Supreme Court nominee by roll call vote, a practice begun in 1967. Justice Kavanaugh was confirmed on a largely party-line vote, 50–48, with Sen. Joe Manchin, D-W. Va., voting for confirmation and Sen. Lisa Murkowski, R-Alaska, voting against. Senator Flake, despite delaying the nomination twice, voted to confirm Kavanaugh.

Unsuccessful Supreme Court nominations are not unusual. Before the unsuccessful Garland nomination in 2016, there had been another unsuccessful Supreme Court nomination as recently as the George W. Bush administration. Over the last two centuries, the Senate has "rejected about 20 percent of all Supreme Court nominees."[59] Most of the rejections occurred in the nineteenth century, with President John Tyler holding the record: Five of his six nominees were rejected by the Senate (see Table 12-2).

The bitter confirmation battles of the present originate with President Ronald Reagan's nomination of conservative Robert H. Bork to the Supreme Court in 1987. A Democratic-controlled Senate rejected Bork, who was perceived as too conservative, by a 58–42 margin. Conservative groups were outraged by the way Bork was treated by the Democratic-controlled Senate. The political campaign mobilized against the nomination gave rise to a new verb, to *bork*.

Since the failed Bork nomination, senators have become increasingly unwilling to support Supreme Court nominees selected by presidents of the opposing party.[60] In 1986, Antonin Scalia was confirmed by the Senate 98–0, even though it was clear that he was a staunch judicial conservative. President Clinton's two nominees in the early 1990s—Ruth Bader Ginsburg in 1993 and Stephen Breyer in 1994—each garnered opposition only from a handful of conservative senators. President George W. Bush's nominees—John Roberts and Samuel Alito—were met with more widespread Democratic opposition, with only half of Senate

TABLE 12-2	Supreme Court Nominations Not Confirmed by the Senate			
Nominee	President	Date of Nomination	Senate Action	Date of Senate Action
William Paterson	George Washington	February 27, 1793	Withdrawn[1]	
John Rutledge[2]	Washington	July 1, 1795	Rejected (10–14)	December 15, 1795
Alexander Wolcott	James Madison	February 4, 1811	Rejected (9–24)	February 13, 1811
John J. Crittenden	John Quincy Adams	December 17, 1828	Postponed	February 12, 1829
Roger Brooke Taney	Andrew Jackson	January 15, 1835	Postponed (24–21)[3]	March 3, 1835
John C. Spencer	John Tyler	January 9, 1844	Rejected (21–26)	January 31, 1844
Reuben H. Walworth	Tyler	March 13, 1844	Withdrawn	
Edward King	Tyler	June 5, 1844	Postponed	June 15, 1844
Edward King	Tyler	December 4, 1844	Withdrawn	
John M. Read	Tyler	February 7, 1845	Not acted upon	
George W. Woodward	James K. Polk	December 23, 1845	Rejected (20–29)	January 22, 1846
Edward A. Bradford	Millard Fillmore	August 16, 1852	Not acted upon	
George E. Badger	Fillmore	January 10, 1853	Postponed	February 11, 1853
William C. Micou	Fillmore	February 24, 1853	Not acted upon	
Jeremiah S. Black	James Buchanan	February 5, 1861	Rejected (25–26)	February 21, 1861
Henry Stanbery	Andrew Johnson	April 16, 1866	Not acted upon	
Ebenezer R. Hoar	Ulysses S. Grant	December 15, 1869	Rejected (24–33)	February 3, 1870

Nominee	President	Date of Nomination	Senate Action	Date of Senate Action
George H. Williams[2]	Grant	December 1, 1873	Withdrawn	
Caleb Cushing[2]	Grant	January 9, 1874	Withdrawn	
Stanley Matthews	Rutherford B. Hayes	January 26, 1881	Not acted upon[1]	
William B. Hornblower	Grover Cleveland	September 19, 1893	Rejected (24–30)	January 15, 1894
Wheeler H. Peckham	Cleveland	January 22, 1894	Rejected (32–41)	February 16, 1894
John J. Parker	Herbert Hoover	March 21, 1930	Rejected (39–41)	May 7, 1930
Abe Fortas[2]	Lyndon B. Johnson	June 26, 1968	Withdrawn	
Homer Thornberry	Johnson	June 26, 1968	Not acted upon	
Clement F. Haynsworth Jr.	Richard M. Nixon	August 18, 1969	Rejected (45–55)	November 21, 1969
G. Harrold Carswell	Nixon	January 19, 1970	Rejected (45–51)	April 8, 1970
Robert H. Bork	Ronald Reagan	July 1, 1987	Rejected (42–58)	October 23, 1987
Douglas H. Ginsburg	Ronald Reagan	October 29, 1987	Withdrawn	
Harriet Miers	George W. Bush	October 3, 2005	Withdrawn	
Merrick Garland	Barack Obama	March 16, 2016	Not acted upon	

Source: Joan Biskupic and Elder Witt, *Guide to the U.S. Supreme Court,* 3rd ed., vol. 2 (Washington, DC: Congressional Quarterly, 1997), 707, authors' notes.

[1]Later nominated and confirmed.

[2]Nominated for chief justice.

[3]Later nominated for chief justice and confirmed.

Democrats voting in favor of Roberts and only four Democrats in favor of Alito. Senate votes on President Obama's Supreme Court nominations—Sonia Sotomayor and Elena Kagan—broke down along party lines, with only nine Republicans voting for Sotomayor and only five Republicans voting for Kagan. Consistent with recent patterns, President Trump's nominees received minimal Democratic support—Gorsuch received three Democratic votes and Kavanaugh only one. "We have shifted from a basic expectation that absent a reason to vote against a nominee members of the opposing party will support a president's nominee," said Benjamin Wittes, senior fellow at the Brookings Institution. "In a very short period of time, that has reversed to a presumption that members of the opposition party will oppose the president's nominee, absent a reason to support him or her. That is a very profound change."[61]

Before more recent nominations, the president's partisan opponents usually preferred to fight Supreme Court nominations on the qualifications issue rather than on ideological grounds. But Judge Garland was unassailable on experience grounds, and Republican senators repeatedly stated that their opposition was not based on the judge himself but on purely ideological considerations. Like Garland, Gorsuch met the historic qualifications for a Supreme Court nominee—he was appointed to the appeals court by President Bush in 2006, after service in the Justice Department and private practice. A graduate of Harvard Law School, Oxford, and Columbia, he possessed unimpeachable academic credentials. Democratic opposition to his nomination was based on his ideological commitments rather than his qualifications. Interestingly, Senator Schumer has been one of the Senate's leading proponents of openly considering nominees' ideology. Long before the Gorsuch nomination, he argued that senators should forthrightly take ideology into account in voting on Supreme Court nominations rather than look for other pretexts for opposing judges with whom they disagree. "For one reason or another, examining the ideologies of judicial nominees has become something of a Senate taboo," writes Schumer. "Unfortunately, the taboo has led senators who oppose a nominee for ideological reasons to justify their opposition by finding non-ideological factors, like small financial improprieties from long ago. This 'gotcha' politics has warped the confirmation process."[62]

The Lower Courts

The politicization of lower-court nominations is arguably one of the more dramatic transformations in U.S. politics in the last generation. Traditionally, presidents tended to defer to home-state senators in making nominations to the federal district and appellate courts, which were really "under the radar" positions. In fact, the Senate itself long enforced the norm of *senatorial courtesy,* under which presidents were expected to consult with home-state senators in making such appointments. Senators would "support an individual senator of the president's party who opposes a nominee to an office in his state."[63] As such, senatorial courtesy placed a heavy weight on the Senate's "advise" power with respect to judicial nominations. The increased salience of such appointments, however, has undercut old norms.[64]

In the last decades, nominations to the federal district and appellate courts have become an issue prominently featured in presidential and congressional campaigns of both parties, though judicial nominations have tended to be a more salient issue for Republicans. Indeed, conservatives with reservations about the Trump presidency often point to his lower-court nominations as a major reason for their continued support of the sometimes-erratic administration.

Two key factors explain the increasingly contentious nature of lower-court nominations. First, the policy making role of the lower courts has come into sharper focus. Starting in the 1980s, the burgeoning conservative movement focused on issues such as abortion and civil rights, turning its attention to the lower courts and their role in deciding controversial issues. Given the small number of cases the Supreme Court hears and decides every term, the courts of appeals have become the courts of last resort on many issues.[65] According to one law professor, the courts of appeals are "the Supreme Courts for their region."[66] The courts of appeals decide tens of thousands of cases annually, "playing a more important role in setting law for vast areas of the country. A decision by the Ninth Circuit, for example, is binding on nine states, where 19 percent of the nation's population lives."[67] Interest groups have also become increasingly sensitive to the discretion of district judges, especially in complex commercial-litigation and employment-discrimination cases. Many of the procedural rulings district judges make are not typically reviewable by appellate courts but can substantially determine the litigation fates of corporate defendants.

Second, some confirmation fights are clearly warm-ups for potential Supreme Court vacancies down the line. The increasing weight given appellate-court experience in Supreme Court nominations has increased the importance of the lower courts as a "bench" for up-and-coming jurists. Defeating a controversial nominee to the court of appeals effectively blocks a later appointment to the Supreme Court.

President Obama's nominations to the lower courts became highly contentious during his second term, resulting in routine obstruction and delay of nominations. The issue eventually came to a head when the Senate GOP blocked three nominees to the U.S. Court of Appeals for the District of Columbia Circuit. Unlike in past disputes over judicial nominations, bipartisan negotiations failed. To break the deadlock, the Democratic Senate majority in 2013 employed the parliamentary maneuver widely termed the nuclear option to eliminate the 60-vote cloture requirement for all executive-branch and judicial-branch nominations, with an exception for Supreme Court nominations.[68] Only four years later, the exception for the Supreme Court was eliminated for the Gorsuch nomination, leading to simple majority cloture on all executive and judicial nominations.

After the deployment of the nuclear option, the Obama administration was able to move judicial nominations, with critics complaining that the president was "pack[ing]" the courts with "far-left" judges.[69] Fully ninety-six judges were confirmed by the Senate after going nuclear,[70] including an incredible twelve judges confirmed on the Senate's last day in session in 2014. At the end of the 113th Congress, 132 district and court-of-appeals judges had been confirmed,[71] and Democratic appointees made up majorities on nine of the thirteen courts of appeals.[72] But Obama's nominees fared poorly in the 114th Congress, after Republicans won majority control of the Senate. Of the nine court-of-appeals nominations President Obama made in the 114th Congress, only five received hearings and two were confirmed. Of Obama's sixty-two district court nominations, forty-six received hearings and eighteen were confirmed.[73] The Republican majority's slow walking of nominations meant that the new administration would have a large number of judicial vacancies to fill.[74]

Given this background, it is no surprise that controversies over judicial nominations arose frequently in the 115th Congress (2017–2018) under President Trump. White House counsel Donald F. McGahn, with considerable assistance from the conservative Federalist Society and its executive vice president, Leonard Leo, headed the administration's efforts.[75]

Many of the controversies in the 115th Congress centered on an important historical mechanism for accommodating senatorial courtesy, the so-called *blue slip*.[76] Under this procedure, before the Judiciary Committee would consider a judicial nominee, the senators from the state in which the judge would serve were issued forms (actual blue slips of paper) on which the senators could signal their approval or disapproval. In recent years, the practice had been for both home-state senators to be consulted through this procedure, regardless of party. The Obama administration worked diligently to secure the blue-slip approval of GOP home-state senators and had a great deal of early success in doing so.[77] That success was undercut, however, by what one observer described as "systematic leadership-led refusal to consent" to moving ahead with nominations.[78]

In the 115th Congress, the Senate Judiciary Committee, chaired by Sen. Charles Grassley, R-Iowa, advanced Trump lower-court nominations even when neither home-state senator had returned a blue slip, a departure from this recent practice.[79] In this manner, the GOP-led Senate circumvented the opposition of Democratic senators to Trump nominees, advancing court of appeals nominees over objections.[80] But the Trump administration also advanced nominees even after little consultation with Republican home-state senators. The Republican-controlled Senate moved forward aggressively with Trump administration judicial nominees despite the limited observance of senatorial courtesy. The Judiciary chair possesses a great deal of discretion over judicial nominations, and Senator Grassley exercised that discretion to expedite judicial confirmations. The Judiciary Committee even held nomination hearings for lower-court nominees while the Senate was on recess in October 2018.

Although Republicans worked with remarkable unity to advance President Trump's judicial nominees, a few senators displayed flashes of independence. Among these, Sen. John Neely Kennedy, R-La., emerged as a player in judicial nominations, raising questions about Trump nominees on key occasions. Senator Kennedy's grilling of Matthew Peterson, a nominee to the District of Columbia district court, went viral, after the senator pointed sharply to the nominee's lack of trial experience and ignorance of the federal rules of procedure.[81] Senator Kennedy's reluctance also helped to stymie the confirmation of another nominee with no trial experience to a district judgeship in Alabama. In committee, Kennedy voted against the nomination of deputy White House counsel Greg Katsas to the U.S. Court of Appeals for the D.C. Circuit, based on possible conflicts of interest. Responding to the nomination of Kyle Duncan to the Fifth Circuit Court of Appeals, based in New Orleans, Kennedy returned his blue slip "undecided," handwriting in that option, which is not provided on the form.[82]

The Duncan nomination highlights the extent of the departure from past practice. Although a home-state senator would normally have been consulted about an appellate nomination in his state, Senator Kennedy had no role in the nomination. In this case, however, the nominee was a prominent conservative litigator who had been lead counsel in the *Hobby Lobby v. Burwell* case, in which the Supreme Court held that private business could refuse, based on the religious beliefs of their owners, to provide contraceptive coverage to female employees. The New Orleans *Times-Picayune* described him as "a darling of right-wing social crusaders."[83] When Duncan was nominated, Kennedy commented that he had never even met the nominee. The senator was critical of White House counsel McGahn, noting in that, "he was on the scarce side, in one conversation, of being polite."[84] The nominee took the unusual step of apologizing to the senator for being "iced out of the process."[85]

Despite the opposition of Senate Democrats—and even, occasionally, Republicans—the Trump administration amassed an impressive record in lower-court nominations through the 115th Congress.[86] The Senate GOP majority's drive to staff the courts with Trump judges is unlikely to slow, as the minority party has few means of slowing the determined effort. As Senator Grassley commented in the 115th Congress, "I think the Democrats now seriously regret that they abolished the filibuster."[87] As with the Gorsuch and Kavanaugh nominations, the Trump administration, the GOP Senate majority, and the conservative movement writ broadly have reshaped the federal judiciary for a generation.

CONCLUSION

Federal courts, like Congress and the president, are central forums for resolving political, social, and economic conflicts in U.S. society. All three branches of government interact constantly to shape the laws under which Americans live. Sometimes, as presidents say, "the buck stops here." In Congress, the buck may stop nowhere, and either elective branch may pass the buck to the courts when it is unable to resolve certain issues. "Through this process of interaction among the branches," writes scholar Louis Fisher, "all three institutions are able to expose weaknesses, hold excesses in check, and gradually forge a consensus on constitutional values."[88]

Interest Group Influence. Video capture from one of the AARP's television advertisements against the 2017 Republican health care legislation. Speaker of the House Paul Ryan, R-Wis., presents the GOP's plan to repeal and replace the Affordable Care Act. Protesters hold signs and shout at lawmakers after the House of Representatives passed the Republican plan.

CONGRESS AND
ORGANIZED INTERESTS

"A bill that's completely opposed by the whole health care establishment is very, very difficult to pass," said John Rother, AARP's top lobbyist for more than two decades.[1] Indeed, Republicans faced a wall of opposition from organized interests as they sought to repeal and replace Obamacare in 2017. The health care industry and patient advocacy groups from the American Heart Association to the March of Dimes all urged lawmakers to oppose the proposed legislation. Summing up the landscape, *Politico* reported, "Just about every major health care group opposes President Donald Trump's health care overhaul."[2]

When Obamacare was developed in 2009–2010, President Obama and congressional Democrats had carefully cultivated support from health insurance companies, doctors groups, hospitals, and the pharmaceutical industry. Deals were cut to accommodate a wide array of affected interests in order to induce their support or at least minimize their opposition to the new federal benefit program. In their repeal effort, however, Trump and Republican leaders did not engage in the same outreach and coalition building. Republicans instead hoped to deal with health care quickly so as to move on to other agenda priorities, such as tax reform. But Republicans were not able to move quickly enough to act before a wide range of groups had mobilized against their legislative effort. "Stakeholders weren't brought in to kind of troubleshoot some of the problem areas of the bill," said Betsy Ryan, CEO of the New Jersey Hospital Association. "Hence, the almost uniform opposition."[3]

AARP was one of the first interest groups to jump into the debate. As the nation's largest organization of older Americans, representing 38 million retirees, the organization immediately perceived a threat to older Americans' health insurance benefits. Over the course of the legislative drive, the AARP's activism on health care policy ran the gamut of tactics interest groups employ to shape public policy. They reached out behind the scenes to policy makers on Capitol Hill, and they publicized their opposition to their members and to television audiences nationwide.

AARP first communicated its position by firing off letters to relevant committee leaders, such as the chair and ranking member of the U.S. House Committee on Energy and Commerce.[4] But AARP's influence campaign did not stop there. The organization spent millions in digital and television demanding that Congress not touch seniors' benefits.[5] "You've earned your Medicare. It was a deal that was made long ago, and AARP believes it should be honored," said a narrator. The organization also called on its members to contact lawmakers on the relevant committees in Congress.[6]

The AARP was just one of many active players in the debate over the fate of the Affordable Care Act. In that sense, the battle over the legislation offers a case study in the diverse ways organized interests make themselves heard in U.S. politics. In the end, the strong and widespread interest group opposition undoubtedly helps explain the ultimate defeat of a majority party's top legislative priority in newly unified government. After devoting nine months to the effort, the 2017 Republicans finally gave up on repealing Obamacare, settled instead for abolishing the ACA's individual mandate to purchase health insurance, and moved on to other legislative priorities.

AMERICAN PLURALISM

The protracted debates over national health care policy since 2009 illustrate the dual nature of American pluralism. On the one hand, a vast array of organized interests, most of them headquartered in the nation's capital, seek to influence government policy. This is the *Washington system* of lobbyists and insider access that incites so much populist rhetoric and public distaste.[7] Narrow profit motives were hardly absent from the health reform debate, as lobbyists sought legislative concessions to line their clients' pockets. When the American Medical Association, the American Nurses Association, and the American Hospital Association all came out in opposition to the Republicans' proposed replacement for the Affordable Care Act, chair of the House Energy and Commerce Committee, Rep. Greg Walden, R-Ore., remarked, "There's a pretty big medical–industrial complex in America, and when you touch it, I've discovered, it touches back."[8]

On the other hand, also weighing in on the debate were patient advocacy and other membership organizations, some of them huge, like AARP. As soon as the Republican bill was released, AARP launched an advertising campaign denouncing its "age tax" that would have permitted health insurance companies to charge older individuals more than five times as much as younger individuals. By means of such organizations, Americans assemble "to petition the government for redress of grievances," in the words of the Constitution's First Amendment. Groups of Americans legitimately concerned about how health care reform might affect the quality, affordability, and accessibility of medical treatments made their concerns known.

The controversy surrounding health care reform illustrates the ambivalence that characterizes both scholarly and journalistic considerations of American pluralism. The world of interest groups prompts fears of a government corrupted by narrow special interests. And yet, organized interests are not only constitutionally protected but also a foundation of civil society and a natural by-product of democratic freedom. President Harry S. Truman, in a wry response to a reporter's question—" Mr. President, would you be against lobbyists who are working for your program?"—remarked, "Well, that's a different matter. We probably wouldn't call these people lobbyists. We would call them citizens appearing in the public interest."[9]

A Capital of Interests

Organized interests wield vast resources—money, connections, personnel, information, and organization—to win passage of legislation they favor, block legislation they oppose, and reward the politicians who help them. Capitol Hill lobbyists, emissaries of these interests, walk the halls of congressional office buildings, request personal meetings with lawmakers and aides, hold informational briefings for members and staff, and jam committee meeting rooms.

Practically every major corporation, trade association, and professional group has Washington lobbyists. Indeed, Washington is home to more national associations than any other city. Numerous law, financial, technology, and public-relations firms also have offices in the District of Columbia. "A financial institution . . . needs to have a Washington office," said the head of one financial trade group. "It puts you at a competitive advantage to have a Washington presence [because you] can have input into the [lawmaking] process."[10]

The lobbying community constitutes one of the largest industry employers in the nation's capital. "The more the government gets involved in an industry's affairs," declaimed an experienced lobbyist, "the more industry hires people to figure that out."[11] When control of one or both houses of Congress moves from one party to another, the changeover often sparks a boost in lobbying hiring and expenditures as organized interests seek out better access to new congressional leaders. "It's standard operating procedure in Washington that whenever there is a shift in power, there is a scramble by companies to make sure they have adequate representation with the new power brokers," explained the head of the Center for Responsive Politics, a D.C.-based think tank.[12] More than $3.3 billion was spent lobbying in 2017.[13] However, it is not possible to track all of the expenditures organizations make to influence policy making. Unlike direct lobbying, other forms of influence peddling are not subject to disclosure, such as funding nonprofit groups, think tanks, and grassroots organizations.[14]

A Nation of Joiners

Americans' zest for joining groups was noted long ago by Alexis de Tocqueville. Americans of all "conditions, minds, and ages daily acquire a general taste for association," he wrote in 1835.[15] Throughout U.S. history, groups speaking for different subsets of "the people" have swayed public policies and politics. The nineteenth-century abolitionists fought to end slavery. The Anti-Saloon League crusaded for the prohibition of alcohol in the 1900s. Activists in the 1960s and 1970s protested the Vietnam War, racial discrimination, and abuse of the environment. In the 1970s and 1980s, interest groups galvanized support for and against equal rights for women. In the 1990s, conservative groups pushed term limits for lawmakers, a balanced-budget amendment, and tax cuts. A wide array of liberal and conservative membership organizations have been prominent in recent U.S. politics, such as anti-abortion groups, immigration reformers, gun rights and gun control advocates, MoveOn.org, Tea Party groups, and Occupy Wall Street.

A free society nurtures politically active groups. "Liberty is to faction what air is to fire," wrote James Madison in *Federalist* No. 10. For decades, interest groups have grown in number and diversity. For example, the American Medical Association dominated health lobbying in the 1950s, but today, hundreds of health advocacy groups woo lawmakers and orchestrate grassroots activity, up from about 90 in 1975 to at least 750 by the early 1990s. "You name a disease, there's probably a Washington lobby for it," said an official of the American Heart Association.[16] Many factors account for the proliferation of interest groups: social and economic complexity; scientific and technological developments; the government's regulatory role; the competition for federal dollars; and the diffusion of power in U.S. national government, which enhances access for outside interests (see Box 13-1 on theories of interest group formation).

Despite the tradition of vibrant associational life in the United States, there is some evidence that Americans' civic engagement has declined since the 1960s. Most famously, Harvard University professor Robert Putnam showed across a wide array of indicators that citizen participation in associations had waned. Fewer Americans were participating in organizations like Cub Scouts, Brownies, PTA, volunteer fire departments, and civic associations, such as Elks and Rotary Clubs. Putnam drew his most famous example from the nation's bowling alleys. His data showed that more people are bowling but doing so outside of traditional bowling leagues, resulting in a drop in the number of bowling leagues.[17] They are, in short, "bowling alone." People "would rather be alone in front of a television set than out with a group," Putnam wrote.[18] Rather than taking personal part in broad-based civic associations, many middle-class citizens now rely on professionally run advocacy groups to speak on their behalf.[19]

In contrast to Putnam, some other scholars have documented growth in newer civic organizations, such as environmental groups and youth soccer leagues. Although membership in older groups such as Lions Clubs or Elks or Moose Lodges has unquestionably declined, other forms of volunteering have increased.[20] Social media also enable the formation of new political communities. With so many people engaging via online and other virtual (rather than face-to-face) interactions, even the meaning of *civic activism* is being transformed.[21]

Biases of Interest Representation

Not all societal interests are organized and represented in the pressure group system. Organizations do not necessarily emerge just because people share a common policy goal or political interest. Economist Mancur Olson Jr. famously analyzed the difficulties of organizing to bring about policy change.[22] Organizing requires time, energy, and money, and individuals know that the small contributions they can make usually will not be decisive or even important. If a group exists and successfully presses for policy changes, the benefits will spread beyond those who worked to bring about the results. If, for example, an environmental group successfully calls for clean-air regulations, urban residents will benefit from the reduced smog, regardless of whether they personally made any contribution to the group's efforts. As a consequence, individuals will prefer to free ride on the work of others.

The issue of the free rider is especially problematic for large groups, where failure to help with the collective effort is totally anonymous. According to Olson's analysis, organizing is easier for small groups with a strong material stake in policy outcomes. In small groups, social pressure can be effectively applied to discourage free riding. In some cases, a single individual or firm will bankroll the cost of organizing because it can benefit even while bearing the costs alone.

The free-rider problem is also less of an obstacle for the many groups that exist as a "by-product" of enterprises organized for other purposes. Businesses, for example, exist to make a profit. But businesses often elect to devote some share of their profits to subsidizing organizations that represent their political interests.

Under Olson's logic, the pressure group system should be tilted toward narrow economic interests that are easier to organize, and it should underrepresent broad public interests. Congress will thus receive more input from narrow groups with a financial stake in policy issues than from groups representing wider public concerns.

Consistent with this theory, there are indeed biases in the composition of the interest group universe. One survey found that business interests make up 72 percent of all groups having Washington representation.[23] The composition of the interest group world also reflects economic inequality. Put simply, it takes money to create and sustain organized interests, so groups representing the well off are more likely to emerge and survive. As political scientist E. E. Schattschneider famously put it, "the flaw in the pluralist heaven is that the heavenly chorus sings with a strong upper-class accent."[24] Frank Baumgartner, a political scientist who was part of a group that studied the lobbying community over a ten-year period, underscored how the poor and less well off are disadvantaged in having their issues advocated on Capitol Hill. "The biggest indictment of the lobbying community is that it amplifies the voice of those who already have the most resources in society and leaves the people with the greatest needs completely voiceless."[25]

The well off and the well educated in U.S. society participate more in politics than the less fortunate, and lawmakers hear disproportionately from them. In her

BOX 13-1 SOME THEORIES ON INTEREST GROUP FORMATION

Scholars have suggested a number of theories to explain the development of interest groups. Special interests have long been a source of fascination, in part because of their ability to influence policy making even though they may not reflect majority sentiment within the country. The case of vocal minorities prevailing over apathetic or disengaged majorities rivets scholarly attention. The implication is that organized interests are more powerful than unorganized interests. Among the various theories of group formation are the following:

- The proliferation hypothesis suggests that as society becomes more complex and interdependent, groups naturally form to reflect the country's intricate array of issues and entities. As new conditions, issues, or forces emerge, new groups are formed to reflect or respond to these developments. "The reasoning behind the proliferation hypothesis is straightforward: groups need a clientele from which to draw members."[1]

- The disturbance hypothesis posits a stable equilibrium among groups. If something disturbs the equilibrium, such as war, technological innovations, or the emergence of new concerns (such as, global warming, school shootings, opioid crisis), then new groups emerge. As two scholars wrote, "Groups organize politically when the existing order is disturbed and certain interests are, in turn, helped or hurt." As an example, they note, "Mobilization of business interests since the 1960s often has resulted from threats posed by consumer advocates and environmentalists, as well as requirements imposed by the steadily growing role of the federal government."[2]

- The exchange hypothesis states that groups form because of the efforts of "entrepreneurs." The argument asserts that "group organizers invest in a set of benefits which they offer to potential members at a price—joining the group. Benefits may be material [private gains], solidarity [camaraderie], or expressive [the reward of belonging to a group with shared values and causes]."[3]

[1]Scott H. Ainsworth, *Analyzing Interest Groups* (New York: W. W. Norton and Co., 2002), 40.

[2]Alan J. Cigler and Burdett A. Loomis, eds., *Interest Group Politics*, 6th ed. (Washington, DC: CQ Press, 2002), 8. See also David B. Truman, *The Governmental Process*, 2nd ed. (New York: Knopf, 1971).

[3]Robert Salisbury, "An Exchange Theory of Interest Groups," *Midwest Journal of Political Science* (February 1969): 1–32.

analysis of legislator–constituent interactions in health care policy, Kristina C. Miler discovered that legislators' perceptions of their constituencies were systematically distorted by the fact that they and their offices interacted so much more frequently with resource-rich groups.[26] The rich and poor are interested in different things. The advantaged talk about taxes, government spending, and social issues, whereas the disadvantaged are primarily concerned about "basic human needs . . . [food], jobs, housing, and health."[27] Elected officials are inundated with messages from groups that represent the politically active (such as the elderly, veterans, and small-business owners). But lawmakers receive comparatively little information about the policy preferences of the needy, who are often only marginally engaged in civic life.

An example of this political reality occurred following the *sequester,* a series of across-the-board spending cuts imposed as a consequence of the Budget Control Act of 2011. One immediate result of these indiscriminate fiscal reductions was nationwide flight delays as numerous air traffic controllers were furloughed from their jobs. Powerful interests—the airlines, businesses, and an angry traveling public—lobbied Congress to get the furloughed controllers back to work. The result was this: A month after the sequester took effect, a law was enacted that ended the furloughs of the air traffic personnel. As a House member noted, "When you [vote for sequester exceptions], what happens is the most politically strong groups with the most lobbyists get relief, at the expense of everybody else. Meals on Wheels, or kids on Head Start, or grants on biomedical research—all of those get left behind."[28]

PRESSURE GROUP METHODS

Pressure groups employ a variety of techniques to influence Congress's decisions. These methods have not always been ethical. Bribes and corruption have periodically fueled public outrage. During the nation's early technological and industrial expansion, railroad interests lobbied for federal funds and land grants to build their routes. Some of these early lobbyists' methods rightfully inspired public ire. In 1874, Sen. Simon Cameron, R-Pa., described an honest politician as one who "when he is bought, stays bought."[29] Samuel Ward, the "king of the lobby" for fifteen years after the Civil War, wrote to his friend Henry Wadsworth Longfellow:

> When I see you again I will tell you how a client, eager to prevent the arrival at a committee of a certain member before it should adjourn, offered me $5,000 to accomplish this purpose, which I did, by having [the member's] boots mislaid while I smoked a cigar and condoled with him until they could be found at 11:45. I had the satisfaction of a good laugh [and] a good fee in my pocket.[30]

But the legislator–lobbyist connection is a two-way street. It is a mistake to envision the relationship as only involving pressure from one direction. Reverse lobbying is pervasive. Lawmakers lobby the lobbyists to achieve their policy priorities.[31] In 2009, for example, Senate Republican leader Mitch McConnell reportedly urged the National Rifle Association to oppose the nomination of Sonia Sotomayor to the U.S. Supreme Court. McConnell knew that NRA opposition would put pressure on conservative Democrats and any Republicans leaning toward support of Sotomayor.[32] Members also try to persuade key groups that are on the fence to back their proposals or at least not publicly oppose them. The passage, in 2003, of a major prescription drug benefit for Medicare enrollees was facilitated by Speaker J. Dennis Hastert's wooing of AARP. Seven years later, congressional Democrats and President Obama succeeded in obtaining AARP's backing for the Affordable Care Act.

Given this interdependence, members and leaders actively reach out to organized interests rather than just passively waiting for group input. For example, House and Senate Democratic leaders and aides schedule regular meetings with their lobbying allies, such as labor unions.[33] The chair of the Senate Democratic Steering and Outreach Committee works "hand in hand with outside advocacy groups to raise public support for bills on the Democratic agenda."[34] Similarly, congressional GOP leaders and their top aides regularly consult with business lobbyists to formulate goals and strategy.[35]

Lobbying relationships have evolved in variety and sophistication. Modern-day lobbying varies according to the nature and visibility of the issue and groups' resources. Among the most important practices are direct and social lobbying, coalitions, grassroots mobilization, and electronic advocacy.

Direct Lobbying

In the traditional method of direct lobbying, lobbyists present their clients' cases directly to members and congressional staff. When a group hires a prominent lawyer or lobbyist, such as Haley Barbour, Ken Duberstein, Heather Podesta, Tom Daschle, or Steve Elmendorf, the direct approach involves personal contact with senators or representatives. An aide to Speaker Thomas P. "Tip" O'Neill Jr., D-Mass. (1977–1987), explained the importance of the personal touch:

[Lobbyists] know members of Congress are here three nights a week, alone, without their families. So they . . . [s]chmooze with them. Make friends. And they don't lean on it all the time. Every once in a while, they call up—maybe once or twice a year [to] ask a few questions. . . . Anne Wexler [a former official in the Carter White House, and later a lobbyist] will call up and spend half an hour talking about . . . politics, and suddenly she'll pop a question, pick up something. They want that little bit of access. That's what does it. You can hear it. It clicks home. They'll call their chief executive officer, and they've delivered. That's how it works. It's not illegal. They work on a personal basis.[36]

Former members of Congress are particularly effective at direct lobbying. A retired twenty-year House member wrote to prospective clients that he could "unravel red tape, open doors, make appointments, work with the Administration or government agencies, influence legislation, and assist in any other service required."[37] Recognizing their value, lobbying firms and clients eagerly enlist the services of former lawmakers. "Each member is part of a network of reciprocity," observed scholar James A. Thurber. "You help me, and I'll help you. That's what a lobbying client is buying."[38]

Member-to-member lobbying can be uniquely effective. No outsider has the same access to lawmakers (and certain precincts of Capitol Hill) that former colleagues have. For example, former GOP senators who may be lobbyists can attend the regularly scheduled Tuesday Republican Policy Committee lunch, "where legislative tactics are plotted on issues ranging from tax cuts to foreign policy—information that gives them a decided edge over other lobbyists."[39] Former representative Jack Kingston, R-Ga. (1993–2015), explained the special advantage of lobbying as a former member. "Policy wonks and knowledgeable people are out there," he said. "The question is, can you get a door opened?"[40] Although ethics rules impose restrictions on the former lawmakers (for example, they may not lobby their colleagues while in the chamber and must wait a year after leaving Congress before actively lobbying), former members still retain privileges denied to others. The longer former members have been out of Congress, however, the fewer personal contacts they have with current lawmakers. Turnover in Congress will render many lobbyists' networks obsolete.

Former top Capitol Hill staff aides are similarly sought after as lobbyists because of their personal knowledge and understanding of key members and congressional processes.[41] The ease with which members and staff rotate from congressional service into lobbying is often referred to as the *revolving door.* According to an analysis by *The Atlantic:* "Of the nearly four dozen lawmakers who left office after the 2016 election, one-fourth stayed in Washington, and one in six became lobbyists."[42] "The Congress-to-K Street connection has been institutionalized," observed Sheila Krumholz of the nonpartisan Center for Responsive Politics. "It's Plan A for former members of Congress."[43] The revolving door also comes full circle in that many former lobbyists also return to take high-ranking staff jobs on Capitol Hill.[44]

A new type of lobbyist is also much sought after these days: the experienced fund-raiser. The talents that some fund-raisers bring to lobbying were summarized as follows:

> The hiring equation for lobby firms is simple: Campaign fund-raisers spend time with lawmakers—often more than policy staffers. They also have the kinds of connections with CEOs and in-house government relations heads that could mean more business for the lobby shop. And they are comfortable making "the ask," not only to sign clients but also to try to get members of Congress and staff to take action on behalf of clients.[45]

Direct lobbying involves many activities beyond meeting with lawmakers. Lobbyists monitor committees; testify (or have their clients appear as witnesses) at hearings; interpret Hill decisions for clients; articulate clients' interests to legislators; draft legislation, speeches, and "Dear Colleague" letters for members; and give campaign assistance. The House offers more occasions for contacting members directly than does the Senate, where lobbyists are more likely to target staff aides.

Taken together, lobbyists are major players in congressional policy making. Members rely heavily on them for information. "[Lobbyists] provide continuity and institutional memory," observed former representative and current lobbyist James P. Moran, D-Va. (1991–2015). "Most of them have been around longer than members."[46] Or as a GOP senator put it, "I would have to say the best information I get in the legislative process comes from people directly involved in the industry that is going to be affected—and from people who represent them: the 'nefarious' lobbyists."[47] "Most members may know one or two issues well, if that," said one financial services lobbyist. "Then you have a 26-year-old kid, maybe he's even 30 and went to a good law school, who's on the staff working 10 hours a day and is supposed to tell his boss how to do derivatives regulation or credit-card reform. Are you kidding?"[48]

Social Lobbying

Lobbying also occurs in social settings, outside the legislative context, such as at dinner parties, receptions, sporting and entertainment events, or on the golf course or tennis court. Successful direct lobbying is grounded in trust.[49] Lobbyists must convince lawmakers that they are credible and knowledgeable before lawmakers will accept advice from or even listen to them. Social interactions are extremely useful for fostering and developing the personal relationships that lobbyists need to be effective. Lobbyists thus seek out opportunities to interact casually with lawmakers, even when no client business will be discussed.

Travel with members of Congress long afforded opportunities for lobbyists to engage in social lobbying, but recent ethics laws have placed restrictions on the practice. Before the 2007 ethics rules were in place, it was not unusual, for example, for legislators to accept flights on corporate jets, reimbursing their sponsors only for the cost of commercial airfare. Now registered lobbyists "may not accompany lawmakers or aides 'on any segment' of a trip."[50] Ethics rules imposed other restrictions on social lobbying, as well. Lobbyists are not permitted to pay for meals for legislators, banning the lobbyist-funded lavish dinners that were the source of so much public distaste. There is, however, the "reception exception" or the "toothpick rule," which permits "members and aides to [eat] food [on toothpicks] at receptions, but bans them from attending sit-down meals with lobbyists."[51] As one lobbyist hosting a reception for legislators ruefully put it, "I'm sitting here as vice president of corporate affairs for the National Association of Manufacturers, and I'm making sure that there's nothing you need a fork for."[52] Members and aides may also attend lobbyist-paid events when carrying out "official duties" and when more than twenty-five people not connected with Congress are in attendance.

A large loophole in all of these ethics rules involves political fund-raising. Social and direct lobbying is unrestricted at campaign events. Many fund-raising events such as golf outings, fishing trips, and sit-down dinners offer wide-open opportunities for casual interactions with lawmakers. For example, Heather Podesta hosted a dinner at her home for five Democratic female senators. The fee for attendees, who, in return, were given a chance to discuss issues with the senators in a private setting, was $30,400 for a "co-chair" of the event, $10,000 for a "vice chair," $5,000 for a "co-host," and $1,000 for an "individual sponsor." Checks, said Podesta, were to be made payable to the Democratic Senatorial Campaign Committee (DSCC).[53] Lawmakers can continue to invite lobbyists to attend "lavish birthday parties in a lawmaker's honor ($1,000 a lobbyist), weekend golf tournaments ($2,500 and up), a Presidents Day weekend at Disney World ($5,000), or parties in South Beach in Miami ($5,000)."[54] Lobbyists end up paying for such events because "they pay a political fund-raising committee set up by the lawmaker. In turn, the committee pays the legislator's way."[55] In short, what is illegal if done directly—such as paying for legislators' meals, travel, or gifts—is legal if done indirectly through campaign contributions.

Coalition Lobbying

To enhance their chances of success, lobbyists often construct coalitions in support of their legislative initiatives. Coalitions bring more resources, contacts, and money to lobbying efforts. When individuals and organizations "band together and support one another," noted former senator John B. Breaux, D-La. (1987–2005), now a Washington lobbyist, it makes for "a smoother and more effective [legislative] operation than if fifty or more voices [are] all arguing for the same principle without any coordination."[56] Examples of such coalitions abound. Dozens of major technology sector companies came together in 2017 as the Coalition for the American Dream to urge Congress and the president to enact legislation allowing the Dreamers—undocumented immigrants brought to the United States as children—to obtain permanent resident status.[57] In 2009, the Pharmaceutical Research and Manufacturers of America (PhRMA) worked successfully with a variety of technology and financial interests to push for more favorable tax treatment of corporate income earned overseas. A study by researchers at the University of Kansas determined that this single tax break earned companies $220 for every dollar they spent lobbying on the issue, "a 22,000 percent rate of return on their investment."[58]

"We have no permanent friends or permanent enemies—only permanent interests." That oft-repeated line helps to explain why "coalitions, like politics, make strange bed fellows."[59] A coalition between the American Petroleum Institute and the Environmental Working Group to fight subsidies to ethanol offers one example. As the head of the environmental group observed, "This is not a sign of any great, broad alliance with the oil industry."[60] Not surprisingly, these marriages of convenience are often difficult to sustain.

Grassroots Lobbying

Instead of contacting members directly, many organizations mobilize citizens in districts and states across the country to pressure their senators and representatives. For example, when eBay, the online auction website, wanted to influence federal telecommunications policy so that phone and cable companies could not favor certain types of Web traffic at the expense of others, it sent an email to more than a million eBay users urging them to contact their members of Congress in support of *network neutrality.*[61] Similarly, Uber aggressively employs its large base of smartphone-wielding customers to pressure government officials.[62] One researcher estimated grassroots lobbying as a "$1-billion-a-year industry."[63]

Interest groups work to activate public opinion on issues and generate communications to members' offices. In addition to older tools, such as email and phone banks, social media has become a particularly valuable tool for this purpose. Interest groups can employ social media to reach supporters and stakeholders who will then, in turn, raise concerns directly to lawmakers. Although lawmakers recognize that lobbying groups orchestrate these campaigns, they also realize they may serve as a rough measure of sentiment and organizational strength behind an issue:

> The congressman has to care that somebody out there in his district has enough power to get hundreds of people to sit down and write a postcard or a letter—because if the guy can get them to do that, he might be able to influence them in other ways. So, a member has no choice but to pay attention. It's suicide if he doesn't.[64]

Lawmakers often try to distinguish between genuine grassroots and fake grassroots (often called "Astroturf") groups. Many so-called grassroots groups are nothing more than front organizations for their financial backers. One group with an environmentally friendly name, the Save Our Species Alliance, was actually pushing "a rewrite of the Endangered Species Act to ease paper and logging business's access to federal lands where those species live."[65] An attractive name can often be a way for a single interest to bankroll an initiative while masking its identity. At times, members may accuse a grassroots lobbying effort of being orchestrated from above; some Republicans beset by protesters defending the Affordable Care Act at town hall meetings in 2017 claimed—with scant evidence—that paid outside agitators were stacking the sessions.

Mass mobilizations have become so common that some firms now specialize in *grass tops lobbying.* Whereas the goal of grassroots lobbying is to mobilize the masses, the goal of grass tops lobbying "is to figure out to whom a member of Congress cannot say no: his chief donor, his campaign manager, a political mentor. The lobbyist then tries to persuade that person to take his client's side" during talks with the lawmaker.[66]

Digital Lobbying

As in most other areas of life, advances in communication technology have transformed lobbyists' work. Smartphones, tablets, and other devices allow lobbyists sitting in a congressional hearing room or office to instantly send out alerts on legislative developments to clients, coalition partners, and their home offices.

Similarly, text messaging, email, and social networking sites such as Twitter, YouTube, and Facebook have all greatly increased the speed with which organized interests can galvanize supporters. For example, a debate over how to deal with online piracy and file sharing triggered, according to one account, the "biggest online protest in history," resulting in 10 million petition signatures, 3 million emails, and 100,000 telephone calls to lawmakers.[67] Social media also allow constituents to communicate to members' offices. Interest groups spur constituents to comment on legislators' Facebook pages or respond to lawmakers on Twitter. Staffers in members' offices, in turn, closely monitor their boss's social media presence, relaying constituent comments and feedback directly to the member.[68] As a result, these sites have emerged as an important portal for member–constituent communications and thereby as a point of interest group access.

The ease, speed, and low cost of digital communications allows interest groups to convey messages immediately to sympathizers anywhere in the country to bring pressure to bear when and where it is most needed. One of the most influential of all lobbying groups, the National Rifle Association, draws much of its political clout from its ability to generate an outpouring of communications to members' offices. According to Sen. Charles Schumer, D-N.Y., the NRA can mobilize "2, 3, 4 million people who care passionately about this issue . . . at the drop of a hat," without facing similar intense and sustained grassroots activism that backs additional gun control legislation.[69]

GROUPS AND THE ELECTORAL CONNECTION

Today, it is often hard to differentiate the roles of interest groups and political parties in electoral politics. "The standard distinction between interest groups and parties used to be that parties were committed to winning elections and that pressure groups let elections happen and then tried to influence the people who got elected," remarked a political scientist. "Now interest groups through their PACs [political action committees] and a variety of other methods are very much involved in the pre-policy arena."[70] As one example, the grassroots operation of the U.S. Chamber of Commerce "has begun to rival those of the major political parties."[71] Unions also train workers to make them more effective advocates, organizers, and potential candidates for elective office.

Some groups are so extensively involved in partisan electoral politics that they are effectively *party allies*—a vital part of their party's "enduring multilayered coalition," in the words of Paul S. Herrnson.[72] For Democrats, group allies include labor unions, environmental and women's rights organizations, and liberal membership groups, such as MoveOn.org. For Republicans, allied groups include the U.S. Chamber of Commerce, pro-life and pro-gun organizations, oil and gas interests, and conservative ideological groups, such as the Club for Growth. Between elections, congressional party leaders and their allied interest groups cooperate to promote their party's message, enhance its public image, and advance its agenda.

Interest groups help elect members to Congress in three principal ways: They raise funds and make financial contributions through PACs; they conduct their own, independent campaigns for or against issues and candidates; and they rate the voting records of legislators.

Groups and Campaign Fund-Raising

Legislators who dislike raising money—almost certainly a majority of them—turn to lobbyists or professional fund-raisers to arrange parties, luncheons, dinners, or other social events to which admission is charged. Lobbyists buy tickets or supply lists of people who should be invited. They even serve as treasurers of members' reelection campaigns or PACs.[73]

Congressional critics—and even legislators and lobbyists themselves—question the propriety of fund-raising practices. A recent study shows that groups that make campaign contributions have an easier time obtaining access to members of Congress. In a field experiment conducted by Joshua L. Kalla and David E. Broockman, local campaign contributors sought to obtain meetings on a legislative issue with members of Congress in 191 congressional districts.[74] The study randomly assigned whether the legislative offices were informed that individuals who would attend the meetings were *local campaign donors* or *local constituents*. When the attendees were revealed to be donors, they obtained access to high-level congressional staffers at three times the rate of attendees who were described as only constituents. Even members of Congress themselves worry about implied obligations when they accept help or money from groups. For their part, lobbyists resent pressure from members to give repeatedly.

Bundling is a widely used fund-raising technique that allows lobbyists and fund-raising entities to raise more money for candidates than they can contribute individually under campaign finance laws. PACs, for example, are limited to giving a candidate $5,000 for use in the primary and general election. There are no limits, however, on "how much a PAC can forward to candidates from other donors."[75] To bundle, a lobbyist or another type of fund-raiser will solicit checks from various sources and then give them all at once to a candidate's campaign committee or to the House and Senate party campaign committees. The candidate knows the bundler's identity because the checks are submitted to the campaign together or, in some cases, because the checks contain identifying information. Lobbyists are not "bundling this cash for altruistic reasons," said the president of a nonpartisan election watchdog group. "They want to get the [lawmakers'] attention and interest."[76]

Groups and Advocacy Campaigns

Interest groups are heavily involved in elections. Incumbents must contend with opposing interests as well as other candidates. Labor unions, for example, spent $60.4 million directly supporting federal candidates in the lead-up to the 2018 elections. But they spent considerably more ($91.6 million) during this period on getting out the vote, persuading union members to support certain candidates, and so on. Such political-mobilization efforts are not required to be reported to the Federal Election Commission.[77] Numerous other groups spend considerable amounts targeting voters in selected states or districts, urging them to vote for or against certain candidates. Here are a couple: The U.S. Chamber of Commerce spent more than $15.5 million on the 2018 elections, and the National Rifle Association spent more than $10 million.[78]

Rating Legislators

About a hundred groups keep pressure on members of Congress by issuing "report cards" on their voting records. Groups select a number of major issues and then publicize members' scores (on a scale of zero to one hundred) based on their "right" or "wrong" votes. Members are often warned by colleagues that certain votes will be scored. "You'll hear this as you walk into the chamber: 'This is going to be a scored vote. The environmentalists are going to score this vote, or the AFL-CIO is going to score this vote,'" explained a House member.[79] Congressional aides sometimes check with lobbying groups to determine whether certain votes will be scored.

To be sure, advocacy groups are not reluctant to announce that they will be grading lawmakers on certain votes. Lawmakers who sign pledges, such as the Taxpayer Protection Pledge, are certain to have their votes monitored closely by outside organizations for any deviations from their promises. If pledges are violated, such as voting for tax hikes, members might face a primary challenge in the next election.[80] Interest groups use scorecards to influence members' decisions on selected issues. The liberal Americans for Democratic Action and the conservative Heritage Action issue score-based ratings that are well known and widely used. The ratings game, however, is always simplistic. The selected votes are often inadequate to judge a member's full record because they are identified with an agenda in mind. Group strategists defend ratings as a means of holding lawmakers accountable and "a shorthand way for voters to tell something about their congressman."[81] After creating these scorecards, interest groups may assign attention-getting names to Congress members who score high or low, such as the "dirty dozen" (from the League of Conservation Voters).

Groups use legislative scorecards to determine which candidates will win endorsement and receive campaign contributions. Interest groups may also canvass door to door in certain areas "to talk to voters about the results" of their scorecards.[82] Incumbents vulnerable to electoral or primary defeat, mindful of the two Congresses, will cast votes carefully to avoid antagonizing powerful interest groups back home. On the other hand, members may also use negative scores in their campaigns. A liberal lawmaker, for example, might "wear bad scores from conservative groups like a badge of honor."[83]

GROUPS, LOBBYING, AND LEGISLATIVE POLITICS

How much influence do organized interests wield over congressional legislation? The U.S. public is convinced that their sway is excessive. Large majorities of survey respondents agree with the statement, "Congress is too heavily influenced by interest groups."[84] Political science research, by contrast, offers no such clarity on this question.[85] But one conclusion is clear: The results of empirical research do not support sweeping populist characterizations of Congress as bought and paid for by moneyed interests. A group of political scientists who examined ninety-eight issues over a ten-year period found that the side with the most PAC donations, lobbyists, money, and members won only half of the time. They concluded, "A better predictor than money in winning or killing legislation was the support of government agency heads, congressmen-turned-lobbyists, high-level congressional and government officials—and best of all—party leaders and the president."[86] The study also pointed out that it is always difficult even for well-resourced interests to change policy because of numerous veto points in the legislative process and the fact that there are usually "people benefiting from the status quo."[87]

The Role of Money

Journalists and campaign reform groups often posit a direct linear correlation between members' votes and the amounts they have received from various groups. Scholarly researchers reject such simple cause-and-effect inferences. Simply correlating the campaign contributions legislators receive with their voting behavior ignores the possibility that members might just as well have voted as they did without any group influence or campaign contributions. Instead, it is necessary to determine whether lawmakers vote differently than we would have expected given their party, ideology, and constituency. The more careful research designs used by scholars frequently fail to find any causal connection between PAC contributions and members' votes.[88] As the manager of a corporate PAC pointed out, money is "only one tool. We use it to defeat people who do not agree with us and elect those who do. I wish we could just 'buy' votes, but we can't. That's not the way it works in the real world."[89]

Rather than altering members' voting behavior, the principal finding of empirical research on interest group behavior is that lobbyists tend to donate to members who are already friendly to their objectives. Labor unions, for example, donate the bulk of their funds to Democrats.[90] Similarly, oil and gas interests contribute primarily to Republicans.[91] Generally speaking, groups do not regard donating to their legislative opponents as a good investment of their campaign money.[92] Furthermore, with the proliferation of interest groups and PACs, candidates have many different groups to which they can turn for fund-raising help. No single group is likely to exert overwhelming financial leverage over any given member of Congress.

In short, the patterns in campaign contributing simply do not conform to crude vote-buying theories. The relationship between lobbyists and legislators rarely resembles a simple economic exchange of money for support. Contributions signal and reinforce a relationship more often than they create one. The influence of money must be weighed along with other considerations influencing members' votes, including constituency pressures, party ties, friendships, personal conscience, idiosyncrasies, and prejudices. As former representative Barney Frank, D-Mass., put it, "Votes will beat money any day. Any politician forced to choose between his campaign contributions and strong public sentiment is going to vote public sentiment. Campaign contributions are fungible, you can get new ones. You can't get new voters."[93]

The enormous sums that interest groups spend on political campaigns undoubtedly affect legislative politics and policy making. Contributions clearly do buy access to legislators. "There is no question—if you give a lot of money, you will get a lot of access. All you have to do is send in the check," explained one corporate executive.[94] On issues that are less visible to the public and where the bulk of money is on one side, there is good reason to think that the playing field will be tilted in favor of those with financial clout. Nevertheless, the linkages between money and policy making are not simple or easy to trace. Under the right circumstances, organized interests can reframe issues, sway members, mobilize support, or demobilize opposition, but there is very little evidence that organized interests are able to convert outright opponents.[95]

Lobbying and Legislation

An open, decentralized institution, Congress presents lobbyists with numerous opportunities to shape the fate of legislation. Groups play a direct or indirect part throughout the congressional process—in individual members' work, committee activities, legislative agenda setting, and floor decision making. Nevertheless, tracing the nature and extent of lobbyists' influence on legislation is no less difficult than untangling the relationship between campaign contributions and lawmaking.

Just as organized interests contribute primarily to their legislative allies, lobbyists also spend most of their time with friendly legislators. Lobbyists rarely target their opponents in Congress; nor do they generally devote significant effort to trying to influence fence-sitters.[96] Instead, they work with lawmakers who share their policy views—providing them with appropriate information, data, and political intelligence that they can perhaps use to persuade wavering colleagues.

Along these lines, many organized interests have ties to sympathetic informal congressional groups. For example, the steel industry maintains links with the Steel Caucus and textile manufacturers with the Textile Caucus. Interest groups are often instrumental in organizing congressional caucuses. These outside organizations assist in setting agendas for caucus meetings. They also help their caucus allies by providing information, research reports, and legislative recommendations.[97] They also sponsor events where lobbyists can mingle with lawmakers.[98]

More broadly, the relationship between lobbyists and legislators is better understood as a *legislative subsidy* than as a simple exchange in which legislators trade policy for political support.[99] Legislators benefit from the help of lobbyists because successful legislating requires so much work and expertise. Lobbyists' primary role is to underwrite the efforts of their legislative allies. Lobbyists provide their congressional supporters with information, legislative language, policy analysis, useful arguments, and political advice. Working with friendly legislators, lobbyists steer policy toward their clients' goals, exerting influence that, in practice, is hard to distinguish from legislators' own policy preferences.

The value of lobbyists to legislators thus extends far beyond campaign contributions. "Essentially, we operate as an extension of congressmen's staff," explained one lobbyist. "Occasionally we come up with the legislation, or speeches—and questions [for lawmakers to ask at hearings]. . . . We look at it as providing staff work for allies."[100]

Lobbyists' information and expertise are thus one of their most valuable assets. A survey conducted by the American League of Lobbyists revealed that lobbyists rated delivering "good information/analysis" as the most effective way to influence a lawmaker.[101] As one lobbyist said, "You have to be armed with facts, precedents and legal points. Sure it's a political environment, but it's much more substantive. The old-style, pat-'em-on-the-back lobbyist is gone, or at least going."[102] Lobbying is substantive because Washington is a town filled with experts and saturated with data, analyses, and reports on all sides of an issue. The result is this: "Facts compete in Washington, just like Democrats and Republicans."[103]

Subgovernments

Many congressional committees deal with policies of concern to specific groups, such as farmers, teachers, or veterans. Lawmakers whose constituencies contain many members of these groups tend to seek seats on the relevant committees.[104] Members from farming areas seek assignment to the agriculture committees; members from states with many users of federal lands (such as ranchers and miners) seek assignment to the natural resources committees. Such committees often form alliances with the bureaucrats and lobbyists who regularly testify before them and with whom members and staff aides frequently meet. At hearings before the House or Senate veterans' affairs committees, for example, the triple alliance is on public view. In attendance are the committee members, along with witnesses from various veterans' organizations (such as the American Legion) and executive officials from the Department of Veterans Affairs. Scholars and journalists use the term *subgovernment* or *iron triangle* for the three-way policy-making alliances of committees, executive agencies, and interest groups.

These cozy, mutually beneficial relationships dominate policy making less today than in the past. Other contending forces (citizens' groups, aggressive journalists, and assertive presidents) have ended their policy monopoly. Term-limited committee chairs also have less time and incentive to cultivate ties with external constituencies.

Still, there is evidence that iron triangles remain influential in various policy domains. A description of such alliances was provided by former defense secretary Robert Gates in a 2009 speech echoing President Eisenhower's 1961 farewell address warning against a *military-industrial complex:*

> First, there is Congress, which is understandably concerned . . . about protecting jobs in certain states and congressional districts. There is the defense and aerospace industry, which has an obvious financial stake in the survival and growth of these programs. And there is the institutional military itself—within the Pentagon, and as expressed through an influential network of retired generals and admirals.[105]

This phenomenon, stated Sen. John McCain, R-Ariz., "should now rightly be called the military–industrial–congressional complex."[106]

REGULATION OF LOBBYING

For more than a hundred years, Congress intermittently considered ways to regulate lobbying—a right protected by the First Amendment's free speech principle and "the right of the people . . . to petition the Government for a redress of grievances." Not until 1946 did Congress enact its first comprehensive lobbying law, the Federal Regulation of Lobbying Act (Title III of the Legislative Reorganization Act). The ineffectiveness of this law finally led to passage of the Lobby Disclosure Act of 1995.[107] In 2007, Congress enacted another major lobbying reform measure, the Honest Leadership and Open Government Act. In general, there have been three main statutory approaches to the regulation of lobbying: defining and prohibiting abusive practices, requiring registration for lobbyists, and providing for disclosure of lobbyists' activities.[108]

The 1946 Lobbying Law

The main objective of the 1946 act was public disclosure of lobbying activities. Persons trying to influence Congress were required to register with the clerk of the House or the secretary of the Senate and to report quarterly the amounts of money they received and spent for lobbying. The law's drafters stressed registration and reporting to enable Congress to evaluate information according to its source:

> The availability of information regarding organized groups and full knowledge of their expenditures for influencing legislation, their membership and the source of contributions to them of large amounts of money, would prove helpful to Congress in evaluating their representations without impairing the rights of any individual or group freely to express its opinion to the Congress.[109]

The lobby law soon proved ineffective. In 1954, the Supreme Court upheld its constitutionality, but the decision (*United States v. Harriss*) significantly weakened the law.[110] First, the Court said that only lobbyists paid to represent someone else must register—exempting lobbyists who spent their own money. Second, the Court held that registration applied only to persons whose "principal purpose" was to influence legislation. As a result, many trade associations, labor unions, professional organizations, consumer groups, and law firms avoided registering because lobbying was not their principal activity. Some lobbyists claimed immunity from the law on the pretext that their job was to inform, not influence, legislators. Finally, the Court held that the act applied only to lobbyists who contacted members directly. This interpretation excluded indirect lobbying activities that, for example, generated grassroots pressure on Congress.

Lawmakers tried repeatedly to plug the 1946 law's loopholes. These attempts foundered largely because it was difficult to regulate lobbying without trespassing on citizens' rights to contact their elected representatives. After repeated efforts to "change the way Washington does business"—a campaign theme that many members advocated—the two parties finally came together to enact the first major overhaul of the 1946 act.

The Lobby Disclosure Act of 1995

The Lobby Disclosure Act of 1995 applied new rules to individuals and firms that lobby Congress and senior executive branch officials. The law broadened the definition of those who must register as lobbyists to include all those who spend at least one-fifth of their time trying to influence lawmakers, congressional aides, or high-level executive officials and who are paid $5,000 or more over a six-month period. Registrations of lobbyists quickly soared.

A study by the Government Accountability Office showed that the number of registered lobbyists more than doubled after the 1995 act went into effect.[111] But the number of registered lobbyists began to fall after 2006.[112] This decline did not necessarily reflect a reduction in the number of people engaged in lobbying. As with the 1946 act, organized interests learned how to exploit loopholes in the 1995 regulations and thus to avoid registering.[113] James Thurber's research suggests that the true number of working lobbyists is closer to 100,000.[114]

Although the 1995 lobby law was an improvement over the old one, it was minimally enforced. A 2005 report by the Center for Public Integrity concluded that the disclosure system was in disarray.[115] Former representative Lee H. Hamilton, D-Ind., described the situation as a lobby disclosure system in name only.[116]

The Honest Leadership and Open Government Act of 2007

Congress revisited issues related to lobbying again in the 110th Congress (2007–2009). Public attention had focused on ethics reform as a result of the Jack Abramoff bribery scandal (2005–2006), which resulted in the convictions of numerous high-ranking officials and staffers, including one member of Congress. Democrats made "draining the swamp" on Capitol Hill a major theme of the November 2006 elections, in which they won majority control of both chambers.[117] Following the elections, Democratic leaders made ethics and lobbying reform a top priority.

Some of the most notable provisions of the 2007 ethics reforms are highlighted in Box 13-2. Allegations of ethical violations are handled by each chamber's ethics committee; lobbying violations are under the purview of the Department of Justice. In March 2008, the House created an Office of Congressional Ethics (OCE), composed of eight private citizens. The OCE may investigate any alleged rules violations by members and report their findings to the House Committee on Ethics for further review. OCE reports are eventually made public, even if the ethics panel chooses to dismiss the cases submitted to them.[118] The OCE's aggressive pursuit of ethics violations made it enemies on Capitol Hill. At the start of the 115th Congress in 2017, congressional Republicans sought to rein in the OCE by putting it under the control of the House Committee on Ethics, but bad headlines, public blowback, and a rebuke from President Trump led them to abandon the effort.[119]

Enforcement of the registration and disclosure requirements under the 1995 and 2007 laws still remains problematic. Some Washington insiders say, "I don't lobby" because they do not meet with lawmakers directly or spend more than 20 percent of their time over three months lobbying for a client.[120] A former Senate party leader does not register as a lobbyist even though he provides clients with lawmaking and other relevant advice. "I provide my clients with analysis, not access," he said.[121]

Foreign Lobbying

Regulations also require those who lobby on behalf of foreign governments and foreign-owned commercial enterprises to register with the Justice Department and file twice-yearly reports on their contacts with lawmakers and federal agencies. Although foreign lobbyists cannot make campaign contributions, one "in every $8 spent lobbying Congress and federal agencies comes from foreign governments."[122] Because of the role of the United States in the global economy and in military security, lobbyists who work for foreign governments and clients spend considerable amounts of time and money promoting their interests on Capitol Hill and with the

BOX 13-2 THE HONEST LEADERSHIP AND OPEN GOVERNMENT ACT OF 2007

Lobby Registration

The clerk of the House and the secretary of the Senate are required to make registration and disclosure forms available, in a searchable and suitable format, on the Internet for public inspection.

Lobbying Disclosure

Lobbyists must file quarterly reports for an electronic database, with a maximum fine of $200,000 for not complying.

Gifts, Meals, and Travel

Lobbyists may not give lawmakers or staff gifts, even those less than $50 in value, and they cannot pay for lawmakers' or staffers' meals or travel expenses.

Members and staff must receive advance approval from the appropriate ethics committee before accepting any travel with any private organization.

Revolving Door

Senators and very senior executive officials are prohibited from lobbying for two years after they leave government; House members are prohibited from lobbying for one year.

Senior staff members who leave Capitol Hill are prohibited from lobbying for one year.

All Senate staff members are prohibited from lobbying the member or committee for whom they worked for one year after leaving.

Campaign Contributions

Registered lobbyists have to reveal all of their political contributions, including bundling of contributions from friends and colleagues.

Lobbying the Executive Branch

Lobbyists who contact executive-branch officials, called *covered officials*, must register with the clerk of the House and secretary of the Senate and disclose their contacts and activities.

Source: Adapted from Jack Maskell, legislative attorney, "Lobbying Law and Ethics Rules Changes in the 110th Congress," Congressional Research Service Report RL34377, September 17, 2007.

broader citizenry. For example, Saudia Arabia significantly stepped up its lobbying expenditures during the Trump administration, in part to manage the fall-out from the assassination of *Washington Post* journalist Jamal Kashoggi in its Istanbul consulate.[123] During the Obama administration, several Washington firms lobbied for the Libyan rebels who led the successful revolt against dictator Muammar Gaddafi.[124]

Globalization of the world's economy also influences congressional lobbying. For example, although Toyota is a Japanese company, it gains political clout from having plants located in fifteen states. In lobbying against the Trump administration's proposed tariff on auto imports, Toyota released a statement touting itself as "an exemplar of the manufacturing might of America."[125] In a globalized economy, Toyota and other multinational corporations point to their U.S. investments and employees to bolster their lobbying efforts.

CONCLUSION

Since the nation's beginning, lobbying and lawmaking have been closely intertwined. Lobbying "has been so deeply woven into the American political fabric that one could, with considerable justice, assert that the history of lobbying comes close to being the history of American legislation."[126]

Contemporary Washington encompasses a vast array of organized groups pursuing their ends on Capitol Hill. In addition to the multitude of industry associations, there are numerous public-affairs lobbies, single-issue groups, PACs, and foreign agents engaged in the influence trade. Many of these groups employ grassroots mobilization and high-tech public-relations techniques. Many victories today are won in Washington because of sophisticated lobbying campaigns waged in home states or districts.

No one questions that groups and lobbyists have a rightful public role, but some aspects of lobbying warrant concern. Groups often push Congress to pass laws that benefit the wealthy few and not the many. Narrow interests can inflate disagreements and hinder compromise. They often misrepresent the voting records of legislators in their rating schemes and pour money into the campaigns of their allies (mainly incumbents). Lawmakers who defy single-issue groups find, at election time, that those organizations are bent on defeating them.

Built-in checks constrain group pressures, however. The immense number of organized interests enables legislators to play one competing group off against another. Knowledgeable staff aides also provide members with information to counter lobbyists' arguments. Lawmakers' own expertise is another informal check on lobbyists. Finally, there are self-imposed constraints. Lobbyists who misrepresent issues or mislead members soon find their access permanently closed off. As Rep. Barney Frank, D-Mass, explained, "I feel better about a position when I can hear from both sides. . . . You can use [lobbyists] to inform you, as long as they know that if they lie, they lose. They will never be allowed to come back to this office."[127]

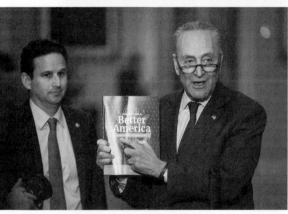

Copies of President Donald Trump's budget for Fiscal Year 2020 delivered to the House Budget Committee. Senate Minority Leader Chuck Schumer, D-N.Y., criticizes President Trump's FY 2020 budget during a question-and-answer session with reporters while Senator Brian Schatz of Hawaii looks on. House Ways and Means Chairman Richard Neal, D-Mass., questions Treasury Secretary Steve Mnuchin during a hearing as Representatives Kevin Brady, Tex., the ranking GOP member, and other panel members, such as John Lewis, D-Ga., listen and await their turn to ask questions.

CONGRESS, BUDGETS, AND DOMESTIC POLICY MAKING

"Dead on arrival" or "dead before arrival" is not about a burial or ordering a stuffed "teddy bear" from Amazon. It's how many lawmakers characterize the president's annual budget, especially if their party affiliation is different from the president's. When President Trump submitted the administration's yearly budget to Congress on March 11, 2019, the most senior Democratic senator, Patrick Leahy of Vermont, declared, "It is not worth the paper it is printed on."[1] Critical comments about presidential budgets have been common for decades because legislative–executive fiscal processes are filled with conflict, contention, and complexity, especially in today's partisan-charged environment.

Even when the president's budget is dismissed by lawmakers, it serves important purposes, such as framing the public debate, serving as a negotiating template, and sharpening areas of legislative–executive agreement and disagreement. Fundamentally, presidential budgets highlight the interests, values, and priorities of the administration. The budget indicates where the administration plans to make fiscal and policy commitments, identifying programs slated to grow, shrink, stay the same, or even be eliminated. Lawmakers, agency officials, interest groups, states and localities, and many other interested parties scour the chief executive's budget to discover its potential impact on their policy and organizational objectives.

President Trump's budget clearly revealed, said an expert, "that he's putting more money into defense, but there's devastating cuts to nondefense that people need to take a look at."[2] The Pentagon would receive a 5 percent increase to $750 billion while the domestic side of the budget would be cut 9 percent, including for departments such as Energy, Education, and Interior, among many others.[3] President Trump's record-high $4.7 trillion budget proposal recommends deep cuts in Medicare, Medicaid, and other health programs. (Recall that during the 2016 campaign trail he promised to protect these programs from cuts.) The president requested $8.6 billion to build a wall on the southern border, an increase from the $5.7 billion that Congress rejected, thereby precipitating a record-setting thirty-five day partial shutdown of the federal government. With 2020 elections underway, the president's budget recommends increases for programs that appeal to his electoral supporters, such as veterans, homeland security, or school vouchers.[4]

None of this is the final word, however. As Sen. Mike Enzi, R-Wyo., chair of the Budget Committee, declaimed: "I've said for decades now that the president's budget is a list of suggestions. Congress is in charge of budgeting."[5] Added Rep. John Yarmuth, D-Ky., chair of the House Budget Committee: "In terms of its ultimate impact, [the president's budget] doesn't have much relevance."[6] Congressional Democrats have very different policy priorities from the president's or many GOP lawmakers. Control of the 116th House means that Democratic legislators will have the largest say in determining for their chamber the appropriate spending levels for agencies and programs.

The "power of the purse" is arguably Congress's most important and powerful constitutional prerogative (to appropriate, borrow, and tax). As James Madison wrote in *Federalist No. 58:* "The power of the purse may, in fact, be regarded as the most complete and effectual weapon with which any constitution can arm the immediate representatives of the people, for obtaining redress of every grievance, and for carrying into effect every just and salutary measure." Madison also recognized that Congress's "power of the purse" engages the president given his constitutional power to veto legislation.

Plainly, conflicts about policies and the money to pay for them lie at the vortex of today's lawmaking process. This chapter will first provide a general overview of the policy-making process. It will then turn to a more detailed discussion of budgeting, which has increasingly come to dominate politics and policy making in Congress.

STAGES OF POLICY MAKING

Public policy is what the government says and does about perceived problems.[7] Policy making normally has four distinct stages: (1) setting the agenda, (2) formulating policy, (3) adopting policy, and (4) implementing policy.

Setting the Agenda

At the initial stage, public problems are spotted and moved onto the national agenda, which can be defined as "the list of subjects to which government officials and those around them are paying serious attention."[8] In a large, pluralistic country such as the United States, the national agenda, at any given moment, is extensive and vigorously debated.

How do problems move onto the agenda? Some emerge as a result of a crisis or an attention-grabbing event—an economic depression, a terrorist attack, a devastating hurricane or earthquake, a series of school shootings, or a high-visibility corruption scandal. For example, in February 2018, a devastating shooting in a high school in Parkland, Florida, led to renewed attention to gun control on the national political agenda. Other agenda items are occasioned by the gradual accumulation of knowledge—for example, rising awareness of an environmental hazard such as global warming. Still other agenda items represent the accumulation of past problems that no longer can be avoided or ignored, such as the safety of the nation's food supply and the crumbling infrastructure.

Agendas are also set in motion by political processes—election results (1964, 1994, 2010, 2016, and 2018 are good examples), turnover in Congress, or shifts in public opinion.[9] For example, the eighty-seven House GOP freshmen elected in 2010, backed by an assertive Tea Party movement, made cost cutting and downsizing government their top priorities. The 2016 election of Donald Trump and Republican majorities in Congress put a border wall with Mexico and new taxes on imports on the congressional agenda. The 2018 mid-term election returned the House to Democratic control. It also produced an activist and diverse class of freshman Democrats, many of whom support progressive policies, such as a "Green New Deal" to address climate change.

Agenda items are pushed by policy entrepreneurs—that is, people who are willing to invest their time and energy in promoting a particular issue. Many of Washington's think tanks and interest groups issue reports that seek to influence the economic, social, or foreign-policy agenda of the nation. Elected officials and their staffs or appointees are more likely to shape agendas than are career bureaucrats.[10] President Trump has used Twitter as a platform to push items of concern to him—such as his demand for a border wall—onto the agenda. Lawmakers are frequently policy entrepreneurs. Party and committee leaders are especially influential. But even rank-and-file members can play the role of entrepreneur. For example, Rep. Alexandria Ocasio-Cortez, who championed the Green New Deal, provoked public debate and won the support of lawmakers who support policy proposals to address global warming. Generally speaking, politicians gravitate toward issues that are visible, salient, and solvable. Tough, arcane, or controversial problems, such as entitlements, may be shunned or postponed because they arouse significant public controversy.

Global climate change is a good example of an issue that will be very difficult for Congress to deal with in a path-breaking way. The vast majority of climate scientists believe that continued high levels of carbon dioxide emissions will generate severe environmental consequences over the next several decades. These consequences likely include more frequent severe weather (e.g., hurricanes, droughts, and wildfires), coastal flooding as sea levels rise, and disruptions to food production. The policy solutions to address climate change are complex, however, and would require changes in national policy that impose real costs on energy producers (and likely consumers), along with international agreements that demand sacrifices by both developed and developing countries. Given that the immediate effects of climate change are not readily apparent to most voters today, forging a political consensus to take on the issue is difficult.[11] Indeed, this kind of creeping crisis is often difficult for members of Congress to grapple with, in part because of the two-Congresses dilemma. As conscientious lawmakers, members might want to forge long-term solutions. But as representatives of their constituents, they must respond to more immediate constituent concerns.

Formulating Policy

In the second stage of policy making, lawmakers and others discuss items on the political agenda and explore potential solutions. Members of Congress and their staffs play crucial roles by conducting hearings and writing committee reports. They are aided by the policy experts in executive agencies, interest groups, legislative support agencies, think tanks, universities, and private-sector organizations. Another term for this stage is *policy incubation,* which entails "keeping a proposal alive while it picks up support, or waits for a better climate, or while a consensus begins to form."[12] Sometimes, this process takes only a few months; more often, it requires years. During Dwight D. Eisenhower's administration (1953–1961), for example, congressional Democrats explored and refined domestic policy options that, while not immediately accepted, were ripe for adoption by the time their party's nominee, John F. Kennedy, was elected president in 1960.[13] The incubation process refines the solutions to problems and brings policies to maturity. The process may break down, however, if workable solutions are not available. The seeming intractability of many modern issues complicates problem solving. Complex topics such as the escalating cost of a college education, stagnating wages, unconventional warfare, cybersecurity, immigration, and transnational criminal gangs are examples of the difficult issues facing contemporary lawmakers. A repertoire of proposals—for example, blue-ribbon commissions, trust funds, or pilot projects—can be applied to a variety of unsolved problems. Problem solvers also must guard against recommending solutions that will be viewed as worse than the problem.

Adopting Policy

Laws often embody ideas whose time has come. The right time for a policy is what scholar John W. Kingdon calls the *policy window:* the opportunity presented by circumstances and attitudes to enact a policy into law. Policy entrepreneurs must seize the opportunity before the policy window closes and the idea's time has passed. After years of effort by lawmakers and outside advocates, in 2019 the House and Senate overwhelmingly passed on a bipartisan basis conservation legislation that, among other things, designated 1.3 million acres of new wilderness areas and created three new national parks.

Once policies are ripe for adoption, they must gain popular acceptance. This is the function of legitimation, the process through which policies come to be viewed by the public as right or proper. Inasmuch as citizens are expected to comply with laws or regulations—pay taxes, observe rules, and make sacrifices of one sort or another—the policies themselves must appear to have been properly considered and enacted. One of the lingering liabilities of the landmark Patient Protection and Affordable Care Act of 2010 is the impression among many Americans that it was rammed through without bipartisan support.

Symbolic acts, such as members voting on the House or Senate floor or the president signing a bill, signal to everyone that a policy was adopted within the traditional practices. Hearings and debates serve to fine-tune policies as well as to cultivate support from affected interests. As for the pace of the overall process, responding to critics of Congress's glacial progress in adopting energy legislation, a senator posed these questions:

> Would you want an energy bill to flow through the Senate and not have anyone consider the impacts on housing or on the automotive industry or on the energy industries that provide our light and power? Should we ignore the problems of the miner or the producer or the distributor? Our legislative process must reflect all of the problems if the public is to have confidence in the government.[14]

Legitimating policies, in other words, often requires a measured pace and attention to procedural details. But a measured pace and painstaking attention to procedural niceties often provide opponents of change with an opportunity to mobilize. In some circumstances, policy makers may be forced to enact bold changes quickly in response to public outcry or demand, knowing that the details will have to be refined and adjusted later. But rushing policy making poses risks to policy legitimation.

Congressional Republicans discovered how a push for rapid action can backfire politically during their effort to repeal the Affordable Care Act in 2017. Their goal was to pass sweeping legislation repealing and replacing Obamacare in the first few months of the new Congress. They pressed forward with no hearings and expedited committee action. But the effort was undermined by the sense among many voters and members that their replacement plan had not been carefully vetted.[15] Noteworthy is that despite years of GOP attacks on Obamacare, a majority of Americans came to appreciate many of the important benefits of the health care law, such as insurance coverage for people with preexisting medical conditions. This issue was compelling in the 2018 mid-term elections, and it contributed to Democrats reclaiming control of the House.[16]

Implementing Policy

In the final stage, policies shaped by the legislature and at the highest executive levels are put into effect, often by a federal agency. Most policies are not self-executing; they must be promulgated and enforced. Congress and the president usually delegate most decisions about implementation to the responsible agencies under broadly worded guidelines. Implementation determines the ultimate effect of policies. Officials of the executive branch can thwart a policy by foot dragging or sheer inefficiency. By the same token, overzealous administrators can push a policy far beyond its creators' intent.

Congress, therefore, must exercise its oversight role. It may require executive agencies to report to or consult with congressional committees or to follow other formal procedures. Members of Congress receive feedback on the operation of federal programs through a variety of channels: media coverage, interest group protests, and even casework for constituents. With such information, Congress can adjust funding, introduce amendments, or recast the legislation on which the policy is based.

TYPES OF DOMESTIC POLICIES

One way to understand public policies is to analyze the nature of the policies themselves. Scholars have classified policies in many different ways.[17] Our typology identifies three types of domestic policies: distributive, regulatory, and redistributive.

Distributive Policies

Distributive policies or programs are government actions that convey tangible benefits—subsidies, tax breaks, or advantageous regulatory provisions—to private individuals, groups, or firms. These benefits are often called *pork,* a derogatory term for program benefits or spending specifically designated for members' states or districts. But pork is often difficult to define objectively. After all, "one person's pork is another person's steak." The projects come in several varieties, including "old-fashioned pork" (bridges and roads), "green pork" (wind, solar, and other alternative-energy projects), "academic pork" (research grants to colleges and universities), or "high-tech pork" (cybersecurity).

Distributive policy making—which makes many interests better off and few, if any, visibly worse off—sometimes comes easily to Congress, an often collegial institution that must build coalitions to function. A classic textbook example—reminiscent of the aforementioned 2019 conservation law—was the $1 billion-plus National Parks and Recreation Act of 1978. Dubbed the "Park Barrel Bill," it created so many parks, historic sites, seashores, wilderness areas, wild and scenic rivers, and national trails that it sailed through the Interior (now Natural Resources) Committee and passed the House 341–61. "Notice how quiet we are. We all got something in there," said one House member after the Rules Committee cleared the bill in five minutes flat. Another member quipped, "If it had a blade of grass and a squirrel, it got in the bill."[18] Distributive politics of this kind throws the two Congresses into sharp relief: national policy as a mosaic of local interests.

The politics of distribution works best when tax revenues are expanding, fueled by high productivity and economic growth. When productivity declines or tax cuts squeeze revenues, it can become difficult to add new benefits or expand old ones. Yet distributive impulses remain strong even in these circumstances, as lawmakers in both parties work to ensure that money is spent for specific purposes in their districts or states. This type of particularistic spending is known by a variety of different names—*pork, spending with a zip code, member projects, congressional-directed spending,* or, more commonly today, *earmarks.* By whatever name, the fundamental purpose of this spending is to "bring home the bacon." Recently, earmarks fell into disfavor, in part because of their cost, political use ("greasing" the legislative wheels), and the circumvention of competitive procedures for funding such constituency-based projects.

Earmark Reform

During the 1990s and early 2000s, the number of earmarks in spending bills increased in number and dollar value. In 1993, there were 892 earmarks worth $2.6 billion; in 1998, there were nearly two thousand earmarks worth $10.6 billion; and by 2005, there were "nearly 14,000 earmarks, costing $27.3 billion."[19] The cost of over nine thousand earmarks peaked at $29 billion in 2006, with a falloff to $15.9 billion (9,500 earmarks) in 2010.[20]

The explosion of earmarking generated significant controversy. Earmarks were criticized as wasteful and unnecessary, especially in an era of rising fiscal deficits. The classic example highlighted by opponents of earmarks was "the bridge to nowhere"—a $230 million bridge connecting a small Alaskan town of eight thousand to an island with fifty residents.[21] Second, there was an unseemly and sometimes corrupt connection between earmarks and campaign contributions. One lawmaker (who ended up in jail) took $2.4 million in bribes from lobbyists to insert earmarks for defense contractors, who would then contribute to his reelection campaign. Third, aggressive watchdog groups, bloggers, and several lawmakers, such as Sen. John McCain, R-Ariz., exposed and challenged on the floor what he viewed as bad earmarks.

Starting in 2007, Congress and the president responded to this public criticism by instituting reforms intended to make the earmark process more transparent and accountable. But the GOP-controlled House went farther by imposing a complete ban on earmarks for all House members in the 112th Congress (2011–2012). Their party regulation stated that "no Member shall request a congressional earmark, limited tax benefit, or limited tariff benefit, as such terms have been described in the Rules of the House." Some House committees also established their own guidelines for excluding earmarks from their measures.[22] The Senate resisted for a time but then moved to ban earmarks. After President Obama declared in his 2011 State of the Union message that he would veto any legislation containing earmarks and the House indicated that it would not pass any bills that contained them, Senate Appropriations chair Daniel Inouye, D-Hawaii, said in a statement, "Given the reality before us, it makes no sense to accept earmark requests that have no chance of being enacted into law."[23]

Many lawmakers, such as then House Appropriations chair Harold Rogers, R-Ky., complained about the loss of congressional power: "The U.S. Constitution directs that all spending must be a product of the House. But the way it is now, we appropriate funds in a general sense for the executive branch and then they, in effect earmark those moneys to where they want to see it go. That really should be the Congress."[24] A plan to restore what advocates euphemistically called "congressionally directed spending" nearly passed the House GOP conference in November 2016 but was quashed by Speaker Ryan, who told his colleagues that "we just had a 'drain the swamp' election and cannot turn right around and bring back earmarks behind closed doors."[25]

When Democrats reclaimed the 116th House, Majority Leader Steny Hoyer, Md., urged the House and Senate to restore earmarks. As he said: "I am working to restore the Congress's constitutional duty to exercise the 'power of the purse' through congressionally directed spending with reforms to ensure transparency and accountability." He added: "I am discussing the issue with members on both sides of the aisle and both chambers."[26] However, Nita Lowey, D-N.Y., the chair of the House Appropriations Committee, said that there was not yet bipartisan and bicameral support for the revival of earmarks. Sen. Richard Shelby, R-Ala., agreed with Lowey and said he would follow her lead. However, both stated that there would be continuing discussions in both chambers and parties "about just how to bring earmarks back."[27]

The debate over earmarks did not end in either chamber for a fundamental two-Congresses reason. As one lawmaker explained, earmarking is "part of the genetic makeup of a legislator," who must try to find a way to help his or her community.[28] In the absence of earmarks, members have turned to other, less transparent means to finance projects back home: earmarks by another name. They include "lettermarking"—lawmakers writing to administrators to urge that home-based projects be funded;[29] "phonemarking"—calling executive officials to request money for projects in their states or districts; and "soft earmarks"—simply "suggesting" to agency officials that money should be spent on the lawmaker's project. Members also might hike the dollar amounts in certain budgetary accounts and "then forcefully request that the agency spend the money on the member's pet project."[30] Some lawmakers continue to solicit funding for earmarked local projects.

To sum up, many lawmakers and analysts contend that eliminating earmarks saves a trivial amount of money and that the lengthy debates over earmarks only detract from the big-budget items that dominate spending, such as entitlements and defense, which need members' attention. Many earmarks are not wasteful and serve worthwhile national purposes, such as repairing decrepit bridges, establishing the Human Genome Project, and requiring the Pentagon to procure more body armor for troops.[31] Some observers have also argued that the earmark ban has made successful negotiation more difficult in Congress, as leaders can no longer use them to build coalitions of support.[32]

Regulatory Policies

Regulatory policies are designed to protect the public from the harm or abuse that might result from unbridled private activity. For example, the Food and Drug Administration monitors standards for foodstuffs and tests drugs for purity, safety, and effectiveness, and the Federal Trade Commission guards against illegal business practices such as deceptive advertising.

Federal regulation against certain abuses dates from the late-nineteenth century, when the Interstate Commerce Act and the Sherman Antitrust Act were enacted to protect against abuses in transportation and monopolistic practices. As the twentieth century dawned, scandalous conditions in slaughterhouses and food-processing plants led to meatpacking, food, and drug regulations. The stock market collapse in 1929 and the Great Depression of the 1930s paved the way for the New Deal's regulation of the banking and securities industries and of labor–management relations. Consumer rights and environmental-protection policies came of age in the 1960s and 1970s. The reversal of some of the protections of the 1930s enactments, plus lax oversight by federal agencies, contributed to the banking crisis of 2008–2009, which, in turn, fueled the Great Recession. Predictably, the fresh wave of Wall Street scandals led to a new round of regulatory fervor. Among its legacies is the Consumer Financial Protection Bureau (P.L. 111–203). Its job is to act as a watchdog for consumers in their purchase of various financial products, such as credit cards or mortgages. Many Democrats and commentators contend that the bureau's consumer watchdog role has been diminished by the Trump administration.[33]

Regulation inevitably arouses controversy. Much of the clean-air debate, for example, involves the basic issue of costs versus benefits: Do the public-health benefits of cleaner air outweigh the financial costs of obtaining it?[34] Environmentalists and health advocates argue that tougher standards for regulating air pollution save the lives of thousands who are afflicted with asthma and other lung diseases. Industries and conservative groups attack these claims, contending that the regulations are unnecessary, too expensive, and produce little health benefit.[35] Similarly, financial regulation pits the goal of protecting consumers against concerns about impeding the smooth operation of credit markets. Responding to critics in the banking industry, the Trump administration has rolled back some of the financial regulations adopted following the Great Recession, arguing that they have undermined the supply of credit for borrowers.

Redistributive Policies

The most difficult of all political feats is redistributive policy—that is, one in which the government purposefully shifts resources from one group to another. Typically controversial, redistributive policies engage a broad spectrum of political actors, not only in the House and Senate but also in the executive branch and among interest groups and the public at large. Redistributive issues tend to be ideological, dividing liberals and conservatives on fundamental questions of equality, opportunity, and property rights. The battle over the Affordable Care Act is an example of a redistributive controversy: paid for largely by taxes on upper-income earners, the law provides substantial subsidies to low- and moderate-income citizens to purchase insurance. Redistribution can even be future oriented: excessive amounts of deficit spending today mean larger financial burdens for the next generation.

Most of the divisive socioeconomic issues of the past generation—civil rights, affirmative action, welfare, immigration, and tax reform—were redistributive problems. A redistributive issue for the twenty-first century is the growing share of the federal budget that goes to the elderly compared with everyone else in society. Spending on entitlement programs, principally Social Security and Medicare, absorbs an ever-increasing proportion of federal dollars, which then are unavailable for other important social, domestic, or security needs.

CHARACTERISTICS OF CONGRESSIONAL POLICY MAKING

As a policy-making body, Congress displays the traits and biases of its membership and structure, as well as those of the larger political system. As for the first, the two houses of Congress have divergent electoral and procedural traditions. As for the second, Congress is representative, especially where geographic interests are concerned, and it is decentralized, having few mechanisms for integrating or coordinating its policy decisions. As for policy itself, Congress is often inclined toward enacting symbolic measures instead of substantive ones. Finally, Congress is rarely ahead of the curve—or the public—tending to reflect conventional perceptions of problems.

Bicameralism

Differences between the House and Senate—their relative sizes, members' terms of office, and the character of their constituencies—shape the policies they make. Six-year terms, it is argued, allow senators some freedom to act as statesmen for at least part of each term before the approaching elections force them to concentrate on fence mending.[36] House and Senate constituencies tend to pull in divergent directions. Homogeneous House districts often promote clear, unambiguous positions on a narrower range of questions than those embraced by an entire state. A senator, then, as a representative of an entire state, must weigh the claims of many competing interests on a broad range of matters.

The sizes of the two chambers dictate procedural biases. House rules are designed to allow majorities to have their way. By contrast, Senate rules give individual senators great latitude to influence action. As a GOP senator once said, "The Senate has the strongest minority of any minority on earth, and the weakest majority of any on earth."[37] In short, the two chambers differ in outlook, constituency, and strategy. This can make forging agreement across the two chambers more challenging and therefore adds to the more general difficulty of changing or terminating existing policies, not to mention passing new legislation.

Localism

Congressional policies respond to constituents' needs, particularly those that can be mapped geographically. Sometimes, these needs are pinpointed with startling directness. For example, an aviation noise control bill required construction of a control tower "at latitude 40 degrees, 43 minutes, 45 seconds north and at longitude 73 degrees, 24 minutes, 50 seconds west"—the very location of a Farmingdale, New York, airport in the district of the Democratic representative who requested the provision.[38] Usually, however, programs are directed toward states, municipalities, counties, or geographic regions. Funds are often transferred directly to local government agencies, which, in turn, deliver the aid or services to citizens. But sometimes, Congress will require states and localities to fund some national priorities without federal assistance. These *unfunded mandates* strain state budgets and rouse the ire of state and local officials.

The No Child Left Behind (NCLB) education law (P.L. 107–110) aroused considerable local controversy. It was approved early in the George W. Bush administration and prescribed mandatory standardized testing in all public schools. School systems in many states complained that the federal government failed to provide enough money to cover the expense of meeting the testing requirement. In 2015, NCLB was rolled back with new legislation allowing states to design and implement their own tests.[39]

National and local policies are necessarily intertwined. National policies can be advanced by state and local governments; in turn, states or localities can develop innovations that spur national action. In many cases, the states serve as testing grounds, or laboratories, for social, economic, and political experiments.

Many policy debates revolve around not only which government level can most effectively carry out a responsibility but also which level best promotes particular values. Liberals tend to prefer that the national government lead in enforcing civil rights and environmental protection. Conservatives support an activist national government on defense and security matters. When it suits their purposes, both liberals and conservatives are capable of advocating either national mandates or local autonomy, depending on which level of government would best serve their objectives.

Piecemeal Policy Making

Policies all too often mirror Congress's scattered and decentralized structure. Typically, they are considered piecemeal, reflecting the patchwork of committee and subcommittee jurisdictions. The structure of a policy frequently depends on which committees have reported it. Working from varying jurisdictions, committees can take different approaches to the same problem. The taxing committees gravitate toward tax provisions to address problems, the appropriations committees will prefer a fiscal approach to issues, the commerce panels typically adopt a regulatory perspective, and so forth. Each approach may be well or ill suited to the policy objective. The approach adopted will depend on which committee is best positioned to promote the bill.

Symbolic Policy Making

Congressional policy making can be more about appearance than substance. Bills are often passed to give the impression that action is being taken, even when the measure adopted is unlikely to have any real impact on the problem. The general public and interest groups continually demand, "Don't just stand there, do something." Doing something is often the only politically feasible choice, even when no one knows exactly what to do or whether inaction might be just as effective.[40] Still, symbolic actions are important to all politicians. This is not the same thing as saying that politicians are merely cynical manipulators of symbols. Words and concepts—*equal opportunity, income inequality, cost of living, amnesty, "wall,"* and *homeland security*—are contested earnestly in committee rooms and on the House and Senate floor. The result, however, is that policy goals are often stated in vague, optimistic language and not spelled out in terms of specific measures of success or failure.

Reactive Policy Making

It would be naive to expect a deliberative body to routinely adopt bold or radical solutions to problems. Elected officials are seldom far ahead of or far behind the collective views of their constituencies. Members know that out-of-the-mainstream views are unlikely to attract widespread public support. Indeed, Congress is essentially a reactive institution. As one House member explained,

> When decision rests on the consent of the governed, it comes slowly, only after consensus has built or crisis has focused public opinion in some unusual way, the representatives in the meantime hanging back until the signs are unmistakable. Government decision, then, is not generally the cutting edge of change but a belated reaction to change.[41]

Ending the statutory "don't ask, don't tell" policy toward gays in the military, for example, came late in 2010—only after public attitudes on the matter had shifted and the Joint Chiefs of Staff had assured lawmakers that the change would not adversely affect military performance.

The reactive character of Congress's policy making is evident in its budget process. Under pressures to reform, Congress embraced formal and informal changes in the way it makes budget decisions. The current budget process, dating from the mid-1970s, was intended to bring coherence to the way standing committees handle the president's budget. It has decisively shaped both Congress's internal decision making and its relations with the executive.

CONGRESSIONAL BUDGETING

Congressional budgeting is a complex process that involves an array of constitutional provisions, laws, rules, and precedents that influence decision making. To illustrate, there are two types of federal spending—discretionary and mandatory (also called direct or entitlement spending). Discretionary spending consists of programs and agencies funded by Congress through annual appropriations bills under the jurisdiction of the House and Senate appropriations committees. Mandatory or entitlement spending consists of obligations embedded in statutes that must be fulfilled unless Congress enacts new legislation revising its earlier commitments. Entitlements are under the purview of the authorizing (or policy-recommending) committees of each chamber.

There are also four types of committees responsible for fiscal decision making, each with their own unique rules and responsibilities—appropriating, authorizing, taxing, and budgeting. In short, virtually all House and Senate members, the president and executive officials, and scores of other participants actively seek to influence Congress's power of the purse. Congressional budgeting is a fragmented and contentious process. Conflict should come as no surprise, considering the high political and policy stakes associated with fiscal decision making.

The Constitution did not prescribe a budgetary system for Congress. The current process evolved to adapt and adjust to new demands, pressures, and circumstances, such as wars, economic crises, budgetary dysfunctions, presidential challenges, and rising deficits. This chapter's focus is to highlight several important features of congressional budgeting, beginning with authorizations and appropriations (see Box 14-1 for some of the terminology used in budgeting).

The discussion then moves forward to examine the rise of "backdoor" spending techniques, which means bypassing the appropriations process; the challenge of entitlements; the cost of "tax expenditures;" interest payments on the national debt; and the basic features of the landmark Congressional Budget and Impoundment Control Act of 1974 (shortened to The 1974 Budget Act), such as the concurrent budget resolution and reconciliation. In addition, there is discussion of several major revisions of the budget process as well as why contemporary lawmakers and outside groups call the budget process "broken" or "dysfunctional."

Authorizations and Appropriations

Congress's budget procedures are shaped by two customary and longtime processes: authorizations and appropriations. Most committees of Congress are

BOX 14-1   A BUDGET GLOSSARY

Appropriations. The process by which Congress provides budget authority, usually through the enactment of twelve separate appropriations bills.

Budget authority. The authority for federal agencies to spend or otherwise obligate money, accomplished through enactment into law of appropriations bills.

Budget outlays. Money that is spent in a given fiscal year, as opposed to money that is appropriated for that year. One year's budget authority can result in outlays over several years, and the outlays in any given year result from a mix of budget authority from that year and prior years. Budget authority is similar to putting money into a checking account. Outlays occur when checks are written and cashed.

Discretionary spending. Programs that Congress can finance as it chooses through appropriations. With the exception of paying entitlement benefits to individuals (see mandatory spending below), almost everything the government does is financed by discretionary spending. Examples include all federal agencies, Congress, the White House, the courts, the military, and programs such as space exploration and child nutrition. About a third of all federal spending falls into this category.

Fiscal year. The federal government's budget year. For example, fiscal year 2020 runs from October 1, 2019, through September 30, 2020.

Mandatory spending. Made up mostly of entitlements, which are programs whose eligibility requirements are written into law. Anyone who meets those requirements is entitled to the money until Congress changes the law. Examples are Social Security, Medicare, Medicaid, unemployment benefits, food stamps, and federal pensions. Another major category of mandatory spending is the interest paid to holders of federal-government bonds. Social Security and interest payments are permanently appropriated. And although budget authority for some entitlements is provided through the appropriations process, appropriators have little or no control over the money. Mandatory spending accounts for about two-thirds of all federal spending.

Pay-as-you-go (PAYGO) rule. This Senate and House procedure requires that all tax cuts, new entitlement programs, and expansions of existing entitlement programs be budget neutral—that is, offset either by additional taxes or by cuts in existing entitlement programs.

Reconciliation. The process by which tax laws and spending programs are changed, or reconciled, to reach outlay and revenue targets set in the congressional budget resolution. Established by the 1974 Congressional Budget Act (P.L. 93–344), it was first used in 1980.

Rescission. The cancellation of previously appropriated budget authority. This is a common way to save money that already has been appropriated. A rescissions bill must be passed by Congress and signed by the president (or enacted over his veto), just as an appropriations bill is.

Revenues. Taxes, customs duties, some user fees, and most other receipts paid to the federal government.

Sequester. The cancellation of spending authority as a disciplinary measure to cut off spending above preset limits. Appropriations that exceed annual spending caps can trigger a sequester that will cut all appropriations by the amount of the excess. Similarly, tax cuts and new or expanded entitlement spending programs that are not offset under the pay-as-you-go law or rule could trigger a sequester of nonexempt entitlement programs.

Source: Adapted from Andrew Taylor, "Clinton's Strength Portends a Tough Season for GOP," *CQ Weekly,* February 6, 1999, 293.

authorizing panels, such as Armed Services, Energy and Commerce, Agriculture, and so on. Generally, legislative rules stipulate that before agencies or programs receive any money, Congress should first pass authorization laws that do three fundamental things: (1) establish or continue (reauthorize) federal agencies and programs; (2) define the purposes, functions, and operations of programs or agencies; and (3) recommend (that is, authorize) the appropriation of funds for programs and agencies. As a Senate leader explained, "Authorizations allow programs to be created and funded. When we pass an authorizing bill, we hope the authorized level will be looked at in [the] appropriations committee—as I did as a longtime member. But we realize there are competing priorities, and full funding doesn't come very often."[42] As an example, the defense authorization bill might authorize the construction of three new submarines and recommend $15 billion for this purpose. Does that mean the Pentagon has the money to build the submarines? No. Congress must enact the defense appropriations bill that would grant the Pentagon legal authority to spend a specific amount of money for the submarines. In short, an authorization can be viewed as a "hunting license" for an appropriation, a law that actually supplies programs and agencies with public funds (budget authority), wherein agencies are granted the legal right to enter into obligations with contractors and to pay them with federal funds.

By custom, the House initiates appropriations bills. The House Appropriations Committee (usually one of its twelve subcommittees) would recommend how much money the Pentagon should receive for the submarines. The amount is called *budget authority* (BA), and it is equivalent to depositing money in a checking account. The *budget outlay* (BO) is the check written by the Pentagon to the contractors hired to construct the submarines. The House Appropriations Committee can provide up to the authorized $15 billion (but not more), propose less funding, or refuse to fund the submarine purchases at all. Assume that the House votes to approve $10 billion. The Senate Appropriations Committee, acting somewhat like a court of appeals, then hears Navy officials asking the Senate to approve the full $15 billion. If the Senate accedes, a House–Senate compromise is worked out, either in a conference committee or by the bicameral exchange of amendments.

The authorization–appropriation sequence is not required by the U.S. Constitution. The dual procedure dates from the nineteenth century and stems from inordinate delays caused by adding riders—extraneous policy amendments—to appropriations bills. "By 1835," wrote a legislator, "delays caused by injecting legislation [policy] into these [appropriations] bills had become serious and [Massachusetts representative] John Quincy Adams suggested that they be stripped of everything save appropriations."[43] Two years later, the House required authorizations to precede appropriations. The Senate followed suit. Both chambers have rules and precedents designed "to segregate decisions about what the government should do [authorizations] from those about how much it can afford [appropriations]." However, policy riders (sometimes called "poison pills" on occasion) are often added to appropriations bills despite the dual procedure.

The Constitution provides that "No Money shall be drawn from the Treasury, but in Consequence of Appropriations made by Law" (Article I, section 9). As a result, appropriations have priority over authorizations. An appropriations measure may be approved even if the authorization bill has not been enacted. Some programs have not been authorized for years, but they still continue to operate. Why? If money is sprinkled on programs or agencies, they continue to exist and function even if their authorization has lapsed. As one House Appropriations subcommittee chair said about the "must-pass" appropriations bills, "It's not the end of the world if we postpone the Clean Air Act or a tax measure. But the entire government will shut down if . . . appropriations [are not enacted annually]."[44]

Authorizations can be annual, multiyear, or permanent. Through the end of World War II, most federal agencies and programs were permanently authorized. They were reviewed annually by the House and Senate Appropriations Committees but not by the authorizing committees (such as Agriculture or Commerce). Since the 1970s, the trend has been toward short-term authorizations, giving the authorizing committees more chances to conduct oversight of agency operations to determine their adequacy and cost effectiveness.[45]

Generally, authorizing committees strive to enact their bills on a timely basis because otherwise they cede their lawmaking power to the appropriating panels. Authorizing panels often are unable to reauthorize their expired measures because of bicameral, political, and policy conflicts. For example, the State Department authorization, until 2016, had not been reauthorized for fourteen years. A lawmaker called agencies and programs that operate without an authorization "zombie" agencies.[46] They continue to operate because they receive appropriations that keep them in business.

A senior member of the Intelligence Committee once exclaimed, "If this committee can't pass authorization bills . . . which give scope and force of law to what we do, we are in fact a paper tiger."[47] But authorizers also try, from time to time, to hitch a ride on an appropriations bill heading to the White House. "Ideally, it's not great to use [appropriations] bills," remarked former representative Barney Frank, D-Mass. "But they may be the only vehicles we can use [for] some [authorization measures] where we're facing a veto or we have problems in the Senate."[48] (In 2018, the Congressional Budget Office (CBO) determined that more than $300 billion had been appropriated for 971 unauthorized agencies, programs, or functions that had expired.[49])

In practice, it is hard to keep the two stages distinct. Authorization bills sometimes carry appropriations, and appropriations bills sometimes contain legislation (or policy provisions). Chamber rules that forbid these maneuvers can be waived. In the House, so-called limitation riders make policy under the guise of restricting agency use of funds. Phrased negatively ("None of the funds may be used for a specified purpose . . ."), such limitation riders bolster congressional control of the bureaucracy.[50] A well-known limitation amendment—barring the use of federal funds for abortions except under limited circumstances—was first adopted in 1976 and has been readopted ever since in appropriations bills. Policy riders can provoke harsh bicameral, party, and legislative–executive disputes.

Whenever Congress cannot complete action on one or more of the twelve regular appropriations bills (generally one for each subcommittee) by the beginning of the fiscal year (October 1), it provides temporary, stopgap funding for the affected federal agencies through a joint resolution known as a *continuing resolution* (CR). Generally, CRs keep the affected agencies funded at the previous year's levels. In the past, continuing resolutions were usually employed to keep a few government agencies in operation for short periods (usually one to three months). In some years, Congress has packaged all the regular appropriations bills into one massive continuing resolution. As polarization and the increased use of the Senate filibuster have made passage of even routine spending bills difficult, it has become common for Congress to rely on continuing resolutions to fund much or all of the government.[51]

To emphasize, traditional practice is that the twelve appropriations bills are to be enacted as stand-alone bills during the fiscal year. This has not happened since 1994 and has happened only four times in forty-one years (1976–2017). There simply is not enough time for Congress to act separately on twelve bills, especially given rancorous partisanship, intense spending disagreements, the use of politically charged limitation (poison pill) amendments, and so on. The result is reliance on packages put together by top party and committee leaders of the majority party. They combine a half dozen or more of the twelve individual measures into an omnibus appropriations bill hundreds or thousands of pages in length. They also create "mini-buses"—for example, four separate appropriations bills packaged into three mini-bus measures. The larger problem, wrote a former House aide, is that "all-or-nothing, several-thousand-page omnibus bills are fed to [rank-and-file] members with no time to read them, no debate, and no open rule that would allow for a fair hearing of amendments."[52] Today, governing by

CRs or omnibus bills is a common occurrence and a source of frustration to many lawmakers. Each year, Congress also passes one or more supplemental appropriations bills to meet unforeseen contingencies.

To sum up, there are three basic types of appropriations: *regular* (made annually), *supplemental* (furnishing funds for unexpected contingencies, such as natural disasters), and *continuing* (providing funds when one or more annual appropriations bills have not been enacted by the start of the fiscal year).

Backdoor Spending Techniques

To sidestep appropriators' abilities to slash their recommended funding levels, authorizing committees evolved backdoor funding provisions to bypass the front door of the two-step authorization–appropriation sequence. Backdoors are authorization laws that mandate rather than simply recommend the expenditure of federal funds. This type of spending legislation, which is reported solely by the authorizing committees, is called mandatory (also called direct or entitlement) spending, as opposed to the discretionary spending recommended annually for agencies by the House and Senate appropriations committees. There are three types of backdoor or direct spending provisions: (1) contract authority permits agencies to enter into contracts that subsequently must be covered by appropriations, (2) borrowing authority allows agencies to spend money they have borrowed from the public or the Treasury, and (3) entitlement programs grant eligible individuals and governments the right to receive payments from the national government.

The fastest-growing of the three types is entitlements, which establish legally enforceable rights for eligible beneficiaries. Spending for entitlement programs (such as Medicare and Social Security) is determined by the number of citizens who qualify and the benefit levels established by law. No fixed dollar amount is established for these programs. Budget wonks sometimes call entitlements "uncontrollable under existing law." Statutory changes are difficult to make because entitlements benefit millions of eligible Americans who often vote, never more so than if their benefits are taken away without an adequate substitute.

The Challenge of Entitlements

Entitlements are the real force behind the escalation of federal spending (see Figure 14-1). Approximately two-thirds of federal spending consists of entitlements that avoid the annual appropriations review process. This ratio of discretionary (determined through yearly appropriations) to mandatory spending represents a dramatic reversal from that of a half century ago. Unlike defense or domestic discretionary programs—for which the appropriations panels recommend annual amounts and on which all lawmakers may vote—entitlement spending occurs automatically under the terms outlined in the statute. It amounts to "auto-pilot" spending: laws that require mandatory payments to all eligible individuals, such as Social Security and Medicare recipients.

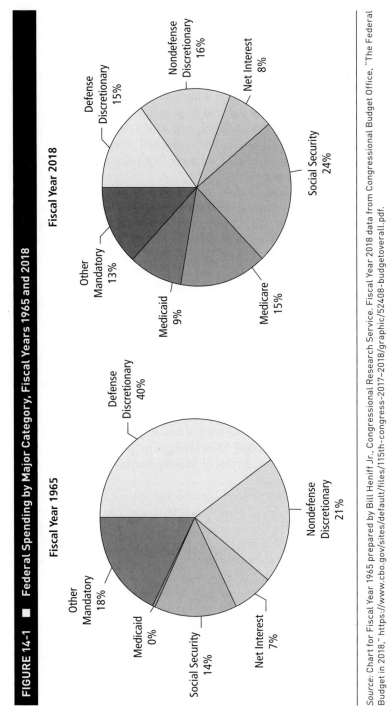

Fiscal Year 2018

Fiscal Year 1965

Source: Chart for Fiscal Year 1965 prepared by Bill Heniff Jr., Congressional Research Service. Fiscal Year 2018 data from Congressional Budget Office, "The Federal Budget in 2018," https://www.cbo.gov/sites/default/files/115th-congress-2017–2018/graphic/52408-budgetoverall.pdf.

Note: Excludes offsetting receipts.

Congress has done a reasonable job of containing discretionary spending, but reining in costly entitlements has proved to be a much more difficult task. In 1996, Congress passed legislation ending a decades-old national welfare entitlement program, Aid to Families with Dependent Children.[53] However, the recipients of the largest share of entitlement spending—senior citizens—are highly protective of these programs and also very likely to vote. A classic example of how hard it is to revamp entitlements occurred in the second term of President George W. Bush. He launched an intense lobbying drive to win public and congressional support for replacing Social Security with individual retirement accounts, but his effort failed to gain any traction. Even many Republicans opposed the plan's reliance on private accounts.

Public officials and analysts have been warning for years—without too much effect—that the projected expenditures of the big three entitlement programs (Social Security, Medicare, and Medicaid) are unsustainable. The long-term demographic challenge confronting these programs is that the United States is an aging society with a population that is living longer, thanks, in part, to advances in often-expensive medical technology. The nation is already witnessing the gradual retirement of the 76 million members of the "baby boom" generation (those born between 1946 and 1964), creating a pool of the largest number of retirees in the history of the country. This development will lead to huge retirement and medical expenditures.

Many proposals have been advanced to deal with the long-term funding challenge, but each is controversial. For Social Security, the proposed changes include raising the retirement age, reducing benefits for future retirees, increasing the payroll tax rate, requiring affluent retirees to pay taxes on their benefits, and raising the amount of income subject to Social Security payroll taxes.[54] Another recommendation to improve the solvency of Social Security is to permit more immigration, both legal and illegal. More immigrants aid the solvency of Social Security because they pay into the Social Security system ($9 billion annually) "but they can't receive benefits."[55]

Many analysts and public officials contend that the real entitlement budget buster of the future is not Social Security but the soaring costs of Medicare and health care in general: "The long-term fiscal problem truly is fundamentally one involving the rate at which healthcare costs grow. . . . Social Security and aging are important, but it is not where the money is," explained a former Obama budget director.[56] Former Speaker Paul Ryan, R-Wisc., once proposed a major overhaul of Medicare—federally subsidized vouchers for seniors so they can purchase health insurance in the private sector—and Medicaid—block grants to the states to care for low-income individuals and families.

Another proposal is the Medicare for All Act that has been introduced in the 116th Congress by many progressive Democrats. It would eliminate the role of private insurance, permit the federal government to be the payer of health care services, and extend health coverage to millions of people who are uninsured. Its fate is uncertain, but from a two Congresses perspective, it seems likely that

Medicare for All and health care generally will be a major 2020 campaign issue in congressional districts and states across the nation. An alterative health care approach favored by moderate Democrats is to improve Obamacare and allow people of a certain age (50 or 55) to buy into Medicare.[57]

Setting aside the Medicare for All Act, Obamacare, and Ryan's health proposals, even the more modest steps "Congress could take now to restrain Medicare's growth are politically perilous. Deny end-of-life care? Restrict eligibility? Reduce treatments? Raise costs?"[58] It is noteworthy on this score that when Congress enacted the Budget Control Act of 2011, it provided for cuts to Medicare at 2 percent annually. The reductions have not aroused controversy, according to an analyst, because they do not hit patients directly and are "miniscule" compared to overall mandatory spending.[59] The costs of providing long-term nursing home or other care for the elderly is "the elephant in the living room that no one's talking about."[60] And Medicaid, a federal entitlement program for indigent and low-income persons that is jointly funded by the national and state governments, has "now surged past Medicare to become the nation's largest health care program."[61]

Two other major components of the budget merit separate mention as well: tax expenditures and interest on the national debt.

Tax Expenditures

Over $2 trillion is consumed by indirect spending, also called tax expenditures or tax preferences. This is the revenue that is forgone through various tax credits, subsidies, or deductions such as the home mortgage interest deduction. Rep. Jim Cooper, D-Tenn., declared that if "there is anything more out of control than entitlement spending," it is tax expenditures.[62] Compared with mandatory or discretionary spending, these expenditures receive scant public attention. One study noted that "much like entitlement programs, [tax expenditures] are on automatic pilot and do not receive sufficient scrutiny as part of the budget process."[63] Significantly, the total value of all tax preferences exceeds the total value of all discretionary spending.

Like other government programs, tax expenditures have their own political constituencies that fight attempts to eliminate or reduce this conglomeration of tax breaks and subsidies. Of the over 200 tax expenditures, most "disproportionately benefit those at the top of the economic ladder."[64] Scholars who study tax expenditures sometimes refer to this form of federal largess as the *submerged state* or the *hidden welfare state.*[65] In contrast to direct spending policies, beneficiaries often do not realize that they are benefiting from a government program, limiting their understanding of the role that the federal government plays in their lives.[66]

Interest on the Debt

"There is a cancer eating away at the budget from within," wrote a journalist, and it is the ever-increasing interest that must be paid to service the national debt.[67] (The debt is the accumulation of annual deficits over time, now over

$22 trillion in 2019 and increasing daily.) The CBO has projected that interest payments will continue to rise from $390 billion in 2019 to $914 billion in 2028. Interest payments are expected to mount to $7 trillion over the next decade. Looming ahead is that interest on the debt could exceed spending for the military, Medicaid, or children's programs."[68]

The rapid increase in interest payments is a combination of various factors, including large tax cuts and higher spending. Higher interest payments mean less money for other programs. The options for Congress to slow the growth of interest payments on the debt appear straightforward, but they are politically controversial and substantively complex: tax more, spend less, combine those two, and foster economic growth. However, the general populace and many public officials, including the president, appear rather unconcerned about escalating deficits and debt. There are fewer "deficit hawks" in Congress, economic times are good, and the president favors deficit spending. Predictions that large deficits and debt harm economic growth have not materialized in a way that arouses broad public concern.

To focus greater attention on issues such as tax expenditures, interest on the debt, entitlements, and much more, Congress passed, more than forty years ago, a landmark budgetary measure, the Congressional Budget and Impoundment Control Act of 1974. The goals of that act included bringing greater coordination and coherence to legislative budgeting and strengthening Congress's power of the purse. However, the results have been at best mixed because it is no easy task to control and monitor federal budgeting.

THE 1974 BUDGET ACT

Congress refocused its budgetary attention in the 1970s after its loose control of the purse strings gave rise to charges of financial irresponsibility. President Richard Nixon blamed Congress for annual deficits, consumer price hikes, high unemployment, and inflation. He also refused to spend monies duly appropriated by Congress, a practice called impoundment. Even though his administration lost every court challenge to the impoundments, Nixon held the political high ground. These diverse pressures prompted Congress to tighten its budget procedures. Among the Act's principal features was the creation of House and Senate Budget Committees as well as the Congressional Budget Office. The nonpartisan CBO prepares economic forecasts for Congress; estimates the costs of proposed legislation; and issues fiscal, monetary, and policy reports. The 1974 act also limited presidential use of impoundments (refusal to spend appropriated funds) and established a timetable for action on authorization, appropriation, and tax measures. The timetable has been changed periodically, and Congress commonly misses some of the target dates (see Box 14-2 for the timetable).

Two central components of Congress's current budget process are the nonbinding concurrent budget resolution as well as reconciliation. The formulation of the budget resolution is the formal responsibility of each chamber's budget panel. Reconciliation is an optional procedure; to be made in order, it requires inclusion in the budget resolutions of both chambers. These two elements compel much of the time-consuming work, attract the attention of many interests and participants clamoring for fiscal resources, and influence policy decisions and outcomes. A third element, the practice of CBO "scoring" of legislative proposals, has become an equally important legacy of the act.

Concurrent Budget Resolution

The core of Congress's annual budget process is adoption of a concurrent budget resolution. Adoption of this resolution by both chambers is supposed to be the start of the annual legislative budget process. This measure is formulated by the House and Senate budget committees, which consider the views and estimates of numerous committees and witnesses.

The resolution consists of five basic parts. First, the budget resolution estimates what the federal government will spend in a fiscal year and for at least the four or nine following fiscal years. For each fiscal year covered by the resolution, the spending is expressed in terms of both budget authority and budget outlays (federal funds spent in a given fiscal year). Second, the total aggregate spending is then subdivided among twenty functional categories, such as defense, agriculture, or energy. For each category, the target indicates what Congress expects to spend in those substantive areas. Third, the budget resolution stipulates the recommended levels of federal revenues needed to pay for the projected spending during each of the fiscal years. Fourth, the budget resolution identifies the estimated deficits (or surpluses should they occur, which is infrequent). Fifth, the total outstanding public debt (savings bonds, Treasury securities, and other government obligations) permitted by law is also specified for at least the five-year period. In effect, the budget resolution sets the overall level of discretionary spending for each fiscal year.

The budget resolution is Congress's fiscal blueprint. It establishes the context of congressional budgeting; guides the budgetary actions of the authorizing, appropriating, and taxing committees; and reflects Congress's spending priorities. A senator described the purposes of the budget resolution: "[The budget] resolution would be analogous to an architect's set of plans for constructing a building. It gives the general direction, framework, and prioritization of Federal fiscal policy each year. Those priorities then drive the individual appropriations and tax measures which will support that architectural plan."[69] In a period of polarized politics, partisan issues dominate debate on these resolutions as Democrats and Republicans battle over spending levels for their competing priorities.

Under the 1974 law, the House and Senate are expected to consider a budget resolution. (Sometimes this does not occur, see below, which gives rise to complaints about "the broken" budget process.) In the House, budget resolutions are typically considered under special rules from the Rules Committee, which limit debate and impose restrictions on the number and types of amendments.

BOX 14-2   THE CONGRESSIONAL BUDGET TIMETABLE

Deadline	Action to be completed
First Monday in February	President submits budget to Congress
February 15	Congressional Budget Office submits economic and budget outlook report to budget committees
Six weeks after president submits budget	Committees submit views and estimates to budget committees
April 1	Senate Budget Committee reports budget resolution
April 15	Congress completes action on budget resolution
May 15	Annual appropriations bills may be considered in the House, even if action on budget resolution has not been completed
June 10	House Appropriations Committee reports last annual appropriations bill
June 15	House completes action on reconciliation legislation (if required by budget resolution)
June 30	House completes action on annual appropriations bills
July 15	President submits mid-session review of his budget to Congress
October 1	Fiscal year begins

Source: Bill Heniff Jr., *The Congressional Budget Process Timetable,* Congressional Research Service Report 98–472 GOV, March 20, 2008.

In the Senate, the 1974 Budget Act sets a fifty-hour limitation for consideration of the budget resolution, unless members accept a unanimous-consent agreement imposing other time restrictions. Amendments can be taken up and voted on after the fifty hours but without debate. This circumstance often leads to "vote-a-ramas," over several days, when senators may "cast back-to-back votes on a dizzying array of dozens of amendments," often with the two Congresses in mind. As national policy makers, members of Congress may have to cast tough but responsible votes, which will "serve as valuable campaign fodder" for opponents in the next election.[70]

When the chambers pass budget resolutions with different aggregate and functional spending levels, House and Senate members usually meet in conference to resolve their disagreements. The conference report is then submitted to both chambers for final action. Because Congress's budget resolution is not submitted to the president, it has no binding legal effect. Instead, it outlines a fiscal framework that enables Congress, through its budget committees, CBO, and other entities, to monitor all budget-related actions taken during the course of a year.

When the House and Senate are late or unable to adopt a concurrent budget resolution, each chamber usually adopts a resolution (H. Res. or S. Res.) reflecting the budget levels and enforcement procedures contained in the resolution adopted by one chamber but not the other. The failure to pass a budget resolution in either chamber has become far more common in recent years amid the fierce partisan warfare over spending and taxes. For example, from 1975 to 1998, Congress never failed to pass a budget resolution. Since that time, until 2018, more than half failed to be adopted by Congress.[71]

In the 116th House, it is unclear whether the House Budget Committee can craft a resolution that will attract majority support. "Doing a budget resolution that can get 218 votes is going to be a difficult task for us," said Budget Chair Yarmuth, "I don't think there's any question about that."[72] One problem he faces is divisions within the majority party. Many progressive Democrats want their priorities recognized in the budget resolution: health care, climate change, more domestic spending, and the like. Some also want explicit reference in the budget resolution to the Green New Deal or Medicare for All, or they might not vote for the budget resolution. Similarly, there are Democrats from swing districts who disfavor promoting those topics in the budget resolution, recognizing they could cause them electoral problems back home.

Senate budget chair Enzi, who did not draft a budget resolution the previous year, decided in 2019 to draft a "realistic" budget resolution. That meant not drafting a resolution that produced a balanced budget after 10 years (a GOP requirement under their party rules) or eliminated deficits and with no guarantee that the measure would reach the floor.[73]

Both budget leaders want to boost the spending caps on discretionary spending embedded in the Budget Control Act of 2011, to avoid a punitive sequester (cancellation of funds) that could occur in 2020: 10 percent for defense and 9 percent for non-defense accounts. (As noted in Chapter 15, the caps for discretionary spending were hiked in 2013, 2015, and 2018.) The current spending cap expires in September 2019. House budget chair Yarmuth said that the "most important thing we have to deal with in the near-term is getting an agreement on the budget caps."[74]

Reconciliation

The 1974 Budget Act established a special procedure called reconciliation, which is an optional process Congress may authorize when it adopts the budget resolution. It is an important process for the Senate because a reconciliation measure needs only a simple majority to pass rather than the usual sixty votes. Its basic purpose is to bring revenue and direct spending (entitlement) legislation into conformity (or reconciliation) with the fiscal targets established in the concurrent budget resolution.[75] This often involves making changes in federal policies that result in budgetary savings. First used in 1980, reconciliation has been employed over twenty-five times since.

Reconciliation is a two-step process. In the first step, Congress adopts a budget resolution containing a provision that usually instructs two or more House and Senate committees to report legislation that changes existing law. The instructions in the budget resolution name the committees required to report legislation; they give each committee the responsibility to change existing laws to comply with the dollar requirement stipulated in the instructions without specifying the policies to achieve those goals; and they establish a deadline for reporting legislation to achieve the savings. In the second step, the House and Senate budget committees compile into an omnibus reconciliation bill the legislative changes in revenue or direct (entitlement) spending programs recommended by the named committees. If the instructions involve only one committee in each chamber, then those panels would bypass the budget committees and report their recommendations to the full House or Senate. On several occasions, reconciliation directives have provided for the maximum of three reconciliation bills during each fiscal year: one involving taxes, another on spending, and a third on raising the statutory debt limit.

Reconciliation in the House is considered under the terms of a rule from the Rules Committee. Procedurally, however, reconciliation is focused on the Senate because measures governed by that optional process are treated differently from other bills or amendments. Reconciliation bills cannot be filibustered (a statutory time limit of twenty hours is placed on debate), passage requires a simple majority instead of the supermajority (sixty votes) needed to stop a talkathon, and amendments must be germane (the Senate has no general germaneness rule). Democratic senator Robert Byrd of West Virginia lamented that reconciliation "can be used by a determined majority to circumvent the regular rules of the Senate in order to advance partisan legislation. We have seen one party, and then the other, use this process to limit debate and amendments on non-budgetary provisions that otherwise may not have passed under the regular rules."[76] To prevent just such a usage of reconciliation bills, senators adopted the so-called Byrd rule (named after Senator Byrd) in the mid-1980s. Under this complex rule, measures cannot be included in the Senate reconciliation package if they are viewed as extraneous provisions that are not primarily budget related. When the parliamentarian rules that a provision violates the Byrd rule, it is dropped from the bill unless sixty senators vote to waive the Byrd rule.[77] Such provisions have been called "Byrd droppings."

The Byrd rule played an important role in the 2009–2010 fight over health care reform. Some Democrats hoped to pass the massive overhaul through reconciliation, but doing so would have resulted in numerous provisions being dropped due to Byrd-rule violations. Democrats passed the overhaul through the standard sixty-vote cloture process in December 2009. However, before House and Senate versions of the bill could go to conference, Democrats lost their filibuster-proof margin in the Senate when Republican Scott Brown pulled off a dramatic upset in a January 2010 special election in Massachusetts.[78] To enact reform, Democrats had to resort to a complicated procedure in which the House adopted the previously passed Senate bill without any amendments, which President Obama signed into law The two chambers subsequently approved a set of changes to the legislation that became law through reconciliation. The latter changes, however, were limited to budget-related adjustments that could pass muster with the Byrd rule.

Reconciliation offers a powerful procedure for fiscal policy, but its effective use these days seems to be limited to circumstances of unified party control. In a classic case, President Ronald Reagan and GOP congressional leaders used it for the first time on a grand scale in 1981, when the House was controlled by Democrats and the Senate controlled by Republicans. During this period, the Democratic party was internally divided: There were liberal and moderate Democrats as well as Reagan Democrats. Despite divided government, budget reconciliation was used to implement Reagan's budget, imposing deep, multiyear reductions (about $130 billion over three years) in domestic spending. Fast forward to today's party polarized era, and it is very doubtful that the Democratic House and GOP Senate could agree to a budget resolution that authorizes the use of reconciliation.

A Revised Budget Process

The growth of budget deficits after 1981 became the prime congressional issue as lawmakers and presidents adapted to a new world: the politics of deficit reduction. Numerous proposals were put forth to deal with the problem. A prominent approach has been to set binding deficit or spending targets, which would be enforced through across-the-board cuts—*sequestration*—if the targets were not met. One difficulty with sequestration, however, was that it could always be forestalled by adoption of a new budget law delaying the pain. Another, more effective strategy, embodied in the Budget Enforcement Act of 1990, was to subject tax and entitlement programs to a new pay-as-you-go (PAYGO) procedure, which required that any tax reductions or any increases in mandatory (entitlement) spending be offset by tax hikes or reductions in other entitlement programs.

Throughout much of the 1990s, the GOP-controlled Congress and President Clinton waged fierce battles over deficit reduction. A fiscal breakthrough soon emerged, however. Indeed, much to the surprise of most observers, an era of budget surpluses arrived in the late 1990s. The robust economy and booming stock market led to much higher federal revenues, and fiscal restraint led to budgetary savings. The end of the Cold War also led to reductions in defense expenditures. "Just about everything broke right that could have broken right," said Robert Reischauer, a former CBO director.[79] The brief era (1998–2002) of surpluses came to a quick end.

What happened to the surplus? It disappeared because the factors that produced it reversed themselves. Instead of defense cutbacks, the nation was paying for military conflicts in Afghanistan and Iraq, reconstruction of those countries, and enhanced homeland security. A record ten years of uninterrupted economic growth ended, and the stock market performed poorly, shrinking federal revenues. The large tax cuts pushed by the Bush administration also contributed to revenue shortfalls. Moreover, Congress's statutory fiscal constraints—spending caps and PAYGO—expired on September 30, 2002. Thus, policy makers were now free to let the deficit increase.

While PAYGO had been effective when it was in place, it clashed with Republicans' goal of cutting taxes since it required finding savings to pay for lost revenues. When Republicans took control of the House in the 112th Congress, they put in place a "cut-as-you-go" (CUTGO) rule, which focused on spending cuts to mandatory (entitlement) programs. Increases in entitlement spending were to be offset only by spending reductions in other mandatory programs. However, tax initiatives were exempt from the CUTGO rule. House Republicans could thus cut taxes without finding offsets for the lost revenue.[80]

When Democrats reclaimed control of the House in the mid-term 2018 elections, they terminated the CUTGO rule and replaced it with PAYGO. Democrats wanted to draw a contrast with Republican control of the House, which witnessed a large spike in the federal deficit. Under the Democratic proposal, mandatory spending or tax cuts would have to be offset with budget cuts to mandatory programs or tax increases. PAYGO quickly aroused the ire of many progressive Democrats. They wanted to know why Democrats are adhering to budgetary constraints when Republicans did not when they controlled the House. As a Democratic member said: "Critical investments in education, health care, and education should not be held hostage to budgetary constraints that Republicans never respected."[81]

A large number of members and outside groups support major reform of the congressional budget process. Reformers point to problems that are widely acknowledged in Congress: missed budget deadlines, reliance on CRs and omnibus bills, the limited authority of the two budget panels, government shutdowns, unauthorized programs, automatic spending via entitlement programs, time-wasting vote-a-ramas in the Senate, and many more.

A central problem for Congress and the White House is determining what set of policies aimed at improving the nation's long-term fiscal prospects can attract the necessary votes. As one analyst observed, on one side are people who stress that being competitive globally and flourishing at home require major government investments in areas such as education, technology, and transportation. On the other side are those who emphasize that excessive federal spending must be curbed first, based on the theory that a nation cannot spend its way to prosperity.[82] To reconcile these competing worldviews underscores the fact that federal budgeting is about more than numbers. It reflects the divergent views of the two political parties about what policies best serve the country's short- and long-term interests.

CONCLUSION

Today, lawmakers are preoccupied with scores of important policy issues: stagnant wages, defense and homeland security, energy sources and usage, and the health of various domestic social programs. Former representative Barney Frank, D-Mass., has posed a question that crystallizes the debate over these various concerns: "What is the appropriate level of public activity in our society?"[83] Democrats and Republicans tend to answer that question differently. Governing, however, means making choices. Future decisions about budgeting and national priorities will surely reflect the values, goals, and interests that result from the confrontations and accommodations inherent in America's pluralist policy-making system.

President Donald Trump addresses the UN General Assembly on September 28, 2018. Senate Armed Services Chairman James Inhofe, R-Okla., and ranking Democrat Jack Reed, R.I., (seated) prepare for a hearing on the nation's defense posture. U.S. Naval Academy midshipmen attend a Senate Armed Services Committee hearing on military readiness. U.S. Secretary of State Mike Pompeo answers questions during a press conference held in Warsaw, Poland.

CONGRESS AND NATIONAL SECURITY POLICIES

On September 25, 2018, President Donald Trump addressed the General Assembly of the United Nations. His speech emphasized several fundamentals of his foreign policy doctrine: "America First," rejection of the "ideology of globalism," and no surrender of "America's sovereignty to an unelected, unaccountable, global bureaucracy." The president expressed long-held views. As an analyst wrote after conducting a thirty-year study of Trump's public statements: "He believes that the U.S. has been taken for a sucker by other countries because of trade deals and security commitments."[1] Thus, each component of the president's doctrine represents a time-for-a-change critique of the interdependent world order that the United States was instrumental in creating after World War II.

With an "America First" foreign policy replacing, in part, the multilateralism of the previous era, it is no surprise that the president is sometimes referred to as the "disrupter in chief" of the status quo. Consider a few examples: The president castigates NATO allies as "free riders" for not paying enough for their own defense and disengages unilaterally from multilateral agreements negotiated by the Obama administration. He withdraws from the Paris Climate Accord (2015), signed by 194 nations to address climate change; the Trans-Pacific Partnership (2015), a twelve-nation pact to establish trading rules for the region; and the Iran nuclear compact (2015) a six-nation accord to constrain Iran's development of nuclear weapons. He launched a number of trade wars with adversaries (e.g., China) as well as allies (e.g., Canada).

President Trump's unconventional leadership style also arouses concern in Congress and many foreign capitals. His impulsive, unpredictable, and visceral decision making, often announced via Twitter, confounds and disturbs congressional members and foreign leaders. For example, he announced in a tweet that

U.S. military forces would withdraw from Syria. When the decision was criticized, he changed course and agreed to keep a small U.S. military force in Syria. President Trump is skeptical of the information and analysis provided by the intelligence agencies. When top intelligence officials affirmed that Iran is adhering to the international agreement to end nuclear weapons development, from which the United States withdrew in 2018, President Trump disagreed and stated that the officials were naïve and ought to go "back to school."[2] Fox News appears to influence his decision making more than the evidence-based analysis of policy experts. His propensity to attack critics (the press as "enemy of the people"), make dubious or false statements, and defend dictators disturbs many public officials here and abroad.

On the other hand, various lawmakers, public officials, and analysts give President Trump credit for taking actions to upend the long-existing world order. Disruption, they say, has fostered a discussion in Congress and elsewhere about forging a new international order to address twenty-first century challenges (e.g., cyber-warfare and mass migration). As Secretary of State Mike Pompeo said, "New winds are blowing across the world. I'd argue that [President Trump's] disruption is a positive development."[3] Former treasury secretary Lawrence Summers stated that President Trump "has China's attention on economic issues in a way that eluded his predecessors. The question is can he use his leverage to accomplish something important."[4]

Walter Russell Mead, an economics professor and writer for the *Wall Street Journal,* opined, "the international rules and institutions developed during the Cold War era must be retooled to withstand new political, economic, and military pressures."[5] Representative Ami Bera, D-Calif., a subcommittee chair of the Foreign Affairs Committee, agreed that President Trump has been a disruptive force. "But in this disruption," Bera said, "he's created an opportunity for us to rethink what diplomacy and development looks like, and what it should look like."[6] Trump's demand that NATO countries must spend more on defense prompted NATO's secretary general Jens Stoltenberg to credit the president for the surge in defense spending from the member states. "We see some real money and some real results. And we see that the clear message from President Donald Trump is having an impact."[7]

Although the GOP-controlled 115th Congress gave President Trump broad support when he made his positions known on legislation and nominations, many Republican lawmakers expressed dismay at President Trump's foreign policy objectives. They sent "messages" of their foreign policy concerns to the White House through floor statements, the introduction of legislation, committee hearings, the adoption of nonbinding resolutions, or the enactment of legislation. A political scientist declaimed that he could not recall "a historical period where you have had the same party control both branches of government and the two branches have been at odds on the basic principles of U.S. foreign policy."[8]

For example, when Secretary of Defense James Mattis resigned in December 2018 in protest at the president's abrupt decision to remove U.S. forces from

Syria, Senate majority leader Mitch McConnell, R-Ky., said: "It's essential that the United States maintain and strengthen the post-World War II alliances that have been carefully built by leaders in both parties. We must also maintain a clear-eyed understanding of our friends and foes, and recognize that nations like Russia are among the latter." He went on say, "I am particularly distressed that [Secretary Mattis] is resigning due to sharp differences with the president on these and other key aspects of America's global leadership."[9]

With Democrats in charge of the 116th House, numerous House committees are subjecting President Trump's foreign policy to intense scrutiny. In his 2019 State of the Union address, the president warned Democrats against conducting partisan investigations. As he said, "If there is going to be peace and legislation, there cannot war and investigation." Undeterred, many House panels commenced investigative oversight of the president and his administration. The chair of the Foreign Affairs Committee said the panel would investigate whether the president's business interests have influenced his foreign policy decisions.

Friction and disagreement between the executive and legislative branch is built into our constitutional system. From the nation's beginning until today, there have been conflicts and compromises between the branches on foreign and defense policies. No issue was more divisive during President George Washington's administration than the question of whether the United States should remain neutral as Britain and France fought for geopolitical supremacy. President Washington ultimately opted for neutrality, even advising in his 1796 Farewell Address that the "great rule of conduct for us, in regard to foreign nations is in extending our commercial relations, to have with them as little political connection as possible. . . . 'Tis our true policy to steer clear of permanent alliances, with any portion of the foreign world." But a series of military mobilizations and interventions launched by presidents—often but not always with congressional support—have transformed the U.S. role such that President Washington's vision bears little resemblance to twenty-first-century conditions. As a world power today, with numerous alliances spanning the globe, the United States and its foreign policies would scarcely be recognized by the nation's founders.

Despite President Trump's actions to reset features of the World War II international order, the United States' vital interests and superpower status require it to be internationally involved. The world is too interconnected for the United States to be an isolationist power—or "America Alone." Although President Trump withdrew from the Trans-Pacific Partnership (Obama's "pivot" to Asia), he signed legislation into law on December 31, 2018, that strengthened the United States' role in Asia (e.g., providing more security and financial development assistance to Indo-China nations). As a scholar at Stanford University wrote, the president's "goal in Asia is consistent with that of previous administrations from both parties: preserving what the Trump administration calls a 'free and open Indo-Pacific.'"[10] There are simply too many issues (immigration, human trafficking, cybercrime, climate change, pandemics, terrorism, and so on) for the United States to resolve alone. They require multilateral cooperation. How the president and Congress move forward to accommodate ever-changing global conditions are complex and chronic challenges.

Formulating and implementing U.S. foreign and national-security policies are not episodic activities but continual obligations. Congress and the president share in these duties—just as in domestic and budgetary matters. Congress has broad constitutional authority to take part in foreign-policy and domestic-security decisions. Even the most decisive chief executives can find themselves constrained by active, informed, and determined policy makers on Capitol Hill.

CONSTITUTIONAL POWERS

The U.S. Constitution is, in noted presidential scholar Edward S. Corwin's classic words, "an invitation to struggle for the privilege of directing American foreign policy."[11] In other words, foreign and military powers are divided between the branches. "While the president is usually in a position to *propose,* the Senate and Congress are often in a technical position at least to *dispose.*"[12] The struggle over the proper role of each branch in shaping foreign policy involves conflict over policy as well as over process.

The President Proposes

The chief executive enjoys certain innate advantages in dealing with foreign affairs. As John Jay wrote in *Federalist* No. 64, the office's unity, its superior information sources, and its capacity for secrecy and dispatch give the president daily charge of foreign intercourse.[13] In Jay's time, Congress was not in session for much of the year, whereas the president was always on hand to make decisions.

The president's explicit international powers are to negotiate treaties and appoint ambassadors (powers shared with the Senate), to receive ambassadors and other emissaries, and to serve as commander in chief of the armed forces. The latter power looms large over the interbranch politics of the modern period, during which presidents have at their disposal huge military, security, and intelligence capabilities.[14] Presidents have claimed not only their explicit prerogatives but also others not spelled out in the Constitution. Whether they are called *implied, inherent,* or *emergency* powers, presidents increasingly invoke them in conducting foreign policy.

The executive branch tends to be favored by foreign-policy specialists, who often denigrate legislative involvement in foreign policy. U.S. leadership in the world, declared a former secretary of state, could be sustained only "if we understand that the president has primary responsibility for the conduct of the nation's foreign policy."[15] Many lawmakers and scholars have a different view. Professor Corwin provided this balanced assessment of the legislative–executive relationship in foreign policy:

> What the Constitution does, *and all that it does,* is to confer on the
> President certain powers capable of affecting our foreign relations, and

certain other powers of the same general kind on the Senate, and still other powers upon the Congress; but which of these organs shall have the decisive and final voice in determining the course of the American nation is left for events to resolve.[16]

Louis Fisher, an expert on legislative–executive relations, emphasized, the "Constitution does not allocate foreign policy to a single branch. It assigns portions to Congress, to the President, and to the president working jointly with the Senate." He added, "The framers deliberately dispersed political functions, including foreign affairs, to avoid concentrating too much power in a single branch."[17]

The boundaries of the president's executive powers received a new test in 2019 when President Trump declared a national emergency at the southern border in order to access funds that Congress had refused to appropriate to build a wall along the border. The president declared that the wall was needed to stop an "invasion" of migrants, gangs, and drugs. In response, the Democratically controlled 116th House passed legislation (H.J. Res. 46) terminating President Trump's emergency declaration.

The Republican-controlled Senate followed suit and approved the House-passed measure by a 59 to 41 vote.[18] President Trump announced in a tweet that he will veto the measure, a first for this president. Should Congress fail to override the veto, the emergency declaration will stand, at least pending judicial review. Plainly, the president's emergency declaration provoked heated debate, legal challenges, bipartisan rejection of a top Trump priority, and legislative initiatives to define the president's emergency powers.[19]

Divided control of the two policy-making branches spurs Congress to cast a more critical eye upon executive actions. Perhaps the most sensible statement of the separation of powers came from Justice Robert Jackson in *Youngstown Sheet and Tube Co. v. Sawyer* (1952). He wrote that "the president might act in external affairs without congressional authority," but he may not act "contrary to an act of Congress."[20] The president's advantages are magnified in times of warfare or crisis. It was Congress's clumsy management of affairs during the Revolutionary War that, among other things, led the founders to champion an independent, energetic executive and to designate the president as commander in chief. Authority tends to become more centralized during wars and crises, so presidential powers reach their zenith at such times. This held true during the Cold War between the United States and the Soviet Union (1947–1989) and the hot wars in Korea (1950–1953) and Vietnam (1964–1975). The same pattern was evident in the period following the terrorist attacks of September 11, 2001. Heightened security fears and wars (Afghanistan and Iraq) and other conflicts in the Middle East (Syria and Yemen, for example) brought new and sometimes unprecedented assertions of executive authority.

Presidential powers usually contract and are subjected to sharper scrutiny from Capitol Hill when tensions ease or when the public tires of a prolonged conflict. As a scholar concluded,

Congress's shifting deference to and defiance of presidential leadership in foreign affairs reflects a political dynamic that stretches back to the beginning of the American republic. Lawmakers are willing to assert their constitutional prerogatives when they believe the United States has little to worry about abroad or the president's proposed course of action threatens to imperil American security. Conversely, when threats are clear . . . , both politics and a sense of good public policy . . . encourage members of Congress to defer to presidential leadership.[21]

In addition to changes in the public mood, partisan incentives also influence the likelihood that Congress will challenge the president's foreign-policy leadership. Divided party control of the two policy-making branches spurs Congress to cast a more critical eye upon executive action.

Congress Reacts

Congress has an impressive arsenal of explicit constitutional duties, such as the power to declare war, to regulate foreign commerce, to raise and support military forces, and to make rules governing military forces, including for "captures on land and water" (Article I, section 8). Paramount is the power of the purse. According to Crabb, Antizzo, and Sarieddine, "It is within the power of Congress to determine the course of American diplomacy, by virtue of its control over expenditures by the federal government."[22]

Congress also wields significant, underestimated influence over the executive branch via its informal powers of debate, investigation, and publicity. Through such mechanisms, Congress can lead public opinion, mobilize political opposition, and thereby constrain the president's choices. An assertive, investigating Congress tends to make presidents think twice before taking bold action in foreign affairs. A recent study, for example, shows that presidents subjected to tougher investigatory scrutiny from Congress tend to take fewer and more limited military actions when faced with international crises than presidents facing a more quiescent Congress.[23]

History demonstrates that neither branch has a monopoly on wisdom and effectiveness in shaping the nation's foreign policy. A challenge for both elective branches is how best to balance national interests with U.S. values, such as the rule of law. A horrific example makes the point.

In 2018, noted journalist Jamal Khashoggi was brutally murdered and dismembered in a Saudi Arabia consulate in Turkey. A sharp critic of the Saudi regime, Khashoggi was called an "enemy of the state" by Saudi Crown Prince Mohammed bin Salman. The CIA concluded that there was sufficient evidence to indicate that the Crown Prince ordered the killing, which the Saudi government denied. President Trump's stance was to question the accusation against the Crown Prince and to emphasize the important strategic role of Saudi Arabia. "It could very well be that the crown prince had knowledge of this tragic event—maybe he did and maybe he didn't," said President Trump. "In any case, our relationship is with the Kingdom of Saudi Arabia."[24] Saudi Arabia is a long-standing ally of the United States in the Middle East, aiding the United States in countering Iran and terrorism as well as in many other ways.

Congressional reaction to the murder of Khashoggi was different, as exemplified by the responses of two GOP Senators. Although Sen. Lindsay Graham of South Carolina aligns closely with the president on many issues, he wrote: "I supported the Saudi regime for years, and I agree with President Trump that Saudi Arabia remains a strategic ally. Yet it is not too much to ask an ally not to abuse civilized norms, and the extrajudicial killing of a journalist in a diplomatic facility is nothing if not uncivilized."[25] At a 2019 hearing on the nominee of a new ambassador to Saudi Arabia, Marco Rubio, Fla., called the crown prince a "gangster," "reckless and ruthless," and "increasingly willing to test the limits of what he can get away with."[26] Even so, the ambassadorial nominee stressed the importance of the U.S.-Saudi relationship and emphasized that engagement was "the best way to change conditions in the Arab kingdom."[27] The reaction of the president and lawmakers in Congress to this issue reflects why the choice between interests and values can be difficult and fraught with uncertainty.

WHO SPEAKS FOR CONGRESS?

Congress is a multitongued institution. There are numerous members, including party and committee leaders, who address the wide-ranging subjects of foreign policy and military affairs. Among them are the lawmakers assigned to the panoply of House and Senate committees that principally deal with international matters. There are also House and Senate panels that consider issues with a tangential bearing on foreign and military policy. The focus here is on the foreign-affairs and national-security panels that are among the most influential on Capitol Hill.

The Senate Foreign Relations Committee considers treaties and the nominations of key foreign-policy officials. It normally regards itself as a working partner and adviser to the president. The committee can also challenge presidential decision making. In the late 1960s and early 1970s, during the height of dispute over the Vietnam War, the committee became a forum for antiwar debate under the leadership of its chair, J. William Fulbright, D-Ark. (1959–1974). A classic example from this period occurred when, at age twenty-seven, John Kerry (former senator, presidential nominee, and secretary of state) became the first Vietnam veteran to testify before the committee. On April 22, 1971, Kerry posed a now famous question: "How do you ask a man to be the last man to die for a mistake?" The panel's jurisdiction includes such matters as foreign economic, military, technical, and humanitarian assistance; declarations of war; treaties and executive agreements; and relations of the United States with foreign nations. For most of its history, the House Foreign Affairs Committee has worked in the shadow of its Senate counterpart. Even so, the House committee tends to attract members with a more global outlook than the House as a whole. It also addresses nearly as wide a range of issues as the Senate committee, including human rights, the nonproliferation of nuclear technology, the United Nations, international economic policy, and intelligence activities relating to foreign policy.

The Senate and House armed services committees, which traditionally have a culture of bipartisanship, oversee the nation's military establishment. Annually, they authorize Pentagon spending for research, development, and procurement of weapons systems; construction of military facilities; and rules for civilian and uniformed personnel. Although global strategy and military readiness are important matters for the committees' members, what also rivets their attention are issues closer to home, such as force levels, military installations, and defense contracts. Thus, constituency politics (the two Congresses) often drive military policy.

Because of their funding jurisdictions, House and Senate appropriations subcommittees exert detailed control over foreign and defense policies. Tariffs and other trade regulations are the domains of the taxing committees (House Ways and Means and Senate Finance). Committees involved in banking handle international financial and monetary policies. And the commerce committees have jurisdiction over foreign commerce generally.

The House and Senate select intelligence committees were created in the late 1970s, following revelations of widespread abuses, illegalities, and misconduct on the part of intelligence agencies, particularly the Central Intelligence Agency (CIA) and the Federal Bureau of Investigation (FBI). The two panels have similar jurisdictional responsibilities, which is oversight of the intelligence community (e.g., the CIA, FBI, and so on), as well as the intelligence activities of other departments and agencies. Moreover, the two panels also report legislation authorizing appropriations for different components of the intelligence community.

The two panels over the years have operated in a generally bipartisan manner. The two leaders of the Senate Intelligence panel—Chairman Richard Burr, R-N.C., and Vice Chair Mark Warner, D-Va.—"have maintained a cooperative bipartisan rapport during the panel's probe into Russia's influence on the 2016 elections."[28] For example, the two issued a joint statement that said: "We see no reason to dispute [the intelligence community's] conclusions" that Russia interfered in the 2016 presidential election with the aim of helping candidate Donald Trump prevail over Hillary Clinton.[29] Bipartisan cooperation on the Russia probe was not evident in the 115th House, however.

The GOP majority on the House Intelligence panel issued a controversial report declaring that there was "no evidence that the Trump campaign [of 2016] colluded, coordinated or conspired with the Russian government," ending the panel's Russia investigation. The Democratic minority viewed the GOP report as partisan (e.g., protecting the president) and incomplete. They continued with their own investigation. With Democrats in control of the 116th House, the Intelligence panel "expanded [the] Russia investigation."[30] Former GOP representative Mike Rogers, Mich., who chaired the House panel for four years (2011–2015), said of the partisan controversies: "I think the sharp-edged partisanship hurts the committee's ability to do traditional and important oversight of the intelligence community. It just becomes a toxic place."[31]

Two other panels are important to note: the House Homeland Security Committee and the Senate Homeland Security and Governmental Affairs Committee. With respect to homeland security, both panels have roughly comparable responsibilities. Both, for example, have legislative and/or oversight jurisdiction over such matters as border and port security, threats to the United States, cybersecurity, the protection of the nation's critical infrastructure, and the Department of Homeland Security.

Faced with a profusion of congressional power centers, executive-branch policy makers complain that they do not know whom to consult when crises arise, that they have to testify before too many committees, and that leaks of sensitive information are inevitable with so many players. But executive-branch officials or their emissaries are often free to consult with as few or as many lawmakers as they choose—in some cases with only the joint party leaders, in others with chairs and ranking members of the relevant committees. And when Congress tries to step in to influence administration policies, executive officers predictably complain about "micromanagement."

TYPES OF FOREIGN AND NATIONAL-SECURITY POLICIES

Foreign policy is the total of decisions and actions governing a country's relations with other nations and consists of national goals to be achieved and resources for achieving them. Statecraft is the art of selecting preferred outcomes and marshaling the appropriate resources to attain them. As former secretary of state Henry A. Kissinger, a foreign-policy pragmatist, put it, "Values are essential for defining objectives; strategy is what implements them by establishing priorities and defining timing."[32]

Defining a nation's goals is no simple matter. The subject has sparked intense conflict both between Congress and the president and within Congress itself. Momentous congressional debates have displayed widely diverging views on subjects such as ties to England and France during the nation's early decades, American expansion abroad, tariff rates, involvement in foreign wars, approaches to combating terrorists, and U.S. involvement in nation building or regime change.

Lee H. Hamilton, D-Ind., a former chair of the House Foreign Affairs Committee and an acknowledged authority on international relations, summarized what he viewed as the major components of the national interest: (1) to preserve the territorial integrity of the United States and the safety and security of its people; (2) to sustain U.S. economic prosperity; (3) to promote democratic values; (4) to promote basic human rights; and (5) to protect the health and welfare of the American people.[33] Today, the national interest has been broadened to include a number of other components that affect the United States' security, such as soaring obesity rates that prevent many individuals from joining the military; the "dysfunction" in Washington that raises questions, noted a defense secretary, "about the capacity of our democracy to respond to crisis"; or illegal fishing because the vessels are used to smuggle arms to terrorist groups and to traffic in drugs and persons.[34]

As for resources for meeting such national goals, military strength and preparedness immediately come to mind. However, other assets, such as wealth, productivity, creativity, political ideals, cultural values, and global credibility, are even more potent in the long run. In balancing national goals and national resources, policy makers confront several different and sometimes overlapping types of foreign and national-security policies. Structural policies involve procuring and deploying resources or personnel; devising strategic policies to advance the nation's objectives militarily or diplomatically; and forging crisis policies to protect the nation from specific foreign or domestic threats.

STRUCTURAL POLICIES

National-security programs involve millions of workers and the expenditure of billions of dollars annually. Decisions about deploying such vast resources are called structural-policy decisions. Examples include choices of specific weapons systems, contracts with private suppliers, the location of military installations, sales of weapons and surplus goods to foreign countries, and trade policies that affect domestic industries and workers. Structural policy making on foreign and defense issues shares important commonalities with distributive policy making in the domestic realm.

Since World War II, the nation has seen a growing imbalance in the military versus nonmilitary elements of foreign policies. In 2019, the U.S. military budget (about $730 billion) was larger than those of the next seven or eight nations of the world combined.[35] But the singular military machine of the United States is, historically speaking, a fairly recent phenomenon. After earlier wars, the United States quickly "sent the boys home" and, under congressional pressure, shrank its armed forces—though each time to somewhat higher plateaus.[36] After World War II, however, the Cold War threat led to unprecedented levels of peacetime preparedness. By 1960, when retiring president Dwight D. Eisenhower, a career military officer, warned against the *military–industrial complex* (his speech draft said *military–industrial–congressional complex*), the new militarism was already deeply embedded in the nation's political and economic system.

After Health and Human Services, Department of Defense (DOD) spending is the biggest discretionary portion of the federal budget. In 2011, Congress enacted the Budget Control Act of 2011 (see Chapter 14) to require fiscal belt-tightening every year for the following ten years for both defense and domestic discretionary spending. In practice, however, Congress has repeatedly enacted legislation (in 2013, 2015, and 2018) to raise the caps to prevent these cuts from taking effect. The 2018 law will expire in September 2020, at which point the Budget Control Act's spending caps will either go into effect or Congress will have to vote to raise them again.

Meanwhile, the Pentagon has also used a separate war account—the Overseas Contingency Operation (OCO), which is exempt from the 2011 law (the Budget Control Act)—as a source of extra funds to ease budgetary pressures. OCO was "originally meant to cover the costs of the wars in Iraq and Afghanistan, but it has grown into an all-purpose funding mechanism for almost anything the Pentagon wants."[37] Various House and Senate committees closely scrutinize the OCO budget to determine if it is the equivalent of a "slush fund" for the Pentagon, used to avoid the statutory spending caps set in the 2011 law and boost funds for a variety of Defense Department initiatives that may be non-war related.

Although spending reductions occur in all of the military services, the Pentagon remains the nation's largest employer, its largest customer, and its largest procurer of equipment and services. DOD controls a huge number of structural outlays, which attract a wide swath of political interests. As a venture capitalist put it, "The military is like a Fortune No. 1 company."[38]

The State Department's 2019 budget and the closely related (but independent) Agency for International Development is just over $50 billion. This budget not only funds diplomatic representation but also foreign development, global health programs, support for peacekeeping missions, refugee resettlement, poverty reduction, humanitarian aid, and many other priorities.[39] The State Department's services and achievements are largely intangible, and in any event, it spends much of its energy and money overseas. It is little surprise, then, that it has few strong domestic clients and, compared with DOD, fewer champions on Capitol Hill. Although State and Defense are typically rivals for resources and influence, Pentagon leaders have urged Congress to provide more money for State. They stress the importance of strengthening national security by better integrating diplomacy and development (soft power) with military action (hard power). Military generals also have supported more money for the foreign aid budget. As an Air Force General stated, "This is better for our country and cheaper in the long run and a lot less blood and treasure."[40] Nonetheless, foreign aid, which accounts for around 1 percent of the annual federal budget, is often targeted for deep spending cuts unless Congress objects.

The Military–Industrial–Congressional Complex

Defense dollars for projects, contracts, and bases, among other things, are sought by business firms, labor unions, and local communities. As champions of local interests, as highlighted by the two Congresses, lawmakers are naturally drawn into the process. The distributive impulse is wholly bipartisan. The perfect weapons system, it is said, is one with a component manufactured in every congressional district in the nation. Recommendations to reduce or eliminate weapons systems or military facilities are typically met with howls of protest from lawmakers whose states and districts would lose jobs. By the same token, the construction of military installations can trigger intense competition between or among states and districts because of the potential for significant job growth in their communities. (Some observers have suggested that a *surveillance–industrial complex* has emerged in the post-9/11 era, in which the government's interception of communications is contracted to private companies.[41])

Weapons Systems

In 2014, the Air Force wanted to retire, for cost-saving reasons, the A-10 Warthog, a jet fighter that provides close (treetop-level) air support to military troops on the ground. Many lawmakers with A-10s located in their states and districts—the two Congresses—quickly mobilized in both chambers to save the A-10. More than thirty lawmakers wrote to the defense secretary, stating, "It would be unconscionable to further cut an asset like the A-10 . . . increasing the risks to our service members."[42] Retired Air Force officers lobbied to save the A-10. In the end, Congress kept the A-10 flying, "forbidding the Air Force from taking it out of service."[43] The Defense Department "opted to use the plane in combat against the Islamic State."[44]

An ostensible replacement for the A-10 and other military jets is the F-35 Joint Strike Fighter, the largest and most expensive Pentagon weapons program in history, estimated at $1.4 trillion in procurement and operating costs over its expected multidecade lifespan.[45] Over fifteen years in the making, the initial estimated cost to build 2,866 F-35s was $233 billion; in 2016, the Pentagon estimated that $379 billion would cover the cost for over 2,457 planes "that come in three models, one each for the Air Force, Navy, and Marine Corps."[46] It is a plane that can travel at the speed of sound and is invisible to radar. However, the F-35 encountered severe problems from design flaws, delays, and growing cost overruns, not to mention being rushed into production before the testing phase was completed. The result was this: engine fires, software issues, a flawed ejection seat that could decapitate pilots, and inadequate cyber protection (from Chinese hackers, for example).

Noteworthy is that despite years of technical deficiencies, delays, and cost over-runs, Lockheed Martin, the F-35s principal designer and builder, was especially strategic in what is called *political engineering.* The company "supports about 133,000 jobs [spread over 1,300 companies] in 45 states and Puerto Rico," which, in turn, has "generated broad bipartisan support [for the F-35] on Capitol Hill."[47]

Military Base Closures

The proliferation and geographic dispersion of military installations is another example of distributive military policy making. In the post–Cold War era, Congress tried to surmount the politically unpalatable problem of closing unneeded military installations. In 1988, it passed a law intended to insulate such decisions from congressional pressure by delegating them to bipartisan Base Realignment and Closing Commissions (BRACs). The BRACs were also intended to eliminate pressure on lawmakers to vote for an administration's programs in exchange for keeping open military bases in their districts. As Rep. Dick Armey, R-Tex., the champion of the BRAC legislation, stated, "The fact is, unfortunate as it is, that historically base closings have been used as a point of leverage by administrations, Democratic and Republican administrations, as political leverage over and above Members of Congress to encourage them to vote in a manner that the administration would like."[48]

Using the defense secretary's recommendations, a BRAC would draw up a list of installations targeted for closure. To make the decisions hard to overturn, the list had to be accepted or rejected as a whole by the president and Congress. The House and Senate each employ so-called expedited (or "fast-track") procedures—a limit on floor consideration and a prohibition on amendments, for example—when they consider base closure legislation. Despite political hurdles, base closures are part of Congress's wider effort to balance the budget by closing unneeded military installations.

Five rounds of BRACs (1988, 1991, 1993, 1995, and 2005) reduced or eliminated hundreds of defense installations. The political pressures were intense. One commission chair was greeted at base entrances by parents holding children who, they said, would starve if the base closed.[49] Anti-BRAC lawmakers from affected areas fought the closure lists and nearly succeeded in overturning them. From the Pentagon's perspective, the closures of excess infrastructure meant that the savings could be spent on higher military priorities. Communities where bases were shuttered looked for new uses for the military facilities, such as the land and buildings and, in some cases, requested federal assistance for the cleanup of environmental contamination at these installations.

Since 2005, there has not been another BRAC. Lawmakers recall that the 2005 BRAC cost more to implement ($35 billion) than the savings ($15 billion) it produced by closing or consolidating facilities. "BRAC is a painful process with questionable cost savings," observed a senator.[50] Asked when there might be another BRAC round, Senate Armed Services chairman Jim Inhofe, R-Okla., replied: '[W]hen the time comes that we feel that we have an adequate funding for our military. I don't know when that time's going to be."[51]

Trade Politics

Another arena for distributive politics is foreign trade. Since the First Congress (1789–1791), the legislative branch's constitutional power to "regulate commerce with foreign nations" and to "lay and collect taxes, duties, imposts, and excises" has been used to protect and enhance the competitive position of U.S. goods and industries, whether cotton, wheat, textiles, or computer software. Until the 1930s, tariff legislation—long the primary source of federal revenue—was contested on Capitol Hill by political parties and economic regions. Northern manufacturers, for example, wanted protectionist tariffs, and southern exporting states wanted low tariffs to avoid other nations' retaliatory tariffs against their agricultural products.

Starting with the Reciprocal Trade Agreements Act of 1934 (P.L. 73–316), however, Congress began to delegate the details of tariff negotiations to the executive branch. The 1974 Trade Act is a key statute that transfers trade-negotiating authority to the president, subject to Congress's ability to approve or disapprove the agreements under expedited procedures (for example, limited floor debate and no amendments in either chamber). Expedited procedures provide assurances to trading partners that Congress will act on any negotiated agreements within a certain time period.

Views on Trade

Trade agreements were a major election issue in the 2016 presidential contest and in numerous congressional races, and they remain an issue today. Trump made dismantling or renegotiating trade accords one of the centerpieces of his successful presidential campaign. The issue was especially significant in the so-called Rust Belt region of the nation (e.g., Ohio and Michigan) where foreign trade agreements are blamed by labor unions and blue-collar workers for the loss of thousands of manufacturing jobs in their states. Once elected, President Trump moved quickly to renegotiate NAFTA (the North American Free Trade Agreement) and to withdraw from TPP (the Trans-Pacific Partnership).

President Trump's view of free trade agreements is different from traditional GOP orthodoxy. Traditional Republicans extol the virtues of open markets, maintaining that "by allowing markets to operate unhindered, nations can boost domestic industries, lift their wages and improve living standards."[52] In contrast, President Trump believes that friendly and unfriendly nations have long engaged in unfair trading practices against the United States (e.g., dumping their products at below cost and establishing high tariffs for U.S.-made products). The United States' mounting trade deficits with other nations—a major concern of the president—is the result of "very stupid trade deals and policies" that allowed other countries to take "advantage of us for years."[53] The president's strategy is to confront and challenge nations for their unfair trading practices.

His prime method is to impose tariffs (taxes) on China and other nations to reduce the trade imbalance and to create a playing field that enhances the trading interests of the United States. (However, the trade imbalance has not narrowed but increased in 2018 to a ten-year high of $621 billion.)[54] "Like no other American president since the 1930s, Trump has employed tariffs as his weapon of choice in a multi-front trade war that he vows will return prosperity to shuttered American factories even as critics complain they will cost several jobs for each one they create."[55] Export-oriented businesses, corporations, and farmers often bear the brunt of "weaponizing" tariffs because the affected nations will impose retaliatory tariffs on exported U.S. products, such as bourbon, soybeans, pork, and hundreds of other products.[56] China's retaliatory tariffs often serve a political purpose: to pressure Trump to stop the trade war by angering GOP constituencies, such "red state" farmers and even Senate majority leader McConnell (tariffs on bourbon, Kentucky's well-known product).

If there are "winners" in trade wars, they are likely to be nations with the greatest bargaining leverage and the capacity to absorb disgruntlement from consumers and businesses paying more for imported products. The United States' huge economy and global influence give President Trump an advantage in making favorable trade deals. In the view of a scholar, "if you're a transactional president and bluster and take every small and big negotiation to the hilt, you can win."[57] The president's success in crafting a new NAFTA provides a glimpse of a zero-sum ("winners and losers"), America First trade world where each nation seeks economic advantages over the other.

President Trump called NAFTA "the worst trade deal ever." He wanted instead a trilateral trade pact with Canada and Mexico that better suited U.S. interests. After many months of negotiations, the president was successful. He used tough talk, threats to walk away from further bargaining, and imposing high tariffs on steel and aluminium from Mexico and Canada to win concessions from the two nations. One account said of the bilateral negotiations between Canada and the United States that "the eleventh hour deal came together as a result of deadline pressure, willingness to compromise and Trump's constant threat of hitting Canada's extensive auto industry with tariffs if it didn't agree to a new deal."[58] The trilateral accord is called the U.S.-Mexico-Canada Agreement (USMCA), the renamed NAFTA and, to some analysts, the new accord is similar to NAFTA.

USMCA requires congressional approval, as well as Canada's and Mexico's, before it can take effect. House Democratic majority leader Steny Hoyer indicated there is "deep disagreement" with the USMCA. For example, Rep. Mark Pocan, D-Wisc., a co-chair of the Congressional Progressive Caucus, said of the new pact: "We want to make sure we have a bill that works for labor, for the environment, for consumers."[59] At this juncture, it is unclear when the administration will transmit the USMCA to Congress for its consideration.

Trade produces winners (cheaper imports for consumers) and losers (displaced workers). Many U.S. workers oppose trade accords, in part because U.S. corporations have moved their businesses overseas to take advantage of low labor costs and lax environmental standards. Worker anger against open trade is also a function of broader discontents and developments, such as globalization and automation. Even so, it seems evident that more needs to be done by the public and private sectors to assist displaced and unemployed workers in states that have lost thousands of jobs. For example, this assistance might include retraining and apprentice programs; financial assistance to attend community colleges and other educational institutions; or computer and digital instruction to give unemployed workers in Rust Belt communities, for example, the skills to win better-paying jobs.[60]

Worth emphasis is that statutory trade agreements and hikes in tariffs require congressional action and cannot be revoked or reversed unilaterally by the president unless the agreement itself authorizes such action. Both Congress and the president shape trade policy. The Constitution (Section 8) grants Congress explicit authority to impose tariffs and to regulate commerce with foreign nations. There are, however, many existing laws that grant the president significant authority to change trade policy.

Section 232 of the Trade Promotion Act of 1962 authorizes the president to impose import tariffs for national security reasons, such as on Canada for steel and dairy products. Wider use of security tariffs, especially when imposed on U.S. allies, has aroused the concern of many lawmakers. They have sponsored legislation that, for example, would "require Congress to pass a resolution of approval before future Section 232 tariffs could take effect."[61] Section 301 of the aforementioned Trade Act of 1974 provides legal authority to the president "to deny U.S. trade benefits or impose import duties in response to foreign trade barriers."[62]

The two Congresses suffuse the politics of trade on Capitol Hill. For example, lawmakers who represent constituents who reside in export-oriented districts or states, such as Iowa or Washington, have lawmakers who champion their cause. Regularly, Iowa GOP senator Charles Grassley talks to Iowans interested in open markets and low tariffs. "It could be agriculture. It could be services. It could be manufacturing. Whether it's John Deere or Vermeer or 3M . . . they're in support of" foreign trade.[63] In much the same way, Democrats from export-oriented Silicon Valley in California also generally argue for reduced trade barriers. In contrast, a Democratic House member from New York City stated, "There's just been a barrage on both sides, from the far left and the far right, in opposition" to free trade.[64]

Fast-Track Trade Negotiations

Having delegated most decisions to the executive, lawmakers who want to review specific trade deals must struggle to get back in the game. The Trade Act of 1974 addressed this dilemma. The president, it said, must actively consult, notify, and involve Congress as he negotiates trade agreements. These agreements would take effect only after an implementing law is enacted, and such legislation would be handled under a fast-track procedure (today called trade promotion authority or TPA). TPA means that Congress delegates authority to the president to negotiate trade agreements subject to an array of required consultations with Congress. In addition, specific requirements are imposed on the president when he submits draft implementing legislation to the Congress.

Most presidents since 1974 have been awarded TPA to negotiate trade pacts subject to up-or-down votes in both houses of Congress within a specified time period and under procedures that promote a final vote on the measure. TPA has lapsed and been renewed several times over the years. For example, in 2002, after a vigorous lobbying effort, President Bush won a five-year renewal of the fast-track procedure. To gain the needed House votes, numerous concessions were made to placate textile workers and citrus growers, among others. The fast-track authority lapsed again in 2007 but was renewed in 2015 for six years.

STRATEGIC POLICIES

To protect the nation's interests, decision makers design strategic policies on spending levels for international and defense programs; total military force levels; the basic mix of military forces and weapons systems; arms sales to foreign powers; foreign-trade inducements or restrictions; allocation of economic, military, and technical aid to developing nations; treaty obligations to other nations; U.S. responses to human rights abuses abroad; and its stance toward international bodies such as the United Nations (UN), the North Atlantic Treaty Organization (NATO), and world financial agencies.

Strategic policies overlap and embrace most important foreign-policy questions. They engage executive decision makers as well as congressional committees. Such debates can express citizens' ideological, ethnic, gender, or economic interests.[65] Strategic issues typically involve broad themes and invoke policy makers' long-term attitudes and beliefs. The key agencies for strategic decision making include the State Department, the Office of the Secretary of Defense, the intelligence agencies, and the National Security Council—all advising the president.

The Power of the Purse

Congress uses its spending power to establish overall appropriations levels for foreign and defense purposes. Under those ceilings, priorities must be assigned among military services; among weapons systems; between uniformed personnel and military hardware; and to economic, cultural, or military aid—to name just a few of the choices. The president leads by presenting the annual budget, lobbying for the administration's priorities, and threatening to veto options deemed unacceptable. Yet if it chooses, Congress also can write its own budget down to the smallest detail. And the omnibus character of many appropriations measures places pressure on the president to accede to the outcome of legislative bargaining on expenditures. To get the largest percentage of the budget the administration wants, the president may have to swallow the smaller percentage he opposes.

Global Threats

Congress responds both to perceived levels of international tension and to shifting public views about global engagement. After the collapse of the Soviet Union, a bipartisan consensus in the Pentagon and in Congress agreed that defense funding and force levels could be cut gradually. That consensus arose either from the belief that a sizable peace dividend could be realized or from the hope that savings could be gained from smarter planning and trimming waste, fraud, and abuse. However, footing the bill for combat operations poses dilemmas for Congress. How much money is needed, and how much freedom should the president have in spending it? President Lyndon B. Johnson gradually deepened U.S. involvement in

Vietnam, but he hesitated to ask Congress to appropriate the needed funds. Thus, the first supplemental funding bill was passed in February 1966, even though Congress had signed on to the war as early as August 1964 (with the Gulf of Tonkin Resolution). Johnson's effort to hide the escalating war costs while maintaining domestic programs elevated both inflation and the federal debt.

After the September 11, 2001, attacks on the United States, Congress acted swiftly to pass a $40 billion supplemental appropriations package, one-fourth of which was under the president's near-total control. Following the U.S. invasion of Afghanistan in October 2001, Congress approved another $30 billion, again featuring flexibility. However, some lawmakers, especially on the funding committees, expressed their doubts. "All presidents want unlimited authority. In any time of conflict, there's a tendency to allow a little more leeway," said an Appropriations subcommittee chair. "We have a responsibility to maintain a balance . . . and we're struggling with that."[66] The power of the purse is a blunt instrument in time of war. In the final analysis, no major foreign or military enterprise can be sustained unless Congress provides money and support. A president can conduct an operation for a time using existing funds and supplies, just as Johnson did at first in Vietnam, but sooner or later, Congress must be asked for funding. The U.S. role in South Vietnam finally ended in 1974, when Congress simply refused to provide emergency aid funds.

Today, a major challenge for defense planners is how to allocate scarce resources among competing security priorities. The threats from hostile nations and nonstate actors are real; the costs of maintaining a volunteer army are high; and budgets for research and development of new weaponry as well as for equipment maintenance are escalating. The bottom line is, should budgetary considerations determine defense strategies, or should the nature of global threats determine, within reason, the Pentagon's spending?

Treaties and Executive Agreements

The Constitution calls for Congress and the president to be partners in a key element of strategic policy: treaties with foreign powers. Under Article VI of the Constitution, all treaties "shall be the supreme Law of the Land" unless the treaty itself requires implementing legislation.

Although the president initiates them, treaties are made "by and with the advice and consent of the Senate." The Senate's consent is signified by the concurrence of two-thirds of the senators present and voting, a quorum being present. Treaty approval by the Senate entails more than a simple up-or-down vote; it is conducted in two steps. First, the Senate takes up the treaty. If it must be amended, an infrequent occurrence, it must be renegotiated with the nations that were parties to it.

Second, the Senate considers a resolution of ratification. Reservations, declarations, or understandings can be added to this document; their adoption by majority vote does not require renegotiation of the treaty. According to one scholar, the "three qualifiers demarcate future U.S. behavior, intent, or policy positions as a result of the treaty. . . . They can also specify U.S. policy on unrelated issues."[67] The Senate, of course, can simply refuse to consider a treaty.

Congress may or may not be taken into the president's confidence when treaties and executive agreements are negotiated. To avoid humiliation like that experienced by President Woodrow Wilson when the Senate rejected the Treaty of Versailles after World War I, modern chief executives typically inform key senators during the negotiation process. Rarely does the Senate reject a treaty outright. In fact, it has turned down only twenty-one treaties since 1789. The most recent was the Senate's rejection of the Convention of the Rights of Persons with Disabilities in December 2012.

A major success for President Obama was winning Senate approval of a major arms control treaty with Russia. Dubbed "New START" (Strategic Arms Reduction Treaty)—the original START treaty was negotiated in the late 1980s— the president won the treaty approval battle after an intensive lobbying campaign:

> He mounted a five-week campaign that married public pressure
> and private suasion. He enlisted the likes of Henry Kissinger, asked
> Chancellor Angela Merkel of Germany to help and sent a team of officials
> to set up a war room of sorts on Capitol Hill. Vice President Joseph R.
> Biden, Jr. had at least 50 meetings or phone calls with Senators.[68]

Worth mention is that President Trump is unilaterally withdrawing from the landmark 1987 Intermediate-Range Nuclear Forces (INF) agreement. The treaty limited the range of land-based cruise missiles (conventional or nuclear). President Trump said that Putin-led Russia had violated the treaty, and that the INF was obsolete because many other nations, such as China, India, and Pakistan, were not signatories to the arms control pact. Noteworthy is that the Constitution requires both the Senate and president to approve a treaty but is silent on withdrawal from a treaty. Presidents assume that the withdrawal prerogative is theirs alone to exercise without congressional involvement.

The demise of the INF has at least three consequences. First, it might spark another dangerous and costly arms race among several nations, such as the U.S., Russia, China, Iran, India, Pakistan, and North Korea. Second, some express concern about ending either bilateral or multi-lateral security treaties. As a former Defense Secretary (William Perry) pointed out: "Our treaties have been a very important vehicle [of dialogue] in the past. They have provisions for discussing the issues, including discussion of disagreements about compliance. When we withdraw from treaties, we are losing this important vehicle."[69] Third, an Air Force general underscored the value of nuclear weapons agreements. His focus was Russia, but the general's proposal could broadly apply to many nations with, or aspiring to have, nuclear weapons. He said that nuclear accords are important. They provide "insight through the verification process" and "that insight is unbelievably important to understand what Russia is doing."[70]

Because of the hurdle of obtaining a two-thirds Senate vote, since World War II, presidents have relied increasingly on executive agreements—international accords that are not submitted to the Senate for its advice and consent. As explained by two legal scholars,

> As a matter of historical practice, the president may also make international agreements if authorized to do so by a law passed by Congress. (These are called "congressional–executive" agreements; the North American Free Trade Agreement is a prominent example.) And in some narrow [usually military] cases, the president may create an international agreement all by himself through his own constitutional powers. [All are] legally binding on the United States and future presidents.[71]

Although the conventional wisdom typically attributes the rise of executive agreements to presidential evasion of the Senate's treaty confirmation role, political scientists Glen S. Krutz and Jeffrey S. Peake argue that executive agreements constitute "a rational response by the president and Congress to the challenges faced by the United States during the daunting complexity brought on by the emergence of its international leadership in the twentieth century" and beyond.[72] Executive agreements go into force more quickly than treaties and offer a much less cumbersome process for management of international affairs—efficiency gains that can benefit Congress as well as the president.

In federal court cases challenging whether such agreements should have been treaties, the justices have invoked the political-questions doctrine and declined to rule on the merits. This doctrine holds that the issue is best left "to the discretion and expertise of the legislative and executive branches."[73]

Other Policy-Making Powers of Congress

In addition to its control of the purse strings, Congress employs an array of other techniques to shape or influence strategic policies. The most common tools of congressional policy leadership are informal advice and legislative prodding through nonbinding resolutions or policy statements; policy oversight and legislative directives or restrictions; and legislative mandates.[74]

Advising, Prodding

Congressional leaders and key members routinely provide the president and other executive officials with informal advice. Sometimes, this advice proves decisive. In 1954, President Eisenhower dispatched Secretary of State John Foster Dulles to meet with a small bipartisan group of congressional leaders to determine whether the United States should intervene militarily in Indochina (Vietnam). The leaders unanimously declined to sponsor a resolution favoring involvement until other nations indicated their support of military action. Lacking assurances from either Congress or foreign allies, Eisenhower decided against intervening.[75]

Congressional speeches are also important in framing media and public opinion. These speeches, two scholars note, can "shape media coverage of prospective uses of force, which in turn impacts public opinion about the war." They add, "All sorts of trouble, political or otherwise, await the president who loses public support for an ongoing military venture."[76]

Oversight

Congress shapes foreign policy through oversight of the executive branch's performance. Hearings and investigations often focus on foreign-policy issues. Recurrent hearings on authorizing and funding State Department and Defense Department programs offer many opportunities for lawmakers to voice their concerns, large and small. Another device is to require that certain decisions or agreements be submitted to Congress before they go into effect. Congress and its committees may also require reports from the executive that "provide not only information for oversight but also a handle for action."[77] Hundreds of foreign- and defense-policy reporting requirements are embedded in current statutes. Oversight in time of war or crisis can be problematic. The president resists intrusions, and lawmakers are often reluctant to impede the administration's actions.

Legislative Mandates

Congress sometimes makes foreign policy by legislative directives—to launch new programs, to authorize certain actions, or to set guidelines. Foreign-policy statutes may include explicit legislative restrictions, which perhaps are Congress's most effective weapon. Often, they are embedded in authorization or appropriations bills. Legislation also shapes the structures and procedures through which policies are carried out. "Congress changes the structure and procedures of decision making in the executive branch in order to influence the content of policy," writes James M. Lindsay.[78] When lawmakers wanted to reform military procurement, they restructured permanent units of the Defense Department to clarify and streamline the process.

CRISIS POLICIES: THE WAR POWERS

An international crisis endangering the nation's safety, security, or vital interests pushes aside other foreign-policy goals. Examples range from Japan's attack on the U.S. naval fleet in Pearl Harbor in 1941 to the al Qaeda attacks of September 11, 2001.

Crisis policies engage decision makers at the highest levels: the president, the secretaries of state and defense, the National Security Council, and the Joint Chiefs of Staff. Congressional leaders are sometimes brought into the picture. More rarely, congressional advice is sought out and heeded—as in President Eisenhower's 1954 decision against military intervention in Indochina. Often, when executive decision makers fear congressional opposition, they simply neglect to inform Capitol

Hill until the planned action is underway. A failed attempt in 1980 to rescue U.S. hostages in Iran, for example, was planned in strictest secrecy, and no legislative consultations were undertaken by the Carter administration. Strict secrecy also surrounded a major success of President Obama's in May 2011: sending special operations forces to kill Osama Bin Laden—the al Qaeda leader and architect of the 9/11 attack on the United States—at his residence in Abbottabad, Pakistan.

Constitutional Powers

War powers are shared by the president and Congress. The president is the commander in chief of the military and naval forces of the United States (Article II, section 2), but Congress has the power to declare (authorize) war (Article I, section 8). The framers vested the power to declare war in Congress because they understood that monarchs and dictators often took their nations to war for personal reasons, such as ambition or military glory, rather than the national interest. As John Jay wrote in *Federalist* No. 4, "These and a variety of other motives, which affect only the mind of the sovereign, often lead him to engage in wars not sanctified by justice or the voices and interests of his people." The framers expected the commander in chief to defend the nation against sudden attacks, implying a limited military role for the president. Lawmakers and scholars have argued for decades about this division of the war powers.

Congress has "enacted eleven separate formal declarations of war against foreign nations in five different wars."[79] The five wars are the following: the War of 1812 (1812–1814), the Mexican War (1846–1848), the Spanish-American War (1898), World War I (1917–1918), and World War II (1941–1945). In four instances, Congress readily assented to the president's call for war, acknowledging in the declaration that a state of war already existed. Only once did Congress delve into the merits of waging war, and that was in 1812, when the vote was close. In two cases—the Mexican and Spanish-American conflicts—lawmakers later had reason to regret their haste.

In an age of undeclared and unconventional wars, more problematic than formal declarations are the hundreds of other instances in which U.S. military forces have been deployed abroad. (The number is uncertain because of quasi-engagements involving military or intelligence advisers.)[80] The examples range from an undeclared naval war with France (1798–1800) to the invasion of Iraq (2003). Since the last declared war—World War II in 1941—numerous military interventions have taken place abroad. Some were massive and prolonged wars: Korea (1950–1953), Vietnam (1964–1975), Afghanistan (2001–), and Iraq (1991, 2003–2011). Still others were short-lived actions, such as rescue or peacekeeping missions—some of which involved casualties (Lebanon, 1983; Somalia, 1992–1993)—or the bombing of Syria for its use of chemical weapons (2018).

Most of these interventions were authorized by the president as commander in chief on the stated grounds of protecting U.S. lives, property, or interests abroad. Some were justified on the grounds of treaty obligations or "inherent powers" derived from a broad reading of executive prerogatives. Others were peacekeeping efforts under UN or NATO sponsorship. There were also humanitarian-relief operations in nations hit by natural disasters, such as the one following the massive earthquake and tsunami in Japan in 2011.

A fundamental change has occurred in the division of war powers between Congress and the president. Congress's constitutional war-declaring authority has migrated to the president. The change occurred in 1950 when President Truman took the nation to war against North Korea, without seeking a declaration of war or any formal congressional authorization. Congress retains an arsenal of tools to challenge the president (such as the purse strings, advice and consent, lawmaking, investigations, and debate), but it often defers to the chief executive rather than asserting its formidable constitutional prerogatives. Federal courts are reluctant to address the constitutionality of presidential war-making actions, preferring to leave the issue to the political branches to work out.

Members of Congress, though wary of armed interventions, are reluctant to halt them: "No one actually wants to cut off funds when American troops are in harm's way," a House leadership aide explained. "The preferred stand is to let the president make the decisions and, if it goes well, praise him, and if it doesn't, criticize him," observed former representative Lee Hamilton.[81] Interventions go well if they come to a swift, successful conclusion, with few American lives lost. Actions that drag on without a satisfactory resolution or that cost many lives will eventually tax both lawmakers'—especially the congressional opposition—and citizens' patience.

The War Powers Resolution

The Johnson and Nixon administrations' conduct of the war in Vietnam left many lawmakers skeptical of presidential war-making initiatives. In 1973, Congress passed the War Powers Resolution (WPR, P.L. 93–148) over President Richard Nixon's veto. This law requires the president to consult with Congress before introducing U.S. troops into hostilities; report to Congress any commitment of forces within forty-eight hours; and terminate the use of forces within sixty days—there is an additional thirty days to ensure a safe withdrawal—if Congress does not declare war, does not specifically authorize the use of force, does not extend the period by law, or is unable to meet.

Presidents commonly issue reports to Congress within forty-eight hours after troops have been deployed abroad. Congress, however, regularly abdicates its responsibility after the sixty-day period to pass legislation supporting U.S. military actions. For example, President Obama reported on March 21, 2011, "consistent with the War Powers Resolution," that he had deployed U.S. military forces in Libya.[82] However, the president missed the sixty-day deadline for securing congressional approval for military operations and thus was evidently required to withdraw U.S. forces. Other presidents have also missed the sixty-day deadline, arguing that the WPR is unconstitutional; that the conflict or intervention is too small or limited to be called a war; or that the United States is not really engaged in hostilities because NATO leaders are in command of the military operation.[83] The WPR has few outright defenders, but lawmakers are not ready to repeal or replace it. Although it diminishes Congress's constitutional power of declaring war, the WPR has some practical virtues. It accommodates the rapid use of armed force without the traditional step of formally declaring war. With respect to some threats, declaring war may not be a viable option, in part because it is difficult to declare war against an array of terrorist groups. Moreover, the WPR gives at least a nodding respect to the framers' belief that Congress, the branch most representative of the people, is the sole source of legal and moral authority for major military enterprises.

The WPR is an awkward compromise of executive and legislative authority, and presidents still intervene as they see fit. Members of Congress tend to sit on the sidelines and allow presidents to ignore the WPR. Yet the WPR stands as a reminder to presidents of the ultimate need to gain congressional approval for major military deployments. That approval did occur when President Herbert Walker Bush came before Congress in 1991 for permission to oust the Iraqi military's occupation of Kuwait; and President George W. Bush did the same in 2001; he received congressional support to depose the Taliban-led government of Afghanistan, which had provided safe haven to the terrorists who planned and carried out the 2001 attack on the United States.

More recently, legislation that was authorized under the expedited procedures of the War Powers Resolution passed the Senate (December 2018). Its purpose was to end U.S. support of the Saudi-led war in Yemen. The House took no action on the measure, but Senate passage indicated the willingness of many Senators to reassert its war-declaring role and challenge the White House for its support of Saudi Arabia, especially after the murder of journalist Jamal Khashoggi.[84]

On February 13, 2019, the House passed (248 to 177) a joint resolution authorized by the War Powers Resolution "directing the removal of United States Armed Forces from hostilities in the Republic of Yemen that have not been authorized by Congress." The Democratic majority argued that a war was underway in Yemen, supported by the United States in various ways, such as intelligence and mid-air refuelling of Saudi bombers that drop U.S.-made bombs on schools, hospitals, funerals, and civilian neighborhoods. GOP lawmakers stated that the War Powers Resolution was fatally flawed. It could not be invoked because U.S. troops were not engaged in "hostilities," which means "firing weapons and dropping bombs."[85] GOP members also noted that presidents have broad authority to assist countries in various ways, short of committing troops to combat. To date, the Senate has not acted on comparable legislation. If both chambers do enact the joint resolution, President Trump is likely to veto the measure.

Recent debates over the war powers involve statutory disagreements over two laws: the 2001 Authorization for Use of Military Force (AUMF) in Afghanistan (P.L. 107–40) and the 2002 Authorization for Use of Military Force in Iraq (P.L. 107–243). The 2001 law authorized the president to use military force against "those nations, organizations, or persons he determines planned, authorized, committed, or aided the terrorist attacks that occurred on September 11, 2001."

The 2002 AUMF authorized the president to use the military to enforce various UN Security Council resolutions and to "defend the national security of the United States against the continuing threat posed [by the Saddam Hussein-led] Iraq," who was wrongly believed to have a cache of weapons of mass destruction.[86] The U.S. military did overthrow the Hussein regime, and Iraq, after several strife-filled years, established its own government.

Since 2001, the United States has been engaged in a seemingly never-ending war against terrorist groups, such as al-Qaeda, that are located anywhere on the planet. (Afghanistan is the nation's longest war, 17 years and counting.[87]) Presidents have used the 2001 AUMF and its elastic language to justify military involvement in scores of nations, such as Yemen, Somalia, Libya, the Philipines, Niger, Nigeria, and Syria, and against terrorist groups that were not in existence in 2001 (e.g., Al Shabab in eastern Africa and the Haqqani Network in Afghanistan and Pakistan). As two House members wrote, the 2001 AUMF "contains no time limits, no geographic constraints and no exit strategy. It has effectively become a blank check for any president, at any time, to wage war without congressional consent."[88]

Lawmakers in both chambers have over the years tried, unsuccessfully so far, to update, abolish, or limit the president's use of the 2001 AUMF. In 2019, for example, senators Tim Kaine, D-Va., and Todd Young, R-Ind., introduced legislation to repeal the AUMFs. As Senator Kaine stated, "They serve no operational purpose, run the risk of future abuse by the president, and help keep our nation at permanent war."[89] On the other hand, there are also lawmakers who support the AUMFs. "What I would hate to do in this time when we have asymmetric threats across the globe," said former House Speaker Paul Ryan, R-Wisc., "is to have an AUMF that ties the hands of the military behind their backs." He added: "The last thing I want to see is an AUMF that makes it much more difficult for our military to respond to keep us safe, because they have that authority right now."[90]

U.S. officials and their allies in Europe and elsewhere worry, too, about domestic Islamic terrorist attacks. Sometimes called lone-wolf strikes, Islamic propagandists radicalize followers in various nations to kill people near their homes. As one told radicalized sympathizers, "Smash his head with a rock, or slaughter him with a knife, or run him over with your car [or truck], or throw him down from a high place, or choke him, or poison him."[91] Homegrown violent terrorist attacks in the United States are infrequent—a tribute to heightened security by local, state, and federal officials.[92] In short, anyone can be a target anywhere in this type of "forever war" where there are no surrender ceremonies and no end in sight to these individual terrorist attacks.[93]

Changes in Warfare

The nature of warfare today has evolved and created new challenges for Congress and the White House. President Trump has even proposed the creation of a new military branch: the Space Force. As Vice President Mike Pence declared, space is a "war-fighting domain" that Russia and China are already active in, such as developing anti-satellite weapons that can destroy the space assets of other nations. Congress must create and fund the new military branch. Increasingly, the future of warfare is being reshaped by at least these five developments.

First, consider that cyber war has replaced the Cold War.[94] Today, the top military threats to the United States are Russia, China, Iran, and North Korea. They have each employed cyber attacks against the United States and other nations and entities to, among other things, gather corporate secrets, steal money and personnel records, sabotage financial institutions, or undermine public trust in the United States' democratic system. Russia and China are especially adept at hacking into public and private facilities. As one account noted, Russia and China "routinely send their professionals and military personnel off to master's programs for degrees in subjects like cyber warfare." To keep up with global cyber arms race, the Pentagon has created an Air Force Cyber College for the military branches to ensure that the United States is not "falling behind peer competitors when it comes to cyber education."[95]

Cyber war raises a number of questions, such as, What is the role of Congress in cyber warfare? Can presidents order cyber attacks on any nation or group without congressional knowledge or approval? Are the United States' enemies in cyber warfare nations, terrorist groups, other nonstate actors, or a combination of all? As a member of NATO, would the United States be obligated to engage in cyber warfare if an alliance state is the target of cyber attacks against, for instance, its electrical grid or military command system? As a noted law professor wrote, "Stealth wars require rules, too." This implies a key role for Congress in defining "the scope of the new war, the authorities and limitations on presidential powers and the forms of review of the president's actions."[96]

Second, there has been a rapid increase in the use of drones: remote-controlled, pilotless vehicles that have become the counterterrorism weapon of choice for the targeted killing of insurgents. Drones are also valuable for gathering intelligence, surveillance, and reconnaissance for the military. The military is exploring the use of swarms of small attack drones that can overwhelm anti-aircraft defenses. The Russian manufacturer of the well-known AK-47 assault rifle (the Kalashnikov) is developing a small and inexpensive drone that terrorists and small armies could purchase.[97] There is concern in the United States that drone technology developed for the military can be used to spy and eavesdrop on Americans, arousing privacy fears among many people. Another concern is how to hold the president accountable for his secret decisions to target and kill individuals abroad, including U.S. citizens, through drone strikes. As Sen. Angus King, I-Maine, put it, "Having the executive being the prosecutor, the judge, the jury and the executioner all in one is very contrary to the traditions and laws of this country."

A third type of modern warfare has its own special vocabulary. Some call it irregular warfare, police actions, asymmetric conflicts, hybrid wars, counterinsurgencies, proxy engagements, peacekeeping (not peacemaking) missions, interventions, or something else.[98] These are "no-win" wars, often against nonstate actors, that can go on for years without the traditional end point of a treaty signing between or among the combatants.

Fourth, participants in the diverse types of warfare are also skilled at peddling disinformation, false data, fake stories, and deepfake videos (the creation of videos that look real) targeted at the United States and other Western nations. The "weaponization of information" is an "integral part of Russian military doctrine" and has, at times, "exceeded the power of force of weapons in their effectiveness" by obfuscating an accurate version of events, promoting policy paralysis, or undermining the decision-making competence of European officials, who are called "American puppets."[99]

Fifth, there is an array of evolving technologies with the capacity to change the way future wars might be fought. Consider the military's focus on robotics where "killer robots," equipped with artificial intelligence, take the place of human soldiers on the battlefield and decide on their own when to fire their weapons; undersea drones that come in multiple sizes, carry diverse payloads, and can operate in shallow water; robotic airplanes that would engage in combat alongside manned aircraft; or hypersonic missiles "that fly at 20 times the speed of sound—about 1 mile per second—to render all missile defense systems obsolete,"[100] and which can reach any target in the world without being seen. As a general said, "You can't defend yourself if you can't see it."[101]

Numerous issues are associated with these weapon developments. For example, what role should humans play in exercising control, or are these machines to be autonomous? Would such weaponry be subject to increased cyber attacks? Who is to blame if a killer robot attacks a hospital? Nonetheless, these types of high-tech weapons aim to ensure that the United States has an advantage over competitors that are engaged in the same type of research.

Together, these five unfolding changes in warfare have heightened the challenge for Congress as its members seek to have ongoing and meaningful influence over the conduct of U.S. national-security policy.

CONCLUSION

Members of Congress cannot avoid foreign and national-security policies. As the world seemingly grows ever more interdependent, even in a period of heightened nationalism, those policies impinge upon every citizen and every local community. Today's legislators know that global developments touch their local constituencies, and they believe (rightly or wrongly) that they will be judged, to some degree, on their understanding of those subjects. It especially behooves lawmakers to debate, challenge, and question presidential war-making policies that could involve the blood and treasure of the nation. As the longest-serving senator in the history of that institution, West Virginia Democrat Robert C. Byrd once stated, "Two constitutional power centers—set up by the framers to check and balance one another—and do battle over politics, policies, and priorities—occupy their distinct ends of Pennsylvania Avenue. What makes it all work for the good of the nation is the character of the individuals who serve."[102]

Citizens and Congress. Tourists in the 1930s gawk at the Capitol's elaborately decorated rooms. Today's tourists can take a Segway tour of Capitol Hill, stopping at the Capitol's East Front plaza. The Capitol Visitor Center informs people about Congress's duties and achievements; guides them toward tours of the building and its chambers; offers food, souvenirs, and restrooms; and treats citizens to an unusual underground view of the Capitol Dome.

16

THE TWO CONGRESSES AND THE AMERICAN PEOPLE

"That meeting was one of the most astounding experiences I've had in my 34 years in politics," remarked Sen. Charles E. Schumer, D-N.Y.[1] Schumer had just emerged from a summit with Treasury Secretary Henry M. Paulson Jr. and Federal Reserve chair Ben Bernanke. House and Senate leaders, along with a group of lawmakers responsible for oversight of financial markets, had assembled at 7:00 p.m. on September 18, 2008. Seated under a portrait of Abraham Lincoln, Bernanke somberly detailed the unfolding financial crisis and warned that the entire economy "was on the brink of a heart attack."[2]

Over the preceding ten days, the government had seized Fannie Mae and Freddie Mac. The investment bank Lehman Brothers had filed for bankruptcy and another firm, Merrill Lynch, had been sold at a fire-sale price. The giant insurance firm American International Group (AIG) had been pulled back from collapse by the federal government's $85 billion emergency loan. Credit markets were frozen, denying credit access to consumers and small businesses throughout the country. "I gulped," said Schumer. "We all realized we're not in normal times."[3] To contain the crisis, the George W. Bush Administration sought immediate congressional support for a plan that would allow the Treasury Department to buy up to $700 billion of the distressed assets weighing down the balance sheets of major financial institutions. To put this request in context, $700 billion was more than the Pentagon's annual budget.[4] The three-page proposal asked for unfettered authority to spend these vast sums, with nothing more than semiannual reports to Congress.

The administration wanted Congress to act in a matter of days. "This is the United States Senate," said then–Senate majority leader Harry Reid, D-Nev. "We can't do it in that time frame."[5] The crisis was so urgent that "the Capital almost had the feel of wartime."[6] Still, lawmakers understandably balked at authorizing so much taxpayer money with so little deliberation. "Just because God created the world in seven days doesn't mean we have to pass this bill in seven days," quipped Rep. Joe Barton, R-Tex.[7] Not all members were willing to trust the administration's claims of impending financial disaster. "Where have I heard this before? The Iraqis have weapons of mass destruction, and they're ready to use them," complained Rep. Gene Taylor, D-Miss. "I'm in no rush to do this."

The bailout proposal was extremely unpopular with constituents, who flooded members' offices with calls that ran as much as 30–1 against.[8] The first effort to pass the bill, on September 30, went down to defeat 228–205 in the House of Representatives.[9] The House's action caused a large-scale sell-off on Wall Street, with the Dow Jones stock index plunging 7 percent in one day.

As days unfolded without a congressional consensus, opinion leaders began to speak of "financial Armageddon" and a "credibility test for Congress."[10] Congress eventually acceded to the administration's $700 billion request, but lawmakers imposed some limits on the administration of the program. They amended the administration's proposal to restrict executive compensation, mandated program oversight, and required aid to Americans in danger of losing homes to foreclosure. The amended proposal was approved by Congress and signed into law on October 3, 2008.[11] In the end, however, Congress's efforts to assert more control over the bailout's implementation failed. In carrying out the program, the administration used the funds not to buy toxic assets but to recapitalize banks. It quickly became clear that the banks could not be held accountable for their use of these funds. Treasury also refused to act on mortgage relief.

Congressional handling of the financial crisis was flawed in many respects, but its action helped stave off a potential second Great Depression. Although the bailout remained highly unpopular with voters, the program proved not nearly as expensive for taxpayers as had been expected.[12] Most of the funds disbursed to financial firms were paid back,[13] and by 2019, investments under the program had actually yielded a $96.6 billion profit to the U.S. Treasury.[14] Many economists later judged that the program helped to stabilize the financial system.[15]

A crisis poses a severe challenge for legislative assemblies. The demand for immediate action compromises deliberation. The congressional process is inherently ponderous, as different perspectives and interests are consulted and majorities are constructed. The United States is not, as some people have claimed, a "presidential nation"; it is a "separated system" marked by the ebb and flow of power among the policy-making branches of government.[16] As former Speaker Newt Gingrich, R-Ga. (1995–1999), said of the nation's complex and frustrating governing arrangements,

> We have to get the country to understand that at the heart of the process
> of freedom is not the presidential press conference. It is the legislative
> process; it is the give and take of independently elected, free people
> coming together to try to create a better product by the friction of their
> passions and the friction of their ideas.[17]

The legislative "give and take" Gingrich described inevitably takes time. But fast-moving crises—all too common in an interconnected world of complex financial and security relationships—often demand that Congress act quickly, frequently without due deliberation.

The U.S. system of government is one of deliberate interplay among institutions. Citizens' ambivalence toward the popular branch of government is yet another reminder of the dual character of Congress—the theme that has pervaded our explanations of how Congress and its members work. The two Congresses are manifest in public perceptions and assessments. Citizens evaluate Congress using standards and expectations that differ from those they use to assess their own senators and representatives.[18] This same duality appears in media coverage: The two Congresses are covered by different sets of reporters working for different kinds of media organizations.

CONGRESS AS POLITICIANS

Lawmakers' working conditions and schedules are far from ideal.[19] The hours are killing, the pay relatively modest when compared to other high-status professions, and the toll on family life heavy. A *Washington Post Magazine* profile of Rep. Joe Courtney, D-Conn., sketched his life as follows:

> Rising, going to hearings, meeting with lobbyists, fundraising, speaking on the House floor, taking more meetings, walking to the apartment, crashing, rising. . . . The [DCCC] continues to send him reminders about his fundraising goals: Get off the Capitol grounds; get to the phone bank; make the call. . . . Another knock. An aide pops in with a reminder: The fundraiser back home is that weekend. . . . "It just never stops. Never."[20]

Courtney's schedule is broadly representative. According to a 2013 study, members of Congress work an average of seventy hours a week when Congress is in session and fifty-nine hours when they're home in the district.[21] Most members sacrifice time with their families to do the job: 85 percent of members' spouses live back home in their district, not in D.C. with them, and 66 percent of members said they had missed an important family event because of their job.[22] "I'm basically single-parenting," said Courtney's wife.[23]

Members' Bonds With Constituents

The public has different expectations for individual members compared with Congress as a whole. From the institutional Congress, the public expects answers to the nation's problems developed in an open and fair policy process. By contrast, in assessing their own representatives, voters take into account far more than lawmakers' work on public policy. They weigh members' service to the state or district, their communication with constituents, and their home style. Voters consider the policy positions their members take, but they have little insight into their member's effectiveness in advancing policy proposals in the legislative process.[24] Put differently, Congress is viewed as a national policy-making institution, but individual members of Congress are only partly assessed in terms of their contributions to policy making. Local representatives are primarily evaluated in light of the personal bonds they forge with constituents and the political positions they take.

Members' high visibility in their states or districts reinforces their local ties. Constituents receive mail from their local representatives, read about them in newspapers and online, and see them on television. Most members cultivate a social media presence today, as well, employing the platforms not just to communicate their own messages but to monitor responses from constituents.[25]

Members maintain a significant staff presence in their districts and states to facilitate responsiveness to constituent requests for assistance. Indeed, just under half of all House staff are based in the district.[26] Incumbents miss few opportunities to do favors for constituents, gestures that are usually appreciated and remembered. Large numbers of citizens report having contacts with their representatives. It is no wonder, then, that constituents view their local representatives in more sympathetic, personal terms than they view the institution of Congress as a whole.

Members and their staffs devote constant attention to generating publicity and local press. "I am never too busy to talk to local TV," said a prominent House member. "Period. Exclamation point."[27] A survey of House press secretaries showed virtually unanimous agreement: "We'd rather get in [the hometown paper] than on the front page of the *New York Times* any day."[28] Local media tend to cast members in a flattering light. Hometown reporters, especially for broadcast media, usually work on general-assignment stories and are ill prepared to question the lawmaker in detail about issues or events. Often, their primary goal is simply to get the legislator on video or audio. This is an ideal situation for politicians, who can express their views in their own words with a minimum of editing and few challenges from reporters.

Senators and representatives thus present themselves to constituents largely on their own terms through advertising, self-promotion, and uncritical coverage by local or regional news media. Members devote countless hours to raising the money they need to craft a public image through paid media.[29] Reflecting on the hundreds of fund-raising calls he makes daily, Representative Courtney said, "You could be Abraham Lincoln, but if you don't have the heart of a telemarketer, you're not going to make it to Congress."[30]

The importance of personal connections and public relations does not mean that constituents are uninterested in their representatives' issue stances. Lawmakers also forge bonds with voters out of mutual agreement on important national issues. At the same time, members' personal ties with voters can help insulate them from disapproval on the occasions when their issue positions diverge from local preferences.

Questions of Ethics

Congressional ethics, however, are perennially in doubt. In a 2018 survey, a mere 8 percent of respondents rated the honesty and ethical standards of Congress members as high or very high.[31] But most political scientists and close observers of the institution have a more favorable assessment of congressional ethics. The conventional wisdom among experts is that the vast majority of lawmakers are dedicated and ethical in their behavior. "Members of Congress behave better than people think," declared former representative Lee H. Hamilton, D-Ind. (1965–1999).[32]

Despite public distrust, lawmakers' behavior today is more transparent and less corrupt than in the past. Members' rising qualifications, more intense media scrutiny, and reforms in campaign finance and ethics procedures have all helped to curtail corruption. Money used to flow freely under the table. "Back in the old days, it was a common occurrence that you walked around with envelopes of cash in your pocket" to hand out to powerful lawmakers, recalled a Washington lobbyist.[33] Today, campaign contributions and direct lobbying expenses are subject to considerably more scrutiny by reporters and civic groups. Although large loopholes remain, financial abuses today are rare by pre-1970s standards.

Why, then, do citizens and commentators remain so contemptuous of lawmakers' ethics? A variety of factors, some of which are beyond members' control, drive public skepticism.

Unethical Behavior

One reason the public distrusts members' ethics is that, unfortunately, unethical behavior persists despite the network of laws and rules intended to restrain it. In 2016, for example, Rep. Chaka Fatah, D-Pa., lost his primary when he was indicted for bribery, money laundering, and fraud relating to a probe into his 2007 campaign for mayor of Philadelphia.[34] Fatah was convicted and sentenced to ten years in federal prison. Staten Island representative Michael Grimm, R-N.Y., resigned from Congress in 2015 after pleading guilty to felony tax fraud. Rep. Aaron Schock, R-Ill., also resigned in 2015 after questions were raised about whether he had fraudulently billed the government for excessive mileage reimbursements.

Scandals, even when they are uncovered and punished, weaken public confidence. Most notable was the megascandal centered on lobbyist Jack Abramoff, who advanced the interests of the gambling industry by means of donations, luxury trips, and favors for some half-dozen lawmakers. In 2006, Abramoff pleaded guilty to fraud, tax evasion, and conspiracy to bribe public officials.[35] The Abramoff scandal ended the political careers of at least six members of Congress, along with those of many congressional staffers and lobbyists. One House member was sentenced to jail for bribery.[36]

Ethics Rules and Processes

Congress's internal processes to police members' ethical violations fail to inspire public confidence. Members typically cringe at passing judgment on their peers. "The House Ethics Committee and the Senate Ethics Committee are structured in a way to protect incumbents rather than to discipline them," observed an ethics lobbyist for Public Citizen. "Members are overseeing each other, and they make sure that nothing comes back to haunt them."[37]

Even energetic ethics enforcement does not improve public perceptions. The House Ethics Committee conducted inquiries into fifty-six members' activities in the 115th Congress (2017–2018) and empaneled subcommittees to investigate cases involving seven members.[38] Despite all of this enforcement activity, Americans continue to rate the ethics of Congress lower than any other profession, even below that of advertisers and car salespeople.[39]

Paradoxically, the intensified regulation of public life actually fuels public distrust. So many rules govern the public activities of lawmakers that they can run afoul of them unintentionally. "High-level public officials are particularly good targets for investigation," explains law professor Cass R. Sunstein, "if only because of the complex network of statutes that regulate their behavior."[40] Elected officials are scrutinized by the Federal Election Commission, the House and Senate ethics committees, the Office of Congressional Ethics, and occasionally by the Justice Department and federal prosecutors (see Box 16-1 on congressional ethics). A number of "watchdog" groups such as Citizens for Responsibility and Ethics in Washington, the Sunlight Foundation, and Public Citizen also closely monitor ethics issues and publicize the results of their investigations.

Changing Standards of Personal Behavior

The contemporary news media exert great enterprise and energy investigating personal indiscretions and ethical violations, a shift from the journalistic norms of earlier eras. The effect on public perceptions is to heighten awareness of congressional shortcomings, regardless of how atypical such failings might be. The diligent work of law-abiding members attracts little attention while an ethical lapse—or even a rumor of one—makes headlines.

In particular, substance abuse and sexual misconduct are far less tolerated today than they were a generation ago. In November 2013, freshman representative Trey Radel, R-Fla., pleaded guilty to buying 3.5 grams of cocaine and was induced to resign his seat.[41] Attitudes toward sexual misconduct have undergone a sea change in recent years. During the 115th Congress (2017–2018), a remarkable number of members resigned because they were accused of unwelcome sexual advances, part of the wave of #MeToo scandals that swept across the worlds of journalism, politics, academia, and entertainment, including representatives John Conyers, D-Mich., Trent Franks, R-Ariz., Blake Farenthold, R-Tex., and Pat Meehan, R-Pa., as well as Sen. Al Franken, D-Minn.[42] In addition, Rep. Elizabeth Etsy, D-Conn., stepped aside rather than run for reelection when it was revealed that she had failed to remove a top staffer accused of sexual harassment. In 2018, Congress adopted new legislation reforming the Congressional Accountability Act of 1995 to establish a better process for congressional employees to report allegations of sexual harassment, to hold members financially liable for harassment settlements, and to make any such settlements more transparent to the public.[43]

Opposition Research

Often scandals are driven by political opponents of the accused. Members of Congress, challengers, and party operatives all opportunistically seize on any ethical miscue, real or manufactured, for political advantage. For example, House Speaker Jim Wright (1987–1989), D-Tex., was forced to step aside because of an ethics scandal that was initially brought to light via opposition research spearheaded by Rep. Newt Gingrich, R-Ga.[44] Later, Gingrich himself, as Speaker of the House, was aggressively investigated for ethics violations. In 1997, he was fined $300,000 for bringing discredit upon the House by using tax-exempt money to promote Republican goals.

In his study of the impact of what he calls the *ethics culture* on federal appointments, G. Calvin Mackenzie writes,

> Instead of getting out of the way so the winners can govern, the losers begin guerrilla operations that never cease, using every weapon and every opportunity to attack, harass, embarrass, and otherwise weaken those who hold office. If you cannot beat them in an election, current practice now suggests, then do everything in your power to keep the winners from governing and implementing their policy priorities.[45]

In other words, ethics charges and countercharges may be nothing more than "politics by other means."[46] Nevertheless, the political payoffs from such accusations encourage political actors to launch them at their opponents at every opportunity, undercutting perceptions of lawmakers generally.

"A Small Class of People"

Do these hazards of public life deter "the best and the brightest" from seeking elective office? It is hard to answer that question. Young people, for example, show lamentably scant interest in government careers.[47] The poor esteem in which the public holds Congress is another deterrent for potential candidates.[48]

U.S. democracy requires that ambitious people put themselves forward as candidates. But many of the ablest individuals decide to sit on the sidelines. Although open seats seem to have little shortage of claimants, parties frequently have difficulty recruiting good challengers to run against officeholders. Indeed, the absence of strong challengers, especially for House seats, is a factor in persistently high incumbent reelection rates. Voters would have better choices if greater numbers of talented individuals were willing to enter the fray.

CONGRESS AS INSTITUTION

Americans expect Congress to be active and productive. Opinion surveys have consistently found that people want Congress to play a strong, independent policy-making role. They look to Congress to vet the president's initiatives carefully.[49]

BOX 16-1 CONGRESSIONAL ETHICS

Members of Congress are bound by the U.S. Constitution, federal laws, party provisions, and House and Senate rules and conduct codes. Although many observers criticize loopholes, the panoply of regulations is extensive.

- **Constitution.** Each chamber has the power to punish its members for "disorderly behavior" and, by a two-thirds vote, to expel a member. Members are immune from arrest during attendance at congressional sessions (except for treason, felony, or breach of peace) and "for any speech or debate in either house, they shall not be questioned in any other place" (Article I, section 6). This latter provision protects lawmakers from any reprisals for expressing their legislative views.

- **Criminal Laws.** Federal laws make it a crime to solicit or accept a bribe; to solicit or receive "anything of value" for performing any official act or service or for using influence in any proceeding involving the federal government; to enter into or benefit from any contracts with the government; or to commit any fraud against the United States.

- **Ethics Codes.** Adopted in 1968 and substantially tightened in 1977, 1989, 1995, 1997, and 2007, the House and Senate ethics codes apply to members and key staff aides. The codes require extensive financial disclosure; restrict members' outside earned income (to 15 percent of salaries); prohibit unofficial office accounts that many members used to supplement official allowances; impose stricter standards for using the frank for mailings; and ban lawmakers from accepting most meals and gifts from lobbyists. The House Committee on Standards of Official Conduct and the Senate Select Ethics Committee implement the codes, hear charges against members, issue advisory opinions, and recommend disciplinary actions.

- **Party Rules.** Congressional parties can discipline members who run afoul of ethics requirements. House Democratic and Republican rules require a committee leader who is indicted to step aside temporarily; a leader who is censured or convicted is automatically replaced.

- **Federal Election Campaign Act Amendments of 1974.** As amended again in 1976 and 1979, the Federal Election Campaign Act imposes extensive requirements on congressional incumbents as well as challengers. Additional rules and penalties were set in the Bipartisan Campaign Reform Act of 2002.

- **Office of Congressional Ethics.** Established by the House of Representatives in 2008, the Office of Congressional Ethics is an independent, nonpartisan board of eight private citizens charged with reviewing allegations of misconduct against House members and staff and, when appropriate, referring matters to the Committee on Standards of Official Conduct.

Policy Success and Stalemate

Although most citizens believe that Congress is an important institution that should share power equally with the president, they lack awareness of the specific ways Congress affects their daily lives. Lee Hamilton tells the following story:

[A] group of [young people] visiting my Indiana office told me that Congress was irrelevant. So I asked them a few questions. How had they gotten to my office? On the interstate highway, they said. Had any of them gone to the local university? Yes, they said, admitting they'd got some help from federal student loans. Did any of them have grandparents on Social Security and Medicare? Well sure, they replied, picking up on where I was headed. Their lives had been profoundly affected by Congress. They just hadn't focused on all of the connections before.[50]

Its poor public reputation notwithstanding, Congress has produced many innovative and effective policies.[51] In an intriguing study, Paul C. Light of the Brookings Institution set out to identify the federal government's most influential actions over a fifty-year period.[52] A survey of historians and political scientists winnowed a preliminary roster of 588 items to a list of fifty "greatest achievements." For the record, the top three successes were judged to be rebuilding Europe after World War II (the Marshall Plan, 1947), expanding the right to vote (Voting Rights Act of 1965), and promoting equal access to public accommodations (Civil Rights Act of 1964).

In every case Light uncovered, Congress played a vital role in the policy's inception, ratification, or implementation. Although Congress was not always the initiator, many programs associated with given presidents—for example, the Marshall Plan (Harry S. Truman) and Medicare (Lyndon B. Johnson)—began as proposals on Capitol Hill.[53]

Despite its past achievements, the contemporary Congress is frequently described as "dysfunctional" and unproductive.[54] Most observers could compile a must-do legislative agenda that would include many items left unaddressed by recent Congresses. Citizens are worried that Congress pays too little attention to long-term problems, such as the cost of entitlements, the public debt, immigration, climate change, and infrastructure maintenance. Setting aside large-scale policy problems, Congress also struggles with routine matters of governance, such as budgeting, appropriations, and appointments.

Assessing the Congressional Process

Congress's institutional shortcomings are numerous and obvious. Beyond its structural and procedural complexities, the quality of its deliberations often falls short of democratic ideals. Lack of comity and bipartisanship, the growth of Senate roadblocks, and questions about appropriate transparency undercut Congress's reputation. Are reforms possible?

Deliberation

The primary function of a legislative assembly is to foster deliberation. "The assembly makes possible a deliberation in which conflicting judgments about the public good . . . can be examined, debated, and resolved," writes Richard Hall. "And through such a process the actions of government achieve legitimacy."[55] Recent developments have undermined the quality and quantity of congressional deliberation.

In order to cope with the pressures of lawmaking in a highly polarized and partisan environment, leaders of both parties tend to "short-circuit regular deliberative procedures in committee, on the floor, and in conference."[56] The legislative process has morphed into a wide variety of highly centralized improvisations—what Barbara Sinclair has termed *unorthodox lawmaking*.[57] Leaders package together disparate policies into omnibus vehicles so bulky that only a small number of staff aides and members know what provisions have been inserted or left out. Outcomes are normally predetermined, especially in the House, where majority party leaders oversee the prefloor negotiations and craft the rules for debate. Most important House measures are considered under restrictive or closed rules permitting few or no amendments.[58] Floor deliberations are just a series of desultory recitations—public speaking in this country has become something of a lost art. Under such circumstances, lawmakers are sometimes embarrassed by provisions they have voted into law.

Committee deliberation has been similarly weakened. Committee meetings are poorly attended, with the outcomes laid out by the chair and the chair's majority party colleagues. Rank-and-file committee members struggle to obtain information about pending legislation and often have little time to offer amendments.[59] Furthermore, leaders may opt to bypass committee consideration altogether, bringing unreported bills directly to the floor.[60] As committees become less consequential policy-making arenas, members have less incentive to develop policy expertise in the matters before their committees.

Congress has also reduced its investments in its own staff capacity to independently develop and evaluate public policy.[61] Staff resources for House and Senate committees were cut by around 45 percent between 1985 and 2015.[62] Legislative-branch appropriations were subjected to tight austerity after 2010 up through 2016, though House and Senate appropriations saw a boost in 2017 and 2018.[63]

Even House–Senate interactions are less deliberative in character. Today's congressional leaders frequently avoid the conference process altogether, convening "pro forma" conferences to ratify deals worked out in leadership offices or exchanging bills back and forth between the chambers. On occasion, House–Senate negotiations have excluded minority party conferees. Such tactics streamline the legislative process but forfeit the benefits of deliberation.

Another factor weakening deliberation is Congress's frantic stop-and-go work schedule. Although earlier members did not live in the nation's capital, most of them stayed in town for weeks at a stretch, their days dominated by extended hearings or deliberations. By the mid–twentieth century, a minority of members—mostly from the eastern corridor—constituted a "Tuesday–Thursday club," spending long weekends at home. Nowadays, nearly all members follow such a schedule. Members arrive in Washington for votes on Tuesday evening and leave after votes conclude on Thursday afternoon. "This truncated schedule," reports a Bipartisan Policy Center commission, "leaves only one full day—Wednesday—for committee hearings, markups, and the other necessary ingredients for fruitful legislating."[64] Extended nonlegislative or "district work periods" surround all the major holidays.

Thirty-four-year House veteran Hamilton offered a blunt assessment of the situation:

> Members of Congress spend too much of their week campaigning, and not enough of it doing the hard work of governing. Building a consensus behind an approach to a national problem is tough; it takes negotiation, extended discussion, and hard study. This is impossible when you spend three days on Capitol Hill and then rush home for an extended weekend of appearances.[65]

One remedy would seem simple: longer sessions (two weeks at least), alternating with periods for constituency work or official travel. Because of the pressures of campaigning in today's highly competitive environment, reforms permitting extended deliberation are not likely.

Comity and Bipartisanship

Another institutional malady is the decline of interpersonal comity. This decline is the product of several converging factors, most notably the escalating cohesion within and polarization between the two parties. Nelson W. Polsby aptly termed the contemporary period an "era of ill feeling" in Congress.[66] Former representative and deputy GOP whip Mickey Edwards of Oklahoma (1977–1993) points to intense party competition for majority control as a key factor undercutting bipartisan cooperation in today's Congress:

> Instead of morphing from candidates to members of Congress on the day they are sworn in, today's legislators engage in permanent campaigning. Neither party is willing to allow the other to gain credit for an achievement that might help it in the next election, so the center aisle that divides Democrats from Republicans in the House has become a wall.[67]

Critics have persuasively faulted the contemporary Congress for engaging in a "destructive form of partisanship" that prevents bipartisan give and take.[68] When the two congressional parties were more internally divided between the 1930s and 1990s, there was greater potential for cross-party coalitions. "Oh, those were frustrating years," recalled former Republican Leader Robert Michel of Illinois, who served in the minority for all of his thirty-eight years in the House (1957–1995):

But . . . I never really felt I was out of the game or that I had no part to play. Under the rules of the House, the traditions of the House . . . there is a role to play for the minority. . . . We struck a deal, we made a bargain [and worked at] bringing dissident factions together . . . to craft good legislation for the country. That was the joy of it![69]

An earlier generation of political scientists had lamented the absence of party government in the United States. They argued in favor of a democratic politics in which parties would run on coherent platforms and command the leadership and unity to enact their programs into law. Key elements of the party government model have now come to pass. The parties are far more internally cohesive; the caucuses meet regularly to decide policy; members' party-line voting presents clear alternatives to voters. But no analyst contends that these changes have increased Congress's legislative capacity. Compared to the less cohesive, centralized parties of the past, today's congressional parties are not more effective at enacting their legislative agendas.[70] Stronger parties result in more policy gridlock, not less.[71]

Fierce and pervasive partisan conflict undermines the public's trust in government. Congressional partisanship has a direct, negative effect on Americans' assessment of the institution.[72] According to one study:

Citizens appear to equate partisan conflict with partisan biases and the notion that members of Congress are avoiding the facts—whatever they may be—when formulating policy. . . . [T]he public perceives partisan conflict as a waste of time and resources that could be spent trying to solve the nation's problems.[73]

Senate Roadblocks

Nowhere has the rise of partisanship created more obstacles for policy making than in the Senate. For much of the Senate's history, filibusters were rare, employed for matters of great constituency or regional importance. Today, they have become a partisan tool. The partisan filibuster—in which most or all of the Senate majority party's agenda is systematically blocked by an organized minority party filibuster—is a recent innovation. Barbara Sinclair's research dates the partisan filibuster to the first two years of the Clinton presidency (the 103rd Congress, 1993–1995), in which Republican-led filibusters obstructed half of all major measures.[74] The practice has escalated since the 1990s.

The emergence of the partisan filibuster has made governance in the Senate exceptionally difficult. "Requiring a supermajority to pass legislation that is at all controversial makes the coalition-building process much more difficult and increases a status quo–oriented system's tendency toward gridlock," writes Sinclair.[75] The widespread use of delaying tactics in the Senate has effects that extend far beyond the highly controversial issues. Delays impede the Senate's ability to manage its routine workload. Similarly, appropriations bills almost never pass on time, denying federal agencies the information they need to plan budgets, evaluate competing contract proposals, and maximize value for taxpayers.[76] Many uncontroversial matters that pass the House never receive Senate consideration simply because of the lack of floor time. Congress regularly fails to conduct basic policy maintenance, allowing programs to languish without needed updates and revisions. One recent study showed that the contemporary Congress was overdue in reauthorizing the major policies in more than half of the public's top priority areas.[77]

Transparency

Another important issue in evaluating Congress is transparency, the ability of the public to monitor and understand congressional proceedings. Questions of transparency present difficult trade-offs for legislative assemblies. On the one hand, a lack of transparency is a major source of public mistrust. People fear that a lack of public access will allow special interests to dominate the legislative process in secret. Generally speaking, the public does not trust legislators to act in the public interest in the absence of public scrutiny and accountability.

On the other hand, transparency can hamper internal legislative bargaining and compromise. It is more difficult for members to accept trade-offs that impose costs on their constituencies when those decisions are made in full public view.[78] Instead, lawmakers have a greater incentive to play to their external constituencies and refuse to engage in meaningful negotiations.[79]

The Perils of Reform

Reforming Congress is often touted as a solution to its organizational or procedural faults. To that end, the House and Senate themselves periodically engage in self-examination. Most recently, the House of Representatives in 2019 voted on a bipartisan basis to establish a Select Committee on the Modernization of Congress, with the aim of developing recommendations to improve congressional resources, information, and staffing, among other goals.

Internal reform efforts are often impeded by the two-Congresses dilemma—that is, reforms can threaten members' electoral interests.[80] In its last major reform effort in 1993 through 1994, for example, Congress refused to adopt any of the recommendations that had been developed to improve and streamline congressional committee jurisdictions. Such changes usually entail loss of power for some members, prompting losers to move to block the reforms.

Despite the difficulties of overcoming institutional inertia, Congress's history nevertheless includes some major planned innovations affecting deliberative processes, committee jurisdictions, and electoral arrangements. At key moments, reformers with different and often conflicting goals—enhancing legislative power and efficiency, gaining partisan or policy advantage, or augmenting individual lawmakers' perquisites—have coalesced around significant changes. Because of the variety of goals involved, however, the results achieved were often different from those anticipated.

Reformers typically find that they must build upon preexisting institutions rather than sweep away current practices and start afresh. An example was the series of new budget procedures piled like so many building blocks on top of the existing authorization–appropriations process by the Congressional Budget Act of 1974. Little wonder that such reforms typically fall short of their sponsors' objectives. Based on a survey of forty-two major institutional innovations over the last century, one author concludes that instead of achieving stable, effective arrangements, congressional reforms result in "a set of institutions that often work at cross-purposes."[81]

Media Coverage

The most open and accessible of the three branches of government, Congress is covered by a large press corps populated by some of the nation's most skilled journalists. Nevertheless, few reporters are able to convey the internal subtleties or the external pressures that shape lawmaking. Moreover, the media best suited to reporting on Congress—serious daily newspapers and magazines—are suffering long-term declines in circulation.[82] In response, newspapers have curtailed their coverage of Congress and national and global politics in general. Pressrooms have been downsized; most foreign bureaus have been closed. Bottom-line pressures on the media threaten the nation's democratic processes by leaving people less informed.

The decline has been equally drastic in television (including the so-called all-news channels). Political news has changed in content as well as coverage. Fewer stories appear on policy issues and more on scandal, wrongdoing, or corruption. Following the canons of investigative journalism, reporters play the role of suspicious adversaries on the lookout for good guys and bad guys, winners and losers. Generally speaking, political radio and TV talk shows are ill-informed, combative, and contemptuous of politicians and their work.

Divergent press coverage—local versus national media—widens the gap between the two Congresses' distinct images. The tone and content of news reporting is more positive for individual members than for the institution. Congress, as an institution, is covered by the national press with lots of skepticism and cynicism while individual lawmakers are covered respectfully by the local media.

Citizens' Attitudes Toward Congress

Citizens' ratings of the job Congress is doing fluctuate with economic conditions, wars and crises, scandals, trust in government overall, and levels of partisan conflict.[83] Approval of Congress surged briefly after it handled the Watergate affair in 1974, after the Republican takeover twenty years later, and after the terrorist attacks of September 11, 2001. The overall trend has been markedly downward since 2002, however, with Congress plumbing historic depths of public dissatisfaction. According to Gallup polling, congressional approval has averaged 17 percent since January 2005. It has not exceeded 29 percent at any point since December 2009. In February 2019, only 1 in 5 respondents approved of the way Congress was handling its job.[84]

The institutional Congress almost always ranks well below respondents' own representatives in public esteem. Since 1992, Gallup has polled respondents on whether various officeholders deserve reelection. Figure 16-1 displays the results comparing answers for the "U.S. representative in your congressional district" as opposed to "most members of Congress." As is evident here, there is variation over time in public opinion assessing whether members of Congress should be reelected. But at any given point, respondents typically rate the case for reelecting their own representative 20 percentage points more highly than the case for reelecting most members of Congress.

To shed light on the reasons constituents evaluate their own members so much more favorably than Congress as a whole, Table 16-1 covers key differences in how voters perceive members and the institution. Congress is not well understood by the average citizen. Partly to blame are the institution's size and complexity, not to mention the arcane twists and turns of the legislative process. But many citizens simply find the whole legislative process distasteful.

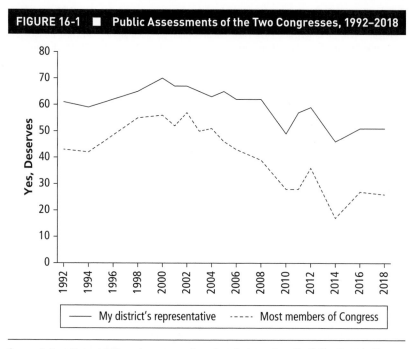

FIGURE 16-1   ■   Public Assessments of the Two Congresses, 1992–2018

Source: Authors' interpolations of survey results, primarily drawn from the Gallup Organization.

Notes: The Gallup Organization question is: "Do the following officeholders deserve reelection?" The plotted points in the figures indicate respondents answering in the affirmative.

TABLE 16-1 ■ High Approval for Members, Low Approval for Congress	
Individual members	**Congress as an institution**
Serve constituents	Resolves national issues only with difficulty or not at all
Run against Congress	Has few defenders
Emphasize personal style and outreach to constituents	Operates as collegial body that is difficult for citizens to understand
Are covered by local media in generally positive terms	Is covered by national media, often negatively (with focus on scandals and conflicts)
Respond quickly to most constituent needs and inquiries	Moves slowly with cumbersome processes that inhibit rapid responses
Are able to highlight personal goals and accomplishments	Has many voices, but none can speak clearly for Congress as a whole

Sources: Timothy E. Cook, "Legislature vs. Legislator: A Note on the Paradox of Congressional Support," *Legislative Studies Quarterly* 4 (February 1979): 43–52; Glenn R. Parker and Roger H. Davidson, "Why Do Americans Love Their Congressmen So Much More Than Their Congress?" *Legislative Studies Quarterly* 4 (February 1979): 53–61; Richard Born, "The Shared Fortunes of Congress and Congressmen: Members May Run From Congress but They Can't Hide," *Journal of Politics* 52 (November 1990): 1223–1241.

Dissension is on display on Capitol Hill to a greater extent than in other branches of government. The president speaks with one voice: Even though there is fierce competition for the president's ear, a statement from the president establishes the administration's position. As for the judiciary, opinions are frequently divided or unclear as judges and justices disagree about law and policy, but their decisions are usually accepted as law. By contrast, no single member—not even the institution's top leaders—speaks for Congress.

The public's ambivalence toward Congress goes far deeper than unhappiness with specific policies or disgust with scandals, according to the sobering conclusions of John R. Hibbing and Elizabeth Theiss-Morse:

People do not wish to see uncertainty, conflicting opinions, long debate, competing interests, confusion, bargaining, and compromised, imperfect solutions. They want government to do its job quietly and efficiently, sans conflict and sans fuss. In short . . . they often seek a patently unrealistic form of democracy.[85]

In other words, people seem to abhor the very attributes that are the hallmarks of robust representative assemblies. As Hibbing and Theiss-Morse observe, Congress "is structured to embody what we dislike about modern democratic government, which is almost everything."[86]

TWENTY-FIRST-CENTURY CHALLENGES

The U.S. Congress is now in its third century. Survival for more than two centuries is no mean feat. Congress has withstood repeated stress and turbulence, including a civil war, political assassinations, terrorist attacks, domestic scandals, and contentious foreign involvement. The U.S. constitutional system is far older than most of the world's existing governments.

Security

The physical setting of the U.S. Capitol now exhibits the stepped-up security arrangements prevalent elsewhere since the September 11, 2001 terrorist attacks. All through the 20th century, visitors and Hill personnel moved freely in and out of the Capitol and surrounding office buildings. Members of the public may still visit most Capitol Hill facilities, but they now encounter uniformed officers, metal detectors, and concrete barriers. One welcome development, however, is the long-needed U.S. Capitol Visitor Center—constructed under the east front that enhances the building's safety while introducing visitors to Congress and its work.

Checks and Imbalances?

The constitutional system of divided powers and competing branches does not yield a stable equilibrium. Powers ebb and flow among the branches. Crises tend to empower the executive branch, whereas more peaceful times are friendlier to congressional power. An activist bench can drive the judiciary into political thickets; at other times, the bench defers to the other branches.

Executive Hubris

Executive-branch encroachments upon legislative prerogatives are neither new nor confined to crisis periods. Most modern presidents have asserted their discretion over program administration, fought for broader leeway in spending appropriated funds, and exploited their freedom to reorganize agencies and redeploy their personnel. Presidents and their appointees naturally seek to control information about what they are doing. There is no question that recent presidents have pushed the boundaries of presidential authority in ways that threaten to eclipse Congress.

Executive dominance is most apparent in military affairs. Throughout the post–World War II era, presidents have regularly embroiled the United States in military conflicts without seeking congressional support. In fact, none of the United States' military actions has been accompanied by a congressional declaration of war since President Truman single-handedly intervened in the Korean War in 1950.[87] Although presidents George H. W. Bush and George W. Bush both asked for congressional authorizations of the use of force in Iraq, they—along with all other contemporary presidents—contended that they did not need congressional approval to act. President Bill Clinton did not ask for any kind of congressional support before launching cruise missiles against the Iraqi intelligence services in 1993; nor did he seek congressional authority before launching air strikes against the Serbs in 1994 and 1995.

The pattern continued in recent administrations. When President Barack Obama decided at a contentious White House meeting in March 2011 to support military action against the Gaddafi regime in Libya, he did so without broadly consulting with Congress or seeking any kind of congressional authorization.[88] Obama also did not seek congressional authorization in 2014 before launching airstrikes in Iraq and Syria as part of a campaign against Islamic State rebels. President Trump did not seek congressional approval in April 2017 before launching 59 Tomahawk cruise missiles at a Syrian airbase in retaliation for a chemical weapons attack against civilians.

Presidents have also become more assertive in denying information to Congress. Recent presidents, including both Barack Obama and George W. Bush, made secrecy a watchword. The Bush White House refused to share documents with Congress, permit certain executive officials to testify before congressional committees, or otherwise cooperate with investigative hearings.[89] In 2012, Congress voted to hold Obama's attorney general, Eric Holder, in contempt of Congress over his refusal to turn over documents relating to the "Fast and Furious Scandal," a failed sting operation managed by the Arizona field office of the U.S. Bureau of Alcohol, Tobacco, Firearms and Explosives.[90]

Despite such complaints, it is also clear that Congress has been complicit in its loss of power. Congress surrendered vast grants of power to the president and the executive branch immediately after the terrorist attacks of 9/11 by approving open-ended military action and the USA Patriot Act. More generally, Congress often prefers to avoid responsibility for difficult decisions.

Party polarization may also have contributed to Congress's refusal to assert its prerogatives more vigorously during recent episodes of unified government. Asked why he opposed investigations into the resignation of Trump's former national security advisor Michael Flynn, Sen. Rand Paul, R-Ky., said, "I just don't think it's useful to be doing investigation after investigation, particularly of your own party."[91] Under unified government in the 115th Congress (2017–2019), the House Intelligence Committee's investigation of Russian interference in the 2016 election was plagued by accusations that Chair Devin Nunes, R-Calif., was acting as a surrogate for the Trump administration rather than seeking out information about potential wrongdoing.[92] Loyalty to a president should be no excuse for congressional timidity. Partisan loyalties did not immunize past presidents, from Franklin D. Roosevelt to Ronald Reagan to Bill Clinton, against probing oversight and sometimes fierce opposition led by their party's leaders on Capitol Hill—even in wartime. If lawmakers do not fiercely defend their prerogatives, they have only themselves to blame when executives ignore them.

Judicial Lawmaking

Congress also faces attacks upon its powers from an activist federal judiciary, which has invalidated congressional enactments in more than thirty cases since 1995. Since the 1990s, the courts have overturned federal laws in areas such as interstate commerce and civil and voting rights, in some cases raising questions that were last litigated in the 1930s. Recent Court rulings have all but eliminated Congress's ability to impose regulations on campaign finance.

The loss of congressional power extends beyond the contemporary Court's propensity to engage in judicial review. The Court also engages in statutory interpretation, sometimes in ways that many members criticize as being at odds with Congress's intent. Even so, congressional party polarization and gridlock make it much more difficult for Congress to reassert its authority by overturning the Court's statutory interpretations.[93] A Congress that cannot act is unable to protect its authority against judicial encroachment.

Members of Congress regularly criticize the courts for "judicial activism," by which they typically mean decisions on a handful of ideological issues, principally involving abortion and religious establishment clause jurisprudence. Meanwhile, fewer members denounce judicial rulings regarding fundamental state and federal authority. The judiciary retains the capacity to constrict legislative powers in much the same way that late-nineteenth-century courts gutted the Civil War constitutional amendments. Senior federal circuit court judge John T. Noonan Jr. explains, "If five members of the Supreme Court are in agreement on an agenda, they are mightier than five hundred members of Congress with unmobilized or warring constituencies."[94]

Is Congress Permanently Damaged?

The Congress of the 1970s sought to reclaim prerogatives that had slipped away during the Cold War period. It passed major reforms designed to reassert congressional power over budgets as well as domestic and foreign policy. In his detailed account, James L. Sundquist sums up that era: "The 1970s were a period of upheaval, of change so rapid and so radical as to transform the pattern of relationships that had evolved and settled into place over the span of half a century or more."[95] The 1970s reform fervor was short lived. Reflecting on the subsequent period, Andrew Rudalevige revisits the question: Is there an imperial presidency? His short answer is yes: "Presidents have regained freedom of unilateral action in a variety of areas, from executive privilege to war powers to covert operations to campaign spending. . . . The default position between presidents and Congress has moved toward the presidential end of the inter-branch spectrum—and irreversibly so."

Is this trend irreversible? As defenders of the constitutional system, we remain cautiously hopeful of the future. After all, partisans of all stripes have a long-term stake in an active, robust legislative branch. Executive initiatives, as popular as they may seem, demand critical review; executive programs must be overseen and evaluated.

What does the future hold? Much depends on a series of questions: Will members of Congress resolve partisan conflicts to make needed progress on pressing problems? Can Congress assert itself to protect its constitutional prerogatives against power-seeking presidents and judges? Unfortunately, no advocate of the framers' constitutional design can offer confident answers.

We conclude with a question for the twenty-first century: Are the two Congresses ultimately compatible, or are they diverging, each detrimental to the other? The burdens placed on both Congresses have become increasingly heavy from an ever-growing and diverse nation in an increasingly complex world. Congress, as an institution, is expected to resolve all kinds of problems. Meanwhile, members are pulled away from their legislative duties by the constant press of fund-raising, party competition, constituency expectations, and short legislative workweeks. Legislators struggle to keep abreast of conflicting demands.

Recent events are not encouraging, but the question remains whether representative democracy will, in the end, be a winning or losing effort. History is only mildly reassuring, and the future poses new and difficult challenges for which the margin of error may be narrower than ever before. And yet representative democracy itself is a gamble. The proposition that representation can yield wise policymaking remains a daring one. As always, it is an article of faith whose proof lies inevitably in the future.

REFERENCE
MATERIALS

APPENDIX A

Party Control: Presidency, Senate, House, 1901–2021

Congress	Years	President	Senate			House		
			D	R	Other	D	R	Other
57th	1901–1903	William McKinley/ Theodore Roosevelt	31	55	4	151	197	9
58th	1903–1905	T. Roosevelt	33	57	—	178	208	—
59th	1905–1907	T. Roosevelt	33	57	—	136	250	—
60th	1907–1909	T. Roosevelt	31	61	—	164	222	—
61st	1909–1911	William Howard Taft	32	61	—	172	219	—
62d	1911–1913	Taft	41	51	—	228	161	1
63d	1913–1915	Woodrow Wilson	51	44	1	291	127	17
64th	1915–1917	Wilson	56	40	—	230	196	9
65th	1917–1919	Wilson	53	42	—	216	210	6
66th	1919–1921	Wilson	47	49	—	190	240	3
67th	1921–1923	Warren G. Harding	37	59	—	131	301	1
68th	1923–1925	Calvin Coolidge	43	51	2	205	225	5
69th	1925–1927	Coolidge	39	56	1	183	247	4
70th	1927–1929	Coolidge	46	49	1	195	237	3
71st	1929–1931	Herbert Hoover	39	56	1	167	267	1
72d	1931–1933	Hoover	47	48	1	220	214	1
73d	1933–1935	Franklin D. Roosevelt	60	35	1	313	117	5
74th	1935–1937	F. D. Roosevelt	69	25	2	319	103	10
75th	1937–1939	F. D. Roosevelt	76	16	4	331	89	13
76th	1939–1941	F. D. Roosevelt	69	23	4	261	164	4
77th	1941–1943	F. D. Roosevelt	66	28	2	268	162	5
78th	1943–1945	F. D. Roosevelt	58	37	1	218	208	4
79th	1945–1947	Harry S. Truman	56	38	1	242	190	2
80th	1947–1949	Truman	45	51	—	188	245	1
81st	1949–1951	Truman	54	42	—	263	171	1
82d	1951–1953	Truman	49	47	—	234	199	1
83d	1953–1955	Dwight D. Eisenhower	47	48	1	211	221	1
84th	1955–1957	Eisenhower	48	47	1	232	203	—
85th	1957–1959	Eisenhower	49	47	—	233	200	—

Congress	Years	President	Senate D	Senate R	Senate Other	House D	House R	House Other
86th[a]	1959–1961	Eisenhower	65	35	—	284	153	—
87th[a]	1961–1963	John F. Kennedy	65	35	—	263	174	—
88th	1963–1965	Kennedy/Lyndon B. Johnson	67	33	—	258	177	—
89th	1965–1967	Johnson	68	32	—	295	140	—
90th	1967–1969	Johnson	64	36	—	247	187	—
91st	1969–1971	Richard M. Nixon	57	43	—	243	192	—
92d	1971–1973	Nixon	54	44	2	254	180	—
93d	1973–1975	Nixon/Gerald R. Ford	56	42	2	239	192	1
94th	1975–1977	Ford	60	37	2	291	144	—
95th	1977–1979	Jimmy Carter	61	38	1	292	143	—
96th	1979–1981	Carter	58	41	1	276	157	—
97th	1981–1983	Ronald Reagan	46	53	1	243	192	—
98th	1983–1985	Reagan	45	55	—	267	168	—
99th	1985–1987	Reagan	47	53	—	252	183	—
100th	1987–1989	Reagan	55	45	—	258	177	—
101st	1989–1991	George H. W. Bush	55	45	—	260	175	—
102d	1991–1993	G. H. W. Bush	57	43	—	268	166	1
103d	1993–1995	Bill Clinton	56	44	—	258	176	1
104th	1995–1997	Clinton	47	53	—	204	230	1
105th	1997–1999	Clinton	45	55	—	207	227	1
106th	1999–2001	Clinton	45	55	—	211	223	1
107th[b]	2001–2003	George W. Bush	50	49	1	210	222	3
108th[b]	2003–2005	G. W. Bush	48	51	1	205	229	1
109th[b]	2005–2007	G. W. Bush	44	55	1	202	232	1
110th[b]	2007–2009	G. W. Bush	49	49	2	233	202	—
111th[bc]	2009–2011	Barack Obama	58	40	2	257	178	—
112th[b]	2011–2013	Obama	51	47	2	193	242	—
113th[b]	2013–2015	Obama	53	45	2	200	233	—
114th[b]	2015–2017	Obama	44	54	2	188	247	—
115th[b]	2017–2019	Donald J. Trump	46	52	2	194	241	—
116th[b]	2019–2021	Trump	45	53	2	235	119	—

☐ Republican control   ☐ Democratic control

Sources: Encyclopedia of the United States Congress, ed. Donald C. Bacon, Roger H. Davidson, and Morton Keller (New York: Simon and Schuster, 1995), 1556–1558; data compiled by authors for 103d through 116th Congresses.

Note: Figures are for the beginning of the first session of each Congress and do not include vacancies, subsequent shifts, or changes in party affiliation.

[a]The House in the 86th and 87th Congresses had 437 members because of an at-large representative given to Alaska and Hawaii prior to redistricting in 1962.

[b]The Senate independents caucused with the Democrats.

[c]For the Senate, we have counted as Democrats Arlen Specter, who shifted parties in April 2009, and Al Franken of Minnesota, who was sworn in on July 7, 2009.

APPENDIX B

Internships: Getting Experience on Capitol Hill

Capitol Hill is an excellent place to obtain first-hand experience with the U.S. government. With 541 lawmakers (representatives, senators, delegates, and resident commissioners); hundreds of committees and subcommittees; scores of informal caucuses; and three congressional support agencies (the Congressional Research Service, Government Accountability Office, and Congressional Budget Office), intern opportunities abound for students interested in experiencing Congress and its members up close and personal.

Undergraduates will find useful information about landing an internship on Capitol Hill in several sources. One is published under the auspices of the American Political Science Association and is titled *Studying in Washington: Academic Internships in the Nation's Capital.* Political scientist Stephen E. Frantzich discusses how to get a good internship, make the most of the experience, and find a place to live in Washington, DC.

From our own years of "soaking and poking" around Capitol Hill, we offer five observations about getting congressional experience. First, no single, central clearinghouse exists for internships. Every congressional office, committee, caucus, and support agency manages its own internship program. Contact information and intern applications may be found on member and committee websites (www.house.gov and www.senate.gov). For example, the House Judiciary Committee's website outlines the application process for undergraduates and law students seeking an internship with the full committee or one of its five subcommittees.

Many intern opportunities are available for minority students, such as through the Congressional Hispanic Caucus Institute (www.chci.org) or the minority access internship program (www.minorityaccess.org). You must be persistent, patient, and determined to find a position that will be a rewarding learning experience. Not only should you find out what duties and functions will be assigned to you as a volunteer intern (it is sometimes possible to secure paid internships), but you also need to remember that you have something useful to offer. Most congressional offices and committees are understaffed and subject to high staff turnover. Although the market for interns is competitive, congressional lawmakers, committees, and staffers want and need your talent.

Second, develop some notion as to where you would like to intern. Do research on the committee, lawmaker, support agency, or caucus that interests you. Remember that every office has its own personality. Senate offices, for example, are often large enterprises with many staff aides, while House offices are generally smaller. Interns thus will have more opportunities for personal, day-to-day contact with House members than with senators. The best way to determine the office environment is by interviewing people who have worked in a particular office, talking with the internship coordinators at your college or university, or visiting the office yourself.

Third, target your own representative and senators. Many congressional members prefer interns from their own state or district, who are likely to be familiar with the geography and concerns of that area. In addition, prospective interns probably will have family and friends who are constituents of the lawmaker. Do not hesitate to use your contacts. You might also volunteer to work in a state or district office of the lawmaker. Before accepting an internship, consider your own views and ideals. If your views are conservative, working for a lawmaker who espouses liberal causes may be difficult. However, if you are tactful and open minded, working for someone whose views differ from yours may be instructive.

Fourth, intern placement opportunities are plentiful. Many colleges and universities sponsor semester programs in Washington, DC. Several schools, including American University, Boston University, Hamilton College, Georgetown University, State University of New York, University of Southern California, University of Illinois, and the University of California system run programs in Washington, DC. Some accept students from other accredited colleges and universities. The Washington Center for Internships and Academic Seminars, in existence since 1975, has placed thousands of students from hundreds of colleges. To be sure, students can Google "congressional internships" and find numerous intern listings to peruse.

Finally, Congress needs and welcomes the influx of new ideas and experiences that interns bring with them. In a recent development, which aims to encourage college students of varying income levels to apply for these positions, House and Senate lawmakers are now provided funds to pay their interns. The work at times may be drudgery—answering mail and telephones, entering information into computers, and running errands—but the opportunity to learn about Congress and to pick up political smarts not easily available from textbooks is nearly without equal. You may even want to keep a private journal of your experiences: what you have done and what you have learned. In sum, an internship on Capitol Hill is likely to be rewarding intellectually and in other ways that are impossible to predict.

Resources

Bailey, Christina M., Jennifer E. Manning, and Kathleen E. Marchsteiner. "Internships, Fellowships, and Other Work Experience Opportunities in the Federal Government." CRS Report 98-654, November 1, 2018.

Best Intern Ever: Roll Call's Guide to Acing Your Internship. Washington, DC: CQ Roll Call Publishing Group, 2014.

The Congressional Intern Handbook. Washington, DC: Congressional Management Foundation, 2006.

Eckman, Sarah, J. "Internships in Congressional Offices: Frequently Asked Questions," CRS Report R44491, October 15, 2018.

Fleishman, Sandra. "The Annual Scramble: Washington Interns Line Up for Their First Lesson—in Housing Supply and Demand." *Washington Post,* May 29, 2004, F1.

Frantzich, Stephen E. *Studying in Washington: Academic Internships in the Nation's Capital.* 5th ed. Washington, DC: American Political Science Association, 2002.

Kane, Paul. "Paid Internships Are a Reality Again in Congress, After a Public Shaming," *The Washington Post,* March 13, 2019, A24.

Lee, Jennifer. "Crucial Unpaid Internships Increasingly Separate the Haves From the Have-Nots." *New York Times,* August 10, 2004, 16.

Maxwell, Bruce. *Insider's Guide to Finding a Job in Washington: Contacts and Strategies to Build Your Career in Public Policy.* Washington, DC: CQ Press, 1999.

Mershon, Erin. "Hill Internships 101: What You Need to Know," *Roll Call,* June 1, 2011 (online version).

Princeton Review. *The Internship Bible,* 10th ed. New York: Random House, 2005.

Reeher, Grant, and Mack Mariani, eds. *The Insider's Guide to Political Internships: What to Do Once You're in the Door.* Boulder, CO: Westview Press, 2002.

Strand, Mark, Michael S. Johnson, and Jerome F. Climer. *Surviving Inside Congress.* Washington, DC: Congressional Institute, 2009.

Washington Center for Internships and Academic Seminars. Website: https://www.twc.edu/programs/academic-internship-program.

Washington Information Directory. Washington, DC: CQ Press. Annual publication that provides information about governmental and nongovernmental groups as well as addresses and phone numbers for congressional offices and committees.

SUGGESTED READINGS

CHAPTER 1

Hibbing, John R., and Elizabeth Theiss-Morse. *Congress as Public Enemy*. Cambridge: Cambridge University Press, 1995.

——. *Stealth Democracy: Americans' Beliefs About How Government Should Work*. Cambridge: Cambridge University Press, 2002.

Mayhew, David R. *Congress: The Electoral Connection*. 2nd ed. New Haven, CT: Yale University Press, 2004.

CHAPTER 2

Binder, Sarah A. *Minority Rights, Majority Rule: Partisanship and the Development of Congress*. Cambridge: Cambridge University Press, 1997.

Jenkins, Jeffery A., and Charles Stewart III. *Fighting for the Speakership: The House and the Rise of Party Government*. Princeton, NJ: Princeton University Press, 2013.

Polsby, Nelson W. *How Congress Evolves: Social Bases of Institutional Change*. New York: Oxford University Press, 2004.

Rakove, Jack N. *Original Meanings: Politics and Ideas in the Making of the Constitution*. New York: Vintage, 1997.

Schickler, Eric. *Disjointed Pluralism: Institutional Innovation and the Development of the U.S. Congress*. Princeton, NJ: Princeton University Press, 2001.

Swift, Elaine K. *The Making of an American Senate: Reconstitutive Change in Congress, 1787–1841*. Ann Arbor: University of Michigan Press, 1996.

Wirls, Daniel, and Stephen Wirls. *The Invention of the United States Senate*. Baltimore: Johns Hopkins University Press, 2004.

CHAPTER 3

Canon, David T. *Race, Redistricting, and Representation*. Chicago: University of Chicago Press, 1999.

Fowler, Linda L., and Robert D. McClure. *Political Ambition: Who Decides to Run for Congress*. New Haven, CT: Yale University Press, 1989.

Jacobson, Gary C., and Samuel Kernell. *Strategy and Choice in Congressional Elections*. New Haven, CT: Yale University Press, 1981.

Lawless, Jennifer L. *Becoming a Candidate: Political Ambition and the Decision to Run for Office*. New York: Cambridge University Press, 2015.

Lawless, Jennifer L., and Richard L. Fox. *Running From Office: Why Young Americans Are Turned Off to Politics*. New York: Oxford University Press, 2015.

Thomsen, Danielle M. *Opting Out of Congress: Partisan Polarization and the Decline of Moderate Candidates*. New York: Cambridge University Press, 2017.

CHAPTER 4

Abramowitz, Alan I. *The Great Alignment: Race, Party Transformation, and the Rise of Donald Trump*. New Haven, CT: Yale University Press, 2018.

Dolan, Kathleen A. *Voting for Women: How the Public Evaluates Women Candidates*. Boulder, CO: Westview Press, 2003.

Fiorina, Morris P., Samuel J. Abrams, and Jeremy C. Pope. *Culture War? The Myth of Polarized America*. 3rd ed. New York: Pearson Longman, 2010.

Fiorina, Morris P. *Unstable Majorities: Polarization, Party Sorting and Political Stalemate*. Stanford, CA: Stanford University Press, 2017.

Herrnson, Paul S. *Congressional Elections: Campaigning at Home and in Washington*. 7th ed. Washington, DC: CQ Press, 2015.

Jacobson, Gary C., and Jamie L. Carson. *The Politics of Congressional Elections*. 9th ed. Lanham, MD: Rowman and Littlefield, 2016.

CHAPTER 5

Arnold, R. Douglas. *Congress, the Press, and Political Accountability*. Princeton, NJ: Princeton University Press, 2004.

Baker, Ross K. *House and Senate*. 4th ed. New York: Norton, 2008.

Burden, Barry C. *Personal Roots of Representation*. Princeton, NJ: Princeton University Press, 2007.

Carnes, Nicholas. *White-Collar Government: The Hidden Role of Class in Economic Policy Making*. Chicago: University of Chicago Press, 2013.

Davidson, Roger H. *The Role of the Congressman*. Indianapolis: Bobbs-Merrill, 1969.

Fenno, Richard F., Jr. *Home Style: House Members in Their Districts*. Boston: Little, Brown, 1978.

Fiorina, Morris P. *Congress: Keystone of the Washington Establishment*. 2nd ed. New Haven, CT: Yale University Press, 1989.

Grimmer, Justin. *Representational Style in Congress: What Legislators Say and Why It Matters*. New York: Cambridge University Press, 2013.

Parker, David C. W. *Battle for the Big Sky: Representation and the Politics of Place in the Race for the U.S. Senate*. Washington, DC: CQ Press, 2015.

Price, David E. *The Congressional Experience: A View From the Hill*. 3rd ed. Boulder, CO: Westview Press, 2004.

Swers, Michele L. *Women in the Club: Gender and Policymaking in the Senate*. Chicago: University of Chicago Press, 2013.

Volden, Craig, and Alan E. Wiseman. *Legislative Effectiveness in the United States Congress: The Lawmakers*. New York: Cambridge University Press, 2014.

CHAPTER 6

Aldrich, John H. *Why Parties? The Origins and Transformation of Party Politics in America*. Chicago: University of Chicago Press, 1995.

Cox, Gary W., and Mathew D. McCubbins. *Setting the Agenda: Responsible Party Government in the U.S. House of Representatives*. New York: Cambridge University Press, 2005.

Curry, James M. *Legislating in the Dark: Information and Power in the House of Representatives*. Chicago: University of Chicago Press, 2015.

Evans, C. Lawrence. *The Whips: Building Party Coalitions in Congress*. Ann Arbor, MI: University of Michigan Press, 2018.

Green, Matthew N. *Underdog Politics: The Minority Party in the U.S. House of Representatives*. New Haven, CT: Yale University Press, 2015.

Harbridge, Laurel. *Is Bipartisanship Dead? Policy Agreement and Agenda-Setting in the House of Representatives*. New York: Cambridge University Press, 2015.

Lee, Frances E. *Beyond Ideology: Politics, Principles, and Partisanship in the U.S. Senate*. Chicago: University of Chicago Press, 2009.

————. *Insecure Majorities: Congress and the Perpetual Campaign*. Chicago: University of Chicago Press, 2016.

Meinke, Scott R. *Leadership Organizations in the House of Representatives: Party Participation and Partisan Politics*. Ann Arbor: University of Michigan Press, 2016.

Pearson, Kathryn. *Party Discipline in the U.S. House of Representatives*. Ann Arbor: University of Michigan Press, 2015.

Peters, Ronald M., Jr. *The American Speakership: The Office in Historical Perspective*. 2nd ed. Baltimore, MD: The Johns Hopkins University Press, 1997.

Rohde, David W. *Parties and Leaders in the Postreform House*. Chicago: University of Chicago Press, 1991.

Rubin, Ruth Bloch. *Building the Bloc: Intraparty Organization in the U.S. Congress*. New York: Cambridge University Press, 2017.

Sinclair, Barbara. *The Transformation of the U.S. Senate*. Baltimore: Johns Hopkins University Press, 1989.

CHAPTER 7

Deering, Christopher J., and Steven S. Smith. *Committees in Congress*. 3rd ed. Washington, DC: CQ Press, 1997.

Evans, C. Lawrence. *Leadership in Committee: A Comparative Analysis of Leadership Behavior in the U.S. Senate*. Ann Arbor: University of Michigan Press, 1991.

Fenno, Richard F., Jr. *Congressmen in Committees*. Boston: Little, Brown, 1973.

Hall, Richard L. *Participation in Congress*. New Haven, CT: Yale University Press, 1998.

King, David C. *Turf Wars: How Congressional Committees Claim Jurisdiction*. Chicago: University of Chicago Press, 1997.

Krehbiel, Keith. *Information and Legislative Organization*. Ann Arbor: University of Michigan Press, 1991.

Maltzman, Forrest. *Competing Principals: Committees, Parties, and the Organization of Congress*. Ann Arbor: University of Michigan Press, 1997.

Wilson, Woodrow. *Congressional Government*. Reprint of 1885 ed. Baltimore: Johns Hopkins University Press, 1981.

CHAPTER 8

Arenberg, Richard A., and Robert B. Dove. *Defending the Filibuster*. Bloomington: Indiana University Press, 2012.

Binder, Sarah A. *Stalemate: Causes and Consequences of Legislative Gridlock*. Washington, DC: Brookings, 2003.

Binder, Sarah A., and Steven S. Smith. *Politics or Principle? Filibustering in the United States Senate*. Washington, DC: Brookings, 1996.

Koger, Gregory. *Filibuster: A Political History of Obstruction in the House and Senate*. Chicago: University of Chicago Press, 2010.

Krehbiel, Keith. *Pivotal Politics: A Theory of U.S. Lawmaking*. Chicago: University of Chicago Press, 1998.

Lawrence, John A. *The Class of '74: Congress After Watergate and the Roots of Partisanship*. Baltimore, MD: Johns Hopkins University Press, 2018.

Longley, Lawrence D., and Walter J. Oleszek. *Bicameral Politics: Conference Committees in Congress*. New Haven, CT: Yale University Press, 1989.

Oleszek, Walter J., Mark J. Oleszek, Elizabeth Rybicki, and Bill Heniff Jr. *Congressional Procedures and the Policy Process*. 11th ed. Washington, DC: CQ Press, 2020.

Schickler, Eric, and Frances E. Lee. *The Oxford Handbook of Congress*. New York: Oxford University Press, 2011.

Sinclair, Barbara. *Unorthodox Lawmaking: New Legislative Processes in the U.S. Congress*. 5th ed. Washington, DC: CQ Press, 2016.

Smith, Steven S. *The Senate Syndrome: The Evolution of Procedural Warfare in the Modern U.S. Senate*. Norman, OK: University of Oklahoma Press, 2014.

Tiefar, Charles. *The Polarized Congress: The Post-Traditional Procedures of Its Current Struggles*. Lanham, MD: University Press of America, 2016.

CHAPTER 9

Arnold, R. Douglas. *The Logic of Congressional Action*. New Haven, CT: Yale University Press, 1990.

Binder, Sarah A. *Stalemate: Causes and Consequences of Legislative Gridlock*. Washington, DC: Brookings, 2003.

Edwards, George C. *At the Margins: Presidential Leadership of Congress*. New Haven, CT: Yale University Press, 1989.

Kingdon, John W. *Congressmen's Voting Decisions*. 3rd ed. Ann Arbor: University of Michigan Press, 1989.

Lapinski, John S. *The Substance of Representation: Congress, American Political Development, and Lawmaking*. Princeton, NJ: Princeton University Press, 2013.

Mucchiaroni, Gary, and Paul J. Quirk. *Deliberative Choices: Debating Public Policy in Congress*. Chicago: University of Chicago Press, 2006.

Sulkin, Tracy. *The Legislative Legacy of Congressional Campaigns*. New York: Cambridge University Press, 2011.

Theriault, Sean M. *Party Polarization in Congress*. New York: Cambridge University Press, 2008.

CHAPTER 10

Binkley, Wilfred. *President and Congress*. New York: Knopf, 1947.

Bond, Jon R., and Richard Fleisher, eds. *Polarized Politics: Congress and the President in a Partisan Era*. Washington, DC: CQ Press, 2000.

Canes-Wrone, Brandice. *Who Leads Whom? Presidents, Policy, and the Public*. Chicago: University of Chicago Press, 2006.

Chafetz, Josh. *Congress's Constitution: Legislative Authority and the Separation of Powers*. New Haven, CT: Yale University Press, 2017.

Edwards, George C., III. *On Deaf Ears: The Limits of the Bully Pulpit*. New Haven, CT: Yale University Press, 2006.

Fisher, Louis. *Constitutional Conflicts Between Congress and the President*. 4th ed. Lawrence: University Press of Kansas, 1997.

Gilmour, John B. *Strategic Disagreement: Stalemate in American Politics*. Pittsburgh, PA: University of Pittsburgh Press, 1995.

Howell, William G. *Power Without Persuasion: The Politics of Direct Presidential Action*. Princeton, NJ: Princeton University Press, 2003.

Kriner, Douglas L., and Eric Schickler. *Investigating the President: Congressional Checks on Presidential Power*. Princeton, NJ: Princeton University Press, 2016.

Mayhew, David R. *Divided We Govern: Party Control, Lawmaking, and Investigations, 1946–2002*. New Haven, CT: Yale University Press, 2005.

Rudalevige, Andrew. *The New Imperial Presidency*. Ann Arbor: University of Michigan Press, 2005.

Thurber, James, and Jordan Tama, eds. *Rivals for Power: Presidential-Congressional Relations*, 6th ed. Lanham, MD: Rowman and Littlefield, 2018.

CHAPTER 11

Aberbach, Joel D. *Keeping a Watchful Eye: The Politics of Congressional Oversight*. Washington, DC: Brookings, 1990.

Arnold, R. Douglas. *Congress and the Bureaucracy: A Theory of Influence*. New Haven, CT: Yale University Press, 1979.

Foreman, Christopher J., Jr. *Signals From the Hill: Congressional Oversight and the Challenge of Social Regulation*. New Haven, CT: Yale University Press, 1988.

Jenkins, Jeffrey, and Eric Patashnik, eds. *Living Legislation: Durability, Change, and the Politics of American Lawmaking*. Chicago: University of Chicago Press, 2012.

Light, Paul C. *A Government Ill Executed: The Decline of the Federal Service and How to Reverse It*. Cambridge, MA: Harvard University Press, 2008.

———. *Government By Investigation: Congress, Presidents, and the Search for Answers 1945–2012*. Washington, DC: Brookings, 2014.

———. *The True Size of Government*. Washington, DC: Brookings, 1999.

Rosenbloom, David. *Building a Legislative-Centered Public Administration: Congress and the Administrative State, 1946–1999*. Tuscaloosa: University of Alabama Press, 2000.

Wilson, James Q. *Bureaucracy: What Government Agencies Do and Why They Do It*. New York: Basic Books, 2000.

CHAPTER 12

Berger, Raoul. *Congress v. The Supreme Court.* Cambridge, MA: Harvard University Press, 1969.

Binder, Sarah A., and Forrest Maltzman. *Advice and Dissent: The Struggle to Shape the Federal Judiciary.* Washington, DC: Brookings, 2009.

Clark, Tom S., *The Limits of Judicial Independence.* New York: Cambridge University Press, 2010.

Fisher, Louis. *Constitutional Dialogues.* Princeton, NJ: Princeton University Press, 1988.

Geyh, Charles Gardner. *When Congress and Courts Collide.* Ann Arbor: University of Michigan Press, 2006.

Katzmann, Robert A. *Courts and Congress.* Washington, DC: Brookings, 1997.

Wittes, Benjamin. *Confirmation Wars: Preserving Independent Courts in Angry Times.* Lanham, MD: Rowman and Littlefield, 2006.

CHAPTER 13

Andres, Gary. *Lobbying Reconsidered.* New York: Pearson Education, 2009.

Baumgartner, Frank R., Jeffrey M. Berry, Marie Hojnacki, David C. Kimball, and Beth L. Leech. *Lobbying and Policy Change: Who Wins, Who Loses and Why.* Chicago: University of Chicago Press, 2009.

Birnbaum, Jeffrey H., and Alan S. Murray. *Showdown at Gucci Gulch: Lawmakers, Lobbyists, and the Unlikely Triumph of Tax Reform.* New York: Random House, 1987.

Hall, Richard L., and Alan V. Deardorff. "Lobbying as Legislative Subsidy." *American Political Science Review 100* (February 2006): 69–84.

Hojnacki, Marie, and David Kimball. "Organized Interests and the Decision of Whom to Lobby in Congress." *American Political Science Review 92* (December 1998): 775–790.

LaPira, Timothy M., and Herschel F. Thomas. *Revolving Door Lobbying: Public Service, Private Influence, and the Unequal Representation of Interests.* Lawrence: University Press of Kansas, 2017.

Loomis, Burdett A., Peter L. Francia, and Dara Z. Strolovich, eds. *Guide to Interest Groups and Lobbying in the United States.* Washington, DC: CQ Press, 2011.

Truman, David B. *The Governmental Process, Political Interests, and Public Opinion.* 2nd ed. New York: Knopf, 1971.

CHAPTER 14

Adler, E. Scott, and John D. Wilkerson. *Congress and the Politics of Problem Solving*. New York: Cambridge University Press, 2013.

Elving, Ronald D. *Conflict and Compromise: How Congress Makes the Law*. New York: Simon and Schuster, 1995.

Hanson, Peter. *Too Weak to Govern: Majority Party Power and Appropriations in the U.S. Senate*. New York: Cambridge University Press, 2014.

Kingdon, John W. *Agendas, Alternatives, and Public Policies*. Boston: Little, Brown, 1984.

Mettler, Suzanne. *The Submerged State: How Invisible Government Policies Undermine Democracy*. Chicago: University of Chicago Press, 2011.

Schick, Allen. *Congress and Money: Budgeting, Spending, and Taxing*. Washington, DC: Urban Institute, 1980.

———. *The Federal Budget: Politics, Policy, Process*. Rev. ed. Washington, DC: Brookings, 2007.

CHAPTER 15

Auerswald, David P., and Colton C. Campbell, eds. *Congress and National Security*. New York: Cambridge University Press, 2012.

Crabb, Cecil V., Jr., Glenn J. Antizzo, and Leila E. Sarieddine. *Congress and the Foreign Policy Process*. Baton Rouge: Louisiana State University Press, 2000.

Fisher, Louis. *Constitutional Conflicts Between Congress and the President*. Lawrence: University Press of Kansas, 2007.

———. *The Constitution and 9/11*. Lawrence: University Press of Kansas, 2008.

Goldsmith, Jack. *The Terror Presidency: Law and Judgment Inside the Bush Administration*. New York: Norton, 2007.

Hinckley, Barbara. *Less Than Meets the Eye: Foreign Policy Making and the Myth of the Assertive Congress*. Chicago: University of Chicago Press, 1994.

Howell, William G., and Jon C. Pevehouse. *While Dangers Gather: Congressional Checks on Presidential War Powers*. Chicago: University of Chicago Press, 2007.

Kriner, Douglas L. *After the Rubicon: Congress, Presidents, and the Politics of Waging War*. Chicago: University of Chicago Press, 2010.

Thorpe, Rebecca U. *The American Warfare State: The Domestic Politics of Military Spending*. Chicago: University of Chicago Press, 2014.

Lindsay, James M. *Congress and the Politics of U.S. Foreign Policy*. Baltimore: Johns Hopkins University Press, 1994.

CHAPTER 16

Adler, E. Scott. *Why Congressional Reforms Fail: Reelection and the House Committee System*. Chicago: University of Chicago Press, 2002.

Cook, Timothy E. *Making Laws and Making News: Media Strategies in the U.S. House of Representatives*. Washington, DC: Brookings, 1989.

Hamilton, Lee H. *How Congress Works, and Why You Should Care*. Bloomington: Indiana University Press, 2004.

Mann, Thomas E., and Norman J. Ornstein, *It's Even Worse Than It Looks: How the American Constitutional System Collided With the New Politics of Extremism*. New York: Basic Books, 2012.

Mayhew, David R. *The Imprint of Congress*. New Haven, CT: Yale University Press, 2017.

Taylor, Andrew J. *Congress: A Performance Appraisal*. Boulder, CO: Westview Press, 2013.

Wolfensberger, Donald. *Congress and the People: Deliberative Democracy on Trial*. Washington, DC: Woodrow Wilson Center Press, 2000.

NOTES

CHAPTER 1

1. Hannah Golden, "28-Year-Old Alexandria Ocasio-Cortez Is Pushing For Millennials' Future Through Politics," *Elite Daily*, June 12, 2018, https://www.elitedaily.com/p/28-year-old-alexandria-ocasio-cortez-is-pushing-for-millennials-future-through-politics-9346653.
2. Ibid.
3. Heather Caygle and John Bresnahan, "Queens Party Boss Angles to Succeed Pelosi as Speaker," *Politico*, April 17, 2018, https://www.politico.com/story/2018/04/17/crowley-pelosi-house-democrats-526994.
4. Shane Goldmacher, "An Upset in the Making: Why Joe Crowley Never Saw Defeat Coming," *New York Times*, June 27, 2018, https://www.nytimes.com/2018/06/27/nyregion/ocasio-cortez-crowley-primary-upset.html.
5. Deepthi Hajela, "Alexandria Ocasio-Cortez, a 28-year-old BU Grad, Just Upset Rep. Joe Crowley in a New York Primary," June 27, 2018, Boston.com, https://www.boston.com/news/politics/2018/06/26/alexandria-ocasio-cortez-joe-crowley-democratic-primary-new-york.
6. David Hawkings, "Joseph Crowley, 56 Years Young and Ready to Succeed the Old Guard," *Roll Call*, April 11, 2018, https://www.rollcall.com/news/hawkings/joseph-crowley-democratic-leadership.
7. Carl Campanille, "Queens Democratic Party Boss Lives in Northern Virginia," *New York Post*, July 8, 2011, https://nypost.com/2011/07/08/queens-democratic-party-boss-lives-in-northern-virginia/.
8. Dennis Saffran, "It's Not Archie Bunker's District Anymore," *City Journal*, June 28, 2018, https://www.city-journal.org/html/joseph-crowleys-defeat-15995.html.
9. Caygle and Bresnahan, "Queens Party Boss."
10. Editorial, *New York Times*, June 19, 2018, https://www.nytimes.com/2018/06/19/opinion/joseph-crowley-alexandria-ocasio-cortez.html.
11. Diana Budds, "The Brilliance of Alexandria Ocasio-Cortez's Bold Campaign Design," *Vox*, July 2, 2018, https://www.vox.com/policy-and-politics/2018/7/2/17519414/ocasio-cortez-campaign-design-campaign-posters-tandem-branding.
12. Kate Aronoff, "Alexandria Ocasio-Cortez on Why She Wants to Abolish ICE and Upend the Democratic Party," *In These Times*, June 25, 2018, http://inthesetimes.com/article/21236/alexandria-ocasio-cortez-ice-new-york-cynthia-nixon-democrats.
13. Paul S. Herrnson, *Congressional Elections: Campaigning at Home and in Washington*, 7th ed. (Washington, DC: CQ Press, 2016), 276.
14. Sam Rayburn, *Speak, Mr. Speaker*, eds. H. G. Dulaney and Edward Hake Phillips (Bonham, TX: Sam Rayburn Foundation, 1978), 263–264. Rayburn was Speaker from 1940 to 1947, 1949 to 1953, and 1955 to 1961.

15. Quoted in Marin Cogan, "Allen West Gets Brushback From Veteran Bishop," *Politico*'s *On Congress: Congressional News and Analysis Blog,* December 21, 2010, www.politico.com/blogs/glenthrush.

16. Michael Thorning, "Healthy Congress Index," Bipartisan Policy Center, July 23, 2018, https://bipartisanpolicy.org/congress/.

17. Frank E. Smith, *Congressman From Mississippi* (New York: Random House, 1964), 127.

18. David R. Mayhew, *Congress: The Electoral Connection* (New Haven, CT: Yale University Press, 1974), 16.

19. Alan Abramowitz, "A Comparison of Voting for U.S. Senator and Representative in 1978," *American Political Science Review* 74 (September 1980): 633–640; Richard F. Fenno Jr., *The United States Senate: A Bicameral Perspective* (Washington, DC: American Enterprise Institute, 1982), 29ff; Frances E. Lee and Bruce I. Oppenheimer, *Sizing Up the Senate: The Unequal Consequences of Equal Representation* (Chicago: University of Chicago Press, 1999), 111–113.

20. U.S. Congress, Joint Committee on the Organization of Congress, *Organization of the Congress, Final Report,* 2 vols., H. Rep. 103–14, 103d Cong., 1st sess., December 1993, 2: 275–287. Also see Table 5–1 in this book.

21. Glenn R. Parker and Roger H. Davidson, "Why Do Americans Love Their Congressmen So Much More Than Their Congress?" *Legislative Studies Quarterly* 4 (February 1979): 53–61; Kelly D. Patterson and David B. Magleby, "Public Support for Congress," *Public Opinion Quarterly* 56 (Winter 1992): 539–540; Randall B. Ripley, Samuel C. Patterson, Lynn M. Mauer, and Stephen V. Quinlan, "Constituents' Evaluations of U.S. House Members," *American Politics Quarterly* 20 (October 1992): 442–456.

22. For how the public's perceptions of the policy process affect Congress's institutional image, see John R. Hibbing and Elizabeth Theiss-Morse, *Congress as Public Enemy: Public Attitudes Toward American Political Institutions* (New York: Cambridge University Press, 1995).

23. Alexander Hamilton, James Madison, and John Jay, *The Federalist Papers,* No. 51, ed. Clinton Rossiter (New York: Mentor, 1961), 322.

24. Hamilton, Madison, and Jay, *Federalist Papers,* No. 52, 327.

25. Edmund Burke, "Speech to Electors at Bristol," in *Burke's Politics,* eds. Ross J. S. Hoffman and Paul Levack (New York: Knopf, 1949), 116.

26. Ibid.

27. Quoted in *Roll Call,* September 9, 1993, 16.

28. *U.S. Term Limits v. Thornton,* 115 S.Ct. 1842 (1995).

29. Quoted in Mark Carl Rom, "Why Not Assume That Public Officials Seek to Promote the Public Interest?" *Public Affairs Report* 37 (July 1996): 12.

30. For an accessible discussion of different voting systems, see Douglas J. Amy, *Behind the Ballot Box: A Citizen's Guide to Voting Systems* (Westport, CT: Praeger, 2000), 65.

31. For a classic analysis of members facing this representational difficulty, see Richard F. Fenno Jr., *Home Style: House Members in Their Districts* (Boston: Little, Brown, 1978), esp. 91–99 and 102–114. For an update, see Justin Grimmer, *Representational Style in Congress: What Legislators Say and Why It Matters* (New York: Cambridge University Press, 2013).

32. Alan I. Abramowitz, *The Disappearing Center: Engaged Citizens, Polarization, and American Democracy* (New Haven, CT: Yale University Press, 2010), 37.
33. Morris P. Fiorina, *Disconnect: The Breakdown of Representation in American Politics,* with Samuel J. Abrams (Norman: University of Oklahoma Press, 2009).
34. Fenno, *Home Style,* 168.
35. Matt Taibbi, "The Worst Congress Ever: How Our National Legislature Has Become a Stable of Thieves and Perverts—in Five Easy Steps," *Rolling Stone,* November 2, 2006, 46.
36. Woodrow Wilson, *Congressional Government* (1885; repr., Baltimore: Johns Hopkins University Press, 1981), 210.
37. Thomas E. Mann and Norman J. Ornstein, *The Broken Branch: How Congress Is Failing America and How to Get It Back on Track* (New York: Oxford University Press, 2006), 141–191.

CHAPTER 2

1. Joseph J. Ellis, *His Excellency George Washington* (New York: Knopf, 2006), 184–186.
2. Alvin M. Josephy Jr., *On the Hill: A History of the American Congress* (New York: Simon and Schuster, 1980), 41–48. For an insightful account of the first Congress, see Fergus M. Bordewich, *The First Congress: How James Madison, George Washington, and a Group of Extraordinary Men Invented the Government* (New York: Simon and Schuster, 2016).
3. Charles A. Beard and John P. Lewis, "Representative Government in Evolution," *American Political Science Review* (April 1932): 223–240.
4. Peverill Squire, *The Evolution of American Legislatures: Colonies, Territories, and States, 1619–2009* (Ann Arbor: University of Michigan Press, 2012).
5. Jack P. Green, ed., *Great Britain and the American Colonies, 1606–1763* (New York: Harper Torch Books, 1970), xxxix. For an analysis of the colonial roots of American separation of powers, see Sean Gailmard, "Building a New Imperial State: The Strategic Foundations of Separation of Powers in America," *American Political Science Review,* 111 (November, 4 2017): 668–685.
6. Edmund C. Burnett, *Continental Congress* (New York: Norton, 1964).
7. *Congressional Quarterly's Guide to Congress,* 5th ed., vol. 1 (Washington, DC: CQ Press, 2000), 9.
8. Burnett, *Continental Congress,* 171. The authors use modern capitalization when quoting the Declaration of Independence (as here) or the Constitution in this volume.
9. Jack N. Rakove, *The Beginnings of National Politics: An Interpretive History of the Continental Congress* (New York: Knopf, 1979), 43.
10. Charles C. Thach Jr., *The Creation of the Presidency, 1775–1789: A Study in Constitutional History* (Baltimore: Johns Hopkins University Press, 1969), 34.
11. James Sterling Young, "America's First Hundred Days," *Miller Center Journal* 1 (Winter 1994): 57.

12. On the framers' general consensus on the need for a stronger national government, see Lance Banning, "The Constitutional Convention," in *The Framing and Ratification of the Constitution*, eds. Leonard W. Levy and Dennis J. Mahoney (New York: Macmillan, 1987); and John P. Roche, "The Founding Fathers: A Reform Caucus in Action," *American Political Science Review* 55 (1961): 799–816.

13. John Locke, *Two Tracts on Government*, ed. Philip Abrams (New York: Cambridge University Press, 1967), 374.

14. For an analysis of how the power of the purse functions in a separation of powers system dating back to England in the 17th century, see Josh Chafetz, "The Power of the Purse," in *Congress's Constitution: Legislative Authority and the Separation of Powers* (New Haven: Yale University Press, 2017), 45–77.

15. Alexander Hamilton, James Madison, and John Jay, *The Federalist Papers*, No. 48, ed. Clinton Rossiter (New York: Mentor, 1961), 322.

16. Ibid., 308.

17. Joseph Story, *Commentaries on the Constitution of the United States*, 5th ed., vol. 1 (Boston: Little, Brown, 1905), 396. For Justice Robert Jackson's comments, see *Youngstown Sheet and Tube Co. v. Sawyer,* 343 U.S. 579, 635 (1952).

18. Mark A. Peterson, "The Three Branches of Government: Powers, Relationships and Checks," in *A Republic Divided*, ed. Annenberg Democracy Project (New York: Oxford University Press, 2007), 105. From his own survey, David R. Mayhew finds the same six out of ten success rate for presidential initiatives in *Partisan Balance: Why Political Parties Don't Kill the U.S. Constitutional System* (Princeton, NJ: Princeton University Press, 2011), 58.

19. In the 2014 case of *NLRB v. Noel Canning* (133 S. Ct. 2550), the Supreme Court restricted the president's ability to circumvent Senate approval of nominations via recess appointments to circumstances when the Senate is not able to transact Senate business. Not all executive nominees require Senate approval. According to the Constitution, "inferior officers" need not be confirmed by the Senate, and Congress can vest the power to appoint inferior officers "in the President alone."

20. William Howell and Jon Pevehouse, "When Congress Stops Wars," *Foreign Affairs* (September/October 2007).

21. In *Nixon v. United States,* 506 U.S. 224 (1993), the Supreme Court refused to review the Senate's procedures. Walter L. Nixon Jr., a formal federal judge, objected that, although he had been convicted by a vote of the full Senate, the evidence in his case had been taken by one of the chamber's committees.

22. *Federalist Papers*, No. 65, 396. See also Cass R. Sunstein, *Impeachment: A Citizen's Guide* (Cambridge, MA: Harvard University Press, 2017).

23. Emily Field Van Tassel and Paul Finkelman, *Impeachable Offenses: A Documentary History From 1787 to the Present* (Washington, DC: Congressional Quarterly, 1999). The only Senate impeachment trial since 1999 was that of Judge G. Thomas Porteous Jr. of the federal district court in Louisiana. See Jennifer Steinhauer, "Senate, for Just the 8th Time, Votes to Oust a Federal Judge," *New York Times*, December 8, 2010.

24. *U.S. v. Rayburn House Office Bldg., Room 2113, Washington, DC, 20515*, 497 F.3d 654 (D.C. Cir. 2007).

25. *Marbury v. Madison*, 1 Cranch 137 (1803).

26. Justia US Law, "Acts of Congress Held Unconstitutional in Whole or in Part by the Supreme Court of the United States," https://law.justia.com/constitution/us/acts-of-congress-held-unconstitutional.html, accessed November 29, 2018.

27. J. Mitchell Pickerill, "Congressional Responses to Judicial Review," in *Congress and the Constitution,* eds. Neal Devins and Keith E. Whittington (Durham, NC: Duke University Press, 2005), 159.

28. *Dred Scott v. Sandford,* 60 U.S. 393 (1856).

29. *Citizens United v. Federal Election Commission,* 130 S.Ct. 876 (2010).

30. *Immigration and Naturalization Service v. Chadha,* 463 U.S. 919 (1983).

31. William N. Eskridge Jr., "Overriding Supreme Court Statutory Interpretation Decisions," *Yale Law Journal* 101 (November 1991): 331–455. Also see R. Shep Melnick, *Between the Lines: Interpreting Welfare Rights* (Washington, DC: Brookings, 1994).

32. See Richard L. Hasen, "End of the Dialogue? Political Polarization, the Supreme Court, and Congress," *Southern California Law Review* 86 (2013): 205–262.

33. Louis Fisher, *Constitutional Dialogues: Interpretation as Political Process* (Princeton, NJ: Princeton University Press, 1988), 275.

34. Quoted in Charles Warren, *The Making of the Constitution* (Boston: Little, Brown, 1928), 162.

35. Quoted in Charles Warren, *The Supreme Court in United States History* (Boston: Little, Brown, 1919), 195.

36. Wendy J. Schiller, "Building Careers and Courting Constituents: U.S. Senate Representation: 1889–1924," *Studies in American Political Development* 20 (Fall 2006): 185–197.

37. See Wendy J. Schiller and Charles Stewart III, *Electing the Senate: Indirect Democracy Before the Seventeenth Amendment* (Princeton, NJ: Princeton University Press, 2014); and Gregory J. Wawro and Eric Schickler, *Filibuster: Obstruction and Lawmaking in the U.S. Senate* (Princeton, NJ: Princeton University Press, 2006).

38. Elaine K. Swift, *The Making of an American Senate* (Ann Arbor: University of Michigan Press, 1996), 5.

39. Joel H. Silbey, *The Partisan Imperative: The Dynamics of American Politics Before the Civil War* (New York: Oxford University Press, 1985).

40. Sarah A. Binder, *Minority Rights, Majority Rule* (New York: Cambridge University Press, 1997), 49.

41. Molly Reynolds, Andrew Rugg, Michael J. Malbin, Norman J. Ornstein, Raffaela Wakeman, and Thomas E. Mann, *Vital Statistics on Congress, 2018* (Washington, DC: Brookings, 2018), https://www.brookings.edu/multi-chapter-report/vital-statistics-on-congress, Table 5–1.

42. See *Jefferson's Manual, and Rules of the House of Representatives,* Section XI, H. Doc. 105–358, 105th Cong., 2d sess., 1999, 145–148.

43. Nelson W. Polsby, "The Institutionalization of the House of Representatives," *American Political Science Review* 62 (March 1968): 146–147.

44. Reynolds et al., *Vital Statistics,* Tables 6–1, 6–2, 6–3, and 6–4.

45. Ibid., Table 6–4.

46. Joseph Cooper and Cheryl D. Young, "Bill Introduction in the Nineteenth Century: A Study of Institutional Change," *Legislative Studies Quarterly* 14, no. 1 (1989): 67–105.

47. Eric Schickler, "Institutional Development of Congress," in *The Legislative Branch*, ed. Paul J. Quirk and Sarah A. Binder (New York: Oxford University Press, 2005), 40; Norman J. Ornstein, Thomas E. Mann, and Michael J. Malbin, *Vital Statistics on Congress, 2001–2002* (Washington, DC: American Enterprise Institute), 149.

48. George B. Galloway, *History of the House of Representatives* (New York: Crowell, 1961), 67.

49. Andrew J. Taylor, "Size, Power, and Electoral Determinants: Exogenous Determinants of Legislative Procedural Choice," *Legislative Studies Quarterly* 31 (August 2006): 338.

50. See Dylan Matthews, "The case for massively expanding the US House of Representatives, in one chart," vox.com, https://www.vox.com/2018/6/4/17417452/congress-representation-ratio-district-size-chart-graph.

51. Schickler, "Institutional Development of Congress," 40.

52. Roger H. Davidson and Walter J. Oleszek, *Congress Against Itself* (Bloomington: Indiana University Press, 1977), 14.

53. Quoted in Eric Schickler, *Disjointed Pluralism: Institutional Innovation and the Development of the U.S. Congress* (Princeton, NJ: Princeton University Press, 2001), 142.

54. James L. Sundquist, *The Decline and Resurgence of Congress* (Washington, DC: Brookings, 1982).

55. Julian E. Zelizer, *On Capitol Hill: The Struggle to Reform Congress and Its Consequences, 1948–2000* (New York: Cambridge University Press, 2004), 153.

56. Roy Swanstrom, *The United States Senate, 1787–1801*, S. Doc. 99–19, 99th Cong., 1st sess., 1985, 283.

57. Jeffery A. Jenkins and Charles Stewart III, *Fighting for the Speakership: The House and the Rise of Party Government* (Princeton, NJ: Princeton University Press, 2013).

58. Ibid.

59. Binder, *Minority Rights, Majority Rule*, 17.

60. Gregory Koger, *Filibustering: A Political History of Obstruction in the House and Senate* (Chicago: University of Chicago Press, 2010).

61. Ibid., 84.

62. David R. Mayhew, *Congress: The Electoral Connection* (New Haven, CT: Yale University Press, 1974), 95.

63. See David W. Rohde, *Parties and Leaders in the Postreform House* (Chicago: University of Chicago Press, 1991); and Nelson W. Polsby, *How Congress Evolves: Social Bases of Institutional Change* (New York: Oxford University Press, 2004).

64. See Sarah A. Binder and Steven S. Smith, *Politics or Principle? Filibustering in the United States Senate* (Washington, DC: Brookings, 1997); Gregory J. Wawro and Eric Schickler, *Filibuster: Obstruction and Lawmaking in the U.S. Senate* (Princeton, NJ: Princeton University Press, 2006); and Sarah A. Binder, Anthony J. Madonna, and Steven S. Smith, "Going Nuclear, Senate Style," *Perspectives on Politics* 5, no. 4 (2007): 729–740.

65. Gregory J. Wawro and Eric Schickler, "Reid's Rules: Filibusters, the Nuclear Option, and Path Dependence in the US Senate," *Legislative Studies Quarterly* 43 (June 2018): 619–647.

66. Schickler, *Disjointed Pluralism*, 13.

67. Ibid., 141–146.
68. Ibid., 213–217.
69. Ibid., 267.
70. Ibid.
71. James Sterling Young, *The Washington Community, 1800–1828* (New York: Harcourt Brace Jovanovich, 1966), 89.
72. Noble Cunningham Jr., ed., *Circular Letters of Congressmen, 1789–1839*, 3 vols. (Chapel Hill: University of North Carolina Press, 1978), 57.
73. Swanstrom, *United States Senate*, 80.
74. Mildred Amer, "Average Years of Service for Members of the Senate and the House of Representatives, First–109th Congresses," Congressional Research Service Report RL32648, November 9, 2005. Earlier studies include Nelson W. Polsby, "The Institutionalization of the House of Representatives," *American Political Science Review* 62 (March 1968): 146–147; and Randall B. Ripley, *Power in the Senate* (New York: St. Martin's Press, 1969), 42–43.
75. Joe Martin, as told to Robert J. Donovan, *My First Fifty Years in Politics* (New York: McGraw-Hill, 1960), 49–50.
76. Robert H. Salisbury and Kenneth A. Shepsle, "U.S. Congressman as Enterprise," *Legislative Studies Quarterly* 6 (November 1981): 559–576.
77. Julie Jennings and Jared C. Nagel, "Federal Workforce Statistics Sources: OPM and OMB," Congressional Research Service Report RL43590, January 12, 2018, Table 3.
78. Cunningham, *Circular Letters of Congressmen*.
79. Martin, *My First Fifty Years*, 101.
80. Colleen J. Shogan, "Blackberries, Tweets, and YouTube: Technology and the Future of Communicating With Congress," *P.S.* 42 (April 2010): 231. See also Matthew E. Glassman, "Tweet Your Congressman: The Rise of Electronic Communications in Congress," in *The Evolving Congress*, Senate Committee on Rules and Administration Prt. 113–130 (Washington, DC: U.S. Government Printing Office, 2014), 95–106.
81. Congressional Management Foundation, *Communicating With Congress: How Citizen Advocacy Is Changing Mail Operations on Capitol Hill* (Washington, DC: Congressional Management Foundation, 2011).
82. For reexaminations of the institutionalization perspective, see Jeffery A. Jenkins and Charles Stewart III, "The Deinstitutionalization (?) of the House of Representatives: Reflections on Nelson Polsby's 'Institutionalization of the House of Representatives' at Fifty." *Studies in American Political Development*, 32 (Fall 2018): 1–22 and Anthony J. Chergosky and Jason M. Roberts, "The De-Institutionalization of Congress," *Political Science Quarterly* 133, no. 3 (2018): 475–495.

CHAPTER 3

1. This number includes sixteen lawmakers who were appointed (two senators) or won special elections (fourteen in the House) in 2017 or 2018 to fill vacancies in their respective chambers.

2. James Varney, "Candidates' Homes Not Even Inside District," *The Washington Times*, October 31, 2018, A5.

3. Arend Lijphart, *Democracies: Patterns of Majoritarian and Consensus Government in Twenty-One Countries* (New Haven, CT: Yale University Press, 1984), 174.

4. Based on data on 2014 population from the U.S. Census Bureau, "National, State, and Puerto Rico Commonwealth Totals Datasets: Population, Population Change, and Estimated Components of Population Change: April 1, 2010 to July 1, 2014," https://www.census.gov/popest/data/national/totals/2014/NST-EST2014-alldata.html. See also David Samuels and Richard Snyder, "The Value of a Vote: Malapportionment in Comparative Perspective," *British Journal's of Political Science* 31, no. 4 (2001): 651–671.

5. See Daniel H. Pink, "Givers and Takers," *New York Times*, January 30, 2004, A21.

6. John D. Griffin, "Senate Apportionment as a Source of Political Inequality," *Legislative Studies Quarterly* 31 (August 2006): 425.

7. Frances E. Lee, "Bicameral Representation," in *The Oxford Handbook of the American Congress, ed.* Eric Schickler and Frances E. Lee (Oxford, UK: Oxford University Press, 2011), 283.

8. The idea is that proportional differences in the number of persons per representative for any pair of states should be kept to a minimum. The first fifty House seats are taken because the Constitution ensures that each state has at least one representative. The question then becomes, Which state deserves the fifty-first seat, the fifty-second, and so forth? The mathematical formula yields a priority value for each seat, up to any desired number. The bottom line is to ensure that states are "entitled to a percentage of representatives equal to [their] portion of the national population."

9. Jeffrey W. Ladewig and Mathew P. Jasinski, "On the Causes and Consequences of and Remedies for Interstate Malapportionment of the U.S. House of Representatives," *Perspectives on Politics* 6 (2008): 90.

10. Sabrina Tavernise, "Racial Projection by the Census Is Making Demographers Uneasy," *New York Times*, November 23, 2018, A1.

11. In 1960, the size of the House was temporarily increased from 435 to 437 members to accommodate the admission of Alaska and Hawaii as states. Three years later, after the 1960 reapportionment, the House reverted back to 435 members.

12. On the role of the Prohibition issue in the congressional failure to reapportion House seats in 1920, see Daniel Okrent, *Last Call: The Rise and Fall of Prohibition* (New York: Scribner, 2010), 239–241, 327–328.

13. *Congressional Quarterly's Guide to Congress,* vol. 2 (Washington, DC: CQ Press, 2000), 898.

14. Clark Bensen, "The Political Impact of Katrina: Apportionment in 2010," POLIDATA Press Release, December 22, 2006, 2.

15. Reid Wilson, "Population Shifts Show Sun Belt Poised to Gain in Congress," *The Hill*, December 21, 2017, online edition.

16. Haya El Nasser, "For 2010 Census, the Counting Gets Tougher," *USA Today*, October 8, 2008, 1A.

17. Kathleen Hunter, "Minority Lawmakers to Ask Leadership to Address U.S. Census Undercounts," *CQ Today,* October 29, 2007, 6.

18. Quoted in Charles Mahtesian, "Dollars and Census," *Government Executive,* December 2007, 50.

19. For a more detailed discussion of districting than is provided here, see Thomas S. Arrington, "Redistricting in the U.S.: A Review of Scholarship and Plan for Future Research," *The Forum* 8 (2010): art. 7.

20. Arizona, California, Hawaii, Idaho, Montana, New Jersey, and Washington have established commissions for drawing congressional district lines.

21. Juliet Eilperin, "The Gerrymander That Ate America," *Slate,* April 17, 2006. Quoted from her book *Fight Club Politics: How Partisanship Is Poisoning the House of Representatives* (Lanham, MD: Rowman and Littlefield, 2006).

22. Sam Wang, "The Great Gerrymander of 2012," *New York Times,* February 3, 2013, SR1.

23. Ibid.

24. Tim Storey and Wendy Underhill, "Red, Wide & Blue," *State Legislatures,* (November/December 2018): 12–14.

25. Reid Wilson, "Democrats Make Legislative Gains Over GOP in Redistricting Battle," *The Hill,* November 27, 2018, online edition.

26. The classic study is still Gordon E. Baker, *The Reapportionment Revolution: Representation, Political Power, and the Supreme Court* (New York: Random House, 1966).

27. L. Paige Whitaker, "Congressional Redistricting: Legal and Constitutional Issues," CRS Report R44199, April 14, 2016, 4.

28. Nolan McCarty, Keith T. Poole, and Howard Rosenthal, "Does Gerrymandering Cause Polarization?" *American Journal of Political Science* 53 (2009): 678.

29. John Sides and Eric McGhee, "Gerrymandering Isn't Evil," *Politico,* June 30, 2015, online edition.

30. Andrew Tan-Delli Cicchi, "Beware the Gerrymander," *The Nation,* February 12/19, 2018, 6.

31. See Jack Fitzpatrick, "Just How Much Gerrymandering Is Unconstitutional? Wisconsin Plaintiffs Want the Supreme Court to Rule," *The Atlantic,* November 1, 2016, online version.

32. Todd Ruger, "High Court Ensures Quick Legal Path in Redistricting Challenges," *CQ News,* December 8, 2015, 2.

33. Material in this paragraph relied on L. Paige Whitaker, "Partisan Gerrymandering: Supreme Court Provides Guidance on Standing and Maintains Legal Status Quo," *Legal Sidebar,* July 2, 2018. *Legal Sidebar* is a publication of the Congressional Research Service, U.S. Library of Congress. Also see Adam Liptak, "Supreme Court Dodges Making Major Ruling On Gerrymandering," *New York Times,* June 19, 2018, A13.

34. Robert Barnes, "Court to Take Up N.C., Md. Gerrymandering Cases," *The Washington Post,* January 5, 2019, A4; Brent Kendall and Jess Bravin, "Supreme Court Takes Up Gerrymandering Again," *Wall Street Journal,* January 5–6, 2019, A3.

35. Sean M. Theriault, *Party Polarization in Congress* (New York: Cambridge University Press, 2008), 83.

36. Nolan McCarty, Keith T. Poole, and Howard Rosenthal, "Does Gerrymandering Cause Polarization?" *American Journal of Political Science* 53 (2009): 678.

37. The sole incumbent defeated in California between 2002 and 2010 was Republican Richard Pombo, who served from 1993 to 2007.

38. Nathan L. Gonzales, "Congress Isn't Perfect but the Politicians Aren't Always to Blame," *Roll Call,* August 8, 2018, online edition.

39. Steven Hill, "Schwarzenegger Versus Gerrymander," *New York Times,* February 19, 2005, A29. See also Steve Lawrence, "Experts Question Redistricting Plan," *Santa Barbara News-Press,* February 20, 2005, A7.

40. Quoted in Bill Bishop, "You Can't Compete With Voters' Feet," *Washington Post,* May 15, 2005, B2. Also see James G. Gimpel and Jason E. Schucknect, *Patchwork Nation: Sectionalism and Political Change in American Politics* (Ann Arbor: University of Michigan Press, 2003); and Bill Bishop, *The Big Sort: Why the Clustering of Like-Minded America Is Tearing Us Apart* (Boston: Houghton Mifflin, 2008).

41. Jowei Chen and Jonathan Rodden, "Unintentional Gerrymandering: Political Geography and Electoral Bias in Legislatures," *Quarterly Journal of Political Science* 8, no. 3 (2013): 239–269.

42. Patrick O'Connor, "House Districts Keep Getting Safer," *Wall Street Journal,* July 29, 2013, A4.

43. Tal Kopan, "Report: Map Shifts Statistics on Congress," *Politico,* July 11, 2013, 6.

44. Definition is from *Shaw v. Reno,* 509 U.S. 630 (1993), quoting *Davis v. Bandemer,* 478 U.S. 109 (1986).

45. Eric Foner, *Reconstruction: America's Unfinished Revolution, 1863–1877* (New York: Harper and Row, 1988), 590.

46. The "retrogression" standard was established in *Beer v. U.S.,* 425 U.S. 130 (1976).

47. Whitaker, "Congressional Redistricting," 3.

48. *Miller v. Johnson,* 515 U.S. 900 (1995).

49. Ibid.

50. Whitaker, "Congressional Redistricting," 9.

51. *Miller v. Johnson,* 515 U.S. 900 (1995).

52. *Easley v. Cromartie,* 532 U.S. 234 (2001).

53. David Lublin, Thomas L. Brunell, Bernard Grofman, and Lisa Handley, "Has the Voting Rights Act Outlived Its Usefulness? In a Word, 'No,'" *Legislative Studies Quarterly* 34 (2009): 547.

54. Ehrenhalt, "Redistricting and the Erosion of Community," 10.

55. David Lublin, *The Paradox of Representation: Racial Gerrymandering and Minority Interests in Congress* (Princeton, NJ: Princeton University Press, 1997).

56. Carol M. Swain, "The Voting Rights Act: Some Unintended Consequences," *Brookings Review* 10 (Winter 1992): 51. See also Lublin, *Paradox of Representation.*

57. Alexander Bolton, "Dems Seek to 'Unpack' Minority Districts," *The Hill,* May 9, 2001, 4.

58. Richard Wolf, "Justices to Rule if Race-Based Districts Legal," *USA Today,* September 2, 2014, online edition.

59. See Adam Liptak, "Justices Side With Black Lawmakers in Alabama," *New York Times,* March 26, 2015, A12; Robert Barnes, "Foes of Alabama Redistricting Get a High Court Win," *Washington Post,* March 26, 2015, A3; and Jess Bravin, "Top Court Questions Alabama Districts," *Wall Street Journal,* March 26, 2015, A6.

60. Louis Sandy Maisel, *From Obscurity to Oblivion: Running in the Congressional Primary* (Knoxville: University of Tennessee Press, 1982), 34.

61. Susan Chira, "Banner Year for Female Candidates Doesn't Extend to G.O.P. Women," *New York Times*, November 16, 2018, A12.

62. The four Capitol Hill campaign committees are the National Republican Senatorial Committee (NRSC), Democratic Senatorial Campaign Committee (DSCC), National Republican Congressional Committee (NRCC), and Democratic Congressional Campaign Committee (DCCC). See Paul S. Herrnson, *Congressional Elections: Campaigning at Home and in Washington*, 4th ed. (Washington, DC: CQ Press, 2004), 90–94.

63. Jennifer L. Lawless, *Becoming a Candidate: Political Ambition and the Decision to Run for Office* (New York: Cambridge University Press, 2012), 137. See also David E. Broockman, "Mobilizing Candidates: A Field Experiment and a Review," *Journal of Experimental Political Science* 1 (Winter 2014): 104–119.

64. Edward Walsh, "To Every Campaign, There Is a Recruiting Season," *Washington Post*, November 12, 1985, A1.

65. C. Douglas Swearingen and Walt Jatkowski III, "Is Timing Everything? Retirement and Seat Maintenance in the U.S. House of Representatives," *Legislative Studies Quarterly* 36 (May 2011): 309–330.

66. David T. Canon, *Actors, Athletes, and Astronauts: Political Amateurs in the United States Congress* (Chicago: University of Chicago Press, 1990), 2–3, 25–31.

67. Jonathan Rauch and Raymond J. La Raja, "Re-Engineering Politicians: How Activist Groups Choose Our Candidates—Long Before We Vote," The Brookings Institution, December 7, 2017, 3.

68. Jonathan Rauch and Raymond J. La Raja, "Politics Shouldn't Be Like Open Mic Night," *New York Times*, January 26, 2018, A21.

69. Michael Janofsky, "Two Congressional Candidates Know They'll Lose, but It's Still Fun," *New York Times*, October 31, 1992, 27.

70. Maisel, *From Obscurity to Oblivion*, 23.

71. This conceptualization is a combination of insights derived from a broad-based, pioneering study of House candidate recruitment by a team of scholars: Cherie D. Maestas, Sara Fulton, L. Sandy Maisel, and Walter J. Stone, "When to Risk It? Institutions, Ambitions, and the Decision to Run for the U.S. House," *American Political Science Review* 100 (May 2006): 195–208; and Walter J. Stone and L. Sandy Maisel, "The Not-So-Simple Calculus of Winning: U.S. House Candidates' Nomination and General Election Prospects," *Journal of Politics* 65 (November 2003): 951–977.

72. Danielle M. Thomsen, "Ideological Moderates Won't Run: How Party Fit Matters for Partisan Polarization in Congress," *Journal of Politics* 76, no. 3 (2014): 786–797.

73. Paul Kane, "Senate Headed for Record Number of Former House Members in Its Lineup," *Washington Post*, July 23, 2014, http://www.washingtonpost.com/poli tics/senate-headed-for-record-number-of-former-house-members-in-its-line up/2014/07/23/31c88518-11e4-11e4-9285-4243a40ddc97_story.html.

74. The seminal work on strategic politician theory is Gary C. Jacobson and Samuel Kernell, *Strategy and Choice in Congressional Elections*, 2nd ed. (New Haven, CT: Yale University Press, 1983).

75. Shira Toeplitz, "Ohio's Limits Tip Races," *Roll Call*, November 20, 2008, 15.

76. L. Sandy Maisel, Cherie D. Maestas, and Walter J. Stone, "The Party Role in Congressional Competition," in *The Parties Respond*, ed. Paul S. Herrnson (Boulder, CO: Westview Press, 2002), 129.

77. Brian D. Feinstein, "The Dynasty Advantage: Family Ties in Congressional Elections," *Legislative Studies Quarterly* 35 (November 2010): 571–598.

78. Evan Harper, "Apps May Aid Upstart Candidates in Next Presidential Race," *Los Angeles Times,* December 3, 2018, online edition.

79. Jamie L. Carson and Jason M. Roberts, "House and Senate Elections," in *The Oxford Handbook of the American Congress,* ed. Eric Schickler and Frances E. Lee (Oxford, UK: Oxford University Press, 2011), 149.

80. Jacobson, *Politics of Congressional Elections,* 23.

81. Ibid., 38.

82. See Walter J. Stone, Sarah A. Fulton, Cherie D. Maestas, and L. Sandy Maisel, "Incumbency Reconsidered: Prospects, Strategic Retirement, and Incumbent Quality in U.S. House Elections," *Journal of Politics* 72 (January 2010): 178–190.

83. Ibid.

84. Maisel, Maestas, and Stone, "Party Role in Congressional Competition," 129.

85. Jennifer L. Lawless and Richard L. Fox, *It Still Takes a Candidate: Why Women Don't Run for Office,* rev. ed. (New York: Cambridge University Press, 2010).

86. The authors thank Jennifer Manning, senior research librarian, Congressional Research Service, for this information.

87. Malanie Zanona, "Women Wield Sizable Power in 'Me Too' Midterms," *The Hill,* September 21, 2018, 13. The 233 figure is from Janet Hook and Julie Bykowicz, "Congress to See Record Number of Women," *Wall Street Journal,* November 15, 2018, A4.

88. Ibid.

89. Ibid., 1.

90. Edward Luce, "The Whole Foods Election," *Financial Times,* November 10–11, 2018, 8.

91. Hook and Bykowicz, "Congress to See Record Number of Women," A4.

92. Tara Golshan, "Midterms 2018: the Reason Republican Women Are on the Decline in the House," www.vox.com, December 4, 2018, 1.

93. Jacobson, *Politics of Congressional Elections,* 19.

94. Bridget Bowman, "Open Primary Pickle Vexes Calif. Dems," *Roll Call,* February 15, 2018,

95. Stephen Ansolabehere, John Mark Hansen, Shigeo Hirano, and James M. Snyder Jr., "The Decline of Competition in U.S. Primary Elections, 1908–2004," in *The Marketplace of Democracy,* ed. Michael P. McDonald and John Samples (Washington, DC: Cato Institute and Brookings, 2006), 74–101.

96. Robert G. Boatright, *Getting Primaried: The Changing Politics of Congressional Primary Challenges* (Ann Arbor: University of Michigan Press, 2013).

97. Ansolabehere et al., "Decline of Competition in U.S. Primary Elections," 81.

98. Alexander Bolton, "Picking 2018 Candidates Pits McConnell vs. GOP Groups," *The Hill,* April 19, 2017, 6.

99. Peter Grier, "How Voters Really Choose," *The Christian Science Monitor Weekly,* August 3, 2015, 31

100. Austin Ranney, "Parties in State Politics," in *Politics in the American States,* ed. Herbert Jacob and Kenneth Vines (Boston: Little, Brown, 1976), 61–99.

101. John F. Bibby, "State Party Organizations," in *The Parties Respond,* 3rd ed., ed. L. Sandy Maisel (Boulder, CO: Westview Press, 1998), 20.

CHAPTER 4

1. Emily Witt, "Beto O'Rourke and Ted Cruz in the Final Stretch of the Texas Senate Race," *The New Yorker,* November 2, 2018, https://www.newyorker.com/news/dispatch/beto-orourke-and-ted-cruz-in-the-final-stretch-of-the-texas-senate-race.

2. Wade Goodwyn, "To Win Texas, Beto O'Rourke Is Running to the Left," National Public Radio, August 17, 2018, https://www.npr.org/2018/08/17/639353916/to-win-texas-beto-orourke-is-running-to-the-left.

3. Patrick Svitek and Abby Livingson, "How the Race Between Ted Cruz and Beto O'Rourke Became the Closest in Texas in 40 Years," *Texas Tribune,* November 9, 2018, https://www.texastribune.org/2018/11/09/ted-cruz-beto-orourke-closest-texas-race-40-years/.

4. Elbert Wang, "Look Up Texas Midterm Turnout in Your County Against Historic Numbers," *Texas Tribune,* November 7, 2018, https://www.texastribune.org/2018/11/07/texas-election-results-turnout-county-look-up/.

5. Gary C. Jacobson, "It's Nothing Personal: The Decline of the Incumbency Advantage in U.S. House Elections," *Journal of Politics* 77, no. 3 (2015): 861–873.

6. See Dena Levy and Peverill Squire, "Television Markets and the Competitiveness of U.S. House Elections," *Legislative Studies Quarterly* 25 (May 2000): 313–325; and James M. Snyder Jr. and David Stromberg, "Press Coverage and Political Accountability," *Journal of Political Economy* 118 (April 2010): 355–408.

7. Theodore E. Jackson Jr., "Brand Marketing in Today's Cluttered Political Marketplace," *Campaigns and Elections* 24 (April 2003): 30.

8. Allison Stevens, "House Candidates in Maryland Striving to Hone Their Messages," *The Hill,* May 8, 2002, 31–32.

9. Quoted in Robin Toner, "In a Cynical Election Season, the Ads Tell an Angry Tale," *New York Times,* October 24, 1994, A1.

10. Parke Skelton, quoted in Mary Clare Jalonick, "How to 'Primary' an Incumbent," *Campaigns and Elections* 22 (May 2001): 35.

11. See Paul S. Herrnson, *Congressional Elections: Campaigning at Home and in Washington,* 7th ed. (Washington, DC: CQ Press, 2016), xviii.

12. The figures cited in this chapter for the 2017–2018 cycle were taken from the website of the Center for Responsive Politics, www.opensecrets.org.

13. Norman J. Ornstein, Thomas E. Mann, and Michael J. Malbin, *Vital Statistics on Congress, 2008* (Washington, DC: American Enterprise Institute, 2008), 75–76.

14. Norah O'Donnell, "Are Members of Congress Becoming Telemarketers," *60 Minutes,* April 24, 2016, transcript, https://www.cbsnews.com/news/60-minutes-are-members-of-congress-becoming-telemarketers/.

15. A survey of members by the Congressional Management Foundation suggests that less time is spent on fund-raising than the DCCC recommends. Members report that they spend roughly 18 percent of their work time on campaign activities, with much of this time devoted to fund-raising (see Ezra Klein, "Congress Spends Too Much Time Fundraising, but It's Less Time Than You Think," *Washington Post,* July 29, 2013, http://www.washingtonpost.com/blogs/wonkblog/wp/2013/07/29/congress-spends-too-much-time-fundraising-but-its-less-time-than-you-think).

16. *Buckley v. Valeo,* 424 U.S. 1 (1976).

17. *McCutcheon v. FEC,* 572 U.S. ___ (2014).
18. See "Self Funding Candidates," Center for Responsive Politics, https://www .opensecrets.org/overview/topself.php.
19. *Citizens United v. Federal Election Commission,* 558 U.S. 310 (2010), slip op. at 44.
20. *Speechnow.org v. Federal Election Commission,* 99 F.3d 686 (2010).
21. Ibid., at 55.
22. David G. Savage, "Corporate Campaign Ads Haven't Followed Supreme Court's Prediction," *Los Angeles Times,* October 27, 2010, online edition.
23. Sean Sullivan, "What Is a 501(c)(4), Anyway?" *Washington Post,* May 13, 2013, https://www.washingtonpost.com/news/the-fix/wp/2013/05/13/what-is-a-501c4-anyway/?utm_term=.e436ebfa64bf.
24. Ray LaRaja, "Why Super PACs: How the American Party System Outgrew the Campaign Finance System," *The Forum* 10, no. 4 (2012): 91–104.
25. Anna Massoglia, "Millions in Masked Money Funnelled Into 2018 Elections," Opensecrets News, Center for Responsive Politics, November 7, 2018, https://www.opensecrets.org/news/2018/11/millions-in-masked-money-funneled-into-2018-elections/.
26. Geoff West and Robert Maguire, "TV Ads in Midterms Up Nearly 90 Percent Fueled by Nondisclosing Groups," Opensecrets News, Center for Responsive Politics, May 7, 2018, https://www.opensecrets.org/news/2018/05/tv-ads-in-midterms-up-nearly-90-percent-fueled-by-nondisclosing-groups/.
27. Under the BCRA, individuals could donate $32,400 to national party committees per calendar year during the 2014 election cycle and $10,000 as a combined limit on contributions to state, district, and local party committees. These amounts are adjusted annually for inflation.
28. Raymond J. LaRaja, "Money in the 2014 Congressional Elections: Institutionalizing a Broken Regulatory System," *The Forum,* 12 no. 4 (January 28, 2015), https://doi .org/10.1515/for-2014-5032.
29. In December 2013, Sen. Mitch McConnell succeeded in adding a provision to a massive spending bill that further loosened the limitations on party fundraising. The new rules allow party organizations to raise up to $97,200 per year from individuals to go into each of three separate accounts. See LaRaja, "Money in the 2014 Congressional Elections."
30. Ibid.
31. The Center for Responsive Politics reports that House and Senate candidates raised $2.74 billion in 2017–2018, but that the total cost of the election was more than $5.19 billion.
32. Quoted in Michael Luo and Stephanie Strom, "Donor Names Remain Secret as Rules Shift," *New York Times,* September 20, 2010, https://www.nytimes .com/2010/09/21/us/politics/21money.html.
33. Campaign data are drawn from the Federal Elections Commission data compiled by the Center for Responsive Politics, www.opensecrets.org/overview/incumbs .php, and by the Campaign Finance Institute http://www.cfinst.org.
34. Gary C. Jacobson and Jamie L. Carson, *The Politics of Congressional Elections,* 9th ed. (New York: Rowman and Littlefield, 2015), 65.

35. For a study documenting the fund-raising advantage of majority party members, see Erik J. Engstrom and William Ewell, "The Impact of Unified Party Government on Campaign Contributions," *Legislative Studies Quarterly* 35 (2010): 543–569.

36. Alexander Fouirnaies and Andrew B. Hall, "The Financial Incumbency Advantage: Causes and Consequences," *Journal of Politics* 76, no. 3 (2014): 711–724.

37. Thomas B. Edsall, "In Tight Races, Early Cash Means Staying Competitive," *Washington Post,* July 14, 1998, A6.

38. Gary C. Jacobson, "The Effects of Campaign Spending on Congressional Elections," *American Political Science Review* 72 (June 1978): 469–491.

39. Gary C. Jacobson, "Money in the 1980 and 1982 Congressional Elections," in *Money and Politics in the United States: Financing Elections in the 1980s,* ed. Michael J. Malbin (Chatham, NJ: Chatham House, 1984), 57.

40. Gary C. Jacobson, *The Politics of Congressional Elections,* 6th ed. (New York: Pearson Longman, 2004), 98.

41. Manu Raju, "How Graham Beat the Tea Party Threat," *Politico,* April 26, 2014, https://www.politico.com/story/2014/04/lindsey-graham-south-carolina-tea-party-105928.

42. David Hinckley, "Average American Watches 5 Hours of TV per Day, Report Shows," *New York Daily News,* March 5, 2014, http://www.nydailynews.com/life-style/average-american-watches-5-hours-tv-day-article-1.1711954.

43. Ann Massoglia, "Ad Wars Escalate Ahead of 2018 Midterm Elections," Opensecrets News, Center for Responsive Politics, September 26, 2018, https://www.opensecrets.org/news/2018/09/ads-war-escalates/.

44. Sara Fischer, "Political Ad Spending Hits New Record for 2018 Midterm Elections," *Axios,* November 6, 2018, https://www.axios.com/record-midterm-ad-spend-explodes-money-was-no-object-1541450836-f92d1767-ad5f-4d85-99ee-96d9847e7691.html.

45. Robin Toner, "In Final Rounds, Both Sides Whip Out Bare-Knuckle Ads," *New York Times,* October 21, 1996, B7.

46. James A. Thurber and Carolyn Long, "Brian Baird's 'Ring of Fire': The Quest for Funds and Votes in Washington's Third District," in *The Battle for Congress,* ed. James A. Thurber (Washington, DC: Brookings, 2001), 188.

47. Brendan Nyhan and Jacob M. Montgomery, "Connecting the Candidates: Consultant Networks and the Diffusion of Campaign Strategy in American Congressional Elections," *American Journal of Political Science* 59, no. 2 (2015): 292–308.

48. Andrew Mayerson, "Campaign Spending Habits: Democrats v. Republicans," Center for Responsive Politics, October 23, 2013, http://www.opensecrets.org/news/2013/10/campaign-spending-habits-democrats-v-republicans.

49. Molly Ball, "'There's Nothing Better Than a Scared, Rich Candidate:' How Political Consulting Works—Or Doesn't," *The Atlantic,* October 2016, https://www.theatlantic.com/magazine/archive/2016/10/theres-nothing-better-than-a-scared-rich-candidate/497522/.

50. Amy Mitchell, Jeffrey Gottfried, Michael Barthel, and Elisa Shearer, "The Modern News Consumer," Pew Research Center, July 2016, http://www.journalism.org/2016/07/07/pathways-to-news.

51. Erika Franklin Fowler generously provided this data. See also Erika Franklin Fowler, "Making the News: Is Local News Coverage Really That Bad?" in *New Directions in Media and Politics,* ed. Travis N. Ridout (New York: Routledge, 2012), 45–60.

52. Quoted in Janet Hook, "Negative Ads a Positive in GOP Strategy," *Los Angeles Times,* September 26, 2006, A10.

53. Stephen Ansolabehere and Shanto Iyengar, *Going Negative: How Attack Ads Shrink and Polarize the Electorate* (New York: Free Press, 1996), 128.

54. Quoted in David S. Broder, "Death by Negative Ads," *Washington Post,* November 3, 2002, B7.

55. Michael Barthel, "Newspapers Fact Sheet," State of the News Media 2018, Pew Research Center, June 13, 2018, http://www.journalism.org/fact-sheet/newspapers/.

56. Amy Mitchell and Jesse Holcomb, "State of the News Media 2016," Pew Research Center, June 15, 2016, http://www.journalism.org/2016/06/15/state-of-the-news-media-2016.

57. Katerina Eva Matsa and Elisa Shearer, "News Use Across Social Media Platforms 2018," Pew Research Center, September 10, 2018, http://www.journalism.org/2018/09/10/news-use-across-social-media-platforms-2018/.

58. Brent Buchanan, "Seven Ways to Effectively Market Your Candidate," *Campaigns and Elections,* April 29, 2015.

59. Rebecca Gale, "Study Finds Congress Is Paying More Attention to Social Media," *Roll Call,* October 14, 2015, http://www.rollcall.com/news/home/new-study-finds-congress-paying-attention-social-media.

60. Dan Morain, "Undercover Campaigning on the Web," *Los Angeles Times,* March 21, 2007, A11.

61. Merle Miller, *Lyndon: An Oral Biography* (New York: Putnam, 1980), 120.

62. "Lessons From Recent GOTV Experiments," GOTV, Yale University, Institution for Social and Policy Studies, http://gotv.research.yale.edu/?q=node/10.

63. Donald P. Green and Alan S. Gerber, *Get Out the Vote!* (Washington, DC: Brookings, 2004), 93–96.

64. Ibid., 40.

65. Dan Glickman, as told to Amy Zipkin, "Landing the Job He Wanted," *New York Times,* April 17, 2005, C10.

66. Paul Houston, "TV and High Tech Send Campaign Costs Soaring," *Los Angeles Times,* October 2, 1986, 121.

67. Jamie Stiehm, "Ben and Jerry's State Offers a Choice of Three Flavors," *The Hill,* November 22, 1995, 26.

68. Glenn R. Simpson, "In Rhode Island, Everyone Goes to Bristol Parade," *Roll Call,* July 9, 1990, 1; Glenn R. Simpson, "Judging From July 4th Bristol Parade in R.I., Chafee Looks Well-Positioned for November," *Roll Call,* July 11, 1994, 21.

69. Leslie Wayne, "Democrats Take Page From Their Rival's Playbook," *New York Times,* November 1, 2008, A15.

70. Press release, "SEIU Members Mobilize Infrequent Voters to Vote for $15, Affordable Healthcare, Opportunity to Join Unions, Drive Historic Midterm Turnout," SEIU, November 7, 2018, http://www.seiu.org/2018/11/

seiu-members-mobilize-infrequent-voters-to-vote-for-15-affordable-health care-opportunity-to-join-unions-drive-historic-midterm-turnout.

71. Michael P. McDonald, "2014 November General Election Turnout Rates," United States Elections Project, accessed January 6, 2016, http://www.electproject .org/home/voter- turnout/voter-turnout-data.

72. Ibid.

73. M. Margaret Conway, "Political Participation in Midterm Congressional Elections," *American Politics Quarterly* 9 (April 1981): 221–244.

74. International turnout figures from the Institute for Social Research, University of Michigan, reported in Pippa Norris, *Electoral Engineering: Voting Rules and Political Behavior* (Cambridge, UK: Cambridge University Press, 2004). A sensible review of the question is found in Martin P. Wattenberg, *Where Have All the Voters Gone?* (Cambridge, MA: Harvard University Press, 2002).

75. Pew Research Center for the People and the Press, "Who Votes, Who Doesn't, and Why," October 18, 2006, 4.

76. "Young People Dramatically Increase Their Turnout to 31%, Shape 2018 Midterm Elections," CIRCLE: The Center for Information and Research on Civic Learning and Engagement, Jonathan M. Tisch College of Citizenship and Public Service, Tufts University, November 7, 2018, https://civicyouth.org/young-people-dra matically-increase-their-turnout-31-percent-shape-2018-midterm-elections/.

77. Pew Charitable Trust, "Why Are Millions of Citizens Not Registered to Vote?" Issue brief, June 21, 2017, https://www.pewtrusts.org/en/research-and-analysis/ issue-briefs/2017/06/why-are-millions-of-citizens-not-registered-to-vote.

78. Joseph D. Rich, "Playing Politics With Justice," *Los Angeles Times,* March 29, 2007, A23. Rich is former chief (1999–2005) of the voting section in the Department of Justice's Civil Rights Division.

79. *Crawford v. Marion County Election Board,* 553 U.S. 181 (2008).

80. Michael Cooper, "After Ruling, States Rush to Enact Voting Laws," *New York Times,* July 5, 2013, http://www.nytimes.com/2013/07/06/us/politics/after-Supreme-Court-ruling-states-rush-to-enact-voting-laws.html?pagewanted=all&_r=0.

81. Jan E. Leighley and Jonathan Nagler, *Who Votes Now? Demographics, Issues, Inequality, and Turnout in the United States* (Princeton: Princeton University Press, 2014).

82. Samuel L. Popkin, *The Reasoning Voter* (Chicago: University of Chicago Press, 1994), 7.

83. National House exit poll, *Washington Post,* http://www.washingtonpost.com/ wp-srv/special/politics/2014-midterms/exit-polls.

84. NBC News Exit Poll, November 6, 2018, https://www.nbcnews.com/card/ nbc-news-exit-poll-first-time-2008-independent-voters-break-n932926.

85. Samara Klar and Yanna Krupnikov, "9 Media Myths About Independent Voters, Debunked," *Vox.com,* January 22, 2016, https://www.vox.com/2016/1/ 22/10814522/independents-voters-facts-myths.

86. Quoted in Richard Morin and Claudia Deane, "How Independent Are Independents?" *Washington Post,* August 2, 2002, A1.

87. Gary C. Jacobson, *The Politics of Congressional Elections,* 5th ed. (New York: Addison, Wesley, Longman, 2001), 108.

88. Martin P. Wattenberg, *The Rise of Candidate-Centered Politics* (Cambridge, MA: Harvard University Press, 1991), 36–39.

89. See Bernard Grofman, William Koetzle, Michael P. McDonald, and Thomas L. Brunell, "A New Look at Split-Ticket Outcomes for House and President: The Comparative Midpoints Model," *Journal of Politics* 62 (February 2000): 34–50.

90. David Nir, "Daily Kos Elections' Presidential Results By Congressional District for the 2016 and 2012 Elections," November 19, 2016, http://www.dailykos.com/stories/2012/11/19/1163009/-Daily-Kos-Elections-presidential-results-by-congressional-district-for-the-2012–2008-elections.

91. Gary Jacobson, *The Politics of Congressional Elections*, 8th ed. (New York: Pearson Longman, 2013), 176.

92. Ibid., 175.

93. James E. Campbell, "The Midterm Landslide of 2010: A Triple Wave Election," *The Forum* 8 (2010): art. 3.

94. Angus Campbell, "Surge and Decline: A Study of Electoral Change," in *Elections and the Political Order*, ed. Angus Campbell, Phillip E. Converse, Warren E. Miller, and Donald E. Stokes (New York: Wiley, 1966), 40–62; Raymond E. Wolfinger, Steven J. Rosenstone, and Richard A. McIntosh, "Presidential and Congressional Voters Compared," *American Politics Quarterly* 9 (April 1981): 245–255.

95. Eric M. Uslaner and M. Margaret Conway, "The Responsible Electorate: Watergate, the Economy, and Vote Choice in 1974," *American Political Science Review* 79 (September 1985): 788–803; Samuel Kernell, "Presidential Popularity and Negative Voting: An Alternative Explanation of the Midterm Congressional Decline of the President's Party," *American Political Science Review* 71 (March 1977): 44–46.

96. Ashley Parker and Josh Dawsey, "'I Am On The Ticket': Trump Seeks to Make the Election About Him, Even if Some Don't Want It to Be," *Washington Post*, October 18, 2018, https://www.washingtonpost.com/politics/i-am-on-the-ticket-trump-seeks-to-make-the-election-about-him-even-if-some-dont-want-it-to-be/2018/10/17/069406f6-d0bc-11e8-a275–81c671a50422_story.html?utm_term=.026d372f29b5.

97. Roberto Alesina and Howard Rosenthal, *Partisan Politics, Divided Government, and the Economy* (New York: Cambridge University Press, 1995). See also Robert S. Erikson, "Congressional Elections in Presidential Years: Presidential Coattails and Strategic Voting," *Legislative Studies Quarterly* 41, no. 3 (2016): 551–574.

98. Joseph Bafumi, Robert S. Erikson, and Christopher Wlezien, "Balancing, Generic Polls and Midterm Congressional Elections," *Journal of Politics* 72 (2010): 705–719.

99. Quoted in Dale Russakoff, "In Tight Arkansas Senate Race, Family Matters," *Washington Post*, August 3, 2002, A1.

100. Jacobson, *Politics of Congressional Elections*, 8th ed., 35.

101. Ibid., 27–28. See Gary C. Jacobson, "Extreme Referendum: Donald Trump and the 2018 Midterm Elections," *Political Science Quarterly* 134 (forthcoming Spring 2019).

102. National Election Studies (now called the American National Election Studies, or ANES), 1980–2002, summarized in Jacobson, *Politics of Congressional Elections*,

122–126; Thomas E. Mann and Raymond E. Wolfinger, "Candidates and Parties in Congressional Elections," *American Political Science Review* 74 (September 1980): 623.

103. Ida A. Brudnick, "Congressional Salaries and Allowances: In Brief," CRS Report for Congress, RL30064, April 11, 2018.

104. Jacobson (2019).

105. Ibid.

106. Michael J. Robinson, "Three Faces of Congressional Media," in *The New Congress*, ed. Thomas E. Mann and Norman J. Ornstein (Washington, DC: American Enterprise Institute, 1981), 91.

107. Jacobson (2019).

108. Paul S. Herrnson and James M. Curry, "Issue Voting and Partisan Defections in Congressional Elections," *Legislative Studies Quarterly* 36, no. 2 (2011): 281–307.

109. Owen G. Abbe, Jay Goodliffe, Paul S. Herrnson, and Kelly D. Patterson, "Agenda Setting in Congressional Elections: The Impact of Issues and Campaigns on Voting Behavior," *Political Research Quarterly* 56 (December 2003): 419.

110. John B. Bader, *Taking the Initiative: Leadership Agendas in Congress and the "Contract with America"* (Washington, DC: Georgetown University Press, 1996).

111. Quoted in Judy Newman, "Do Women Vote for Women?" *Public Perspective* 7 (February–March 1996): 10.

112. Janie Velencia, "The 2018 Gender Gap Was Huge, and It Helped Democrats Win the House." FiveThirtyEight, November 9, 2018, https://fivethirtyeight.com/features/the-2018-gender-gap-was-huge/.

113. Karen M. Kaufmann and John R. Petrocik, "The Changing Politics of American Men: Understanding the Sources of the Gender Gap," *American Journal's of Political Science* 43 (July 1999): 864–887.

114. Quoted in Barbara Vobejda, "Fragmentation of Society Formidable Challenge to Candidates, Report Says," *Washington Post,* March 7, 1996, A15.

115. Frances E. Lee, *Insecure Majorities: Congress and the Perpetual Campaign* (Chicago: University of Chicago Press, 2016), chap. 2.

116. Morris P. Fiorina, "An Era of Tenuous Majorities," Hoover Institution Essays on Contemporary American Politics, September 7, 2016, https://www.hoover.org/sites/default/files/research/docs/fiorina_final_essay1.pdf#overlay-context=research/era-tenuous-majorities-historical-context. See also Morris P. Fiorina, *Unstable Majorities: Polarization, Party Sorting, and Political Stalemate* (Stanford, CA: Hoover Institution Press, 2017).

117. See, for example, Nathaniel Rakich, "The Senate Will Be Competitive Again In 2020, But Republicans Are Favored," FiveThirtyEight, November 28, 2018, https://fivethirtyeight.com/features/the-senate-will-be-competitive-again-in-2020-but-republicans-are-favored/.

118. For a discussion of these reversals, see Gary Miller and Norman Schofield, "Activists and Partisan Realignment in the United States," *American Political Science Review* 97 (May 2003): 245–260.

119. Jacobson, *Politics of Congressional Elections,* 6th ed., 249–253.

120. Ronald Brownstein, "The Two Americas Just Lurched Further Apart," CNN Politics, November 8, 2018, https://www.cnn.com/2018/11/08/politics/election-2018-two-americas-brownstein/index.html.

121. Delegates to the parties' national conventions were analyzed in a classic study by Herbert McCloskey, Paul Hoffman, and Rosemary O'Hara, "Issue Conflict and Consensus Among Party Leaders and Followers," *American Political Science Review* 54 (1960): 406–427.

122. The "middlingness" of the citizenry is vigorously argued in Morris P. Fiorina, *Culture War? The Myth of a Polarized America,* with Samuel J. Abrams and Jeremy C. Pope (New York: Pearson-Longman, 2005). See also Samara Klar and Yanna Krupnikov, *Independent Politics: How American Disdain for Parties Leads to Political Inaction* (New York: Cambridge University Press, 2016).

123. Alan I. Abramowitz, *The Great Alignment: Race, Party Transformation, and the Rise of Donald Trump* (New Haven, CT: Yale University Press, 2018). See also Pew Research Center for the People and the Press, "The Partisan Divide on Political Values Grows Even Wider," survey report, October 5, 2017, http://www.people-press .org/2017/10/05/the-partisan-divide-on-political-values-grows-even-wider/.

124. David W. Brady, "Electoral Realignments in the U.S. House of Representatives," in *Congress and Policy Change,* ed. Gerald C. Wright Jr., Leroy N. Reiselbach, and Lawrence C. Dodd (New York: Agathon Press, 1986), 46–69.

125. See Table 5 in Jennifer E. Manning and R. Eric Peterson, "First-Term Members of the House of Representatives and Senate, 64th–114th Congresses," Congressional Research Service Report for Congress, R41283, March 7, 2016. The average freshman class size between 1950 and 2016 was 60 members.

126. Warren E. Miller and Donald E. Stokes, "Constituency Influence in Congress," *American Political Science Review* 57 (March 1963): 45–57.

127. Tracy Sulkin, *Issue Politics in Congress* (New York: Cambridge University Press, 2005), 2.

128. Ibid., 177.

CHAPTER 5

1. Sarah Yager, "Jon Tester Bets the Farm," *The Atlantic,* October 25, 2018, https://www .theatlantic.com/politics/archive/2018/10/democrat-jon-tester-fights-keep-montana-senate-seat/573820/.

2. Ibid.

3. David C. W. Parker, *Battle for the Big Sky: Representation and the Politics of Place in the Race for the U.S. Senate* (Washington, DC: CQ Press, 2015), p. 101.

4. Parker, pp. 103–04.

5. Kevin Robillard, "'I Don't Think They Can Beat Who I Am,'" *Politico,* April 18, 2018, https://www.politico.com/story/2018/04/18/jon-tester-montana-democrat-senate-531524.

6. Yager, "Jon Tester Bets the Farm."

7. Ibid.

8. Robillard, "'I Don't Think They Can Beat Who I Am.'"

9. Ibid.

10. Ida Brudnick, "Congressional Salaries and Allowances," Congressional Research Service Report No. RL30064, Updated April 11, 2018.

11. *Roll Call,* "Wealth of Congress Index," February 27, 2018, http://www.rollcall.com/wealth-of-congress.

12. John Stuart Mill, *Considerations on Representative Government* (London: Longmans, Green, 1967 [1861]), quoted in Lisa Schwindt-Bayer and William Mishler, "An Integrated Model of Women's Representation," *Journal of Politics* 67 (2005): 413.

13. Hannah Finichel Pitkin, *The Concept of Representation* (Berkeley: University of California Press, 1967), 166.

14. See David T. Canon, *Race, Redistricting, and Representation: The Unintended Consequences of Black Majority Districts* (Chicago: University of Chicago Press, 1999); Michele L. Swers, *The Difference Women Make* (Chicago: University of Chicago Press, 2002); and Vanessa Tyson, *Twists of Fate: Multiracial Coalitions and Minority Representation in the U.S. House of Representatives* (Oxford, UK: Oxford University Press, 2016).

15. See Claudine Gay, "Spirals of Trust? The Effect of Descriptive Representation on the Relationship Between Citizens and Their Government," *American Journal of Political Science* 46 (2002): 717–732; John D. Griffin and Michael Keane, "Descriptive Representation and the Composition of African American Turnout," *American Journal of Political Science* 50 (2006): 998–1012; Katherine Tate, "The Political Representation of Blacks in Congress: Does Race Matter?" *Legislative Studies Quarterly* 26 (2001): 623–638; and David Broockman, "Black Politicians Are More Intrinsically Motivated to Advance Blacks' Interests," *American Journal of Political Science* 57 (2013): 521–536.

16. Data on characteristics of members are found in Jennifer E. Manning, "Membership of the 116th Congress: A Profile," Congressional Research Service Report No. xx, 2019.

17. Alan Ehrenhalt, *The United States of Ambition: Politicians, Power, and the Pursuit of Office* (New York: Times Books, 1992), 16.

18. Casey Burgat and Charles Hunt, "Congress in 2019: The 2nd Most Educated and Least Politically Experienced House Freshman Class," *Brookings Fixgov Blog,* December 28, 2018, https://www.brookings.edu/blog/fixgov/2018/12/28/congress-in-2019-the-2nd-most-educated-and-least-politically-experienced-house-freshman-class/.

19. William T. Bianco, "Last Post for 'The Greatest Generation': The Policy Implications of the Decline of Military Experience in the U.S. Congress," *Legislative Studies Quarterly* 30 (February 2005): 85–102.

20. Nicholas Carnes, "Does the Numerical Underrepresentation of the Working Class in Congress Matter?" *Legislative Studies Quarterly* 37, no. 1 (2012): 5–34.

21. Ibid. See also Nicholas Carnes, *White-Collar Government: The Hidden Role of Class in Economic Policy Making* (Chicago: University of Chicago Press, 2013).

22. Betsy Rothstein, "Congresswomen Press Women's Health Issues," *The Hill,* February 24, 1999, 19; Maureen Dowd, "Growing Sorority in Congress Edges Into the Ol' Boys' Club," *New York Times,* March 5, 1993, A1, A18.

23. Kerry L. Haynie, "African Americans and the New Politics of Inclusion: A Representational Dilemma?" in *Congress Reconsidered,* 8th ed., ed. Lawrence C. Dodd and Bruce I. Oppenheimer (Washington, DC: CQ Press, 2005).

24. Thomas L. Brunell, Christopher J. Anderson, and Rachel K. Cremona, "Descriptive Representation, District Demography, and Attitudes Toward Congress Among African Americans," *Legislative Studies Quarterly* 33 (2008): 223–242.

25. Tate, "The Political Representation of Blacks in Congress," 631.

26. Janet M. Box-Steffensmeier, David C. Kimball, Scott R. Meinke, and Katherine Tate, "The Effects of Political Representation on the Electoral Advantages of Incumbents," *Political Research Quarterly* 56 (September 2003): 264.

27. See Canon, *Race, Redistricting, and Representation*; Broockman, "Black Politicians Are More Intrinsically Motivated"; Katrina L. Gamble, "Black Political Representation: An Examination of Legislative Activity Within U.S. House Committees," *Legislative Studies Quarterly* 32 (2007): 421–448; Michael D. Minta, "Legislative Oversight and the Substantive Representation of Black and Latino Interests in Congress," *Legislative Studies Quarterly* 34 (2009): 193–218.

28. Inter-Parliamentary Union, "Women in National Parliaments," December 1, 2018, http://archive.ipu.org/wmn-e/classif.htm.

29. The pioneering study of this subject is Irwin N. Gertzog, *Congressional Women: Their Recruitment, Treatment, and Behavior* (New York: Praeger, 1984). Two more-recent studies are Barbara C. Burrell, *A Woman's Place Is in the House* (Ann Arbor: University of Michigan Press, 1994); and Richard Logan Fox, *Gender Dynamics in Congressional Elections* (Thousand Oaks, CA: Sage, 1997).

30. Quoted in Sheryl Gay Stolberg, "Working Mothers Swaying Senate Debate, as Senators," *New York Times*, June 7, 2003, A3.

31. Jamie Stiehm, "In Senate, Sisterhood Can Override Party," *The Hill*, November 22, 1995, 16.

32. Emily Moon, "Martha McSally's Experience With Sexual Assault in the Military Is Part of a 'Silent Epidemic,'" *Pacific Standard*, March 7, 2019, https://psmag.com/news/martha-mcsallys-experience-with-sexual-assault-in-the-military-is-part-of-a-silent-epidemic.

33. See Swers, *The Difference Women Make.*

34. Jeremy Peters, "Objections by Women Open Rift in G.O.P.," *New York Times*, January 22, 2015, http://www.nytimes.com/2015/01/23/us/politics/house-gop-discards-bill-banning-abortion-at-20-weeks-but-passes-another-restriction.html?_r=0.

35. See Kathleen A. Dolan, *Voting for Women: How the Public Evaluates Women Candidates* (Boulder, CO: Westview Press, 2003); Leonie Huddy and Nayda Terkildsen, "Gender Stereotypes and the Perception of Male and Female Candidates," *American Journal of Political Science* 37 (1993): 119–147.

36. Michele Swers, "Building a Reputation on National Security: The Impact of Stereotypes Related to Gender and Military Experience," *Legislative Studies Quarterly* 32 (2007): 559–595.

37. Kirk Victor, "Still an Old Boys' Club?" *National Journal*, March 12, 2005, 750, 752.

38. Niels Lesniewski, "Feinstein Unveils CIA Torture Report," *Roll Call*, December 9, 2014.

39. Donald P. Haider-Markel, Mark R. Joslyn, and Chad J. Kniss, "Minority Group Interests and Political Representation: Gay Elected Officials in the Policy Process," *Journal of Politics* 62 (2000): 568–577.

40. Quoted in Erika Niedowski, "Four Walk Out of the Closet and Toward the House," *CQ Weekly,* April 25, 1998, 1051.

41. Manning, "Membership of the 116th Congress: A Profile."

42. Ibid.

43. Ibid.

44. Ibid., 6. For tenure figures, see Figure 2–1.

45. Charles S. Bullock and Burdett A. Loomis, "The Changing Congressional Career," in *Congress Reconsidered,* 3rd ed., ed. Lawrence C. Dodd and Bruce I. Oppenheimer (Washington, DC: CQ Press, 1985), 66–69, 80–82.

46. Jennifer Wolak, "Strategic Retirements: The Influence of Public Preferences on Voluntary Departures From Congress," *Legislative Studies Quarterly* 32 (May 2007): 285–308.

47. Quoted in Shailagh Murray, "GOP Lawmakers Gird for Rowdy Tea Party," *Washington Post,* July 18, 2010, A3.

48. Frances E. Lee and Bruce I. Oppenheimer, *Sizing Up the Senate: The Unequal Consequences of Equal Representation* (Chicago: University of Chicago Press, 1999), 20–23. Also see Robert A. Dahl, *A Preface to Democratic Theory* (New Haven, CT: Yale University Press, 1956).

49. John D. Griffin, "Senate Apportionment as a Source of Political Inequality," *Legislative Studies Quarterly* 31 (2006): 405–432.

50. Bruce I. Oppenheimer, "The Representational Experience: The Effect of State Population on Senator–Constituency Linkages," *American Journal of Political Science* 40 (1996): 1280–1299.

51. Frances E. Lee, "Representation and Public Policy: The Consequences of Senate Apportionment for the Geographic Distribution of Federal Funds," *Journal of Politics* 60 (1998): 34–64. Also see Stephen Ansolabehere, Alan Gerber, and James M. Snyder Jr., "Equal Votes: Equal Money: Court-Ordered Redistricting and the Distribution of Public Expenditures in the American States," *American Political Science Review* 96 (2002): 767–777.

52. Robert Weissberg, "Collective vs. Dyadic Representation in Congress," *American Political Science Review* 72 (1978): 535–547.

53. Jane Mansbridge, "Rethinking Representation," *American Political Science Review* 97 (November 2003): 515–528.

54. Barry C. Burden, *Personal Roots of Representation* (Princeton, NJ: Princeton University Press, 2007).

55. Richard F. Fenno Jr., *The Making of a Senator: Dan Quayle* (Washington, DC: CQ Press, 1989), 119.

56. Quoted in Adam Nagourney, "Upbeat Schumer Battles Polls, Low Turnouts, and His Image," *New York Times,* May 16, 1998, A14.

57. Frank E. Smith, *Congressman From Mississippi* (New York: Pantheon, 1964), 129–130.

58. Donald R. Matthews, *U.S. Senators and Their World* (Chapel Hill: University of North Carolina Press, 1960), chap. 5; Ross K. Baker, *House and Senate,* 3rd ed. (New York: Norton, 2001), chap. 2.

59. Barbara Sinclair, *The Transformation of the U.S. Senate* (Baltimore: Johns Hopkins University Press, 1989).

60. Herbert B. Asher, "The Learning of Legislative Norms," *American Political Science Review* 67 (June 1973): 499–513.

61. Rachael Bade and Heather Caygle, "Exasperated Democrats try to rein in Ocasio-Cortez," *Politico,* January 11, 2019, https://www.politico.com/story/2019/01/11/alexandria-ocasio-cortez-democrats-establisment-1093728.

62. Quoted in Thomas E. Cavanagh, "The Two Arenas of Congress," in *The House at Work,* ed. Joseph Cooper and G. Calvin Mackenzie (Austin: University of Texas Press, 1981), 65.

63. Daniel M. Butler, Christopher F. Karpowitz, and Jeremy C. Pope, "A Field Experiment on Legislators' Home Styles: Service Versus Policy," *Journal of Politics* 74 (April 2012): 474–486.

64. David C. W. Parker and Craig Goodman, "Making a Good Impression: Resource Allocation, Home Styles, and Washington Work," *Legislative Studies Quarterly* 34 (November 2009): 493–524. See also Justin Grimmer, Sean Westwood, and Solomon Messing, *The Impression of Influence: Legislator Communication, Representation, and Democratic Accountability* (Princeton, NJ: Princeton University Press, 2014).

65. Box-Steffensmeier et al., "Effects of Political Representation," 266.

66. Kenneth M. Bickers and Robert M. Stein, "The Electoral Dynamics of the Federal Pork Barrel," *American Journal of Political Science* 40 (November 1996): 1300–1326.

67. Robert M. Stein and Kenneth M. Bickers, "Congressional Elections and the Pork Barrel," *Journal of Politics* 56 (May 1994): 377–399.

68. Quoted in Louis Jacobson, "For Arkansas, No Abundance of Clout," *National Journal,* February 20, 1999, 475.

69. Quoted in Scott MacKay, "Chafee's New Book Is Tough on Pro-War Democrats, Republicans, President Bush," *Providence Journal,* January 27, 2008.

70. Marian Currinder, *Money in the House: Campaign Funds and Congressional Party Politics* (Boulder, CO: Westview Press, 2009); Eric S. Heberlig, "Congressional Parties, Fundraising, and Committee Ambition," *Political Research Quarterly* 56 (2003): 151–161; Anne H. Bedlington and Michael J. Malbin, "The Party as Extended Network: Members Giving to Each Other and to Their Parties," in *Life after Reform,* ed. Michael J. Malbin (Lanham, MD: Rowman and Littlefield, 2003), 121–140.

71. Patrick Sellers, *Cycles of Spin: Strategic Communication in the U.S. Congress* (New York: Cambridge University Press, 2010).

72. Solomon Messing and Rachel Weisel, "Partisan Conflict and Congressional Outreach," *Pew Research Report,* February 23, 2017, http://www.people-press.org/2017/02/23/partisan-conflict-and-congressional-outreach.

73. Roger H. Davidson, *The Role of the Congressman* (New York: Pegasus, 1969), 98; U.S. Congress, Senate Commission on the Operation of the Senate, *Toward a Modern Senate,* S. Doc. 94–278, 94th Cong., 2nd sess., committee print, 1997, 27; U.S. Congress, House Commission on Administrative Review, *Final Report,* 2 vols., H. Doc. 95–272, 95th Cong., 1st sess., December 31, 1977, 2: 874–875.

74. Richard L. Hall, *Participation in Congress* (New Haven, CT: Yale University Press, 1998).

75. Ross A. Webber, "U.S. Senators: See How They Run," *Wharton Magazine* (Winter 1980–1981): 38.

76. Quoted in Richard E. Cohen, "Member Moms," *National Journal,* April 7, 2007, 17, 21.

77. U.S. Congress, Senate Commission on the Operation of the Senate, *Toward a Modern Senate.*

78. Quoted in Lindsay Sobel, "Former Lawmakers Find Trade Association Gold," *The Hill,* November 26, 1997, 14.

79. Center for Responsive Politics, *Congressional Operations: Congress Speaks—A Survey of the 100th Congress* (Washington, DC: Center for Responsive Politics, 1988), 47–49. See also Congressional Management Foundation, *Life in Congress: The Member Perspective* (Washington, DC: Congressional Management Foundation, 2013).

80. Quoted in *Washington Post,* October 18, 1994, B3.

81. U.S. Congress, Joint Committee on the Organization of Congress, *Organization of Congress* 2 (December 1993): 281–287; Luke Rosiak, "AWOL on Hill: Fundraising Trumps Voting," *Washington Times,* February 20, 2013, A1.

82. Quoted in Vernon Louviere, "For Retiring Congressmen, Enough Is Enough," *Nation's Business,* May 1980, 32.

83. John R. Hibbing, *Congressional Careers: Contours of Life in the U.S. House of Representatives* (Chapel Hill: University of North Carolina Press, 1991), 117.

84. Craig Volden and Alan E. Wiseman, *Legislative Effectiveness in the United States Congress* (Cambridge, UK: Cambridge University Press, 2014).

85. Ibid., 126, 128.

86. Gerard Padro I. Miquel and James M. Snyder Jr., "Legislative Effectiveness and Legislative Careers," *Legislative Studies Quarterly* 31 (August 2006): 348.

87. Ibid.

88. Gary W. Cox and William C. Terry, "Legislative Productivity in the 93rd–105th Congresses," *Legislative Studies Quarterly* 33 (2008): 613. See also Volden and Wiseman, *Legislative Effectiveness in the United States Congress.*

89. William H. Riker, *The Theory of Political Coalitions* (New Haven, CT: Yale University Press, 1962), 24–38.

90. Pitkin, *Concept of Representation,* 166.

91. Steven Kull, *Expecting More Say: The American Public on Its Role in Government Decision-Making* (Washington, DC: Center on Policy Attitudes, 1999), 13–14.

92. Henry J. Hyde, "Advice to Freshmen: 'There Are Things Worth Losing For,'" *Roll Call,* December 3, 1990, 5.

93. Quoted in Jamie Stiehm, "Ex-Rep Mike Synar, Who Fought Lobbyists, Succumbs to Brain Tumor," *The Hill,* January 10, 1996, 5.

94. Thomas E. Cavanagh, "The Calculus of Representation: A Congressional Perspective," *Western Political Quarterly* 35 (March 1982): 120–129.

95. John W. Kingdon, *Congressmen's Voting Decisions,* 3rd ed. (Ann Arbor: University of Michigan Press, 1989), 47–54.

96. Lawrence N. Hansen, *Our Turn: Politicians Talk About Themselves, Politics, the Public, the Press, and Reform,* part 2 (Washington, DC: Central Public Accountability Project, 1992), 9.

97. Richard F. Fenno Jr., *Home Style: House Members in Their Districts* (New York: Pearson Longman, 2003), 1.

98. See the discussion of senators' varied constituencies in Lee and Oppenheimer, *Sizing Up the Senate,* chap. 3.

99. Fenno, *Home Style,* 4–8.

100. John F. Bibby and Thomas M. Holbrook, "Parties and Elections," in *Politics in the American States: A Comparative Analysis,* 7th ed., ed. Virginia Gray, Russell L. Hanson, and Herbert Jacob (Washington, DC: CQ Press, 1999), 66–112. Also see Thomas L. Brunell, *Redistricting and Representation: Why Competitive Elections Are Bad for America* (New York: Routledge, 2008).

101. Ballotpedia, "United States House of Representatives Elections, 2018," https://ballotpedia.org/United_States_House_of_Representatives_elections,_2018.

102. James L. Payne, "The Personal Electoral Advantage of House Incumbents, 1936–1976," *American Politics Quarterly* 8 (October 1980): 465–482; Robert S. Erikson, "Is There Such a Thing as a Safe Seat?" *Polity* 8 (Summer 1976): 623–632.

103. We classify a winning incumbent as having received a warning sign if he or she received 55 percent or less of the two-party vote.

104. Thomas E. Mann, *Unsafe at Any Margin: Interpreting Congressional Elections* (Washington, DC: American Enterprise Institute, 1978).

105. Fenno, *Home Style,* 8–27.

106. Thomas P. O'Neill Jr., *Man of the House,* with William Novak (New York: St. Martin's Press, 1987), 25.

107. Nancy Bocskor, "Fundraising Lessons Candidates Can Learn from Tom Sawyer . . . and Other Great American Salesmen," *Campaigns and Elections* 24 (April 2003): 33.

108. Richard F. Fenno Jr., *Senators on the Campaign Trail* (Norman: University of Oklahoma Press, 1996), 131–132.

109. David E. Price, *The Congressional Experience,* 3rd ed. (Boulder, CO: Westview Press, 2004), 10.

110. Fenno, *Home Style,* 153.

111. Ibid., 56.

112. Anthony Champagne, *Congressman Sam Rayburn* (New Brunswick, NJ: Rutgers University Press, 1984), 28.

113. Parker and Goodman, "Making a Good Impression," 517.

114. See Justin Grimmer, *Representational Style in Congress* (New York: Cambridge University Press, 2014).

115. Kingdon, *Congressmen's Voting Decisions.*

116. Brian J. Fogarty, "The Strategy of the Story: Media Monitoring Legislative Activity," *Legislative Studies Quarterly* 33 (August 2008): 445–469.

117. See Christian R. Grose, Neil Malhotra, and Robert P. Van Houweling, "Explaining Explanations: How Legislators Explain Their Policy Positions and How Citizens React," *American Journal of Political Science* 59 (2015): 724–743.

118. Heather Caygle, "Crowley Defeat Puts Spotlight on Pelosi's Future," *Politico,* June 27, 2018, https://www.politico.com/story/2018/06/27/joe-crowley-defeat-pelosi-speaker-678807.

119. See Congressional Management Foundation, "Life in Congress: The Member Perspective," 2013, http://www.congressfoundation.org/storage/documents/CMF_Pubs/life-in-congress-the-member-perspective.pdf.

120. Quoted in Jim Wright, *You and Your Congressman* (New York: Coward-McCann, 1965), 35.

121. Betsy Rothstein, "Hey, Congressman! Someone Is Blocking My Driveway!" *The Hill*, June 9, 2004, 18–19.

122. See Melinda N. Ritchie and Hye Young You, "Legislators as Lobbyists," *Legislative Studies Quarterly* 44 (February 2019): 65–95.

123. Parker, *Battle for the Big Sky*, pp. 103–105.

124. Lee and Oppenheimer, *Sizing Up the Senate*, 56.

125. The National Election Study is now the American National Election Study (ANES). Warren E. Miller, Donald R. Kinder, Steven J. Rosenstone, and the National Election Study, *American National Election Study, 1990: Post-Election Survey*, 2nd ed. (Ann Arbor, MI: Inter-University Consortium for Political and Social Research, January 1992), 166–170.

126. Ida A. Brudnick, "Members' Representational Allowance: History and Usage," Congressional Research Service Report 40962, Updated January 8, 2019.

127. Congressional Management Foundation, *2004 House Staff Employment Study*; and Congressional Management Foundation, *2001 Senate Staff Employment Study*. See also Emily Goodin, "Congressional Staffers Say Low Pay, Long Hours Has Them Eying New Jobs," *The Hill*, September 9, 2013.

128. Molly Reynolds, Andrew Rugg, Michael J. Malbin, Norman J. Ornstein, Raffaela Wakeman, and Thomas E. Mann, *Vital Statistics on Congress, 2018* (Washington, DC: Brookings, 2018), tables 5–1, 5–3, 5–4, https://www.brookings.edu/multi-chapter-report/vital-statistics-on-congress.

129. Cited in C. Simon Davidson, "Congressional Office Off-Limits for Members' Campaigns," *Roll Call*, April 16, 2007, 8.

130. Charles Bosley, "Senate Communications With the Public," in U.S. Senate, Commission on the Operation of the Senate, *Senate Communications With the Public*, 94th Cong., 2nd sess., 1977, 17.

131. See Justin Grimmer, *Representational Style in Congress: What Legislators Say and Why It Matters* (Cambridge, UK: Cambridge University Press, 2013), 125–132.

132. R. Douglas Arnold, *Congress, the Press, and Political Accountability* (Princeton, NJ: Princeton University Press, 2004).

133. For descriptions of the studios, see Michael J. Robinson, "Three Faces of Congressional Media," in *The New Congress*, ed. Thomas E. Mann and Norman J. Ornstein (Washington, DC: American Enterprise Institute, 1981), 62–63; and Martin Tolchin, "TV Studio Serves Congress," *New York Times*, March 7, 1984, C22.

134. Tolchin, "TV Studio Serves Congress."

135. Cokie Roberts, "Leadership and the Media in the 101st Congress," in *Leading Congress: New Styles, New Strategies*, ed. John J. Kornacki (Washington, DC: CQ Press, 1990), 94.

136. Markus Prior, "The Incumbent in the Living Room: The Rise of Television and the Incumbency Advantage in U.S. House Elections," *Journal of Politics* 68 (August 2006): 657–673. See also Brian F. Schaffner, "Local News Coverage and the Incumbency Advantage in the U.S. House," *Legislative Studies Quarterly* 31 (November 2006): 491–511.

137. Brian Wingfield, "The Latest Initiative in Congress: Blogging," *New York Times*, February 24, 2005, E4; Jennifer Bendery, "Social Media Goes Viral on Capitol

Hill," *Roll Call,* February 7, 2011, 1; Michael D. Shear, "G.O.P. to Open House to Electronic Devices," *New York Times,* December 25, 2010, A16.

138. E. Scott Adler, Chariti E. Gent, and Cary B. Overmeyer, "The Home Style Homepage: Legislator Use of the World Wide Web for Constituency Contact," *Legislative Studies Quarterly* 23 (November 1998): 585–595.

139. "Congress on Social Media in 2018," *Quorum,* December, 11, 2018, https://www .quorum.us/data-driven-insights/congress-social-media-2018/412/.

140. Michael Kruse, "The Most Important New Woman in Congress Is Not Who You Think," *Politico Magazine,* February 15, 2019, https://www.politico.com/ magazine/story/2019/02/15/congress-house-democrats-freshmen-mikie- sherrill-aoc-225054.

141. Ibid.

142. Bob Benenson and Jonathan Allen, "It's Looking Like Blue Skies All Over Again," *CQ Weekly Report,* November 26, 2007, 3541.

143. Fenno, *Home Style,* 99.

CHAPTER 6

1. Nathaniel Rakich and Perry Bacon Jr., "Why Nancy Pelosi Isn't Guaranteed the Speakership," fivethirtyeight.com, November 8, 2018, https://fivethirtyeight .com/features/why-nancy-pelosi-isnt-guaranteed-the-speakership/.

2. Sheryl Gay Stolberg, "Nancy Pelosi's Path to House Speaker May Be Complicated by a 'Pink Wave,'" *New York Times,* November 15, 2018, https://www.nytimes .com/2018/11/15/us/politics/pelosi-house-speaker.html.

3. Rachael Bade, Heather Caygle, and John Bresnahan, "'We were shocked as sh—': How Pelosi Crushed the Dem Rebels," *Politico,* December 13, 2018, https:// www.nytimes.com/2018/11/15/us/politics/pelosi-house-speaker.html.

4. Ibid.

5. Ibid.

6. Ibid.

7. Heather Caygle and John Bresnahan, "House Democrats Postpone Vote on Leadership Term Limits," *Politico,* February 13, 2019, https://www.politico.com/ story/2019/02/13/house-democrats-leadership-term-limits-1168425.

8. Ibid.

9. *Wall Street Journal,* January 30, 1985, 5.

10. The seminal work on the collective-action problem is by Mancur Olson, *The Logic of Collective Action, Public Goods, and the Theory of Groups* (Cambridge, MA: Harvard University Press, 1965).

11. Matthew N. Green, *The Speaker of the House: A Study of Leadership* (New Haven, CT: Yale University Press, 2010), 4.

12. Aaron Blake, "John Boehner Just Endured the Biggest Revolt Against a House Speaker in More Than 100 Years," The Fix, *Washington Post* weblog, January 6, 2016, http:// www.washingtonpost.com/blogs/the-fix/wp/2015/01/06/boehner-could-face- biggest-speaker-defection-since-1923.

13. See Graeme Browning, "The Steward," *National Journal*, August 5, 1995, 2004–2007.

14. For an excellent discussion of this era, see Gregory Koger, *Filibustering: A Political History of Obstruction in the House and Senate* (Chicago: University of Chicago Press, 2010).

15. Quoted in *U.S. News and World Report*, October 13, 1950, 30.

16. See, for example, Barbara Sinclair, *Majority Leadership in the U.S. House* (Baltimore: Johns Hopkins University Press, 1983).

17. Tom Kenworthy, "House GOP Signals It's in a Fighting Mood," *Washington Post*, December 26, 1988, A8.

18. See Barbara Sinclair, *Unorthodox Lawmaking: New Legislative Processes in the U.S. Congress*, 3rd ed. (Washington, DC: CQ Press, 2007), Table 6.4, 123.

19. The GOP had wandered in the "wilderness of the minority" for forty years. A. B. Stoddard, "Rejuvenated Gingrich Mounts Media Offensive," *The Hill*, July 10, 1996, 24.

20. Ibid., 165–176.

21. Quoted in Cannon Centenary Conference, *The Changing Nature of the Speakership*, H. Doc. 108–204 (Washington, DC: Government Printing Office, 2004), 62.

22. Ben Pershing, "Smith Spars With Leaders," *Roll Call*, March 26, 2003, 13.

23. Sarah A. Binder, Thomas E. Mann, Norman J. Ornstein, and Molly Reynolds, *Mending the Broken Branch: Assessing the 110th Congress, Anticipating the 111th*, Brookings, January 2009, www.brookings.edu/papers/2009/0108_broken_branch_binder_mann.aspx.

24. Major Garrett, "A Politician's Politician," *National Journal*, January 7, 2011.

25. Molly K. Hooper, "Boehner to Members: Leadership Is Watching Your Voting Patterns," *The Hill*, December 6, 2012.

26. Jonathan Allen, "The A-hole Factor," *Politico*, December 13, 2012.

27. Mike DeBonis, Robert Costa, and David Fahrenthold, "The Rise and Fall of a Nominee," *Washington Post*, October 9, 2015, A8.

28. Erin Kelly, "Republicans Nominate Paul Ryan for Speaker," *USA Today*, October 29, 2015, online edition.

29. Alexander Burns and Jonathan Martin, "Roiling the G.O.P., Ryan Turns Focus to House Control," *New York Times*, October 11, 2016, A1.

30. Noland D. McCaskill, "Trump Refuses to Back Off Attacks on Ryan," *Politico*, October 19, 2016, 4.

31. See, for example, John H. Aldrich and David W. Rohde, "The Transition to Republican Rule in the House: Implications for Theories of Congressional Politics," *Political Science Quarterly* 112 (Winter 1997–1998): 541–567.

32. John H. Aldrich and David Rohde, "The Logic of Conditional Party Government: Revisiting the Electoral Connection," in *Congress Reconsidered*, 7th ed., ed. Lawrence Dodd and Bruce Oppenheimer (Washington, DC: CQ Press, 2001), 275–276.

33. See "The House in Sam Rayburn's Time," in Nelson W. Polsby, *How Congress Evolves: Social Bases of Institutional Change* (New York: Oxford University Press, 2003).

34. See Keith Krehbiel, *Pivotal Politics: A Theory of U.S. Lawmaking* (Chicago: University of Chicago Press, 1998).

35. Randall Strahan, *Leading Representatives: The Agency of Leaders in the Politics of the U.S. House* (Baltimore: Johns Hopkins University Press, 2007), xii.

36. See, for example, Green, *Speaker of the House;* Ronald M. Peters Jr., *The American Speakership: The Office in Historical Perspective,* 2nd ed. (Baltimore: Johns Hopkins University Press, 1997); and D. B. Hardeman and Donald C. Bacon, *Rayburn: A Biography* (Austin: Texas Monthly Press, 1987).

37. Sometimes exceptions are made to the general norm that top party leaders do not chair committees. During the 107th Congress (2001–2003), Majority Leader Dick Armey, R-Tex., chaired the Select Committee on Homeland Security, which reported the bill signed into law by President George W. Bush creating the Department of Homeland Security.

38. Christopher Madison, "Message Bearer," *National Journal,* December 1, 1990, 2906.

39. Floyd M. Riddick, *Congressional Procedure* (Boston: Chapman and Grimes, 1941), 345–346.

40. Mike DeBonis, "Rewarded for Early Loyalty, McCarthy Emerges as Key House Liaison," *The Washington Post,* February 6, 2017, A3.

41. See Charles O. Jones, *The Minority Party in Congress* (Boston: Little, Brown, 1970), 23.

42. See Frances E. Lee, "Presidents and Party Teams," *Presidential Studies Quarterly* 43, no. 4 (2013): 775–791.

43. Quoted in Jackie Kucinich, "New Whips Work in Tag Team," *Roll Call,* December 6, 2010.

44. Quoted in Jennifer Yachnin, "No 'Sharp Elbows' for Whip Clyburn," *Roll Call,* December 11, 2006, 36. Also see Richard Cohen, "A Different Kind of Whip," *National Journal,* January 20, 2007, 42–44.

45. Michael Doyle, "House GOP's Vote-Getter Off to a Rough Start," McClatchy Washington Bureau, February 11, 2011.

46. Heather Caygle and Sarah Ferris, "Pelosi's Freshmen Fracture Amid GOP Pressure," *Politico,* February 14, 2019, https://www.politico.com/story/2019/02/14/house-democrats-freshmen-voting-gop-1169554.

47. Ibid.

48. "'This Is Not a Day at the Beach': Pelosi Tells Moderate Dems to Stop Voting With GOP," *Politico,* February 28, 2019, https://www.politico.com/story/2019/02/28/nancy-pelosi-house-democrats-1195854.

49. Emma Brown, "Senate Votes in Favor of DeVos," *Washington Post,* February 8, 2017, A1.

50. Woodrow Wilson, *Congressional Government* (Boston: Houghton Mifflin, 1885), 223.

51. David J. Rothman, *Politics and Power: The United States Senate, 1869–1901* (Cambridge, MA: Harvard University Press, 1966), 5–7.

52. See Gerald Gamm and Steven S. Smith, "Emergence of Senate Leadership: 1833–1946," in *U.S. Senate Exceptionalism,* ed. Bruce I. Oppenheimer (Columbus: Ohio State University Press, 2002), 212–238.

53. Margaret Munk, "Origin and Development of the Party Floor Leadership in the United States Senate," *Capital Studies* 2 (Winter 1974): 23–41; Richard A. Baker and Roger H. Davidson, eds., *First Among Equals: Outstanding Senate Leaders of the Twentieth Century* (Washington, DC: Congressional Quarterly, 1991).

54. See Robert Caro, *Master of the Senate* (New York: Random House, 2002).

55. Rowland Evans and Robert Novak, *Lyndon B. Johnson: The Exercise of Power* (New York: New American Library, 1966), 104.

56. See John G. Stewart, "Two Strategies of Leadership: Johnson and Mansfield," in *Congressional Behavior*, ed. Nelson W. Polsby (New York: Random House, 1971), 61–92; William S. White, *Citadel: The Story of the United States Senate* (New York: Harper and Bros., 1956); Joseph S. Clark, *The Senate Establishment* (New York: Hill and Wang, 1963); and Randall B. Ripley, *Power in the Senate* (New York: St. Martin's Press, 1969).

57. *Congressional Record*, 96th Cong., 2nd sess., April 18, 1980, S3294.

58. Mitch McConnell, *The Long Game: A Memoir* (New York: Sentinel, 2016), 254.

59. Paul Kane, "For McConnell, Gorsuch's Nomination to the Supreme Court Is a Personal Victory," *Washington Post*, February 19, 2017, A5.

60. Alexander Bolton, "Trump to Sign Border Deal, Declare National Emergency," February 14, 2019, *The Hill*, https://thehill.com/homenews/senate/430070-mcconnell-trump-to-sign-border-deal-declare-national-emergency.

61. Quoted in *The Hill*, February 22, 2017, 21.

62. See Frances E. Lee, *Beyond Ideology: Politics, Principles, and Partisanship in the U.S. Senate* (Chicago: University of Chicago Press, 2009).

63. Kirk Victor, "Deconstructing Daschle," *National Journal*, June 1, 2002, 610.

64. Kirk Victor, "Getting to 60," *National Journal*, January 13, 2007, 37.

65. Quoted in Carl Hulse and Adam Nagourney, "Senate G.O.P. Leader Finds Weapon in Unity," *New York Times*, March 16, 2010.

66. Carl Hulse, "As Trump Era Dawns in America, Schumer Says Democrats Must Be the 'Barrier,'" *New York Times*, November 20, 2016, 25.

67. McConnell, *The Long Game*, 2.

68. Naomi Lim, "Schumer: GOP Won't Embarrass Democrats by Voting on 'Green New Deal,'" *Washington Examiner*, February 14, 2019, https://www.washingtonexaminer.com/news/schumer-gop-wont-embarrass-democrats-by-voting-on-green-new-deal.

69. Ibid.

70. Francine Kiefer, "Trump's Democratic Dance Partner," *Christian Science Monitor Weekly*, December 5, 2016, 22. For a list of the expanded Democratic leadership team, see Ben Geman, "Senate Leadership: Sanders Wants to Help His Base Storm Congress," *National Journal Daily*, December 8, 2016, 7.

71. Kirk Victor, "Short on Surprises," *National Journal*, October 28, 2006, 37.

72. Quoted in Jill Zuckman, "Dick Durbin's Passion Ignites Foes' Ire," *Chicago Tribune*, June 17, 2005, online edition.

73. *New York Times*, December 6, 1988, B13.

74. David Truman, *The Congressional Party* (New York: Wiley, 1959).

75. Stephen Jessee and Neil Malholtra, "Are Congressional Leaders Middlepersons or Extremists? Yes," *Legislative Studies Quarterly* 35 (2010): 361–392.

76. David S. Joachim, "Louisianan Extends His Rapid Rise in the House G.O.P.," *New York Times,* June 19, 2014.

77. David Grant, "Women Step Up in House GOP Leadership. Why That's Just a Start," DC Decoder Wire, *Christian Science Monitor,* November 15, 2012, www.csmonitor .com/USA/DC-Decoder/Decoder-Wire/2012/1115/Women-step-up-in-House-GOP-leadership.-Why-that-s-just-a-start.

78. Sinclair, *Majority Leadership in the U.S. House.*

79. *Congressional Record,* 98th Cong., 1st sess., November 15, 1983, H9856.

80. Quoted in Thomas B. Rosenstiel and Edith Stanley, "For Gingrich, It's 'Mr. Speaker!'" *Los Angeles Times,* November 9, 1994, A2.

81. *Congressional Record,* 94th Cong., 1st sess., January 26, 1973, S2301.

82. Niels Lesniewski and Lindsey McPherson, "GOP Seeks Brotherly Love," January 25, 2017, 8.

83. Richard E. Cohen, Jake Sherman, and Simmi Aujla, "GOP Taps Freshmen for Prime Spots," *Politico,* December 9, 2010, www.politico.com/news/sto ries/1210/46216.html.

84. Matt Canham, "Sen. Mike Lee Joins Republican Leadership Team He Has Often Defied," *Salt Lake Tribune,* January 23, 2015, http://www.sltrib.com/ news/2026476-155/sen-mike-lee-joins-republican-leadership.

85. Emma Dumain, "GOP Moves Forward With Sweeping Steering Panel Changes," November 17, 2015, CQ.com, online version.

86. Neil MacNeil, *Dirksen: Portrait of a Public Man* (New York: World, 1970), 168–169.

87. Mark Preston, "Daschle May Write Book Chronicling His Times as Leader," *Roll Call Daily Issue,* e-newsletter, May 20, 2002, 3.

88. Sidney Waldman, "Majority Leadership in the House of Representatives," *Political Science Quarterly* 95 (Fall 1980): 377.

89. Patrick Sellers, *Cycles of Spin: Strategic Communication in the U.S. Congress* (New York: Cambridge University Press, 2010).

90. *New York Times,* June 7, 1984, B16.

91. Noelle Straub and Melanie Fonder, "GOP Shifts Strategy for New Minority Status," *The Hill,* July 18, 2001, 6.

92. Mark Preston, "Lott Showcases Senators Facing Re-election," *Roll Call,* March 15, 2001, 3.

93. Eric Heberlig, Marc Hetherington, and Bruce Larson, "The Price of Leadership: Campaign Money and the Polarization of Congressional Parties," *Journal of Politics* 68 (2006): 992–1005. See also Eric Heberlig and Bruce Larson, *Congressional Parties, Institutional Ambition, and the Financing of Majority Control* (Ann Arbor: University of Michigan Press, 2012), esp. 159–196.

94. Marian Currinder, "Nancy Pelosi and Steny Hoyer: How Their Past Rivalry Helped Shape the Future of Leadership Races," Legbranch.org, May 3, 2018, https:// www.legbranch.org/2018-5-2-k5aye55cylrsoi8zuilz74hhqk20gq/.

95. Stephen Gettinger, "Potential Senate Leaders Flex Money Muscles," *Congressional Quarterly Weekly Report,* October 8, 1988, 2776.

96. Sinclair, *Majority Leadership in the U.S. House,* 96–97.

97. Gail Russell Chaddock, "Two House Health Care Reform Votes," *Christian Science Monitor,* March 20, 2010.

98. House Democrats disbanded their policy committee at Pelosi's direction. In its place, she established a revamped Steering Committee, which has a policy component (headed by George Miller of California) and a committee assignment component (chaired by Rosa DeLauro of Connecticut). See Erin Billings, "Pelosi Revamps the Steering Committee," *Roll Call,* March 13, 2003, 3.

99. Quoted in Fred Barnes, "Raging Representatives," *New Republic,* June 3, 1985, 9.

100. See Logan Dancey and Geoffrey Sheagley, "Heuristics Behaving Badly: Party Cues and Voter Knowledge," *American Journal of Political Science* 52, no. 2 (2013): 312–325; and Marc J. Hetherington, "Resurgent Mass Partisanship: The Role of Elite Polarization," *American Political Science Review* 95, no. 3 (2001): 619–631.

101. Jim Hoagland, "The Price of Polarization," *Washington Post,* May 5, 2005, A25.

102. Quoted in Elizabeth Shogren, "Will Welfare Go Way of Health Reform?" *Los Angeles Times,* August 10, 1995, A18.

103. Frances E. Lee, *Beyond Ideology: Politics, Principles, and Partisanship in the U.S. Senate* (Chicago: University of Chicago Press, 2009), 4.

104. See V. O. Key Jr., *Politics, Parties, and Pressure Groups,* 5th ed. (New York: Crowell, 1964); and Austin Ranney and Willmoore Kendall, *Democracy and the American Party System* (New York: Harcourt Brace, 1956).

105. See Harold W. Stanley and Richard G. Niemi, *Vital Statistics on American Politics, 2007–2008* (Washington, DC: CQ Press, 2007), Tables 1–10 and 1–11.

106. Robert Draper, "The Obamacare Operation," *New York Times Magazine,* February 19, 2017, 35.

107. Ibid., 36.

108. See Andrew Siddons, "House Democrats Plan Local Events to Counter Obamacare Repeal," *CQ News,* December 22, 2016, online version; and Dan Goldberg, "Schumer Calls Republican Health Care Plans A 'War on Seniors,'" *Politico Pro Budget & Appropriations Brief,* February 8, 2017, online version.

109. Quoted in Ben Weyl, "The Tables Have Turned," *CQ Weekly,* November 6, 2014, 7.

110. *Congressional Record,* 104th Cong., 1st sess., October 11, 1995, E1926. Rep. Lee H. Hamilton, D-Ind., who made the comment, strongly opposed the overuse of omnibus bills.

111. Lee H. Hamilton, *A Creative Tension: The Foreign Policy Roles of the President and Congress,* with Jordan Tama (Washington, DC: Woodrow Wilson Center Press, 2002), 33.

112. Quoted in Richard E. Cohen, "Byrd of West Virginia: A New Job, a New Image," *National Journal,* August 20, 1977, 1294.

113. Quoted in Emma Dumain, "Democrats Irrelevant? Don't Be So Sure, Pelosi Promises," *Roll Call* weblog, December 7, 2014, http://blogs.rollcall.com/218/nancy-pelosi-democrats-irrelevant-just-watch/?dcz=.

114. Ed O'Keefe, "Boehner Appearing on Leno: GOP Is to Blame for Shutdown," Post Politics, *Washington Post* weblog, January 24, 2014, http://www.washingtonpost.com/blogs/post-politics/wp/2014/01/24/john-boehner-appears-on-the-tonight-show-with-jay-leno.

115. Bob Levey, "14-Year House Minority Leader Reached Across the Aisle," *Washington Post,* February 18, 2017, B5. The quotation was cited in Michel's obituary and the quoted material is from his first speech as GOP leader, which he delivered on December 8, 1980, to his GOP colleagues.

CHAPTER 7

1. Woodrow Wilson, *Congressional Government: A Study in American Politics* (Boston, MA: Houghton Mifflin and Co., 1885), 79.

2. *Washington Post,* May 14, 1987, A23.

3. *Congressional Record,* 100th Cong., 1st sess., June 25, 1987, H5564.

4. The House has five delegates (American Samoa, District of Columbia, Guam, Northern Mariana Islands, and Virgin Islands) and one resident commissioner (Puerto Rico).

5. Quoted in *New York Times,* July 11, 1988, A14.

6. See, for example, Kenneth A. Shepsle and Barry R. Weingast, "The Institutional Foundations of Committee Power," *American Political Science Review* (March 1987): 85–104.

7. John W. Ellwood, "The Great Exception: The Congressional Budget Process in an Age of Decentralization," in *Congress Reconsidered,* 3rd ed., ed. Lawrence C. Dodd and Bruce I. Oppenheimer (Washington, DC: CQ Press, 1985), 329. For the classic discussion of committee and member roles, see Richard F. Fenno Jr., *Congressmen in Committees* (Boston: Little, Brown, 1973).

8. See Keith Krehbiel, *Information and Legislative Organization* (Ann Arbor: University of Michigan Press, 1991); and Bruce Bimber, "Information as a Factor in Congressional Politics," *Legislative Studies Quarterly* (1991): 585–606.

9. Roy Swanstrom, *The United States Senate, 1787–1801,* S. Doc. 87–64, 87th Cong., 1st sess., 1962, 224.

10. Lauros G. McConachie, *Congressional Committees* (New York: Crowell, 1898), 124.

11. DeAlva Stanwood Alexander, *History and Procedure of the House of Representatives* (Boston: Houghton Mifflin, 1916), 228; George H. Haynes, *The Senate of the United States: Its History and Practice,* vol. 1 (Boston: Houghton Mifflin, 1938), 272; Ralph V. Harlow, *The History of Legislative Methods in the Period Before 1825* (New Haven, CT: Yale University Press, 1917), 157–158.

12. *Cannon's Procedures in the House of Representatives,* H. Doc. 80–122, 80th Cong., 1st sess., 1959, 83.

13. Quoted in *Wall Street Journal,* May 3, 1979, 1.

14. John Bresnahan, "The Demise of One of the Best Gigs in Congress," *Politico,* January 31, 2018, 1.

15. Ibid., 10

16. Amanda Northrop, "The Tennessee Senator, Who Still Believed in Compromise in Trump's Washington, Is Stepping Down at the End of His Term," *Vox.Com,* December 17, 2018.

17. Alan K. Ota, "Reid's New Panel Ratios Meet GOP Resistance," *Roll Call,* November 14, 2012, online edition. Sens. Angus King of Maine and Bernie Sanders of Vermont, neither of whom ran as Democrats, are considered Democrats because they caucus with that party.

18. Ibid.

19. Marianne LeVine, "Kamala Harris to Keep Her Spot on Judiciary Panel, Schumer says," *Politico,* December 12, 2018, 13. See Todd Ruger, "Diversity Boost for Senate Judiciary," *Roll Call,* January 10, 2018, 3.

20. Heather Caygle, Bernie Becker, and Rachael Bade, "Panel Adds Member After Hispanic Dems' Complaints," *Politico,* January 16, 2019, 4.

21. Committees permitted extra subcommittees including the committees on Appropriations, no more than thirteen, although the panel typically creates a dozen; Armed Services, Financial Services, Foreign Affairs, and Oversight and Reform, each no more than seven subcommittees; and no more than six subcommittees for Agriculture and Transportation and Infrastructure.

22. *Congressional Record,* 104th Cong., 1st sess., January 4, 1995, H33.

23. Theo Emery, "Controversial King Denied Top Immigration Slot," *CQ Today,* January 10, 2011, 5.

24. See, for example, Mike DeBonis, "GOP Leaders Block Iowa Lawmaker From House Panels," *The Washington Post,* January 15, 2019, A8; and Trip Gabriel, Jonathan Martin, and Nicholas Fandos, "G.O.P. Leaders Condemn King Over Comments," *New York Times,* January 15, 2019, A1. On January 15, 2019, the House adopted overwhelmingly a resolution rejecting "White nationalism and White supremacy." The first clause of the resolution (H. Res. 41) referenced the rhetoric of Representative King, who voted for the resolution. House GOP rules require indicted members to resign from their committees until legal matters are resolved. Under this rule, two GOP members of the 116th House resigned from their committee assignments. See Melanie Zanona, "Trio of House Republicans Face Life in Exile," *Politico,* February 5, 2019, 1.

25. Nick Bowlin and Geof Koss, "Nelson Concession Could Prompt Committee Leadership Shuffle," *Greenwire,* November 19, 2018, 2.

26. David Hawkings, "House 'A' Committees—Ways and Means, Approps, and Energy & Commerce)—Welcome New Members," *Roll Call,* January 10, 2017, 1.

27. Humberto Sanchez and Niels Lesniewski, "Spending Panel Loses Its Luster," *Roll Call,* December 21, 2012, 1.

28. Kate Ackley, "Dollar Bills: A Quiet Push Is On to Restore Earmarks to Give Lawmakers a Greater Stake in Governing," *CQ Weekly,* February 11, 2019, 14–19.

29. Alex Isenstadt, "The Lucre of Landing a Key Committee," *Politico,* January 19, 2011, 20.

30. Zachary Warmbrodt and Heather Caygle, "Fiery Freshmen Put Under Care of 'Auntine Maxine,' *Politico,* January 17, 2019, 15. Also see "AOC [Alexandria Ocasio-Cortez], Other Firebrands Poised to Take on Wall Street," *The Hill,* January 17, 2015, 1.

31. James Bornemeier, "Berman Accepts Seat on House Ethics Panel," *Los Angeles Times,* February 5, 1997, B1; *CQ Daily Monitor,* December 11, 1999, 1. Also see Hannah Hess, "House Ethics: An Isolating Gavel to Hold," *Roll Call,* December 9, 2014, 3.

32. Fenno, *Congressmen in Committees.* Also see Heinz Eulau, "Legislative Committee Assignments," *Legislative Studies Quarterly* (November 1984): 587–633.

33. Christopher J. Deering and Steven S. Smith, *Committees in Congress,* 3rd ed. (Washington, DC: CQ Press, 1997), 61–62, 78.

34. Shirley Chisholm, *Unbought and Unbossed* (Boston: Houghton Mifflin, 1970), 84, 86.

35. Jerry Hagstrom, "The Freshman Farm Caucus," *National Journal Daily,* December 6, 2018, p. 9.

36. Quoted in Ethan Wallison, "Freshman Democrats Get Panel Waivers," *Roll Call,* June 21, 1999, 20.

37. Hawkings, "When Committees Boost Careers," 3.

38. Joseph A. Califano, Jr., *Our Damaged Democracy* (New York: Touchstone, 2017), 53.

39. Ibid. See Appendix A for the information.

40. Ken Buck, *Drain the Swamp* (Washington, DC: Regnery, 2017), 74. The top tier committees, Buck said, are Appropriations, Energy and Commerce, Financial Services, Rules, and Ways and Means.

41. Deirdre Shesgreen and Christopher Schnaars, "Some in Congress Cry Party Extortion," *USA Today,* May 26, 2016, online edition.

42. Andrew Beadle, "First Lady's Résumé Won't Impress Seniority System," *CQ Daily Monitor,* November 20, 2000, 9.

43. Pelosi and Hoyer's quotes are from Mike Lillis, "Pelosi's Pick Wins Round 1 for Energy Panel," *The Hill,* November 19, 2014, 10.

44. Ella Nilsen, "Term Limits: Pelosi Might be Open to Term Limits for Committee Chairs," *Vox.com,* December 6, 2018, 2.

45. Mike Lillis, "Black Caucus Chairman Pushes Back Against Committee Term Limits," *The Hill,* December 7, 2018, online edition.

46. Nancy Ognanovich, "GOP Rules, Losses Seen Triggering New Senate Lineups," *Daily Report for Executives,* October 31, 2016, online edition.

47. Paul Gigot, "Mack Uses Knife on Old Senate Order," *Wall Street Journal,* July 14, 1995, A12.

48. Chris Frates, "Trust Fall," *National Journal,* February 2, 2013, 35.

49. Connor O'Brien, "Chairman Thornberry Turns 'Delegator-in-Chief,'" PoliticoPro .com, March 1, 2016, online edition.

50. Quoted in *Washington Post,* November 20, 1983, A9.

51. John T. Bennett, 'Bulldog' Jim Jordan Still in Position to Fight for Trump," *Roll Call,* December 3, 2018, online edition.

52. Jennifer Shutt, "Sanders Will Use New Clout to Question Republican Budget," *CQ News,* November 16, 2016, online edition.

53. See David King, *Turf Wars* (Chicago: University of Chicago Press, 1997).

54. Allison Stevens, "No Ordinary Power Grab: Chairman Complains of 'Bold' Power Grab," *CQ Today,* June 23, 2004, 1, 9.

55. Quoted in Bob Pool, "Survivors Take Stock of Gains Against Cancer," *Los Angeles Times,* May 30, 1997, B1.

56. Ralph Vartabedian, "Senate Panel Is Ready to Take IRS to Task," *Los Angeles Times,* September 22, 1997, A1.

57. "Dodd-Frank" refers to Sen. Christopher Dodd, D-Conn., who chaired the Banking, Housing, and Urban Affairs Committee, and Rep. Barney Frank, D-Mass., who headed the Financial Services Committee. Senator Dodd retired at the end of the 111th Congress. Frank served as the ranking member on Financial Services because of GOP control of the House in the 112th Congress; he retired at the end of that Congress.

58. Darlene Superville, "Congressional Panels Seek 'Real People,'" *Los Angeles Times,* March 25, 2007, online edition.

59. Elizabeth Brotherton, "Webcasting Goes Mainstream Among House Committees," *Roll Call,* March 7, 2007, 3.

60. Sean Piccoli, "Hill Samples 'Third Wave,'" *Washington Times,* June 13, 1995, A8.

61. Warren Leary, "When Astronauts Brief Congress, a Little Levity Goes a Long Way," *New York Times,* June 15, 2005, A16.

62. *Congressional Record,* 107th Cong., 2nd sess., July 16, 2002, S6849.

63. Quoted in *Washington Post,* November 25, 1985, A4. Also see Richard L. Hall, *Participation in Congress* (New Haven, CT: Yale University Press, 1998).

64. Quoted in "CQ Midday Update Email," December 14, 2004, 1, www.cq.com.

65. Eric Redman, *The Dance of Legislation* (New York: Simon and Schuster, 1973), 140.

66. Hugh Heclo, "Issue Networks in the Executive Establishment," in *The New American Political System,* ed. Anthony King (Washington, DC: American Enterprise Institute, 1978), 87–124. Also see David E. Price, "Policy Making in Congressional Committees: The Impact of 'Environmental Factors,'" *American Political Science Review* (Fall 1978): 548–574.

67. Molly Hopper, "House Judiciary Committee Seeks Bipartisan Touch," *The Hill,* January 18, 2011, 8.

68. Norris Cotton, *In the Senate* (New York: Dodd, Mead, 1978), 65.

69. See E. Eric Petersen and Sarah J. Eckman, "Staff Tenure in Selected Positions in House Committees, 2006–2016," CRS Report R44683, November 9, 2016, 7, and by the same two authors, "Staff Tenure in Selected Positions in Senate Committees, 2006–2016," CRS Report R44685, November 9, 2016, 7.

70. Rep. Bill Pascrell Jr., "Why Is Congress so Dumb?" *The Washington Post,* January 13, 2019, B1

71. *Washington Post,* March 20, 1977, E9.

72. David Whiteman, *Communication in Congress: Members, Staff, and the Search for Information* (Lawrence: University Press of Kansas, 1995). A good article on the role of staff is Steven T. Dennis, "Nabors Is the 'Glue' Between WH, Congress," *Roll Call,* May 10, 2012, 1.

73. Quoted in *Washington Post,* November 20, 1983, A13.

74. Josephine Hearn, "House Staffers Follow Bosses' Footsteps on the Campaign Trail," *The Hill,* October 18, 2006, 4.

75. Nick Sobczyk, "Pelosi Promises to Reinstate Select Committee," *E&E Daily,* December 13, 2018, 1.

76. Anthonly Adragna, John Bresnahan, and Heather Caygle, "Pelosi Looks to Soothe Chairs-to-Be Over Climate Panel," *Politico,* December 12, 2018, 6.

77. Sobczyk, "Pelosi Promises to Reinstate Select Committee," 2.

78. Brian Dabbs, "Climate Panel Stirs Conflict in House GOP," *National Journal Daily,* January 29, 2019, 1.

79. Ibid., 2.

80. Quoted in Roger H. Davidson and Walter J. Oleszek, *Congress Against Itself* (Bloomington: Indiana University Press, 1977), 263.

81. E. Scott Adler, *Why Congressional Reforms Fail* (Chicago: University of Chicago Press, 2002), 11.

82. Paul Glastris and Haley Sweetland Edwards, "The Big Lobotomy," *Washington Monthly,* June/July/August 2014, 57.

83. Quoted in Peter Kaplan and David Mark, "With Election Day Over, the Campaign Begins in the House," *CQ Daily Monitor,* November 20, 2000, 3.

84. John Boehner, "What the Next Speaker Must Do," *Wall Street Journal,* November 5, 2010, A19.

85. Don Wolfensberger, "House Need Not Reinvent the Wheel to Reform," *The Hill,* March 23, 2016, online edition.

86. Carl Hulse, 'You Control Nothing': House G.O.P. Braces for Life in the Minority," *New York Times,* December 30, 2018, 18.

87. David Drucker and Emily Pierce, "Reid to Baucus: Stop Chasing GOP Votes on Health Care," *Roll Call,* July 7, 2009, online edition.

88. David Nather, "Daschle's Soft Touch Lost in Tough Senate Arena," *CQ Weekly,* July 20, 2002, 1922.

89. *National Journal Congress Daily AM,* January 30, 2007, 15.

90. Both quotations in this paragraph are from Ronald Brownstein, "Gangmen Style," *National Journal,* May 11, 2013, 9.

91. The information in this paragraph is largely from Emma Dumian, "Diaz-Balart and the Art of an Immigration Deal Undone," *Roll Call,* January 14, 2015, 1.

92. Nather, "Daschle's Soft Touch Lost."

93. Paul Kane, "Committee Chairs Seek to Reassert Power in Congress," *Washington Post,* February 17, 2013, A4.

94. *Committee Structure,* Hearings Before the Joint Committee on the Organization of Congress (Washington, DC: Government Printing Office, 1993), 779.

95. Curt Suplee, "The Science Chairman's Unpredictable Approach," *Washington Post,* October 15, 1991, A21.

CHAPTER 8

1. *Constitution, Jefferson's Manual, and Rules of the House of Representatives,* H. Doc. 111–157, 111th Cong., 2011, 129. The rules of the Senate are contained in *Senate Manual,* S. Doc. 107–1, 107th Cong., 2002.

2. See Barbara Sinclair, *Unorthodox Lawmaking: New Legislative Processes in the U.S. Congress,* 3rd. ed. (Washington, DC: CQ Press, 2007).

3. Paul Kane, "History Professor Landed a Privileged Perch to See How Harry Reid Works," *The Washington Post,* May 5, 2016, A17.

4. In 2011, the GOP leadership in both chambers successfully forced President Barack Obama to accept deep spending cuts in exchange for Republican support in hiking the government's borrowing authority so it could pay its debts. In the process, Standard and Poor's—a major credit rating agency—for the first time ever downgraded the creditworthiness of the United States after an acrimonious partisan battle between Congress and the president. In 2019, President Donald Trump took responsibility for the longest government shutdown in history (35 days) in his unsuccessful attempt to force Congress to provide $5.8 billion to build a wall on the nation's border with Mexico.

5. Lee H. Hamilton, *How Congress Work and Why You Should Care* (Bloomington, ID: Indiana University Press, 2004), 58.

6. Donald R. Matthews, *U.S. Senators and Their World* (Chapel Hill: University of North Carolina Press, 1960), chap. 5.

7. See Barry C. Burden, *Personal Roots of Representation* (Princeton, NJ: Princeton University Press, 2007).

8. Quoted in John Solomon, "Family Crisis Shifts Politics," *USA Today*, August 16, 2001, 15A.

9. Matt Fuller, "Members Offer Rare Display of Emotion With ABLE Act," *Roll Call*, December 4, 2014; see http://blogs.rollcall.com/218/disability. ABLE stands for "Achieving a Better Life Experience." It allows individuals with disabilities to create tax-exempt savings accounts that will allow them to prepare for future financial needs.

10. *National Journal*, April 10, 1982, 632.

11. Reid Wilson, "Partisan Roles Don't Keep Van Hollen, Sessions From Reaching Across the Aisle," *The Hill*, March 12, 2009, 3.

12. Quoted in Julie Rovner, "Senate Committee Approves Health Warnings on Alcohol," *Congressional Quarterly Weekly Report*, May 24, 1986, 1175.

13. Woodrow Wilson, *Congressional Government* (Boston: Houghton Mifflin, 1885), 320.

14. Theodore Sorensen, *Kennedy* (New York: Harper and Row, 1965), 184.

15. *Wall Street Journal*, June 2, 1988, 56.

16. David A. Fahrenthold, "Rep. Andrews, Leaving With No Laws, Cites Successes," *Washington Post*, February 5, 2014, A6.

17. *Congressional Record*, 95th Cong., 1st sess., May 17, 1977, E3076.

18. Richard Simon, "Congress Turns Bill Titles Into Acts of Exaggeration," *Los Angeles Times*, June 19, 2011, online edition.

19. Ibid.

20. For information on the drafting process, see Lawrence E. Filson, *The Legislative Drafter's Desk Reference* (Washington, DC: Congressional Quarterly, 1992).

21. *CQ Monitor*, July 24, 1998, 5.

22. Lawrence J. Haas, "Unauthorized Action," *National Journal*, January 2, 1988, 20.

23. Brianna Ehley and Jennifer Haberkorn, "Tough Reelection: Sponsor an Opioid Bill," *Politico Pro Health Care*, June 16, 2018, www.politicopro.com.

24. Stacy Kaper, "Bob Corker Charts Leadership Course," *National Journal Daily*, April 13, 2013, 5.

25. T. R. Reid, *Congressional Odyssey: The Saga of a Senate Bill* (San Francisco: W. H. Freeman, 1980), 17.

26. Paul Singer, "More Bills, More Lawyers for Leg. Offices," *Roll Call*, March 28, 2007, 22.

27. Carroll J. Doherty, "Lots of Inertia, Little Lawmaking as Election '98 Approaches," *CQ Weekly*, July 18, 1998, 1925.

28. Quoted in Margaret Kriz, "Still Charging," *National Journal*, December 6, 1997, 2462.

29. Michael Teitelbaum, "The Path Unclear for 'Consensus Bill,'" *CQ Weekly*, March 25, 2019.

30. David M. Drucker, "Trump Brings Opportunities, Challenges," *Washington Examiner*, January 30, 2017, 32.

31. Christopher M. Davis, "How Legislation Is Brought to the House Floor: A Snapshot of Parliamentary Practice in the 113th Congress (2013–2014)," Congressional Research Service Report, February 13, 2015, 4.

32. Martin Gold et al., *The Book on Congress* (Washington, DC: Big Eagle Publishing, 1992), 124.

33. Donald R. Wolfensberger, "Suspended Partisanship in the House: How Most Laws Are Really Made," paper prepared for the annual meeting of the American Political Science Association, Boston, August 29–September 1, 2002, 11.

34. *Congressional Record*, 112th Cong., 1st sess., January 5, 2011, H29.

35. Davis, "How Legislation Is Brought to the House Floor," 6.

36. Privileged business under House rules includes such items as committee assignment resolutions, adjournment resolutions, or "rules" from the Rules Committee.

37. See Jason Roberts, "The Development of Special Orders and Special Rules in the U.S. House of Representatives, 1881–1937," *Legislative Studies Quarterly*, August 2010, 307–336.

38. Quoted in Jonathan Salant, "Under Open Rules, Discord Rules," *Congressional Quarterly Weekly Report*, January 28, 1995, 277.

39. *National Journal*, January 21, 1995, 183.

40. Lizette Alvarez, "Campaign Finance Measure Soundly Rejected by House," *New York Times*, June 18, 1998, A26.

41. Michael S. Lynch, Anthony J. Madonna, and Jason M. Roberts, "The Cost of Majority-Party Bias: Amending Activity Under Structured Rules," *Legislative Studies Quarterly* 41, no. 3 (2016): 633–655.

42. "Switched Votes for Gas Bill," *Congressional Quarterly Weekly Report*, February 14, 1976, 313.

43. Daniel Newhauser, "GOP Leaders Drop Hammer on Rules Rebels," *National Journal Daily*, June 17, 2015, 3.

44. *Congressional Record*, vol. 162, February 1, 2017, H7339. Speaker Ryan's comments are in the *Congressional Record*, October 29, 2015, H7339.

45. Ibid., vol. 165, January 26, 2019, H620.

46. The Bipartisan Policy Center's "Healthy Congress Index" tracks patterns in House floor amending rules, among other data about congressional procedure and activity. See "114th Congress: 114th Congress Improves, but Gridlock Overshadows," Bipartisan Policy Center, January 19, 2017, http://bipartisanpolicy.org/congress/#house-floor-amendment-process-rules.

47. Don Wolfensberger, "Why Are Restrictive Rules Ratcheting Up?" *Roll Call*, July 24, 2015, online edition.

48. Molly Hooper, "Leaders Push Back on Farm Bill Vote," *The Hill*, September 19, 2012, 8.

49. Lindsey McPhearson, "House GOP Tries New Tact," *Roll Call*, March 28, 2019, 1.

50. Information courtesy of Richard Beth, specialist in legislative process, Congressional Research Service, Library of Congress.

51. Derek Willis, "As Pelosi Takes Over, an Attempt to Revive the 'Lost Art' of Legislating," the *New York Times*, January 2, 2019, online edition.

52. William McKay and Charles W. Johnson, *Parliament & Congress: Representation & Scrutiny in the Twenty-First Century* (New York: Oxford University Press, 2010), 429.

53. *National Journal's Congress Daily PM,* January 13, 1995, 4.

54. John F. Bibby, ed., *Congress off the Record* (Washington, DC: American Enterprise Institute, 1983), 2.

55. Heather Caygle and Sarah Ferris, "Pelosi's Freshmen Fracture Amid GOP Pressure," *Politico.com.,* February 15, 2019, 4.

56. *Congressional Record,* vol. 165, February 15, 2019, H1554.

57. Sheryl Gay Stolberg, "Republicans Hope to Sway Voters With Labels That Demonize Democrats," *New York Times,* February 18, 2019, A12.

58. Mike DeBonis, "Blowup in House Over Votes by Moderate Democrats," *The Washington Post,* March 1, 2019, A6; Catie Edmondson, "Pelosi Quells Rebellion to Pass Second Gun Control Bill," *New York Times,* March 1, 2019, A15; and Natalie Andrews and Joshua Jasmerson, "Pelosi Struggles Over Party Unity," *Wall Street Journal,* March 1, 2019, A5.

59. Sen. J. Bennett Johnston, D-La. (1972–1997), quoted in *New York Times,* November 22, 1985, B8.

60. Quoted in "Democrats to Forgo Control in Brief Edge," *Washington Times,* November 29, 2000, A4.

61. Charles Homan, "Mitch McConnell Got Everything He Wanted. But the President He Helped Elect Has Turned Out To Be the One Thing He Can't Control," *New York Times Magazine,* January 27, 2019, 39.

62. *Congressional Record,* 101st Cong., 2nd sess., July 20, 1990, S10183.

63. Susan F. Rasky, "With Few Bills Passed or Ready for Action, Congress Seems Sluggish," *New York Times,* May 14, 1989, 24.

64. *Congressional Record,* 111th Cong., 2nd sess., September 21, 2010, S7251.

65. Elizabeth Drew, *Senator* (New York: Simon and Schuster, 1979), 158.

66. *Congressional Record,* 97th Cong., 2nd sess., May 20, 1982, S5648.

67. Mary Dalrymple, "Democrats Say They Are Unified in Opposition Platform," *CQ Today,* January 29, 2002, 5.

68. James Wallner, "McConnell Follows In Reid's Footsteps," *Legislative Procedure* (blog), February 12, 2019. Also see Wallner, "McConnell Maintains Firm Grip Despite Pledging to Restore the Senate," *WashingtonExaminer.com,* February 11, 2019.

69. Christopher M. Davis, "Filling the Amendment Tree in the Senate," CRS Report RS22854, February 2, 2011, 2.

70. *Congressional Record,* 107th Cong., 2nd sess., April 17, 2002, S2850.

71. Eleanor Van Buren, "Not Everyone Wants the Internet in Their Home," January 28, 2019, 7.

72. Robert C. Byrd, *The Senate, 1789–1989,* vol. II (Washington, DC: U.S. Government Printing Office, 1991), 163.

73. Gail Russell Chaddock, "Limits on Filibusters Are Already Pervasive," *Christian Science Monitor,* May 24, 2005, 2.

74. See comments by Alan Cranston of California, then Senate Democratic whip, in *New York Times,* July 17, 1986, A3.

75. David Herszenhorn, "Thrust and Parry on the Senate Floor," *New York Times,* November 22, 2009, E3.

76. U.S. Congress, *Operations of the Congress: Testimony of House and Senate Leaders*, hearing before the Joint Committee on the Organization of Congress (Washington, DC: Government Printing Office, 1993), 50.

77. Doug Obey, "Alaska," *The Hill*, July 10, 1996, 27.

78. Sixteen additional cloture motions were filed but not voted upon. Two of the sixteen, however, were agreed to by unanimous consent. Information for the 109th Congress compiled by the U.S. Senate Library.

79. Data compiled by the Senate Library.

80. *Congressional Record*, 111th Cong., 2nd sess., September 15, 2010, S7120.

81. Steven S. Smith, *The Senate Syndrome: The Evolution of Procedural Warfare in the Modern U.S. Senate* (Norman, OK: The University of Oklahoma Press, 2014), 265, 8.

82. Valerie Heitshusen, "Majority Cloture for Nominations: Implications and the 'Nuclear' Option," Congressional Research Service Report, R43331, 5. For the procedural details associated with establishment of the new precedent, see *Congressional Record*, November 21, 2013, S8416–S8418.

83. *Congressional Record*, November 21, 2013, S8420.

84. Shawn Zeller, "Rule Here To Stay?" *CQ Weekly*, October 13, 2014, 1286.

85. Burgess Everett, "Breakthrough on Trump's Cabinet After 2 a.m. Vote," *Politico Pro Budget and Appropriations Brief*, February 20, 2017, online edition.

86. Ibid.

87. John Bresnahan and Burgess Everett, "Senate 'Coming Apart,' Appears Unlikely to Heal Soon," *Politico*, February 7, 2017, 8.

88. Carl Hulse, "Ghost of Garland Lingers as G.O.P. Brandishes 'Nuclear Option' Again," *New York Times*, February 21, 2019, A14. Carl Hulse, "In Altering Debate Time, Senate Steadily Hands Reins to Majority Party," *New York Times*, April 4, 2019, online edition.

89. See Barbara Sinclair, "Ping Pong and Other Congressional Pursuits: Party Leaders and Post-Passage Procedural Choice," in Jacob Strauss, ed., *Party and Procedure in the United States Congress* (Lanham, MD: Rowman and Littlefield, 2012), 231–252.

90. Jonathan Allen and John Cochran, "The Might of the Right," *CQ Weekly*, November 8, 2003, 2762.

91. Barbara Sinclair, *Unorthodox Lawmaking: New Legislative Processes in the U.S. Congress*, 4th ed. (Washington, DC: CQ Press, 2012).

92. Barber B. Conable, "Weaving Webs: Lobbying by Charities," *Tax Notes*, November 10, 1975, 27–28.

CHAPTER 9

1. Deborah Barfield Berry and Eliza Collins, "Criminal Justice Bill Passes House, Heads to President Trump for His Signature," *USA Today*, December 20, 2018, https://www.usatoday.com/story/news/politics/2018/12/20/criminal-justice-reform-bill-passes-congress-goes-president-trump/2373992002/.

2. German Lopez, "The First Step Act, Explained," Vox.com, February 5, 2019, https://www.vox.com/future-perfect/2018/12/18/18140973/state-of-the-union-trump-first-step-act-criminal-justice-reform.

3. Eliza Collins and Deborah Barfield Berry, "Criminal Justice Overhaul: An Inside Look at How Donald Trump and Congress Got to 'Yes,'" *USA Today*, December 17, 2018, https://www.usatoday.com/story/news/politics/2018/12/17/how-congress-got-yes-criminal-justice-reform-bill/2288578002/.

4. Ibid.

5. Ibid.

6. Ibid.

7. Ibid.

8. Richard L. Hall, *Participation in Congress* (New Haven, CT: Yale University Press, 1998), 27–30.

9. Amanda H. Allen and Stacy Goers, "Obscure Caucus: The Quiet Men of Congress," September 6, 2013. The listing omits senators: "Senators are by definition not obscure, although there are several who seem to strive for it." To be listed in the Obscure Caucus, House members must have served at least two full terms.

10. Quoted in *The Hill*, November 15, 2000, 16.

11. David Price, *Who Makes the Laws?* (Cambridge, MA: Schenkman Publishing, 1972), 297; David E. Price, *The Congressional Experience*, 3rd ed. (Boulder, CO: Westview Press, 2004), chap. 6.

12. Quoted in Bernard Asbell, *The Senate Nobody Knows* (Garden City, NY: Doubleday, 1978), 210.

13. Richard F. Fenno Jr., "Observation, Context, and Sequence in the Study of Politics," *American Political Science Review* 80 (March 1976): 3–15.

14. Lindsay Sobel, "Early Fast-Track Support Cost Members Leverage," *The Hill*, November 12, 1997, 33.

15. Matthew Daly, "Indians Benefited in 111th Congress," *Washington Times*, December 30, 2010, A4.

16. Peter W. Stevenson, "The Iconic Thumbs-Down Vote That Summed Up John McCain's Career," *Washington Post*, August 27, 2018, https://www.washingtonpost.com/politics/2018/08/27/iconic-thumbs-down-vote-that-summed-up-john-mccains-career/?utm_term=.ab68128b4daf.

17. Cited in Philippe Shepnick, "Moynihan Is Champion Bill Writer," *The Hill*, March 10, 1999, 6.

18. Brianna Ehley and Jennifer Haberkorn, "Tough Reelection? Sponsor an opioid bill," *Politico*, June 16, 2018.

19. These data are from the 109th Congress (2005–2006) and were calculated by Laurel Harbridge. For a valuable analysis of cosponsorship dynamics in recent decades, see Harbridge, *Is Bipartisanship Dead? Policy Agreement and Agenda-Setting in the House of Representatives* (New York: Cambridge University Press, 2015).

20. Jacob R. Straus, "Use of 'Dear Colleague' Letters in the US House of Representatives: A Study of Internal Communications," *Legislative Studies Quarterly* 19 (2013): 60–75.

21. *Porgy and Bess*, music and lyrics by George Gershwin, Ira Gershwin, and DuBose Heyward, 1935.

22. Julie Grace Brufke and Scott Wong, "House GOP Reverses, Cancels Vote on Dem Bill to Abolish ICE," *The Hill*, July 16, 2018, https://thehill.com/homenews/house/397331-house-gop-reverses-canceling-vote-on-dem-bill-to-abolish-ice.

23. Hall, *Participation in Congress*, 139; also see 119.

24. Ibid., 126–127.

25. Ibid., 102.

26. See James M. Curry, *Legislating in the Dark: Information and Power in the House of Representatives* (Chicago: University of Chicago Press, 2015).

27. See Craig Volden and Alan E. Wiseman, *Legislative Effectiveness in the United States Congress* (Cambridge, UK: Cambridge University Press, 2014).

28. Gary Mucchiaroni and Paul J. Quirk, *Deliberative Choices: Debating Public Policy in Congress* (Chicago: University of Chicago Press, 2006), 197.

29. "Final Word," NationalJournal.com, June 5, 2012, 4.

30. Rachel Bade, "Ryan Breaks Record for Shutting Down Floor Debate," *Politico*, November 7, 2017.

31. John D. Wilkerson, "'Killer' Amendments in Congress," *American Political Science Review* 93 (September 1999): 535–552. See also Charles J. Finocchiaro and Jeffery A. Jenkins, "In Search of Killer Amendments in the Modern U.S. House," *Legislative Studies Quarterly* 33, no. 2 (2008): 263–294, which identifies five successful killer amendments in the House from 1953 to 2004.

32. Quoted in Peter Gosselin, "Paulson Will Have No Peer Under Bailout Deal," *Los Angeles Times*, September 29, 2008, online edition.

33. Dave Cook, "'Brutal Vote' Ahead on Whether to Raise the National Debt Ceiling," *Christian Science Monitor*, November 19, 2010, online edition.

34. "2017 Vote Studies: Voting Participation," *CQ Magazine*, February 12, 2018.

35. Niels Lesniewski and Stacey Skotzko, "Members Go to Great Lengths for Voting Stats," *Roll Call*, July 16, 2012, 5.

36. Dan Friedman, "A Rare 'Present' Vote for Schumer," NationalJournal.com, July 16, 2012.

37. John B. Gilmour, *Strategic Disagreement: Stalemate in American Politics* (Pittsburgh: University of Pittsburgh Press, 1995), 41.

38. Quoted in Ramesh Ponnuru, "Division on the Right," *National Review*, November 21, 2003.

39. David C. King and Richard J. Zeckhauser, "Congressional Vote Options," *Legislative Studies Quarterly* 28 (August 2003): 400–401.

40. Quoted in Eric Schmitt, "House Votes to Bar Religious Abuse Abroad," *New York Times*, May 15, 1998, A1.

41. Albert R. Hunt, "Balanced-Budget Measure Is Likely to Pass Senate Next Week, Faces Battle in House," *Wall Street Journal*, July 30, 1982, 2.

42. "2017 CQ Vote Studies: Party Unity," *CQ Magazine*, February 12, 2018.

43. Ibid.

44. Emily Cadei, "Paul Ryan Faces Uphill Battle Cleaning Up the House," *News-week*, October 29, 2015, https://www.newsweek.com/challenges-new-speaker-paul-ryan-388419.

45. Ibid.

46. Shankar Vedantam, "My Team vs. Your Team: The Political Arena Lives Up to Its Name," *Washington Post*, September 29, 2008, A6.

47. For an extended analysis of partisan interests as a source of party cohesion and conflict, see Frances E. Lee, *Beyond Ideology: Politics, Principles, and Partisanship in the U.S. Senate* (Chicago: University of Chicago Press, 2009).

48. Gary C. Jacobson, *The Politics of Congressional Elections,* 7th ed. (New York: Pearson Longman, 2009), 135–144.

49. See Frances E. Lee, *Insecure Majorities: Congress and the Perpetual Campaign* (Chicago: University of Chicago Press, 2016).

50. John Breaux, "Congress's Lost Art of Compromise," *Roll Call,* April 19, 2005, 17.

51. Gary W. Cox and Mathew D. McCubbins, *Setting the Agenda: Responsible Party Government in the U.S. House of Representatives* (New York: Cambridge University Press, 2005), 18.

52. See John W. Kingdon, *Congressmen's Voting Decisions* (New York: Harper and Row, 1981); and Randall B. Ripley, *Party Leaders in the House of Representatives* (Washington, DC: Brookings, 1967), 139–159.

53. Donald R. Matthews and James A. Stimson, *Yeas and Nays: Normal Decisionmaking in the U.S. House of Representatives* (New York: John Wiley, 1975), 95.

54. Quoted in Morton Kondracke, "Who's Running the House? GOP Freshmen or Newt?" *Roll Call,* December 18, 1995, 5.

55. See Gary W. Cox and Mathew D. McCubbins, *Legislative Leviathan: Party Government in the House* (Berkeley: University of California Press, 1993); Gary W. Cox and Keith T. Poole, "On Measuring Partisanship in Roll-Call Voting: The U.S. House of Representatives, 1877–1999," *American Journal's of Political Science 46,* no. 3 (2002): 477–489; and Sean M. Theriault, *Party Polarization in Congress* (New York: Cambridge University Press, 2008).

56. *Congressional Record,* 100th Cong., 1st sess., June 23, 1987, S8438.

57. David Fahrenthold, "In Political Gamble, Reid Holds Senate Votes He Knows He'll Lose," *Washington Post,* December 9, 2010, A3.

58. Glenn Thrush and Maggie Haberman, "Trump Becomes Ensnared in Fiery G.O.P. Civil War," *New York Times,* March 26, 2017, A1.

59. Lindsey McPherson, "New Democrat Coalition Elects Derek Kilmer as New Chairman," *Roll Call,* November 30, 2018, https://www.rollcall.com/news/politics/new-democrat-coalition-elects-derek-kilmer-as-new-chair.

60. For discussion of the "creative class," see Richard Florida, "The Rise of the Creative Class," *Washington Monthly,* May 2002. For extended treatment of these different sources of electoral support for the Democratic Party, see John B. Judis and Ruy Teixeira, *The Emerging Democratic Majority* (New York: Simon and Schuster, 2004).

61. John F. Manley, "The Conservative Coalition in Congress," *American Behavioral Scientist* 17 (December 1973): 223–247; Barbara Sinclair, *Congressional Realignment: 1925–1978* (Austin: University of Texas Press, 1982); and Mack C. Shelley, *The Permanent Majority: The Conservative Coalition in the United States Congress* (Tuscaloosa: University of Alabama Press, 1983).

62. See, for example, William A. Galston, "Can a Polarized American Party System Be 'Healthy'?" *Issues in Governance Studies* (Brookings), April 20, 2010, 1; and Thomas E. Mann and Norman J. Ornstein, *It's Even Worse Than It Looks: How the American Constitutional System Collided With the New Politics of Extremism* (New York: Basic Books, 2012), 51–58.

63. Stephen Gettinger, "R.I.P. to a Conservative Force," *CQ Weekly,* January 9, 1999, 82–83.

64. Sarah A. Binder, "The Disappearing Political Center," *Brookings Review* 15 (Fall 1996): 36–39. An extended analysis of the problem and its results is found in

Sarah A. Binder, *Stalemate: Causes and Consequences of Legislative Gridlock* (Washington, DC: Brookings, 2003).

65. Keith T. Poole and Howard Rosenthal, "Patterns of Congressional Voting," *American Journal of Political Science* 35 (February 1991): 228–278; Keith T. Poole and Howard Rosenthal, *Congress: A Political-Economic History of Roll-Call Voting* (New York: Oxford University Press, 1997). See Norman J. Ornstein, Thomas E. Mann, and Michael J. Malbin, *Vital Statistics on Congress, 2008* (Washington, DC: Brookings, 2008), 160–161.

66. Using different measures of similar data, the same point is made in Morris P. Fiorina, *Culture War? The Myth of a Polarized America,* 2nd ed., with Samuel J. Adams and Jeremy C. Pope (New York: Pearson Longman, 2006), 16–21, and fig. 2–2.

67. Sean M. Theriault, "The Case of the Vanishing Moderates: Party Polarization in the Modern Congress" paper presented at the 2003 annual meeting of the Western Political Science Association, Denver, fig. 1. Ideology scores from similar years (1969–1970 and 1999–2000) yield virtually the same results. Binder, *Stalemate,* 23–26.

68. Quoted by E. J. Dionne Jr., "The Real Pelosi," *Washington Post,* April 9, 2009, A17.

69. Binder, "Disappearing Political Center," 37. Binder defines centrists as those members who are closer to the ideological midpoint between the two parties than to the ideological center of their own party.

70. These estimates are based on Professor Keith Poole's DW-NOMINATE scores for senators and House members provided on his website, http://voteview.com/dwnomin.htm.

71. The South includes the eleven states of the former Confederacy.

72. David W. Rohde, "Electoral Forces," in *Parties and Leaders in the Postreform House* (Chicago: University of Chicago Press, 1991), esp. 34–40.

73. Jeffrey M. Stonecash, Mark D. Brewer, and Mack Mariani, *Diverging Parties* (Boulder, CO: Westview Press, 2002).

74. David Wasserman, "The Bittersweet Mosaic," *National Journal,* April 14, 2012, 27.

75. Ibid., 30. Also see Naftali Bendavid, "Southern White Democrats Face End of Era in Congress," *Wall Street Journal,* August 9, 2012, A1; and Ed O'Keefe, "White Democratic Congressmen in the South Are Becoming an Endangered Species," *Washington Post,* September 7, 2012, A9.

76. See "2017 Vote Studies: Party Unity," *CQ Weekly,* February 12, 2018.

77. Ibid.

78. R. Douglas Arnold, *The Logic of Congressional Action* (New Haven, CT: Yale University Press, 1990).

79. Ibid., 68.

80. Ibid., 84.

81. It is worth noting that recent presidents have taken stands on fewer issues. See Ornstein, Mann, and Malbin, *Vital Statistics on Congress, 2008,* 144–145.

82. "2017 CQ Vote Studies: Presidential Support—Trump Divided, Conquered," *CQ Magazine,* February 12, 2018.

83. "2017 CQ Vote Studies: Presidential Support—Trump Divided, Conquered," *CQ Magazine,* February 12, 2018.

84. Shawn Zeller, "Victory From Defeat," *CQ Weekly,* January 21, 2013, 120.

85. This pattern is even sharper when Congress is polarized along partisan lines. See Daniel Paul Franklin and Michael P. Fix, "The Best of Times and the Worst of Times: Polarization and Presidential Success in Congress," *Congress & the Presidency* 43 (2016): 377–394.

86. John W. Kingdon, *Congressmen's Voting Decisions,* 3rd ed. (Ann Arbor: University of Michigan Press, 1989).

87. Quoted in John F. Bibby, ed., *Congress Off the Record* (Washington, DC: American Enterprise Institute, 1983), 22.

88. Roger H. Davidson, *The Role of the Congressman* (Indianapolis: Bobbs-Merrill, 1969), 22–23.

89. Robert L. Peabody, "Organization Theory and Legislative Behavior: Bargaining, Hierarchy, and Change in the U.S. House of Representatives," paper presented at the 1963 annual meeting of the American Political Science Association, New York.

90. Carl J. Friedrich, *Constitutional Government and Democracy,* 4th ed. (Waltham, MA: Blaisdell Publishing, 1967), 269–270.

91. Quoted in Claudia Dreifus, "Exit Reasonable Right," *New York Times Magazine,* June 2, 1996, 26.

92. Meredith Shiner, "The Speaker of the Unruly," *CQ Weekly,* September 10, 2012, 1834.

93. Debra J. Saunders, "Farm bill Shows That Republicans and Democrats Can Spend Harmoniously," *Las Vegas Review-Journal,* December 14, 2018, https://www.reviewjournal.com/opinion/opinion-columns/debra-saunders/farm-bill-shows-that-republicans-and-democrats-can-spend-harmoniously-1551564/.

94. Elliott Abrams, "Unforgettable Scoop Jackson," *Reader's Digest,* February 1985. Quotation cited in *Congressional Record,* 99th Cong., 1st sess., February 20, 1985, E478.

95. Quoted in David E. Rosenbaum, "The Favors of Rostenkowski: Tax Revision's Quid Pro Quo," *New York Times,* November 27, 1985, B6.

96. Alexander Bolton, "Broken Health-Care Pledge Tests Collins-McConnell Relationship," *The Hill,* December 21, 2017, https://thehill.com/homenews/senate/365922-broken-health-care-pledge-tests-collins-mcconnell-relationship.

97. Quotes from Jonathan Allen, "Effective House Leadership Makes the Most of Majority," *CQ Weekly,* March 29, 2003, 751.

98. See, for example, Chris Frates, "Payoffs for States Get Reid to 60," *Politico,* December 19, 2010, online edition.

99. Gilmour, *Strategic Disagreement,* 4.

100. Gary W. Cox and Jonathan N. Katz, "Gerrymandering Roll Calls in Congress, 1879–2000," *American Journal's of Political Science* 51 (January 2007): 117.

101. See William H. Riker, *The Theory of Political Coalitions* (New Haven, CT: Yale University Press, 1962), 32. Theorists define legislative bargaining situations formally as n-person, zero-sum games in which side payments are permitted—that is, a sizable number of participants are involved; when some participants win, others must lose, and participants can trade items outside the substantive issues under consideration.

102. John G. Stewart, "Two Strategies of Leadership: Johnson and Mansfield," in *Congressional Behavior,* ed. Nelson W. Polsby (New York: Random House, 1971), 67.

103. Russell Hardin, "Hollow Victory: The Minimum Winning Coalition," *American Political Science Review* 79 (December 1976): 1202–1214.

104. Breaux, "Congress's Lost Art of Compromise," 17.

105. Binder, *Stalemate,* 127.

106. Robert J. Dole, quoting Dirksen, in remarks to the Senate, March 29, 2000. Dole quoted in *The Hill,* April 5, 2000, 32.

CHAPTER 10

1. Doyle McManus, "Trump's Looking for Trouble by Threatening New Shutdown," *Los Angeles Times,* January 30, 2019, https://www.latimes.com/politics/la-na-pol-trump-shutdown-congress-20190130-story.html.

2. Burgess Everett, "'Get This Done': McConnell Moves to Avoid New Shutdown," *Politico,* January 30, 2019, https://www.politico.com/story/2019/01/30/mcconnell-government-shutdown-1137750.

3. Philip Rucker, Josh Dawsey, and Seung Min Kim, "Inside Trump's Shutdown Turnaround," *Washington Post,* January 25, 2019, https://www.washingtonpost.com/politics/prisoner-of-his-own-impulse-inside-trumps-cave-to-end-shutdown-without-wall/2019/01/25/e4a4789a-20d5-11e9-8b59-0a28f2191131_story.html?utm_term=.cd6c391dd820.

4. Donald J. Trump, @realDonaldTrump, Twitter, January 24, 2019, 8:16AM, https://twitter.com/realDonaldTrump/status/1088470495312400384.

5. Rachel Bade, Heather Cygle, and John Bresnahan, "'She's Not One to Bluff': How Pelosi Won the Shutdown Battle," *Politico,* January 25, 2019, https://www.politico.com/story/2019/01/25/pelosi-latest-government-shutdown-1128577.

6. Heather Caygle, Andrew Restuccia, and Rachel Bade, "Dems Spurn Trump on Shutdown Talks," *Politico,* January 15, 2019, https://www.politico.com/story/2019/01/15/democrats-refuse-trumps-meeting-shutdown-1101486.

7. Rucker, Dawsey, and Kim, "Inside Trump's Shutdown."

8. Burgess Everett and Andrew Restuccia, "'Complete, Total Surrender': Why Trump Waved the White Flag," *Politico,* January 25, 2019, https://www.politico.com/story/2019/01/25/trump-goverment-shutdown-over-1128594.

9. Rucker, Dawsey, and Kim, "Inside Trump's Shutdown."

10. Ibid.

11. David R. Mayhew, *America's Congress: Actions in the Public Sphere, James Madison Through Newt Gingrich* (New Haven: Yale University Press, 2002).

12. David R. Mayhew, *The Imprint of Congress* (New Haven: Yale University Press, 2017).

13. Alexander Hamilton, "*Federalist 70,*" *The Project Gutenberg Ebook of The Federalist Papers,* https://www.gutenberg.org/files/1404/1404-h/1404-h.htm#link2H_4_0070.

14. Charles O. Jones, *Separate but Equal Branches: Congress and the Presidency* (Chatham, NJ: Chatham House, 1995), 138–157.

15. Woodrow Wilson, *Congressional Government* (Boston: Houghton Mifflin, 1885), 52.

16. Meghan M. Stuessy, "Regular Vetoes and Pocket Vetoes: In Brief," Congressional Research Service Report RS22188, August 2, 2016. Updates after 2009 available from the U.S. Senate Library, http://www.senate.gov/reference/reference_index_subjects/Vetoes_vrd.htm.

17. The American Presidency Project at the University of California, Santa Barbara, also tracks presidential vetoes as well as signing statements, executive orders, and many other data and documents. See http://www.presidency.ucsb.edu.

18. Tim Groseclose and Nolan McCarty, "The Politics of Blame: Bargaining Before an Audience," *American Journal's of Political Science* 45, no. 1 (2001): 100–119.

19. Alexis Simendinger, "The Veto-Free Zone," *National Journal,* December 17, 2005, 3888.

20. Sheryl Gay Stolberg and Michael D. Shear, "Senators Strike Bipartisan Deal on Immigration Despite Veto Threat," *New York Times,* February 14, 2018, https://www.nytimes.com/2018/02/14/us/politics/trump-immigration-veto-threat.html.

21. Hans J. G. Hassell and Samuel Kernell, "Veto Rhetoric and Legislative Riders," *American Journal of Political Science* 60, no. 4 (2016): 845–859.

22. Ibid.

23. Dave Boyer, "For Obama, Veto Isn't Overriding Concern," *Washington Times,* December 26, 2012, A1.

24. Several court decisions, such as *Kennedy v. Sampson* (1974), established the principle that pocket vetoes are not to be used during congressional sessions but only after Congress's final adjournment at the end of its second session.

25. Louis Fisher, "The Pocket Veto: Its Current Status," Congressional Research Service Report RL30909, March 30, 2001, summary.

26. *Los Angeles Times,* March 18, 1988, part I, 4.

27. *Clinton v. New York,* 524 U.S. 417 (1998). Helen Dewar and Joan Biskupic, "Line-Item Vote Struck Down: Backers Push for Alternative," *Washington Post,* June 26, 1998, A1.

28. Louis Nelson, "Trump, Unhappy With Omnibus Bill, Calls on Congress to Reinstate Line-Item Veto," *Politico,* March 23, 2018, https://www.politico.com/story/2018/03/23/trump-line-item-veto-482192.

29. Ibid.

30. See Kenneth Mayer, *With the Stroke of a Pen: Executive Orders and Presidential Power* (Princeton, NJ: Princeton University Press, 2001). Presidents also justify their issuance of executive orders and memorandums by citing their constitutional "executive Power" authority, role as "Commander in Chief," and right to "take Care That the Laws be faithfully executed." For a review of the difference between executive orders and presidential memorandums, see Gregory Korte, "How Obama Became the Go-It-Alone President," *USA Today,* December 17, 2013, online edition; Glenn Kessler, "Claims About Obama's Use of Executive Orders and Presidential Memorandums," *Washington Post,* January 4, 2015, A4; and Kenneth S. Lowande, "After the Orders: Presidential Memoranda and Unilateral Action," *Presidential Studies Quarterly* (December 2014): 724–741.

31. See, for example, Richard P. Nathan, *The Administrative Presidency* (New York: John Wiley, 1983); and Robert R. Durant, *The Administrative Presidency Revisited* (Albany: State University of New York Press, 1992).

32. William G. Howell, *Power Without Persuasion: The Politics of Direct Presidential Action* (Princeton, NJ: Princeton University Press, 2003). The Obama administration has abandoned the term *enemy combatant* for those held at Guantánamo Bay, Cuba. See David Savage, "No More 'Enemy Combatants' at Guantánamo Bay," *Los Angeles Times*, March 14, 2009, online edition.

33. Jacqueline Klimas, "Trump Going for Full-Blown Space Force, White House Memo Reveals," *Politico*, November 29, 2018, https://www.politico.com/story/2018/11/29/space-force-military-branch-999528.

34. William G. Howell and David E. Lewis, "Agencies by Presidential Design," *Journal of Politics* (November 2002): 1096.

35. John M. Donnelly, "Obama Spoils for Fight Over Gitmo," *CQ News*, January 7, 2015, online edition. Also see Charles Hoskinson, "Obama Sidesteps Congress in Releasing Gitmo Prisoners," *Washington Examiner*, January 12, 2015, 8. When Gitmo opened in 2002, it held 779 prisoners.

36. Ibid., 1100.

37. Terry M. Moe and William G. Howell, "The Presidential Power of Unilateral Action," *Journal of Law, Economics, and Organization* 15, no. 1 (1999): 132–179.

38. Elizabeth Shogren, "President Plans Blitz of Executive Orders Soon," *Los Angeles Times*, July 5, 1998, A11.

39. Linda Feldmann, "Faith-Based Initiatives Quietly Lunge Forward," *Christian Science Monitor*, February 6, 2003, 2.

40. Michael D. Shear, "Trump Will Withdraw U.S. From Paris Climate Agreement," *New York Times*, June 1, 2017, https://www.nytimes.com/2017/06/01/climate/trump-paris-climate-agreement.html.

41. Anne Gearan, Paul Sonne, and Carol Morello, "U.S. to Withdraw From Nuclear Arms Control Treaty With Russia, Raising Fears of a New Arms Race," *Washington Post*, February 1, 2019, https://www.washingtonpost.com/world/national-security/us-to-withdraw-from-nuclear-arms-control-treaty-with-russia-says-russian-violations-render-the-cold-war-agreement-moot/2019/02/01/84dc0db6-261f-1-1e9-ad53-824486280311_story.html?utm_term=.007940d5a40d.

42. Glenn Thrush, "Trump's Use of National Security to Impose Tariffs Faces Court Test," *New York Times*, December 19, 2018, https://www.nytimes.com/2018/12/19/us/politics/trump-national-security-tariffs.html.

43. Rick Gladstone and Satoshi Sugiyama, "Trump's Travel Ban: How It Works and Who Is Affected," *New York Times*, July 1, 2018, https://www.nytimes.com/2018/07/01/world/americas/travel-ban-trump-how-it-works.html.

44. David Nakamura and Josh Dawsey, "'I Can Do It If I Want': Trump Threatens to Invoke Emergency Powers to Build Border Wall," *Washington Post*, January 4, 2019, https://www.washingtonpost.com/politics/i-can-do-it-if-i-want-trump-threatens-to-invoke-emergency-powers-to-build-border-wall/2019/01/04/992a129c-105b-11e9-8938-5898adc28fa2_story.html?utm_term=.26700aed324f.

45. Brad Plumer, "If Trump Wants to Dismantle Obama's EPA Rules, Here Are All the Obstacles He'll Face," *Vox*, December 8, 2016, http://www.vox.com/energy-and-environment/2016/12/7/13855470/donald-trump-epa-climate-regulations.

46. Lisa Friedman and Brad Plumer, "E.P.A. Announces Repeal of Major Obama-Era Carbon Emissions Rule," *New York Times,* October 9, 2017, https://www.nytimes.com/2017/10/09/climate/clean-power-plan.html.

47. Robert Barnes, "Trump Can't Immediately End DACA, Appeals Court Panel Says, Setting Up Supreme Court Fight," *Washington Post,* November 8, 2018, https://www.washingtonpost.com/politics/courts_law/trump-cant-end-daca-appeals-court-says-setting-up-supreme-court-fight/2018/11/08/4a76f928-e386-11e8-ab2c-b31dcd53ca6b_story.html?utm_term=.5d3d9fd28cdd.

48. See T. J. Halstead, "Presidential Signing Statements: Constitutional and Institutional Implications," Congressional Research Service Report RL33667, April 13, 2007.

49. Dan Friedman, "On the Other Hand," *National Journal,* March 28, 2009, 54.

50. Laura Meckler, "Obama Shifts View of Executive Power," *Wall Street Journal,* March 30, 2012, A12; Charlie Savage, "Trump Claims Power to Bypass Limits Set by Congress in Defense Bill," *Washington Post,* August 14, 2018, https://www.nytimes.com/2018/08/14/us/politics/trump-signing-statements.html.

51. Richard Berke, "Courting Congress Nonstop, Clinton Looks for an Alliance," *New York Times,* March 8, 1993, A1.

52. Mayhew, *America's Congress,* x.

53. Ibid., 9.

54. See Stephen Wayne, *The Legislative Presidency* (New York: Harper and Row, 1978).

55. W. Lance Bennett, "Toward a Theory of Press–State Relations," *Journal of Communication* 40, no. 2 (1990): 103–125.

56. Richard E. Neustadt, *Presidential Power* (New York: John Wiley, 1960), 23.

57. Ibid., 16.

58. Ibid., 50.

59. Ibid., 53.

60. Paul C. Light, *The President's Agenda* (Baltimore: Johns Hopkins University Press, 1982), 230–231.

61. Matthew N. Beckmann, "Up the Hill and Across the Aisle: Discovering the Path to Bipartisanship in Washington," *Legislative Studies Quarterly* 41, no. 2 (2016): 269–295; and *Pushing the Agenda: Presidential Leadership in US Lawmaking,* 1953–2004 (New York: Cambridge University Press, 2010).

62. Tim Alberta, "Inside the GOP's Health Care Debacle: Eighteen Days That Shook the Republican Party—and Humbled a President," *Politico,* March 24, 2017, http://www.politico.com/magazine/story/2017/03/obamacare-vote-paul-ryan-health-care-ahca-replacement-failure-trump-214947.

63. John A. Farrell, *Tip O'Neill and the Democratic Century* (Boston: Little, Brown, 2001), 553.

64. Lyndon B. Johnson, *The Vantage Point* (New York: Popular Library, 1971), 448.

65. Johnson, *Vantage Point,* 448.

66. Jack Valenti, "Some Advice on the Care and Feeding of Congressional Egos," *Los Angeles Times,* April 23, 1978, 3.

67. Burgess Everett and Lauren French, "Coburn Leaves Brasher Bomb-Throwers in Wake," *Politico,* July 9, 2014, 14.

68. See, for example, Carl Hulse, Jeremy Peters, and Michael Shear, "Obama Is Seen as Frustrating His Own Party," *New York Times,* August 18, 2014, http://www.nytimes.com/2014/08/19/us/aloof-obama-is-frustrating-his-own-party.html.

69. Anne Gearan, Mike DeBonis, and Seung Min Kim, "Trump Surprises Lawmakers in Backing Some Tougher Gun Controls," *Washington Post,* February 28, 2018, https://www.washingtonpost.com/powerpost/democrats-rally-around-universal-background-checks-ahead-of-white-house-meeting/2018/02/28/13c4a5d2-1ca4-11e8-9de1-147dd2df3829_story.html?utm_term=.062020b4b879.

70. Maggie Haberman and Yamiche Alcindor, "Pelosi and Schumer Say They Have Deal With Trump to Replace DACA," *New York Times,* September 13, 2017, https://www.nytimes.com/2017/09/13/us/politics/trump-dinner-schumer-pelosi-daca-obamacare.html.

71. Alan Gomez, "What Is President Trump's Policy on DREAMers? It Keeps Changing," *USA Today,* February 7, 2018, https://www.usatoday.com/story/news/politics/2018/02/07/what-president-trumps-policy-dreamers-keeps-changing/312783002/.

72. Jordain Carney, "Trump Shutdown Moves Leave GOP Senators in Disbelief," *The Hill,* December 20, 2018, https://thehill.com/homenews/senate/422329-trump-shutdown-moves-leaves-gop-senators-in-disbelief.

73. Rachel Bade, "McCarthy Rebrands Himself," *Politico,* October 11, 2018, https://www.politico.com/story/2018/10/11/mccarthy-trump-immigration-populists-890085.

74. Donald J. Trump, @realDonaldTrump, *Twitter,* August 10, 2017, https://twitter.com/realdonaldtrump/status/895599179522650112?lang=en.

75. Ashley Parker and Robert Costa, "One Administration, Two Styles: Trump the Brawler and Pence the Cajoler," *Washington Post,* January 6, 2017, https://www.washingtonpost.com/politics/one-administration-two-styles-trump-the-brawler-and-pence-the-cajoler/2017/01/05/65e93554-d370-11e6-945a-76f69a399dd5_story.html?utm_term=.0b434380cc50.

76. Peter Baker, "Washington Worries About Its New Power Couple," *New York Times,* November 10, 2010, A18.

77. Roy P. Basler, ed., *The Collected Works of Abraham Lincoln,* vol. 3 (New Brunswick: Rutgers University Press, 1953), 27.

78. Samuel Kernell, *Going Public: New Strategies of Presidential Leadership,* 3rd ed. (Washington, DC: CQ Press, 2006), 2. Also see James Ceaser et al., "The Rise of the Rhetorical Presidency," *Presidential Studies Quarterly* 21 (Spring 1981): 158–171.

79. Richard M. Pious, *The American Presidency* (New York: Basic Books, 1979), 194. Also see George C. Edwards III, *The Public Presidency* (New York: St. Martin's Press, 1983).

80. See Kernell, *Going Public.*

81. Farrell, *Tip O'Neill and the Democratic Century,* 553.

82. John Harwood, "After 15 Months in Office, Policy vs. Politics for Obama," *New York Times,* April 26, 2010, A13.

83. Chuck Lindell, "Cornyn: Trump's Tweets Undermine Agenda, But Gains Still Made, *Austin-American Statesman,* January 2, 2018, https://www

.statesman.com/news/20180102/cornyn-trumps-tweets-undermine-agenda-but-gains-still-made.

84. Bastien Inzaurralde, "This Linguist Studied the Way Trump Speaks For Two Years. Here's What She Found," *Washington Post,* July 7, 2017, https://www.washingtonpost.com/news/the-fix/wp/2017/07/07/this-linguist-studied-the-way-trump-speaks-for-two-years-heres-what-she-found/?noredirect=on&utm_term=.8c8b20445f87.

85. Caitlin E. Dwyer and Sarah A. Treul, "Indirect Presidential Influence, State-Level Approval, and Voting in the U.S. Senate," *American Politics Research* 40, no. 2 (2012): 355–379.

86. Russell Berman, "Where Trump's Popularity Matters—And Where It Doesn't," *The Atlantic,* March 15, 2017, https://www.theatlantic.com/politics/archive/2017/03/trump-approval-rating-39-percent-republican-congress/519555.

87. George C. Edwards III, *On Deaf Ears: The Limits of the Bully Pulpit* (New Haven, CT: Yale University Press, 2003); *Governing by Campaigning: The Politics of the Bush Presidency* (New York: Pearson Longman, 2008).

88. Brandice Canes-Wrone, "The President's Legislative Influence From Public Appeals," *American Journal of Political Science* 45 (2001): 313–329.

89. George C. Edwards III, *The Strategic President: Persuasion and Opportunity in Presidential Leadership* (Princeton, NJ: Princeton University Press, 2009).

90. Ibid., A20.

91. Jonathan Martin, "Obama Wants Filter-Free News," *Politico,* March 24, 2009, 17.

92. The figures for both the informal and formal press sessions are cited in Donovan Slack, "Obama Lags in First-Term Press Conferences," *Politico,* January 16, 2013, 11. On the other hand, the president has given numerous TV interviews. See George E. Condon Jr., "Tuned Out," *National Journal,* November 5, 2011, 26–33.

93. Sheryl Gay Stolberg, "Obama Makes History in Live Internet Video Chat," *New York Times,* March 27, 2009, A15.

94. Cecilia Kang, "Obama to Hold First Twitter Town Hall," *Washington Post,* July 6, 2011, A4; and Hayley Peterson, "Obama to Field 'Tweets' on Jobs, Economy," *Washington Examiner,* July 6, 2011, 12.

95. Chris Cillizza, "Three Lessons for Obama From His First Four Years," *Washington Post,* January 21, 2013, A2.

96. Quoted in Walter Pincus, "More From Nixon the Political Scientist," *Washington Post,* January 26, 2010, A13.

97. Mayhew, *America's Congress,* 78.

98. Matthew E. Glassman, "Tweet Your Congressman: The Rise of Electronic Communications in Congress," in *The Evolving Congress,* Committee on Rules and Administration, United States Senate. (Washington, DC: U.S Government Printing Office, 2014), 95–106.

99. Douglas L. Kriner and Eric Schickler, "Investigating the President: Committee Probes and Presidential Approval, 1953–2006," *Journal of Politics* 76, no. 2 (2014): 521–534.

100. See Brandice Canes-Wrone and Scott De Marchi, "Presidential Approval and Legislative Success," *Journal of Politics* 64, no. 2 (2002): 491–509; and Beckmann, *Pushing the Agenda.*

101. Douglas L. Kriner and Eric Schickler, *Investigating the President: Congressional Checks on Presidential Power* (Princeton, NJ: Princeton University Press, 2016).

102. John Zaller, *The Nature and Origins of Mass Opinion* (New York: Cambridge University Press, 1992).

103. Aaron Wildavsky "The Two Presidencies," *Transaction* 4, no. 2 (1966): 7–14.

104. Ibid., 9.

105. Ronald Brownstein, "Strategies Shift as Bush Drops in Polls," *Los Angeles Times,* July 5, 2001, A9.

106. John Harwood and Jeanne Cummings, "Bush's Approval Rating Slips to 50%, a 5-Year Presidential Low," Wall Street Journal, June 28, 2001, A18.

107. Ron Faucheux, "Presidential Popularity: A History of Highs and Lows," *CQ Daily Monitor,* February 7, 2002, 14.

108. Nolan D. McCaskill and Louis Nelson, "Polls: Majority Support Missile Strikes Against Syria," *Politico,* April 10, 2017, https://www.politico.com/story/2017/04/poll-syria-missile-strikes-237067.

109. Brandice Canes-Wrone, William Howell, and David E. Lewis, "Toward a Broader Understanding of Presidential Power: A Reevaluation of the Two Presidencies Thesis," *Journal of Politics* 70, no. 1 (2008): 1–16.

110. Mayhew, *America's Congress.*

111. See Douglas L. Kriner, *After the Rubicon: Congress, Presidents and the Politics of Waging War* (Chicago: University of Chicago Press, 2010); and William G. Howell and Jon C. Pevehouse, *While Dangers Gather: Congressional Checks on Presidential War Powers* (Princeton, NJ: Princeton University Press, 2007).

112. See Frances E. Lee, "How Party Polarization Affects Governance," *Annual Review of Political Science* 18 (2015); and *Insecure Majorities: Congress and the Perpetual Campaign* (Chicago: University of Chicago Press, 2016).

113. See Jon R. Bond and Richard Fleisher, *The President in the Legislative Arena* (Chicago: University of Chicago Press, 1992); and Canes-Wrone, "The President's Legislative Influence From Public Appeals."

114. George C. Edwards, III, *At the Margins: Presidential Leadership of Congress* (New Haven, CT: Yale University Press, 1990).

115. Glenn Thrush, "With the 111th, the Age of Pelosi Dawns," *Politico,* January 6, 2009, 16.

116. Peter Baker, "An Unlikely Partnership Left Behind," *Washington Post,* November 5, 2007, A1.

117. Tim Alberta, "Conservatism in the Age of Trump," *National Review,* December 21, 2016, http://www.nationalreview.com/article/443236/donald-trump-conservatism-right-wing-future.

118. Carl Hulse and Adam Nagourney, "Senate G.O.P. Leader Finds Weapon in Unity," *New York Times,* March 17, 2010, A13.

119. Ibid.

120. Frances E. Lee. "Dividers, Not Uniters: Presidential Leadership and Senate Partisanship, 1981–2004," *Journal of Politics* 70, no. 4 (2008): 914–928; and *Beyond Ideology: Politics, Principles and Partisanship in the U.S. Senate* (Chicago: University of Chicago Press, 2009).

121. Frances E. Lee, *Beyond Ideology,* 76–77.

122. William G. Howell and Jon C. Pevehouse, "When Congress Stops Wars," *Foreign Affairs*, September/October 2007, https://www.foreignaffairs.com/articles/iraq/2007-09-01/when-congress-stops-wars.

123. Douglas L. Kriner, *After the Rubicon*.

124. David Mayhew, *Divided We Govern* (New Haven, CT: Yale University Press, 1991), 198.

125. See Sarah A. Binder, *Stalemate: Causes and Consequences of Legislative Gridlock* (Washington, DC: Brookings Institution Press, 2003); and William Howell, Scott Adler, Charles Cameron, and Charles Riemann, "Divided Government and the Legislative Productivity of Congress, 1945–94," *Legislative Studies Quarterly* 25, no. 2 (2000): 285–312.

126. R. Douglas Arnold, "Explaining Legislative Achievements" in *Congress and Policy Making in the 21st Century*, ed. Jeffery A. Jenkins and Eric M. Patashnik (New York: Cambridge University Press, 2016).

127. William Howell et al, "Divided Government and the Legislative Productivity of Congress," 299.

128. Mayhew, *Divided We Govern,* 162.

129. See, for example, Stephen J. Wayne, "Great Expectations: What People Want From Presidents," in *Rethinking the Presidency,* ed. Thomas E. Cronin (Boston: Little, Brown, 1982), 185–199.

130. Dean Scott, "Next President Likely to Have Limited Chance for Passage of Emission Caps, Senator Says," *Daily Report for Executives,* August 4, 2008, A-15.

131. Arthur M. Schlesinger Jr. and Alfred De Grazia, *Congress and the Presidency: Their Role in Modern Times* (Washington, DC: American Enterprise Institute, 1967), 1.

132. Leonard D. White, *The Federalists* (New York: Macmillan, 1948), 55.

133. Leonard D. White, *The Jeffersonians* (New York: Macmillan, 1951), 35.

134. Wilson, *Congressional Government;* Burns, *Presidential Government.*

135. See Joseph S. Clark, *Congress: The Sapless Branch* (New York: Harper and Row, 1964); and Arthur Schlesinger Jr., *The Imperial Presidency* (Boston: Houghton Mifflin, 1973).

136. Andrew Restuccia, "Cantor Assails Obama's 'Imperial Presidency,'" *Politico,* October 24, 2012, 28.

137. Nicole Gaudiano and Eliza Collins, "Exclusive: Nancy Pelosi Vows 'Different World' for Trump, No More 'Rubber Stamp' in New Congress," *USA Today,* January 3, 2019, https://www.usatoday.com/story/news/politics/2019/01/03/nancy-pelosi-trump-can-expect-different-world-new-congress/2391622002/.

CHAPTER 11

1. Chris Mooney, Brady Dennis, and Steven Mufson, "Trump Names Scott Pruitt, Oklahoma Attorney General Suing EPA on Climate Change, to Head EPA," *Washington Post,* December 8, 2016.

2. Josh Dawsey and Andrew Restuccia, "Trump Planning to Give Cabinet Unusually Wide Latitude," *Politico,* January 9, 2017, http://www.politico.com/story/2017/01/donald-trump-cabinet-233333.

3. Quoted in E. J. Dionne Jr., "Back From the Dead: Neoprogressivism in the '90s," *American Prospect,* September–October 1996, 25.

4. Richard E. Neustadt, "Politicians and Bureaucrats," in *The Congress and America's Future,* 2nd ed., ed. David B. Truman (Englewood Cliffs, NJ: Prentice Hall, 1973), 199. See also Louis Fisher, *The Politics of Shared Power: Congress and the Executive,* 3rd ed. (Washington, DC: CQ Press, 1993).

5. See Harold Relyea, "Executive Branch Reorganization and Management Initiatives: A Brief Overview," Congressional Research Service Report RL33441, May 30, 2006.

6. *Congressional Record,* 109th Cong., 1st sess., February 15, 2005, S1437.

7. Keith Koffler, "Confirmation Wars Could Be Thing of the Past," *Roll Call,* November 21, 2008, 10.

8. Charlie Savage, Nicholas Fandos and Katie Benner, "Barr Vows to Let Mueller Finish and to Protect Justice Dept. Integrity," *New York Times,* January 15, 2019, https://www.nytimes.com/2019/01/15/us/politics/mueller-barr.html.

9. Steven V. Roberts, "In Confirmation Process, Hearings Offer a Stage," *New York Times,* February 8, 1989, B7.

10. Norman Ornstein, "Confirmation Process Leaves Government in Serious Gridlock," *Roll Call,* March 25, 2009, 6.

11. Edward Luce and Krishna Guha, "Appointments Bottleneck at Treasury Tightens," *Financial Times,* March 19, 2009, 4.

12. Jennifer Steinhauer and Steve Eder, "Republicans, Facing Pressure, Postpone Hearings for Four Trump Cabinet Nominees," *New York Times,* January 11, 2017, p. A10.

13. Doyle McManus and Robert Shogun, "Acrid Tone Reflects Long-Term Trend for Nominations," *Los Angeles Times,* March 9, 1997, A6.

14. Alan K. Ota, "A Capital's Empty Chairs," *CQ Weekly,* July 5, 2010, 1604.

15. See Clay Johnson and Mack McLarty, "A Better Way to Govern," *The Aspen Idea* (Summer 2012): 64–66.

16. Partnership for Public Service, "Political Appointee Tracker," https://ourpub licservice.org/issues/presidential-transition/political-appointee-tracker.php, accessed March 26, 2017; and https://ourpublicservice.org/political-appointee-tracker/, accessed January 4, 2019.

17. Julie Pace, Zeke Miller, and Jonathan Lemire, "Turnover, Investigations Have Trump Administration Adrift," *US News,* March 2, 2018.

18. *"Noel Canning* Would Have Nixed Hundreds," *Daily Report for Executives,* February 6, 2013, A-10.

19. 573 U.S. ___ (2014).

20. See Alex Ward, "The Strongest Case for—and Against—Matthew Whitaker's Appointment," vox.com, November 21, 2018. https://www.vox.com/policy-and-politics/2018/11/21/18103517/matthew-whitaker-appointment-legal-con stitution-vacancy-act.

21. See, for example, Will Englund, "Czar Wars," *National Journal,* February 14, 2009, 16–24.

22. Bruce Ackerman, "A Role for Congress to Reclaim," *Washington Post,* March 11, 2009, A15.

23. On Bannon, see Daniel Victor and Liam Stack, "Stephen Bannon and Breitbart News, in Their Words," *New York Times,* November 15, 2016, A14; on Kushner's potential conflicts of interest, see Susanne Craig and Maggie Haberman, "Jared Kushner Will Sell Many of His Assets, but Ethics Lawyers Worry," *New York Times,* January 10, 2017, A10.

24. Bonnie Berkowitz and Kevin Uhrmacher, "It's Not Just the Cabinet: Trump's Transition Team May Need to find About 4,100 Appointees," *Washington Post,* updated Dec. 5, 2018, https://www.washingtonpost.com/graphics/politics/trump-transition-appointments-scale/.

25. Andrew Rudalevige, "The Cabinet Was the Easy Part. Staffing (and Steering) the Bureaucracy Takes Much More Work," *Monkey Cage* (blog), Washington Post, https://www.washingtonpost.com/news/monkey-cage/wp/2017/01/10/the-cab inet-was-the-easy-part-staffing-the-bureaucracy-takes-much-more-work.

26. See Henry Hogue, "Statutory Qualifications for Executive Branch Positions," Congressional Research Service Report RL33886, February 20, 2007.

27. *Congressional Record,* 105th Cong., 1st sess., September 12, 1996, S10367.

28. Shankar Vedantam, "Who Are the Better Managers—Political Appointees or Career Bureaucrats?" *Washington Post,* November 24, 2008, A6.

29. Joe Davidson, "The Do's and Don'ts on Political Activity," *Washington Post,* October 31, 2013, A17.

30. Alyssa Rosenberg, "Minding the Hatch Act," *Government Executive,* October 2008, 76.

31. Joe Davidson, "Guidelines on Hatch Act and Social Media Are 'Rules of the Road' for Upcoming Elections," *Washington Post,* August 24, 2010, B3.

32. For example, under the Honest Leadership and Open Government Act of 2007, high government officials and senators are subject to a two-year cooling-off period after leaving office; House members must comply with a one-year cooling-off period. See Bart Jansen, "Details of the Lobbying Rules Law," *CQ Weekly,* September 17, 2007, 2693.

33. Zachary A. Goldfarb, "Regulators See Chance to Cash In," *Washington Post,* December 30, 2010, A11.

34. This order built upon restrictions issued by President Obama. See Michael S. Schmidt and Eric Lipton, "Trump Toughens Some Facets of Lobbying Ban and Weakens Others," *New York Times,* January 29, 2017, A16.

35. Quoted in Vic Hallard, "In Defense of Legislatures," *Council of State Governments,* February 1, 1996, 9.

36. Bart Jensen, "Who has security clearance? More than 4.3M people," *USA Today,* June 6, 2017, https://www.usatoday.com/story/news/2017/06/06/who-has-security-clearance/102549298/.

37. Craig Whitlock, "Thousands of Defense Jobs to Be Eliminated," *Washington Post,* August 10, 2010, A4.

38. Ellen Nakashima, "Pentagon Hires Out More Than In," *Washington Post,* April 3, 2001, A19.

39. Ibid.

40. Paul C. Light, "The True Size of Government: Tracking Washington's Blended Workforce, 1984–2015," The Volker Alliance, https://www.volckeralliance.org/publications/true-size-government.

41. Joe Davidson, "Defining 'Inherently Governmental' and Role of Contractors in War," *Washington Post,* June 22, 2010, B3.
42. *Congressional Record,* 100th Cong., 1st sess., July 29, 1987, S10850.
43. Richard S. Beth, "The Congressional Review Act and Possible Consolidation Into a Single Measure of Resolutions Disapproving Regulations," Congressional Research Service Report R40163, January 26, 2009, 8. Worth noting is that since the start of 2012, the "Obama administration, either because of bureaucratic oversight or because they were considered too minor to be reported" has failed to report many rules to the House and Senate and to the GAO. About 1,800 regulations have not been reported to Congress or the GAO as the law requires. See Juliet Eilperin, "Study: Hundreds of Rules Passed by Obama Administration Are Technically Illegal," *Washington Post,* July 30, 2014, online edition.
44. Tim Devaney, "GOP Finds Secret Weapon Versus Obama Regulations," *The Hill,* January 20, 2015, 6; and Daren Bakst and James L. Gattuso, "Stars Align for Congressional Review Act," *Issue Brief #4640 on Regulation,* Heritage Foundation, December 16, 2016, http://www.heritage.org/research/reports/2016/12/stars-align-for-the-congressional-review-act.
45. Maeve P. Carey, Alissa M. Dolan, and Christopher M. Davis, "The Congressional Review Act: Frequently Asked Questions," Congressional Research Service Report 7–5700, November 17, 2016.
46. Paul Bedard, "MAGA List: 205 'Historic Results' Help Trump Make Case for 2020 Re-election," *Washington Examiner,* December 31, 2018.
47. Kimberly Kindy, "Legislative Rollback of Obama-Era Worker Safety Rules Awaits Trump's Signature," *Washington Post,* March 22, 2017, https://www.washingtonpost.com/news/politics/wp/2017/03/22/legislative-rollback-of-obama-era-worker-safety-rules-awaits-trumps-signature.
48. Rebecca Adams, "Republicans Dust Off a Little-Used Tool to Go After Overhaul Rules," *CQ Today,* November 29, 2010, 3.
49. Gautham Nagesh, "Agencies Flooded by Comments on New Rules," *Wall Street Journal,* September 4, 2014, A4.
50. Matthew Wald, "Court Voids a Bush Move on Energy," *New York Times,* January 14, 2004, A12.
51. Cyril Zaneski, "Escape Artist," *Government Executive,* March 2001, 29. The U.S. Supreme Court is also considering whether agency "guidance" documents are being employed to reinterpret and implement statutory requirements. At issue is "whether federal agencies increasingly preferred to issue interpretive rules instead of regulations to avoid the drawn-out process that includes public notice and comment periods," as required by the Administrative Procedures Act. See Erica Martinson, "Justices Probe Basis of Some Regulatory Efforts," *Politico,* December 2, 2014, 13.
52. See Brad Plumer, "If Trump Wants to Dismantle Obama's EPA Rules, Here Are All the Obstacles He'll Face," *Vox,* December 8, 2016, http://www.vox.com/energy-and-environment/2016/12/7/13855470/donald-trump-epa-climate-regulations.
53. Susan Dudley, "Government Regulations: Rhetoric vs. Reality," *Politico,* September 13, 2012, 28. Also see Jia Lynn Yang, "Do Federal Regulations Really Kill Jobs?" *Washington Post,* November 14, 2011, A1.

54. Larry Margasak, "GOP Agenda: Major Impact May Be on 2012 Election," *Washington Examiner,* January 3, 2011, 13.

55. "A Coming Assault on the E.P.A.," *New York Times,* December 25, 2010, A20.

56. Amy Harder, "House GOP Push on EPA Running Out of Steam," *National Journal Daily,* December 6, 2012, 8.

57. Benjamin Goad, "GOP: We Will Gain From Backlash on Regulation," *The Hill,* September 29, 2014, 8.

58. Brady Dennis and Juliet Eilperin, "Trump Signs Order at the EPA to Dismantle Environmental Protections," *Washington Post,* March 28, 2017.

59. Umair Irfan, "EPA Analysis of Its Own New Climate Proposal: Thousands of People Will Die," vox.com, August 21, 2018, https://www.vox.com/2018/8/21/17763916/epa-clean-power-plan-affordable-clean-energy.

60. Frank Ackerman, Lisa Heinzerling, James K. Hammitt, and Milton C. Weinstein, "Balancing Lives Against Lucre," *Los Angeles Times,* February 25, 2004, A17. Ackerman and Heinzerling are economists, and Hammitt and Weinstein are risk analysis experts.

61. *Congressional Record,* July 11, 1995, S9705.

62. Ibid., S9697.

63. Joseph S. Clark, *Congress: The Sapless Branch* (New York: Harper and Row, 1964), 63–64.

64. David B. Frohnmayer, "The Separation of Powers: An Essay on the Vitality of a Constitutional Idea," *Oregon Law Review* (Spring 1973): 330.

65. David B. Truman, *The Governmental Process,* rev. ed. (New York: Knopf, 1971), 439.

66. Woodrow Wilson, *Congressional Government* (Boston: Houghton Mifflin, 1885), 297.

67. Lisa Rein, "Conversations: Gene L. Dorado," *Washington Post,* December 30, 2010, B3.

68. David Rogers, "Sen. Lott Becomes GOP's New Standard-Bearer, but His Style Will Be Tested in the Next Congress," *Wall Street Journal,* November 15, 1996, A16.

69. Jennifer Steinhauer and Robert Pear, "Republicans, Sensing Weakness in Health Law Rollout, Switch Tactics," *New York Times,* October 24, 2013, A19.

70. Wilson, *Congressional Government,* 303.

71. Rochelle Stanfield, "Plotting Every Move," *National Journal,* March 26, 1988, 796.

72. *Watkins v. United States,* 354 U.S. 178 (1957). See also James Hamilton, *The Power to Probe* (New York: Vantage Books, 1976).

73. William S. Cohen and George J. Mitchell, *Men of Zeal: A Candid Inside Story of the Iran-Contra Hearings* (New York: Viking Penguin, 1988), 305.

74. See Douglas L. Kriner and Eric Schickler, *Investigating the President: Congressional Checks on Presidential Power* (Princeton, NJ: Princeton University Press, 2016).

75. See Jason A. MacDonald and Robert J. McGrath, "Retrospective Congressional Oversight and the Dynamics of Legislative Influence Over the Bureaucracy," *Legislative Studies Quarterly* 41 (2016): 899–934.

76. Louis Fisher, in *Extensions* (Carl Albert Congressional Research and Studies Center newsletter) (Spring 1984): 2.

77. John R. Johannes, "Study and Recommend: Statutory Reporting Requirements as a Technique of Legislative Initiative—A Research Note," *Western Political Quarterly* (December 1976): 589–596.

78. Guy Gugliotta, "Reporting on a Practice That's Ripe for Reform," *Washington Post*, February 11, 1997, A19.

79. John T. Bennett, "Fewer Reports to Congress? DoD Move Could Backfire, Experts Warn," *Federal Times*, October 18, 2010, 11.

80. Ibid.

81. Michael W. Kirst, *Government Without Passing Laws* (Chapel Hill: University of North Carolina Press, 1969).

82. Joseph A. Davis, "War Declared Over Report-Language Issue," *Congressional Quarterly Weekly Report*, June 25, 1988, 1752–1753; David Rapp, "OMB's Miller Backs Away From Report-Language Battle," *Congressional Quarterly Weekly Report*, July 9, 1988, 1928.

83. Sen. Chuck Grassley, "The Federal Government Needs an IG in Chief," *Politico*, July 22, 2009, 30. Also see Charles S. Clark, "Into the Limelight," *Government Executive*, March 2011, 17–24. There are instances when IGs fail to do their job. According to one account, the IG at the Department of Veterans Affairs "did not sound the alarm that a 'systemic' nationwide fraud was being perpetrated against veterans seeking medical care until [2014], despite finding the schemes at multiple facilities since 2005." See Mark Flatten, "Inspector General Missed Warning Signs for a Decade," *Washington Examiner*, October 6, 2014, 30; and Peter H. Schuck, "The VA's Problem? Congress," *Washington Post*, May 30, 2014, A15.

84. Heather Kuldell, "The Pentagon Doesn't Know All the Software on Its Networks—And That's a Problem," *DefenseOne*, December 20, 2018, https://www.defenseone.com/technology/2018/12/pentagon-doesnt-know-all-software-its-networksand-s-problem/153669.

85. Frank Konkel, "Agencies Increase FITARA Scores," Nextgov, December 11, 2018, https://www.nextgov.com/cio-briefing/2018/12/agencies-increase-fitara-scores/153439/.

86. Jared Allen, "'Personal Pain' Is Teed Up for Head of HUD," *The Hill*, July 30, 2010, 8.

87. Greta Wodele, "DHS Facing Appropriators' Wrath for Missing Deadlines," *National Journal's CongressDaily PM*, February 17, 2005, 2.

88. Slade Gorton and Larry Craig, "Congress's Call to Accounting," *Washington Post*, July 27, 1998, A23.

89. Jason A. MacDonald, "Limitation Riders and Congressional Influence Over Bureaucratic Policy Decisions," *American Political Science Review* (November 2010): 781. Also see Jessica Tollestrup, "The Appropriations Process and Limitation Amendments: A Case Study of Party Politics on the House Floor," in *Party and Procedure in the United States Congress*, ed. Jacob Strauss (Lanham, MD: Rowman and Littlefield, 2012), 61–99.

90. *Congressional Record*, 95th Cong., 1st sess., April 30, 1975, E2080.

91. Alan Baron and Michael Gerhardt, "Porteous Impeachment: A First," *National Law Journal*, January 17, 2011, 34.

92. See Joel D. Aberbach, *Keeping a Watchful Eye: The Politics of Congressional Oversight* (Washington, DC: Brookings, 1990); and James Q. Wilson, *Bureaucracy: What Governmental Agencies Do and Why They Do It* (New York: Basic Books, 1991).

93. Richard Cohen, "King of Oversight," *Government Executive*, September 1988, 17.

94. David Nather, "Congress as Watchdog: Asleep on the Job?" *CQ Weekly,* May 22, 2004, 1190.

95. Greg Miller and Karoun Demirjian, "Chairman and Partisan: The Dual Roles of Devin Nunes Raise Questions About House Investigation," *Washington Post,* March 26, 2017, http://wapo.st/2nUNvJZ?tid=ss_tw.

96. Lesley Clark, "'The Time for Accountability Has Arrived as Democrats Put White House Under Microscope," *McClatchy News,* January 1, 2019, https://www .mcclatchydc.com/news/politics-government/congress/article223252835.html.

97. Ibid.

98. Joel D. Aberbach, "The Congressional Committee Intelligence System: Information, Oversight, and Change," *Congress and the Presidency* 14 (Spring 1987): 51–76; Mathew McCubbins and Thomas Schwartz, "Congressional Oversight Overlooked: Police Patrol Versus Fire Alarm," *American Journal of Political Science* (February 1984): 165–177.

99. Bill Myers, "'Google Your Government' Database Bill Signed Into Law," *Examiner,* September 29, 2006, 17.

100. Jennifer Martinez, "GOP to Public: We Want to Know What You'd Cut," *Politico,* January 20, 2011, 6.

101. Lyndsey Layton, "'Citizen Regulators' Take Toy Safety Testing Into Their Own Hands," *Washington Post,* December 26, 2010, A3.

102. Louis Fisher, "Micromanagement by Congress: Reality and Mythology," paper presented at a conference sponsored by the American Enterprise Institute, Washington, DC, April 8–9, 1988, 8. See also David S. Broder and Stephen Barr, "Hill's Micromanagement of Cabinet Blurs Separation of Powers," *Washington Post,* July 25, 1993, A1.

CHAPTER 12

1. See Dexter Perkins and Glyndon Van Deusen, *The United States of America: A History,* vol. 2 (New York: Macmillan, 1962), 560–566.

2. See, for example, Dylan Mathews, "Court-Packing, Democrats' Nuclear Option for the Supreme Court, Explained," https://www.vox.com/2018/7/2/17513520/court-packing-explained-fdr-roosevelt-new-deal-democrats-supreme-court.

3. Alexander Bickel, *The Least Dangerous Branch* (Indianapolis, IN: Bobbs-Merrill, 1962), 1.

4. Alexis de Tocqueville, *Democracy in America* (New York: American Library, 1956), 72.

5. 567 U.S. ___ (2012).

6. 759 F. 3rd 358 (2014).

7. *King v. Burwell,* 576 U.S. ___, (2015).

8. *Marbury v. Madison,* 5 U.S. (1 Cranch) 137 (1803).

9. Charles Gardner Geyh, *When Courts and Congress Collide: The Struggle for Control of America's Judicial System* (Ann Arbor: University of Michigan Press, 2006), 229.

10. *District of Columbia v. Heller,* 554 U.S. 570 (2008).

11. See, for example, Robert Schlesinger, "Sotomayor Hearings Remind Us the Republicans Can Be Judicial Activists, Too," *U.S. News and World Report,* July 22, 2009, www.usnews.com.

12. *Kelo v. City of New London,* 545 U.S. 469 (2005). See, for example, an editorial in the July 11, 2005, *New Republic* praising the *Kelo* decision as one that "defenders of judicial constraint, particularly liberals, should applaud" (p. 7).

13. For example, Sen. John McCain singled out *Kelo* as an example of judicial activism in a speech at Wake Forest University on May 6, 2008. Sen. Jeff Sessions made the same point in a *Washington Post* op-ed on May 7, 2010, A25.

14. Sandra Day O'Connor, "The Threat to Judicial Independence," *Wall Street Journal,* September 27, 2006, A18.

15. *National Federation of Independent Business v. Sebelius,* 567 U.S. ___ (2012).

16. 550 U.S. 618 (2007)

17. See, for example, the House debate on the Lilly Ledbetter case, *Congressional Record,* 111th Cong., 1st sess., January 9, 2009, H113–H138.

18. See Robert A. Katzmann, ed., *Judges and Legislators* (Washington, DC: Brookings, 1988); and Robert A. Katzmann, *Courts and Congress* (Washington, DC: Brookings, 1997).

19. *New York Times,* May 12, 1983, B8.

20. See, for example, Antonin Scalia, *A Matter of Interpretation* (Princeton, NJ: Princeton University Press, 1997).

21. Jonathan Kaplan, "High Court to Congress," *The Hill,* February 5, 2003, 21.

22. 759 F. 3rd 358 (2014).

23. *King v. Burwell,* 576 U.S. ___, ___ (2015) (Scalia, J., dissenting).

24. Stanley I. Kutler, *Judicial Power and Reconstruction Politics* (Chicago: University of Chicago Press, 1968).

25. Howard Gillman, "How Political Parties Can Use the Courts to Advance Their Agendas: Federal Courts in the United States, 1875–1891," *American Political Science Review* 96 (September 2002): 511–524.

26. Quoted in Stephen Dinan, "DeLay Threatens to Curb Courts' Jurisdiction," *Washington Times,* March 6, 2003, A4.

27. For an account of the congressional politics of court-curbing, see Alyx Mark and Michael A. Zilis, "Restraining the Court: Assessing Accounts of Congressional Attempts to Limit Supreme Court Authority," *Legislative Studies Quarterly* 43 no. 1 (2018): 141–169.

28. Tom S. Clark, "The Separation of Powers, Court Curbing, and Judicial Legitimacy," *American Journal of Political Science* 53 (October 2009): 971–989.

29. Joan Biskupic and Elder Witt, *Guide to the U.S. Supreme Court,* 3rd ed., vol. 2 (Washington, DC: CQ Press, 1997), 720.

30. William H. Rehnquist, *Grand Inquests: The Historic Impeachment of Justice Samuel Chase and President Andrew Johnson* (New York: William Morrow, 1992), 132.

31. Russell R. Wheeler and Robert A. Katzmann, "A Primer on Interbranch Relations," *Georgetown Law Journal* (April 2007): 1172.

32. Rehnquist, *Grand Inquests,* 114.

33. "History of the Federal Judiciary: Impeachments of Federal Judges," Federal Judicial Center, www.fjc.gov/history/home.nsf/page/judges_impeachments.html.

34. Biskupic and Witt, *Guide to the U.S. Supreme Court*, 717.

35. Ibid., 718.

36. Carol Leonning, "New Rules for Judges Are Weaker, Critics Say," *Washington Post,* December 17, 2004, A31; David Von Drehle, "Scalia Rejects Pleas for Recusal in Cheney Case," *Washington Post,* February 12, 2004, A35; Eileen Sullivan, "Courts Order Review of Judges' Security," *Federal Times,* March 21, 2005, 12.

37. Tony Mauro, "Kennedy Talks Tough on Salaries, Cameras," *Legal Times,* February 19, 2007, 14.

38. Nathan Koppel, "Kagan Says 'Yes' to Cameras in the Courtroom," Law Blog, *Wall Street Journal,* June 29, 2010, http://blogs.wsj.com/law/2010/06/29/kagan-says-yes-to-cameras-in-the-courtroom.

39. Tony Mauro, "Unlike Other Nominees, Kavanaugh Hesitates About Cameras in Supreme Court," *National Law Journal,* September 6, 2018, https://www.law.com/nationallawjournal/2018/09/06/unlike-other-nominees-kavanaugh-hesitates-about-cameras-in-supreme-court/?slreturn=20181107082613.

40. Seth Stern, "A Career as Federal Judge Isn't What It Used to Be," *Christian Science Monitor,* January 22, 2002, 1.

41. Mark Sherman, "Big Money Depletes Judges' Ranks," *Washington Times,* December 30, 2008, B3. Also see Adam Liptak, "The State of Courts, and a Plea for a Raise," *New York Times,* January 1, 2009, A13. The current (and past) salary figures are available at http://www.uscourts.gov/judges-judgeships/judicial-compensation.

42. Linda Greenhouse, "Chief Justice Advocates Higher Pay for Judiciary," A14. Also see editorial, "There Oughta Be a Law," *USA Today,* January 9, 2007, 12A.

43. See Paul Bland, "Justice Kennedy: Are Judges Abandoning the Bench?" Consumer Law and Policy Blog, pubcit.typepad.com/clpblog/2007/02/justice_kennedy.html.

44. *Chisholm v. Georgia,* 2 U.S. 419 (1793).

45. *Dred Scott v. Sandford,* 60 U.S. 393 (1857).

46. See Louis Fisher, *American Constitutional Law,* 6th ed. (Durham, NC: Carolina Academic Press, 2005), 1072.

47. Jennifer Dlouhy, "Congress Reluctant to Change Constitution," *CQ Today,* February 11, 2003, 9.

48. *Texas v. Johnson* 491 U.S. 397 (1989)

49. Norman Ornstein, "To Break the Stalemate, Give Judges Less Than Life," *Washington Post,* November 28, 2004, B3.

50. Tony Mauro, "Profs Pitch Plan for Limits on Supreme Court Service," *Legal Times,* January 3, 2005, 1. Also see Robert Barnes, "Legal Experts Propose Limiting Justices' Powers, Terms," *Washington Post,* February 23, 2009, A15.

51. Burgess Everett and Glenn Thrush, "McConnell Throws Down the Gauntlet: No Scalia Replacement Under Obama," *Politico,* February 13, 2016, http://www.politico.com/story/2016/02/mitch-mcconnell-antonin-scalia-supreme-court-nomination-219 248#ixzz47snW8YnJ.

52. Adam Liptak, "Trump's Supreme Court List: Ivy League? Out. Heartland? In." *New York Times,* November 15, 2016, A21, http://www.nytimes.com/2016/11/15/us/politics/trump-supreme-court-justices.html?_r=0.

53. Terri L. Peretti, "Where Have All the Politicians Gone? Recruiting for the Modern Supreme Court," *Judicature* (November–December 2007): 120. Also see Paul A. Sracic, "Politician on Court Isn't a Bad Thing," *USA Today,* March 30, 2005, 13A.

54. Jeff Zeleny, "A Premium on Secrecy in Vetting of Court Pick," *New York Times,* May 13, 2009.

55. Michael D. Shear, "Supreme Court Justice Anthony Kennedy Will retire," *New York Times,* June 27, 2018, https://www.nytimes.com/2018/06/27/us/politics/anthony-kennedy-retire-supreme-court.html.

56. Emma Brown, "California Professor, Writer of Confidential Brett Kavanaugh Letter, Speaks Out About Her Allegation of Sexual Assault," *Washington Post,* September 16, 2018, https://www.washingtonpost.com/investigations/california-professor-writer-of-confidential-brett-kavanaugh-letter-speaks-out-about-her-allegation-of-sexual-assault/2018/09/16/46982194-b846-11e8-9-4eb-3bd52dfe917b_story.html?noredirect=on&utm_term=.f0485928e81e.

57. Erica Werner, "Some GOP Senators Concede Ford's Credibility, but Point to Lack of Corroboration," *Washington Post,* September 27, 2018, https://www.washingtonpost.com/business/economy/some-gop-senators-concede-fords-credibility-but-point-to-lack-of-corroboration/2018/09/27/6d97c484-c287-11e8-b338-a3289f6cb742_story.html?utm_term=.b18779d908f6.

58. Sheryl Gay Stolberg and Nicholas Fandos, "Brett Kavanaugh and Christine Blasey Ford Duel With Tears and Fury," *New York Times,* Sept. 27, 2018, https://www.nytimes.com/2018/09/27/us/politics/brett-kavanaugh-confirmation-hearings.html.

59. Ralph Neas, "United States Needs More Discussion of Judicial Philosophy," *Roll Call,* May 9, 2002, 10.

60. Seth Stern, "Senate Shows Supreme Decline in Deference," *CQ Weekly,* July 12, 2010, 1635.

61. Quoted in ibid.

62. Charles E. Schumer, "Judging by Ideology," *New York Times,* June 26, 2001.

63. Harold W. Chase, *Federal Judges: The Appointing Process* (Minneapolis: University of Minnesota, 1972.), 7.

64. Sarah A. Binder and Forrest Maltzman, "The Limits of Senatorial Courtesy," *Legislative Studies Quarterly,* 29 no. 1 (2004): 5–22.

65. Linda Greenhouse, "Case of the Dwindling Docket Mystifies the Supreme Court," *New York Times,* December 7, 2006, A1.

66. Ibid.

67. Elizabeth Palmer, "Appellate Courts at Center of Fight for Control of Judiciary," *CQ Weekly,* February 23, 2002, 534.

68. For an account of this institutional change, see Gregory J. Wawro and Eric Schickler, "Reid's Rules: Filibusters, the Nuclear Option, and Path Dependence in the US Senate," *Legislative Studies Quarterly* 43, no. 4 (2018): 619–647.

69. Orrin Hatch, "Don't Change the Filibuster Again," *Politico,* December 8, 2014, http://www.politico.com/magazine/story/2014/12/orrin-hatch-filibuster-113388.html#.VI3ghSda9FU.

70. Niels Lesniewski, "How the Nuclear Option Changed the Judiciary," *Roll Call,* December 19, 2014, http://blogs.rollcall.com/wgdb/nuclear-option-judiciary-nominations.

71. Ibid.

72. Francine Keifer, "One Year Later, the 'Nuclear Option' Has Worked. Is That Good?" *Christian Science Monitor,* December 9, 2014, http://www.csmonitor.com/USA/DC-Decoder/2014/1209/One-year-later-Senate-s-nuclear-option-has-worked.-Is-that-good-video.

73. Data retrieved from the Department of Justice's judicial nominations website, https://www.justice.gov/olp/114th-congress-judicial-nominations-list.

74. Philip Rucker and Robert Barnes, "Trump to Inherit More Than 100 Court Vacancies, Plans to Reshape Judiciary," *Washington Post,* December 26, 2016, A1, https://www.washingtonpost.com/politics/trump-to-inherit-more-than-100-court-vacancies-plans-to-reshape-judiciary/2016/12/25d190dd18-c928-11e6-85b5-76616a33048d_story.html?hpid=hp_hp-top-table-main_trumpjudges805 p%3Ahomepage%2Fstory&utm_term=.ec27e47a97bc.

75. Jason Zengerle, "How the Trump Administration Is Remaking the Courts," *New York Times Magazine,* August 22, 2018.

76. Mitchel A. Sellenberger, The History of the Blue Slip in the Senate Committee on the Judiciary, 1917–Present," http://congressionalresearch.com/RL32013/document.php.

77. Sheldon Goldman, Elliot Slotnick, and Sara Schiavoni, "Obama's Judiciary at Midterm," *Judicature* 94, no. 6 (2011): 267.

78. Quoted in ibid., 268.

79. David Lat, "Good Riddance to 'Blue Slips,'" *New York Times,* May 8, 2018 https://www.nytimes.com/2018/05/09/opinion/senate-judicial-nominees-blue-slips.html (nomination of Ryan Bounds to 9th Circuit).

80. Grassley adhered to the blue slip procedure in the case of nominees for district court judgeships but not for appellate judgeships. In a November 16, 2017, press release, he explained, "I'm less likely to proceed on a district court nominee who does not have two positive blue slips from home-state senators. But circuit courts cover multiple states. There's less reason to defer to the views of a single state's senator for such nominees."

81. Derek Hawkins, "Trump Judicial Nominee Fumbles Basic Questions About Law," *Washington Post,* December 15, 2017, https://www.washingtonpost.com/news/morning-mix/wp/2017/12/15/trump-judicial-nominee-fumbles-basic-questions-about-the-law/?noredirect=on&utm_term=.49be5bc7321f.

82. Zoe Tillman, "A Republican Senator Is Getting in the Way of One of Trump's Biggest Successes," *Buzzfeed News,* November 30, 2017, https://www.buzzfeed-news.com/article/zoetillman/a-republican-senator-is-getting-in-the-way-of-one-of-trumps#.erDokePVZ.

83. Drew Broach, "Kyle Duncan Confirmed in Tight Senate Vote for 5th Circuit Court Judgeship," *New Orleans Times-Picayune,* April 24, 2018, http://www.nola.com/national_politics/2018/04/kyle_duncan_confirmed_senat.html.

84. Karoum Demirjian, "Republican Senator Suggests Trump Is Strong-Arming Judicial Nominees Through Congress," *Washington Post,* November 29, 2017, https://www.washingtonpost.com/powerpost/republican-senator-suggests-trump-is-strong-arming-judicial-nominees-through-congress/2017/11/29/584 2d74c-d51e-11e7-95bf-df7c19270879_story.html?utm_term=.25eda02ada26.

85. Ibid.

86. Li Zhou, "Trump Has Gotten 66 Judges Confirmed This Year. In His Second Year, Obama Had Gotten 49," *Vox*, December 27, 2018, https://www.vox .com/2018/12/27/18136294/trump-mitch-mconnell-republican-judges.

87. *Congressional Record*, S7285, November 16, 2017.

88. Louis Fisher, "Congressional Checks on the Judiciary," in *Congress Confronts the Court*, ed. Colton C. Campbell and John F. Stack Jr. (Lanham, MD: Rowman and Littlefield, 2001), 35.

CHAPTER 13

1. Adam Cancryn, Sarah Karlin-Smith, and Paul Demko, "Deep-Pocketed Health Care Lobbies Line up Against Trump," *Politico*, May 5, 2017.

2. Ibid.

3. Ibid.

4. Jonathan Cohn, "Another Warning Sign for Republicans Trying to Repeal Obamacare," *The Huffington Post*, February 3, 2017, http://www.huffingtonpost .com/entry/aarp-obamacare-affordable-care-act_us_589280eee4b070cf8b80 ab63?0yets3im5vlhaor.

5. Jessie Hellman, "AARP Launches Ad Campaign Urging Republicans to 'Protect' Medicare," *The Hill*, January 30, 2017, http://thehill.com/policy/ healthcare/316799-aarp-launches-ad-campaign-urging-republicans-to-pro tect-medicare.

6. Cohn, "Another Warning Sign."

7. See John R. Hibbing and Elizabeth Theiss-Morse, *Congress as Public Enemy: Public Attitudes Toward American Political Institutions* (New York: Cambridge University Press, 1995).

8. Brian Naylor, "Medical, Hospital Groups Oppose GOP Health Care Plan," NPR, March 9, 2017, http://www.npr.org/2017/03/09/519450642/medical-hospital-groups- oppose-gop-health-care-plan.

9. Joel Jankowsky and Thomas Goldstein, "In Defense of Lobbying," *Wall Street Journal*, September 4, 2009, A15.

10. Bill Swindell, "Industry's Increased D.C. Presence Reflects New Reality," *National Journal's CongressDaily AM*, July 28, 2010, 1, 14. *CongressDaily* is pub- lished by *National Journal*, a Washington-based journal.

11. Ibid., 14.

12. Baa Vaida, "Brisk Business for K Street in 2010," *National Journal*, July 24, 2010, 44. Many lobbying groups have their offices on K Street in the District of Columbia.

13. Lobbying Database, Center for Responsive Politics, https://www.opensecrets .org/lobby. See also Lee Drutman, *The Business of America Is Lobbying: How Corporations Became Politicized and Politics Became More Corporate* (New York: Oxford University Press, 2015).

14. Alexander Becker, "Spending on Lobbying Is Actually Falling. Or Is It?" Post Politics, *Washington Post* weblog, August 19, 2014, http://www.washingtonpost.com/blogs/ post-politics/wp/2014/08/19/spending-on-lobbying-is-actually-falling-or-is-it.

15. Alexis de Tocqueville, *Democracy in America,* ed. Phillips Bradley (New York: Knopf, 1951), 119.

16. Janny Scott, "Medicine's Big Dose of Politics," *Los Angeles Times,* September 25, 1991, A15.

17. Robert Putnam, "The Strange Disappearance of Civic America," *American Prospect* (Winter 1996): 35.

18. Quoted in Suzi Parker, "Civic Clubs: Elks, Lions May Go Way of the Dodo," *Christian Science Monitor,* August 24, 1998, 1.

19. Theda Skocpol, *Diminished Democracy: From Membership to Management in American Civic Life* (Norman: University of Oklahoma Press, 2003).

20. Everett Carll Ladd, "The American Way—Civic Engagement—Thrives," *Christian Science Monitor,* March 1, 1999, 9.

21. See, for example, "CIRCLE Poll: So Much for Slacktivism, As Youth Translate Online Engagement to Offline Political Action," Center for Information and Research on Civic Learning and Engagement, Tufts University, October 15, 2018, https://civicyouth.org/circle-poll-so-much-for-slacktivism-as-youth-translate-online-engagement-to-offline-political-action/.

22. Mancur Olson Jr., *The Logic of Collective Action: Public Goods and the Theory of Groups* (Cambridge, MA: Harvard University Press, 1965).

23. Kay L. Schlozman and John T. Tierney, *Organized Interests and American Democracy* (New York: Harper and Row, 1986).

24. E. E. Schattschneider, *The Semi-Sovereign People* (New York: Holt, Rinehart and Winston, 1960), 35.

25. Melinda Burns, "K Street and the Status Quo," *Miller-McCune,* September–October 2010, 65. Also see Frank R. Baumgartner et al., *Lobbying and Policy Change: Who Wins, Who Loses, and Why* (Chicago: University of Chicago Press, 2009).

26. Kristina C. Miler, "The View From the Hill: Legislative Perceptions of the District," *Legislative Studies Quarterly* 32 (November 2007): 597–628.

27. Sidney Verba, Kay Lehman Schlozman, and Henry Brady, "The Big Tilt: Participatory Inequality in America," *American Prospect* (May/June 1997): 78.

28. Greg Sargent, "Democrats' Sequester Conundrum," *Washington Post,* April 30, 2013, A13. Also see Darren Samuelsohn, "Sequester Exemptions as Earmarks," *Politico,* April 23, 2013, 1.

29. Elise D. Garcia, "Money in Politics," *Common Cause,* February 1981, 11.

30. Jeffrey H. Birnbaum, "Lobbyists: Why the Bad Rap?" *American Enterprise,* November/December 1992, 74. Also see Jeffrey H. Birnbaum, *The Lobbyists* (New York: Times Books, 1992).

31. David Karol, "Party Activists, Interest Groups, and Polarization in American Politics," *American Gridlock: The Sources, Character, and Impact of Political Polarization,* ed. James Thurber and Antoine Yoshinaka (New York: Cambridge University Press, 2015).

32. "NRA Threats Fail to Sway Senators on Sotomayor," *Washington Times,* August 2, 2009, http://www.washingtontimes.com/news/2009/aug/2/nra-threats-fail-to-sway-senators-on-sotomayor/?page=all.

33. Tory Newmyer, "Majority Formalizes K St. Ties," *Roll Call,* February 15, 2007, 23.

34. Alexander Bolton, "Dems Enlist Help to Push Their Agenda," *The Hill*, February 14, 2007, 1.

35. Emily Pierce, "GOP Taps Thune to Get Cozy with K St.," *Roll Call*, January 22, 2009.

36. Quoted in Hedrick Smith, *The Power Game* (New York: Random House, 1988), 232.

37. Ronald J. Hrebenar and Ruth K. Scott, *Interest Group Politics in America* (Englewood Cliffs, NJ: Prentice Hall, 1982), 63.

38. Quoted in Alan K. Ota, "Democratic Foot in Revolving Door," *CQ Weekly*, June 25, 2007, 1900.

39. Mark Preston, "Ex-GOP Senators Get Special Access," *Roll Call*, April 3, 2003, 1, 24.

40. Russell Berman, "An Exodus From Congress Tests the Allure of Lobbying," *The Atlantic*, May 1, 2018, https://www.theatlantic.com/politics/archive/2018/05/lobbying-the-job-of-choice-for-retired-members-of-congress/558851/.

41. Chris Frates, "Hill Experience Gives Lobbyists a Leg Up," *Politico*, May 17, 2007.

42. Russell Berman, "An Exodus From Congress."

43. Fredreka Schouten, "Ex-Lawmakers Go to Lobbying-Related Jobs," *USA Today*, March 25, 2013, http://www.usatoday.com/story/news/politics/2013/03/25/former-lawmakers-lobbying-jobs/2011325.

44. R. Jeffrey Smith and Dan Eggen, "More Former Lobbyists Flocking to Jobs on Hill," *Washington Post*, March 18, 2011, A1.

45. Anna Palmer, "Help Wanted: Lobbyists Who Can Raise Cash," *Politico*, May 21, 2012, 15.

46. Quoted in Sam Walker, "Who's In and Who's Out Among Capitol Lobbyists," *Christian Science Monitor*, November 8, 1995, 3.

47. Quoted in *National Journal's CongressDaily PM*, March 15, 2002, 8.

48. Steven Brill, "On Sale: Your Government," *Time*, July 12, 2010, 32.

49. Bertram J. Levine, *The Art of Lobbying: Building Trust and Selling Policy* (Washington, DC: CQ Press, 2008).

50. John Cochran and Martin Kady II, "The New Laws of the Lobby," *CQ Weekly*, February 26, 2007, 594.

51. Eliza Newlin Carney and Bara Vaida, "Shifting Ground," *National Journal*, March 31, 2007, 27.

52. Quoted in Cochran and Kady, "New Laws of the Lobby," 594.

53. Joseph Curl, "Big Money Buys Seats at Lawmakers' Dinner Tables," *Washington Times*, November 3, 2009, A1.

54. David Kirkpatrick, "Congress Finds Ways of Avoiding Lobbyist Limit," *New York Times*, February 11, 2007, 1.

55. Ibid.

56. John Breaux, "Effective Coalitions for Coalitions," *The Hill*, March 21, 2007, 18.

57. Harper Neidig, "Tech Forms New Group to Lobby for 'Dreamers': Report," *The Hill*, October 20, 2017, https://thehill.com/policy/technology/356417-report-tech-to-form-new-coalition-to-lobby-for-dreamers.

58. Dan Eggen, "Investments Can Yield More on K Street, Study Indicates," *Washington Post*, April 12, 2009, A8.

59. Ernest Wittenberg, "How Lobbying Helps Make Democracy Work," *Vital Speeches of the Day*, November 1, 1982, 47.

60. Ellyn Ferguson, "An Unexpected Alliance Fights Ethanol Expansion," *CQ Today*, July 26, 2010, 7. Also see Anna Palmer, "Lobbying Coalition Calls for Congressional Hearing on Ethanol," *Roll Call*, August 25, 2010, online edition.

61. Martin Kady II, "Keeping Grass-Roots Lobbying Under Wraps," *CQ Weekly*, March 26, 2007, 877.

62. Rosalind S. Helderman, "Uber's Aggressive Tactics Push Change," *Washington Post*, December 14, 2014, A1.

63. Edward T. Walker, "Grass-Roots Mobilization, by Corporate America," *New York Times*, August 10, 2012, http://www.nytimes.com/2012/08/11/opinion/grass roots-mobilization-by-corporate-america.html?_r=0.

64. John T. Tierney and Kay Lehman Schlozman, "Congress and Organized Interests," in *Congressional Politics*, ed. Christopher J. Deering (Chicago: Dorsey, 1989), 212.

65. Kady, "Keeping Grass-Roots Lobbying Under Wraps," 877.

66. Alison Mitchell, "A New Form of Lobbying Puts Public Face on Private Interest," *New York Times*, September 30, 1998, A14. Also see Ken Kollman, *Outside Lobbying: Public Opinion and Interest Group Strategies* (Princeton, NJ: Princeton University Press, 1998).

67. David Gelles, "Lobbying Scuttles U.S. Piracy Laws," *Financial Times*, January 21–22, 2012, 1.

68. Bradford Fitch and Kathy Goldschmidt, "#SocialCongress2015," Congressional Management Foundation Report, 2015, http://www.congressfoundation.org/ social-congress-2015-download.

69. Matea Gold, Joseph Tanfani, and Lisa Mascaro, "NRA Clout Rooted More in Its Tactics Than Its Election Spending," *Los Angeles Times*, July 29, 2012, online edition.

70. Jeffrey Birnbaum, "The Forces That Set the Agenda," *Washington Post*, April 24, 2005, B5.

71. Tom Hamburger, "U.S. Chamber of Commerce Grows Into a Political Force," *Los Angeles Times*, March 8, 2010, online edition.

72. Paul S. Herrnson, "Party Organizations, Party-Connected Committees, Party Allies, and the Financing of Federal Elections," *Journal of Politics* (November 2009).

73. Brody Mullins, "Growing Role for Lobbyists: Raising Funds for Lawmakers," *Wall Street Journal*, January 27, 2006, A1.

74. Joshua L. Kalla and David E. Broockman, "Campaign Contributions Facilitate Access to Congressional Officials: A Randomized Field Experiment," *American Journal of Political Science* 60 (2015): 545–558.

75. Fredreka Schouten, "Polled PAC Donations Add $33M Punch to Races," *USA Today*, August 17, 2010, 5A.

76. Manu Raju, "Members Get Bundles of Lobbyist Cash," *Politico*, February 16, 2010, 1.

77. Tom McGinty and Brody Mullins, "Political Spending by Unions Far Exceeds Direct Donations," *Wall Street Journal*, July 10, 2012, A1, A7.

78. Data from Center for Responsive Politics, https://www.opensecrets.org/.

79. John Brinkley, "Members of Congress Perform Under Judging Eyes of Lobbyists," *Washington Times*, March 16, 1994, A16. Also see John Cochran, "Interest Groups Make Sure Lawmakers Know the 'Score,'" *CQ Weekly*, April 19, 2003, 924–929.

80. See Robert L. Reynolds, "A Pledge to End All Pledges," *Wall Street Journal*, December 24, 2012, A13; and Grover Norquist, "The Case for the Tax Pledge: Political Accountability," *USA Today*, December 13, 2012, 8A.

81. Bill Whalen, "Rating Lawmakers' Politics by Looking Into Their Eyes," *Insight*, October 20, 1986, 21.

82. "Environment," *National Journal's CongressDaily PM*, February 21, 2006, 10.

83. Eliza Newlin Carney, "Keeping Score," *CQ Weekly*, January 21, 2013, 118–119.

84. Hibbing and Theiss-Morse, *Congress as Public Enemy*, 63–65.

85. Frank R. Baumgartner and Beth L. Leech, *Basic Interests: The Importance of Groups in Politics and in Political Science* (Princeton, NJ: Princeton University Press, 1998), 13.

86. Burns, "K Street and the Status Quo," 64; and Baumgartner et al., *Lobbying and Policy Change*.

87. Interview with Prof. Marie Elizabeth Hojnacki, *CQ Weekly*, September 6, 2010, 2005.

88. Janet M. Gretzke, "PACs and the Congressional Supermarket: The Currency Is Complex," *American Journal of Political Science* 33 (1989): 1–24; Lawrence S. Rothenberg, *Linking Citizens to Government: Interest Group Politics at Common Cause* (New York: Cambridge University Press, 1992); John R. Wright, "Contributions, Lobbying, and Committee Voting in the U.S. House of Representatives," *American Political Science Review* 84 (1990): 417–438.

89. Gary J. Andres, *Lobbying Reconsidered* (New York: Pearson Longman, 2009), 159. Worth noting is that the House Office of Congressional Ethics has investigated the "propriety of [lawmakers] using a vote as a fundraising opportunity by hosting events in close proximity to a major vote." See Edward Epstein, "Outside Panel in for Insider Criticism," *CQ Weekly*, August 9, 2010, 1911.

90. See the labor union profile at the Center for Responsive Politics, www.opensecrets.org. The center is a nonprofit research organization that tracks the role of money in politics.

91. James G. Gimpel, Frances E. Lee, and Michael Parrott, "Business Interests and the Party Coalitions: Industry Sector Contributions to U.S. Congressional Candidates," *American Politics Research* 42 (2014): 1034–1076; and Karol, "Party Activists, Interest Groups, and Polarization."

92. Richard L. Hall and Frank W. Wayman, "Buying Time: Moneyed Interests and the Mobilization of Bias in Congressional Committees," *American Political Science Review* 84 (September 1990): 800. See also their review of the literature on patterns in campaign contributions on pages 799–800.

93. Quoted in Claudia Dreifus, "And Then There Was Frank," *New York Times Magazine*, February 4, 1996, 25.

94. Don Van Natta Jr., "$250,000 Buys Donors 'Best Access to Congress,'" *New York Times*, January 27, 1997, A1.

95. See Richard A. Smith, "Advocacy, Interpretation, and Influence in the U.S. Congress," *American Political Science Review* 78 (1984): 44–63; and Hall and Wayman, "Buying Time." Also see Eric Lipton and Kevin Sack, "Fiscal Footnote: Big Senate Gift to Drug Maker," *New York Times*, January 20, 2013, A1.

96. Marie Hojnacki and David C. Kimball, "Organized Interests and the Decision of Whom to Lobby in Congress," *American Political Science Review* (December 1998): 775–790.

97. Susan Webb Hammond, *Congressional Caucuses in National Policymaking* (Baltimore: Johns Hopkins University Press, 2001).

98. Paul Singer, "The Tax-Payer-Funded Caucus Is Still Thriving," *Roll Call,* May 18, 2010, 4; Fredreka Schouten, "Lobbyists Get Power Access Via Caucuses," *USA Today,* July 24–26, 2009, 1A.

99. Richard L. Hall and Alan V. Deardorff, "Lobbying as Legislative Subsidy," *American Political Science Review* (February 2006): 69–84.

100. *Wall Street Journal,* October 5, 1987, 54.

101. Mary Lynn Jones, "Survey Says Lobbyists Find Information Rules the Hill," *The Hill,* November 18, 1998, 8.

102. Kirk Victor, "New Kids on the Block," *National Journal,* October 31, 1987, 2727.

103. Burns, "K Street and the Status Quo," 66. As an example, see Patrice Hill, "Facts Spin on Small-Business Tax," *Washington Times,* August 31, 2010, A1.

104. E. Scott Adler and John S. Lapinski, "Demand-Side Theory and Congressional Committee Composition: A Constituency Characteristics Approach," *American Journal of Political Science* 41 (1997): 895–918; and E. Scott Adler, "Constituency Characteristics and the 'Guardian' Model of Appropriations Subcommittees, 1959–1998," *American Journal of Political Science* 44 (2000): 104–114.

105. *Congressional Record,* December 15, 2011, S8629.

106. *Congressional Record,* December 15, 2011, S8629. See also Rebecca U. Thorpe, *The American Warfare State: The Domestic Politics of Military Spending* (Chicago: University of Chicago Press, 2014).

107. The "Guide to the Lobbying Disclosure Act" can be found on the website of the clerk of the U.S. House of Representatives: http://clerk.house.gov.

108. William Luneburg and Thomas Susman, *The Lobbying Manual,* 3rd ed. (Washington, DC: American Bar Association, 2005), 7.

109. U.S. Congress, *Organization of the Congress,* H. Rept. 1675, 79th Cong., 2nd sess., 1946, 26.

110. *United States v. Harriss,* 347 U.S. 612 (1954).

111. Francesca Contiguaglia, "GAO Finds That Lobbyist Registration Has Soared," *Roll Call,* May 14, 1998, 14.

112. Alec Goodwin and Emma Baccellieri, "Number of Registered Lobbyists Plunges as Spending Declines Yet Again," Center for Responsive Politics, August 9, 2016, https://www.opensecrets.org/news/2016/08/number-of-registered-lobbyists-plunges-as-spending-declines-yet-again.

113. Data from Center for Responsive Politics, October 27, 2014, https://www.opensecrets.org/lobby.

114. Lee Fang, "Where Have All the Lobbyists Gone?" *The Nation,* February 19, 2014, http://www.thenation.com/article/178460/shadow-lobbying-complex#.

115. Alex Knott, *Special Report: Industry of Influence Nets Almost $13 Billion* (Washington, DC: Center for Public Integrity, 2005), 1–4.

116. Lee H. Hamilton, "Lobbying Murkiness Undermines Our Trust in Congress," Center on Congress at Indiana University, April 11, 2005, 2, http://congress.indiana.edu.

117. Eric Garcia, "A History of 'Draining the Swamp,'" *Roll Call,* October 18, 2016, https://www.rollcall.com/news/politics/history-of-draining-the-swamp.

118. See John D. McKinnon and Brody Mullins, "Lawmakers Face Ethics Probe," *Wall Street Journal,* September 1, 2010, A4.

119. Kyle Cheney and John Bresnahan, "What Is the Office of Congressional Ethics and Why Does It Matter? *Politico,* January 3, 2017, http://www.politico.com/story/2017/01/office-of-congressional-ethics-what-does-it-do-233128.

120. Kate Ackley, "Unlobbyists Give Real Lobbyists a Bad Name," *Roll Call,* February 13, 2012, 1.

121. Chris Frates, "When a Lobbyist Isn't a Lobbyist," *Politico,* July 26, 2010, 1, 12.

122. Janie Lorber and Kate Ackley, "Tracking Lobbyists for Other Countries," *Roll Call,* October 2, 2012, 3. Also see Arnd Jurgensen and Renan Levine, "Foreign Lobbying," in *Guide to Interest Groups and Lobbying in the United States,* ed. Burdett Loomis (Washington, DC: CQ Press, 2012), 321–332.

123. Theodoric Meyer, Lorraine Woellert, and Marianne Levine, "Diplomatic Crisis Spotlights Saudi Arabia's Spending in Washington," *Politico,* October 16, 2018, https://www.politico.com/story/2018/10/16/saudi-arabia-spending-washington-909882.

124. Kevin Bogardus, "First DC Firm to Sign With Libyan Rebels Is Rewarded With Contract," *The Hill,* April 4, 2012, 20.

125. Jill Cowan and Tom Benning, "Toyota Responds to Trump Tariffs," *Dallas Morning News,* June 29, 2018, https://www.dallasnews.com/business/toyota/2018/06/28/toyota-says-tariffs-increase-cost-every-vehicle-sold-united-states-manufacturing-trump.

126. Edgar Lane, *Lobbying and the Law* (Berkeley: University of California Press, 1964), 18.

127. Brill, "On Sale: Your Government," 32.

CHAPTER 14

1. Caitlin Emma and Jennifer Scholtes, "Trump's Budget Sets Up Another Shutdown Battle: President's Plan Seeks Deep Cuts to Agencies Like HHS, EPA and the State Department," *Politico,* March 12, 2019, 12.

2. Jeff Dufour, "Wednesday Q&A," *National Journal Daily,* March 13, 2019, 6.

3. See, for example, Kellie Mejdrich, "Nondefense Programs Cut 9 Percent on Average in Trump Budget," *CQ News,* March 11, 2019, online edition; David Lerman, "Spending Cuts, Growth Outpace Tax Cuts, Military Increases," *CQ News,* March 11, 2019, online edition; and Paul M. Krawzak and David Lerman, "Battle of the Bulge," April 8, 2019, entire issue.

4. Jim Tankersley and Michael Tackett, "Record Budget Is Trump's Shot Across the Bow," *New York Times,* March 12, 2019, A1.

5. David Sherfinski, "Trump's Federal Budget Plan Arriving Without Much Fanfare," *The Washington Times,* March 11, 2019, A4.

6. Ibid.

7. Randall B. Ripley and Grace A. Franklin, *Congress, the Bureaucracy, and Public Policy,* 5th ed. (Pacific Grove, CA: Brooks/Cole, 1991).

8. John W. Kingdon, *Agendas, Alternatives, and Public Policies* (Boston: Little, Brown, 1984), 3.

9. Ibid., 17–19.

10. Ibid., chap. 2.

11. See Justin Gillis, "U.N. Panel Issues Its Starkest Warning Yet on Global Warming," *New York Times*, November 2, 2014, http://www.nytimes.com/2014/11/03/world/europe/global-warming-un-intergovernmental-panel-on-climate-change.html; and William Nordhaus, *The Climate Casino* (New Haven, CT: Yale University Press, 2013).

12. Nelson W. Polsby, "Strengthening Congress in National Policymaking," *Yale Review* (Summer 1970): 481–497.

13. James L. Sundquist, *Politics and Policy: The Eisenhower, Kennedy, and Johnson Years* (Washington, DC: Brookings, 1968).

14. American Enterprise Institute, *The State of the Congress: Tomorrow's Challenges?* (Washington, DC: AEI, 1981), 8.

15. John Bresnahan and Rachael Bade, "Ryan Wounded by Health Care Fiasco," *Politico*, March 25, 2017, http://www.politico.com/story/2017/03/paul-ryan-future-health-care-obamacare-trump-236480.

16. See, for example, Noam N. Levey, "Elections Deliver Robust Validation of Obamacare," *Los Angeles Times*, November 9, 2018, online edition; Jennifer Haberkorn, "GOP Feeling Health Law's Sting," *Los Angeles Times*, January 1, 2019, online edition; and Sarah Jones, "Running on Obamacare," *The New Republic*, November 2018, 4–6.

17. Theodore Lowi, "American Business, Public Policy, Case Studies, and Political Theory," *World Politics* (July 1964): 677–715; Theodore Lowi, "Four Systems of Policy, Politics, and Choice," *Public Administration Review* (July–August 1972): 298–310; Samuel P. Huntington, *The Common Defense* (New York: Columbia University Press, 1961); Ripley and Franklin, *Congress, the Bureaucracy, and Public Policy*.

18. Mary Russell, "'Park-Barrel Bill' Clears House Panel," *Washington Post*, June 22, 1978, A3.

19. George E. Condon Jr., "Bending Congress's Ear(marks)," *National Journal's CongressDaily*, February 11, 2011, 5.

20. Stephen Dinan, "Earmarks End for One Year, but Perk Still Potent on Hill," *Washington Times*, February 10, 2011, A6.

21. *Congressional Record*, 111th Cong., 1st sess., May 6, 2009, H5279.

22. Frank Oliveri, "McKeon Lays Out Rules for Keeping Earmarks Out of Defense Authorization Bill," *CQ Today*, March 28, 2011, 2.

23. Raymond Hernandez, "A House District Liked Its Earmarks, and Then Elected Someone Who Didn't," *New York Times*, February 5, 2011, A16.

24. Ibid.

25. Megan R. Wilson, "Ryan Stops Vote on Bringing Back Earmarks," *The Hill*, November 16, 2016, http://thehill.com/homenews/house/306443-ryan-stops-vote-on-bringing-back-earmarks.

26. Kate Ackley, "Dollar Bills?" *CQ Weekly*, February 11, 2019, 14–19.

27. See Jennifer Shutt, "Earmarks Won't Be Back This Year, at Least in the House," *CQ News*, March 1, 2019, online edition; and Jennifer Shutt, "Senate to Follow House, Keep Earmarks Out of Spending Bills," *CQ News*, March 4, 2019, online edition.

28. Eliza Newlin Carney, "The Earmarks Paradox," *National Journal's CongressDaily*, February 14, 2011, 5.

29. Russell W. Mills, Nicole Kalaf-Hughes, and Jason A. MacDonald, "Agency Policy Preferences, Congressional Letter-Marking and the Allocation of Distributive Policy Benefits," *Journal of Public Policy* 36, no. 4 (2016): 547–571.

30. Ron Nixon, "Earmarks Ban May Loom, but Lawmakers Find Ways to Finance Pet Projects," *New York Times*, December 28, 2010, A11.

31. Condon, "Bending Congress's Ear(marks)," 5.

32. Jonathan Rauch, "The Case for Corruption: Why Washington Needs More Honest Graft," *The Atlantic*, February 19, 2014, http://www.theatlantic.com/magazine/archive/2014/03/the-case-for-corruption/357568.

33. Jesse Eisinger, "The Consumer Financial Protection Bureau's Declaration of Independence," *Pro Publica*, February 15, 2018, online edition.

34. See, for example, Margaret Kriz, "Heavy Breathing," *National Journal*, January 4, 1997, 8–12.

35. Joby Warrick, "White House Taking a Hands-On Role in Writing New Clean Air Standards," *Washington Post*, May 22, 1997, A10.

36. See, for example, Kenneth A. Shepsle, Robert P. Van Houweling, Samuel J. Abrams, and Peter C. Hanson, "The Senate Electoral Cycle and Bicameral Appropriation Politics," *American Journal of Political Science* 53 (2009): 343–359; Jeffrey Lazarus and Amy Steigerwalt, "Different Houses: The Distribution of Earmarks in the U.S. House and Senate," *Legislative Studies Quarterly* 34 (2009): 347–373; and Robert A. Bernstein, Gerald C. Wright Jr., and Michael B. Berkman, "Do U.S. Senators Moderate Strategically?" *American Political Science Review* 82 (1988): 237–245.

37. Donald Lambro, "Steady GOP Rebound Strategy," *Washington Times*, June 7, 2001, A17.

38. Judy Sarasohn, "Money for Lat. 40 N, Long. 73 W," *Congressional Quarterly Weekly Report*, May 12, 1979, 916.

39. See Maggie Severns, "How Congress Finally Killed No Child Left Behind," *Politico*, December 11, 2015, http://www.politico.com/story/2015/12/paul-ryan-congress-no-child-left-behind-216696.

40. "Don't Just Do Something, Sit There," *The Economist*, December 23, 1995–January 5, 1996, 11–12.

41. Barber Conable, "Government Is Working," *Roll Call*, April 19, 1984, 3. Congress has initiated change many times. A classic example is the Thirty-seventh Congress (1861–1863), which drafted "the blueprint for modern America" by enacting measures to finance the Civil War, build the transcontinental railroad, eradicate slavery, promote the land-grant college movement, provide settlers with homestead land, and create the Department of Agriculture. See James M. McPherson, *Battle Cry of Freedom: The Civil War Era* (New York: Ballantine, 1988), 452.

42. *Congressional Record*, 110th Cong., 2nd sess., September 22, 2008, S9173.

43. Robert Luce, *Legislative Problems* (Boston: Houghton Mifflin, 1935), 426. Also see Louis Fisher, "The Authorization-Appropriation Process in Congress: Formal Rules and Informal Practices," *Catholic University Law Review* (Fall 1979): 51–105; Richard F. Fenno Jr., *The Power of the Purse* (Boston: Little, Brown, 1966).

44. Richard Munson, *The Cardinals of Capitol Hill* (New York: Grove Press, 1993), 6.

45. See Louis Fisher, "Annual Authorizations: Durable Roadblocks to Biennial Budgeting," *Public Budgeting and Finance* (Spring 1983): 23–40.

46. Curt Mills, "The Walking Fed: Killing Off All 'Zombie' Agencies," *WashingtonExaminer.Com*, April 18, 2016, 14.

47. Chris Strohm, "Tensions Arise Over Revised Intel Measure," *National Journal's CongressDaily*, March 16, 2011, 16.

48. Quoted in Alan Ota, "Spending Bills May Be Democrats' Plan B," *CQ Today*, April 27, 2007, 8.

49. CBO's March 14, 2019, "Expired and Expiring Authorizations of Appropriations: Fiscal Year 2019," can be found at www.cbo.gov.

50. Jason A. MacDonald, "Limitation Riders and Congressional Influence Over Bureaucratic Policy Decisions," *American Political Science Review* 104, no. 4 (2010): 766–782.

51. See Peter Hanson, *Too Weak to Govern: Majority Party Power and Appropriations in the U.S. Senate* (Cambridge, UK: Cambridge University Press, 2014).

52. Corie Whalen, "Sloshed With Spending," *Washington Examiner*, February 19, 2019, 24.

53. Jason DeParle, "U.S. Welfare System Dies as State Programs Emerge," *New York Times*, June 30, 1997, A1.

54. David R. Francis, "Social Security: A Contrarian View," *Christian Science Monitor*, February 26, 2007, 17.

55. Alexia Fernandez Campbell, "Social Security Crisis: Why Baby Boomers Need Immigrants to Fund Retirement," *Vox.com*, August , 2018.

56. David Cook, "Rising Healthcare Costs Pose Fundamental Risk to U.S.," *Christian Science Monitor*, September 18, 2007, online edition.

57. Kimberly Leonard, "The Turncoat Lobbyist Pushing 'Medicare for All,' *Washington Examiner*, February 19, 2019, 27.

58. William Welch, "Medicare: The Next Riddle for the Ages," *USA Today*, March 17, 2005, 10A.

59. Paul M. Krawzak, "The Cuts No One Notices," *CQ Weekly*, February 11, 2019, 26.

60. Quoted in Julie Rovner, "The Real Budget Buster," *National Journal's CongressDaily AM*, April 5, 2001, 5.

61. Donald Kettl, "Looking for a Real Crisis: Try Medicaid," *Governing*, April 2005, 20.

62. Jonathan Nicholson, "Do Tax Expenditures Really Work? Experts Say Not Enough Data to Tell," *Daily Report for Executives*, October 25, 2010, J-1.

63. Ibid.

64. N. Gregory Mankiw, "The Blur Between Spending and Taxes," *New York Times*, November 21, 2010, B5. Also see Nicholson, "Do Tax Expenditures Really Work?" J-1.

65. See Suzanne Mettler, *The Submerged State: How Invisible Government Policies Undermine American Democracy* (Chicago: University of Chicago Press, 2011); and Christopher Howard, *The Hidden Welfare State: Tax Expenditures and Social Policy in the United States* (Princeton, NJ: Princeton University Press, 1997).

66. Mettler, *Submerged State*.

67. Gerald F. Seib, "As Budget Battle Rages On, a Quiet Cancer Grows," *Wall Street Journal*, March 8, 2011, A4.

68. Nelson D. Schwartz, "What May Soon Exceed Cost of U.S. Military? Interest on U.S. Debt," *New York Times*, September 26, 2018, p. A1.

69. *Congressional Record*, 106th Cong., 2nd sess., March 2, 2000, S1050.

70. Mark Preston, "'Vote-a-Rama' Keeps Wearing Senate Down," *Roll Call*, March 26, 2003, 1.

71. Bill Heniff Jr., "Congressional Budget Resolutions: Historical Information," *CRS Report RL30297*, November 16, 2015. More recent information was provided by Meghan Lynch, CRS budget expert.

72. Ibid.

73. Paul M. Krawak, "Enzi Moving Ahead With 'Realistic" Budget Resolution," *CQ News*, March 7, 2019, 1. Also see Alexander Bolton, "Will Senate GOP Try To Pass a Budget This Year," *The Hill,* February 7, 2019, 8.

74. Caitlin Emma, "Politico Pro Q&A: House Budget Chair John Yarmuth," *Politico Pro.Com*, February 26, 2019, 2.

75. *Congressional Record*, 107th Cong., 1st sess., February 15, 2001, S1532.

76. Testimony of Sen. Robert C. Byrd, Senate Budget Committee, *Senate Procedures for Consideration of the Budget Resolution/Reconciliation*, February 12, 2009, 3.

77. David Rosenbaum, "Democratic Filibuster Hopes Fade," *New York Times*, November 18, 2002, A15; David Baumann, "The Octopus That Might Eat Congress," *National Journal's*, May 14, 2005, 1470–1475.

78. The election was to fill the vacancy due to the death of Democrat Ted Kennedy.

79. Quoted in ibid., 27.

80. Lori Montgomery, "House GOP Passes New Rules on Tax and Spending Legislation," *Washington Post*, January 6, 2011, A7.

81. Tara Golshan, "The PAYGO Fight Roiling House Democrags, Explained." *VOX.com*, January 3, 2019, 3.

82. Matt Bai, "Sure Recipe for Decline: Neglect and Gluttony," *New York Times*, February 17, 2011, A17.

83. *Congressional Record*, 107th Cong., 2nd sess., July 16, 2002, H4749.

CHAPTER 15

1. "Allies and Interests," *The Economist,* December 17, 2016, 52.

2. "Trump vs. Intelligence, Again," *Los Angeles Times,* January 31, 2019,s online edition.

3. Dave Boyer, "Pompeo to Forum: 'New Winds Are Blowing,' *The Washington Times,* January 23, 2019, A8.

4. Lawrence Summers, "Washington May Bluster But Cannot Hold China Back," *Financial Times,* December 4, 2018, 9.

5. Walter Russell Mead, "Pompeo on What Trump Wants," *Wall Street Journal*, June 26, 2018, A15.

6. Harrison Cramer, "New Panel Eyes Trump Foreign Policy," *National Journal Daily*, February 27, 2019, 4.

7. Nahal Toosi, "Skeptics Give Trump Grudging Credit on Foreign Policy," *Politico*, February 6, 2019, 14.

8. John M. Donnelly, "GOP Congress Tries to Rein In Trump on Foreign Policy," *Roll Call,* August 6, 2018, online edition.

9. Nicholas Fandos, "Fresh Concerns Divide G.O.P. and the President," *New York Times,* December 21, 2018, A12.

10. Michael Auslin, "Trump's Successful Pivot to Asia," *Wall Street Journal,* January 16, 2019, A17.

11. Edward S. Corwin, *The President: Office and Powers, 1787–1957,* 4th ed. (New York: New York University Press, 1957), 171. Also see Cecil V. Crabb Jr. and Pat M. Holt, *Invitation to Struggle: Congress, the President, and Foreign Policy,* 4th ed. (Washington, DC: CQ Press, 1992).

12. Corwin, *The President,* 171 (emphasis in the original).

13. Alexander Hamilton, James Madison, and John Jay, *The Federalist Papers,* ed. Clinton Rossiter (New York: Mentor Books, 1961), 391–393.

14. On how the growth of the security state has affected interbranch relationships, see Rebecca U. Thorpe, *The American Warfare State: The Domestic Politics of Military Spending* (Chicago: University of Chicago Press, 2014).

15. Testimony before the House International Relations Committee, January 12, 1995. Reported by Maureen Dowd, *New York Times,* January 13, 1995, A1.

16. Corwin, *The President,* 171 (emphasis in the original).

17. Louis Fisher, *The Politics of Shared Power: Congress and the Executive,* 4th ed. (College Station, TX: Texas A&M University Press, 1998), 177.

18. Erica Werner, Seung Min Kim, and John Wagner, "Senate Rebuffs President's Border Action," *The Washington Post,* March 15, 2019, A1.

19. See, for example, Kurtis Lee, "What Constitutes an Emergency?" *Los Angeles Times,* January 8, 2019, online edition; Alexander Bolton, "GOP Wants President to Back Off on Emergency," *The Hill,* March 7, 2019, 1; and Margaret Taylor, "Declaring an Emergency to Build a Border Wall: The Statutory Arguments," *LawfareBlog,* January 7, 2019.

20. *Youngstown Sheet and Tube Co. v. Sawyer,* 343 U.S. 636 (1952).

21. James Lindsay, "Deference and Defiance: The Shifting Rhythms of Executive–Legislative Relations in Foreign Policy," *Presidential Studies Quarterly* (September 2003): 545.

22. Cecil V. Crabb Jr., Glenn J. Antizzo, and Leila E. Sarieddine, *Congress and the Foreign Policy Process* (Baton Rouge: Louisiana State University Press, 2000), 4.

23. Douglas L. Kriner and Eric Schickler, *Investigating the President: Congressional Checks on Presidential Power* (Princeton, NJ: Princeton University Press, 2017).

24. Mark Landler, "Trump Stands With Saudis Over Murder of Khashoggi, View Ignores C.I.A. and Stirs Outrage on Capitol Hill," *New York Times,* November 21, 2018, A1.

25. Lindsay Graham, "Congress Gets Tough on the Saudis," *Wall Street Journal,* December 4, 2018, A17

26. Nahal Toosi, "Rubio: Saudi Crown Prince Has Gone 'Full Gangster,'" *Politico,* March 7, 2019, 7.

27. Ibid.

28. Burgess Everett and Elana Schor, "Senate Republicans Shun 'Spygate,'" *The Hill,* May 24, 2018, 11. Also see Olivia Beavers and Morgan Chalfant, "Drama Hits Senate Intel Panel's Russia Inquiry," *The Hill,* February 14, 2019, 10.

29. Karoun Demirjian, "Russia Favored Trump in 2016 Election, Senate Panel Says," *The Washington Post*, May 17, 2018, A2.

30. Chris Megerian, "One Committee, Two Conclusions," *Los Angeles Times*, April 28, 2018, online edition. Also see Jason Zengerle, "How Devin Nunes Turned the House Intelligence Committee Inside Out," *NYTimes.com*, April 24, 2018, and Morgan Chalfant and Jordan Fabian, "Trump and Dems Clash Over Probes," *The Hill*, February 7, 2019, 1, 12.

31. Ibid., Megerian.

32. Henry A. Kissinger, "Implementing Bush's Vision," *Washington Post*, May 16, 2005, A17.

33. *Congressional Record*, 105th Cong., 2nd sess., March 2, 1998, E252.

34. Johan Bergenas, "Why Illegal Fishing Is a National Security Issue," *Politico*, September 13, 2016, 29.

35. Fareed Zakaria, "A Pentagon Out of Control," *Washington Post*, December 5, 2014, A17.

36. Christopher J. Deering, "Congress, the President, and Military Policy," *The ANNALS of the American Academy of Political and Social Science* 499, no. 1 (September 1988): 136–147.

37. William D. Hartung, "The Pentagon's Mystery Money," *Los Angeles Times*, August 15, 2014, online edition.

38. Quoted in Matt Richtel, "Trade Investors Cull Start-Ups for Pentagon," *New York Times*, May 7, 2007, C8.

39. *Budget of the United States Government, Fiscal Year 2006*, Historical Tables (Washington, DC: Government Printing Office, 2005), table 3.2.

40. Rachel Oswald, "Ex-Generals Visit Capitol Hill to Stump for Foreign Aid," *CQ News*, March 16, 2016, online edition.

41. Christopher Dickey, "The Surveillance--Industrial Complex," review of *The Shadow Factory: The Ultra-Secret NSA From 9/11 to the Eavesdropping on America* by James Bamford, *New York Times Book Review*, January 11, 2009, 11.

42. Rowan Scarborough, "Firestorm After 'Friendly Fire,'" *Washington Times*, October 30, 2014, A13.

43. Charles Hoskinson, "Unloved Warthog Lives On to Fight Another Day," *Washington Examiner*, December 8, 2014, 4.

44. Jeremy Herb and Connor O'Brien, "McCain's Reelection Pivot: Bringing Home the Bucks," *Politico*, October 19, 2016, 6.

45. William D. Hartung, "How Not to Audit the Pentagon," *Los Angeles Times*, April 10, 2016, online edition.

46. John M. Donnelly, "Significant Cyber Vulnerabilities, Other Woes Bedevil F-35 Jets," *CQ News*, April 26, 2016, online edition.

47. Rajiv Chandrasekaran, "Too Big to Bail," *Washington Post*, March 10, 2013, A8, A9. Also see Tony Capaccio, "Pentagon Cuts Plan for F-35 Jet Order," *Washington Post*, February 17, 2014, A17.

48. *Congressional Record*, 100th Cong., 2nd sess., July 7, 1988, 17072.

49. Karl Viox, "It's Closing Time for Base Commission," *Washington Post*, December 29, 1995, A21. Scholars regard this as an intriguing example of blame avoidance politics. See, for example, Christopher J. Deering, "Congress, the President, and

Automatic Government: The Case of Military Base Closures," in *Rivals for Power: Presidential–Congressional Relations*, ed. James A. Thurber (Washington, DC: CQ Press, 1996).

50. Megan Scully, "Military Plan Hits BRAC Wall," *CQ Weekly*, February 6, 2012, 235.
51. Gregory Hellman, "Politico Pro Q&A: Sen. Jim Inhofe," *PoliticoPro.com*, December 18, 2017, 12.
52. Ana Swanson, "Trump's Isolationist Approach Is Unnerving Free Trade Republicans," *New York Times*, November 16, 2017, A15.
53. Paul Kiernan and Josh Zumbrun, "Trade Deficit in Goods Hits Record," *Wall Street Journal*, March 7, 2019, A5. Of course, there are many reasons for trade deficits. For example, the U.S. economy is healthy, in part because of large tax cuts and more spending by the government. Thus, many people have more money in their pockets and are spending it on imported goods. Or as two noted economists stated: "If a country consumes more than it produces, it must import more than it exports. That's not a rip-off; that's arithmetic." George P. Shultz and Martin Feldstein, "The Deficit That Matters," *The Washington Post*, May 7, 2017, A21.
54. Paul Kiernan and John Zumbrun, "Trade Deficit in Goods Hits Record," *Wall Street Journal*, March 7, 2019, A1.
55. Ibid., A6.
56. See, for example, Jacob Bunge and Lucy Craymer, "Hit by Tariffs, U.S. Pork Struggles To Compete," *Wall Street Journal*, October 19, 2018, A1.
57. Don Lee, "Downside of Trump Tactics," *Los Angeles Times*, October 14, 2018, online edition.
58. Alexander Panetta and Adam Behsudi, "How Trump Got To 'Yes' on the New NAFTA Deal," *Politico*, October 3, 2018, 9.
59. Sabrina Rodriguez, "Lighthizer Must Sell New NAFTA to Skeptical Democrats," *Politico*, March 13, 2019, 6.
60. Katherine S. Newman and Hella Winston, "Make America Make Again: Training Workers for the New Economy," *Foreign Affairs*, January/February 2017, 114–121.
61. Joshua Jamerson, "President's Trade Authority in Crosshairs," *Wall Street Journal*, February 15, 2019, A10.
62. Bruce Hirsh, "Trump May Use Obscure Law as Club on Trading Partners," *Politico*, December 6, 2016, 21. See also Justin Wolper, "Presidents Have Surprising Power to End Trade Deals," *New York Times*, September 20, 2016, A3.
63. John T. Bennett, "Public Anger, Business Angst," *CQ Weekly*, July 11, 2016, 15.
64. Ibid., 16.
65. Charles McC. Mathias Jr., "Ethnic Groups and Foreign Policy," *Foreign Affairs* 59 (Summer 1981): 975–998.
66. Joseph J. Schatz, "Has Congress Given Bush Too Free a Spending Hand?" *CQ Weekly*, April 12, 2002, 859.
67. David P. Auerswald, "Advice and Consent: The Forgotten Power," in *Congress and the Politics of Foreign Policy*, ed. Colton C. Campbell, Nicol C. Rae, and John Stack (Upper Saddle River, NJ: Prentice Hall, 2003), 47–48.
68. Peter Baker, "Gamble by Obama Pays Off With Final Approval of Arms Control Pact," *New York Times*, December 23, 2010, A6.

69. Jamie McIntyre, "A Farewell to Arms Control," *Washington Examiner*, February 19, 2019, 37.

70. Jamie McIntrye, "Nuclear Commander Defends Deterrence," *Washington Examiner*, March 5, 2019, 34.

71. Quoted in Gail Russell Chaddock, "Off-Radar Tax Breaks Draw New Scrutiny," *Christian Science Monitor*, March 9, 2005, 11.

72. Glen S. Krutz and Jeffrey S. Peake, *Treaty Politics and the Rise of Executive Agreements: International Commitments in a System of Shared Powers* (Ann Arbor: University of Michigan Press, 2009), 10.

73. Jeanne J. Grimmett, "Why Certain Trade Agreements Are Approved as Congressional–Executive Agreements Rather Than as Treaties,"CRS Report 97–896, February 17, 2009, 5.

74. This section draws on the invaluable summary of congressional policy initiation in Ellen C. Collier, "Foreign Policy Roles of the President and Congress," CRS Report 93–20F, January 6, 1993, 11–17.

75. The classic account of this incident is Chalmers M. Roberts, "The Day We Didn't Go to War," *Reporter*, September 14, 1954, 31–35.

76. William G. Howell and Jon C. Pevehouse, *When Danger Lurks: Congressional Checks on Presidential War Powers* (Princeton, NJ: Princeton University Press, 2007), 223.

77. Ellen C. Collier, "Foreign Policy by Reporting Requirement," *Washington Quarterly* 11 (Winter 1988): 75.

78. James M. Lindsay, "Congress, Foreign Policy, and the New Institutionalism," *International Studies Quarterly* 38 (June 1994): 281–304.

79. Jennifer K. Elsea, "Defense Primer: Congress's Constitutional Authority With Regard to the Armed Forces," *In Focus*, Congressional Research Service, November 13, 2018, p. 2. During World War II, there were separate declarations of war against Nazi Germany's allies, such as Rumania and Bulgaria. It is common in many textbooks and articles to cite the five rather than name all eleven.

80. Richard F. Grimmett, "Instances of Use of United States Armed Forces Abroad, 1798–2006," CRS Report RL32170, January 8, 2007.

81. Quotes from Helen Dewar, "Congress's Reaction to TV Coverage Shows Ambivalence on Foreign Policy," *Washington Post*, October 9, 1993, A14; and Helen Dewar, "Clinton, Congress at Brink of Foreign Policy Dispute," *Washington Post*, May 16, 1994, A1.

82. Richard F. Grimmett, "War Powers Resolution: Presidential Compliance," CRS Report RL33532, March 25, 2011. Also see Richard Grimmett, "The War Powers Resolution After Thirty-Six Years," CRS Report R4119, April 22, 2010.

83. See David A. Fahrenthold, "Obama Misses Deadline for Approval of Libya Operations," *Washington Post*, May 21, 2011, A3; and John C. Yoo and Robert J. Delahunty, "Libya and the War Powers Resolution," *Wall Street Journal*, May 20, 2011, A15.

84. Tracy Wilkinson and Jennifer Haberkorn, "Senate Takes Step Toward a Rebuke of War in Yemen," *Los Angeles Times*, December 13 2018, A3.

85. *Congressional Record*, vol. 165, February 13, 2019, H1535.

86. Matthew C. Weed, "The War Powers Resolution: Concepts and Practice," CRS Report R42699, December 11, 2018, 48–49.

87. Thomas Gibbons-Neff and Julian E. Barnes, "Pentagon Plan Sees U.S. Clear Of Afghanistan," *New York Times*, March 3, 2019, A1.

88. Rep. Barbara Lee (D-Calif.) and Justin Amash, (R-Mich.), "Congress Owes the American People a Debate Over War Authorization," *The Hill*, February 28, 2018, 27.

89. Kristina Peterson, "Bill Seeks to Limit Executive War Power," *Wall Street Journal*, March 7, 2019, A4.

90. Mike Lillis, "Ryan: No Need for Congress to Authorize Syria Strikes," *The Hill*, April 12, 2018, online edition.

91. Sam Jones, "Islamists Lone-Wolf Strikes on the Rise as ISIS Taps Pool of Vulnerable Radicals," *Financial Times*, July 27, 2016, 4. Also see Rukmini Callimachi, "Not 'Lone Wolves' After All," *New York Times*, February 5, 2017, A1.

92. Rowar Scarborough, "Top Counterterror Chief Warns of Vast Global Army," *Washington Times*, September 28, 2016, A7.

93. Gabriel Schoenfeld, "The Fog of Forever War," *Wall Street Journal*, August 9, 2016, A11.

94. David Ignatius, "The Cyber War Has Replaced the Cold War," *Washington Post*, September 16, 2016, A15.

95. Martin Matishak, "The Cyber College That Wants to Train the Entire Military," *Politico*, October 31, 2016, online edition.

96. Jack Goldsmith, "Stealth Wars Require Rules, Too," *Washington Post*, February 6, 2013, A17. Goldsmith also includes covert action, special forces, drone surveillance and targeting, and other stealthy means within his call for new rules for a new type of war. Also see David E. Sanger, "In Cyberspace, New Cold War," *New York Times*, February 25, 2013 A1.

97. Liz Sly, "Like that AK-47? Kalashnikov Has a Kamikaze Drone for You," *The Washington Post*, February 24, 2019, A17.

98. Sam Leith, "Saying Nothing Is Not an Option," *Financial Times*, October 10–11, 2014, 19.

99. Neil MacFarquhar, "Russia's Powerful Weapon to Hurt Rivals: Falsehoods," *New York Times*, August 29, 2016, A1.

100. Ben Wolfgang, "Putin to Deploy New Hypersonic Missile System," *The Washington Times*, December 27, 2018, A1.

101. Jamie McIntyre, "Nuclear Commander Defends Deterrence," *Washington Examiner*, March 5, 2019, 34.

102. Robert C. Byrd, *Losing America* (New York: Norton, 2005), 23.

CHAPTER 16

1. Quoted in Carl Hulse and David M. Herszenhorn, "Behind Closed Doors, Warnings of Calamity," *New York Times*, September 20, 2008, C5.

2. Jonathan Weisman, David Cho, and Paul Kane, "With No Plan B, House Reluctantly Passes Politically Risky Measure," *Washington Post*, October 4, 2008, A1.

3. Quoted in ibid.

4. David M. Herszenhorn, "Administration Is Seeking $700 Billion for Wall Street in Possible Record Bailout," *New York Times*, September 21, 2008, A1.

5. Quoted in Joe Nocera, "36 Hours of Alarm and Action as Crisis Spread," *New York Times*, October 2, 2008, A1.

6. Jackie Calmes, "Dazed Capital Feels Its Way, Eyes on Nov. 4," *Washington Post*, September 20, 2008, A1.

7. Quoted in Lori Montgomery, Paul Kane, and Neil Irwin, "Bailout Proposal Meets Bipartisan Outrage; Lawmakers Balk as Officials Press Case for Quick Action," *Washington Post*, September 24, 2008, A1.

8. David M. Herszenhorn, "Word Reaches Congress: As the Market Goes Down, So Goes the Electorate," *New York Times*, October 2, 2008, C10.

9. Jonathan Weisman, "House Rejects Financial Rescue, Sending Stocks Plummeting," *Washington Post*, September 30, 2008, A1.

10. "Bailout Breakdown," *New York Times*, September 25, 2008, A18; David S. Broder, "Credibility Test for Congress," *Washington Post*, September 25, 2008, A19.

11. For a first-hand account of these events, see John Lawrence, "When America Stared Into the Abyss: The Untold Story of How America's Political Leaders Crossed the Aisle to Stave Off Financial Collapse in 2008," *The Atlantic*, January 7, 2019, https://www.theatlantic.com/ideas/archive/2019/01/john-lawrence-inside-2008-financial-crash/576574/. See also Robert G. Kaiser, *Act of Congress: How America's Essential Institution Works, and How It Doesn't* (New York: Knopf, 2013), 13–26.

12. Andrew Kohut, "Pessimistic Public Doubts Effectiveness of Stimulus, TARP," Pew Research Center for the People and the Press, April 28, 2010, http://people-press.org/reports/pdf/608.pdf.

13. Paul Kiel and Dan Nguyen, "Bailout Tracker," ProPublica (updated January 22, 2019), http://projects.propublica.org/bailout/.

14. Tim Massad, "The Response to the Financial Crisis—in Charts," *Treasury Notes*, U.S. Department of the Treasury, April 13, 2012, www.treasury.gov/connect/blog/Pages/financial-crisis-response-in-charts.aspx.

15. Steven Pearlstein, "Unfairly Rewarding Greedy Bankers, and Why It Works," *Washington Post*, January 14, 2009, D1.

16. See Charles O. Jones, *The Presidency in a Separated System* (Washington, DC: Brookings, 1994).

17. *Congressional Record*, 105th Cong., 1st sess., May 21, 1997, H3072.

18. Glenn R. Parker and Roger H. Davidson, "Why Do Americans Love Their Congressmen So Much More Than Their Congress?" *Legislative Studies Quarterly* 4 (February 1979): 53–61.

19. See Roger H. Davidson, "The House of Representatives: Managing Legislative Complexity," in *Workways of Governance: Monitoring Our Government's Health*, ed. Roger H. Davidson (Washington, DC: Governance Institute and Brookings, 2003), 24–46; and Sarah A. Binder, "The Senate: Does It Deliberate? Can It Act?" in Davidson, *Workways of Governance*, 47–64.

20. Michael Leahy, "House Rules: Freshman Congressman Joe Courtney, Elected by a Margin of 83 Votes, Is Learning That the First Requirement of Power Is Self-Preservation," *Washington Post Magazine*, June 10, 2007, W12.

21. Congressional Management Foundation and the Society for Human Resource Management, *Life in Congress: The Member Perspective*, 2013, http://www

.congressfoundation.org/storage/documents/CMF_Pubs/life-in-congress-the-member-perspective.pdf.

22. Ibid.

23. Quoted in Leahy, "House Rules," W12.

24. Philip Edward Jones, "Which Buck Stops Here? Accountability for Policy Positions and Policy Outcomes in Congress," *Journal of Politics*, 73 (2011): 764–782.

25. Congressional Management Foundation, "Communicating With Congress: Perceptions of Citizen Advocacy on Capitol Hill," 2011, http://www.congressfounda tion.org/storage/documents/CMF_Pubs/cwc-perceptions-of-citizen-advocacy.pdf.

26. Brookings Institution, "House Staff Based in District Offices, 1970–2016," *Vital Statistics on Congress*, Table 5–3, https://www.brookings.edu/multi-chapter-report/vital-statistics-on-congress/.

27. Bob Benenson, "Savvy 'Stars' Making Local TV a Potent Tool," *Congressional Quarterly Weekly Report*, July 18, 1987, 1551–1555.

28. Timothy Cook, *Making Laws and Making News: Media Strategies in the U.S. House of Representatives* (Washington, DC: Brookings, 1989), 82–83.

29. Tim Roemer, "Why Do Congressmen Spend Only Half Their Time Serving Us?" *Newsweek*, July 15, 2015, http://www.newsweek.com/why-do-congressmen-spend-only-half-their-time-serving-us-357995.

30. Quoted in ibid.

31. Gallup, "Honesty/Ethics in Professions," December 3–12, 2018, http://www.gal lup.com/poll/1654/honesty-ethics-professions.aspx.

32. Lee H. Hamilton, "Ten Things I Wish Political Scientists Would Teach About Congress," Pi Sigma Alpha Lecture, American Political Science Association, August 31, 2000, 7. Also see Hamilton's thoughtful book, *How Congress Works and Why You Should Care* (Bloomington: Indiana University Press, 2004).

33. Quoted in T. R. Goldman, "The Influence Industry's Senior Class," *Legal Times*, June 16, 1997, 4.

34. Theodore Meyer, "Fatah Becomes First House Primary Loser of 2016," *Politico*, April 26, 2016, http://www.politico.com/story/2016/04/rep-chaka-fattah-loses-primary-222502.

35. Susan Schmidt and James V. Grimaldi, "Abramoff Pleads Guilty to 3 Counts," *Washington Post*, January 4, 2006, A1.

36. Paul Blumenthal, "Abramoff Investigation Continues Apace," Sunlight Foundation weblog, February 2, 2009, http://sunlightfoundation.com/blog/2009/02/02/abramoff-investigation-continues-apace.

37. Scott Higham, "Congressional Ethics Committees Protect Legislators, Critics Say," *Washington Post*, October 7, 2012, www.washingtonpost.com/investigations/congressional-ethics-committees-protect-legislators-critics-say/2012/10/07/a313e59c-e251–11e1-ae7f-d2a13e 249eb2_story.html.

38. Ethics Committee, U.S. House of Representatives, "Summary of Activities 115th Congress," January 2, 2019, https://www.govinfo.gov/content/pkg/CRPT-115hrpt1125/pdf/CRPT-115hrpt1125.pdf.

39. Megan Brenan, "Nurses Again Outpace Other Professions for Honesty, Ethics," Gallup, December 20, 2018, https://news.gallup.com/poll/245597/nurses-again-outpace-professions-honesty-ethics.aspx.

40. Cass R. Sunstein, "Unchecked and Unbalanced," *American Prospect* 38 (May–June 1998): 23. Sunstein served as head of the Office of Information and Regulatory Affairs in the Office of Management and Budget during President Obama's first term.

41. Ashley Parker, "Congressman in Drug Case Resigns Seat in Florida," *New York Times*, January 27, 2014, http://www.nytimes.com/2014/01/28/us/politics/flor ida-congressman-facing-pressure-after-cocaine-charge-to-resign.html?_r=0.

42. Nathaniel Rakich, "We've Never Seen Congressional Resignations Like This Before," *FiveThirtyEight*, January 29, 2018, https://fivethirtyeight.com/features/more-people-are-resigning-from-congress-than-at-any-time-in-recent-history/.

43. Katherine Tully-McManus, "Donald Trump Signs Overhaul of Anti-Harassment Law for Members of Congress, Staff," *Roll Call*, December 21, 2018, https://www.rollcall.com/news/politics/donald-trump-signs-overhaul-anti-harassment-law-members-congress-staff.

44. John M. Barry, *The Ambition and the Power: The Fall of Jim Wright* (New York: Viking, 1989).

45. G. Calvin Mackenzie with Michael Hafken, *Scandal Proof: Do Ethics Laws Make Government Ethical?* (Washington, DC: Brookings, 2002), 158.

46. Benjamin Ginsberg and Martin Shefter, *Politics by Other Means: Politicians, Prosecutors, and the Press From Watergate to Whitewater*, 3rd ed. (New York: Norton, 2002).

47. Jennifer L. Lawless and Richard L. Fox, *Running From Office: Why Young Americans Are Turned Off to Politics* (New York: Oxford University Press, 2015). See also Paul C. Light, "Measuring the Health of the Public Service," in Davidson, *Workways of Governance*, 96–97.

48. Jennifer L. Lawless, *Becoming a Candidate: Political Ambition and the Decision to Run for Office* (New York: Cambridge University Press), 166–170.

49. David R. Mayhew, *The Imprint of Congress* (New Haven: Yale University Press, 2017), 7–8. See also Diane Hollern Harvey, "Who Should Govern? Public Preferences for Congressional and Presidential Power," PhD dissertation, University of Maryland, 1998.

50. Hamilton, "Ten Things I Wish Political Scientists Would Teach About Congress," 3.

51. For a comprehensive analysis of Congress's contributions to national government, see David R. Mayhew, "Congress as a Handler of Challengers: The Historical Record," *Studies in American Political Development* 29, no. 2 (2015): 185–212.

52. Paul C. Light, *Government's Greatest Achievements: From Civil Rights to Homeland Security* (Washington, DC: Brookings, 2002).

53. Ibid., 63.

54. See, for example, the collection of essays in Nathaniel Persily, ed., *Solutions to Political Polarization in America* (New York: Cambridge University Press, 2015).

55. Richard Hall, *Participation in Congress* (New Haven, CT: Yale University Press, 1996), 2.

56. Binder et al., "Mending the Broken Branch," 7.

57. Barbara Sinclair, *Unorthodox Lawmaking: New Legislative Processes in the U.S. Congress*, 5th ed. (Washington, DC: CQ Press, 2016).

58. Ibid.

59. James M. Curry, *Legislating in the Dark: Information and Power in the House of Representatives* (Chicago: University of Chicago Press, 2015).

60. William Bendix, "Bypassing Congressional Committees: Parties, Panel Rosters, and Deliberative Processes," *Legislative Studies Quarterly* 41, no. 3 (2016): 687–714.

61. Lee Drutman and Steven Teles, "Why Congress Relies on Lobbyists Instead of Thinking for Itself," *Atlantic Monthly*, March 10, 2015, https://www.theatlantic.com/politics/archive/2015/03/when-congress-cant-think-for-itself-it-turns-to-lobbyists/387295.

62. Brookings Institution, *Vital Statistics on Congress*, https://www.brookings.edu/multi-chapter-report/vital-statistics-on-congress/, Table 5–5, May 2018.

63. Ida A. Brudnick, "Legislative Branch: FY2017 Appropriations," CRS Report for Congress, R44515, June 2, 2016.

64. Commission on Political Reform, "Governing in a Polarized America: A Bipartisan Blueprint to Strengthen Our Democracy," Bipartisan Policy Center, June 24, 2014, http://bipartisanpolicy.org/wp-content/uploads/sites/default/files/files/BPC%20CPR%20Governing%20in%20a%20Polarized%20America.pdf. See also Michael Thorning, "Final Analysis: 114th Congress Improves, but Gridlock Overshadows," Bipartisan Policy Center, January 19, 2017, http://bipartisanpolicy.org/blog/114th-congress-improves-but-gridlock-overshadows.

65. Lee Hamilton, "We Can't Wait Much Longer to Fix Congress," *Comments on Congress*, December 15, 2005.

66. Nelson W. Polsby, *How Congress Evolves: Social Bases of Institutional Change* (New York: Oxford University Press, 2004), 130–137.

67. Mickey Edwards, "Wanted: A Congress With a Backbone," *Los Angeles Times*, August 29, 2006, B13.

68. Binder et al., "Mending the Broken Branch," 7.

69. Quoted by David S. Broder, "Role Models, Now More Than Ever," *Washington Post*, July 13, 2003, B7.

70. James M. Curry and Frances E. Lee, "Non-Party Government: Bipartisan Lawmaking and Party Power in Congress," *Perspectives on Politics* 17 (1, 2019): 47–65.

71. Sarah A. Binder, "Polarized We Govern?" Center for Effective Public Management, Brookings Institution, May 2014, https://www.brookings.edu/research/polarized-we-govern/.

72. Laurel Harbridge and Neil Malhotra, "Electoral Incentives and Partisan Conflict in Congress: Evidence From Survey Experiments," *American Journal's of Political Science* 55 (July 2011): 494–510.

73. Mark D. Ramirez, "The Dynamics of Partisan Conflict on Congressional Approval," *American Journal of Political Science* 53 (July 2009): 683.

74. Sinclair, *Unorthodox Lawmaking*.

75. Sinclair, *Unorthodox Lawmaking*, 270.

76. Peter C. Hanson, "Abandoning the Regular Order: Majority Party Influence on Appropriations in the U.S. Senate," *Political Research Quarterly* 67 (2014): 519–532.

77. Suzanne Mettler, "The Policyscape and the Challenges of Contemporary Politics to Policy Maintenance," *Perspectives on Politics* 14 no. 2 (June 2016): 369–390.

78. Frances E. Lee and Sarah A. Binder, "Making Deals in Congress" in *Solutions to Political Polarization in America*, ed. Nathaniel Persily (New York: Cambridge University Press, 2015), 240–261.

79. For an extended analysis of these dilemmas, see John B. Gilmour, *Strategic Disagreement: Stalemate in American Politics* (Pittsburgh: University of Pittsburgh Press, 1995).

80. E. Scott Adler, *Why Congressional Reforms Fail: Reelection and the House Committee System* (Chicago: University of Chicago Press, 2002), 11.

81. Eric Schickler, *Disjointed Pluralism: Institutional Innovation and the Development of the U.S. Congress* (Princeton, NJ: Princeton University Press, 2001), 268.

82. Michael Barthel, "Newspapers: Fact Sheet," Pew Research Center, June 13, 2018, http://www.journalism.org/fact-sheet/newspapers/.

83. Jessica C. Gerrity, "Understanding Congressional Approval: Public Opinion From 1974 to 2014," in *The Evolving Congress,* U.S. Senate Committee on Rules and Administration, S. Prt. 113–30, 189–216.

84. Huffpost Pollster, "Congress Job Approval," February 23, 2017, http://elections.huffington post.com/pollster/congress-job-approval.

85. John R. Hibbing and Elizabeth Theiss-Morse, *Congress as Public Enemy* (Cambridge, UK: Cambridge University Press, 1995), 147.

86. Gerrity, "Understanding Congressional Approval," 210.

87. See Louis Fisher, *Presidential War Power,* 2nd ed. (Lawrence: University Press of Kansas, 2004).

88. Josh Rogin, "How Obama Turned on a Dime Toward War," The Cable, *Foreign Policy* weblog, March 18, 2011, http://thecable.foreignpolicy.com/posts/2011/03/18/how_obama_turned_on_a_dime_toward_war.

89. Quoted in Kirk Victor, "Congress in Eclipse," *National Journal,* April 5, 2003, 1068.

90. John Bresnahan and Seung Min Kim, "Attorney General Eric Holder Held in Contempt of Congress," *Politico,* June 28, 2012, http://www.politico.com/news/stories/0612/77988.html.

91. Andrew Kaczynski, "Rand Paul on Flynn: 'Makes No Sense' to Investigate Fellow Republicans," CNN Politics, February 14, 2017, http://www.cnn.com/2017/02/14/politics/kfile-rand-paul-republican-investigations.

92. Andrew Prokop, "The Devin Nunes Tape Tells Us What We All Knew: His Investigation Is About Protecting Trump," Vox.com, August 9, 2018, https://www.vox.com/2018/8/9/17670930/devin-nunes-tape.

93. Richard L. Hasen, "End of the Dialogue? Political Polarization, the Supreme Court, and Congress," *Southern California Law Review* 86, no. 2 (2013): 139.

94. James L. Sundquist, *The Decline and Resurgence of Congress* (Washington, DC: Brookings, 1981), 482–483.

95. Andrew Rudalevige, *The New Imperial Presidency: Renewing Presidential Power After Watergate* (Ann Arbor: University of Michigan Press, 2005), 261.

INDEX

A-10 Warthog, 438

AARP, 373–374, 380

Abbe, Owen G., 96

ABC News, 133

"A Better Way" Platform, 96

Abortion rights, 69, 80, 112, 473

Abramoff, Jack, 393, 459

Abramowitz, Alan I., 9

Absentee balloting, 86

Ackerman, Bruce, 329

ACLU (American Civil Liberties Union), 262

Active players, in Congress, 265

Adams, John, 13, 37

Adams, John Quincy, 412

Adams, Samuel, 16

Additional initial referral, of bills, 202

Adelson, Sheldon, 85

Administrative Procedure Act (APA) of 1946, 301, 334

Adopting policy, 400–401

Advertising:

AARP campaign against "age tax," 374

    campaign strategy and, 70

    constituent outreach vs., 133

    consulting firms to conduct, 81

    deceptive, 405

    digital, 80, 83

    local, 132

    negative, 82–83

    nondisclosing outside groups and, 76

    raising money for, 57

    television, 79

    See also Media

Advise-and-consent role of Senate, 327–329

Advocacy campaigns, 386

Affordable Care Act of 2010. See Patient Protection and Affordable Care Act of 2010

African Americans:

    Black Caucus, 194

    Black Lives Matter, 3

    Chisholm, Shirley, 188–190

    gerrymandering to disempower, 53

    Legislative Black Caucus, 56

    legislators as, 111–112

Agency for International Development, 437

Agenda setting, in policy making, 398–400

Age of legislators, 113

Agriculture, Nutrition, and Forestry Committee, 230

Aid to Families with Dependent Children, 416

AIG (American International Group), 455

Air Force Cyber College, 452

Alabama Legislative Black Caucus v. Alabama (2015), 56

Alaska Delegation Report, 133

Alexander, DeAlva Stanwood, 178

Alexander, Lamar, 179, 247

Alito, Samuel, 49, 365, 368

al Qaeda, 311, 448, 451

Alsop, Richard, 51

Amash, Justin, 268, 282

Amendments:

    "amendment tree filling," 250–251

    bill process stage, 242–243

    decision making in Congress and, 268–269

"America First" foreign policy of Donald Trump, 427

American Community Survey, 50

American Heart Association, 373, 375

American Hospital Association, 374

American International Group (AIG), 455

American League of Lobbyists, 390

American Medical Association, 374–375

American National Election Study
(ANES), 95
American Nurses Association, 374
American people, two Congresses and,
455–474
citizen attitudes toward, 468–471
constituents, bonds with, 457–458
damage to, 473–474
ethics and, 459–462
executive branch encroachment,
471–473
institution, Congress as, 461
judicial lawmaking, 473
media coverage of, 468
overview, 455–457
policy successes, 463
process shortcomings, 463–468
security at Congress, 471
American Petroleum Institute, 383
American Political Science
Association, A5
Americans for Democratic Action, 387
American University, A6
ANES (American National Election
Study), 95
Anti-Saloon League, 376
Antizzo, Glenn J., 432
Apalachicola National Forest, 230
APA (Administrative Procedure Act) of
1946, 301, 334
Apportionment, in House of
Representatives, 41–42
Appropriating standing committees, 179
Appropriations:
authorizations and, 409–414
bureaucracy and process of, 342–343
Committee for, 179, 181
Appropriations Subcommittee on
Transportation, 199
Aristotle, 108
Armed Services Committee, 193, 264
Armey, Dick, 264, 439
Arnold, R. Douglas, 133, 282–283, 316
Article I of U.S. Constitution, 18–20, 23, 296
Article II of U.S. Constitution, 21–22,
295–296, 343, 361

Article III of U.S. Constitution, 350
Articles of Confederation, 16–17, 25
Asher, Herbert B., 115
Assignments to Committees. *See*
Committees
Asymmetric polarization, 278
Atlantic, The, 381
Authorization for Use of Military Force
in Iraq of 2002, 450
Authorization for Use of Military Force
(AUMF) of 2001, 450–451
Authorizations and appropriations,
409–414
Authorizing standing committees, 179

BA (budget authority), 410–411
Backdoor spending techniques, 414
Baird, Brian, 80
Balance theory of midterm election
loss, 92
Baldwin, Tammy, 112
Banking, Housing, and Urban Affairs
Committee, 199
Bannon, Steve, 329
Barbour, Haley, 380
Barenblatt v. United States (1959), 338
Barr, William, 323, 328
Barton, Joe, 336, 456
Base Realignment and Closure (BRAC)
Commissions, 264, 439
Baumgartner, Frank, 376
Beckmann, Matthew N., 305
Bee, Samantha, 10
Bennett, W. Lance, 304
Bera, Ami, 428
Bernanke, Ben, 455
Bicameralism, 25–26, 406–407
Biden, Joseph R., Jr., 193, 212, 306, 445
Bill of Rights, 20. *See also* U.S. Constitution
Bills:
cosponsorship of, 266
extracting from committee, 239–240,
247–249
introducing, 222–228
shortcuts for minor, 229–231
See also Voting in Congress

Binder, Sarah A., 31, 290
bin Laden, Osama, 311, 448
Bipartisan Campaign Reform Act of
	2002, 83
Bipartisan Policy Center, 465
Bipartisanship, 465–466
Bishop, Rob, 5
Black, Hugo, 46
Blackburn, Marsha, 182
Black Caucus, 194
Black Lives Matter, 3
Blackstone, William, 14
"Blue Dog" Democrats, 279, 281
Blue-slip approval of lower court
	nominations, 370
Blunt, Roy, 225, 314
BO (budget outlay), 410–411
Boehner, John:
	centralized leadership of, 145
	committee assignments made by, 162
	experience of, 140
	followers of, 172
	presidential relationships with,
		307, 339
	procedural votes of, 241
	"regular order" preference of, 212
	women as committee leaders
		under, 192
Bolton, John, 329
Bono, Mary, 265
Booker, Cory, 262
Border security:
	budget submission for, 398–399
	DHS policies for, 344–345
	Trump agenda for, 146, 301
Bork, Robert H., 365
Boston Tea Party (1773), 15
Boston University, A6
Boxer, Barbara, 337
BRAC (Base Realignment and Closure)
	Commissions, 264, 439
Brand New Congress, 3
Brat, David, 214
Breaux, John B., 383
Brennan, William J., 47
Brewster, Owen, 29

Breyer, Stephen, 365
Brigham Young University, 89
Brinkmanship tactics, 220
Broadcasts, from legislators, 133
Bronx Progressives, 3
Broockman, David E., 386
Brookings Institution, 144, 368, 463
Brown, Michael, 330
Brown, Scott, 423
Brown v. Board of Education, 359
Buck, Ken, 193
Buckley v. Valeo (1976), 74
Budget Act of 1974:
	authorization-appropriations process
		in, 468
	concurrent budget resolutions,
		419–421
	overview, 418–419
	reconciliation, 247, 422–423
	revised budget process, 423–425
Budget authority (BA), 410–411
Budget Committee, 198
Budget Control Act of 2011, 379, 417,
	421, 436–437
Budget Enforcement Act of 1990, 423
Budgeting in Congress, 409–425
	authorizations and appropriations,
		409–414
	backdoor spending techniques, 414
	Budget Act of 1974, 418–425
	entitlements, 414–418
	See also Policy making in Congress
Budget outlay (BO), 410–411
Bundling, in fund raising, 386
Burden, Barry C., 114
Bureaucracy, 321–348
	appropriations process and, 342–343
	civil service under authority of
		Congress, 329–333
	Congressional vetoes of, 340–341
	hearings and investigations of, 340
	impeachment process and, 343
	inspectors general and, 342
	mandatory reports from, 341
	micromanagement by Congress, 346
	nonstatutory controls over, 342

oversight by Congress, 338–339, 344–346
overview, 321–322
rulemaking process, 333–338
Senate confirmation of presidential appointees, 323–329
Burke, Edmund, 7–8
Burkean ideal, 121
Burr, Richard, 434
Bush, George H. W., 90, 124, 319, 450, 472
Bush, George W.:
  Congressional seat losses, 90
  Great Recession of 2008-2009, 455–456
  Hurricane Katrina and, 330
  Iraq, use of force in, 472
  No Child Left Behind (NCLB) education law, 314, 407
  Office for Homeland Security created by, 300
  Republican government of, 318–319
  September 11, 2001 attacks and, 308–309
  signing statements of, 302
  Social Security privatization failure, 416
  Texas voting turnout for, 70
  trade promotion authority (TPA) won by, 442
  two-presidencies thesis relevant to, 311–312
  veto power used by, 296
  War Powers Resolution and, 450
Bypassing committees, 214–215
Byrd, Robert C., 156, 161, 171, 252, 259, 422, 453
Byrd rule, in budget reconciliation, 422–423

Calendar of Business, in Senate, 245
Calendar Wednesday rule, to dislodge bills from committee, 239
Calhoun, John C., 154
Califano, Joseph, 193
Cameron, Simon, 379
Campaigns:
  advocacy, 386
  Bipartisan Campaign Reform Act of 2002, 83

corporate contributions to, 188
Democratic Congressional Campaign Committee (DCCC), 73
Democratic Senatorial Campaign Committee (DSCC), 383
organized interest groups and fund raising for, 386
See also Elections; Recruitment and candidacy
Campbell, James E., 90
Candidacy, recruitment and. See Recruitment and candidacy
Canes-Wrone, Brandice, 312
Cannon, Joseph G., 142, 232
Canon, David T., 60
Cantor, Eric, 214
Cantwell, Maria, 186
Capito, Shelley Moore, 163, 294
Capuano, Michael, 65
Career politicians, 110
Careers:
  Congressional, 33–34
  Congressional service, 119–120
  constituency, 127
  internships and, A5–A7
"Carpetbagger caucus," 40
Carson, Jamie L., 77
Carter, Jimmy, 304, 448
Castor, Kathy, 210
Caucuses, party, 138, 165, 196–197
Cavanagh, Thomas E., 121
CBO (Congressional Budget Office), 29, 208, 413, 418
CBS, 60 Minutes, 73
Census, Congressional apportionment based on, 41–44
Center for Public Integrity, 393
Center for Responsive Politics, 375, 381
Chafee, Lincoln, 117
Chavez, Cesar, 3
Chen, Jowei, 52
Cheney, Richard B. "Dick," 167
Chisholm, Shirley, 188–190
Chisholm v. Georgia (1793), 360
CIA (Central Intelligence Agency), 432, 434

Citizens for Responsibility and Ethics in Washington, 460
Citizenship status, in census data, 43–44
Citizens United v. Federal Election Commission (2010), 24, 75
Civil service, 329–333. *See also* Bureaucracy
Civil War, 19, 24
Clark, James B. "Champ," 142
Class Action Fairness Act of 2005, 357
Clay, Henry, 28, 154, 318
Clean Power Plan regulations, 301–302, 336
Cleaver, Emanuel, 116
Climate change:
    Clean Power Plan to address, 301
    climate crisis select committee in House, 184, 209–211
    national policy agenda for, 399–400
    Trump dismantling of regulations to address, 336
Clinton, Bill:
    Congressional seat losses with, 90
    COPS program of, 315
    deficit reduction budget battles of, 423
    executive orders of, 301
    Garland appointed federal judge by, 363
    government shutdowns, 144
    impeachment trial of, 23
    legislative branch conflicts with, 319
    military force used by, 472–473
    public issues championed by, 309
    Republican filibusters and, 466
Clinton, Hillary, 69, 90, 96, 145, 198, 434
Closed Rule, 235
Closure of military bases, 438–439
Cloture, 252–257, 369
Cluster-voting rule, 231
Clyburn, James E., 56, 149–151, 244
Coalition for the American Dream, 383
Coalition lobbying, 383
Coalitions, building, 169–171
Coattails, elections and, 90
Coburn, Tom, 306
Cohen, William S., 322
Colbert, Stephen, 10

Cole, Tom, 82, 236
Collective-action problem, 139, 286
Collective representation, 114
Collins, Doug, 262
Collins, Susan, 101, 112, 170, 265, 270, 282, 288
Columbia University, 368
Commerce, Science and Transportation Committee, 186, 199
Commerce Clause of U.S. Constitution, 18–19
Committee on Homeland Security, 185
Committee on Oversight and Government Reform, 198
Committees, 175–218
    authority of chairs of, 211–213
    biases in assignments to, 196
    bills referred to, 203–206
    bypassing, 214–215
    climate crisis select committee, 209–211
    conference, 185–186
    congressional, 27–28
    environment of policy making in, 206
    evolution of, 177–179
    formal criteria in assignments to, 190–192
    generalizations about, 215–216
    informal criteria in assignments to, 192–193
    joint, 185
    leadership of, 197–198
    multiple referrals in policy making in, 202
    overlapping jurisdictions in policy making in, 199–201
    overview, 175–176
    party, 165–166
    party caucus and chamber approval in assignments to, 196–197
    party task forces and "gangs," 213–214
    pecking order in assignments to, 186–188
    preferences and politicking in assignments to, 188–190
    purposes of, 177

select or special, 184–185
seniority in assignments to, 193–196
staff of, 207–208
standing, 179–184
See also Leaders and parties
Committee of the Whole House on the state of the Union, 241–244
Common carriers, reform initiatives and, 32
Communication styles, in Congress. *See* Hill *versus* home styles
Compound Rule, 234, 236
Conceptual markups, 205
Concurrent resolutions, 223
Conditional party government theory, 146–148
Conference committees, 185–186, 258
Conflict-of-interest concerns, 326
Congress, evolution of, 13–38
    antecedents of, 14–17
    bicameralism in, 25–26
    branches of government, 20–23
    executive branch conflicts with, 29
    first meeting of, 13–14
    individual member interests in, 31–33
    judicial review of, 23–25
    legislator's job evolution, 33–36
    limitations of, 20
    overview, 37
    partisan interests in, 30–31
    powers of, 17–20
    size of, 28–29
    workload of, 26–28
    See also House of Representatives; Senate
Congresses, two separate:
    comparing, 8–10
    Crowley/Ocasio-Cortez primary of 2018 (NY), 1–3
    divergent views of, 10–12
    dual nature of, 3–8
    tensions from, 152
    See also American people, two Congresses and
Congressional Accountability Act of 1995, 460

Congressional Budget Act of 1974. *See* Budget Act of 1974
Congressional Budget and Impoundment Control Act of 1974, 29. *See also* Budget Act of 1974
Congressional Budget Office (CBO), 29, 208, 413, 418
Congressional government, periods of, 318
Congressional Hispanic Caucus, 194, A5
Congressional Progressive Caucus, 441
Congressional Record, 236, 270
Congressional Research Service, 208, 328
Congressional Review Act (CRA), 333
Congress: The Electoral Connection (Mayhew), 5
Connolly, Gerry, 345
Consensus Calendar, 228–229, 239
Conservative coalition, 147, 278
Conservative Democratic Forum, 305
Constituencies:
    bonds with, 127, 457–458
    casework on, 128–129
    explaining activity to, 126–127
    geographic and demographic, 122–124, 148
    impact on Congressional voting of, 281–283
    independent judgment *versus* opinion of, 120–121
    legislative-executive conflicts from differences in, 316–317
    overview, 121–122
    political and personal, 124–125
Constitution. *See* U.S. Constitution
Constitutional Convention of 1789, 40
Constitutional powers of presidents:
    administrative, 299–303
    line-item veto, 299
    overview, 295–296
    veto bargaining, 296–299
Consumer Financial Protection Bureau, 328, 405
Continuing resolution, in budgeting, 413–414

"Contract with America" party
platform, 143
Convention of the Rights of Persons
with Disabilities of 2012, 445
Conyers, John, 460
Cook Political Report (Wasserman), 63-64
Coons, Chris, 65
Cooper, Jim, 417
COPS program, 315
Cordray, Richard, 328
Cornyn, John, 159, 293, 308
Corporate campaign contributions, 188
Corwin, Edward S., 430
Cosponsorship of bills, 266
Cotton, Tom, 262
Courtney, Joe, 457-458
Courts, Congress and, 349-372
    federal courts, 350-351
    judicial nominees and, 361-363
    lower court nominees and, 368-371
    overview, 349-350
    U.S. Supreme Court. *See* U.S.
        Supreme Court
Cox, Gary, 276
CRA (Congressional Review Act), 333
Crabb, Cecil V., Jr., 432
Cracking and packing techniques of
    gerrymandering, 47-48, 56
Credit defaults, 220
Crisis policies, 447-453
Crowley, Joseph, 1-3, 65, 127
Crowley/Ocasio-Cortez primary of 2018
    (NY), 1-3
Cruz, Ted, 69-70
C-SPAN (Cable Satellite Public Affairs
    Network), 204, 258
Cue-givers in Congressional voting, 285
Cummings, Elijah, 198
Cut-as-you-go (CUTGO) rule, 424
Cyber war, 452

DACA (Deferred Action for Childhood
    Arrivals), 301-302
Daines, Steve, 191
Daschle, Tom, 380
Davis v. Bandemer (1986), 48

DCCC (Democratic Congressional
    Campaign Committee), 73
Deadline lawmaking, 220
Debt, interest on, 417-418
Decision making in Congress, 261-292
    amendments and, 268-269
    bargaining in, 285-289
    choices in voting, 269-270
    constituency impact on voting,
        281-283
    cue-givers and roll call voting, 285
    ideology impact on voting, 277-281
    leadership in, 266
    meaning in voting, 270-271
    overview, 261-263
    participation in, 267-268
    party impact on voting, 272-277
    power to choose, 263
    presidency impact on voting,
        283-285
    specialized decisions, 264-265
    timing of, 265
Declaration of Rights and Grievances
    (Stamp Act Congress, 1765), 15
DeFazio, Peter, 210
Deferred Action for Childhood Arrivals
    (DACA), 301-302
DeLay, Tom, 357
DeMint, Jim, 264
Democracy in America
    (de Tocqueville), 351
Democratic Caucus:
    committee chair elections by, 143
    Hoyer as chair of, 149
    Pelosi and, 138
    Rayburn and, 147
    subcommittee chairs and, 183
Democratic Congressional Campaign
    Committee (DCCC), 73
Democratic Policy and Communications
    Center (DPCC), 163
Democratic Senatorial Campaign
    Committee (DSCC), 383
Demographic constituencies, 122-124
Demographics, changes in, 2
Descriptive representation, 109, 208

Development, Relief, and Education for Alien Minors (DREAM) Act, 225
DeVos, Betsy, 152, 256, 321
Diaz-Balart, Mario, 214
Dickinson, John, 16
Digital lobbying, 385
Dingell, John D., 197, 211–212, 228, 339
Direct lobbying, 380–382
Dirksen, Everett M., 163, 290
Discharge petition, to dislodge bills from committee, 239–240
Discretionary spending, 410
Distributive policies, 402–404
Distributive theory of committees, 177
Districting, in House of Representatives:
  gerrymandering, 47–53
  majority-minority, 53–57
  malapportionment, 45–47
  overview, 44–45
District of Columbia v. Heller, 353
Disturbance hypothesis of interest group formation, 378
Dodd, Chris, 111
Dodd-Frank Wall Street Reform and Consumer Protection Act of 2012, 203, 331
Dole, Bob, 110, 214
Domenici, Pete, 227
Donnelly, Joe, 282
"Don't ask, don't tell" policy, 408
Door-to-door canvassing, 84
Dorgan, Byron, 265
Double filibusters, 252
Dow Jones Index, 456
DPCC (Democratic Policy and Communications Center), 163
DREAM Act (Development, Relief, and Education for Alien Minors), 225
Dred Scott v. Sandford (1857), 24, 360
Dromm, Danny, 2
Drones, military use of, 452
DSCC (Democratic Senatorial Campaign Committee), 383
Duberstein, Ken, 380
Dulles, John Foster, 446

Duncan, Kyle, 371
Durbin, Richard J., 159, 261–262, 317

Early deciders, in Congress, 265
Early Money Is Like Yeast (EMILY's List), 59, 80
Earmarks, 187, 403–404
Easley v. Cromartie (2001), 55
eBay.com, 384
Economy, globalized, 393, 395
Edsall, Thomas B., 77
Education of legislators, 109
Edwards, George, 308–309
Ehrenhalt, Alan, 47, 57, 109
Eisenhower, Dwight D., 155, 391, 400, 436, 446–447
Elections, 69–106
  allocating resources in, 79–80
  campaign finance regulations, 74–77
  campaign organization in, 80–81
  campaign resources in, 72–73
  campaign strategies in, 70–72
  candidate appeal in, 93–96
  close contact appeals in, 83–85
  Cruz v. O'Rourke (Texas, 2018), 69–70
  election outcomes, 99–104
  incumbents *versus* challengers, 77–79
  issue voting in, 96–98
  legislation timing affected by, 226–227
  mass appeals in media in, 81–83
  parallel campaigns in, 85
  party loyalties in, 88–93
  voting patterns in, 85–88
Electoral College, census and, 43
Eleventh Amendment to U.S. Constitution, 360
Elmendorf, Steve, 380
Emanuel, Rahm, 2
EMILY's List (Early Money Is Like Yeast), 59, 80
Emmers, Tom, 64
Energy and Commerce Committee, 202, 209–210
Energy and Natural Resources Committee, 186, 230
Entitlements, 414–418

Entrepreneurs, policy, 399–400
Environmental Working Group, 383
Environment and Public Works
Committee, 199
Enzi, Mike, 398, 421
Ernst, Joni, 182
Eshoo, Anna, 194
Eskew, Carter, 72
Ethics in Congress, 459–462
Etsy, Elizabeth, 460
Evenwel, Sue, 49
Evenwel v. Abbott (2016), 49–50
Exchange hypothesis of interest group
formation, 378
Executive agreements, 444–445
Executive branch of government, 29,
471–473. *See also* Bureaucracy;
Presidents and Congress
Executive Calendar, in Senate, 245
Executive orders, 300–301
Executive privilege, doctrine of, 23
Explicit bargaining, 286–287

Facebook, 2, 69, 83, 134, 309–310,
331, 385
Face-to-face canvassing, 84
Fannie Mae (Federal National Mortgage
Association), 455
Farenthold, Blake, 460
Farewell Address of 1796
(Washington), 429
"Fast and Furious Scandal" of
2012, 472
Fast-track trade negotiations, 442
Fatah, Chaka, 459
Federal Bureau of Investigation (FBI),
325, 365, 434
Federal Communications Commission
(FCC), 252, 335
Federal courts, 350–351
Federal Election Campaign Act
Amendments of 1974, 462
Federal Election Commission (FEC), 74,
83, 387, 460
Federal Emergency Management
Agency (FEMA), 330

Federal Funding Accountability and
Transparency Act of 2006, 346
Federal Home Loan Mortgage
Corporation (Freddie Mac), 455
Federalist Papers, 6, 20, 29, 40, 361, 376,
398, 430, 448
Federalist party, 30
Federalist Society, 370
Federal National Mortgage Association
(Fannie Mae), 455
Federal Register, 333–337
Federal Regulation of Lobbying Act of
1946, 391–392
Federal Reserve, 455
Feingold, Russ, 82
Feinstein, Dianne, 112
Female candidates for office, 62–64
Fenno, Richard F., Jr., 10, 114, 122,
124–125, 188, 265
Fifteenth Amendment to U.S.
Constitution, 19, 53
Filibusters:
cloture invoking stopped by, 251–252
increase in, 253–254
nuclear option and, 254–256
Republican, of 2013, 32
weaponization of, 254
Finances, election. *See* Elections
Financial Services Committee,
188, 196, 199
Financing government, as
Congressional power, 18
Fiorina, Morris P., 100, 129
First Amendment to U.S. Constitution,
20, 74
First Continental Congress (1774), 15–16
First Step Act, 261–263, 290
Fiscal year, federal, 410
Fischer, Deb, 163
Fisher, Louis, 24–25, 298, 346, 431
Fiske, John, 51
Flake, Jeff, 364–365
Floor procedures:
House of Representatives, 240–245
legislative process and, 31
Senate, 249–256

Flynn, Michael, 329, 472
Foley, Thomas S., 143
Ford, Christine Blasey, 364–365
Ford, Gerald R., 110
Foreign Affairs Committee, 428–429
Foreign Relations Committee, 193
Formulating policy, 400
Fourteenth Amendment to U.S.
    Constitution, 19, 43, 45, 49, 54, 360
Fourteenth Congressional District of
    New York, 2
Fox News, 428
Frank, Barney, 112, 389, 395, 413
Franken, Al, 460
Franking privilege, 131–132
Franks, Trent, 460
Frantzich, Stephen E., A5
Freddie Mac (Federal Home Loan
    Mortgage Corporation), 455
Freedom Caucus, 145, 167, 198, 277, 307
Freedom's Watch, 85
Free-rider problem, 376
French and Indian War, 15
Frumin, Alan S., 230
Fudge, Martha, 137–138
Fulbright, J. William, 433
Fund raising:
    campaign focus on, 70, 73–75, 77, 79
    candidate ability in, 61–62
    committee assignments and, 193
    lobbyists in, 381, 383
    organized interest groups and
        campaign, 386
    time spent on, 118

Gaddafi, Muammar, 395
Gallup polling, 469
"Gang of eight" in 113th Senate, 214
Gannon, Joseph G., 178
GAO (Government Accountability Office),
    208, 339, 392
Garfield, James A., 329
Garland, Merrick, 156, 350, 363, 368
Garrett, Scott, 82
Gates, Robert, 341, 391
Gavin, James, 224

Gender:
    leadership positions and, 160
    voting and gap in, 98
    women legislators, 111–112
Gentrification, demographics of, 2
Geographic constituencies, 122–124
Georgetown University, A6
Gerber, Alan S., 84
Gerry, Elbridge, 47, 51
Gerrymandering:
    Arizona, 46
    cracking and packing techniques of,
        47–48
    majority-minority districts in, 53–57
    origins of, 51–52
    partisan, 48–50
    pro-incumbent, 52–53
Get-out-the-vote (GOTV) drives, 71, 84–85
Gingrich, Newt:
    administrative reforms of, 140
    centralized control of committees by,
        212–213
    committees abolished by, 161, 195
    committee staffs reduced by, 207
    "Contract with America,"
        96, 143–144, 226
    ethics violations of, 461
    frustration with governing
        arrangements, 456–457
    persuasion approach of, 276
Ginsburg, Ruth Bader, 46, 49, 355, 365
Glickman, Dan, 84
Globalization, 393, 395
Glorious Revolution of 1688 (England), 14
Goldstein, Kenneth, 82–83
Goldwater, Barry, 89
Goodyear Tire and Rubber, 355
Gorsuch, Neil, 32, 256, 363, 368
Gottheimer, Josh, 82
GOTV (get-out-the-vote) drives, 71, 84–85
Government Accountability Office (GAO),
    208, 339, 392
Government shutdowns, 220
Graham, Bob, 230
Graham, Lindsey, 79, 306, 433
Grandy, Fred, 119

Grassley, Charles E.:
  "holds" explained by, 252
  "nuclear option" explained by, 255
  president pro tempore of Senate, 154
  rulemaking process and, 333
  Senate confirmation of presidential
    appointees and, 323, 327
  Senate Judiciary Chair, 262, 268
  trade politics and, 442
  Trump lower-court nominations
    advanced by, 370–371
Grassroots lobbying, 384
Grass tops lobbying, 384
Great Depression of 1930s, 405
Great Recession of 2008-2009, 405, 455
Great Society programs, 318–319
Green, Donald P., 84
Green, Matthew N., 139
"Green New Deal," 159, 399
Grimm, Michael, 459
Guantánamo Bay, Cuba, prison for
  terrorists built at, 300
Gun control, on national policy
  agenda, 398
Gutierrez, Luis V., 128

Hall, Richard L., 267, 464
Hamilton, Alexander, 17, 23, 29–30, 295,
  318, 331, 361
Hamilton, Lee H., 393, 435, 449, 459,
  463, 465
Hamilton College, A6
Harding, Warren, 296
Hard-to-contact populations,
  census and, 43
Harrington, James, 14, 17
Harris, Kamala, 181
Harvard University, 368, 375
Hassell, Hans J. G., 297
Hastert, Dennis, 144, 185, 212, 241
Hastert, J. Dennis, 380
Hatch, Carl, 331
Hatch Act of 1939, 331
Hatfield, Mark, 214
Hawley, Josh, 192–193
Haynes, George H., 178

Health, Education, Labor, and Pensions
  Committee, 213
Hearings, on bills, 203
Heitkamp, Heidi, 282
Hensarline, Jeb, 196
Heritage Action, 262, 387
Herrnson, Paul S., 4, 72, 386
Hibbing, John R., 119, 470
Hidden welfare state, 417
Higgins Brian, 138
Hill versus home styles, 107–135
  allocating time, 118–119
  backgrounds of legislators, 108–114
  careers in Congressional service,
    119–120
  constituency bonds in, 127
  constituency demographics in,
    121–125
  explaining activity, 126–127
  independent judgment versus
    constituency opinion in, 120–121
  legislative offices in, 127–131
  media and, 131–134
  overview, 107–108
  roles of legislators, 114–118
  self-presentation, 125–126
Hispanic Caucus, 194, A5
Hispanic legislators, 182
Hit the Ground Running (McCarthy), 190
Hobbes, Thomas, 290
Hobby Lobby v. Burwell, 371
Holder, Eric, 472
Holds, 252
Honest Leadership and Open
  Government Act of 2007, 393–394
Honeymoon effect, of new presidents, 284
House Administration Committee, 181
House Armed Services Committee, 341
House Calendar, 228
House Committee on Agriculture, 188,
  190, 267
House Committee on Appropriations,
  176, 411
House Committee on Energy and
  Commerce., 374
House Committee on Ethics, 181, 393

House Committee on Oversight and Government Reform, 342
House Committee on Rules, 230–234, 239–240
House Democratic Caucus, 138, 231
House Energy and Commerce Committee, 336, 339
House Ethics Committee, 144, 460
House Foreign Affairs Committee, 433–434, 435
House Homeland Security Committee, 435
House Intelligence Committee, 472
House Judiciary Committee, A5
House of Representatives:
 apportionment in, 41–44
 floor leaders, 149–150
 incumbency advantage in, 95
 party control of, A2–A3
 size of, 28–29
 Speaker of the House, 139–149
 Ways and Means Committee of, 1, 29, 145
 whips, 150–152
 See also Congress, evolution of; Rules and procedures
Howell, William G., 300, 312, 315
Hoyer, Steny:
 committee assignment support of, 194
 constituencies and, 192
 earmarks restored by, 404
 experience length of, 149
 motions to recommit, 151, 244
 Pallone backed by, 194
 Pelosi versus, 164
 Pence and, 307
 USMCA and, 441
Huerta, Delores, 3
Hugin, Bob, 75
Human Genome Project, 404
Hussein, Saddam, 312
Hyde, Henry J., 121, 242

IGs (inspectors general) offices, 342
Immigration and Customs Enforcement agency (ICE), 3, 152, 266

Immigration and Naturalization Service v. Chadha (1983), 24
Immigration issues, 43, 214
Impeachment:
 bureaucracy and, 343
 judges and, 358–359
 process of, 22–23
Imperial presidents, 318
Implementing policy, 401–402
Implicit bargaining, 286
Incubation, of policy, 400
Incumbency:
 advantage of, 93–95, 100
 gerrymandering to support, 52–53
 legislative scorecards and, 387–388
 margins of safety of, 123–124
 out-of-touch stereotype of, 2
 seat winnability and, 61–62
Independent model, legislative-executive relations as, 295
Indirect spending, 417
Influence district, 56
Information, weaponization of, 453
Informational theory of committees, 177
Inhofe, Jim, 439
Inouye, Daniel, 403
Inspectors general (IGs) offices, 342
Instagram.com, 2, 83, 134
Interest on debt, 417–418
Interests, organized or special. See Organized interests
Intermediate-Range Nuclear Forces (INF) Treaty of 1987, 301, 445
Internal Revenue Code, Section 501c(4) of, 76
Internal Revenue Service (IRS), 203, 356
International affairs committees in Congress, 433–435
International Arabian Horse Association, 330
Internet, as news source, 83
Internships on Capitol Hill, A5–A7
Interstate Commerce Act, 405
Intolerable Acts, 15
Iran-Contra investigation (1987), 340
Iran nuclear compact of 2015, 427

Iraq war hearings (2007), 340
Iron triangles (committees, federal
    departments, and pressure
    groups), 206, 391
Irregular warfare, 452
IRS (Internal Revenue Service), 203, 356
Issue-oriented style, 126
Issue uptake, 104
Issue voting, 96–98

Jackson, Henry M. "Scoop," 288
Jackson, Robert, 21, 431
Jackson, Ronny, 108
Jacobson, Gary C., 62, 77, 79, 95
Jay, John, 430, 448
Jefferson, Thomas, 30, 219–220, 247, 296
Jeffries, Hakeem, 262
Johnson, Andrew, 23
Johnson, Lyndon B.:
    campaign tactics of, 83
    committee assignments by, 190
    Great Society program of, 318
    majority leader, 155–156
    military force used by, 443–444
    presidential relationships with, 305–306
    vote counting of, 289
"Johnson Treatment," 155
Joint Chiefs of Staff, 447
Joint Committee on the Organization of
    Congress, 215
Joint committees, 185
Joint resolutions, 223
Jolly, David, 73
Jones, Charles O., 295
Jordan, Jim, 150, 198
Judicial branch of government:
    Congressional actions reviewed by,
        23–25
    judicial activism, 353
    judicial review, 353
    lawmaking by, 473
    statutory creation of, 19
Judiciary Act of 1789, 23
Judiciary Committee, 202
Judiciary Subcommittee on Immigration
    and Citizenship, 183

Kagan, Elena, 359, 364, 368
Kaine, Tim, 193, 451
Kalla, Joshua L., 386
Karcher v. Daggett (1983), 47
Kashoggi, Jamal, 395
Kavanaugh, Brett M., 348–349, 359–360,
    363–365, 368
Kelo v. City of New London, 353
Kennedy, Anthony M., 75, 349, 359, 364
Kennedy, John F., 110, 224, 232, 300,
    319, 400
Kennedy, John Neely, 370–371
Kennedy, Ted, 224
Kent, Samuel B., 359
Kernell, Samuel, 297, 307
Kerry, John, 433
Keystone XL oil pipeline, 335
Khashoggi, Jamal, 432, 450
Kimmel, Jimmy, 10
King, Angus, 59, 169, 452
King, Peter T., 265
King, Steve, 183
Kingdon, John W., 285, 400
Kingston, Jack, 381
King v. Burwell, 352–353, 356
Kissinger, Henry, 435, 445
Klobuchar, Amy, 348–349
Koch brothers, 262
Koenig, Andy, 321
Krumholz, Sheila, 381
Krutz, Glen S., 446
Kushner, Charles, 262
Kushner, Jared, 262, 329

Labor unions, as interest groups,
    387–388
Laden, Osama bin, 311, 448
Lake, Celinda, 98
Landford, James, 191
Landrieu, Mary, 289
Late deciders, in Congress, 265
Leaders and parties, 137–174
    activities of, 160–164
    coalition building, 169–171
    decision making in Congress and, 266
    House floor leaders, 149–150

House whips, 150–152
overview, 137–139
party caucuses, 165
party committees, 165
party conflict, 167–168
party groups, informal, 165–167
selection of, 159–160
Senate floor leaders, 154–159
Senate presiding officers, 152–154
Speaker of the House, 139–149
two-party system, 168–169
See also Committees
Leadership Conference on Civil and
    Human Rights, 262
League of Conservation Voters, 387
Leahy, Patrick, 397
Ledbetter, Lily, 355
Ledbetter v. Goodyear Tire and Rubber
    (2007), 355
Lee, Mike, 163, 261, 364
Legal training, of legislators, 109
Legislative Black Caucus, 56
Legislative-executive conflict and
    cooperation:
    constituency differences, 316–317
    partnership *versus* independent
        model in, 295
    party loyalties, 313–315
    public expectations, 315–316
    rulemaking, 335–336
    timetables, 317
Legislative Reorganization Act of 1946,
    29, 32–33, 128, 209, 338
Legislative Reorganization Act of
    1970, 243
Legislative subsidy, lobbyist-legislator
    relationship as, 390
Legislators:
    job evolution of, 33–36
    popular image of, 5–6
    rating, 387–388
    tasks of, 4–5
    See also Hill *versus* home styles
Lehman Brothers, 455
Leighley, Jan E., 88
Leo, Leonard, 370

Lewis, David E., 300, 312
Light, Paul C., 326, 463
Lincoln, Abraham, 307, 331
Lindsay, James M., 447
Lobby Disclosure Act of 1995, 392–393
Lobbying:
    coalition, 383
    digital, 385
    direct, 380–382
    Federal Regulation of Lobbying Act of
        1946, 391–392
    foreign, 393, 395
    grassroots, 384
    Honest Leadership and Open
        Government Act of 2007, 393–394
    legislation and, 389–390
    Lobby Disclosure Act of 1995, 392–393
    social, 382–383
    upper-class orientation of, 377
Localism, policy making affected by, 407
Locke, John, 14, 17–18
Lockheed Martin, 438
Logrolling, 287–288
Long, Russell, 227
Longfellow, Henry Wadsworth, 379
Lott, Trent, 113
Lower court nominees, 368–371
Lower status occupations, 110
Lowey, Nita M., 111, 404
Low-information rationality, in voting
    decisions, 88
Lublin, David, 56

Mackenzie, G. Calvin, 461
Madison, James, 6, 20–21, 25, 29–30,
    376, 398
Magleby, David, 89
Magnuson, Warren, 288
Mail, legislative use of, 131–132
Maisel, L. S., 60
Majority-minority districting, 53–57
Malapportionment in House of
    Representatives, 45–47
Manchin, Joe, 159, 186, 192–193, 252,
    282, 365
Mandatory minimum sentences, 19

Mandatory spending, 410

Marbury v. Madison (1803), 23–24, 353

March of Dimes, 373

Markey, Edward, 159

Markups of bills, 204–205

Marshall, John, 23, 350

Martin, James D., 36

Mason, George, 25

Massachusetts Bay Company, 15

Massachusetts state constitution, 17

Matthews, Billy, 128

Matthews, Donald R., 115

Mattis, James, 428–429

Mayhew, David R., 5, 31–32, 303, 310, 315–316

Mazur, Mark J., 327

McBath, Lucy, 222

McCain, John, 170, 265, 391, 403

McCarthy, Kevin, 145–146, 150, 164, 190, 210, 306

McCarthy, Nolan, 52

McCaskill, Claire, 192–193, 268

McConnell, Mitch:

  agenda controlled by, 283

  amendments offered by, 268

  "amendment tree filling" by, 251

  appropriations negotiations of, 171

  cabinet nominees and, 256

  campaign finance reform and, 76

  committee assignments made by, 163, 181–182

  criminal justice reform and, 262

  "electable" candidates and, 65

  GOP 2017 Philadelphia retreat, 162

  Kavanaugh hearings and, 350

  National Rifle Association connections to, 379–380

  national security and, 429

  partial government shutdowns and, 293–294

  party politics of, 277, 314–315

  power to schedule of, 245–246

  refusal to consider Obama Supreme Court nominees, 363

  Senate majority leader, 156–159

  task forces formed by, 214

  tax cuts of 2017, 288

  Trump unpredictability and, 306

McCormack, John W., 178

McCubbins, Mathew, 276

McDonald, Jason A., 343

McGahn, Donald F., 370–371

McGovern, Jim, 233, 236

McHenry, Patrick, 229

Mead, Walter Russell, 428

Meadows, Mark, 145, 307

Media:

  Congress covered by, 468

  legislators and, 131–134

  party leaders and, 169–171

  See also Advertising

Medicaid, 354, 417

Medicare for All Act, 3, 416–417

Meehan, Pat, 460

Meek, Carrie P., 110

Megabills, 171, 225–226, 228

"Member Day Hearings," 205

Menendez, Bob, 75

Merkel, Angela, 445

Merrill Lynch, 455

Message bills, 336

MeToo movement, 63, 111, 460

Michel, Bob, 172

Micro-targeting, in elections, 84

Midterm elections, 90–93

Mikva, Abner J., 355

Miler, Kristina C., 378

Military background of legislators, 110

Military base closures, 264, 438–439

Military-industrial complex, 391

Military-industrial-Congressional complex, 436–439

Mill, John Stuart, 109

Miller, Carol, 63

Miller, Warren E., 104

Missouri Compromise of 1820, 24

Money, organized interests use of, 388–389

Monroe, James, 302

Montesquieu, Baron de, 14, 17

Moran, James P., 382

Morris, Gouverneur, 25

MoveOn.org, 376, 386

Mr. Smith Goes to Washington
(1939 film), 251

Mucchiaroni, Gary, 268

Mueller, Robert, 323, 325, 328, 344

Muhlenberg, Frederick A. C., 13

Multiple-Step Rule, 238

Mulvaney, Mick, 307

Murkowski, Lisa, 170, 265, 365

Murray, Patty, 111, 159

Murtha, John P., 289

Muskie, Edmund S., 264–265

"Must-pass" debt ceiling, 269

Nadler, Jerrold, 344

NAFTA (North American Free Trade
Agreement), 440–441

Nagler, Jonathan, 88

National Association of
Manufacturers, 382

National debt ceiling, 269

National Defense Authorization Act,
215–216

National Election Study, 129

*National Federation of Independent
Business v. Sebelius,* 351–354

National Labor Relations Board
(NLRB), 328

National Parks and Recreation Act of
1978, 402

National Rifle Association (NRA), 306,
379–380, 385, 387

National Rifle Association Legislative
Action Fund, 76

National security. *See* Security policies

National Security Council, 447

Native Americans, health care of, 265

NATO (North Atlantic Treaty
Organization), 427–428, 443, 446

Navarro, Peter, 329

NCLB (No Child Left Behind education
law), 314, 407

Nelson, Ben, 289

Nelson, Bill, 76, 186

Nelson, Garrison, 84

Network neutrality, 384

Neustadt, Richard E., 304

New Deal, 29, 99, 319, 349, 405

New Democrat Coalition, 167, 278

New Freedom programs, 319

New Frontier program, 232

Newhouse, Neil, 98

New Jersey Hospital Association, 373

New Orleans *Times-Picayune,* 371

News outlets, 132–133

Newspapers, dropping circulation of, 83

"New START" (Strategic Arms
Reduction Treaty), 445

New York's Fourteenth Congressional
District, 2

New York state constitution, 17

New York Times, 2, 365, 458

Nielsen, Kirstjen, 344

Nixon, Richard M., 29, 89, 110, 299, 310,
319, 418

NLRB (National Labor Relations
Board), 328

NLRB v. Noel Canning, 328

No Child Left Behind (NCLB) education
law, 314, 407

Nominating procedures, 64–66

Non-governmental organizations. *See*
Organized interests

Noonan, John T., Jr., 473

North American Free Trade Agreement
(NAFTA), 440–441

North Atlantic Treaty Organization
(NATO), 427–428, 443, 446

North Carolina General Assembly, 120

NRA (National Rifle Association), 306,
379–380, 385, 387

Nuclear option (majority cloture),
254–255, 369

Nunes, Devin, 344, 472

Obama, Barack:
AARP support of ACA and, 380
bills drafted during administration
of, 225
Boehner and, 145
communication skills of, 308–309
confirmation of appointees of, 326

Congress and, 306
Congressional difficulties of, 283, 335–336
Congressional seat increases with, 90
Congressional support of, 314
Congress working with, 319
Deferred Action for Childhood Arrivals (DACA) program of, 301
earmarks vetoed by, 403
executive orders used by, 302, 318
Garland nominated to Supreme Court by, 363
Guantánamo Bay, Cuba, prison and, 300
healthcare plan support cultivated by, 373
legislative involvement of, 212
Libya military operations of, 449
lower court nominations of, 369–370
McConnell and, 156
military force used by, 472
"New START" (Strategic Arms Reduction Treaty) success of, 445
party caucuses and, 165
recess appointments of, 328–329
signing statements used by, 302
special operations to kill Osama bin Laden, 448
veto power used by, 296, 298
Obamacare. *See* Patient Protection and Affordable Care Act of 2010
Obey, David, 135
"Obscure Caucus," 264
Ocasio-Cortez, Alexandria:
Crowley constituency problems and, 127
food implications of political issues, 190
Green New Deal, 159
New York primary of 2018 won by, 1–3, 59, 63, 65
policy entrepreneurship of, 399
primary challenges threatened by, 116
social media following of, 134
Occupations of legislators, 109–110
Occupy Wall Street, 376
OCO (Overseas Contingency Operation), 437
O'Connor, Reed, 352

O'Connor, Sandra Day, 353, 364
Office for Homeland Security, 300
Office of Congressional Ethics (OCE), 393, 462
Office of Diversity and Inclusion, 208
Office of Information and Regulatory Affairs (OIRA), 336
Office of Management and Budget (OMB), 29, 296, 336, 342
Oliver, John, 10
Olson, Mancur, Jr., 376
Omar, Ilhan, 134
Omnibus bills, 171, 225–226, 228
100th Meridian rule, 230
O'Neill, Thomas P. "Tip," Jr.:
centralized committee control of, 143
committee realignment plans and, 211
importance of timing explained by, 226
inner circle of, 124–125
lobbyists and, 380
Reagan dealings with, 305
Rules Committee and, 233
scheduling power of, 161
"One person, one vote" principle, 45
Open Rule, 235
Open seats, 61–62
Opinion leaders, 98, 310–311
Oppenheimer, Bruce, 52
Opposition research, 461
Oregon v. Mitchell (1970), 360
Organized interests, 373–396
electoral connection to, 385–388
lobbying, legislation and, 389–390
lobbying regulations on, 391–395
money, role of, 388–389
overview, 373–374
pluralism, 374–379
pressure groups, methods of, 379–385
subgovernments, 390–391
Ornstein, Norman, 325
O'Rourke, Beto, 69–70
Outsourcing, in government bureaucracy, 331–332
Overseas Contingency Operation (OCO), 437
Oxford University, 368

Packing and cracking techniques of gerrymandering, 47–48, 56

PACs (political action committees). *See* Political action committees (PACs)

Pallone, Frank, 194

Parallel campaigns, 85

Paris Climate Accord of 2015, 427

Participation in decision making in Congress, 267–268

Partisan gerrymandering, 48–50

Partisan interests in Congress, 30–31

Partisan theory of committees, 177

Partnership model, legislative-executive relations as, 295

Party politics:
    Congressional voting affected by, 272–277
    control of presidency, Senate, and House, A2–A3
    early, 30–31
    federal employees restricted in, 331
    legislative-executive conflict and cooperation based on, 313–315
    legislator role in, 117–118
    loyalties to, 88–93
    nominations and, 65
    See also Leaders and parties

Pascrell, Bill, Jr., 207

Patient Protection and Affordable Care Act of 2010:
    court challenges to, 351–352
    late decider impact on, 265
    legitimation questions about, 400–401
    organized interests and, 374
    Republican attempt to repeal, 169–170, 305

Patronage, 303

Paul, Rand, 306, 472

Paulson, Henry M., Jr., 455

Pay-as-you-go (PAYGO) rule, 410, 423–424

Peace Corps, 224

Peake, Jeffrey S., 446

Pelosi, Nancy:
    Affordable Care Act supported by, 170
    committee assignment support of, 194

decentralization and, 213

election challenges to, 137–138

first female Speaker of the House, 111

House experience of, 140

House floor leaders and, 149

House party leadership described by, 172

ideology in voting, 279

Office of Congressional Ethics created by, 161

partial government shutdowns and, 293–294

party discipline enforced by, 151–152

power centralization under, 144–145

Republican negative advertising against, 85

"rubber stamp Congress" *versus*, 318

Rules Committee and, 241

Select Committee on Climate Crisis supported by, 209–210

"Six for '06" initiatives of, 96

Trump border wall funding *versus*, 146

Trump unpredictability and, 306

Pence, Mike, 152, 162, 307, 451–452

Perlmutter, Ed, 138

Permanent Select Committee on Intelligence, 183

Perry, Rick, 321

Perry, William, 445

Personal and political constituencies, 124–125

Personal staffs of legislators, 129–131

Person-to-person style, 125–126

Persuasive power of presidents, 304–307

Peterson, Matthew, 370

Pevehouse, Jon C., 315

Pew Research Center, 83

Pharmaceutical Research and Manufacturers of America (PhRMA), 383

Piecemeal policy making in Congress, 407–408

Pitkin, Hannah, 109, 120

Pivotal voter theory, 148

Plato, 39

Pluralism, organized interests and, 374–379

Plurality vote, 8
Pocan, Mark, 441
Pocket veto, 298
Podesta, Heather, 380, 383
Policy entrepreneurs, 264
Policy making by committees:
  bills referred to, 203–206
  environment of, 206
  multiple referrals in, 202
  overlapping jurisdictions in, 199–201
Policy making in Congress, 397–409
  bicameralism impact on, 406–407
  distributive policies, 402–404
  localism impact on, 407
  overview, 397–398
  piecemeal, 407–408
  reactive, 408–409
  redistributive policies, 405–406
  regulatory policies, 405
  stages of, 398–402
  successes, 463
  symbolic, 408
  See also Budgeting in Congress
Policy window, 400
Political action committees (PACs):
  campaign contributions of, 74–75
  organized interest groups use of, 385–386
  refusal to accept contributions from, 188
Political and personal constituencies, 124–125
Political engineering, 438
Politico, 373
Politics. See Leaders and parties;
  Party politics
Pollock v. Farmers' Loan and Trust Co. (1895), 18, 360
Polsby, Nelson W., 26
Pompeo, Mike, 428
Poole, Keith T., 52, 278
Popkin, Samuel L., 88
Pork barrel politics, 36
"Pork" spending, 187
Porteous, Thomas, Jr., 359
Porter, Katie, 188

Portman, Rob, 163, 264
Post-Katrina Emergency Management
  Reform Act of 2006, 330
Postveto action, 298–299
"Power of the purse," 18, 29, 398, 443–444
Preference outliers, committee
  members as, 177
Presidential government, periods of, 318
Presidential Succession Act of 1947, 139
President pro tempore of Senate, 152–154
Presidents and Congress, 293–320
  balance of power, 317–319
  constitutional powers, 295–299
  elections of, 90–93
  impact of, on Congressional voting, 283–285
  imperial, 473–474
  legislative-executive conflict and
    cooperation, 313–317
  opinion leadership, 310–311
  overview, 293–295
  party control of, A2–A3
  party leaders and, 162
  persuasive power, 304–307
  rhetorical power, 307–310
  Senate confirmation of presidential
    appointees, 323–329
  "two presidencies," 311–312
Press, local, 132–133
Pressley, Ayanna, 65, 134
Pressure groups. See Organized interests
Price, David E., 125, 264
Price, Tom, 160, 256
Primary election system, 65–66
Private Calendar, 228
Private school vouchers, 321
Privatizing government bureaucracy, 331–332
Procedures in Congress. See Rules and
  procedures
Process shortcomings in Congress, 463–468
Professionalization, in Congress, 34–36.
  See also Recruitment and candidacy
Progressive Caucus, 167
Progressive era, 30

Progressive movement, 25
Progressive Party of early 20th
   century, 169
Prohibition, 41–42
Pro-incumbent gerrymandering, 52–53
Proliferation hypothesis of interest
   group formation, 378
Property norm, in committee
   assignments, 192
Proportional representation, 8–9
Pruitt, Scott, 321
Pryor, David, 93
P.S. (Political Science and Politics), 99
Public Citizen, 460
Public expectations of legislative-executive
   conflicts and cooperation, 315–316
Public policy issues, 98
Public relations, party leaders'
   involvement in, 169–171
Purdue, David, 306
Putin, Vladimir, 326
Putnam, Robert, 375

Queen-of-the-Hill Rule, 238
Quirk, Paul J., 268

Race of legislators, 110–111
Radel, Trey, 460
Radical Republicans (Civil War), 19
Rakoive, Jack N., 16
Rankin, Jeannette, 111
Rayburn, Sam, 4, 125, 142–143, 147, 232
Reactive policy making in Congress,
   408–409
Reagan, Ronald:
   agenda control by, 304–305
   appointments of, 328, 365
   assassination attempt on, 308
   Congress working with, 319
   media-savviness of, 307–308
   oversight and, 473
   reconciliation of budgets and, 423
   southern strategy voters for, 89–90
   veto of 1988 civil rights bill by, 299
Reapportionment, in House of
   Representatives, 41–42

Recess appointment option, 328
Reciprocal Trade Agreements Act of
   1934, 440
Reconciliation, in budgeting, 410,
   422–423
Reconstruction, after Civil War, 53
Reconstruction Acts of 1867, 358
Recruitment and candidacy, 39–68
   amateurs and professionals, 59–61
   called or chosen, 57–59
   formal rules of, 40–44
   gerrymandering and, 47–53
   majority-minority districting, 53–57
   malapportionment in districting, 45–47
   nominating procedures, 64–66
   overview, 44–45
   quality candidates, 61–64
   voting affected by, 93–96
Redistributive policies, 405–406
Redistricting, 2, 46
Reed, Thomas Brackett, 31
Reed, Thomas "Czar," 142
Reed's Rules, adoption of (1890), 31, 37
Reelection, goal of, 5
Referral of bills to Committees:
   Committees receiving, 203–206
   decline in, 228
   multiple, 202, 227
   phraseology affecting, 227
   rules and, 230
   Senate bypassing of, 247, 250
Reforming Congress, 467–468
Regulatory policies, 405
Regulatory review of agencies, 336–338
Reid, Harry, 213, 251, 255, 265,
   276, 289, 455
Reischauer, Robert, 424
Religion of legislators, 112–113
Reorganization plans, 300
Reports on legislation, 205–206
Republic (Plato), 39
Republican National Committee, 336
Republican party, Federalists *versus*, in
   early U.S., 30
Republican Study Committee, 145, 167
Rescission, in budgeting, 410–411

Resolutions, 223
Revenues, in budgeting, 411
Revere, Paul, 16
Revolutionary War, 16
Revolving door from Congress to lobbying firms, 381
Reynolds v. Sims (1964), 45, 49
Rhetorical power of presidents, 307–310
Richmond, Cedric, 194
Right of first recognition, of majority leaders, 250–251
Road-tripping, by legislators, 127–128
Roberts, Cokie, 133
Roberts, John, 46, 53–54, 365, 368
Roberts, Pat, 205
Robinson, Michael J., 95
Robotics, military use of, 453
Rodden, Jonathan, 52
Rodgers, Cathy McMorris, 160
Rogers, Harold, 404
Rogers, Mike, 434–435
Rogers, Will, 10
Rohrabacher, Dana, 145
Roll Call magazine, 264
Roll call voting, 285
Rooney, Francis, 210
Roosevelt, Franklin D., 90, 319, 331, 349–350, 473
Rosendale, Matt, 108
Rosenthal, Howard, 52, 278–279
Ross, Wilbur, 44
Rother, John, 373
Rubio, Marco, 326, 433
Rudalevige, Andrew, 473
Rules and procedures, 219–260
    bills, dislodging from committee, 239–240
    bills, introducing, 222–228
    bills, shortcuts for minor, 229–231
    bureaucracy involvement in, 333–338
    Congressional committee on, 181, 232–234
    creative, 234–239
    House floor procedures, 240–245
    House-Senate differences, resolving, 257–259

    overview, 219–222
    scheduling in Senate, 245–249
    Senate floor procedures, 249–256
    Senate scheduling, 245–249
Russell, Richard B., 155
Rust Belt, loss of House seats of, 42–43
Rutherford., Matthew J., 327
Ryan, Betsy, 373
Ryan, Paul:
    adoption of rules of, 241
    agenda control of, 283
    AUMF and, 451
    Authorization for Use of Military Force of 2001 and, 268
    closed rules of, 236
    committees and, 212–213
    earmarks discouraged by, 404
    experience length of, 140
    GOP 2017 Philadelphia retreat, 162
    GOP Steering Committee revamped by, 163
    Medicare overhaul proposed by, 416
    partial government shutdowns and, 293
    party orientation of, 272
    Speaker of the House, 145–146
Ryan, Tim, 137

Salman, Mohammed bin, 432
Sanders, Bernie, 3, 59, 84, 159, 169, 198
Sarieddine, Leila E., 432
Sarpalius, Bill (D-Tex.), 7
Satellite feeds, from legislators, 133
Save Our Species Alliance, 384
Scalia, Antonin, 48–49, 156, 356, 363, 365
Scalise, Steve, 160, 210
Schattschneider, E. E., 376
Scheduling in House of Representatives:
    bills, dislodging from committee, 239–240
    bills, shortcuts for minor, 229–231
    committee on rules, role in, 232–234
    creative rules and, 234–239
Scheduling in Senate, 245–249
Schiller, Wendy, 265
Schlesinger, Arthur M., Jr., 317–318
Schock, Aaron, 459

Schroeder, Pat, 119
Schumer, Charles E.:
  Affordable Care Act supported by, 170
  committee assignments by, 193
  committee assignments made by,
    181–182
  committee system and, 176–177
  Democratic Policy and Communications
    Center chair, 163
  experience length of, 115
  financial crisis of 2008, 455
  Gorsuch nomination and, 363
  ideology considerations for
    nominees, 368
  lobbying concerns of, 385
  "present" vote by, 270
  Senate minority leader, 158
  Tester *versus*, 107
  Trump unpredictability and, 306
Sclafani, Jennifer, 308
Scott, Rick, 76, 186
Scott, Tim, 110
Second Continental Congress (1775), 16
Security policies, 427–454
  Congressional, 471
  Constitutional powers on, 430–433
  crisis policies, 447–453
  international affairs committees in
    Congress, 433–435
  military-industrial-Congressional
    complex, 437–439
  overview, 427–430
  strategic, 443–447
  trade politics, 439–442
  types of, 435–436
SEIU (Service Employees International
  Union), 85
Select Committee on Energy Independence
  and Global Warming, 209
Select Committee on the Climate Crisis,
  184, 209–211
Select Committee on the Modernization
  of Congress, 185, 467
Select or special committees, 184–185
Self-executing Rule, 238
Self-presentation, by legislators, 125–126

Senate:
  advise-and-consent role of, 327–329
  apportionment, 40–41
  floor leaders of, 154–159
  growth of, 28–29
  incumbency advantage in, 95
  partisanship as roadblock in, 466–467
  party control of, A2–A3
  popular election to, 6
  presidential appointees confirmed by,
    323–329
  presiding officers of, 152–154
  unlimited debate rules of, 32
  See also Congress, evolution of; Rules
    and procedures
Senate Appropriations Committee, 412
Senate Democratic Steering and
  Outreach Committee, 380
Senate Ethics Committee, 460
Senate Foreign Relations Committee,
  318, 433
Senate Homeland Security and
  Governmental Affairs Committee, 435
Senate Intelligence Committee, 112
Senate Intelligence panel, 434
Senate Judiciary Committee, 359
Senate Steering Committee, 167
Sentences, mandatory minimum, 19
Separation-of-powers framework, 22–23
September 11, 2001 attacks, 311, 323
Sequester spending cuts, 379, 411, 423
Service Employees International Union
  (SEIU), 85
Sessions, Jeff, 256, 262, 328
Seventeenth Amendment to U.S.
  Constitution, 6, 25
Sexual assault, 111–112
Sexual orientation of legislators, 112
Shelby, Richard, 404
Shelby County v. Holder (2013), 53–54, 86
Sherman Antitrust Act, 405
Shoe-leather campaigning, 84
Shrinking center, in Congress, 279
Signing statements (proclamations),
  302–303
Simpson, Alan, 269, 287

Simpson, Mike, 179

Sinclair, Barbara, 115, 464, 466

Sinema, Kyrsten, 112

Sixteenth Amendment to U.S. Constitution, 18, 360

Smith, Christopher H., 144, 212

Smith, Howard W. "Judge," 232

Snell, Bertrand, 150

Snowe, Olympia J., 168

Social class, voting and, 88

Social lobbying, 382–383

Social media:

    elections and, 83

    guidelines for federal employee use of, 331

    Ocasio-Cortez reliance on, 2–3

    organized interests use of, 385

    O'Rourke use of, 69

    political communities formed on, 375

    reliance on, for news, 134

    Trump use of, 310

Soltz, Jon, 138

Sorensen, Theodore, 224

Sotomayor, Sonia, 368, 380

Spatial theory, 200

Speaker of the House:

    cluster-voting rule and, 231

    contemporary, 143–146

    influence of, 146–149

    multiple referrals of bills to, 202

    role of, 139–142

    Rules Committee and, 232–234

Special interests. *See* Organized interests

Specialized decision making in Congress, 264–265

Speechnow.org v. Federal Election Commission (2010), 75

Split-ticket voting, 90

Staffs, legislative, 129–131

Stamp Act Congress, 15

Stamp Act of 1765, 15

Standing committees, 179–184

Stanford University, 429

State government, federal government relationship with, 322

State of the Union address, 21

State University of New York, A6

Stauber, Pete, 82

Steel Caucus, 390

Stevens, John Paul, 7, 356

Stewart, Potter, 55

Stokes, Donald E., 104

Stoltenberg, Jens, 428

STOP Act (Synthetics Trafficking and Overdose Prevention), 225

Strahan, Randall, 148–149

Strategic Arms Reduction Treaty (START), 445

Strategic security policies, 443–447

Strict scrutiny standard, 54–55

Structured Rule, 234–235, 238

Studying in Washington: Academic Internships in the Nation's Capital (American Political Science Association), A5

STUPIDITY Act (Stop Shutdowns Transferring Unnecessary Pain and Inflicting Damage In The Coming Years)., 225

Styles, in Congress. *See* Hill *versus* home styles

Subgovernments, organized interests as, 390–391

Submerged state, 417

Substantive representation, 109

Sulkin, Tracy, 104

Summers, Lawrence, 428

Sun Belt, gain of House seats of, 42–43

Sundquist, James L., 473

Sunlight Foundation, 460

Sunstein, Cass R., 460

Supermajority rule, in Senate, 245

Surge and decline theory of midterm election loss, 91

Surveillance–industrial complex, 438

Suspension Day Rule, 238

Suspension-of-the-rules procedure, 229

Swers, Michele, 112

Swift, Elaine K., 26, 37

Symbolic policy making in Congress, 401, 408

Synar, Mike, 121

Tariffs, 301, 434, 440–442
Tate, Katherine, 111
Tax Cut and Jobs Act (TCJA) of 2017, 352
Tax expenditures or preferences, 417
Taxing, as Congressional power, 18
Taxpayer Protection Pledge, 387
Taylor, Gene, 456
Taylor, John, 30
Tea Act, 15
Tea Party movement, 65, 113, 145, 376, 398
Teapot Dome inquiry (1923), 340
Tennant v. Jefferson County Commission (2012), 47
Tenure of legislators, 113
Term limits, 138, 361
Tester, Jon, 107–108, 129, 264
Texas v. United States (2017), 352
Textile Caucus, 390
Theiss-Morse, Elizabeth, 470–471
Theriault, Sean M., 52
Thirteenth Amendment to U.S. Constitution, 19, 360
Thomas, Clarence, 55–57
Thornberry, Mac, 264
Thune, John, 159
Thurber, James A., 381, 392
Thurmond, Strom, 224
Tillerson, Rex, 326
Time and timing:
    allocating, 118–119
    decision making in Congress, 265
    legislative-executive conflicts from differences in, 317
Tisdale, Elkana, 51
Titus, Dina, 85
Tlaib, Rashida, 134
Tocqueville, Alexis de, 351, 375
Toyota Corp., 395
Trade Act of 1974, 440, 442
Trade Promotion Act of 1962, 442
Trade promotion authority (TPA), 442
Trade relations, 434, 439–442
Trans-Pacific Partnership of 2015, 427, 429, 440
Transportation and Infrastructure Committee, 176

Transportation Security Agency, 293
Travel ban, presidentially imposed, 301
Treaties, 444–445
Treaty of Versailles, 445
Truman, David B., 338
Truman, Harry S., 184, 300, 375, 449, 472
Trump, Donald J.:
    Affordable Care Act repeal attempts, 373
    border wall agenda of, 431
    budget submission for 2019, 397–398
    bureaucracy targeted by, 321–322
    climate change regulations dismantled by, 336
    communication of, 308
    Congress and, 283, 306–307
    filibusters discouraged by, 252
    First Step Act and, 261–262
    foreign policy of, 427–429
    free trade agreements and, 440–441
    GOP 2017 Philadelphia retreat, 162
    Gorsuch nominated by, 32
    Intermediate-Range Nuclear Forces (INF) agreement of 1987 withdrawal by, 445
    Jim Jordan and, 198
    Khashoggi killing, reaction to, 432–433
    line-item veto, 299
    lower court nominations of, 369–370
    midterm elections and, 92
    military force used by, 472
    Montana voting for, 107–108
    partial government shutdowns and, 293–294
    polarizing actions of, 52
    Republican retirements and, 96
    Russian support of election of, 434–435
    Ryan and, 145–146
    seat losses with, 90
    Senate advise-and-consent role bypassed by, 328–329
    signing statements used by, 302
    social media used by, 310
    Space Force proposal of, 300, 451–452
    Supreme Court nominees of, 364
    tax cuts of 2017, 288
    Twitter use by, 399

two-presidencies thesis relevant to, 312
unilateral power used by, 301–302
veto power used by, 296–297
women's marches and, 63
Tuesday Group, 145, 167
Tuesday Republican Policy Committee, 381
Tunney, John, 29
Twain, Mark, 10
Twenty-Sixth Amendment to U.S.
    Constitution, 360
Twitter.com, 2, 83, 134, 309, 331, 385
Two-party system, 168–169
Two-presidencies thesis, 311–312
Tyler, John, 365

Uber, Inc., 384
Udall, Morris K., 355
Unanimous consent agreements,
    231, 246–248
Unfunded mandates, 407
Unintentional gerrymandering, 52
Union Calendar, 228
United Nations (UN), 443
United States Statutes at Large, 313
United States v. Harris (1954), 392
University of California system, A6
University of Illinois, A6
University of Kansas, 383
University of Nevada-Las Vegas, 85
University of Southern California, A6
Unlawful enemy combatants, legal
    system for handling, 300
Unorthodox lawmaking (Sinclair), 464
Unruh, Jess, 72
Upton, Fred, 336
USA Patriot Act of 2001, 472
USASpending.gov, 346
U.S. Bureau of Alcohol, Tobacco,
    Firearms and Explosives, 472
U.S. Capitol Visitor Center, 471
U.S. Chamber of Commerce, 76, 385–387
U.S. Constitution:
    Article I of, 18–20, 23, 296
    Article II of, 21–22, 295–296, 343, 361
    Article III of, 350
    Commerce Clause of, 18–19

dual nature of Congress in, 6
Eleventh Amendment to, 360
Fifteenth Amendment to, 19, 53
First Amendment to, 20, 74
Fourteenth Amendment to, 19, 43, 45,
    49, 54, 360
security policies in, 430–433
Seventeenth Amendment to, 6, 25
Sixteenth Amendment to, 18, 360
Thirteenth Amendment to, 19, 360
Twenty-Sixth Amendment to, 360
U.S. Department of Defense, 436–437
U.S. Department of Education, 321
U.S. Department of Energy, 321
U.S. Department of Homeland Security
    (DHS), 112, 185, 323, 343, 435
U.S. Department of Housing and Urban
    Development (HUD), 342
U.S. Department of Justice, 393, 460
U.S. Department of State, 437
U.S. Department of the Treasury, 455–456
U.S. Environmental Protection Agency,
    301, 321, 335–336
U.S. Food and Drug Administration, 405
U.S.-Mexico-Canada Agreement
    (USMCA), 441
U.S. Office of Special Counsel, 331
U.S Supreme Court:
    Arizona redistricting (2015), 46
    citizenship question on census, 44
    Commerce Clause, 18–19
    Congressional term limits and, 40
    federalism of, 354
    gerrymandering in North Carolina
        and Maryland (2019), 52
    judicial activism of, 353
    legislative checks on judiciary, 356–361
    Line-Item Veto Act, 299
    New Deal legislation invalidated by,
        349–350
    nominees to, 363–368
    overview, 351–353
    pocket veto, 298
    Sotomayor nomination opposed by
        NRA, 380
    statutory interpretation by, 354–356

U.S. Supreme Court cases:
  *Alabama Legislative Black Caucus v.
    Alabama* (2015), 56
  Barenblatt v. United States (1959), 338
  Brown v. Board of Education, 359
  Buckley v. Valeo (1976), 74
  Chisholm v. Georgia (1793), 360
  *Citizens United v. Federal Election
    Commission* (2010), 24, 75
  Davis v. Bandemer (1986), 48
  District of Columbia v. Heller, 353
  Dred Scott v. Sandford (1857), 24, 360
  Easley v. Cromartie (2001), 55
  Evenwel v. Abbott (2016), 49–50
  Hobby Lobby v. Burwell, 371
  *Immigration and Naturalization Service
    v. Chadha* (1983), 24
  Karcher v. Daggett (1983), 47
  Kelo v. City of New London, 353
  King v. Burwell, 352–353, 356
  Ledbetter v. Goodyear Tire and Rubber
    (2007), 355
  Marbury v. Madison (1803), 23–24, 353
  *National Federation of Independent
    Business v. Sebelius*, 351–354
  NLRB v. Noel Canning, 328
  Oregon v. Mitchell. (1970), 360
  Pollock v. Farmers' Loan and Trust Co.
    (1895), 18, 360
  Reynolds v. Sims (1964), 45, 49
  Shelby County v. Holder (2013), 53–54, 86
  *Speechnow.org v. Federal Election
    Commission* (2010), 75
  *Tennant v. Jefferson County
    Commission* (2012), 47
  Texas v. United States (2017), 352
  United States v. Harris (1954), 392
  Vieth v. Jubelirer (2004), 48–50
  Watkins v. United States (1957), 338, 340
  Wesberry v. Sanders (1964), 45
  Wisconsin v. Gill (2018), 50–51
  *Youngstown Sheet and Tube Co. v.
    Sawyer* (1952), 431

Value in Electing Women, 59
Vanderbilt University, 52

Van Hollen, Chris, 2, 314
Veterans' Affairs Committee, 107, 190, 212
Vetos:
  bargaining based on, 296–299
  Congressional, 340–341
  line-item, 299
Vice president, Senate presided over
    by, 152
Vieth v. Jubelirer (2004), 48–50
Violence Against Women Act, 225
Vitter, David, 269
VoteVets lobbying group, 138
Voting in Congress:
  candidate appeal in, 93–96
  choices in, 269–270
  constituency impact on, 281–283
  cue-givers and roll call, 285
  ideology impact on, 277–281
  issues as reasons for, 96–98
  meaning in, 270–271
  party impact on, 272–277
  party loyalties in, 88–93
  polarization in, 102
  presidency impact on, 283–285
Voting Rights Act (VRA) of 1965, 53–54,
    56, 86

Walden, Greg, 374
Wall Street executive bonuses, taxpayer
    funded (2009), 340
Wall Street Journal, 428
Ward, Samuel, 379
Warner, Mark, 434
War powers, 447–453
War Powers Resolution of 1973, 449–451
Warren, Earl, 340, 364
Washington, George, 13, 17, 21, 323, 429
Washington Center for Internships and
    Academic Seminars, A6
Washington Post, 395
Washington Post Magazine, 457
Washington system of lobbyists and
    insider access, 374
Wasserman, David, 63
Wasserman-Schultz, Debbie, 118
Watergate hearings (1973-1974), 340

CONGRESSIONAL TIME LINE: **1789–1932**

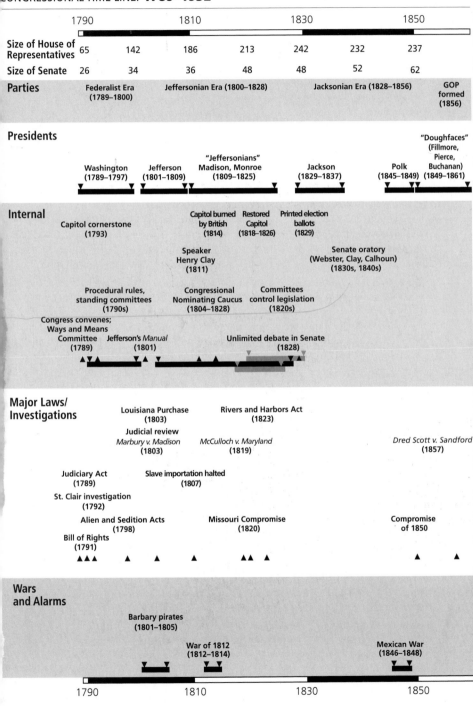

	1790		1810		1830		1850	
Size of House of Representatives	65	142	186	213	242	232	237	
Size of Senate	26	34	36	48	48	52	62	

Parties

Federalist Era (1789–1800)   Jeffersonian Era (1800–1828)   Jacksonian Era (1828–1856)   GOP formed (1856)

Presidents

Washington (1789–1797)   Jefferson (1801–1809)   "Jeffersonians" Madison, Monroe (1809–1825)   Jackson (1829–1837)   Polk (1845–1849)   "Doughfaces" (Fillmore, Pierce, Buchanan) (1849–1861)

Internal

Capitol cornerstone (1793)

Capitol burned by British (1814)   Restored Capitol (1818–1826)   Printed election ballots (1829)

Speaker Henry Clay (1811)

Senate oratory (Webster, Clay, Calhoun) (1830s, 1840s)

Procedural rules, standing committees (1790s)

Congressional Nominating Caucus (1804–1828)

Committees control legislation (1820s)

Congress convenes; Ways and Means Committee (1789)   Jefferson's *Manual* (1801)

Unlimited debate in Senate (1828)

Major Laws/ Investigations

Louisiana Purchase (1803)

Rivers and Harbors Act (1823)

Judicial review *Marbury v. Madison* (1803)

McCulloch v. Maryland (1819)

Dred Scott v. Sandford (1857)

Judiciary Act (1789)

Slave importation halted (1807)

St. Clair investigation (1792)

Alien and Sedition Acts (1798)

Missouri Compromise (1820)

Compromise of 1850

Bill of Rights (1791)

Wars and Alarms

Barbary pirates (1801–1805)

War of 1812 (1812–1814)

Mexican War (1846–1848)

| 1790 | 1810 | 1830 | 1850 |